A history of Newfoundland, from the English, colonial, and foreign records

D W. Prowse

H.M. QUEEN VICTORIA IN 1838.

A

HISTORY OF NEWFOUNDLAND

FROM THE

English, Colonial, and Foreign Records

BY

D. W. PROWSE, Q.C., LL.D.,

Judge of the Central District Court of Newfoundland

WITH NUMEROUS ILLUSTRATIONS AND MAPS

SECOND EDITION REVISED AND CORRECTED

London

EYRE AND SPOTTISWOODE

1896

LONDON:
EYRE AND SPOTTISWOODE
Her Majesty's Printers

CONTENTS.

CHAPTER I

CHAPTER II.

CHAPTER III.

CHAPTER IV.

a 2

CHAPTER X.

CHAPTER XI

CHAPTER- XII.

CHAPTER XIII.

CHAPTER XIX.

CHAPTER XX.

CHAPTER XXI.

CHAPTER XXII.

PLATES.

PREFACE

SECOND EDITION.

In preparing the first edition of this History, notwithstanding all my efforts to bring the work within moderate compass, it grew into a ponderous volume, and a costly one. In the present issue, whilst preserving all the essentials of the original, I have so reduced its size, and lessened its price, as to place it within the reach of all. Slight errors in the text have been corrected; some recently acquired information added to the notes; and, in order to bring the History up to date, a concluding chapter has been written on the events of the year 1895, and the future prospects of the Colony.

The publication of this new edition gives me an opportunity of performing two very pleasant tasks, to record the advance and prosperity of the Colony during the past year. and to thank my reviewers everywhere for the generous praise they have bestowed upon my first attempt at authorship. I thank them not only for myself, but on behalf of my fellow colonists; the kindly notice they have taken of my volume is not so much due to any small merits in the work, it is far more the expression of kindly interest so universally felt for England's most ancient Colony, whose sad eventful history I have endeavoured truthfully to relate.

In the introduction to my first edition I mentioned the friendly helpers who assisted me in its preparation; in the present volume I wish briefly to record my thanks to those who aided me in its publication.

b

My friend Mr. Edmund Gosse's graceful introductory note gained many readers. Mrs. John Richard Green, the eminent historian, and the late Right Hon. Sir John Cowell, K.C.B., Master of the Household, a distinguished scholar, and one of the Queen's most trusted advisers, gave me great encouragement and most welcome sympathy. I am under deep obligations to my gentle critics, Mr. and Mrs. A. R. Whiteway, and the most efficient of Private Secretaries, my friend and guide in literary London, H. F. Wilson. I have also to thank Lord Ripon, the officials of the Colonial Office, Sir Henry G. Bergne, K.C.M.G., and the Librarian of the Foreign Office, for much courtesy.

The Government of Newfoundland have given liberal assistance in the production of both editions. The responsibility of seeing the work through the press has been undertaken by my son, G. R. F. Prowse. To my fellow Newfoundlanders who have given my History such a cordial reception, and especially to those who have bought the book, my best thanks are due.

D. W. P.

St. John's, July, 1896.

CHAPTER I.

THE PRE-COLUMBIAN DISCOVERY OF AMERICA.

THE history of America is a modern history. Authentic annals of the New World cover only four centuries, and commence from its discovery by Columbus in 1492. Prior to this great and ever-memorable adventure, there are stories of voyages, islands, discoveries, allusions in Aristotle, Plato, and Seneca to a great country dimly seen beyond the western ocean. Nearly every European country had some such obscure tradition ; the Spanish Basques, the Bretons, the Italians, with their story of the brothers Zeno, the Irish Saint Brendan, the trip across the Atlantic of a Welsh prince in a ship of glass, with an able crew of twelve harpers,—all these stories are interesting and romantic, some, perhaps, authentic, at present, however, they lie outside the sober domain of history, in the dim regions of myth and fable

The Atlantic voyages of the Northmen stand on quite a different footing Mixed up with a shadowy mythology we have a large portion of real history. The discovery of North America by the Icelanders in the tenth and eleventh centuries of our era is now recognised by scholars as being as true and well ascertained as the landing of William the Conqueror in England, 1066. The Icelanders claim to have discovered Greenland[1] in 982. Here they established a number of settlements,

[1] In the year 834 the Norwegians were acquainted with a country in the north called Groneland, commonly called *Old Greenland,* to distinguish it from Spitzbergen. In the charter of the Emperor Ludovicus Pius to St Ansgharius, first Archbishop of Hamburg, dated 834, published by Lindenbrogius in 1706 (p. 125), (which also includes Adam of Bremen's work) we read —"We make known to the present and future sons of God's Holy Church that, in our days, by the divine grace, a door is opened for preaching the Gospel in the northern regions, viz , Denmark, Sweden, Norway, *Greenland,* Halingalandon [most probably Lapland], Iceland, and Scredevindon [no doubt Finland] "

Pope Gregory varies the names of some of these northern people who were included in this new diocese so much that some can scarcely be recognised now The Danish Chronicle, it seems, makes Groneland to have been discovered as early as 770 , but according to the Iceland Chronicle, not before 982 it being by this last account peopled by a Norwegian who had fled to Iceland The

built churches, forts, and houses.   Most minute particulars about these
are given in the saga of Eric Raude or Red.   Dr. Rinke, in his History
of Greenland, says :—

> "In a country where no tree can grow, the faintest trace of former buildings
> can be made out. . . . . Kakortok Church contains three separate entrances;
> the principal one is covered with very large flat regular stone, measuring about
> twelve feet in length.   In the opposite or eastern wall is a window most skilfully
> arched, but apparently likewise constructed from rough stones."

About a hundred places have been found scattered along the coast

of Greenland, and these
localities can be identi-
fied by reference to the
ancient sagas.

The daring character
of the Northmen is
shown by the fact that
in their small crazy
craft they made Arctic
voyages.   Four miles
beyond Uppernavick,
at Kingitoarsuk, a stone
has been found with a
Runic inscription, stat-
ing that it was raised
by Erling, the son of
Sigvat, and Enride
Oddsven, in 1133.

When these ad-
venturous Northmen
reached Greenland, the
most eastern part of
North America, their
discovery of Labrador

STATUE OF ERIC IN BOSTON, ERECTED BY PROF. HORSFORD.

and Newfoundland would certainly follow.   The first north-easter would
drive their small unweatherly vessels on to the coasts of Labrador.
Their finding North America is not only inherently probable, but is
proved to us absolutely by the direct testimonies of the ecclesiastical
historian Adam of Bremen and of Oderic Vital, and by a brief of Pope

writers of both chronicles, it is evident, had
no knowledge of the charters of the Pope and
Emperor. In 1070, Adam of Bremen says
that Albert Archbishop of Hamburg sent
missionaries to Greenland and to other parts;
his geography is very obscure for Nineteenth-
Century students.   The Danish and Norwegian Histories give 1348 as the year in
which the colony of Greenland was lost.—I
am indebted to Mr. Reddan for this note.

Nicholas V., dated 1448, addressed to two bishops of Iceland urging them to take measures for the support of the Church in Greenland. Adam of Bremen, who died in 1076, wrote a history of the diocese of Hamburg and Bremen between A.D. 988 and 1072. He mentions the names of Green-land bishops and the discovery of Vinland by the Icelanders.

Gudrid, the widow of Thor-finn Karlsefne, one of the most distinguished of the Icelandic explorers of America, actually visited Rome on a pilgrimage after the death of her husband, about 1028 or 1030.

Beyond stat-ing these brief facts, it does not concern our His-tory further to dwell upon the pre - Columbian voyages. In

MAP OF THE ICELANDER STEPHANIUS, 1570.[2]

From Torfaeus' "Gronlandia Antiqua," 1706.

America the colonisation of the Icelanders entirely disappeared—"like the baseless fabric of a vision, left not a rack behind." Their transitory occupation left no result or influence on the New World, of which they were the first European settlers.[1]

---

[1] In the *Studies on the Vineland Voyages,* by Gustav Storm, *Memoires de la Société Royale des Antiquaires du Nord,* 1888, New-foundland is recognised as the "Markland" of the Sagas. There is an interesting article by Sir D. Wilson, LL.D., *The Vineland of the Northmen,* in the *Trans. of Royal Society of Canada,* vol. viii., sec. ii., p. 109.

[2] The strong resemblance between the Greenland of this map, J. de la Cosa's, and Ruysch's, point to some common source, either Norse or English, prior to, or as the result of, Cabot's voyage; more likely the former. A. "This is where the English have come, and has a name for barrenness, either from sun or cold." B. "This is near where Vinland lies which . . . . . is called good. Our countrymen [Icelanders] have thought that to the south it ends with the wild sea, and that a sound separates it from America." C. "Land of the giants." For other references *see* WINSOR'S *N. & C. H. of America,* I., 130.

CHAPTER II.

REIGN OF HENRY VII.

1485–1509.

1492 —First voyage of Columbus; sailed 3rd August, discovered America 12th October, 1492

1496.—On the Petition of John Cabot, a patent granted on 5th March by King Henry VII to him and his sons to discover new lands

1497 —John Cabot's voyage in the ship *Matthew*, of Bristol discovered North America and Newfoundland, sailed from Bristol 2nd May, returned 6th August, grant of £10 on 10th August to the discoverer of the new island; letters on 23rd August from Pasqualigo, also on 24th August and 18th December from Soncino, describing the voyage. Same year, Vasco de Gama, Portuguese navigator, doubled Cape of Good Hope, Africa. Pension of £20 per annum to John Cabot on revenues of Bristol on 13th December, passed Great Seal, 28th January 1498

1498 —Warrant on 3rd February to John Cabot to take up six ships, Cabot sailed along the east coast of North America; arrived home with a cargo of fur and fish, probably in June 1499. Possible exploration of Newfoundland by an independent English expedition anticipating Cabot's arrival on part of the coast Loans to Carter, Thirkill, and Bradley on 22nd March and 1st April by Henry VII Letter on 25th July from Puebla and Ayala to the Spanish Sovereigns announcing departure of Cabot's second expedition.

1500.—Gaspar Cortereal, a Portuguese, probably made a voyage to America; his patent is dated 12th May, it refers to former unsuccessful explorations Juan de la Cosa's map

1501 —English progress southwards mentioned in Hojeda's charter. 19th March, Charter from Henry VII to Richard Warde, John Thomas, John Fernandez, &c for ten years, Portuguese, being aliens, to be charged extra duties. Authentic voyage of Cortereal, sailed on 15th May to the Labrador coast; fifty natives brought home on 8th October; King of Portugal said they were the best slaves he had seen, Cortereal never returned, letters from Lisbon on 17th, 18th, 19th October by Cantino and Pasqualigo about the expedition

1502 —Grant on 7th January to Bristol men that found "Thistle" Grant on 15th January to Miguel Cortereal, who fitted out an expedition to search for his brother; probably sailed on 10th May; Miguel never returned Three Indians at the Court of Henry VII Cantino's map of Cortereal's voyage, 19th November 9th December, Charter to Ashenhurst, Fernando, Eliot, and Gonzalo for forty years, freedom from duties for five years, &c , alien clause omitted.

. .1503 —Further expedition in search of the Cortereals. Grant on 30th September to Bristol merchants who have been in the Newfoundland, and to one who brought hawkes from thence

1504 —Probable date of the French expedition to Cape Breton Grant on 8th April to an English priest going to the New Island. A number of French, Breton and Norman, English and Portuguese vessels resorting to the Newfoundland fishery. From this period onward, for a hundred years following, Newfoundland was visited every year by an annually increasing number of English, French, and Portuguese fishermen, subsequently also by Spaniards.

1505 —Popyngais and cats brought from Newfoundland

1506 —Jean Denys of Harfleur fishing in Newfoundland

1508 —Ruysch—first engraved map showing America Aubert, pilot of Dieppe, voyaged to Newfoundland, brought back two Indians Act severing Fish and Stock-fishmonger's Companies.

The latter part of the fifteenth century forms one of the great epochs of history, the veritable renaissance, the new birth of the world. At this period begins the history of America, the modern history of England, and practically the present history of Europe.

Many remarkable events combined to make this age illustrious; the invention of printing, the general use of gunpowder and artillery in war, and the capture of Constantinople by the Turks. This last event put to flight numerous Greek scholars, who bore their precious manuscripts to Italy, and thus inaugurated the new learning—commenced in England by an Oxford scholar, Grocyn, bringing Greek writings to his ancient university.

HENRY VII.
From an engraving after contemporary portrait.

The advent of Henry Tudor to the Throne, his marriage with the beautiful Elizabeth of York, the destruction or impoverishment of the great feudal houses in the Wars of the Roses, combined with the vigorous manner in which the astute Henry curtailed their power, effaced them for ever as the promoters of domestic war. In place of robber barons and the bloody civil feuds they fomented, for the first time there appears conspicuous upon the stage of our modern history the power of the commoner, the merchant princes of England, and the sure growth of commerce.

But of all the causes, great and powerful, working at this wonderful period for the progress of the world, undoubtedly the greatest influence of all was the daring maritime enterprise which simultaneously discovered

CARAVELS OF COLUMBUS.
After drawings in the Spanish Admiralty Office.

New Continents in both East and West. The immediate effect was a great expansion of thought, a great stirring up of the imagination, all wonderful things seemed possible to the generation that found a New World. The discovery of America by Columbus, and the doubling of the Cape of Good Hope by Vasco de Gama, gave the Old World new Europes in Asia, Africa, America, and subsequently Australia.

The voyage of Columbus is one of the grandest events in history. it doubled the habitable portion of the globe, and gave Europe new fields for enterprise Columbus believed the lands he had discovered were a part of Asia, and it took nearly three more centuries to map out the whole configuration of America

The life of the great Genoese sailor is, and always will be, the grandest romance of history, age cannot wither it, time cannot stale it, nothing can lessen the importance of this splendid achievement As the brilliancy of a splendid jewel is enhanced by its fine setting, so the picturesque story of the great Italian navigator, devoted son of the Church, the last of the crusaders, has been set in a halo of glory by the most brilliant writers of our age

The tale is ever fresh and delightful, whether set forth in the graceful pages of Irving, the terse pellucid English of Helps, or the grand sonorous Castilian of Emilio Castelar

The world has lately been ringing with his praises, the critics have fought over his forty portraits, and the dozen Islands, scene of his veritable landfall.

. Alas ! for the glory of our Island, for the praise of our discoverer, there are no portraits to discuss, no noble Isabella la Catolica, no devoted friar. No golden haze of romance surrounds our earliest annals The story of the discovery of Newfoundland and North America, as told by the Cabots, is as dull as the log of a dredge-boat Every picturesque element is eliminated from it, and the great voyage, so pregnant with moral and material results, is brought down to the low level of a mere trading adventure But though the tale is dull, and still shrouded in mystery, it must remain one of the greatest events in history, it gave North America to the English by indefeasible right of discovery How different might have been the future of this great Continent— the home of nearly seventy millions—where, under orderly and settled government, freedom broadens slowly down—where mighty industry and bright intelligence have built up one of the richest, fairest, and freest lands the sun ever shone upon ? What might have been our destiny had Columbus, not Cabot with his West of England sailors, discovered Northern America ? Heaven only knows what would have been our fate—possibly a great Spanish possession, with chronic revolutions, disordered finances, pronunciamentos, half-breeds, and fusillades.

Until quite recently the history of the discovery of North America by the English could not be written It is not derived from English records It can now, however, be told with a fair degree of accuracy, thanks to the labours of Rawdon Brown and other eminent scholars We derive our main facts from the Calendars of Venice, and that great mine of history, the Archives of Simancas, in Spain. John

Cabot was a Genoese navigator and merchant adventurer, experienced and skilled in all the nautical knowledge of those days. Italy—home of art, science, literature, commerce, and navigation—gave to Spain, France, and England Columbus, Verrazano, and Cabot. Very few facts are known about John Cabot's life; he was made a citizen of Venice in 1476; he had been to Mecca, where he saw the caravans arriving from the far East with spices, &c. The date of his arrival in England is uncertain. Stachey says, in 1496 he was naturalized ("idenized"), and living within Blackfriars, probably only while he was pressing his suit at Court

VENICE ABOUT 1620.[1]
From an old print.

There was an important colony of Italian merchants and money lenders in London during this reign, who may have helped our explorer with the king; Lombard Street perpetuates their memory. All that we do know positively is that Giovanni Gabotto, or Cabotta, or Gabote (anglicised into John Cabot), some time before 1496, was living in Bristol, then the chief city of the West. At this period Bristol did a large trade with Iceland, exchanging the famous West of England cloth, hats, caps, hosiery, and small wares for Iceland[2] stock-fish. The grand old church, St. Mary's Redcliffe, still bears testimony to the munificence of her princely merchant, William Canynge.

The city[3] had twice given Henry VII. a cordial reception, and the king looked with favourable eyes on her merchants. Some years before the discovery, Cabot was brought under the notice of the sovereign, and employed in negotiating with the King of Denmark about the English trade with Iceland.[4] Doubtless, on his voyages to the island, the shrewd, clever Italian sailor would hear all about

[1] It is just possible that Lion's Den, in Bonavista Bay, is the place where Cabot erected the arms of Venice, the winged lion, on his first voyage.

[2] See Appendix, p. 24, THE ICELAND FISHERY.

[3] Henry IV. had given exemptions to Bristol from certain dues, and a separate

Admiralty jurisdiction, on account of the many voyages undertaken by her merchants and the great expense they had incurred.

[4] ANSPACH'S *History of Newfoundland*, 1819, p. 25. I have not been able to trace Anspach's authority, but there is no reason to doubt the accuracy of the statement.

the Icelandic expeditions to America. In 1493, when Columbus returned from his famous voyage, "All men at the Court of Henry VII.," says Sebastian Cabot, "affirmed it to be a thing more divine than "human to sail by the West to the East." Cabot approached the King with a Petition for discovering new lands :—

"To the king, our sovereigne Lord. Please it your Highnes of your most noble and habundant grace to graunt unto John Cabotto citizen of Venes Lewes, Sebastyan and Sancto his sonneys your gracious letters patentes under your grete sele in due forme to be made according to the tenour hereafter ensuying [the draft charter is lost] and they shall during their lyves pray God for the prosperous continuance of your most noble and Royale Estate, long to enduer."

This is the earliest document definitely connecting England with the New World. William of Wyrcester and Ayala do indeed mention voyages made at the expense of Bristol in 1480, and from 1491 to 1496, but if they bore any results they were kept secret.

The records tell us that the monarch gave him very little encouragement. At last, however, through the influence of the Bristol merchants, he was prevailed on to grant the Genoese a charter, but solely on the condition that he was to have a royal share of the profits, but on no account to bear any of

SEAL OF HENRY VII.

the expenses. It is dated 5th March 1496 (11th year of the reign) :—

" Henry by the Grace of God, &c., &c. . . . Be it known to all, that we have given and granted to our well-beloved John Cabot, citizen of Venice, and to Lewis, Sebastian and Sanctus, sons of the said John, and to their heirs and deputies, full authority, &c., &c., . . . to sail to all parts, countries and seas of the East, of the West and of the North, under our banner and ensigns, with five ships, and to set up our banner on any new-found-land, as our vassals and lieutenants . . . upon their own proper costs and charges, to seek out and discover whatsoever isles . . . of the heathen and infidels, which before the time have been unknown to all Christians . . . to pay to us the fifth part of the capital gain so gotten for every then voyage; and to return to the port of Bristol."

Cabot, like a wise man, inserted the names of his sons in order to extend the duration of the charter to the full extent of their young lives, but there is no record to show that any of them accompanied him

On the second of May 1497 John Cabot set sail from Bristol on his famous voyage, accompanied by a Burgundian and sixteen English sailors, in a little West of England vessel, about fifty tons, called the *Matthew* We read —

"This year (1497) on St John the Baptist's Day, the land of America was found by the merchants of Bristowe, in a ship of Bristowe called the *Matthew*, the which said ship departed from the port of Bristowe the 2nd of May, and came home again 6th of August following " [1]

We can picture to ourselves the scene as the brave little ship leaves the Avon, and the wind fills her broad lug sails as she rounds the picturesque coast of North Devon on a fair day in the shining month of May, and steers down the Irish sea, and then on to the great waste of waters and the far unknown ocean. What were the hopes and prospects of the bold Italian navigator and his little crew of sturdy English sailors ? Most likely he argued, " My countryman has found land at the south " of this great western sea   The Icelanders found it on the north   It is all " part of Asia. I will strike it somewhere, sailing west " Many writers consider that John Cabot could not have made the voyage out and home in so short a time   I cannot see the force of the argument. Easterly winds generally prevail in the North Atlantic in early May   Given a fair wind, these little vessels, with their flat floors, and broad lug sails, could easily go five to six knots before the wind. Fifty-three days out from Bristol to Newfoundland, and forty-two days home, would not be a record-breaking passage, even for those days   We learn from Soncino, that on this voyage Cabot first sailed around Ireland, then towards the north, and finally steered west   On the 24th June, at early morn, an inscription on the Cabot map says, they first sighted the New World

There has been much learned discussion regarding this landfall, and after the whole matter has been thoroughly threshed out, there is no absolute certainty as to the exact point first seen   Strong arguments have been put forward in favour of Labrador by Mr J P. Howley, F R.G S, and others. The inscription on the map of 1544, attributed to Sebastian Cabot,[2] has led many writers to place the landfall at Cape Breton, but

---

[1] *Fust MSS, Hull Court, Gloucestershire.* See *Encl. Brit*, 9th edit., vol iv, p. 350 The word America shows it is not a contemporary document, and its genuineness has been doubted.

[2] The Cabot mappemonde is now in the Paris National Library; it came from Germany. M. Harrisse suggests that S. Cabot placed the English landfall on Cape Breton when the French had begun to colonise

there is no other evidence to support this claim, in fact it is at variance with contemporary accounts of the voyage, and the inferences to be drawn from the earliest maps

In this colony an unbroken tradition points to Cape Bonavista, Newfoundland, as the first land seen[1] This tradition is confirmed by an English map of Newfoundland made by John Mason, a distinguished captain in the Royal Navy of England about 1616; opposite to Cape Bonavista he writes these words, probably copying the wording of an older map : "*First found by Cabot*"—"*A Caboto primum reperta*"[2] On this ground, and for other reasons, as a Newfoundlander, I claim for Cape Bonavista the honour of being the first land seen in North America. In all probability, St John's was also discovered either on Cabot's first or second voyage[3]

It is possible that although John Cabot discovered Cape Bonavista, he did not so name it. Some of the Portuguese associated in 1501 with Eliot's company were from the Azores, and may have called the headland after Bonavista in the Cape de Verd Islands; but against this

Canada in order to gain the favour of the English and secure his return, and that his call in 1547 was the result of this piece of duplicity ; the map could not have been published much before 1546. Mr Justin Winsor, the American historian, says "The map, in its confused nomenclature and antiquated geographical notions throughout, indicates that the draft was made by a 'prentice hand—probably by some Italian map fabricator"

Two things are quite clear, the landfall of Cabot was either on the Labrador or Eastern Newfoundland coast, and this map is not the original one made by John Cabot

[1] " Bonavista ! Oh ! good sight !" is the natural exclamation the old Italian might make, as after his long and dangerous voyage he first caught sight of land, bright and green with the springing grass of June. There is no other cape with the same name on the eastern shore of North America.

Cortereal struck this part of the coast on his voyages, and, curiously enough, Cartier made Cape Bonavista on his first voyage (1534). Sailing vessels coming to Newfoundland from Northern Europe nearly always sight Cape Bonavista. Supposing Cabot to be steering towards Labrador, he would meet ice and run south, and be very likely to make in with the land at this point, or even without meeting the ice the Labrador current would drag his vessel south Tradition, probability, and the certain evidence of Mason's map of Newfoundland, made 278 years ago, demonstrate almost to a certainty Cape Bonavista as the landfall of John Cabot. Cape Race—Capo Rasso, Cape Spear—Cabo Spera or Espera, Bonavista and Bonaventura, are among the earliest names on ancient maps

The Reverend George Paterson furnishes very valuable information concerning the Portuguese explorations, and their attempted settlement in Cape Breton I think his enthusiasm carries him rather far when he makes out nearly all the names on our east coast as Portuguese Conception Bay is so, but *Buonavista* is distinctly Italian (so is *Buona Ventura*—good find! lucky hit!) In Spanish it would be *Buena Vista* ; in Portuguese *Boa Vista*. *Raso* is also Italian, it means shaved, cut off—an excellent description of our famous headland The English word razor is from the same source Cabot made at least two voyages to Newfoundland, he was a skilled seaman and map-maker, and though the originals of his maps have all disappeared, there can be no doubt that he made a running survey of the coast, named the headlands, and marked them on charts. The *King* map, 1502, is the earliest to contain a name that has survived (unless the supposition that the Cape English of J de la Cosa and modern maps are identical is correct) ; its Capo Raso is distinctly Italian, although the map was probably made in Portugal, thus showing strong presumptive evidence of its being copied from a Cabotian chart.

[2] *See p* 106

[3] I feel convinced Cabot saw our capital in all its primitive beauty, the bold outlines of the surrounding hills clothed to the water's edge with the dark verdure of the forest, it must have been a beautiful scene, his navigator's eye would specially note its unique value as a land-locked harbour, the most perfect of its kind in the world

argument is the fact that in most Portuguese maps Bonavista does not appear, whilst in the map of Gaspar Viegas in 1534 it is given as *Boavista*, a translation into Portuguese from the original Italian *Buonavista*. Viegas and others appear to have received the name from sailors on the coast, and not from the geographers

On his return to England, August 6th, 1497, the old Venetian navigator was received with great rejoicing. On the 23rd of August, seventeen days after his arrival, Pasqualigo, a Venetian in London, writing to his brother in Venice, says ·—

" The English run after him like mad. His name is Zuan Cabot, and they call him the great Admiral " [1]

The most interesting account of the voyage is contained in an amusing letter from Raimondo di ¦Soncino, London, to the Duke of Milan, 18th December 1497 :—

" The king has gained a great part of Asia without a stroke of the sword. In this kingdom is a popular Venetian called Zoanne Caboto, a man of considerable ability, most skilful in navigation, who having seen the most serene kings, first him of Portugal, then him of Spain, that they had occupied unknown islands, thought to make a similar acquisition for His Majesty [Henry VII]. And having obtained the royal privileges which gave him the use of the land found by him, provided the right of possession was reserved to the Crown, he departed in a little ship from Bristol with 18 persons, who placed their fortunes with him. Passing Ibernia [Ireland] more to the west, and then ascending towards the north, he began to navigate the eastern part of the ocean, leaving for some days the north to the right hand, and having wandered enough he came at last to firm land, where he planted the royal banners, took possession for his Highness, made certain marks, and returned

" The said Messer Zoanne, as he is a foreigner and poor, would not be believed if his partners who are all Englishmen, and from Bristol, did not testify to the truth of what he tells. This Messer Zoanne has the description of the world in a chart, and also in a solid globe which he has made, *and he shows where he landed;* and that going toward the east he passed considerably beyond the country of the Tanais . . The sea is full of fish which are taken not only with the net but also with a basket in which a stone is put so that the basket may plunge into water . . And the Englishmen, his partners, say that they can bring so many fish that the kingdom will have no more business with Islanda [Iceland], and that from this country *there will be a very great trade in the fish they call stock fish*

" They say, now they know where to go, the voyage will not take more than 15 days if fortune favours them after leaving Ibernia. . . . The Admiral, as Messer Zoanne is already styled, has given his companion, a Burgundian, an island, and has also given another to his barber, a Genoese, and they regard themselves as Counts, and my lord the Admiral as a Prince. And I believe that some poor Italian friars will go on the voyage, who have the promise of being Bishops. And I, being a friend of the Admiral, if I wished to go, could have an Archbishoprick." [2]

[1] *Venetian Calendars,* i. 262.
[2] This letter, in the State archives of   Milan, was first published in 1865 in the *Annuario Scientifico*

The king does not seem to have been much moved by the enthusiasm of his subjects In an entry in the Privy Purse expenses of the monarch, this item is found · "August 10th, 1497 To hym that found the new isle, 10*l*." [1] This may have been paid to the great Admiral, though more probably it was a gratuity to the sailor who first sighted land However, on the 13th December of the same year, a pension of 20*l*. a year was granted to John Cabot, payable half-yearly. This was sealed on the 28th January following (1498) On the 3rd of February 1498, the following warrant was issued to John Cabot —

" To all Men to whom theis presentes shall come greting Know ye that We of our Grace especiale and dyvers causes us moving, We have given and granten, and by these presents géve and graunte, to our well beloved John Kabotto, the Venecian, sufficiente auctorite and power that he by him, his Deputie or Deputies, sufficient may take at his pleasure VI Englishe shipes in any Porte or Portes, or other places within this, our Realme of England or Obeisance, so that, and if the said shippes be of the burthen of CC tonnes, or under, with their apparail requisite and necessarie for the safe conduct of the said shippes, and them convey and leade to the *Londe and Isles of late founde by the said John*, in our name and by our commandment Paying for them and every of them as if we should in or for our own cause pay and none otherwise."

This would enable him to take up six ships on the same terms as if for the use of the Royal Navy, but he has still to pay for them himself, and even the noble pension of 20*l* is to be taken out of the revenue of Bristol, not from the king's own ample means. In the spring of the next year (1498) John Cabot went on a second voyage Mindful of the immense quantities of fish seen about our island on the first voyage, other masters also came out this year provided with fishing gear and fishermen, from the following Records we learn that Bristol and London merchants fitted out ships with hats, caps, and hosiery, and the famous West of England blankets and cloth, to barter and trade ; also, that some money was received from the king, probably by way of loan ·—

" 1498 —This year one Sebastian Gaboto, a Genoa's son, born in Bristow, . . caused the king to man and victual a ship at Bristow to search for an island which he knew to be replenished with rich commodities In the ship divers merchants of London adventured small stocks, and in the company of this ship sailed also out of Bristow three or four small ships fraught with sleight and grosse wares, as coarse cloth, caps, laces, points, and such other." [2]

" April 1st, 1498, a reward of £2 to James Carter, for going to the new isle."

" To Lanslot Thirkill, of London, upon a prest for his shipp going towards the new Ilande, 22nd March, 1498, £20."

" Delivered to Launcelot Tirkill going towards the New Ile in prest £20."

" April 1st, 1498, to Thomas Bradley and Launcelot Thirkill, going to the new Isle, £30." [3]

---

[1] BENTLEY'S *Excerpta Historica*, 1831, p 113

[2] STOWE'S *Annales*, 1615, p. 482.

[3] BENTLEY'S *Excerpta Historica*, p. 116.

In 1500 we have unmistakeable evidence from Spanish sources of English discoveries, in the map of Juan de la Cosa.[1] Cape Race, or, possibly, Cape English, in St. Mary's Bay, is represented by the "Cavo de Ynglaterra" ("English Cape"); further west on the same map is an inscription, "Mar descubierta por Ingleses" ("Sea discovered by the English"). This map probably shows the results of Cabot's second voyage.[2]

The pension and warrant are the last records of the famous explorer, John Cabot. He utterly disappears from history about this period; whether he died or left England, we cannot tell.[3] He discovered a new continent, and no man knows his grave.

In March 1501 John Cabot's patent seems to have been cancelled, and a new charter granted to three substantial merchants — Thomas Ashenhurst, Richard Warde, and John Thomas, and three Portuguese from the Azores — John Gonzalo and John and Francis Fernando. In December of the

The Custom-house upon ẏ Back of Bristoll

Quæ Cæsaris sunt Cæsari.

CUSTOM HOUSE, BRISTOL.
From Millerd's Map, 1671.

---

[1] JUAN DE LA COSA was a distinguished Biscayan navigator and geographer, native of Santoña. In the list of the crew of Columbus' vessel — the *Santa Maria* — he is mentioned as "Maestre," or "Sailing Master." He was a member of the celebrated Contractation House of Seville for the promotion of navigation and the examination and the licensing of pilots for the Indies.

[2] Pedro de Ayala's letter about this voyage is given at p. 29.

[3] According to the Spanish writers, John Cabot was a kind of second-class Columbus, and had been both to Lisbon and Seville trying to get aid for his scheme of Transatlantic discovery. They admit, however, that there is no very reliable authority for this statement. It is very likely that he may have been in these cities many times in the course of his regular business as a merchant. As the originator, probably, of great-circle sailing, John Cabot showed himself a man of great originality, no mere servile imitator of Columbus; he noticed also the variation of the compass. The knowledge of these two facts seems to have constituted the life-long stock-in-trade of his son Sebastian. It is suggested by Bristol writers that Cathay Street commemorates the voyages of Cabot.

same year another patent was drawn out in favour of Hugh Eliot
and Ashenhurst, and two Portuguese—John Gonzalo and Francis Fernando.   This new charter gave the patentees the very largest powers, and

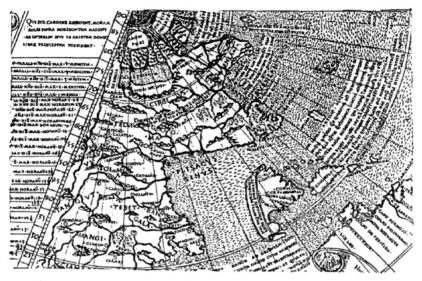

RUYSCH'S MAP, 1508.[1]

From the Ptolemy published at Rome, 1508.

a monopoly of trade to the new land for forty years.   There is a special
reservation in favour of the King of Portugal,[2] whose subjects we shall
find, later on, were the most friendly and liberal to Gilbert.   As far as
we can learn, Henry's charters for the new isle were so much waste
paper.

In the year 1501 we have an account of the first Portuguese voyage
to North America, made by the noble and intrepid navigator, Gaspar
Cortereal.   He came on this coast with a charter from the King of
Portugal to possess the land, and for many years after his death his
relatives held the hereditary title of Governor of Terra Nova.[3]   The
accounts of the first voyages, in which he sailed along the Greenland

[1] This is the first engraved map to show
Newfoundland. Ruysch says he sailed to
the new country in an English ship; he has
been thought to be the Burgundian who went
in Cabot's first voyage; this map, however,
was composed, it is evident, at a somewhat
later period.

[2] Possibly the Portuguese granted Eng-

lishmen freedom to trade in the Brazils and
elsewhere in exchange for the right of fishing
in Newfoundland.

[3] Spain and Portugal claimed the new
world as their own; they looked upon the
English as poachers on their preserves. Pope
Alexander VI., in 1493, drew a line of demar-
cation 100 leagues west from the Azores and

coast and made this island and Labrador, are shadowy His voyage in 1501 is given by Pasqualigo, the Venetian Ambassador, and Alberto Cantino. Two of his vessels brought home fifty or sixty natives The king was much pleased with the description of the country, on account of the timber, and he said the captives—probably Montagnais —were the best slaves he had ever seen The daring Gaspar was lost on the Labrador coast.

The Rev. George Patterson, in his very able and learned paper—"A Lost Chapter in American History"—informs us that —

"Immediately after Gaspar Cortereal's first voyage—1500 or 1501—fishing companies were formed in Viana, Aveiro, and Terceira, Portugal, for the purpose of founding establishments in Terra Nova In 1506 the King of Portugal gave orders that all fishermen returning from Newfoundland should pay a tenth part of their profits at the Custom House. At different times Aveiro alone had 60 vessels sailing to Newfoundland, and in 1550 150 fishing vessels. Equal numbers sailing from Oporto and other ports, gave a large increase of revenue." [1]

This is not the only or, to us, the most important of the "lost chapters" of our history. As regards England's share in this great Transatlantic codfishery, most writers have declared that, for the first half of the sixteenth century—from 1500 to 1560—there were no English fishermen or traders in Newfoundland As I read the testimony of the Records, this is absolutely an incorrect view of history. The silence of historians on such a subject is no evidence whatever. Such a vulgar subject as the fishery and fishermen was quite beneath the dignity of history The annals of the kingdom were the acts of princes. The destiny of nations was truly, in these times, the sport of kings; consequently, we have every vagary, religious and matrimonial, of Henry the VIIIth, the cut of Elizabeth's ruffs, and the colour of her petticoats, while there is not a word about the daring fishermen who left little obscure western ports to found our Colonial Empire The public—the common people who formed the British nation—seem to be entirely

Cape Verde Islands, measured from a point midway between the two ; all west of this line to belong to Spain, all east to Portugal It is doubtful whether the Pope originally intended to grant the Peninsular Powers territory in America north of Spanish latitudes, especially when we consider that England was still a Roman Catholic country and friendly with Spain ; certainly by his charters Henry VII repudiated any such interpretation, perhaps the divorce of Catherine and Henry's quarrel with the Pope caused the Spanish to claim all America west of the line I think the Portuguese claimed our island at first under pretence of prior discovery, and not by virtue of the Papal decision. In the earlier maps Newfoundland was placed much too far to the east to come within the Portuguese jurisdiction. Ribero, the Spanish official cartographer, gives Greenland only to the English, whilst our island is marked Tiera Nova de Cortereal, and the United States as Tiera de Esteva Gomez In the Maiollo map our island is marked Cortereal In the fine map of Mercator (1569) we have much fuller geographical information, and the Portuguese and Spanish pretensions as owners of the whole new world are no longer maintained

[1] Trans. Royal Society of Canada, vol. viii, sec. ii, p 145, 1890. The Portuguese on the north-east coast of America, &c, by Rev. G. PATTERSON, D D.

ignored. Take the very latest English Histories on the Tudor Period, and you will find about three lines on the discovery of North America and a hundred pages devoted to Anne Boleyn The true history of the period can only be found in the Records and the grand old Acts of Parliament It is on the undoubted evidence of these ancient documents that I base my argument that England governed Newfoundland and participated in her fishery continuously from the earliest period. It is certain that Cabot made two, if not three voyages, and that the second was partly for trading. The following entries show that there were English or Anglo-Portuguese trading voyages to the new isle in the first years of the sixteenth century —

"1502, January 7.—To men of Bristoll that founde Thisle, £5

"1502, Sep. 30.—To the merchants of Bristoll that have bene in the Newe-founde Launde, £20

"17th Nov. 1503 —To one that brought haukes from the Newfounde Island, £1

"8th April 1504 —To a Preste that goeth to the New Islande, £2" [1]

"1505, 25 August —To Clays going to Richmond with wylde catts and popyngays of the Newfound Island for his costs 13/4

"25 September [?] —To Portzugales that brought popyngais and catts of the mountaigne with other stuf to the kinges grace [2]

"This year [3] (1502) were brought unto the king three men taken in ye Newfound Islands by Sebastian Gabote before-named, in Anno Domini 1498 These men were clothed in beast skins and eate raw flesh, but spake such a language as no man could understand, of the which three men two of them were seen in the king's court, at Westminster, two yeeres after They were clothed like Englishmen, and could not be discerned from Englishmen." [4]

We have further proof that the West of England was foremost in these enterprises Will anyone for a moment believe that these Devonshire fishermen—the most pugnacious and pertinacious race in all the three kingdoms—ever entered upon a most profitable business and then gave it up? This argument, strong as it may appear to anyone acquainted with West Countrymen, is not all or even the strongest proof, the unanswerable argument is contained in the Acts of Henry VIII, 1541, and Edward VI, 1548 (referred to in my next chapter), where the Newfoundland fishery is classed with old-established trades like the Iceland and Orkney fisheries Then we have the statements of Hayes and Parkhurst about the ancient and established rule of the English in the Colony How could it be established or ancient if English fishermen were absent from Newfoundland from 1500 to 1560? A late

[1] BENTLEY's *Historia Excerpta*, 1831, pp 126, 129, 131, 133

[2] Cf *M[onte] de Gatto* in the Maiollo map, and the numerous Cat Bays, &c on our coast This animal was the Canadian lynx, called in Newfoundland "wild cat" it was very common in the early days, and Head-Constable O'Reilly informs me they are still abundant on the west coast Popinjay is from a Portuguese word, "papagayo," for a bright-coloured bird, probably an owl or hawk, these birds are very abundant on the island, and in great variety,

[3] It is generally thought that these natives were brought over in 1502, and that Sebastian Cabot's name was an erroneous interpolation of some late transcriber

[4] STOW's *Annales*, 1615, p. 485.

English writer—J A Doyle—"The English in America," speaks of the English sailors of this time as "jeopardizing their lives on the dreary " coast of Labrador, and bringing home strange birds and savage men " to amuse the citizens of London" Does Mr. Doyle suppose the Devonshire fishermen let the French and Portuguese reap all the benefits of this splendid and profitable fishery, which Raleigh declared in his day was the mainstay and support of the western countries, and content themselves with catching hawks and capturing Indians? Truly, this would not be the West Country way '

From contemporary records we can now state pretty accurately when the various nations began to fish in Newfoundland The English in 1498; the records show their continuous operations from that date The Portuguese appear to have commenced the fishery in 1501. The first account of the French is in 1504. There is a record of a voyage of Jean Denys, of Harfleur, to Newfoundland in 1506,[1] he is said to have made a map of the Island, which has been lost In the Paris National Library the following record has been found by M. Harrisse :—

"Let a note be made of the mark of my boats and barks which I leave in Newfoundland in the haven of Jean Denys' called Rougnoust."[2]

As we have seen, the first and chief result of the discovery of North America was the immediate establishment of a great fishery. In all ages of the world the fishery has been the mother of commerce, the parent of navigation The cod fishery, pursued by Englishmen first in Iceland, and afterwards on a larger scale in Newfoundland, made Englishmen sailors, and Britain a great maritime Power De Witt says ·—

"The navy of England became formidable by the discovery of the inexpressible rich fishing bank of Newfoundland "

It was this industry that first started the early colonisation of North America; the fishery was the powerful incentive that bound England to the New World for a century. The first attempted settlement of New England by Gosnold and Brereton in 1602 was to prosecute this fishery.

It is amongst the popular fictions of American history that when the Pilgrim Fathers moored their barque on the wild New England shore, their sole object was to worship God in their own way, and to kill Quakers after their own fashion, but sober history tells quite a different tale In Winslow's "Brief Narration of the True Grounds or Causes of " the first Planting of New England," it is stated that when the Puritans sent agents from Leyden to the High and Mighty Prince James to gain

[1] RAMUSIO's *Delle Navigationi*, 1550, vol. iii , p. 423, &c   [2] *Paris National Library*, *MSS Français*, 24,209.

B

his consent to their going to America, the king at once asked, "What profit might arise?" They answered in one single word—"Fishing" "So God have my soul," said the royal Solon, "'tis an honest trade, 'twas the Apostles' own calling"; and so they obtained leave to go They sought a place for their settlement convenient for cod fishing and whaling, and in 1624 they sent to England a ship laden with salt-codfish.

The time of the discovery of Newfoundland was a fortunate period for England Henry's love of money kept him from war, and under his peaceful reign Britain began, as it were, to gird up her loins for the great onward race that was to commence in the succeeding reigns In order to understand the importance of the discovery of the New World to England, we must first try to realise the contemporary history of the Mother Country

At this distance of time it is difficult to picture to ourselves how small and unimportant England then was. She had a comparatively small foreign trade, principally in wool. To encourage this manufacture, it was made law that everyone dying should be buried in wool. Even this small commerce was principally in the hands of foreigners Fancy an age that had neither tea nor coffee, when potatoes and tobacco were unknown. Except for very rich people, who had game, there was no fresh meat to be had all through the winter.[1] Fish, fresh and salted, formed the chief article of winter diet. To our forefathers of that age, therefore, the discovery of the fishing grounds of Newfoundland was a veritable God-send—a piscatorial El Dorado Codfish was gold in these old days[2] The History of Newfoundland, especially its earliest annals is essentially a history of the cod fishery

It is a strange feature in those turbulent times, amidst wars and rumours of wars, to find fishermen sailing unnoticed from little harbours

---

[1] PRICES OF MEAT AND BEER —The price of meat in the Tudor age : 1 cwt of beef, 4s 8d ; beef and pork, about ½d per lb ; mutton, 3 farthings per lb , when the quarter of malt was 2s , ale was one half penny per gallon; when it rose to 4s , the gallon of ale was one penny. Spaniards were astonished at the English food. "They live in poor houses," said the lordly dons, "but they fare as well as a king" These prices should be multiplied several times to bring them up to modern money value.

[2] PRICE OF FISH, 1512 to 1525 —EARL PERCY'S HOUSEHOLD EXPENSES "Item to be paid to the said Richard Gowge and Thomas Percy to make provision for cxl stock-fish for the expenses of my house for a hole yere

after yd obol the pece by estimacion And so the hole somme for full contentacion for the said stock-fish for one hole yere is xxxiii jd (33s 3d)
Same account for her-
   rings for a year - £4 10s. 0d.
Salt fish cod for one
   year - - - 18 4s 0d
Red herrings - - 3 3s. 4d
Salt salmon - - 5 0s 0d"
Newfoundland fish, in the days of Queen Elizabeth, was sold at 10s per 100 fish—equal to 50s per qtl This would be quite up to the old West Countryman's toast in Newfoundland—"the Pope and ten dollars"—a price per quintal often got in Spain early in this century

in Northern Spain, Portugal, France, and the West of England, spring after spring, daring the dangers of the western seas, the fogs, the thick-ribbed ice, and, worse than all, the erring captains—as old Whitbourne called the rovers, pirates, and sanguinary sea-robbers of that wonderful age—to gather a harvest in the new-found-land

These traders escaped the notice of kings and chroniclers, their humble calling ensured their safety for the first half century. In Newfoundland, besides the fisheries, they carried on a great free trade, oils and wines, and fruits of France, Spain, and Portugal, were exchanged for English cutlery and West of England cordage, cloth-hats, caps, and hosiery[1] The business was most profitable all round; it built up the West of England. Each year these old mariners came out with the easterly winds in the spring. Of the French and Portuguese, some fished on the banks and brought their fish home green, but the majority met in St. John's every year, spring and autumn. From this harbour they spread themselves out, north and south, to carry on the shore fishery, each nationality going together in small companies of from four to six ships; returning to St John's as a rendezvous each nation's ships sailed home together in convoy[2]

Whilst the cod-fisher pursued his calling in some snug harbour—Spaniard's Bay, Portugal Cove, Biscayan Cove, Frenchman's Cove, English Harbour—the more daring spirits, chiefly the Biscayans, chased the seal and the walrus in the Gulf, and followed the dangerous trade of the whale fishery. The head-quarters of the latter were the Ramea Islands (the present Magdalen Islands), the Straits of Belle Isle, and the north-east portion of the Gulf of St. Lawrence. They followed their quiet avocations armed to the teeth. Each vessel mounted cannon,

[1] Two articles in which the West of England were pre eminent in the days of Elizabeth (and for which Devon and Dorset are still celebrated in the reign of Victoria) were West of England cloth and Bridport cordage. Even in our time, the Spaniards bought Gundry's lines, twines, and cordage in St John's to take back to Spain.

[2] The names on the east coast of New-foundland, especially about Conception and Trinity Bay, all prove the early occupation of these localities by the English There is not a solitary foreign name in Trinity Bay. To escape the exactions of the English, who ruled over all from the very commencement of the fishery, the Portuguese spread themselves south, west, and north Cartier met Portuguese vessels in the Straits of Belle Isle, and we see from the Basque records (page 48) that the hardy Biscayans fished together in small companies of two and three vessels. The list given of the various ports frequented by them, shows how widely spread were their operations. Their great object was to avoid contact as much as possible with the over-bearing English, their poor ragged hireling crews had no chance in a fight with the Devonshire freebooters In the south of Newfoundland, it is made part of a fisher-man's agreement that "a share of a wreck" shall form part of his compensation, and in the Elizabethan days the spoils of a Spaniard was considered as regular an incident in the fishery as the share of cod All foreigners made St. John's their rendezvous for convoy. The end of August was a usual time for sailing, and the presence of so many Portuguese and other foreign vessels in St John's during Gilbert's visit is thus accounted for. The great Portuguese fishing fleet, which in the Elizabethan age employed several thousand men, is now represented by two banking schooners, and about fifty fishermen.

B 2

and his rude arms always lay alongside the fisherman as he plied his oar and cast his net But they were merry souls amidst all the dangers of the seas, wars, pirates, and rovers Each week the Admiral of the port retired, and at every change the new official gave a feast to all. The cheap and generous wines of Europe would then be freely circulated, and the sombre woods of the little port be enlivened, perchance, by the chanson of the French or the rattling of the castanets and lively airs on the Spanish guitar If it was a Basque port the fun would be fast and furious—there would be the national Gaita (the bag-pipes) and song, dance, and single-stick with broken heads, to enliven the feast

If there were English there they would be admirals and rulers over all, and woe betide the foreigner who disobeyed the West Countryman's orders, or dared to do anything on Sunday but drink and feast

We are indebted to a French lawyer, Lescarbot,[1] who was one of the first French explorers of Nova Scotia, for a graphic description of the surroundings of these ancient fishermen. He says one old master, Captain Savalet, of the little French frontier seaport of St. Jean de Luz—

"Received us with all the kindness in the world The good honest man told me that the same voyage was the forty-second voyage that he had made in those parts, and nevertheless the Newfoundland men do make but one a year He was marvellously pleased with his fishing, and told me, moreover, that he took, every day, fifty crownes worth of fish, and that his voyage would be worth £1,000 He paid wages to sixteen men and his vessel was of eighty tunnes and would carry 100,000 dry fishes "[2]

Besides this description we have an ancient picture of the mode of fishing, the stage, the ram's horn or trough, the splitting-table, the pews, the flakes, the hand barrows, all are exactly like those to be found to this day around our shores. The hook used was very large, and the barb shaped like a harpoon. The dress of the fisherman is quaint; each worker is represented with a long bib—the barvel—reaching from his neck to his toes, tied in at the waist, long boots, a sort of mop cap, or something like a soft felt with the brim turned down, or else the "borra" copied from the Basque, like the bonnet or Tam-O'Shanter of the Highlander. All wore broad leather belts, braces are quite a modern invention I have never seen a barvel myself, but an old friend, Mr. John Pike of St. Lawrence, tells me he can remember when all the fishermen used them, they were made of sheep skin, with the wool inside, the outside

[1] MARC LESCARBOT—" Avocat en Parlament "—came out to Annapolis (the French Port Royal) with Poutrincourt in 1606. He was a jovial fellow, who enjoyed the rough life with the Indians, fishing, shooting, and camping out He helped to found the first settlement in Nova Scotia (Acadie) For a promenade in the winter he built a covered verandah to their house. We owe to this whole-souled lawyer "The History of New France"

[2] LESCARBOT'S Nova Francia, London, 1609, p. 129.

coated with tar—long aprons, like the dress of the ancient fishermen, fastened with a belt. This was before the invention of oil clothes. Barvels were used by fishermen all along the North American coast

The shore codfishery, known amongst the French as "*La pêche sedentaire*," was pursued very much in the same manner as it is carried on to-day. The boats went out before dawn, returned with their loads, the fish were thrown up at the stage heads, split, and salted. The splitting table, the trough, known as the Ram's Horn (for washing out the fish after salting), the flakes (stages raised on piles and covered with boughs), were all in general use from the very commencement of this great industry

The bank or deep sea codfishery was carried on very differently from our modern methods. The men all fished from the ship, each in a sort of gangway hung over the side of the vessel, as depicted in the engraving

In those early days, when bultows were unknown and traps undreamed of, the old-fashioned fishermen, with their primitive hook as big as a small killock, with a huge lump of lead or iron for a sinker, and a rough strong hemp line, caught codfish galore. Some of the early writers stated that the fish were so abundant that the bears used to catch them; I have heard an old planter declare that the cod crowded into the land so in his time that he has seen a dog catch fish; Jukes, in his "Excursions in Newfoundland," mentions a dog of George Harvey's, Isle-aux-Morts, which caught sculpins. Although the early cod catchers fished mostly with hook and line, they had nets in addition, for the capture of herring, and were acquainted with the use of seines, for the taking both of bait and larger fish.

The English was entirely a shore fishery, on the principle of shares, the owners of the vessel receiving two-thirds of the catch, the crew one-third[1] The Bretons and Normans also divided the proceeds of the voyage. The French and Spanish Basques and the Portuguese all paid their men wages. The Portuguese were partly shore fishermen, partly bankers. The Spanish Basques, or Biscayans, shore fishermen, whalers, and sealers. The French were mostly bankers, and carried their fish home, as they do now, green, to be afterwards dried and made in France; many, however, were engaged in the shore fishery.

At first the English had very small vessels, their average size being less than fifty tons; by Whitbourne's time they had increased to about eighty tons. From the very earliest period the English had a carrying fleet (sack ships); as the small over-crowded fishing ships were not able

---

[1] This was a custom long before Newfoundland was discovered (cf PALMER's *Manship*, vol. ii, p 88)

to convey the product of their voyage, so larger vessels took the dried
fish to the Mediterranean markets. The Bretons and Normans, who
were deep-sea fishermen, braved the dangers of the Atlantic in wretched
little tubs. Much larger craft were employed by the Basques and

Portuguese; we read of Basque vessels of four hundred tons, manned by
forty men.

Besides carrying on a shore fishery the fishermen did a barter trade
with the Indians for furs, and like good Christians they tried to convert
the dusky savages. When one of the chiefs was being taught the Lord's

prayer, he came to a full stop when he was told to say, "Give us this day our daily bread ", he asked if he prayed for bread alone, would he get any fish or moose meat? " I am afraid," says Lescarbot, " the sincerity of their conversion is very questionable."

The uncouth West Country name—The New-founde-lande—which has remained the designation of our Island, applied in the sixteenth century not only to this Colony, but also to Nova Scotia, New Brunswick, Cape Breton, Prince Edward's Island, and the islands and coasts of the Gulf of St Lawrence, even down to the State of Maine   Foreigners called these countries by the generic name of the " Baccalaos "—the land of dried-cod-fish.

By 1509, Henry VII was gathered to his fathers ; he never dreamed of the mighty empire in the West which his subjects were founding— the New England that was to be. Ignoble and inglorious, however, as were the days of his reign, they served as a peaceful preparation for the coming time—the golden age of his descendant, Queen Elizabeth.

APPENDIX TO CHAPTER II.

I. The Iceland Fishery.

The Iceland trade and fishery is frequently mentioned in the Records; I think it embraced, as the Newfoundland fishery did in later times, a much wider area than the name implied. Probably fishermen frequently brought their products to Westmaney, not only from "Gunnbeorn's Skerries" and the east coast of Greenland, but also from Wardhouse, beyond Cape North, and from the Luffoden Islands, the higher prices realised for the cure of the real Iceland fish making it profitable to bring fish from other localities to be re-sold as "Iceland." The extent and ramifications of the trade and exchange formerly carried on in Iceland and the adjacent seas, and England's share in it, are not fully realised by historians. The mention of a "*Blobei house*" in the will of John Sparks, of Cromer, in 1483 (RYE's *Cromer, Past and Present,* p 51), and the depiction of an English ship whaling in OLAUS MAGNUS' *Carta Marina,* 1539 (*see* WINSOR's *N. & C. H. of A.,* i 123), look as if Englishmen, as well as Biscayners, were engaged in the fifteenth century in whaling. Mr Palmer says the English merchants went to Wardhouse for herrings, I suppose for bait (PALMER's *Manship,* i 311).

English fishermen, accustomed to range over the whole north-eastern littoral of the Atlantic, would not be likely to allow the new opening in the west to remain long undeveloped. There seems some ground for supposing that the Labrador section of our fishery, reached by way of Cape Farewell, was at first reckoned as a part of the Iceland voyage, and the catch sold as Iceland fish (Cf ZIEGLER's map of *Gronlandia and Terra Bacallaos,* 1532, we read [from East Greenland], "Inde continuator littori terræ Baccallaos")

Robert Bacon, a mariner of Cromer, who captured James I of Scotland in 1405, claims to have been the discoverer of Iceland (RYE's *Cromer, Past and Present,* p 49), this, probably, only means that he was the first Cromer man who engaged in the trade.

In 1400 England had fishery rights around the Island (*Cotton MSS*), but even in 1360 it must have been a regular voyage, for one Nicolas of Lynn had been five times there, on one occasion making the voyage in a fortnight (ZARTMANN's *Nouvelles Annales*). There is an undated MS at Hatfield, No 186 72, about "the privilege

of ancient fishing in Iceland" Kohl, in his *Discovery of Maine* (p 113), quoting from Magnuesen, says that in one snowstorm in April 1419, as many as 25 English vessels were wrecked, and their crews drowned; the disaster was attributed to the treachery of the islanders, and an armed force was sent from England to take revenge. Kohl also says that Englishmen frequently landed and fortified themselves in Iceland, and acted as if they intended to retain permanent possession of the island. This statement is borne out by a map made about 1520, marked No 4 in Knntsmann's atlas, which shows the English standard on the island.

The following records from Rymer's *Fœdera* show to some extent the course of English commerce in the north in the thirteenth, fourteenth, and fifteenth centuries

FROM RYMER'S *Fœdera*

Letter in 1217, from Henry III to the King of Norway, saying he will gladly promote commercial intercourse with that realm. Letter from the King of Norway in 1284, asking Edward to protect the Norse merchants from the Germans while in England. In 1309, Edward II. told the King of Norway he would be glad to renew the ancient friendships between the realms. In 1311, compensation was claimed for injuries committed on the sailors of an English ship wrecked in Norway. In 1313 there are two complaints from Edward II to the King of Norway, that certain English sailors were imprisoned in Norway, and Edward asks the Norwegian king to listen to the petition of the English merchants; and later on, in the same year, he requests the restoration of the goods of the Englishmen. In 1316, compensation was claimed for injuries done to some merchants of Berwick by Norwegians. In 1361, Edward III. demanded restitution to W. de Stokesby and other English merchants whose ship was plundered at Cost, in Norway. In 1408 license was granted to the English merchants in Norway, Sweden, and Denmark, to elect *governors*.

In 1411, Henry IV. informed the council of North Berne [Bergen], that he had forbidden the Hanse merchants to leave England in consequence of the injuries done to English merchants; he also informed them that he had granted licenses to nine merchants at St Botolph to leave England. In 1412, the merchants of Lenn (Lynn) were illtreated by the Hanse, Henry IV. desired the Lynn and Hanse merchants to investigate the matter. On 28th November 1415, the English king forbade fishermen going to Iceland and the other islands of Norway and Denmark, except in accordance with *ancient customs*. In 1416, a ship was granted to the Danish ambassador to return home. In 1432 there is a resolution to send ambassadors to Denmark.

On 28th January 1438, a license was given to John Bp of Shalholt in Iceland, to take a ship to Iceland and send it back with merchandise [? fish] for the payment of his creditors. Similar license to John Bp of Holar. On 26th February a license to John Secheford and John Candeler, to export corn and other victuals to Iceland for the use of the Bp. of Scalhelte, confessor of the King of Denmark. On 12th May 1444, there is a proclamation to the sheriffs of London, Norfolk, and six other places to forbid all persons going to Iceland or other parts prohibited by the King of Denmark. On 4th December 1445, there is a safe-conduct to Godsum, Bp. of Shalholt, to go to Iceland, and return. In the spring of 1450, all ships were debarred from going to Iceland except two of Canynge's. In 1447, the Dean of Salisbury went as ambassador to Denmark, and in 1449, Sir R. Shottisbroke. On 4th July 1450, there is the exemplification of a safe-conduct until Michaelmas 1451 from the King of Denmark to English merchants, and of a license from the marshall and master of the chamber of the King of Denmark to John Wolffe, of England, to trade to Iceland.

Danish ambassadors were in England in 1464, and a treaty was made in 1465 with Denmark, at Hamburgh. In 1473, Edward IV promised to keep the treaty for two years, and hold a diet to settle differences. The King of Denmark himself proposed to or did come to England this year, for a safe-conduct was granted to him. In 1476, the treaty was renewed to 1478, and again to 1480, during which time a diet was to be held. A fresh treaty was signed in 1479. On 22nd October 1478, there is a license to John and Thomas Alcok to trade to Iceland, and on April 24th, 1483, a further license to Robert Alcok, of Kingston-on-Hull, to send a ship laden with merchandise to Iceland.

In the course of the negotiations in 1600, Rymer notices the exemplification of a treaty made in 1489-90; this was evidently the basis of all arrangements during the sixteenth century. It must have been in settling this treaty, or in the further discussion which took place about 1492, that Cabot was employed by Henry VII (cf. ANSPACH's *H of Newfoundland*, p. 25; no authority given).

In 1531 the Danes complained of injuries done to their subjects, and Henry VIII made a counter-complaint that 30 Englishmen had been killed that year in Ireland, and Cromwell in 1534 has a "remembrance" of the losses of a Mr Honyng there (*Records*). The English also had many conflicts with their rivals, the Hanse merchants. This fishery had another special danger; the Scotch used to lay in wait for the ships on their way home and capture them—they did this even late in Elizabeth's reign (*Records*, 1584), for this reason we constantly read of ships being sent to "waft" the Iceland fleet past the Scottish coast (*Records*, 1523). It was the custom at Yarmouth, at a Corporation dinner given on Black Friday (before Palm Sunday), to remind the mayor to write for a convoy for the Iceland fleet (PALMER's *Manship*, ii 62).

The following interesting Icelandic Annals, which Mr. York Powell has very kindly literally translated for me, give a graphic picture of the early fishing, and show the close social, ecclesiastical, and commercial connexion which existed between the two countries in the fifteenth century. Mr. York Powell says there are several notices of the Iceland fishery in COOPER's *Appendix to the Fœdera.*

ENTRIES IN THE ICELANDIC ANNALS.

"1336 Arne abbot of Lysa beheaded off England and all his ship's crew by the Duggars and all cast overboard.

"1349 At that time a cog sailed out of England with many folk aboard and laid in off Bergen-bay and was but little unladen when all the folk died on board and as soon as the goods came into the town off the ship the townfolk straightway began to die. Then the sickness went all over Norway and laid it so waste that there did not survive one-third part of the people of the land. England's cog sunk with nigh all the goods and the dead and it was not unladen. More ships and busses sunk with their cargo and men yet unladen.

"1412 A ship came from England east of Deerholmsey; they rowed out to them, and they were fishermen out of England; that same fall there were five of the Englishmen that parted from their companions and came ashore east of Horn out of a boat and said they wished to buy food saying that they had starved on the boat many a day. These five Englishmen were here the winter over, for their ship was away when they went back for her and all aboard her.

"1413 A merchant ship came out of England to Iceland. The skipper was named Richard New. he had the king of Norway's letters to let him sail in his realm with his merchant ship freely . . . many bought wares of him down at the sound [Hafnafiord] but many wise men took it ill. He sailed a short while after, he never came back to Iceland. Vigus Ivarsson took an oath from him that he would be faithful and true to the country. The five Englishmen that had been here over the winter sailed with him.

" Fishermen from England came north off Iceland and took some meat off a yeoman and left money instead thereof *Item* the English seized in the Eastfirths some sheep in Papey off Elfetfirth. There sailed hither out of England that summer 30 fishing boats or more

" There came 5 English ships to Iceland and lay inside the Westmanneys. There came out a letter sent from the English king to the Commonalty and the best men in the country to allow leave of trade to his men, especially in the ship that belonged to him At first they talked about the Bergen tariff but the Englishmen would not take part therein Afterwards they traded each man as it suited him best

" Two nights before Allhallowsmass there was a fire at Bergen The fire broke out first in the *Englishmen's yard*

" 1415 That same summer 6 ships from England lay near Hafnarfirth Franklin Vigfus Iwarsson sailed out to England, and he had with him 60 lasts of dried fish and a good deal of pure silver

" 1419 On Thursday there came such a bad gale with snow that far and wide round the land English ships were wrecked no fewer than 25, all the men were lost but the goods and pieces of the ships were washed up The storm came on a little before daymeal and did not last till high day.

" The Icelanders wrote this year to King Eric of Pomerania respecting foreign traders and fishers.

" 1420 Thorleif Arnason sailed hence and fought with the English at sea and made Norway safely

" 1425. There were taken on the Westmanneys Baltazar and Sir Hamos and flitted over to England, few thought that a loss

" 1426 Baltazar came out and was greeted as Governor by all. He sailed back to England that same summer, with them that he had come with

" 1427 Bishop John Johnson of Holar came out to Hafnarfirth with the English

" 1428 Many shipwrecks by reason of the great storms at sea 18 ships wrecked at Acreness Two sexareens were cast up at Musarness far on to the mire, all unhurt

" 1429 The Lord Bishop John Johnson came to Holar from England [He had gone back to England for a while in 1427.]

" 1430. In that same year there came out hither to this country Bishop John Geridsson Bishop of Sealholt he came with his ship to Hafnarfirth Wednesday next after the mass of John the Baptist. The lord bishop came out of England where he had stayed the winter before . . . two priests came out hither with Lord John Bishop of Shalholt one named Matthew the other Nicholas Priest Nicholas sailed back that same summer later on and with him many lasts of dried fish in the bishop's name, for it was easy for him to get fish and other things

for the people of this country favoured the bishop rather.

" 1467 The end was that Sir Biorn was slain by the English at Rif . . . and in vengeance thereof afterward in the summer she [the Lady Olaf] had all the English slain and she had twelve of them bound with a rope and all their heads cut off

" 1510 In the days of Bishop Stephen was a fight at the Westmanneys between Englishmen and the men of Side [an Icelandic district]. There fell 14 Englishmen and one priest of the Icelanders Sir John by name and he was called ' butter-nose.' . . . Some years after in 1518, or thereabout, there was a fight between the English and the Hamburgers in Hafnarfirth.

" 1530 Erland of Strand and his men fought with the English in Grindwick . . . he also slew two Englishmen guiltless . . . one named John Dalton . . . the other was called Nicholas

" In the days of Bishop Gredmund the Dutch [Germans] and English fought at Grindwick . . . The Dutch came on them unawares and drunken There fell 14 Englishmen and their skipper Ricki Bray

" 1520 Sir Martein sailed nine winters with the English. . . he first sailed with Robert that married his sister Gudlang Emas's daughter here The bridal was at the eut of the English The English brought a tun of wine out of every ship and there lay 9 ships there. The feast lasted half a month. They sailed thence that same summer and Sir Martein with them, he went to an English school [university]."

Bristol at one time took a leading position in the Iceland trade In 1436 Henry VI. granted a license to John, the Bishop of Holar, who was then in London from Iceland, in which he authorised him to engage John May [of Bristol], with his ship the *Katherine*, for a voyage to Iceland May was to act as the bishop's attorney, and to transact his business, as the bishop did not wish to leave England (RYMER's *Fœdera*)

In 1450, all ships were " stayed " from the Iceland and Finmark voyages, exception only being made in favour of two ships of William Canynge, who had lent the king money (cf SEYER and GALLAWAY). For the next fifty years at least, Bristol, through Canynge's enterprise, was the chief market for dry-cod, and her historians claim the most important port in Europe; from her wharves the products of the Northern fisheries were distributed all over the Latin States The merchant marine of the Atlantic seaboard was employed largely in carrying for this trade, Columbus in 1477 and, no doubt, Cabot and Cortereal engaged in it, in fact, Cabot must have had great experience in Iceland to be entrusted to conclude an agreement about the fishery with Denmark

Though the trade up to the discovery of America had been controlled by Bristol merchants, I can only find one occasion recorded in which West Country ships went to Iceland during the sixteenth century (*Records*, 1594). This does not by any means prove that no other ships went, but the marked absence of the names of western ports from the lists of those that sent ships to Iceland is significant.

In 1510 Henry VIII. repealed an Act, 8 Henry VI cap ii, 1429, by which it was agreed that all Englishmen going to buy fish were required, upon pain of forfeiture of all goods, to go to the "staple" town of North Bergen, where they would enjoy the same rights as the Hanse, the Act of Henry VI was to prevent the great disorders then occurring at the fishery Henry VI. was a nephew of the King of Denmark

The repeal of this old agreement with Denmark was probably to give relief to the east coast traders, who were already feeling the effect of Newfoundland competition.

In 1517 there were 300 English traders in one port, Hafnar Fiord, but in 1581 the entire fleet apparently numbered only 200, probably all from Suffolk and Norfolk (23 Eliz cap vii) In 1533, for some reason, only 85 ships, all from the east coast, appear to have composed the Iceland fleet; they paid £414 duty on their catch (*Records*)

In 1523 we appear to have further evidence that the opening up of our fishery was affecting this trade, for we find Christian II. asking Henry VIII if he wished to trade to Iceland (*Records*) The frequent changes also in the Charters of the Stock-fishmongers would seem to indicate that there was a disturbing element felt in London in the early part of the sixteenth century (cf. HERBERT's *Twelve Livery Co's*)

In 1512 the cost of "great dry Hisselonde fish" was 38s 4d for every 124, next year it was sold to Government for the army at 53s 9½d per 100' (*Records*) This shows indirectly the enormous profits which must have been made in the Newfoundland fishery for the first half of the century Later, when these high prices could no longer be maintained owing to the Reformation and the increasing supply of Newfoundland fish, we have constant complaints from merchants about false counting, especially of cod fish imported in barrels (*Lansdowne MSS*, 1583, &c; 5 Eliz V made it illegal to import cod in barrels). It is interesting to notice a petition in 1568 (when no doubt the market was flooded with Newfoundland fish) which states that badly dried fish was being brought in and sold as "*Iceland*" fish. (*Hatfield MS*) I think this refers to Labrador fish. The profits of the Eastlanders, who had clung to the Iceland trade, were evidently dwindling away, they could not afford to sell their fish at 10s per 100.

As the Newfoundland trade monopolized the energies of the West and South coast of England, very little attention was paid to Iceland by the Government; Eastlanders, feeling the effect of low prices, ceased to pay their license fees to the King of Denmark In 1580 the merchants of Eastland complained of Dr Rodgers' unjust demands (*Hatfield MS*) Rodgers was evidently asking for dues owing to the King of Denmark, as he is the same person who, in 1592, requested the renewal of the Commercial Treaty mentioned below. In 1585, however, the merchants' remonstrance appear to have been attended to, as there is an Order in Council on July 25, "for redressing the wrongs of the English in Iceland" (*Records*)

On the 21st June 1590, the King of Denmark wrote that he had received the charge of C. Perkins, the Queen's ambassador, but must defer replying thereto as his counsellors are absent (RYMER.)

A further petition was presented by the East Coast traders in 1591 —

"Time out of mind we have proceeded to Iceland for the buying of stock fish and taking of green fish such as codd, ling &c. Now are prevented at Westmancy [Iceland] from pitching booths or buying fish Used to pay when we had booths 5 marks, if only for fishing one angel and a barrel of salt or a barrel of beare no more" (*Hatfield MS*)

The loss of revenue was evidently keenly felt in Denmark. We find a warrant in 1586 allowing the king himself, in his own ships, to import a cargo of fish duty free to Harwich, and take away some Wiltshire woollen goods and tin (*Hatfield MS*)

Matters reached a climax in 1592, when the agreement allowing the English to fish in Iceland had not been renewed for twelve years, though terminable every seven years, and the King of Denmark was "offended" (*Records*); the reason seems to have been that the trade was carried on at a loss, for Raleigh next year said the Newfoundland was the only profitable fishery, "the Newfoundland voyages are the only ones making any profit" (*Hatfield MS*)

On the 8th July 1595, the King of Denmark wrote to Elizabeth to say he could permit Englishmen to fish in Iceland except at Westmaney, which is reserved for the Court; he complained of the conduct of English fishermen. (RYMER.)

In 1598 the senate of Denmark advised Sir T. Egerton, Lord Buckhurst, and the Earl of Essex, to use moderation and prudence in settling the differences between the two kingdoms (RYMER)

This year Dr Perkins was sent to Denmark to make fresh arrangements with the Danish king (*Hatfield MS*), whose "remonstrances" were considered next year by the English Council (*B.M. M.S. Vesp. CXIV.*) In 1600 there were apparently some further attempts at a settlement (cf. RYMER's notice of the 1479 treaty in this year)' In February 1600, Elizabeth complained that her fishermen had been forbidden by Danish officers to fish in the "deep sea" in the north. (RYMER) No terms seem to have been arrived at, for in 1602 the King again prohibited fishing in Iceland to all strangers without license (*Lansdowne MS*)

In the same year complaint was made of injuries done to Englishmen, Christian IV. justified the seizure of vessels from Hull, and complained of the capture of Danish vessels On July 15th Elizabeth said she would send commissioners to Bremen by September 25th to treat of commercial matters The commissioners met in October, but returned home on hearing of the death of the queen. A treaty was ratified in 1621 (RYMER)

A careful perusal of the Records seems to show that the Iceland voyage was gradually deserted by all but the Norfolk and Suffolk fishermen, who were frequently consulted about the decaying character of the trade (*Hatfield MS*, Aug 7, 1602)

In 1594 the inhabitants of Beeson and Sherringham are mentioned incidentally as being the chief traders to Iceland (*Records*)

The relative insignificance of this fishery in the latter half of the sixteenth century is shown in a petition in 1586 against the importation of foreign fish, the petition speaks of the time "*when the Iceland voyage was most frequented*" (*Hatfield MS*) It evidently was not then, nor had been for some time, any longer the dominating factor in the stock-fish market, and the statement of Parkhurst in Hakluyt, made eight years before, which has led many writers astray, that it was still the chief English fishery must be wrong

It is only fair to state that Mr Palmer says (*Manship*, ii 89) —"During the reign of Charles I the Iceland and North Sea fisheries for cod, &c, which had long been prosecuted with success, attained their greatest prosperity. About 150 vessels were then employed in the North Sea fishery off the coast of Norway and about 20 vessels went annually to Iceland. The half doles from these fisheries alone from 1645–49, averaged £300 per annum, but shortly afterwards they fell off, the fisheries became unsuccessful, and in 1740 only one vessel went to Iceland and doled £47 . . . . . In 1607 the half dole only produced £135 on an average" If the £414 paid by 85 ships in 1533 was this same dole, the east coast fishery, or at any rate the Iceland section of it, can hardly be said to have reached its highest point in the seventeenth century I suggest that the merchants of Norfolk and Suffolk were encouraged to re-embark in this trade on account of an unusual demand for fish caused by the civil war and the consequent cessation of agriculture, &c.

Two special causes helped to increase the Newfoundland fishery to the detriment of the Iceland traders One was the advantage taken by the West Countrymen of the Act 5 Eliz cap V to embark in a large export trade to make up for the diminishing demand in the home market; the "*poor inhabitants of Norfolk and Suffolk*" petitioned in 1568 against "*the new evil of the priviledge of exporting fish free of duty*" (*Records.*) The Act 23 Eliz VII (1580) recites — "Where[as] the merchauntes of divers places of this realme [? West Countrymen] have for their private gaynes ingrossed unto their hands great quantities of fish taken by aliens, being in goodness farre inferiour to the fysh taken by Englishmen [? Eastlanders] in the Island voyages .   there be of late decayed, not onely the number of two hundred sayle or more ot good ships that yearly traded to Island for taking fish usuallye solde in this realme but also the number of maryners "

The other cause which militated against treeless Iceland (Englishmen were not allowed to fish in Norway —PALMER'S *Manship*, i 311) was the abundance of wood in Newfoundland for making stages and barrels Though the question of barrelled fish, which was so much agitated in the trade from 1560 onwards for many years (cf 5 Eliz V and *Lansdowne MSS*. from 1580 forwards), partly related to Dutch herrings and Cornish pilchards, the demand for licenses by West Countrymen like Downing (*Lansdowne MS*, 1583) and Sir William Gorges (*Lansdowne MS*, 1586) to import barrelled fish, and the prohibition in the Act 5 Eliz cap V. against importing cod in barrels, show, I think, that the practice of packing Newfoundland fish in this way was in use at this early period, and the facility it gave for easy distribution was no doubt one of the many causes which helped to transfer the English interest from Iceland to Newfoundland The wording of sec. 7 of 5 Eliz V, that "forasmuche as ther ys much deceiptful Packing used in Codd brought in Barralles into this Realme," all fish must be brought in "loose in Bulke and by Tale" refers, I venture to think, to dry fish as well as green

The barrelling of cod fish must not, however, be understood to have originated at this time. In 1482 by 22 Edw IV c. 2, and in 1495 by 11 Henry VII c 23, most stringent regulations were laid down for barrelled fish, prescribing the size of the barrels, the size of the fish, the manner of splitting, boning, and packing; there were to be no "broken belied" fish; salmon and other fish were to be "xxvij inches from the bone of the fyn to the iij joynte of the taille, the bone to be taken away into the navel, the fyshe splatted [split] down to a handful [within a span] of the taile and not to be packed double in the barrel"; searchers and gaugers were to be appointed to see the Act was carried out properly.

This note is simply a compilation of old records Certain points are mere conjecture A closer examination of the documents quoted may prove that they will not bear the interpretation put upon them , the history of early English commerce has yet to be written. A study of the Iceland fishery is interesting to Newfoundlanders , it helps to some extent to throw light upon the way in which our own was carried on at first, to fill a blank in our Island history Englishmen seem to have " commanded all there," to have fearlessly traversed the northern seas to reap a golden harvest which built up the ancient towns of Norfolk and Suffolk

This fishery is again receiving the attention of Englishmen , fast steam trawlers are now supplying the English markets with fresh fish from Iceland

II. Pedro de Ayala's letter to Spain.

[Original in cipher]

25 July 1498.

"I well believe that your Highnesses have heard how the King of England has equipped a fleet to discover certain Islands and mainland that certain persons who set out last year for the same have testified that they have found I have seen the chart which the discoverer has drawn, who is another Genoese like Columbus, and has been in Seville and in Lisbon procuring to find those who would help him in this enterprise .

.   .   .   .   The King determined to despatch an expedition, because he had the certainty that they had found land last year. The fleet consists of five ships provisioned for one year. . . . .   The Genoese went on his course I have seen the course and distance he takes, think that the land they have found or seek is that which your Highnesses possess, for it is the end of that which belongs to your Highnesses by the convention with Portugal It is hoped that they will return by September .   . . .   I believe the distance is not 400 leagues And I told him that I thought they were the Islands discovered by your Highnesses, and I even gave him a reason, but he would not hear it , as I believe your Highnesses now have intelligence of all, as well as the chart or mappe-monde that this Genoese has made, I do not send it now, though I have it here , and to me it seems very false, to give out that they are not the said Islands "

III. Sebastian Cabot.

No history of Newfoundland will be considered complete without allusion to John Cabot's well-known son, although we have absolutely nothing to thank him for, quite the reverse

Sebastian's friend, Martyr, was forced to admit that the Spaniards denied his claim to be the discoverer of North America

The members of the Drapers Company in 1521, replying to a request of the king and Wolsey for ships to explore the Newfoundland (a general name then for all North America), said " We think it were to sore adventure to jopard V ships with men and goods unto the said Island uppon the singular trust of one man callyed as we understand Sebastyan which Sebastyan as we here say *was never in that land* hymself all if he makes reports of many things as he hath heard his Father and other men speke in tymes past."

It is stated that he offered his services to the king for a voyage of discovery, but was refused In 1512 he made a chart for Henry VIII of the coast of Gascony and Guienne, in France, and in the same year took service with Spain as a reviser of maps and charts He was specially engaged on account of his supposed exclusive knowledge of our coast King Ferdinand wrote to Sebastian on 12th September 1512 . "Sabeis que en Burgos os hablaron de mi parte Conchillos i el Obp de Palencia sobre la navegacion á los Baccalos e ofrecistes servirnos " (HARRISSE'S *Disc of N. America*, p 20.) In 1518 he was appointed to examine all pilots for America

In 1524, just before the Congress of Badajos, he came to England on some secret mission to Henry VIII , 43s 4d was paid to J Goderick for bringing him over In 1526 he ascended the Paraguay, in South America, in command of an expedition in which Robert Thorne had adventured a large share. In 1547 he was again brought to England, at a cost of £100 In answer to three very urgent demands from Charles V. for his return to Spain—"a very necessary man for the Emperor, whose servant he was, and had a pension of him " — on 21st April 1550 the English Privy Council replied. "He of himself refused to go either to Spain or to the Emperor, and that he being of that mind, and the king's subject, no reason or equity that he should be forced against his will " — (*Harl*, 523, folio 6) In 1553 he was an active promoter and governor of the Muscovy Company. He is supposed to have died in 1557.

He claimed amongst the scientific navigators of the age the very highest position as an authority on all geographical questions, but appears to have gradually fallen into discredit

Unfortunately, he was a great liar, every fresh record that is hunted up fixes him with a fresh falsehood He told Eden that his father died, leaving him very rich, soon after the discovery of Columbus ; his father was alive in 1498, and in the receipt of a pension, and very poor He told his English friends he was Bristol born ; he made Contarini believe he was a Venetian, he declared he could tell the distance at sea by the compass He lied to Spain, to Italy, and to England Edward VI gave him a handsome pension—£166 13s 4d —but less than the splendid salary he had in Spain In Queen Mary's time he had, no doubt at the instance of her husband, Philip II, to divide his pension with Worthington, and, between them, all his maps disappeared   Doubtless he was forced to sell them to the Spanish Government, and this may account for their total loss to the world

Sebastian Cabot's instructions to Sir Hugh Willoughby show his character "There is to be no dicing, carding, tabling, morning and evening prayers are to be said" On the other hand, "the natives of strange countries are to be enticed aboard and made drunk with your beer and wine, for then you shall know the secrets of their hearts" They were also to be "cautious about certain creatures with men's heads and the tails of fishes, who swim, with bows and arrows, about the fords and bays, and live on human flesh"

In their insular pride, Englishmen believed Sebastian Cabot, their countryman, was the great explorer who had found the new world They gloried in his wonderful exploit, and resolutely ignored the real discoverer, his illustrious father.

The works of Biddle, Justin Winsor, Desimoni, and Harrisse contain the fullest documentary records of the Cabots. Recently there have been several new contributions to the history of John and Sebastian Cabot—books by Sr. F Tarducci, an Italian, and E Madero of Buenos Ayres—and a review in "La Espana Moderna," by Captain Fernandez Duro of the Royal Spanish Navy. They throw very little fresh light on the lives of the Cabots   Duro brands Sebastian as a traitor to Spain; Tarducci exalts him as a patriot   The name of Sebastian's Spanish wife is given— Catalina Medrano—and his daughter Elizabeth, and a last letter shortly before his death to Charles V Captain Duro, a very well-informed writer, considers that Sebastian was not in the first voyage, and that he was a great schemer.

The latest work on the Cabots is by Dr. S. E Dawson, published in "The Transactions of the Royal Society of Canada," 1894, it is very able and exhaustive Dr. Dawson sets out with the theory that John Cabot's landfall in 1497 was at Cape Breton, which he identifies with the "Cavo descubierta" of Cosa; he cleverly arranges his facts to suit this theory, which forces him to argue that Cabot sailed from west to east along the southern coast of Newfoundland, as far as Cape Race, the author, however, ignores the fact that the old pilots in naming

the coast followed the calendar. The position of Cape St Jorge (April 23rd) and C. St Lucia (December 13th) *west* of St. Nicholas (December 6th) show conclusively that the navigator whose voyage Cosa's map records sailed from east to west In addition to the arguments in favour of Cape Bonavista as the landfall of John Cabot, contained at p. 10, there may be added the names near the Cape, of "King's Cove," in the foreign maps Royal Port, showing probably where the Genoese erected the royal-arms, and "*Keels*" or Keels strand, where the first boat landed.

Mr Harrissé prints, in his new book "John Cabot," for the first time, the following Warrant from Henry VII for the payment of John Cabot's pension, and proves pretty conclusively the Cabots to be Genoese; the rest of the book deals mainly with the life of Sebastian and his claim to be considered a scientific cosmographer and practical seaman

1498.

22nd February

Henry by the Grace of God, King of England, and of France, and lord of Ireland, to the Tresourer and Chaubrelaines of oure Eschequer greting. Whereas we, by oure warrant under oure signet, for certain consideracions have geven and graunted unto John Caboote xxli [£20] yerely during oure pleasure to be had and prayyed by the hands of our custumers in oure poorte of Bristowe, and as we be euformed, the said John Caboote is delaied of his payement because the said custumers have no sufficient matier of discharge for their indempnitie to be yolden at their accompt before the Barons of our Eschequer. Wherefore we wol and charge you that ye oure said Tresourer and Chaubrelaines that now be and hereafter shalbe that ye unto suche tymes as ye shall have from us otherwise in comandement do to be levied in due fourme in several tailles every of them conteignyng xli upon the customers of the revenues in oure said poorte of Bristowe at two usual termes of the yere whercof oon taill to be levied at this time conteignyng xli of the revenues of oure said poorte upon Richard Meryk and Arthure Kemys, late custumers of the same. And the said taill or tailles in due and sufficient fourme levied ye delyver unto the said John Caboote to be had of our gift by way of rewarde without prest or eny other charge to be sette upon hym, or any of them, for the same   And thes our lettres shal be youre sufficient warrant in that behalf   Geven undre oure prive seal at oure Manor of Shene the xxii of ffebruary, the xiii yere of oure reign (H HARRISSE's *John Cabot*, 1895, p 394)

CHAPTER III.

REIGN OF HENRY VIII

1509-1547

1510.—Repeal of 8 Henry VI c II., 1429, about trading to Iceland and Norway

1511 —Agramonte's voyage to America

1512 —Rut in command of ships in the Royal Navy. Sebastian Cabot, engaged by the Spanish King on account of his supposed knowledge of Newfoundland, leaves England for Spain "Great dry Iselande" fish selling for 38s 4d per 124

1513.—Iceland fish sold at 53s. 9½d. per 100 to the Government.

1515 —First printed account of Cabot's voyage in Peter Martyr's *Decades.*

1517 —Three hundred English traders at Hafnae Fiord in Iceland

1518.—Lescarbot says Baron-de-Lery sailed to America, landed cattle at Canso and Sable Island, and thus made the first attempt at settlement of North America

1520 —Kuntsman No. 4 map assigning Iceland to the English

1521 —Portuguese patent to Fagundez, showing a knowledge of our south coast

1522 —Sabine says there were forty or fifty houses in Newfoundland at this time

1523 —Verrazano, sent by Francis I, King of France, made land at Carolina, sailed north to Cape Breton   Grant of two fisheries on the U.S. Coast to Ayllon

1525 —Gomez reports Newfoundland sea full of fish   Paulo Centurione, a Genoese, engaged by Henry VIII. for a voyage of discovery, failed through the death of Centurione.

1526 —Tyson acting as Thorne's agent in the West Indies.

1527.—Robert Thorne's expedition, John Rut wrote his celebrated letter from St John's to Henry VIII, found 14 vessels, 11 sail of Norman, one Brittaine, and two Portugal barks, fishing in St John's Harbour, Rut receives a pension   Maiollo map.

1529 —Acknowledgment by Ribero in his map of discoveries by Bristol men.

1531.—Fifty Englishmen killed in Iceland

1532 —Ziegler states that the "Baccalaos" country is a continuation of Greenland

1534 —Jacques Cartier's celebrated voyage, made Newfoundland, and then sailed up St Lawrence to Bay Chaleur   Gaspar Viegas' map shows Bonavista for the first time on our coast.

1535.—Cartier's second voyage; sailed up to Montreal, founded French Empire in North America.

1536 —Expedition of Master Hoare, of London, and a number of gentlemen and lawyers; disastrous voyage; stole a French ship in Newfoundland, and came home. Stockfish and Saltfishmongers Companies reunite

1539 —Olaus Magnus' map showing an English ship whaling near Iceland

1541.—Cartier's third voyage; built a fort near Quebec, called Charlesbourg. 33 Henry VIII c II., first Act of Parliament relating to America. Roberval arrived in St. John's, "found 17 ships of fishers"; met Jallobert and Noel there returning to France Sixty French ships in Newfoundland

1542.—John Rotz presents a map, showing the New World, to Henry VIII.

1544 —Two French ships left for Newfoundland every day in January and February

1545 —Probable commencement of Basque fishing in Newfoundland on a large scale   No French ships go to Canada for fear of the Spaniards

In tracing the course of our Island History during this remarkable reign one of the great debatable grounds of English History, we are fortunately not concerned in any way with the fierce controversial war that wages around this period   Luckily our subject is piscatorial and not polemical

The enthusiasm aroused by the great discoveries of the last reign had not sensibly abated   Henry was stirred up to make several futile attempts to discover the north-west passage to India   France came late in the field, but, though last, her explorers, Verrazano and Cartier, were not least amongst the world's great navigators and discoverers

The age produced no great coloniser like Raleigh to arouse and direct the energy of the nation towards founding Greater Britains beyond the sea ; the thought of a great Colonial Empire in America never entered the minds of the two first Tudor sovereigns   To Henry VIII , however, belongs the credit of founding the Royal Navy ; he fully realised that England should be a great naval power, supreme at sea.   Under his fostering care colleges were founded for navigation, hospitals for retired seamen ; he passed a law fixing the rate of wages for shipwrights, and gave a bounty of five per cent. for shipbuilding ; he employed Italian shipwrights to teach his subjects the art of naval construction.   In consequence of these measures, during this period English trade and navigation made wonderful strides ; English ships were larger and better built, and large sums were spent on coast defence   England reaped the benefit of these preparations in the Armada year   There were also regular voyages to Spain, the Mediterranean, and the Brazil   Though he regulated shipbuilders' wages, when a new man-of-war was to be laid down the ships' carpenters were corralled like so many cattle, and kept in durance vile until their work was completed ; the only difference was that they were paid properly for their work whilst prisoners   Hawkins, in the enlightened age of Elizabeth, carried out the same course of pressing men to work in the dockyards.

According to his lights, the king did his best to make England mistress of the seas   Under his rule, paternal government was carried to the very extreme of absurdity ; he not only prescribed his subjects' religion, but he regulated their diet, the price of meat, and their dress ; he was specially strenuous in directing all matters about the fishery, and preventing "regrating and forestalling." in the sale of fish,[1] an old-fashioned expression for cornering the market To this laudable desire on the part of the king we are indebted for a most valuable bit of historical information concerning this Colony it is contained in an Act, which, as a specimen of legislation, is unique A modern Act of Parliament is as bare and bald as a Blue Book, but these old enactments, "the statutes at large," are the very essence of English History : contained in the quaintest language, their absurd arguments and their extraordinary negation of all our modern notions of political economy make them simply delightful Amongst these wonderful productions the following is a fairly choice specimen :—

"ACT 33 HENRY VIII c. XI

" *The Bill conceryning bying of fisshe upon the see.*

" WHEREAS many and dyvers townes and portes by the see side have in tymes past bene in great welthe and prosperitie well buylded by using and exercysing the crafts and feate of fisshing by the whiche practise it was not onelie great strengthe to this Realme by reason of bringing up and encreasing of Maryners whensoever the King's Grace had nede of them but also a greate welthe to the Realme and habundance of suche wherebie oure sovereigne Lorde the King the Lords Gentilmen and Comons were alwais well served of fisshe in Market townes of a reasonable price and also by reason of the same fisshing many men were made and grewe riche and many poure Men and Women had therebie there convenyent lyving,—to the strengthe encreasing and wellthe of this realme

" And Whereas many and dyvers of the saide fissherman for their singular lucre and advantage doe love the saide crafte of fisshing and be confederate wt Pycardes Flemynghes Norman and Frenchemen and sometyme sayle over into the costes of Pycardie and Flaunders and sometyme doo meete the said Pycardes and Flemynges half the see over.

" Penalty on subjects bying fishe in Flaunders &c , or at sea to be sold in England £10.

" And be it furder enacted by the auctoritie aforesaide that it shall be lawfull to all and every fissher estrannger to come and to sell

" Provided furthermore that this Act or any thing therin conteyned shall not extende to any person whiche shall bye eny fisshe in any parties of Iseland Scotlands Orkeney, Shotlande, Irelande, or *Newland—*[Newfoundland] "

---

[1] There are regulations on this subject (RYE's *Cromer, Past and Present*, pp 45, 46), dating as far back as 1358 At first it was ordered that no fish should be landed until the masters of the ships had settled a price with the merchants, so that the fish should be sold at a reasonable price at the fairs It was found, however, that the merchants, conniving amongst themselves, refused to buy except at an unprofitable price, and the fish rotted. To remedy this, the fishermen were allowed after six days, if no price was settled, to land their fish, and sell as best they could. Mr Rye thinks they must have had wells to keep their fish alive

In PALMER's *Manship* (ii 81) there is further information on this subject. Mr Palmer also says —

" A practice seems to have grown up at an early period for the fishermen to leave the sale of their fish to the ' hosts ' or parties with whom they lodged in the town, who thus acted as brokers, paying dues and demands, and being accountable for the price If we may judge by the numerous ordinances made for their regulation, we must suppose that they attempted to monopolize the trade and to take undue advantage of their position, by appropriating to themselves too large a share of the profits

Here we have an explanation of the expression "Half seas over"—when the English met the Picardes there would be a big carousal.

The Bill is the first English Act of Parliament relating to America; it seems to have escaped the attention of American and English historical cholars; it is most invaluable for our History, as it completely establishes my argument that the English carried on the Newfoundland fishery continuously from the very discovery of the Island; our fishery, by this Act, is placed on a par with such well-established trades as the Icelandic,

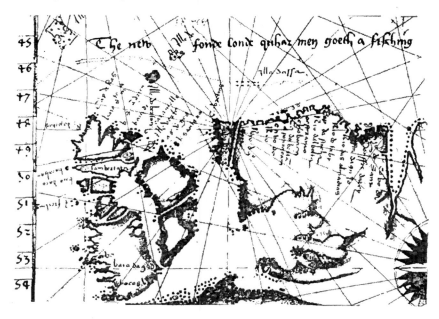

ROTZ MAP, 1542.[1]
From B.M. MS. Reg. 20 E. IX.

Irish, and Shetland fisheries. This view of the subject is further confirmed by the Act of Edward VI., and corroborated by Anthony Parkhurst, who had made four voyages to Newfoundland; writing to Hakluyt, in 1578, he said :—

"The English are commonly lords of the harbour where they fish, and use all strangers' help in fishing if need require, according *to an old custom of the country,*

[1] This map was presented to Henry VIII. by Rose (so I learn from M. Harrisse the name should be spelt), a French pilot. The map is of a composite character, based upon Cabot's and Cortoral's voyages and the French expedition to Cape Breton, but not showing the French explorations on our east and northeast coasts. The inscription, "The new fonde londe quhar men goeth a fisching," is not the work of the map maker, but has been added by some Englishman.

which thing they do willingly, so that you take nothing from them more than a boat or two of salt in respect of your protection of them against rovers or other violent intruders, who do often put them from good harbours "

In 1583, Hayes, in his narrative, also says :—

"The English merchants that were, and always be, admirals by turns interchangeably over the fleets of fishermen within the same harbour, *for our English merchants command all there.*"

How could they speak of English dominion and usage in the Colony in 1578 as an ancient custom if the English did not participate in the fishery during these past seventy or eighty years ? True, History is silent on the subject, but this furnishes no argument ; the fishery was quite beyond the scope of history as then understood, and we know, from the records, that no account was kept of the movements of fishing vessels.

The Collector was the dire enemy alike of the Devonshire, the Basque, the Norman, and the Portuguese fishermen ; concealment of both their voyages and their prosperity was a settled policy , like the poor fellaheen and the ryots, they hid their treasures from the harpies of the Government It was only when the English Admiralty officers became too outrageous in their rapacity that complaints were made to the Crown, and an Act passed in 1547 to restrain them

These adventurous old Devonshire sailors, year by year, left their little ports to reap the harvest of the seas across the Atlantic.

Each autumn the forest resounded to the woodman's axe as he felled the giant oaks to build the fishing-ship ; with skill and patient labour the sturdy little craft took form and mould , the obscure West Country haven was busy with riggers, and caulkers, and sailmakers , the hills resounded with the clang of the anvil as they forged the goodly anchor, and made the cable on which hung the lives of men

Devonshire not only reared true men, but she built good ships , every bit of timber and every nail and treenail that was driven was real honest work done by skilled hands, in the sight of all the village critics , they were not built for "yachting over summer seas," but for encounters with the ice and the hard knocks and rough voyages of the Atlantic

M Oppenheim says of the Elizabethan sailor —

" It speaks well for his seamanship afloat, and the skill and good workmanship of shipwrights ashore, that not one ship was lost by stress of weather, by fire, or by running aground During those same years, and sometimes during the same gales which the English ships weathered successfully, whole Spanish fleets foundered at sea "[1]

[1] *English Historical Review.*

Year by year, as the wealth from the far-off fishery was poured into the western counties, more ships were made and old ones repaired.

Until 1580 there are but sparse accounts of the English ships that fished in Newfoundland, but we know from contemporary history, and the Act of Henry VIII. and the further Act of Edward VI., that England carried on from Devonshire a considerable fishery in Newfoundland; the west was the great centre of maritime enterprise in England; her seamen the most daring and most numerous; all the great Elizabethan seamen—Drake, Hawkins, Raleigh—were Devonshire men.

They sailed the ships as well as they built them; their models were not our models, nor their ways our ways in the modes of shipbuilding; to use the old sailors' phrase, they built their vessels "for beasts of burthen, not for birds of passage." They had great beam, were low in the waist, high forward and aft, and had great sheer, without fore and aft sails; they were no good on a wind, but sailed fairly well going free; above all they were excellent sea-boats.

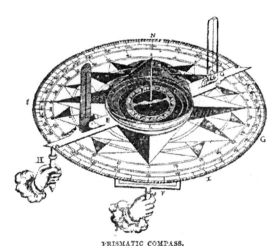

PRISMATIC COMPASS.
From Dudley's "Arcano del Mare," 1646.

The type of ship, of course, varied according to the purpose for which she was designed. In a paper by William Borough, in the reign of Elizabeth, three orders are described:—

"1. The shortest, broadest, and deepest order. To have the length by the keel double the breadth amidships, and the depth in hold half that breadth.

"This order is used in some merchant ships made for most profit.

"2. The mean and best proportion for shipping for merchandise, likewise very serviceable for all purposes. Length of keel, 2 or 2¼ that of beam. Depth of hold, ¼¼ths that of beam.

"3. The largest order for galleons or ships for the wars, made for the most advantageous of sailing. Length of keel, 3 times the beam. Depth of hold, ⅖ths of beam."

Men-of-war had high poops and deck cabins, which Raleigh condemned as "sluttish dens that breed sickness in peace"; ordinary fishing vessels in the beginning of the sixteenth century had flush decks, three masts, the foremast very far forward, and the mizzen very far aft ; the sails were three big lug sails ; the ballast carried was always sand, and the cook-room, a solid structure of brick and mortar, was built on the ballast.   Hawkins was the inventor of movable top-masts—fishing vessels were rigged low, and their masts were single spars until late in the sixteenth century.

Top-masts or top-gallant sails are not mentioned in official papers till 1618. Studding sails were not those now known by that name. They were called "bonnets" and "drablers"; the bonnet laced on to the foot of the ordinary sail, the drabler on to the foot of the bonnet.   The invention of the log line is claimed for an Elizabethan Englishman, named Humphrey Cole, but it appears to have been in use as early as 1521, on board Magellan's ships. Chain pumps, capstans, and other improvements were made only in the reign of Elizabeth. Even in this reign no large vessel had fore and aft canvas.

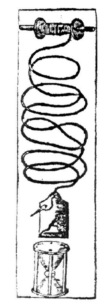

LOG LINE.

From Champlain's Voyages, 1632.

We have very few records of official voyages to the New World by Englishmen during Henry VIII.'s reign. Ships of the courtiers and gallant gentlemen, like Hore's and Gilbert's, nearly always came to grief, whilst the bluff-bowed, square, extraordinary little tubs, handled by the rough fishermen, who trusted to "latitude, lead, and look-out," made their voyages continuously for forty and fifty years [1] without losing a rope yarn ; never a mishap, nor a claim on the Insurance Company, for probably none existed then for fishing ships. [2]

In 1523 four ships were sent out by Francis I. of France, under the command of Giovanni Verrazano, a Florentine navigator ; three put back damaged, so Verrazano proceeded in the *Dolphin* alone; he cruised along the whole Atlantic coast from Carolina to Cape Breton, and on the strength of this voyage the

[1] The French Basque, Savalet, told Lescabot he had then made forty-two voyages ; and Echevete, the Spanish Basque, says he made twenty-eight.

Depositions were taken in 1667 from several seamen at Dartmouth who had been going to Newfoundland for between fifty and fifty-five years.

[2] Marine Insurance was carried on by Lombards and Flemings earlier than this ; in Elizabeth's reign it passed into the hands of Englishmen.

See Appendix, p. 84, for an Insurance effected in 1604 on a Newfoundland freight of fish to France.

French claimed a right to the countries visited by him, but the claim had no solid foundation, and was never recognised by England.[1]

The first official voyage that we know of—actually made under the direct orders of Henry VIII.—was in 1527; connected with this adventure there are many difficulties arising from the extremely scanty information obtainable on the subject. Hakluyt, our chief authority, wrote many years after the event.

There can be no doubt that the expedition was urged upon the king by Robert Thorne, of Bristol, living at Seville, who "exhorteth the " King with very waighty and substantial reasons to set forth a

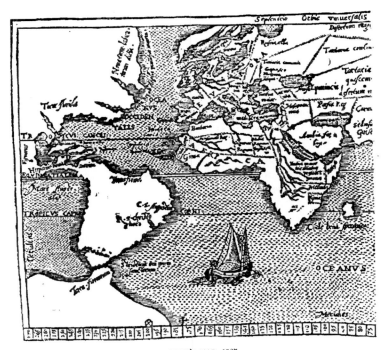

THORNE'S MAP, 1527.

From Hakluyt's "Divers Voyages," 1587.

" discouerie euen to the North Pole"; he sent a "little Mappe or Carte of the Worlde" to illustrate his views. It was clearly a royal expedition to find the north-west passage to India. John Rut,[2] the rough

---

[1] Fishermen and traders had penetrated south of Cape Breton before this; Verrazano found the natives quite prepared to trade, and able to drive a good bargain.

[2] Rut, of the Royal Navy, and the master of several ships for Henry VIII., was in the *Gabriell Royall* and *Maria de Loreta*, from 1512 to 1513; he was a yeoman of Ratcliffe; had a pension of £10 per annum, dated Hampton Court, 24 May, 19 Henry VIII.—(*Records.*)

seaman, whose letter gives us the most information about the voyage, was an old master in the navy, and when the expedition failed, through the loss of his consort, he brought home a cargo of fish.

Royal ships often traded in this reign, and were hired for commerce [1] and adventure ; there was practically no difference between the armed merchantman of those days and the Tudor Royal Navy ; there was no uniform, nothing to mark the distinction between the services.

A difficulty about this voyage arises from Hakluyt's mention of " The Canon of Saint Paul " The diligent chronicler, in his collection of " Diverse Voyages," after speaking of " worthy Master Robert Thorne's " large discourse to the King," tells us " that he was informed by " Masters Hall and Grafton that Henry sent forth two faire ships, well " victualled and manned, on the 20th of May 1527, and after making " enquiries he is told by Sir Francis Frobisher and Richard Allen that " a learned and wealthy canon of Saint Paul's went on the expedition, " that one of the ships was called the *Dominus Vobiscum*, and that " one of the ships was cast away in the Straits of Belle Isle."

It is clear that this refers to the voyage of Rut and his consort ; the dates are the same, these ships were sent by the king, and one was wrecked northward, just as the *Sampson* was.

Former writers have jumped to the conclusion that the Albert de Prado [2] who wrote a letter to Cardinal Wolsey, of the same tenour as Rut's, was a Canon of Saint Paul's, London There may have been a Canon of Saint Paul's on board, but his name was not Albert de Prado, for the Records at St. Paul's contain no such name as De Prado, Field (Prado is Spanish for field), or anything like it. That the expedition was a royal one, and fitted out by Wolsey, is shown by Lord Edward Howard's letter to the Cardinal, saying he " would be " glad to be employed in the expedition to be made to Newfoundland, " and so find his wife and children meat and drink." [3] As a voyage of discovery the expedition was a failure, but Rut's letter is invaluable, as it gives us information about the Island ; it was probably not old John's first voyage to Newfoundland, as he seems to be well acquainted with the points of land. Master Grube's two ships from Plymouth appear to have made about the same sort of passage as John Cabot's ; evidently these vessels, sailing so late, were not fishing ships, and this is another clear proof of the large English fishery then carried on in Newfoundland ; they were sack ships going out to trade and

---

[1] In 1526 we find in the *Records* a proposition to use the idle men-of-war as merchant ships to Iceland, &c

[2] The *Records* show Prado's debts were paid by the Royal Treasurer, but I can find no other information about him ; it seems likely that he was the son of a Spanish-American trader, perhaps he himself had sailed under Gomez

[3] *Records*

bring back a cargo of fish, oil, furs, and produce The regular time of sailing for the fishing would be February or March, some French vessels used to leave even in January.

Sabine, in his history of the fishery,[1] relying apparently upon Oviedo or Herrara, says that in 1517 there were only fifty ships— English, French, Spanish,[2] and Portuguese—fishing in Newfoundland, but according to the Portuguese records this must be an error; as regards the English ships, we can rest assured that Master Grube's two barques and Rut's ships were not the only English vessels there

Purchas says :—

" King Henry VIII. set forth two ships for discouerie one of which perished in the north parts of Newfoundland the Master of the other John Rut writ this letter to King Henrie in bad English and worse writing over it was this superscription.

" Master Grubes two ships departed from Plymouth the 10th day of June, and arrived in the Newfoundlands the 21 day of July and after we had left the sight of Selle [Scilly Islands] we had never sight of any land till we had sight of Cape de Bas.[3]

JOHN RUT'S LETTER

" Pleasing your Honourable Grace to heare of your servant John Rut with all his company here in good health thanks be to God and your Graceship— The *Mary of Gilford*,[4] with all her . . . . . . thanks be to God—and if it please your honourable Grace we ranne in our course to the Northward, till we came into 53 degrees, there we found many great Islands of ice and deepe water, we found no sounding, and then we durst not go no further to the Northward for feare of more ice [evidently making for a north-west passage], and then we cast about to the Southward, and within foure dayes after we had one hundred and sixtie fathom and then we came into 52 degrees and fell with the mayne land and within ten leagues of the mayne lande we met with a great Island of ice and came hard by her for it was standing in deep water and so went in with Cape de Bas[3] a good Harbour and many small Islands and a great fresh river going up farre into the mayne land and the mayne land all wilderness and mountains and woodes and no naturall ground but all mosse and no inhabitation nor no people in these parts, and in the woods we found footing of divers great beasts but we saw none not in ten leagues—And please your Grace the *Sampson* and wee kept company all the way till within two dayes before we met with all the Ilands of ice; that was the first day of July at night and there arose a great and a marvallous great storme and much foul weather—I trust in the Almightie Jesu to heare good newes of her—and please your Grace we were considering and a writing of all our order, how we would wash us, and what course we would draw and when God doe send foule weather, that with the Cape de Sper shee should go—and he that come first should tarry the space of sixe weeks one for another, and watered at Cape de

---

[1] SABINE'S *Report of the principal Fisheries of the American Seas.* Washington, 1853.

[2] See Note 2, p. 43, about Spaniards not being mentioned in Oviedo's narrative.

[3] Cape de Bas—probably Cape de Grace —Cape Bauld, the north-east point of New-foundland. It may have been the Cape de Raz shown on old maps near Cape Bauld.

[4] " Account of the victuals and wages of *Mary Guildford*, per master and purser, £19 14s 4d Lode manage and premage to master and crew at 6d per ton "

Bas ten days ordering of your Grace and fishing, and so departed to the Southward to seek our fellowe, the third day of August we entered into a good Harbour called St John and there we found Eleuen Saile of Normans and one Brittaine [Breton] and two Portugall Barks all a fishing and so we are ready to depart towards Cape de Bas that is 25 leagues as shortly as we have fished and so along the Coast until we may meete with our fellowe and so with all diligence that lyes in me toward parts to that Ilands that we are commanded at our departing [it is evident he had strict instructions to make a vigorous attempt to find a N W passage, instead of doing so he was making up a cargo of fish], and thus Jesu save and keepe your Honourable Grace and all your Honourable Reuer.

"In the Hauen of St John the third day of August written in haste 1527, by your servant John Rut to his uttermost of his power"[1]

It seems likely that Rut and Albert de Prado wrote their letters hastily to catch one of Master Grube's ships returning to Europe with her freight of fish

The only outside evidence[2] of any kind which has come down to us about this voyage is the mention by Cartier of a Cape Prato[3] in the Gulf of St. Lawrence, showing that perhaps the *Mary of Guildford* penetrated there; whether the information was given to Cartier by the vessels which were fishing in the Gulf as he passed along, or he got it from a map showing Prado's discoveries, cannot now be ascertained.

The natural curiosity of the human mind, and the spirit of adventure which leads all sorts and conditions of men, even in the present day, to Africa and the wilds of Asia, prompted in the reign of bluff King Hal one of the most extraordinary wild-cap expeditions it has ever been the lot of the historian to describe, it is recorded by the industrious Hakluyt as—

"The voyage of Master Hore and divers other gentlemen to Newfoundland and Cape Briton in the yere 1536

"Master Hore, of London, a man of goodly stature and of great courage, and given to the study of Cosmographie, in the yere of our Lord 1536, encouraged divers gentlemen and others, being assisted by the king's favour and good countenance, to accompany him in a voyage of discoverie upon the north west parts of America, wherein his persuasions tooke such effect that within a short space many gentlemen of the Inns of Court and of the Chancerie, and divers others of good worship desirous to see the strange things of the world, very willingly entered into the action with him . . . . The whole number that went in the two tall ships the *Trinitie* and the *Minion* were five score persons, whereof 30 were gentlemen, which all were mustered in warlike manner at Gravesend, and after the receiving of the sacrament they embarked themselves in the ende of April 1536"[4]

[1] PURCHAS' *His Pilgrims*, 1625

[2] When we remember that Thorne had an agent, Tyson, in the Spanish West Indies, selling armour for him, it seems quite unnecessary to connect (BARRETT and CORRY) the arrival of an English three-master at Porto Rico with this expedition. English ships were, I believe, frequently in the Brazils, and along the coast of Maine, even as early as this, and the fact that the ship mentioned by Herrera was armed, had come from the Bacallaos, crossed the Gulf Stream, and lost a Piedmont pilot in a fight with the natives, need in no way apply to Rut's expedition

[3] This may have been, however, only a natural name (Prado—a field) applied to the beautiful grass-covered Magdalen Islands

They appear to have been so badly victualled that they were guilty of cannibalism; they had no pilot, otherwise they would have gone on the well-known track to Newfoundland. What thirty idle gentlemen and briefless barristers expected to find or do in these unknown regions it is impossible to conjecture. They did not lose the two tall ships, but they were so starved and impoverished that, but for the timely arrival of a French ship in some part of the south-western coast of Newfoundland, probably White Bear Bay, they would all have perished. The only advantage of having so many lawyers aboard

CASTALDI'S MAP, ABOUT 1550.[1]

From Ramusio's "Le Navigationi."

appears at this juncture, for, says Hakluyt:—

"When in their dire extremity, and as they were going to cast lots who should be killed, such was the mercie of God, that in the same night there arrived a French ship in that port well furnished with vittaile, and *such was the policie of the English* [acting, no doubt, on the advice of their learned counsel] that they became masters of the same, and, changing ships and vittailing them, they set sail to come into England."

This ill-fated expedition, product of the enthusiasm and ignorance of the age, is one of the many wrecks with which our history is strewn; court gallants and hair-brained lawyers are poor substitutes for practical seamen in dangerous exploring voyages; Gilbert's disastrous expedition is a still more striking example of the utter folly of putting landsmen in charge of ships.

[1] This is the first engraved map specially devoted to Newfoundland.

In the magnificent work of Navarrete, " Colleccion de los Viages &c.," recounting all the discoveries of the Spaniards up to the sixteenth century, he describes the voyage in 1525 of Estevan Gomez, a Spaniard from Corunna, who took with him a crew of hardy Basque fishermen, and explored the American coast, certainly as far north as Cape Race, on the strength of this expedition Diego Ribero marks all the present United States as the land of Stephen Gomez, " Tierra de Estevan Gomez," and therefore belonging to Spain Navarrete says he found the sea full of fish, and there can be no doubt he was in Newfoundland.

It is clearly proved, as well as any remote historical event can be substantiated, that the English, Portuguese, Bretons, and Normans were the first fishermen in Newfoundland. The Spanish Basques or Biscayans did not engage regularly in the fishery until about 1545, previous to that period they carried on a very extensive fishery in Ireland; gradually this was reduced, and the Biscayans turned their attention to the great Transatlantic fishery ; we have abundant evidence that besides the codfishery they carried on a very extensive whale and seal fishery, both in the Gulf of St Lawrence and to the northward Their head-quarters were in the gulf and straits known in those ancient times as the Grand Bay The splendid harbour of Port-Aux-Basques still commemorates their presence on our shores The Biscayans used to continue their operations until December. From these hardy and daring fishermen England had to obtain harpooners when she first began whaling

We seem to have proof of the commencement of the Spanish fishery in the Colony in a very complete form. First there is the Spanish permission given in 1511 by Ferdinando el Catolico to Juan de Agramonte to take two ships :—

" Á descobrir cierta tierra nueva en los limites que a nos pertenescen—to discover certain new land within the limits [fixed by the Pope] which belong to us. [The charter goes on to state that the crew must be Spaniards] with the exception of two pilots, who may be Bretons, or of other nation who have been there—á excepcion de dos pilotos, que permitia fueran *Bretones* o de otra nacion que alla hayan estado " [1]

Agramonte sailed to North America, found no gold, but captured some slaves , his voyage was not repeated. [2]

---

[1] DURO, p. 310.
[2] In 1523 Lucas Vasques de Ayllon was granted the title of Adelantado, fifteen leagues square of land, and two codfisheries in the country discovered by him. De Ayllon received a charter in this year to search for a strait north of Florida, but was required to avoid Portuguese possessions (Newfoundland was placed within their limits) I think these fisheries were much further south than our Island

Oviedo—a Spaniard and contemporary of Gomez—mentions no Spanish vessels in Newfoundland. Herrara, a much later *compiler*, does—apparently about 1527.

Then we have in the English Calendar of State Papers (vol v., 443) 1535 :—[1]

"Sir A St. Leger said that as many as 200 to 300 sail of Spanish fishermen might sometimes be seen at one time in Valentia Harbour [in Ireland]"

In the Spanish Naval Records edited by Captain C. Fernandez Duro, of the Royal Spanish Navy, there is a—

"Memorial from the son of Matias de Echevete saying that he was the first Spaniard who went to the Newfoundland fishery in a French vessel 1545, and afterwards made 28 voyages up to 1599, being the founder of the Basque fishery there —Memorial del hijo de Matias de Echevete diciendo que este fuè el primer Espanol que fuè a la pesca de Terra Nova en nao Francesca el ano 1545 y despues hizo 28 viages hasta el de 1599 siendo fundador de la pesca de los Vascongados "[2]

And in 1561 Sir T. Chamberlain said :—

"The Spanish had found a trade to Newfoundland which previously they did not occupy so much "[3]

If the memorial of Echevete is not absolutely true, it represents substantially the truth, for Navarette does not claim a very early participation in our fishery for his countrymen, but considers probably the report of Gomez gave an impetus to the fishery, he mentions the Biscayan lawsuit in 1561, at San Sebastian, when evidence was given by sailors having been forty years in the trade, but Navarette does not lay much stress upon this, and it seems most likely their fishing in Newfoundland did not assume a national character till about 1545 ; judging from the accounts of the Spanish historians, it is not unlikely that individual ships came upon the coast to trade from the earliest times, possibly bringing salt and returning with fish.[4]

But the question appears to be completely settled by the following account by Captain Duro of this lawsuit, taken from the Records of San Sebastian —

"In 1561 a dispute arose about the payment to the Church of Two per cent on the products of the Newfoundland fishery, at which time witnesses were asked if they knew if the Newfoundland fishery had been followed for only a few years Amongst the declarants were some old men of seventy, who all agreed that this fishery was not more than from seventeen to twenty years established before then. That is to say that they frequented Newfoundland from 1541 to 1545, and on account of the very much gain in these voyages they had abandoned their fishery in Flanders England and other places   Some of the witnesses said that the fishery of Newfoundland had been discovered since the year 1526 and that the Guipuscoans carried it on since 1540."

"En el pleito seguido en San Sebastian el año 1561 con los maestres de Naos, sobre pagar à las iglesias el dos por ciento de los productos de la pesca de Terra Nova en el cual se preguntó a los testigos   Si saben que la pesqueria de Tierranueva ha seido hallada y usada de pocos años y tiempo à esta parte; y habiendo entre

[1] Records   Probably exaggerated
[2] Duro's Arca de Noé, p 313
[3] Records.

See HARRISSE's Discovery of North America, 1892.

los declarantes algunos ancianos hasta de setenta años tódos estuvieron conformes en que la pesca no contaba mayor antiguedad que de diez y seis á veinte años a la fecha: es decir, que se frecuentaba desde 1541 ó 1545 y que por la mucha ganancia que producian estos viages se habian abandonado los to Flandes, Inglaterra y otros partes, &c.[1]

The celebrated voyages of Jacques Cartier in 1534, 1535, and 1541, gave France the title to Canada. Cartier had probably been an old fisherman on the Newfoundland coast; his native port, St. Malo, every year sent out fishermen to the New World. It is to Cartier that we owe the first description of the noble river St. Lawrence, and a true configuration of our island; although his enterprise was barren of results and his attempts at colonising Canada failed, he greatly enlarged our knowledge of the New World, and laid the foundation of the mighty empire of New France.

Sieur Jean Francis de la Roche, Seigneur de Roberval, who had sailed in August 1541 with three ships with two hundred persons and

JACQUES CARTIER.

After an old portrait.

" divers gentlemen of quality," affords another example like Hore, of the failure of landsmen in naval affairs. On his way to Quebec he met Jallobert and Noel, two of Cartier's captains, in St. John's.[2] His expedition to New France was a series of disasters. In the autumn of 1543 he and all his followers abandoned the Colony. The account of Roberval's voyage is very meagre, and we can only gather from it that our harbour of St. John's, even in that early age, was the capital and head-quarters of the Transatlantic fishery. On his arrival, Roberval tells us that he found seventeen ships of fishers in the harbour; unfortunately he does not give us their nationality. He also had a dispute with some Portuguese fishermen in the Straits of Belle Isle. Clearly these old cod smacks had discovered all around the St. Lawrence long before the court gallants and their grand expeditions. Cartier's patent was strenuously opposed at Court by the Breton merchants, who considered these exploring expeditions would injure their fishing rights in the Gulf, and even when he obtained his grant, they were able to

---

[1] C. F. Duro's *Arca de Noé*, p. 314.
[2] Hakluyt's statement that Roberval met Cartier is disproved by Gosselin. Roberval's arrival at St. John's was most likely in the autumn of 1541; this may account for the small number of vessels he met there.

prevent his getting a crew until the king sent peremptory orders to
the authorities at St. Malo. Cartier mentions meeting French fisher-

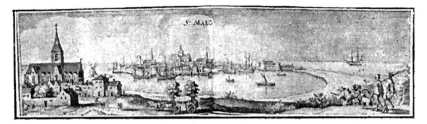

ST. MALO ABOUT 1620.
From an engraving of Merian's.

men in the Gulf, probably at Brest—Entre du Golf—from the very
earliest times the northern head-quarters of the Gulf fishery.

DIEPPE ABOUT 1620.
From an engraving of Merian's.

There is little to note concerning our Island history during this
reign. Far from the jarring strife of Europe, the fishermen pursued
their humble trade in Newfoundland ; year by year they built up a
great business, which grew and prospered and enriched England.

Both the great Tudor monarchs were statesmen—men of energy and
ability—yet both failed to grasp the idea of a Colonial Empire ; just as
in our days parish politics in the Colonies and narrow views at home
obscure from our countrymen the grand idea of Imperial Federation.

APPENDIX TO CHAPTER III.

I. The Basque Fishery.

The words "Biscayan" and "Guipuscoan" occur frequently in the old writers, they refer to two divisions of the Basque provinces in Spain, the third province, "Alava," being inland, is not mentioned.

The Spanish Basques were amongst the most adventurous navigators in Europe, they were the great whalers of ancient days. There are very early notices of their codfishing; a treaty was made between them and Edward III, signed 1st August 1351, which conceded to them the right to fish on the English coast for certain payments during twenty years Navarrete, vol 1, p 48, says —

"El padre Las Casas, que poseyó los papeles de Colon, digo que el Admirante, tenia apuntado en su libro de memorias, entre otros indicios de la existencia de tierras al Occidente, que un marinero tuerto, en el puerto de Santa Maria, y otro Gallego, en Murcia, le habian dicho, que un viage que hicieron á Irlanda, desviados de su derrota, navegaron tanto al N O, que avistaron una tierra que imaginarion ser la Tartaria, y era Terra Nova"

"Father Las Casas, who had possession of Columbus' papers, says that the Admiral had an entry in his note book, amongst other indications of the existence of lands in the West, that a cock-eyed sailor in St Mary's Port and another, Gallego, in Murcia, had told him that on a voyage which they had made to Ireland, thrown out of their course, they sailed so far to the north-west that they saw land, which they imagined to be Tartary and was Newfoundland."

This is a very doubtful story If land was seen, it was most probably Greenland, which appeared upon maps before Columbus' voyage, and was undoubtedly visited by traders, most likely Biscayan whalers, before Cabot's discovery. The name Labrador (given apparently to all the land north of Newfoundland at first) has been claimed as that of a Biscayan whaling captain Scoresby's book contains much information on this whale fishery.

The facts given in the text are strongly against the claim that these men fished in Newfoundland before 1497. Juan de la Cosa, a Biscayan, and the highest authority of his day, does not appear to know our coast, nor do there appear to be any names of a Biscayan source on the earliest maps. '

A Spanish writer, Tomé Cano, declares, that since the Spaniards lost this fishery 487,500 qtls have been annually consumed in Spain, costing £600,000.

Bad government has been the curse of Spain, and of all the Spanish colonies, it fell most heavily on these fair Basque provinces. All the industry, both by sea and land, of these hardy toilers, these brave industrious Cantabrians, could make no headway against kings, who, notwithstanding repeated royal promises to respect their rights, laid an embargo on their ships and took their labourers and seamen to man the royal fleets

There is no more piteous story in European history than the decay and impoverishment of this great Basque nation by Spanish misgovernment. A witty proverb well expresses this chronic cause of national decay. The saintly Alfonso was in such high favour in Heaven that the Holy Virgin could not refuse his prayers, he supplicated that the Spaniards might be the bravest, and their women might be the most lovely, and their country the most fertile, all was granted "One more favour, Holy Mother," said the king, "give Spain a good government" "No, my son," said the Virgin, "if Spain had a good government I would not be able to keep an angel in Heaven a day longer."

Echevete gives an account of the Spanish fishing and whaling fleet being caught in the autumn of 1577 and frozen up in some port in Newfoundland or Labrador (in the original record the name is left blank), that five hundred and forty men died, and that seventeen of the best sailors of Zarauz were amongst them. We know from Whitbourne and Guy's instructions that the Biscayans remained in Newfoundland until very late in December. With their poor appliances for heating and ragged clothing they may have succumbed to the rigours of an unusually hard winter By a sudden change of weather, very common in this country, they may have been frozen up. A number of English crews were caught in this way in the winter of 1817 as far south as Renews

The Basques had fine vessels. In 1586 Bingham mentions the capture of one off Ireland of four hundred tons with a large crew, mostly boys, and very ragged.

We learn from the Spanish Records that, in 1549, a Biscayan Catholic priest ministered to the spiritual wants of his devout countrymen in Newfoundland, the Spanish Basques, like the noble Bretons, being distinguished for their loyalty to the Church The Basques in our times are celebrated as Catholics,

Conservatives, and Carlists. "Dios, Patria, y Rey," is the provincial war cry

"1549, Marzo 23 Memorial de Jacobo de Ibiceta Maestro de Nao previendo para la pesca de Terra Nova pidiendo ornamentos para que un clerigo que lleva a bordo puede decir misa en aquella Tierra."—(*Collec. Vargas. Ponce, ley III*)

The Spanish Records state that during the reign of Philip II. two hundred ships and six thousand men were employed in Newfoundland The king wished them to have a convoy of ships of war; in 1553 there was a Royal ordinance to this effect The Biscayans thanked the king for his solicitude about their interests, but they did not wish to have his ships with them, theirs were ready to sail, and they had expended two hundred thousand ducats fitting them out The order was revoked The Biscayans argued that they were safer going together in twos and threes than in a fleet

They were very jealous of their provincial rights, and rebelled against the requisitions made on them by Philip II. for ships and men.

We have preserved the report to the queen of a conversation of Sir T Chamberlain with the King of Spain, 1561 —

"In Biscay they had for a long time felled timber for building ships, and planted none, so there was scarcely any now, and that double the price it was 30 years ago Those of Biscay frankly declared that their ships had been so often stopped for the king's service and so badly paid, that they had to turn to other trades He [Chamberlain] alleged another reason to prove the country was not destitute of shipping by their trading further off, and that they, the Spanish, have found a trade unto the Newfoundland for fish, which they did not previously occupy so much"

As the result of Sir B Drake's expedition in 1585, the fishermen did not propose to go to Newfoundland in 1586 (*Advertisements from Spain*), and in fact a general embargo was laid on the whole fleet

In 1587 (year before the Armada), 24 June, St Jehan de Luce, Shute wrote to Walsingham —"In Spain it seems they are in hopes of peace with Her Majesty and along the coasts adjoining France it is much desired insomuch as they are not pressing forward the rigging of ten large ships, he gave Walsingham advice of And whereas it was prohibited in all the Ports of La Provence and Biscay that none should go forth unto the Newland a fishing, of late it is permitted and they are preparing as they of custom have done hitherto"—(*Hatfield MS*)

This is confirmed by the Spanish Records A royal order forbade any ships to sail to Newfoundland without license; the ships were wanted for the Armada, then preparing. It was only on the 15th July that instructions were sent to release them, with a warning to go

well armed, and be careful about English pirates from Rochelle

The scare of the impending conflict virtually destroyed the Biscayan fishery From this time forward the Newfoundland fishery was principally in English hands The great Spanish fleet dwindled down in a few years from one hundred and fifty sail to less than ten For we learn in 1593, from Sylvester Wyat, who made a voyage from Bristol to Newfoundland, that he found only eight Spanish vessels in a fleet of upwards of eighty sail of French and English.

The Spanish fishery not only suffered from the war, but from the excessive duties imposed on their products It was the most flourishing industry in Spain, but the impecunious Government, instead of encouraging it, helped to destroy it by a load of taxation and severe restrictions, especially the monopoly of salt.

In 1602 seven Basque vessels went to Newfoundland for whaling, and many more for fishing

In 1631 the Biscayan fishery to Newfoundland was in very low water, in 1632 only six ships went out, in 1638 thirty ships were in the business

In 1681, however, from the Port of Passage alone, there were 13 vessels of 2,810 tons and 550 men for codfishing in Newfoundland, and nine vessels of 2,060 tons for whaling; they carried from 5 to 20 guns

In 1681 the French prohibited the Basques from fishing in Newfoundland I do not think this order was ever really carried out. From the English Records it appears very distinctly that the Biscayans fished with the French, and were on the most friendly terms The Spanish and French Basques were always most closely allied

In 1690, according to the Spanish Records, the French again refused to allow them to fish there any more, as it was a French colony

From a resumé of the sworn testimony taken at St Sebastian in 1697, given in Captain Duro's book, we have fuller information on the subject of the French excluding the Biscayans from Newfoundland

The first witness called was Captain Martin De Sapiain His testimony is as follows —

"Que en el tiempo de su memoria, que la tiene de cuarenta y ocho años à esta parte, habia visto que los naturales de esta provincia han ido à las islas y costas de Terra Nova à hacer pesca de bacallao en cualquier puerto, como son Traspas, Santa Maria, Cunillas Placencia, Petit Placencia, Petit Paradis, Martiris, Buria Chumea, Buria Andia, San Lorenz Chumea, San Laurenz Andia, San Pierre, Fortuna, Miquele Portu, Chasco Portu, Señoria, Opot Portu, Tres Islas, Portuchoa y Echaide Portu que este ultimo lo descubrio Juan de Echaide."

Having thus stated that, within his memory of forty-eight years, he has seen that Biscayans had gone to the islands and coasts of Newfoundland to fish in any port, such as the following [as above], and at Echaide Portu, which was discovered by Juan Echaide, a native of St. Sebastian, Sapiain says —

"He knew Echaide, who died forty years ago [1650], being then eighty years old. That in none of these ports had there ever been any embargo or impediment by the subjects of the King of France or of any other kingdom, and that, without distinction or preference, whoever occupied first in the harbour had the preference, according to immemorial custom, whereof the memory of man runneth not to the contrary, and he has seen this until the present year, when they have been interrupted by the French"

With the products of successful whaling, fishing, and sealing in Newfoundland, the Spanish Basques built the stately old houses which are the admiration of travellers, amidst the green hills and lovely vales of Alava, Viscaya, and Guipuscoa, the fairest scenes in all Northern Spain

Many of the old Biscayan families have a whale in their coats of arms, showing that the founders made their fortunes in the fishing and whaling business. Clements R Markham, C B, F R S, in his paper on the Basque whale fishery, shows that the Basques captured the whale (*Balæna Biscayensis*) from time immemorial in boats; that Baffin and the first English whaling vessels were in the habit of shipping boats' crews of Basques to harpoon the whales; also that the word "harpoon" is derived from the Basque word "*arpoi*," the root being "*ar*," to take quickly; the Basque "*harpoinari*" is a harpooneer

Viscaya (Biscay) and Guipuscoa and Alava had free institutions long before England

II. The French Newfoundland Fishery.

The French have always been our great rivals in the Newfoundland fishery, and twice they have overrun the Colony and completely defeated the English

Their fishermen, the Normans and Bretons, were amongst the first to carry on the great Transatlantic trade in Newfoundland; Parkhurst said these daring old mariners had very small, poorly fitted out vessels, yet they fished on the banks in the most stormy month of the year; Whitbourne mentions meeting them on his way out in the spring.

In 1523 a Captain Coo took several French prizes, amongst them a ship of Rouen, with Newfoundland fish, fisher boats, crays, &c The Frenchmen seem to have made a stubborn resistance, for it cost £6 18s to heal sixteen men *burnt* in taking this Newfoundland ship

In 1529, in consequence of robberies by Bristol's barks, no Breton or Portuguese ships dare come to Milford, but in 1537 we find the tables turned and French and Spanish openly plundering English fishing vessels and entering harbours, and as late as 1558 we learn that the trade of Bristol was thoroughly crippled on account of great losses from enemies who had taken their best ships

In 1542 there is a letter from the Privy Council to the Mayor of Bristol to discharge a French ship laden with fish out of Newfoundland, which was arrested for certain considerations in that port.

In 1531 the *La Barbara*, of "Seynt Bridgeon," John Callaye, master, with fish from Newfoundland *Island*, was stranded at "Rammersgate."

French fishing in Newfoundland was so flourishing in 1540 that the authorities of St. Malo had to stay ships in order to get Cartier a crew. In 1541 and 1542 no less than sixty French ships were fishing in Newfoundland (Gosselin) In 1546 we have the report of John Francis of Roan (Rouen) being spoiled by an English pirate of Newland fish In January and February 1544 from Havre, Rouen, Dieppe, and Harfleur about two ships left every day for the fishery In 1545 no ship of France left for Canada for fear of the Spaniards

By the foreign intelligence from France we learn that the English agent found at St Malo on the 15th April 1560 twenty-five ships waiting for a fair wind for Newfoundland, and at Carcolle five ships ready to start with those of St Malo.

From the Records in 1561 we know that thirty ships left for Newland from the little towns of Jumieges, Vaterville, and La Bonille, and that the tonnage had risen from seventy to one hundred and fifty tons for these ships, and that many of them were "well appointed" Neither of these statements agree with Parkhurst's description.

Elizabeth's Government seem to have been always eager for information about the French Newfoundland fleet On April 20 1561 Throckmorton reported to the queen —

"The Constable of France said that he knew no more about the rigging of a ship than about the day of judgment, nor of army, men, munitions or artillery for these ships; that now was the time their men used to prepare to go to Newfoundland for fishing, and per-adventure some would go to *Rome* [a neat hit at the Protestant Walsingham]. That they made three notable voyages in the year, in the spring to Newfoundland fishing, in August to the Bourbage, and in October to Rochelle and Bordeaux for wines"

The French fishing fleet was by far the largest during the early period from 1504 to 1580. Owing probably to the wars and the distracted state of France, the French fishing declined during the reign of Elizabeth, and on

D

the advent of James to the throne, out of 400
vessels engaged in the trade, the English had
250 and later 270; of the remaining 150
vessels there were not probably more than
70 or 80 French. In 1645 the French were
the only rivals of the English in Newfoundland, their numbers were then reckoned at
100 sail.

In the following chapters I shall refer to
this important subject more at length, in order
to show the great change which took place in
the relative positions of the great contending
parties. During the reign of the Tudors,
until the occupation of Placentia by the
French, and even for a few years later, they
fished, in common with the English, all about
the coast, but chiefly on the north part of the
Island, called by them "Petit Nord," extending from White Bay to Quirpon, and on the
south and west extending from Cape Race to
Cape Ray.

CHAPTER IV.

REIGN OF EDWARD VI.

1547–1553.

1547.—2nd & 3rd Edward VI., Act of Parliament punishing officers of the Admiralty for taking bribes from the fishermen of Newfoundland, Iceland, and Ireland

1549 —A priest accompanies the Basque fleet to Newfoundland

1550 —Map, B M MSS , 17,938*b*, showing English influence

REIGN OF MARY

1553–1558.

1553 —Spanish ordinance that the Basque Newfoundland fleet should be convoyed , order revoked upon protest of the merchants.

REIGN OF ELIZABETH.

1558–1603.

1560 —Twenty-five vessels at St Malo, waiting for a fair wind for Newfoundland, and five at Carcolle

1561 —Sir T. Chamberlain's report on Basque shipping The Constable of France's report upon the movement of French ships, thirty ships go from Jumieges, Vaterville, and La Bouille to Newfoundland, dispute about payment of tithes to the church of St Sebastian by Basque Newfoundland fishermen

1562 —Act confirming 2nd & 3rd Edward VI

1564 —5 Eliz c v , Act forbidding cod to be imported in barrels

1565.—Hawkins, on his way from West Indies, stopping on the banks to fish Frobisher's voyage of discovery for a north-west passage , names Frobisher's straits

1568.—Petition against importation of dried fish falsely marked as " Iceland "

1577 —Basque fleet frozen up in Newfoundland or Labrador , five hundred and forty men perished

1578 —Anthony Parkhurst's voyage and description of the country, fifty English vessels engaged in Newfoundland fishery, France and Spain, one hundred and fifty sail each, Portuguese, fifty. Sir H Gilbert's first voyage, stayed a short time ; lost a ship and a bold captain, Miles Morgan , defeated by Spaniards

1579 —Whitbourne's first voyage to Newfoundland, in a ship of Master Cotton's, of Southampton ; loaded in Trinity.

1580 —Demand of Denmark for payment of usual licence fees in Iceland Charter-party for Newfoundland fish at 10s per 100, and oil at £12, freight to Bordeaux 38s

1581.—Only two hundred traders going to Iceland , 23 Eliz c vii , relating to the fishery

1582 —Voyage of Sir Thomas Hampshire to Newfoundland with five ships , settled the tenure of ships' rooms

1583 —Sir Humphrey Gilbert's last voyage, came to St John's to get supplies ; took possession of the Colony ; made several grants of land, lost on passage home First important description of the country by Hayes, the captain of the only surviving vessel of the expedition Peckham's Brief Discourse Over two hundred sail of Spanish Basques fishing, whaling, and sealing on our coasts and Labrador Petition of Downing to import barrelled fish ; further petition in 1586 of Sir Wm Gorges on the same subject

1585 —Sir Walter Raleigh's first colonisation at Roanoke, in Virginia, colony destroyed Sir Bernard Drake, with a commission from Elizabeth, seized several Spanish and Portuguese vessels in Newfoundland, met Whitbourne in St John's.

1586—Indenture of Newfoundland fish for the army in Ireland at 20s per 100. Basque fleet forbidden to go to Newfoundland Drake reports "the Passage" full of Newfoundland fish, "new and very good"

1587.—Embargo on Basque fleet not withdrawn this year till 15th July

1588.—Spanish Invincible Armada defeated by the English; English Newfoundland fleet stayed at home to fight; great fleet of Spanish Basques practically disappears from Newfoundland from this date

1589—Only 10,000 Newfoundland fish on the market in the West of England. Merchants of the West prohibited from trading to Brittany (then in the hands of the Leaguers), and ordered to go to Jersey and Guernsey instead.

1591—Petitions of P de Hody and Harques for restitution of ships and fish captured by Bristol privateers Petition about ancient right of English to fish in Iceland, upon payment of merely nominal licences.

1592—Twenty Spanish ships-of-war off Scilly trying to intercept the English Newfoundland fleet.

1593—Richard Strange made a voyage to prosecute seal fishery; head-quarters at Ramea, Gulf of St Lawrence. Sylvester Wyet from Bristol found only eight Spanish ships in a fleet of eighty; statement in the House of Commons by Raleigh, on 19th February, that the Newfoundland fishery was the stay and support of the West of England; there is also a letter of Raleigh's of this year, stating that the Newfoundland " voyages " were the only ones making any profit

1594.—Captain Rice Jones, of Bristol, made a voyage to Newfoundland, and prosecuted the fishery at St. Pierre. Guernsey destitute of provisions and Newfoundland fish Newfoundland fleet in danger from three Spanish men-of-war; Raleigh writes to Cecil, that all the Newfoundland fleet of one hundred sail may be taken, " *the greatest calamity which could befall England* "

1595—Supplies from Newfoundland for army in Ireland

1596.—French pirate, Michel de Sancé, captured English vessel commanded by Richard Clark

1597.—Charles Leigh and Abraham Von Herwic, London merchants, came out to do business in Newfoundland June 15th to 24th—Sir Anthony Shirley re-victualled in Newfoundland on his way to England Dutch, Irish, and French ships at Plymouth in September, waiting to buy fish when the English Newfoundland fleet arrived

1598—Large cargoes of Newfoundland fish brought to Southampton and Poole; greater part sold by October to go to Spain, by way of France.

1599—Licence to Bowgan to export 60,000 Newfoundland fish from England.

1600—Sir Walter Raleigh, Governor of Jersey, inaugurated trade between the Island and Newfoundland; Jersey a free port. Newfoundland fish selling in Bayonne at 14 to 18 royals, " according to goodness."

1601.—Spanish vessels attempting to intercept the Newfoundland fleet

1602—Spanish Newfoundland fleet reported to be kept back to take troops to Ireland, seven Basque vessels go to Newfoundland for whaling, and many more for fishing from St Jean de Luz Gosnold's voyage to New England.

1603.—Attack on an English ship in Newfoundland by seven French vessels; damage £949.

During the reigns of Edward VI. and Mary—times of great religious and political excitement—commerce and maritime adventure languished. There was, however, already a considerable Brazil trade, and much commerce to the Levant and Spanish America. Sir John Hawkins in

1562 began the traffic in negroes between Africa and South America—
"the commodious and gainful voyage to the Brazils," as Hakluyt calls

ELIZABETH.

*From an engraving after the
Newcome picture.*

this inhuman trade. Up to the end of
Mary's reign the trade to Spanish America
was partly open to the English; in her
time trade between England and Russia
also commenced. There are, however, no
recorded voyages to this Colony. The
Newfoundland fish trade had for some
time been a settled business. Not only a
large fishery, but a large trade was carried
on in Newfoundland, as shown by the
presence of merchant ships, like Mr. Grube's
two vessels, noticed in the last chapter.
The most important information about the
island in this reign is contained in the
following Act of Edward VI., proving
conclusively the magnitude and continuity
of the English fishery transactions and trade to the new land :—

"2nd & 3rd Ed., Cap. VI., A.D. 1548.

*" An Act against the Exacting of Money or other Thing by any Officer for License to
traffick into Ireland, &c.*

"FORASMUCH as within these few Years now last past there hath been
levied, perceived and taken by certain of the officers of the Admiralty, of such
Merchants and Fishermen as have used and practised the Adventures and
Journeys into *Iseland, Newfoundland, Ireland,* and other Places commodious
for Fishing and the getting of Fish, in or upon the Seas or otherwise, by way
of Merchandise in those parts, divers great Exactions, as Sums of Money, Doles,
or Shares of Fish, and such other like Things, to the great Discouragement and
Hindrance of the same Merchants and Fishermen, and to no little damage to the
whole Commonweal: And whereof also great Complaints have been made and
Informations also yearly to the King's Majesty's most Honourable Council:
For Reformation whereof, and to the Intent also that the said Merchants and
Fishermen may have Occasion the rather to practise and use the same Trade
of Merchandise and Fishing freely without any such Charges or Exactions as
is before limited, whereby it is to be thought that more plenty of Fish shall
come into this Realm, and thereby to have the same at more reasonable prices:

"Be it therefore enacted by the King our Sovereign Lord, and the Lords
and Commons in this present Parliament assembled, and by the Authority of the
same, that neither they, nor any Officer or Minister, Officers or Ministers of the
Admiralty for the Time being, shall in any wise hereafter exact, receive or take
by himself, his Servant, Deputy, Servants or Deputies, of any such Merchant or
Fisherman, any Sum or Sums of Money, Doles or Shares of Fish, or any other
Reward, Benefit, or Advantage whatsoever it be, for any Licence to pass this
Realm to the said Voyages or any of them, nor upon any Respect concerning
the said Voyages or any of them: upon Pain to forfeit for the first Offence
treble the Sum, or treble the Value of the Reward, Benefit, or Advantage that
any such Officer or Minister shall hereafter have to take of any such Merchant

or Fisherman; for the which Forfeiture the Party grieved, and every other Person or Persons, whatsoever he or they be, shall and may sue for the same by Information, Bill, Plaint or Action of Debt, in any of the King's Courts of Record, the King to have the one Moiety, and the Party complaining the other Moiety: In which suit no Essoin, Protection or Wager of Law shall be allowed: And for the second Offence the Party so offending not only to lose or forfeit his or their Office or Offices in the Admiralty, but also to make fine and Ransom at the King's Will and Pleasure."

During the whole Tudor Period up to the earlier years of Elizabeth's reign, England, as an ally of Spain, made no effectual opposition to her exclusive dominion in America. Under a spirited sovereign, however, like Elizabeth, Englishmen could no longer endure the galling yoke and jealous exclusiveness of the Spaniards in South America. In Newfoundland the Devon fishermen learnt how to measure their strength with them, to conquer and to rule the Biscayan and the Basque. Soon the English, following the example of the hardy seamen of Brittany, began to infest the Spanish West Indies. The smuggling piratical trade begun by the French was followed up by Drake, Hawkins, and countless other daring West Country adventurers. English historians do not acknowledge the fact, but it is quite clear that the first lesson in taming the Spaniard was learnt by the courageous Devonshire fishermen in Newfoundland.

"The spacious days of Great Elizabeth" form the most brilliant period of English history. To this golden age our Island story is united by imperishable bands—linked for ever with the Immortals who have made the Elizabethan age the wonder and the glory of all time. The nursing mother of our infant Colony was the Divine Gloriana. The great Bacon was not only a shareholder in Guy's plantation, but with his powerful influence he strongly advocated in a pamphlet the policy of settlement; he speaks of "The Gold Mines " of the Newfoundland Fishery, of which there " is none so rich." Spenser—Raleigh's greatest friend—was united with him in his colonisation schemes, and it needs no stretch of the imagination to picture to ourselves the greatest English man of action—explorer, warrior, statesman, above all poet—expounding with glowing eloquence to Shakespeare his vast schemes of the Plantation in the Newfoundlands and the building up of a greater England beyond the seas.

SIR FRANCIS DRAKE.
From a print in the B.M.

In this age of Elizabeth we seem to breathe a freer and a nobler air. The chains of feudalism have been cast off for ever. Compared with former reigns, Shakespeare's time seems strangely modern. The plays that delighted the subjects of the virgin queen still charm the subjects of Victoria. Cecil, Prime Minister of Elizabeth, has a direct and still more illustrious descendant in Lord Salisbury, Prime Minister of our own time. No other Government in Europe can show such stability and continuity as this. And then the great queen herself is strangely familiar to us, ever in public, graceful, majestic, ready to make a speech on all occasions. The fierce light that beats upon a throne has brought out all her follies and frivolities. Granted that her speech and manner would not suit our modern sensibilities, still she will ever remain a great personality, the most picturesque figure in English history—"the Pilot that weathered the storm"—the great sovereign that ever sought the public weal—"that wrought her people lasting good"

Our own history in this age also opens up more clearly. We are no longer groping in the dark, with obscure records and contradictory testimony. From the illustrious writers of the period we are able now to give "the very age and body of the time his form and pressure"

In the first years of her reign Raleigh was a boy, and neither Elizabeth nor her councillors had any thought of American colonisation; she was, however, most favourable to voyages of discovery. She gave substantial aid to the daring Frobisher in his arctic voyage to discover a north-west passage to India.[1]

She was her father's daughter, and her masculine mind thoroughly realised that England should be mistress of the seas. To this end she encouraged the fisheries as the true foundation on which naval supremacy must rest. One of her first acts (1562) was to confirm the law of Edward VI. protecting the Newfoundland fishermen from the plundering officials of the Admiralty. She further encouraged their business by passing a law to compel everyone to eat fish on Wednesdays and Saturdays ——

ACT 5 ELIZABETH, c V

" Touching certain politick constitutions for the maintenance of the Navy."

Sec. XIV. sets out "And for the increase of the provisions of fish by the more usual and common eating thereof Be it further enacted, by the authority aforesaid, that from the Feast of Saint Michael the Archangel 1564, every Wednesday in every week throughout the whole year which heretofore hath not

---

[1] The idea of a north-west passage to India through some strait north of Labrador was not unnatural. The Elizabethan seamen argued, if there was a passage south, which Magellan had found, there must also be one in a corresponding position north. They never realised the immense northern extension of America. Though the whole three voyages of Frobisher are most fantastic, there can be no question about his daring. Frobisher Straits is a perpetual monument to his memory.

by the laws or customs of the realme been used and observed as a fish day shall be hereafter observed and kept as Saturdays in every week be or ought to be upon pain that every person offending herein shall forfeit three pounds for every time he or they shall offend or else suffer three months' close imprisonment without bail or mainprise.

Sec XXXIX. "And because no manner of person shall misjudge of the intent of this estatute limiting orders to eat fish and to forbear eating of flesh but that the same is purposely intended and meant politickly for the increase of fishermen and mariners and repairing of ports towns and navigation and not for any superstition to be maintained in the choice of meats.

Sec. XL "Be it enacted, that whosoever shall, by preaching, teaching, writing or open speech notify that any eating of fish or forbearing of flesh mentioned in this estatute is of any necessity for saving the soul of man or that it is the service of God, otherwise than as other politick laws are and be, that then such person shall be punished as the spreaders of false news are and ought to be.

These old Acts are not only quaint and full of a certain dry humour, they contain also the very pith and marrow of English history.

This politic and ingenious device to create a Protestant Lent, and compel Englishmen to eat fish for a hundred days in the year, was a dismal failure. The proud stomachs of our ancestors have always resented interference with their beef and beer ; like Falstaff, they would not feast or fast upon compulsion. Fishmongers petitioned Her Majesty that the fish days were not observed, and so, after eighteen years' struggle, like a wise sovereign, she bowed before the inevitable, her legalised fast was left to die out.

By 23 Eliz Cap. VII. (1581), a most drastic measure, however, was soon passed prohibiting the importation of foreign-caught fish by Englishmen, and imposing a duty on all foreign fish See VI enacted :—

"Provided always that this Act or anything therein contained shall not extend or be prejudicial to any providing or bringing of fish in or out of the country of Iceland, Shetland or Newfoundland or any parts or seas thereto adjoining or on the Scottish Seas, nor to any fish that shall be killed taken and salted by the Queen's Natural Subjects, anything in this Act to the contrary notwithstanding."

Newfoundland, as in former statutes, is specially mentioned.

During this remarkable reign English commerce increased by leaps and bounds. Devonshire, however, still remained pre-eminent as the great centre of maritime enterprise—as the Iceland and Irish fish trades declined the Newfoundland enterprise increased The records show us clearly that the old mariners from Dartmouth and Bideford, and a score more of little West Country coast towns, knew every port and place and headland in Newfoundland ; Cape Race, Cape St. Francis, and Baccalieu were as familiar to Devon sailors as Berry Head and the Land's End.

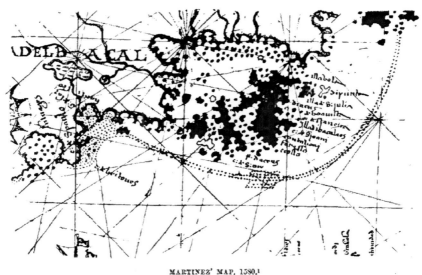

MARTINEZ' MAP, 1580.[1]

B.M. MSS., Harl.

Long before Gilbert's famous adventure, the trip to our Island was an everyday voyage, and no longer an expedition of discovery. All around the coast of Newfoundland, the Gulf, and Cape Breton, down to the State of Maine, English and foreign fishermen fished and explored. It is expressly stated by Hayes, the survivor of Gilbert's miserable, ill-fated expedition, that they went by way of our Island to get a supply of victuals, and not on a voyage of discovery, or to take possession of the Island. Sir Anthony Shirley re-victualled in Newfoundland on his way to England in 1597, and Raleigh's fleet called there on his last voyage from Guiana for the same purpose. Hayes says :—

"The last place of our assembly before we left the coast of England was in Cawsand Bay, near unto Plymouth, then resolved to put unto the sea with shipping and provision, such as we had, before our store yet remaining, but chiefly the time and season of the year, were too far spent. Nevertheless it seemed first very doubtful by what way to shape our course and to begin our intended discovery, either from the South northward, or from the North southward. The first—that is beginning South—without all controversy was the likeliest, wherein we were assured to have commodity of the current [the Gulf Stream] which from the

<hr>

[1] This map is of Spanish-Italian origin, and represents, probably, the ideas of Cartier's explorations in the Gulf of St. Lawrence current in Spain and Italy; it is similar to the map given in Bishop Howley's *Ecclesiastical History.* Newfoundland is split up into islands.

Cape of Florida setteth northward, and would have furthered greatly our navigation, discovering from the aforesaid Cape along towards Cape Breton. . . . . . These and other like reasons alleged in favour of the southern course first to be taken, to the contrary was inferred that for as much as both our victuals and many other needful provisions were diminished and left insufficient for so long a voyage and the wintering of so many men, we ought to shape a course most likely to minister supply, and that was to take the Newfoundland in our way, . . . where being usually at that time of the year until the fine of August a multitude of ships repairing thither for fish, we should be relieved abundantly with many necessaries."

I think I have conclusively proved the continuous dominion and possession of the English in Newfoundland. It appears quite clear that, taking one year with another, twenty years before Gilbert's voyage, at least fifty English vessels engaged in the Transatlantic fishery, as these old ships carried about a man to a ton, they would give from two thousand five hundred to three thousand men engaged in this business. But besides the actual fishing vessels, there were also merchant ships from London, Southampton, and other ports engaged in the trade as freighters. The little fishing vessels, after a good voyage, could not carry all their fish to market, so these freighters, known in the trade as "sack ships," traded and carried, probably the name was derived from sack (sherry), because these vessels often brought salt and a supply of the good wines of Xeres to Devonshire and Newfoundland. That St. John's was a great place for trade—a great mart—is shown by the Irish Government sending out two ships to get fish and *other supplies* in 1595 [1]

It will thus be clearly seen that the prevailing idea about Gilbert's expedition being a voyage of discovery to Newfoundland is entirely erroneous, he came to St John's because it was a well-known port, where his poor, half-starved company would be sure of an ample supply of food and necessaries

During nearly all the Tudor Period, England was a close ally of Spain, and the English fishing ships had the run of all the Spanish and Italian ports. The Peninsula has always been our greatest customer. At one time Spain consumed half a million quintals of Newfoundland fish, later in Elizabeth's reign, when she was at war, Devonshire became the great depôt for dried cod, and Dutch and sometimes English ships freighted it to France, and thence to the Mediterranean. In the Appendix will be found a charter-party for freighting a cargo of fish from Chester to France, and a licence to export fish in 1599 [2]

---

[1] In the *Irish State Papers* Sir G Fenton writes in 1595 to Burghley, that "he has sent out again two ships to Newfoundland for fish and other provisions for the army in Ireland, and the people, and the ships being to touch at Poole or some other part of the West Country, he hopes they will not be detained by some general restraint of shipping"

[2] P 84

We cannot fix the precise year in which settlement commenced in Newfoundland ; Sabine states that in 1522 there were forty or fifty houses in Newfoundland ; but, from scattered information contained in the records, and narratives of voyages, it is clear that, from a very early period, a few crews were left behind every winter to cut timber for building cook-rooms, stages, train vats, wharves, and for the construction of boats. Hayes speaks of the weather observed in December, and of the boats built in Newfoundland.

No doubt it was a daring experiment for the first Devon crew that put up their winter house and did their lumbering and sporting in the lonely isle ; but there were no dreaded savages on the eastern coast between Cape St. Francis and Cape Race.

SHOOTING WHITE BEARS.

From De Veer's Waerachtighe, 1605.

After the first successful venture, regular crews would be fitted out, with their master carpenters and blacksmiths and boat builders. Game was so prodigiously abundant, good timber close at hand and plentiful, that there never would be wanting volunteers for this work. Whitbourne gives us quite a homily on the necessity of winter crews ; and it is obvious to anyone acquainted with our shore fishery that it could not be carried on to any extent successfully without winter men. It is no argument that history does not inform us about these first residents ; their presence here would not be mentioned. No lists were kept of fishing vessels or their crews—at any rate from Devonshire—all through the Tudor Period ; and no notice would be taken of the doings of those obscure fishermen in the far-off land.

The earliest narrative in the reign of Elizabeth about the ancient Colony is contained in a letter from Anthony Parkhurst, a merchant of Bristol, to Hakluyt, dated November 13th, 1578. He says:—

"He had made four voyages to Newfoundland, and had searched the harbours, creeks, and lands, more than any other Englishman. That there were generally more than 100 sail of Spaniards taking cod, and from 20 to 30 killing whales; 50 sail of Portuguese; 150 sail of French and Bretons, mostly very small; but of English only 50 sail. Nevertheless [he adds] *the English are commonly lords of the harbours where they fish, and use all strangers help in fishing*, if need require, *according to an old custom of the country*; which thing they do willingly, so that you take nothing from them more than a boat or two of salt, in respect of your protection of them against rovers or other violent intruders, who do often put them from good harbours."

KILLING WALRUS.
From De Veer's Waerachtighe, 1605.

The arrogance of the old West Country buccaneer is amusing—the cool way in which he speaks about plundering the inoffensive foreign fishermen; evidently the Portuguese had better ships and stronger crews, for the bold Antonie abuses them as "Vile Portingals, descending of the Jews and Judas kind." After enumerating the various kind of fish in Newfoundland, he says: "The mussels all contain pearls; that " he had heard of a Portugal that found one worth 300 ducats."—"That " in half a day he could take as many lobsters as would find 300 men " with a day's meat." Of the trees, he says: "The trees is most fir, " yet plenty of pine-apple trees; few of those two kinds meet to mast a " ship of three score and ten tons."

The important expedition of Sir Thomas Hampshire to Newfoundland, in 1582, shows the wise and enlightened policy of the great queen; before Sir Thomas's arrival it had been the custom for the first comer in each harbour to seize any piece of foreshore he might select sufficient to cure and dry his codfish. This custom gave rise to endless disputes. The queen authorised Hampshire to make a new rule: Whatever room

TRINITY HARBOUR.
From a photograph by Mr. White, Trinity.

or space of foreshore a master of a vessel selected, he could retain it so long as he kept up his buildings on it, and employed it for the use of the fishery.

This wise regulation largely increased the Newfoundland fishery, gave the western men a more permanent interest in the country, and augmented the number of wintering crews; permanent fishing establishments, wharves, flakes, stayes were built and winter guardians appointed, small plots of land were cultivated, simply gardens; thus settlement and a planter's shore fishery began in the colony. The first of these scattered settlements were between Cape St. Francis and Cape Race, and around Conception Bay.

The people who began as part of a winter crew often became the first permanent settlers. Born hunters, restless roaming spirits, like the Daniel Boones and Kit Carsons of western fame, they produced a race still famous for their woodcraft, their sporting skill, and their daring courage on the ice floes.[1]

[1] Newfoundlanders have been conspicuous from the earliest times for their skill at woodcraft and sealing.

Devonshire, with its wonderful variety of hill and dale and moorland, has always been famous for game and hunting. To the old West Countrymen Newfoundland was a very sportsman's paradise, abounding in fin, fur, and feather. Hayes speaks of the innumerable quantity of game, how their

Two of the most interesting figures in our early history are Gilbert[1]
and Whitbourne[2]; both were on the Island together in 1583 Sir
Humphrey came as the queen's representative, and Whitbourne, as a
common sailor, took part in the function, and watched the ceremonious
taking possession of the Colony, in whose affairs he afterwards played
such a leading part   One was a gallant gentleman, soldier, courtier,
descended of an ancient family, with all respect for the courtly knight,
Richard Whitbourne, West Country sailor, our historian, and Newfoundland's steadfast friend, is more to us and dearer to our hearts as colonists
than even the brave and most unfortunate Sir Humphrey.   Poor
Richard, afterwards Sir Richard, had no friends at Court, he rose from
the ranks, a sturdy lad made into a smart sailor by the hard usage and
rope's-ending, the training by which every Devon mariner rises from the
forecastle to the cabin   His first experience in the country was as a
hand before the mast, or perhaps as mate "in a worthy ship of the
" burthen of 300 tons, set forth by one Master Cotton, of Southampton."

men killed partridges with cudgels   Dr
Vaughan, about 1620, tells of one man
killing 300 partridges (willow grouse)   Abbé
Baudoin (1696) speaks with wonder of the
marvellous woodcraft of the Newfoundlanders.   These colonial hunters were the
lineal descendants of the old Devonian
hunters and poachers, keen-eyed, untiring,
they took to woodcraft as a duck takes to
water
    As a sealer the Newfoundlander has
always been without a rival   Nothing
astonished the Dundee whalers more when
they first came to the Colony than to see
our men jump over the side of the ship and
skip from pan to pan over the loose ice,
locally known as "copying"   Sandy thought
them "vara wild men," but now he is
learning to imitate them   The Scot, however,
is a long way behind the genuine native, who
has been practising it from a small boy,
copying, jigging tomcods, and going in the
woods trouting, being the popular amusements
of the native boy.
    Islanders are proverbially conservative
in their habits and customs, the familiar
Newfoundland snow shoes—known as pot
racquets, the punts, and the long single
barrel gun—known as the Poole gun (as
shown in De Vere's picture, p 59)—are all
copies of those used in the old Dorset sea
port, and figure as part of a wild fowler's
equipment in Colonel Hawker's well-known
old book on shooting, published during the
last century, from generation to generation
the old familiar patterns have remained
unchanged
    [1] Sir Humphrey Gilbert was born in
1539; he died in 1583   He was second
of three sons of Otto Gilbert, of Green-

way, Devon   His mother, a Champernoun,
relative of the great family of the
Carews, became the third wife of Captain
Walter Raleigh, and by him had two sons,
the youngest of whom was the great Sir
Walter Raleigh   Her three children by
Gilbert were all knighted, John, Humphrey,
and Adrian   Humphrey was educated at
Eton and Oxford, served in Ireland and
the Netherlands   In 1576 was published
his famous tract, "Discourse of a Discoverie
for a new Passage to Cataia"   In 1578 he
received his large patent from the queen,
authorising him "to discover, occupy, and
possess such remote heathen lands not
actually possessed of any Christian Prince
or people as should seem good to him"
(This patent and his agreements with
Peckham will be found in Mr Sainsbury's
Colonial Papers Addenda, 1574–1674)
Gilbert disposed of nearly all his patrimony
in fitting out his first expedition, 1578, which
was a total failure   June 11th, 1583, began
his famous voyage to Newfoundland, in
which he perished, with all the crew of his
little vessel   Gilbert was an enthusiast, a
dreamer, a man with no executive ability,
no command of men, of dauntless courage,
and undoubtedly pious after the fashion of
the age   He did splendid service to England
as a pioneer of colonisation   His character
has been well portrayed by Kingsley as a
weak-headed enthusiast, a totally unfit
commander for the rough work of exploring
and settlement of new lands   Both expeditions show nothing but disorder, incapacity,
and predestined failure
    [2] See pp 114 to 118 for further account
of Whitbourne.

The young sailor, in the beautiful land-locked harbour of Trinity, amidst all the hurry and bustle of the shore fishery, first saw the "natural inhabitants,' as he called the Beothics or Red Indians ; he says :—

" They are few in number, and as something rude and savage people having neither knowledge of God nor living under any kind of civil government. In their habits, customs, and manners they resemble the Indian of the continent from whence, I suppose, they come," [still they are said to be] " an ingenious and tractable people, being well used," [and as] " ready to assist in the whale fishery for even small reward."

Whaling was successfully prosecuted by the Biscayans, and Cotton's ship was to have been engaged in the same daring enterprise Whitbourne says :—

" We were bound to the Grand Bay (which lieth on the north side of that land) purporting there to trade then with the savage people (for whom we carried sundry commodities), and to kill whales and to make trayne oil as the Biscaines do there yearly in great abundance. But then our intended voyage was overthrowne by the indiscretion of our captaine and faintheartednesse of some gentlemen of our company, whereupon we set saile from thence and bare with Trinity Harbour in Newfoundland, where we killed great store of fish, deere, beares, beavers, scales, otters, and such like, with abundance of sea-fowle, and so returning to England we arrived safe at Southampton ' :

Throughout these early narratives there are notices of the aborigines of Newfoundland, the Beothics Whitbourne speaks of them as tractable if well used. The French everywhere in America seem to have had more friendly relations with the Indians than any other Europeans, in the very beginning of the fishery the French were assisted by the Indians in curing their fish and a considerable barter trade was carried on with them, the Biscayans also in their whaling operations had help from the Indians. With the other Indian tribes of the continent, Cape Breton, &c, the French kept up the most amicable relations, only with the native Indians of the Colony, called indifferently Beothicks, Beothucks, and Bethicks, was there always dire hostility, brought about by a terrible act of treachery on the part of the Indians, related by Kirke, they first attacked a small party of French who were alone and unarmed, murdered them all, and then dressing up in the Frenchmen's clothes they allured another party of French fishermen and killed twenty-one of them. Like all savages they were inveterate thieves. Whitbourne says :—

" Many of them secretly every yeere come into Trinity Bay and Harbour in the night time purposely to steal sailes, lines, hatchets, hookes, knives, and such like "

On this subject it is unfortunate that we have only the white man's story, and the red man is unheard, the French may have given them great provocation and revenge is part of the creed of an Indian.

Old Whitbourne himself, much as we love and admire him, admits having shared in a most outrageous spoliation of the poor savages :—

" The Indians have great store of redoaker which they use to colour their bodies, bowes and arrowes, and canowes withal; they use the rinds of spruce trees

HENLEY ISLAND.
From a drawing by the Hon. and Rev. W. Gray.

round and deepe in proportion like a brass kettle to boyle their meat in, which hath been well proved by three mariners of a ship riding at anchor by mee who being robbed in the night by the savages of their apparel and divers provisions, came suddenly upon them where they had set up their tents and were feasting . . . . by shooting off a musket they all ran away naked without any apparel . . . . all their three cannowes, their flesh skinnes, yolkes of egges, targets, bowers and arrowes, and much fine okar and divers other things were brought away and shared, and they brought to me the best cannowe, bowes and arrowes . . . . which may seem to invite us to find out some other trade with them."

Charles I. issued a proclamation in 1630, prohibiting disorderly trading with Red Indians. The most hopeful effort to establish friendly relations with these poor savages was made in 1612, when Guy and Captain Whittington met the Indians. Purchas says :—

" They met at Random in Trinity Bay, eat and drank together, and exchanged furs and skins for hatchets and knives, appointed a meeting for next year by a sign when the grass should be of such a height to bring down all their furs and skins for traffick with the English. At the time appointed for their meeting, instead of Captain Whittington and other agents, there came a fisherman to this place to make a voyage; seeing Indians and not knowing the reason of their coming, he let fly a shot from aboard; Indians ran off, imagining they were Guy's men, and now will not trade."[1]

NATIVES OF CANADA.

From Champlains' Voyages, 1632.

Thus, unfortunately, there was an end to the overtures which might have resulted in renewed amity and peace with these poor persecuted savages. With Mic-Mac and Eskimos, Europeans easily established cordial relations, but during the whole period there never seems to have been peace between the English settlers and these unfortunate Boethics. The account of their extinction and the efforts made to promote intercourse with them, will be given later on. The story of the Red Indian is a sad, dismal tale of wanton cruelty, suspicion, and treachery.

To write the complete history of English colonisation in this Island is quite beyond the limits of my work. I can only shortly state a few salient points. It does seem strange to us that for nearly a century England made no official attempt to colonise her new possession. The voyages of Rut and Hoare were distinctly for exploration, to discover a north-west passage; Sir Humphrey Gilbert was full of the same idea, and wrote a tract and made a map to promote an expedition for that purpose.

In the age of Elizabeth, though old conceptions were passing away, credulity, superstition, and the fantastic ideas of bygone days still lingered. All competent authorities now agree that in those days one man alone in England realised the benefits of colonisation. It was the transcendent mind of Raleigh, with the vivid imagination of a poet and the profound wisdom of a statesman, that first expounded to the Elizabethan age the plan of English colonisation, the foundation of greater Englands in the New World; knowing the temper of the time

---

[1] Purchas' *His Pilgrims.*

he had to proceed warily; he held out gold as an inducement for his new projects. Fishermen were urged to capture Indians, to bring home

GILBERT'S MAP, 1578.

From Winsor's N. and C. H. of America.

strange birds and beasts, and products of America. All these things captivated the credulous mind of the public, and, says Raleigh, "helped "forward the Plantation mightily." Whilst he encouraged in every way the working of the gold mine of the Newfoundland fishery, in his emphatic words "the main stay and support" of his own Devon and western counties, his mind was set on gaining the whole vast continent, and on this grand idea he spent a fortune (equal to £200,000 or a million dollars). His half brother, Sir Humphrey Gilbert, a pale reflection of his great relative, assisted in these projects; years before the actual expedition sailed the brothers worked together to expedite their plans. Raleigh's influence at Court procured the charter from Elizabeth; the dread of Spain, then an ally of England, had to be overcome; the Queen agreed to everything, only refusing to allow her favourite courtier to leave England.

The expedition of 1583 was not Gilbert's first attempt; in 1578, with the connivance of the Court, he sailed from England with two ships. His object is disclosed thus :—

" A discourse how Her Majesty may annoy the King of Spain by fitting out a fleet of shippes of war under pretence of a voyage of discovery, and so fall upon the enemies shippes and destroy his trade in Newfoundland and the West Indies, and possess the country."

This paper is still extant;[1] the signature is thought to be Gilbert's; one passage arguing against delay, "for the wings of a man's life are plumed with the arrows of death," shows that, if penned by him, it was conceived and dictated by Raleigh.

"I will [it continues] undertake to fit out ships well armed for Newfoundland, where they will meet with all the great ships of France, Spain, and Portugal; the best I will bring away and burn the rest; commit us afterwards as Pirates if you will, but I shall ruin their sea force, for they depend on their fishermen for their navies."

Poor Sir Humphrey was a dreamer, an enthusiast; the expedition was a complete failure; he arrived out in Newfoundland, and, probably in a fight with the Spaniards, lost a tall ship and a bold captain, Miles Morgan.

Gilbert was terribly crippled and impoverished, but sooner than forfeit his large patent, which was for six years, and would expire next year, 1584, he sold a large part of his estate, and with the aid of Raleigh (who furnished one ship), Peckham, Hayes, and others, a little fleet of five vessels and two hundred and fifty men were got together.[2] They were of all trades; "hobby horses and morris dancers, and many like conceits

THE NARROWS, ST. JOHN'S.

"were provided to win the savage people by all fair means possible." Gilbert's crew consisted partly of the off-scourings of the jails, and the result, as might be anticipated, was most disastrous; one ship took to piracy, and a great portion of his villainous followers deserted. On the 3rd of August 1583, Gilbert arrived at St. John's with two ships and a pinnace—the *Delight*, Admiral's ship, 120 tons, the *Golden Hind*, 40 tons, and the *Squirrel*, 10 tons.

[1] *Records.*
[2] Davy Ingram's account of the country through which he passed seems to have had some influence in gaining Gilbert the support of Peckham and others.

Before the entrance of the harbour they found the little *Swallow*, of 40 tons, at anchor, which the English merchants would not permit to enter :—

"These English merchants that were and always be admirals by turn interchangeably over the fleet of fishermen within the same harbour"

In reading this narrative we are forcibly impressed with the dominion exercised by these extraordinary English merchant adventurers in Newfoundland : they looked upon the whole island as their own dominion, gained by their own valour, without the slightest assistance from the English Government   They therefore resented the entrance of a mere courtier into their domain.   They knew full well that they had only their own strong right arms and stout hearts to depend upon, in those days there was no such thing as international justice.   If by chance a French vessel captured one of ours, there was no redress, they would be fortunate to escape with their lives from a howling French mob   To be captured by a Spaniard was to fall into the very gate of death, a captured Frenchman had a show of justice in England, but no substantial recompense for injury.   There are many cases in the records like the following :—

"April 18, 1591.   Petition from Bayonne to the Privy Council that a ship of Peter de Hody of Bayonne from Newfoundland with 108,000 dry fish, 4,000 green. 14 hhds of Train oil, total value 6,000 crowns, had been taken by a ship of Sir W. Raleigh, and brought to Uphill near Bristol." [1]

Hody spent five hundred crowns, but got no redress from the rich victuallers of Bristol, who had received the proceeds of the merchandise, and kept the ship; so he returned to France

"Sept 1591   The *Eliza*, *Beneventure* and *Dudley* took a ship *The Holy Ghost* from M. de Harques of St Jean de Luz with 15,000 dry fish, 60 hhds of train, and 48 men whom they stripped to their shirts.   De Harques and his two brothers have been suitors in England for past eight months' [1]

The ship was afterwards ordered to be given up, but the owners did not get her—*she ran ashore*—a regular West Country trick.

In our day these daring adventurers would be dubbed "pirates" The only way they exercised dominion was by a reckless dare-devil courage, which made the very name of Englishman a terror to the Spaniards   It was the almost fiendish cruelty to English prisoners that stirred the whole nation against Spain   They have a proverb in the Peninsula expressing the highest tribute to the valour of our ancestors :—

"Con todo el mundo guerra,
Mas paz con Inglaterra"

"War with all the world, but peace with England".

[1] *Records*

Mr. Oppenheim, in the " English Historical Review," says :—

" It speaks sufficiently for the courage of the Elizabethan sailor that during the whole of the reign but two English men-of-war, the *Jesus of Lubeck* and the *Revenge*, were captured by the Spaniards, and then only after desperate fighting against overwhelming odds."

We realise the power of Elizabeth, when even in remote Newfoundland the moment the merchants knew of her commission they obeyed Gilbert's orders. This narrative will also disabuse our minds of the idea of the Newfoundland trade as carried on by a few poor fishermen. It comes

PISTOLET'S MAP, 1587.[1]
B.M. MSS. Eg. 4513-8.

out clearly in this History that nearly a century before any English colony was founded in North America, England had a great trade and

[1] This map is of French origin, and differs very little from that of Descellier, given at p. 40, John Dee's at p. 59, and Vallard's made at Dieppe. It shows the results of early French explorations in Newfoundland and Labrador, particularly from Notre Dame Bay to the Straits of Belle Isle. The English standard is shown near Hamilton Inlet.

fishery in Newfoundland   In 1594, Sir Walter Raleigh said that if any harm should happen to the Newfoundland fleet it would be the greatest calamity which could befall England.[1]

The entertainers of Sir Humphrey were merchants   St. John's was even then an important free port, a large international trade was carried on, the owners coming out with their masters, and superintending it themselves   It is also expressly told us that they had houses, for the General lived ashore with them for the three weeks he stayed in St John's.

The character of this business will be easily understood ; it was an absolutely free trade ; no Custom House officer to trouble the merchant's pocket or his conscience   The principal traffic consisted in selling for cash—or bartering for fish and oil—Mediterranean products, salt, olive oil, fruits, wines, also West of England cordage, cloth hats, caps, hosiery, Sheffield wares, and general English merchandise   The master and his crew fished, the merchant had his store and traded ; considering the large number of fishermen of all nations, probably about fifteen thousand, resorting to Newfoundland, it must have been an extensive and, I need not add, a lucrative trade.

There are three narratives of Gilbert's expedition—Hayes', Peckham's, and Clark's.   Hayes says :—

" Saturday, 3rd August, we made ready our fights and prepared to enter the harbour, any resistance to the contrary notwithstanding, there being within of all nations to the number of 36 sail.

" But first the General [Gilbert] despatched a boat to give them knowledge of his coming for no ill intent, having commission from Her Majesty for this voyage we had in hand ; and immediately we followed with a slack gale, and in the very entrance, which is but narrow, the Admiral fell upon a rock [Cahill's Rock] on the larboard side, by great oversight

" After the English merchants had been shown our commission they were all satisfied.   The merchants with their masters departed.   They caused forthwith to be discharged all the great ordinance of their fleet in token of our welcome."

Afterwards arrangements were made to fit out this poor, ill-provided expedition with necessary food and supplies   Hayes continues —

" Commissioners were appointed, part of our own company and part of theirs to go into other harbours adjoining (*for our English merchants command all there*) to levy our provision, whereunto the Portugals (above all other nations) did most willingly and liberally contribute.

" In so much as we were presented (above our allowance) with wines, marmalades, most fine rusk or biscuits, sweet oils, and sundry delicacies ; also, we wanted not of fresh salmons, trouts, lobsters, and other fresh fish brought daily unto us

[1] *Hatfield MS.*

ST. JOHN'S, FROM RIVERHEAD, IN 1891.

From a photograph by S. H. Parsons.

" Moreover as the manner is in fishing every week to choose their Admiral anew, or rather they succeed each in orderly course, and have weekly their Admiral's feast solemnized, even so the General, captains and masters of our fleet were continually invited and feasted.

" Next morning being Sunday, 4th August, the General and his company were brought on land by the English merchants, who showed unto us their accustomed walks into a place they called ' the garden.' [1] But nothing appeared more than nature itself without art, who confusedly hath brought forth roses abundantly wild, but odoriferous, and to sense very comfortable Also the like plenty of raspberries, which do grow in every place "

It is quite evident that Gilbert and his companions had a very jovial time in St John's, then, and now, famous for its hospitality

It seems, says Hayes, speaking of St John's—

" A place very populous and much frequented."

And Sir George Peckham says that the English merchants—

" Before endeavouring to fraughte themselves with fish repayred unto Sir Humphrey and assisted him in his designs "

Hayes continues :—

" Upon Monday being the fifth of August the General caused his tent to be set up on the side of an hill [2] in the viewe of all the flete of English men and strangers, which were in number between thirty and forty sail, then, being accompanied by all his Captains, Masters, Gentlemen and Soldiers he caused all, the Masters and principall officers of the shippes as well Englishmen as Spaniards Portugals and all other nations to repayre into his tent and then and there in the presence of them all he did cause his commission under the great seal of England to be openlie and solemnlie reade unto them whereby was graunted unto him his heyres and assignes by the Queen's most excellent Majestie many great and large royalties liberties and priviledges

' The effect whereof being signified unto the strangers by an interpreter he took possession of the said lande in the right of the Crown of England by digging up a turfe and receiving the same with a hazell wande delivered unto him after the manner of the lawe and custome of England

" Then he signified unto the company both strangers and others that from thenceforth they were to live in that land as the territories appertayning unto the Crowne of England and to be governed by such lawes as by good advise should be set down which in all points (so neero as might be) should be agreeable to the Lawes of England and for to put the same in execution presentlie he ordained and established three lawes ·

" 1 Establishment of the Church of England

" 2 Any attempt prejudicial to Her Majesty's rights in the territory to be punished as in a case of High Treason.

[1] The late Sir R J Pinsent and several others have discussed the site of "ye ancient garden" It is difficult to define its exact position, but it was probably somewhere about Cherry Garden, on the banks of Waterford Bridge River, the most picturesque walk about St John's A path would go along there into the woods. It is in the direction in which sailors would naturally take a stroll on a Sunday afternoon.

[2] The hill would be, probably, Garrison Hill, the centre of the harbour In Hatton and Harvey's History the General is described as standing on the beach of St John's Harbour to perform the ceremony, and the pillar as being set up near the water edge. Peckham's narrative shows that it was on the hill

" 3. Anyone uttering words of dishonour to Her Majesty should lose his ears and have his goods and ship confiscated.

" All men did verie willingly submit themselves to these lawes.

" Then he caused the Queen's Majesties arms to be engraved and set upon a pillar of wood not far from the tent with great solemnity.

" After this divers Englishmen made suit unto Sir Humphrey to have of him by inheritance theyre accustomed stages standings and drying places in sundry parts of that land for theyre fish as a thing they do make great accompte of. Which he granted unto them in fee farme.

" And by this means he hath possession mayntained for him in many parts of that country.

" To be briefe he dyd lette, sette, give and dispose of many things as absolute Governor there by virtue of Her Majesty's letter patent."[1]

He gave title to a great many English merchants for their fishing places in St. John's and the neighbouring harbours. Some of the St. John's merchants wanted larger grants of land.

" Now [says Hayes] he became contrarily affected, refusing to make any so large grants, especially of St. John's, which certain English merchants made suit for, offering to employ their money and travail [work] upon the same ; yet neither by their own suit nor of other of the company whom he seemed willing to pleasure, it could be obtained."[1]

GILBERTDS quos aliena deduxit in orbem
Quo CHRISTI imbuerit barbara colla iugo   B.
SIR HUMPHREY GILBERT.
From Holland's Herwologia.

The merchants evidently contemplated permanent settlement and cultivation, and only wanted to be secure in their tenure ; and it tells somewhat against the gallant knight that his " contrariety" helped to retard the progress of the Colony.

The splendid harbour of St. John's and its unique position, midway between Cape Bonavista and Cape Race, where at first all the English fishing operations were carried on, made our capital, from the very beginning, the metropolis and head-quarters of the Newfoundland fish trade, both English and foreign.

It was a grave misfortune for the Colony that the first great

---

[1] HAKLUYT.

colonisation scheme fell into the hands of a poor, bankrupt, incapable man like Gilbert, to use Hayes' words—

"He thrust himself into the action for which he was not fit, presuming the cause pretended on God's behalf would carry him to the desired end." [1]

What shall we say of a great patentee like Gilbert, owner of half a continent, refusing the English merchants in St. John's a title to land around the infant capital, on which they were willing to spend their money, time, and labour Later on, when an official settlement was made under Guy, he was directed by the patentees to go to Conception Bay, not to St John's. The directors of the company seem to have been well acquainted with the Newfoundland fishery, full directions are given to him about the fish trade, &c, clearly, long before that time, all the chief and best places in the good harbours of the east coast had been appropriated by merchants and fishermen.

Gilbert had with him a Saxon ore refiner named Daniel, he was so impressed with the mineral wealth of the Colony that he proposed to . leave the settlement and discovery of the south to Hayes, for, he said, " I am now become a northern man altogether, and my heart is set on " Newfoundland"

Our Colony undoubtedly possesses great mineral wealth, this has been proved · whether Sir Humphrey and his miner really found anything but the glittering iron pyrites known as "fool's gold" cannot now be ascertained, as ore, papers, and everything else were lost at sea

The end of this ill-organised expedition was dire disaster, on the 29th of August their Admiral's ship *Delight* was lost off Cape Sable, through utter carelessness and bad seamanship; the little frigate *Squirrel* and the *Golden Hind* escaped, on the 31st of August they bore up for England Poor Gilbert has been painted for us as so complete an angel that it is a relief to find him at times giving way to human infirmities and acting like an ordinary man After they had passed Cape Race on their return voyage, Gilbert came aboard the *Hind* to get a wound in his foot dressed, afterwards, on a fair day, he came aboard again " to " make merry, together with the captain, master, and company, and ' continued there from morning until evening," no doubt drinking the good wine they had received in St. John's On the same day, for the loss of some mineral specimens, " he was not able to contain himself, but " beat his boy in a great rage."

Lest I should be charged with misrepresenting the qualities of this most unfortunate adventurer, read his character drawn by Kingsley in the fascinating pages of " Westward Ho": "a philosopher—says Amyas —but not so much of a general, not able to control men."

[1] HAKLUYT

The death of Sir Humphrey was as sad and tragic an end as ever befell a hero   It seems the Knollys or some of his enemies had questioned his courage on ship board, seamanship he had none, so to prove his mettle he refused to leave the wretched little tub of a *Squirrel* (10 tons)   He said :—

"'I will not forsake my little company going homewards with whom I have passed so many storms and perils,' albeit [says Hayes] this was rather rashness than advised resolution, to prefer the wind of a vain report to the weight of his own life."[1]

Unfortunately he was no sailor or he might have known her condition, overweighted on deck with "fight's netting and small artillery," cumbersome for so small a boat to pass through the ocean at that period of the year.

On Monday, 9th September, in the afternoon—

"The frigate *Squirrel* was near cast away oppressed by waves, yet at that time recovered ; and giving forth signs of joy, the General [Gilbert] sitting abaft with a book in his hand, cried out to us in the *Hind* (so oft as we did approach within hearing), 'We are as near Heaven by sea as by land,' reiterating the same speech well beseeming a soldier, resolute in Jesus Christ, as I can testify he was.

"Suddenly on Monday night we lost sight of the *Squirrel's* light   Our watch cried out the General was cast away, which was too true, for in that moment the frigate was devoured and swallowed up of the sea."[1]

Poor Gilbert! probably he was so disheartened by failure and losses that he almost courted death.   Hayes, a practical sailor, by his skill, and the good seamanship of Master Cox, of Limehouse, arrived safe in England, and to him we are indebted for probably the most interesting narrative contained in the voluminous collection of Hakluyt, the Story of the Unfortunate Expedition to Newfoundland

Hayes concludes with a fitting tribute to the piety and courage of his unfortunate leader :—

"But such is the infinite bounty of God, who from every evil deriveth good For besides that fruit may grow in time of our travelling into these north-west lands the crosses, turmoils, and afflictions, both in the preparation and execution of this voyage, did correct the intemperate humours which before we noted to be in this gentleman, and made unsavoury and less delightful his other manifold virtues.   Then, as he was refined and made nearer drawing unto the image of God, so it pleased the Divine will to resume him unto himself, whither both his and every other high and noble mind have always aspired "[1]

Almost immediately after the death of Gilbert, the burthen of colonising America, which had been too heavy for his poor weak

[1] HAKLUYT

shoulders, fell on his illustrious half-brother Raleigh.[1] His plans for founding Virginia were not successful in his lifetime, but with untiring energy and dauntless courage he persisted in his endeavours and spent his substance; he sowed the seed, others reaped the fruit. To Raleigh, above all men in this great age, is due the honour and glory of founding England's Colonial Empire. He was all-powerful in Devon; we find him always mindful of her interests, and urging the Government to buy salt fish for the army and navy.[2]

In the Records the supplying of this fish is very frequently mentioned. It was almost always scarce. The merchants dealt with the Government on sound commercial principles, charging them twenty

SIR WALTER RALEIGH.

From an engraving after an old portrait.

---

[1] Raleigh was born in 1552, at a small farmhouse called Hayes, near Budleigh, Devon. His father, Walter Raleigh, married for his third wife the widow of Otto Gilbert, of Compton Castle. His mother, a Champernoun, was connected with the illustrious family of the Carews. Young Walter had an experience of life given to few. As a Devonshire boy he had all the usual practice and expereince of seamanship, boating, and sailing. At seventeen he left Oxford with his uncle for the wars in France, where he was distinguished for courage and military skill. He next studied law. Next we find him at Court, and a soldier in Ireland. He represented his native county in Parliament. Amongst his compeers his marvellous eloquence is the trait most dwelt upon; but, besides being an orator and a statesman, he was an able general, one of the most accomplished and scientific sailors of his age. He planned the strategy which conquered the Invincible Armada. As a voluminous writer he takes high rank, even in the age of Bacon and Shakespeare. No other Englishman showed genius in so many different capacities as Raleigh. Our own age is astonished at the remarkable conjunction of financier, scholar, debater, and politician exhibited in such marvellous combination by Mr. Gladstone. Our hero possessed all these gifts in equal degree. But whilst our Grand Old Man's chief manual exploit in active life is cutting down trees, Raleigh was soldier, sailor, ship-builder, and colonizer.

In this age the mists of sectarian prejudice are clearing away. We no longer see Raleigh and Elizabeth through a glass darkly. To us their patriotism shines out clearly, whilst their faults and crimes are not hidden. In the supreme hour of danger Raleigh largely contributed to the salvation of England. In the days of monopolies he was a pronounced free-trader. Every honest Englishman execrates the memory of Henry VIII. for the murder of the noble Catholic Sir Thomas More. Our feelings are still stronger against the drivelling James Stuart for the death of the grandest Englishman of action of all time—Raleigh. His memory has been worthily commemorated by a tablet in Westminster Abbey, erected by Americans to "Raleigh, the Founder of the English Empire in America."

[2] As early as 1338 there is an order from Edward III. to his clerk to provide *stockfish*, presumably for the army in France. —(RYMER'S *Fœdera*.)

shillings per hundred fish when the regular trade price was ten shillings We find in 1586 :—

"An Indenture of bargain whereby the Commissioner at Chester takes up for Her Majesty's service in Ireland 20,000 Newfoundland fish at 20/- per 100"

In his latter years Raleigh was Governor of Jersey. St. Heliers was a free port, and under his fostering care the trade of the little Norman Isles was vastly increased; he encouraged the islanders to participate in the great Newfoundland fish trade, in which Jersey and her adventurous sons have always played a most prominent part.[1]

In 1583, immediately after the death of Gilbert, Sir George Peckham, a London merchant, who had been chief adventurer with the unfortunate Sir Humphrey, published the first printed book on Newfoundland, entitled —

A TRVE REPORTE,

Of the late difcoueries,

and poffefsion, taken in the right of the Crowne of Englande, of the New-found Lander by that valiant and worthe Gentleman Sir Humfrey Cilbert Knight

Wherein is also breefely fette downe, her highneffe lawfull Tytle thereunto, and the great and manifolde Commodities, that is likely to grow thereby, to the whole Realme in generall, and to the Adventurers in particular. Together with the eafines and fhortnes of the Voyage

Seene and allowed.

At London, Printed by I.C. for Iohn Hinde, dwelling in Paules Church yarde, at the figne of the golden Hinde. Anno 1583

TITLE PAGE OF PECKHAM'S BOOK.

From a copy of the first edition in the B M

"A true report of the late discoveries and possession taken in the right of the Crown of England of the Newfoundlands by that valiant and worthy gentleman Sir Humphrey Gilbert, Knight Wherein is also briefly set down her highness lawful title thereunto and the great and manifold commodities that are likely to grow thereby to the whole realm in general, and to the adventurers in particular. Together with the easiness and shortness of the voyage written by Sir George Peckham, Knight, the chief adventurer and furtherer of Sir Humphrey Gilbert's voyage to Newfoundland."[2]

In an age when there were no newspapers and no interviewers, the only chance of obtaining publicity was to write a pamphlet. This work is in the nature of an Elizabethan advertisement, and is worthy of the genius of a modern company promoter. It sets out most truthfully the great internal resources of the new Colony·—

"By establishing a safe harbour and head-quarters, and it is well known to all men of sound judgment that this Newfoundland voyage is of greater importance

---

[1] "Guernsey, April 1594 —Guernsey destitute of provisions for soldiers except 60,000 Newland fish, a barque of herrings, and 40 tuns of cider' Jersey must have had a much larger share at this time in the Newfoundland trade than her smaller sister island.

[2] This is the title of a later edition than the one illustrated.

and will be found more beneficial to our country than all other voyages at this day in use and trade amongst us."

The work is a most sensible, clear-headed, business document, and the author shows himself as a shrewd trader, he offers attractions to everyone— sport for the gentles and nobles, fishing for all, a north-west passage to India from Newfoundland for the scientific and adventurous The hundred pound subscriber was to have sixteen thousand acres of land with authority to keep Court Leet and Court Baron, to be chosen one of the Council to make laws, to pay one half-penny an acre for the building of forts, towns, churches, &c. The smallest contributions were accepted, even the subscriber of ten shillings had his rights and lands in proportion.

The whole pamphlet is an ingenious attempt to get money from the public and to keep Gilbert's charter alive Sir John Gilbert maintained his brother's shadowy claim for years after, as I find some Devon fishermen complaining of being prevented by him from going to Newfoundland, probably for claims due under Gilbert's charter As we proceed with this history we shall see other instances of the extraordinary and fantastic way in which kings and potentates flung away islands and continents to adventurers and Court favourites All the very early ones came to naught, the later ones caused strife and difficulty everywhere.

This book marks the great advancement of the age, the resources of the island are set forth, perhaps, in too glowing terms, but its immense advantage to England is not in any way exaggerated. The proposal to make St Johns a fortified town was thoroughly practical; it would have secured our capital from the attacks and destruction it afterwards suffered from the French

Besides the patriotic endeavours of Sir George Peckham to encourage settlement and relieve the distressed poor of England by emigration, the gallant Sydney and Carlile, sons-in-law of Walsingham, wrote and advocated the planting of colonies in Newfoundland and North America. Their only effect was to encourage the prosecution of the fishery, which increased by leaps and bounds.

We have an account in Hakluyt of Strange's prosecution of the seal and whale fishery in the Gulf of St Lawrence, of Rice Jones's fishing at St Peter's

Piracy was prominent, Cecil and Raleigh engaged in it under the guise of privateering A notable French pirate, De Sauce, behaved very cruelly to one Richard Clark, which is duly recorded as follows, but

little is said of the constant raids made by Englishmen on ships of all
nations :—

"1596. Report of Richard Clarke and others concerning the piracy committed
by three French ships at St. John's Newfoundland. The Captain of the Admiral
[commodore of the three ships] was named Michel de Sancé; the Master of the
Vice-Admiral Martin de Sancé. Having been used with kind entertainment and
invited to breakfast on the 25 September, in requital he invited the Frenchman
aboard his ship the next day. The captain of the Admiral feigned an excuse and sent
for Clarke to visit him in his sickness; upon a sudden the French fell on Clarke
and his men, calling out 'rendez vous, rendez vous.' He and nine men were
kept prisoners nine days and their ships pillaged. Witnesses: Ric. Clarke,
Matt Ryoes and Phil. Fabyan, Mate Sam Clarke, Surgeon, and seventeen others."[1]

The most interesting of these voyages is the adventure of Charles
Leigh, a London merchant; in Cape Breton he lost one of his ships,
the *Chancellor*, and came into collision with a big Biscayan ship, whose
captain, surrounded by his countrymen, dared to treat him ill. The
Englishman wanted to fight, but the Biscayan ran off. Next he captured a Spanish ship in the St. Lawrence. A comrade vessel came to
her rescue, so Leigh had to give up his prize and prisoners in order to

SMEATON'S LIGHTHOUSE.   MOUNT EDGECOMBE.
        PENLEE POINT.   ARMADA MEMORIAL.
            DRAKE'S ISLAND.
                    THE HOE, PLYMOUTH.
        From a photograph by A. B. Prowse, Esq., M.D., of Clifton.

rescue his prize crew. Finally, to avenge himself for all these mishaps,
he attacked a big French vessel in St. Mary's, captured her after a hard
fight, and so returned with two ships and a valuable cargo. The whole
story exhibits the daring, reckless character of the English adventurers
of the day, and the extraordinary difficulties under which business was
carried on.

Though nominally at peace, still for all practical purposes England
and Spain were at war between 1584 and 1588. Elizabeth openly aided
the Hollanders in their struggles against Philip: Drake plundered the

[1] *Records.*

Spanish main and captured the great treasure ships, his Royal mistress sharing the plunder   When the haughty Mendoza remonstrated with her she sent him packing out of England.   Elizabeth and her advisers knew that war with Spain was inevitable, she never shrank from the contest or tried to conciliate the irritated Spanish monarch, on the contrary, she carried the war into the enemy's country   It was a tremendously bold policy for a little country like England with the present population of London and a revenue of half a million, to attack a colossal power like Spain   In 1585 the most daring blow of all was made on the Spanish fishing fleet in Newfoundland   Whitbourne records the arrival of Sir Bernard Drake in St John's that year with a commission from the Crown   He also mentions the seizure of several Portuguese vessels by Drake.   Portugal at that time formed part of Philip's dominions. Doubtless these vessels were taken in St John's whilst the Biscayans were away north and south sealing, whaling, and catching cod

A number of English ships had been seized and confiscated in Spain and their crews treated with great cruelty, one vessel had been capriciously confiscated because an edition of " Cato " was found aboard.

The secret history of this expedition is told in the Records. Mr Froude says Sir J. Hawkins devised it, arguing, " half the sailors of " the Peninsula went to Newfoundland each year, he proposed to " capture them, and leave their ships to rot in the Harbours " Elizabeth seems to have been opposed to it at first

On June 20th of this year Walsingham completed the plan (the details are in his handwriting) " for annoying the Spaniard by seizing " their ships in Newfoundland," and on the same date a commission was issued to Sir Bernard Drake " to proceed thither to warn all English " vessels about the seizures in Spain, and prevent them making sale of " their fish there, and to take all Spanish ships and subjects, and to " bring them into some of the western ports of England, without " disposing of any part of the lading until further orders."

The following minute shows he was successful ·——

" Oct 10, 1585   Council to Sir John Gilbert advising of the capture of Spanish ships and sailors at Newfoundland   Returns allowed to 600 Spanish prisoners, allowance reduced from 3s 4d per week to 3d per day per man in consequence of ill-treatment of Englishmen in Spain ; to be paid out of the fish taken and the rest distributed in prize money " [1]

The Spaniards were so dismayed by this bold stroke that the next year their fishing fleet did not go to Newfoundland.

All this large quantity of fish, probably fifty to sixty thousand quintals, was smuggled into France and Spain afterwards, as we find

Records

complaints about the Custom House officers having exacted illegal fees upon its export.

It is perfectly marvellous how well Elizabeth knew every movement of her enemies; every intrigue against her was keenly watched by her ubiquitous agents and spies; if Mary Stuart cast an amorous glance at Bothwell it was duly reported; if Philip II. moved a man, or a ship was rigged in Biscay, immediately the queen had word.

Considering the difficulties of communication in those days—the dangers from floods, robbers, pirates—how successfully her intelligence

WHALING

From Bernard's Recueil, 1700.

department must have been served. For us, "heirs of all the ages," many secrets of the Courts of Spain and England have now been laid bare. Elizabeth's reputation as a sovereign rests on her success, but an imperishable monument to her memory has been raised in her *Statutes.* The State Papers preserved at Hatfield show her talent as a politician, how cleverly and boldly she played the game against Philip. Posing as a Protestant champion, whilst a Catholic at heart—

simply because they forced her hand—she was all the time planning and preparing for the great struggle with Spain

Elizabeth's policy in defying and fighting Spain was no rash reckless undertaking, it was a settled policy, based, as I have just said before, on knowledge most varied and intimate of the true position of Spain, besides, it was the only policy the high-spirited English nation would permit, the submission of James Stuart to Spain in the next reign helped to turn the national feeling against him. Out of this great conflict with the colossal power of Philip, England emerged as not only the conqueror, but as Mistress of the Seas—the true genius of the English people had found its occupation.

From the secret history of the reign we get the true state of affairs, we realise the power and activity of the Spanish people, and what they might have done against us if they had been free and well led. There were two to three hundred Spanish vessels on the coast of Ireland in Henry VII and Henry VIII.'s reigns, and about one hundred and fifty in the early part of Elizabeth's reign, catching bacalao,[1] and whaling in Newfoundland and the Gulf of St. Lawrence The result of the successful Spanish war was to give England complete control of the Transatlantic cod-fishery; the great Newfoundland Spanish fleet never came again after that terrible defeat, although stray Biscayans, protected by the French, continued to fish in Newfoundland up to a much later date We shall see subsequently that they claimed the fishery as a right, which Pitt declared he would not acknowledge, even if the enemy were in possession of the Tower of London. From the Armada year until 1630 the English held the Newfoundland fishery practically without a rival, out of the whole number of fishing vessels England had more than double the fleet of her rivals, and all quietly submitted to her control[2]

1588 is the ever-memorable year of the Invincible Armada, all through this season its coming had been threatened, and many of the Newfoundland fishing ships stayed at home to take part in the battle. Bideford had seven ships in the great fight, and later on the little north of Devon town boasted of having more ships in the northern and

[1] This is the general word in Spanish for dried cod, probably derived from the Basque "bacailaba", the correct Castilian for codfish is "abadejo" "Del abadejo, la cabeza y el pellejo" means the head and the skin are the best of the fish "Bacalao" was used in Spain long before the discovery of Newfoundland. It is referred to in *Don Quixote* in the queer scene between Maritornes and the arriero

In the sixteenth century, and later on, "bacalao" was used as a trade word by all the European nations, just as we now use the words "guano" and "tobacco"—both Spanish words which have come into general use

[2] In April of next year, 1589, Moys writes to Lord Burghley from Plymouth.— "The whole country cannot supply above a hundred thousand Newland fish for the fleet." In ordinary years the stock on hand was twenty times this amount—two million fish a striking illustration of the destructive influence of war on commerce

Newfoundland trade than any port in England, save London or Topsham, says Kingsley in "Westward Ho!":—

"It is to the sea life and labour of Bideford and Dartmouth, and Topsham and Plymouth (then a petty place), and many another little western town that England owes the foundation of her naval and commercial glory. It was the men of Devon, the Drakes and Hawkins, Gilberts and Raleighs, Greuvilles and Oxenhams, and a host more of 'forgotten worthies,' whom we shall learn one day to honour as they deserve, to whom she owes her commerce, her colonies, her very existence."

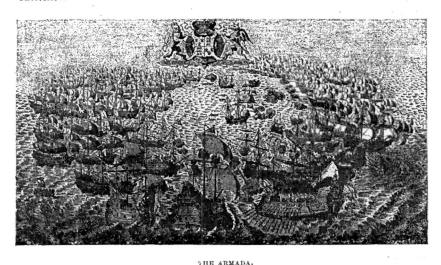

THE ARMADA.
From Pine's engraving, 1738.

Whitbourne was there in his own large ship, and some smaller vessels fitted out entirely at his own expense; Bristol, Bideford, Dartmouth, Plymouth, Topsham, Bridport, Exmouth, Poole, all had their share in the fight.

The Royal fleet, even in Elizabeth's reign, was less than the tonnage of the *Teutonic*, but the English ships were wonderfully strong and well built, thanks to old Hawkins and his father; they were practical seamen as well as shipbuilders. Kingsley states that Young and Prowse, who fired the Spanish fleet in the Calais Roads—"Let their names live long in the land"—were both Devonshire men; the records, however, declare that Young belonged to Chichester. Prowse was undoubtedly from Devonshire, and probably connected with the New-foundland trade. Like Whitbourne, their valour was their own reward. The action in the fireships was a most gallant exploit, and had the most decisive results. These daring old merchant captains received no honour save the imperishable glory of being recorded in history as the saviours of England.[1]

The defeat of the Armada left England supreme mistress of the seas[2], the terrible nightmare of Spanish conquest had no longer any terror for the bold islanders; they mocked at all Philip's later attempts to subdue them. The benefits of Elizabeth's bold policy to trade were simply incalculable. Besides the exclusive control of the transatlantic cod-fishery, England now traded everywhere, and mightily increased in wealth, material prosperity, and territory.

Nearly all the great British possessions were gained without the aid of Government. India was won and held for a long time by a trading company, so were America and Australia, and by the same means in our days England will gain a great empire in Africa, such efforts suit the particular genius of Englishmen.

The landing of the Pilgrim Fathers, their dangers and privations, on the wild New England shore, has been an inexhaustible theme for the poets and historians of the United States, but the earlier conquest of North America, the more wonderful exploits of the daring West Country fishermen, who alone and unaided maintained the English sovereignty in Newfoundland and North America against all comers, a century before the *Mayflower*, are still unhonoured and unsung, and really unknown.

In the whole eventful history of English adventure there are no events more remarkable than the doughty deeds of these Devon men, who for a hundred and fifty years kept this colony for England and ruled over the thousands of foreign fishermen who resorted to the island. The consequences of this early dominion were widespread. It has coloured the whole of our history.

Having won the country, the Western adventurers believed they had a right to keep it as a perpetual possession for fishing, and nothing more, for this reason, after the death of Elizabeth, they banded together to resist settlement. Had France or any foreign power over-mastered the Devonshire men and gained Newfoundland, how would New England and Virginia have fared? If once France had possessed the island with her twenty thousand hardy fishermen she would have held the key of North America, and with her sea and land forces the colonies would have ceased to exist as independent communities.

[1] *See* note in Appendix to this Chapter
[2] About 800 Spanish and Dutch ships were destroyed or captured in the years immediately following 1588.

APPENDIX TO CHAPTER IV.

I. Charter Party and Sale of Newfoundland Fish.

26 Sept 1580.

" It is agreed this day betwixt Wm Massie and Thomas Tetlow, merchants of city of Chester, of the one part, and Wm. Dale, master of ye good ship called *ye William of London*, of the other part, and doth bargain and sell 34,000 Newland fish, merchauntable at 10*s* the 100, current money in England, also foure tonnes traine at £12 per tonne. In consideration the said fish and traine to pay £120 at once, and rest at Lady day in Lent next ensuing. Provided always that the said shippe shall goe for Rochelle and Bordeaux at 38*s* per ton, or for Bordeaux at 42*s* per ton, and to stay in one or both places 30 days at the will and pleasure of said merchants or their factors, and for the freight to be paid after the safe arrival and full discharge in Chester water, the one half within three days, and the rest within 20 days after, and be the full payment with the safe arrival of ye said ship, the residue of the fish money within 20 days after the payment of the whole freight "

II. Licence to Export Newfoundland Fish.

" Whereas Her Majestie is pleased at the humble suit of Nicholas Bowgan, that he be licensed to transport out of the Realme three score thousand of Newland fishe, whereof there is at this present good quantitie in the most partes. This is straitly to will and charge you to suffer him to buy and transport from thens the said quantitie of fish, to carry the same to what countrey or place he shall think best for his best market, and therefore you shall not nede to take any bondes of him in that behalf, permitting him also to transport the same in a French bottome or any other straunge bottome whatsoever, not increasing any custome unto him in that behalf. And this I charge you to so accomplished towards him with all favourable and good despatch, for so is Her Majesties pleasure, he paieing such custome only as others Her Majesties subjects are wont to doe. This 17 Sepr 1599.

" Lord Treasurer, F. Buckhurst.

" To all justices of the peace, maiors, bailifes, and other hed officers. As likewise to all customers, controllers, governors, and surveyors of portes in the counties and portes of Devon and Cornwall "

III. Insurance Policy on Newfoundland Fish in 1604

An Assurance.

" In the name of God Amen. Be it known unto all men by theis presentes that A. J of London Merchaunte and Company doe make assurance and cause themselves and euery of them to be assured Loste or not Loste, knowne or not knowne, from the newe founde Land to Toulone and Marcelleze uppon fishe already Laden or to be Laden in the good shippe called the *Hopewell* of London of the burthen of 120 tonnes or thereaboutes whereof is Master under God in this presente voyage B G or whosoeuer els shall goe for Master in the said shippe or by whatsoeuer other name or names the same shippe or the Mr thereof is or shalbe named or called. Beginninge the adventure from the day and hower of the lading of the said Fishe aboorde the said shippe in the newe found land aforesaid and so shall continewe and endure untill suche time as the same shippe with the same fishe shalbe arived at Toulone and Marcelleze and the same their dischardged and laid on Land in good safetye. Touching the adventures and perilles which wee the assurers hereafter named are contented to beare and doe faithfully promise, by theis presentes, to take uppon us in this presente voyage, are of the Seas men of warre, Fier, Enemies, Pirates, Robers, Theeves, Jettesons, Letters of Mark and counter Mark forrestes, Restraintes, and detaynements of kinges and princes and of all other persons, barratrye of the Master and Marriners of all other perilles, Losses and misfortunes whatsoeuer they be, or howsoeuer the same at any time before the date hereof haue channced or hereafter shall happen or come to the hurte detriment or damage of the said Fishe or of any parte or parcell thereof. Although newes of any Losse hath alreadie come or by the computacion of one League or three Englishe Miles to one hower might haue come to London before the subscribing hereof, any order, Custome, or usage *heretofore had or made in Lumbard streete* or nowe within the Royall Exchange in London to the contrary in any wise notwithstanding. And that in case of any misfortunes, it shall and may be Lawfull to the assured, their factors, servauntes or assignes or to any of them to serve, Labor, and travell for, in and aboute the defence, safeguard, and recouery of the said fishe or of any parte or parcell thereof without any prejudice to this assurance. To the charges whereof, wee the assurers shall contribute eche one, according to the rate and quantitie of his some herein assured. Yt is to be understood that this presente writing and assurance being made and registred according to the Queenes Majesty's order and appointment, shalbe of asmuch fforce, strength, and effecte as the best and moste surest pollecy or writinge of assuranch which hath beene euer hertofore used to be made, Loste or not Loste, Knowne or not knowne in the foresaid streete or Royall Exenange in London And so we the assurers are contented and doe promise and binde ourselves and euery of us, our heires, executors and goodes by theis presentes to the assurede, their Executors, Administrators and assignes for the true performance of the premisses, Submitting ourselves, as well the assurede as the assurers to the order, determinacion and judgment of suche Merchants as nowe be, or heareafter shalbe sworne and aucthorised by the Ld Maior of this Cittie of London for the time being for the deciding and ending of causes of assurances, confessing our selves fully satisfied, contented and paid of and for the consideracion dewe to us for this assurance by theis presentes at the handes of A J after the rate of Seaven per Centu And in testimony of the truth, wee the assurers haue hereconto seuerally subscribed our names and somes of money assured yeouen in the office of assurance within the Royall Exchange in London 3 O 1604

"R C F R"

(From a Petworth MS by permission of the Right Hon Lord Leconfield)

The above is the oldest known record of English marine insurance, the earliest mentioned by Mr Martin is in 1613 The Act referred to was passed in 1601 to create a court to settle underwriters' disputes and regulate assuranceing, which the Act recites had been "tyme out of mynde an usuage amongste "merchants of this realme and forraine "nacyons"

The rates varied About 1560 Sir Thomas Gresham paid five per cent for a cargo of warlike material from Hamburgh to London, insuring to half the value. The above insurance was at seven per cent, but the following entry shows that the rate fell as low as fourper cent under the firm foreign policy of Cromwell —

| Bartholme Laine from Newfoundland. | 16 Oct. 1654 Tho Griffith from Newfoundland to Naples in the *Naptes Merchant* cd at 4 per ct. | - 4-00-00 |

(Rawlinson MS, Bodleian Lib)

Whilst the owners of sack ships from London and the larger ports used the above comparatively modern method of paying premiums against loss, it seems likely that the much more primitive form of Bottomry was employed by the West Countrymen in the fishing trade This system is thought to have been in use amongst the Phœnicians, and is referred to in the Hanseatic articles at Wisby about 1300, and was highly developed at Bruges in the XIV century Instead of paying a premium, the ship owner *received a* sum of money by way of mortgage upon the hull or *bottom* of the ship, if she was lost the mortgagor forfeited all his advance, but when she returned safely he received back his capital with an additional bonus Bottomry is frequently mentioned in connection with our trade during the XVII century Insurance frauds were very common even in the fourteenth century (For fuller information, see Mr F Martin's *History of Lloyd's*)

IV Lawrence Prowse.

Lawrence Prowse, who figures in this daring adventure, was one of the most noted sea captains of that wonderful age, his exploits on the Spanish Main with Amyas Preston are set forth in "Westward Ho" James I imprisoned him at the instance of the Spaniards for piracy, but English feeling would not brook the execution of the man who fired the Spanish fleet, and the bold Lawrence was discharged. The family of Prowse is one of the most ancient in Devonshire, it is spelt in a dozen different ways—Pruz, Prust, Proust, Prouz, and, finally, Prowse Prince's "Worthies of Devon" and many other local h stories contain references to this "clarous and dignous" family. They sent Members to the House of Commons continuously, from 1295 to 1763 there was always a Prowse in Parliament They figured in all the great naval battles from the Armada to Trafalgar, where that old one-legged hero, Captain Prowse, of H M S *Sirius*, showed himself a lineal descendant of Lawrence Prowse. Captain Prowse fought more single ship actions than any other man in the Navy; his life is now being prepared for the Naval Records Society by Professor Layton

In the Armada Memorial at Plymouth the centre shield contains the Prowse Arms in honour of their share in that great victory I am indebted to the distinguished Antiquarian, Dr A B Prowse, FRCS, Clifton, and Mrs Bloomfield, Yeovil, Somerset, for information about this now widespread old Devonshire family

CHAPTER V.

REIGN OF JAMES I.

1603–1625.

1603.—Martin Pring's voyage to New England from Bristol.

1604.—Insurance on a freight of Newfoundland fish at seven per cent

1605.—Two hundred and fifty English ships in Newfoundland according to Sir J Child; fish sold at 8s. per 100 Henry Hudson's third voyage

1608.—Foundation of Guy's Company

1609.—Sir George Somers and others wrecked at Bermuda.

1610.—Charter to Lord Bacon and others; instructions to Guy, arrival of Guy at Cupids with colonists, &c, built "Sea Forest" house Baudoin reports a man being born at Harbour Grace this year who was alive about 1697. The Newfoundland catch at this period valued by Mr W Monson at £100,000

1611.—Guy writes to Slancy in May from Cuper's Cove, proclaimed laws; returns to England

1612.—Peter Easton, pirate, in Newfoundland Guy returns to Newfoundland with the Rev Erasmus Stourton, writes to England in July, attempts to trade with the Beothics. Don Pedro de Cuñega advising King of Spain to destroy English colonies in America

1613.—Colston's letter, announces birth of a boy on March 27th Guy abandons Newfoundland, leaving William Colston in charge of the Colony

1614.—Captain John Smith's voyage to New England Whitbourne meets the privateer Sir Henry Mainwaring with five ships in St John's Complaint of French Ambassador to James I. about injuries done to Frenchmen in Canada, &c.

1615.—Whitbourne holds Vice-Admiralty Court Captain John Mason, R N, Governor of Guy's Plantation

1616.—Sir William Vaughan purchases part of Guy's Grant Letter from Dermer, dated Cuper's Cove, 9th September Damage to fishermen in Newfoundland by Flemish and English pirates to the extent of £1,700.

1617.—First colonists sent to Vaughan's Colony at Trepassey Letter from Mason to Scott Mason's map made

1618.—Whitbourne sent out to Vaughan's Colony at Trepassey Colony of Bristol's Hope founded at Harbour Grace Death of Raleigh. Plunder of Whitbourne's ships by Raleigh's captains on return voyage Petition of the Western Ports against the Planters, &c Squantum taken to Cupid's where he meets Dermer. Ordinance for Jersey rectifying the abuse of taking powder for ships sailing to Newfoundland to reset there

1619.—Great fire in Conception Bay, 5,000 acres burnt mauriously by the fishermen.

1620.—Great disturbances in St. John's, Petty Harbour, between English and Portuguese. Commission to Mason to take up ships to suppress piracy. Landing of Pilgrim Fathers. Publication of Mason's book on Newfoundland.

1621.—Colony founded by Baltimore; twelve men came out with Capta'n Wynne, Governor. Saw mill and grist mill at Clarke's Beach damaged by fishermen. Mason leaves Newfoundland. Jacobsen's map of Newfoundland. Act for freer fishing in Newfoundland and Virginia thrown out.

1622.—Wynne's and Powell's letters of 28th July to Baltimore; further letters from Wynne and "W. H." to Baltimore in August. Great forest fire near Ferryland noticed by "W. H.," who made a sporting excursion inland. Publication of Whitbourne's book on Newfoundland. Sir William Alexander's Nova Scotia colonists winter in Newfoundland.

1623.—First account of cargo of fish sent from Newfoundland to Virginia. Baltimore's charter. Lord Falkland's advertisement gives 400 French, Biscayans, and Portuguese, and 250 English in Newfoundland; English catch valued at £120,000; fish selling at £4 per 1,000, and oil at £12 per tun; salt costing 20d. per bushel. Two men-of-war convoy the English fleet.

The early part of this reign marks the commencement of the colonisation period in English history. All the grand schemes, alike of ignorant enthusiasm, of noble aims, and of statesmanlike projects, in Elizabeth's reign had come to nought; neither England, nor France, at the beginning of the Stuart period, possessed a single settlement on the American continent. The Calendar of State Papers at the beginning of this century is full of applications from all sorts and conditions of adventurers, claiming to be the fortunate discoverers of new islands and territories, teeming with gold and valuable commodities; the craze of the seventeenth century was colonisation. The pages of the Records read more like some fantastic mediæval romance than the dull folios of official papers. From this period dates the foundation of our great American colonies; the creation of French dominion in America; the formation of New France and Acadie. In 1607 the London Company made the first settlement in Virginia, at James Town. New England, first known as Northern Virginia, was brought into notice by the successful voyages of Gosnold, Brereton and Archer 1602; followed by Martin

JAMES I.
From an engraving after Vandyke.

Pring, 1603; Weymouth, 1605; Popham and Raleigh Gilbert's settlement at the mouth of the Kennebec, 1607; and the celebrated Captain John Smith's adventure in 1614.

The result of all these voyages was the establishment of a large English trade and fishery on the New England coast, carried on by London and Devonshire adventurers in the same manner, but on a much smaller scale than the Newfoundland trade and fishery, which was then entirely in the hands of the English, and employed two hundred and fifty ships and over ten thousand men. It cannot be doubted that it was the great success of the English in Newfoundland that tended to encourage fresh enterprise in the same direction on the North American continent.[1]

CAPTAIN SMITH.
From his History of Virginia, 1620.

These English plantations were watched with jealous eye by the Spaniards. Foreigners, and especially Frenchmen, always endeavour to gain an advantage over England when the country is under a weak sovereign and a vacillating ministry. It was to please the king of Spain that Raleigh was executed, and the plan of his last expedition betrayed. Though humiliated and beaten, Spain still with proud persistence claimed all that had been given to her by the Bull of

---

[1] New Englanders showed great jealousy of Newfoundland. Gosnold says of Cape Cod, which he first named, "Surely I am persuaded that in the mouths of March, April, and May, there is upon the coast better fishing, and in as great plenty, as in Newfoundland." . . . Brereton predicts, "For as much as merchants are diligent inquisitors after gains, they will soon remove their trade from Newfoundland to New England."

In 1605 James Rosier writes of Weymouth's adventure, "Would warrant (by the help of God) in a short voyage, with a few good fishers, to make a more profitable return from hence [New England] than from Newfoundland, the fish being so much greater, better fed, and abundance with train [large livers for more oil]."

The most spiteful of all our detractors,

and the most jealous of Newfoundland's success, is the great eccentric Captain John Smith; he writes:—"If Newfoundland doth yearly freight near 800 sail of ships, with a silly, lean, skinny poor-john and coor fish, and those who adventure there can gain tho' they draw meat, drink, and clothes, and all their necessary gear and outfits, from second, third, fourth, or fifth hand, and from so many parts of the world, ere they come together to be used in the voyage, and if Hollande, Portugall, Spainard, French, or other, do much better than they, why doubt of success in going to New England, where there is victual to feed us, wood of all sorts to build boats, ships, or barques, the fish at our doors, pitch, tar, masts, and yards." All these fine arguments did not stop the Newfoundland trade.

Donation; Bermuda,[1] Virginia, and Newfoundland she maintained rightly belonged to her. In 1612 we find Don Pedro de Cuñega advising the King of Spain :—

"It will now be an easy matter to remove these people from Virginia [he was well aware of the weak state of the New Colony], and now will be to the purpose to punish them, for they boldly attempt further plantations, having already begun another in Terra Nova."

"[March 10, same year.] Further complaints from Spain about Virginia. The ambassador says may prove of so much inconvenience to the King of Spain."[2]

"1613. Further hot dispute with Spain about England's rights to Bermuda and Virginia."

The landing of the Pilgrim Fathers in New England in 1620 has been so idealised, so woven round with poetry and fancy, that it almost savours of sacrilege to dwell upon its plain prosaic aspect, a fishing adventure combined with a colonisation scheme.

The Puritan element is to-day the backbone of much that works for good in America, both politically and morally. New England was colonised by a pure, unmixed race of Englishmen, mostly from East Anglia; the same stock that carried out the great English revolution, ruled the new Colony. These sober, self-reliant, deeply religious settlers were led and ruled by the same class that charged at Marston Moor, and gave England freedom.

BERMUDA.
From Smith's Virginia, 1620.

To the Puritan party is mainly due modern English Parliamentary Government. In the new world they achieved almost a greater result;

---

[1] In 1609, July 28th, the *Sea Venture*, with Sir Geo. Somers, Sir Thomas Gates, and Captain Newport on their way to Virginia, was wrecked on the Bermudas. They took possession of the Islands for the English Crown. They were divided and settled in an orderly manner, and have a continued and very interesting history from that date. Their early annals do not concern our history save that the object and destination of every runaway from the Plantations both in Virginia and its dependency Bermuda was to reach Newfoundland. These Islands were originally discovered by Bermudez, a Spanish Captain, in his vessel *La Garza*—"The heron." The Spaniards called the Islands "La Garza," the English sometimes "The Somers Islands" after the gallant Sir George, but finally the old euphonious Spanish name of Bermuda became the permanent designation of these beautiful islands.
Records.

as clear-headed, practical Englishmen, they inherited the national genius for government. They laid the keel of the constitution of the United States in the compact, written in a crabbed hand aboard the *Mayflower*, with a boldness and cunning worthy of the progenitors of the Yankees; they maintained an absolutely free Republican Government against all the English sovereigns, and developed a great English colonisation, which has outstripped every other attempt of the kind, ancient or modern.

The American historian, especially a New England writer, dwells on this marvellous story with pardonable pride, he expatiates on the spiritual and moral aspect of the Pilgrims and their genius for government, but, like his English prototype, he ignores altogether the plain, simple fact proved by the clearest evidence, that his ancestors, mostly humble, God-fearing people, came to New England to earn their living by fishing; and whilst their great political success was chiefly due to the circumstance that the best settlers, gentlemen like Winthrop, governed, their unexampled material prosperity was laid in the fishery. Great commercial nations have everywhere, in the history of the world, risen from the same humble foundation, witness Carthage, Venice, Holland, England; and clearly and directly New England's commerce, and her great maritime prosperity, which, at one time, bid fair to outstrip England, was primarily due to her fishing and whaling.[1]

The history of these great North-Eastern States is closely interwoven with our own; the early intercourse between the two dependencies had immense influence on Newfoundland, and, to clearly

---

[1] In addition to the entries in the Records much information on this subject is to be derived from a number of works on New England, but chiefly from the admirable report of Lorenzo Sabine. Besides the evidence given in Winslow's narrative about the interview with King James I we have the fact that New England before 1620 was chiefly known as a good fishing country. In Rota's map, presented to Henry VIII, 1542 (p. 34), the sea south of Newfoundland is called "the Newfoundlande where men go a fishing" Gosnold's and Smith's histories refer principally to this industry. Weston, one of the chief supporters of the Pilgrims, advised them to settle near Cape Cod for fishing. Their crazy bark the *Speedwell* was bought for that purpose'

' Captain John Smith says :—"At last, upon these inducements [fishing] some well disposed Brownists [a name for the Pilgrims] as they are teamed, with some gentlemen and merchants of Leyden and Amsterdam, to save charges, would try their own conclusions, tho' with great loss and much misery, till time had taught them

to see their owne error, for such humorists will never beleeve well till they bee beaten with their owne rod"

In the next chapters he refers to their prosperous condition (1624) "Since they have made a salt worke whereby they preserve all the fish they take, they have fraughted this yeere a ship of 180 tons" The records show their sojourn at Cape Cod The "Shoal Hope," of Gosnold, was for fishing After they had held a solemn consultation respecting their final settlement, some were disposed to select Cold Harbour, because it offered some advantages for whale and cod fishing. Others insisted they should proceed to Agwam (now Ipswich), a harbour which was known to fishermen who had been on the coast. In 1625 the Colony despatched two vessels with fish and furs, one was captured by Turkish pirates off the English Coast In 1628 they were selling fish and corn to the Dutch at New York; by 1643 they were shipping fish to Malaga, and in 1645 their first vessel visited Bay Bulls to fish and trade

understand our history, it is absolutely necessary to comprehend theirs. The New Englander of to-day is the strongest advocate of temperance and abolition, his Puritan ancestors were just as loud in their claim to export fire rum to Newfoundland, to send their refuse fish to the West Indian negroes, to smuggle, and defy the British navigation laws, to trade with this ancient colony, notwithstanding all restrictions, and to steal the Devonshire men's servants. This last point will probably be denied by American historians, but the fact is too clearly proved by official documents, of which space only allows me to quote a few

The second period of our colonial annals commences with the reign of James I. of England and VI. of Scotland. In studying this period of English history, all feel more or less the glamour of the Stuarts; the beautiful Queen of Scots has to this day votaries from all lands, and ardent and enthusiastic souls are still the champions and defenders of King Charles the Martyr. The subtle, all-pervading influences of art and poetry have shed such a halo of glory around these unfortunate sovereigns, that neither the hard logic of facts, nor time, nor reason, have been able to deaden or destroy the almost universal sympathy for this picturesque dynasty. Even for the slobbering, shuffling, uncouth pedant, with his nameless vices, the first English Stuart, "the most sagacious, high, and mighty Prince James," there is still some sympathy In his policy to Newfoundland he appears, at first sight, in a favourable light; he was guided, in the early years of his reign, by Elizabeth's minister, Cecil, Lord Salisbury, and his colonial policy was the liberal and enlightened policy of his great predecessor, his advances to Guy's associates were liberal, and in marked contrast to his tyrannical and treacherous dealings with the Virginia Company. James, the pupil of the great scholar, George Buchanan, had undoubtedly a love of learning; his life-long friendship and strong attachment to his great chancellor, Bacon,[1] is one of the redeeming features of his reign. The illustrious English philosopher is known to us by his glorious works, to his contemporaries his chief characteristic was eloquence, this is the theme of "rare Ben Jonson's" discourse on him How could a vain pedant

[1] Lord Chancellor in the reign of James I, the father of English philosophy, whose reputation is world wide, took a deep interest in colonisation schemes; he wrote his celebrated Essay on Plantations to further the settlements in America, he showed special interest in Guy's Plantation by becoming a shareholder and subscriber to the company On no subject does the genius of Bacon show to greater advantage than in his Essay on Plantations; one passage alone proves how far he was ahead of the age of monopolies in which he lived —"Let there be freedom from customs till the plantation be of strength, and not only freedom from custom, but freedom to carry their commodities where they may make the best of them, except there be some special cause of caution" Bacon, like Raleigh, preached, even then the doctrine of free trade Bacon strongly advocated settlement in the Colony, and described in his elegant and glowing, language the inestimable value of our fisheries to England

like James resist the adroit flattery, the eloquent adulation, of
such a subject as Bacon? It was entirely due to the great chancellor's
influence that the king granted the advances and issued the charter
to Bacon and his associates in Guy's Newfoundland Colonisation
Company.

BACON.
From an old portrait.

We shall find that all the
other patents granted during
this reign for the settlement of
colonies were given to the Court
party, personal friends of the
monarch. Both Sir William
Vaughan and his brother, Lord
Carberry, were great allies and
supporters of the king's political
views. The first Lord Falkland
was his deputy in Ireland, an
honourable and enlightened man,
and, strange to relate, a friend
of James'. Eternal disgrace
rests upon our colonisers, Bacon
and Baltimore. Bacon—"the
wisest, brightest, meanest of mankind," the last English statesman
to use the rack and to pervert
justice,——to please his master
used all his great influence and genius against English liberty and
parliamentary government, to further the divine right and absolute
authority of the king. Baltimore—in private life an amiable, enlightened
man, a sincere and honest Catholic—earned his sovereign's gratitude in
the Spanish marriage question, and as a parliamentary tool to bribe,
bully, and argue in the House against the great Coke and the noble
band of patriots who strove to give England a free Parliament.

Soon after the accession of James the early chaotic period of our
history comes to an end. England began at last to give more attention
to her ancient Colony. A rude attempt was made to govern and settle
the island by means of a Royal chartered company, like the East
African schemes of our own day. This was part of the policy of
Elizabeth; Bacon, Peckham, Guy, Falkland, and Baltimore were all
simply adopting the projects of Raleigh and Gilbert. I have called this
period, 1610 to 1711, the fishing admiral period, simply because of the
baneful rule of these ignorant tyrants under the sanction of the Home

Government; the century might also be called the colonisation period. Through evil report and good report, amidst the fiercest opposition from the Devonshire ship fishermen, small bands of settlers had, for years before Guy's arrival, been settled on the eastern coast, between Cape Race and Cape Bonavista. The first of these colonies were planted in the neighbourhood of St. John's, and gradually extended around Conception Bay, thence north to Cape Bonavista, and south to Cape Race.

The story of the formation of Guy's Colony, called by the founder "Sea forest plantation," is one of the most interesting episodes in our early annals; as there is no detailed information about it in any extant history of Newfoundland, I have set forth all the facts that can now be gathered from the contemporary records. Young Alderman John Guy is a striking personality, shrewd, pushing, energetic, and full of ambition. The company consisted of most of the men of light and leading in James's Court. Bacon was undoubtedly the guiding spirit in the enterprise, whilst Guy and Roberrow were the working members.

We find the same individuals who were in Peckham and Gilbert's company members of Guy's association. They had become so impoverished by the dismal failure of Gilbert's unfortunate adventure and Raleigh's colonisation schemes, that when John Roberrow, John Guy, and others, were appointed a committee to confer with their London associates, they decided that the scheme was quite feasible, and would be profitable and of great value to the kingdom, but a portion of the charges should be borne by the Government. As far as we can ascertain, this took place in 1607. Undoubtedly the company was the outcome of the various projects put forward by Sir George Peckham and afterwards by Sir Philip Sidney and Carlyle, who were Walsingham's sons-in-law. It was only by immense Court influence that money was obtained from the Government. The Stuarts as a dynasty were perennially impecunious, and it took three years' pleading and all Bacon's influence to get the desired subsidy; it must have been considerable, as

ARMS OF THE LONDON AND BRISTOL COMPANY
FOR COLONISING NEWFOUNDLAND.

Mr. Alderman Guy and his shrewd merchant associates appear to have only put in a nominal sum, less than £100 each, payable in five yearly instalments. In 1610 the charter to Bacon and his associates was issued under the Great Seal.[1] This instrument is very full and comprehensive, it is a far more practical and statesmanlike document than the loose grants of Elizabeth; the extent of territory covered by the charter is defined—from Cape St. Mary's to Cape Bonavista. The public right to the fishery is specially reserved. Guy's instructions show clearly that the charter was a dishonest attempt to give away to Court favourites land occupied and possessed by Englishmen long anterior to the grant.

SEAL OF JAMES I.

After obtaining his title deeds, Guy sailed from Bristol, May 1610, with his brother Philip, his brother-in-law Colston, and thirty-nine persons, in three ships. From the records of Bristol and other sources we are able to give a pretty accurate account of their proceedings. They had carefully chosen the site for their new colony. Old Newfoundland traders were evidently connected with the company, and all their arrangements were planned by persons well acquainted with the trade. There remains a MS.[2] containing the——

"INSTRUCTIONS to JOHN GUY from the Associates of his Company, 1610.

"You shall furnish yourself with at least twelve months victualles with munition nets and with all manner of tooles and implements [and you shall make choice of the] skill and manuall arts of such as are to go with you that you shall think important for the advancement [of the colonie].

"As the benefit and use of domestic creatures without whom not onlie any desolate countrie but also a [civilized countrie] could not well be inhabited we

---

[1] See appendix to this chapter.

[2] I was fortunate enough to find this most interesting document -the instructions from Guy's associates about the management of the plantation; the paper has been partially burnt, but the principal part of the contents have been preserved.—*B.M. MSS. Otto E.*, VIII. 5.

would have you take with you a small number of evrie kind of them male and female water and other things needful for their transportation not [placing them on the sea shore] but either by islands or necks of lands between Bayes where togethei with the care of a herdsman they shall escape from wild beasts and so increase and multiplie of which number [we would] not have anyone killed without great and urgent cause

" When it shall please God to send you and your Companie into the Newfoundland we would have you make choice of some place which you shall find fittest within the limits of the country assigned unto us in order to plant our said colonie. The Baye of Concepsion we prefer before other places for the first attempt

" Upon your first arrival there the sooner to operate our patent and to prevent ye murmuring of suspicious and jealous persons that perhaps will not [fail] to spread abroad that this enterprize wilbe to the prejudice of ye fishermen as well of our nation as others We do hould it expedient that you call an assembly of all the fishermen that shall be nere thereabouts and there in their presence openlie and distinctlie cause to be read the graunt under the King's Majesties great seal which you shall have along with you, that by the tenour of it they may be satisfied that there is no intent of depriving them of their former right of fishing which being done you shall declare in the presence of them all that you enter upon that place to take actuall seazin and possession (never by grace and assistance of God to be discontinued) in ye name of the whole country comprehended within the said giant to the use of us and our associates our heirs and assigns to be holden of our sovereign Lord the King by the rents and services secured by the said graunte and that by such your acte the King's Majestie of England is actually invested with the title and supreme dignitie next under God of the said country

" How you are to spend your time there we need not particularlie [put] you in mind of being in good hope that according to the opinion we do conceive of you all matters shall be carefullie providently and paynofullie ordered and that there shall be no wasting of the victualles nor time misspent in idleness but all industrious courses practised to set forward the enterprize as namelie buildings to be erected for habitation. . .

". (text burnt) . [With the] returne of the ships after the fishing is ended all fish [which you have] made [and shall] not need for your own use [re]ceive to be transported to England and if it may be [bought?] you may also send some quantity of that wine which you . that trial may be made of it as also of the zansaparilla [to see if it] be good and what else you shall judge fit to be sent

. " If you can buy any train [cod oil] for eight pounds the tonne or [thereabouts] we would have you to deale for it for the use of the Companie and charge us by exchange for the payment of it and to take or send to Bristoll and failing thereof to keep it in your warehouses until we do send for it in the winter time for we doubt not that ships may harbour themselves there in the winter in Januarie or Februarie seeing out of the Grand Bay being 4 degrees to the northward it is a thing yearly experimented that ye Biscainers remain until December If you can buy there 60,000 of good dry fish reasonable you may likewise do it and charge us home by exchange and place it in our warehouses until we send a bark thither to take it in and to go with it there home to Spain which coming there alone may sell better than that which came first the great glut marring oftentimes that market

. " You shall as soon as may be conveniently done make choice and bring to the sea shore a ships lading of masts sparres and deal boards to be in a readines to reload any ship that shall happen to be sent unto you with salt which you shall unloade and lay it in your warehouses to be readie there for our use to be used in fishing or to be sold to ye fishermen By employing of shipping of great buiden the trade between Bristoll and Newfoundland may be profitable. We are in good hopes that you shall find sufficient cargo there with which the said ship shall be reloaden   .

" And if any persons employed in this service shall be found to be seditious mutinous or in any manner unfit you shall by the next returne of any ship from there home send them home to be discharged giving advertisement of their behaviour.

" And for the succession of the principal or head of this enterprize if it should please God to take him away it is thought meete that such person shall succeed him as the said John Guy shall nominate under his hand writing and for default thereof the successor shalbe there unto elected by most of votes of the persons that shall survive and if equal votes the lot to be cast whether of them shalbe preferred.

" And we would have you to assay by all good meanes to [capture] one of the savages of the country and to intreate [him well and] to keepe him and teach him our language that you may after obtayne a sale and free commerce with them which [are] strong there.

" We learne that there is found there and no question [fernes ?] whereby may be gathered that yt workmen experte to [make glass ? were] now sent with you with such foreine simples as the mixture of mettall requireth you might presently rase glase to . . . . . nevertheless for more certaintie we now forbear onlie would have you send home some of the fearne [i e kelp] dryed and some . . . [that] it may be considered of.

" Every ship that resorteth thither to fishing bringeth with them [sawyers ?] to make or mend their fishing boates which may well be supplied [by you with] pine boards whereof you shall have plentie when ? the saw is set up.

" Such ashes as you make keep and send to Bristoll that we may have tryall of them and that thereby it may be the [better proved] whether such sope ashes as come out of the Sound may [not be sent from] there home

' And to the end that God may bless this attempt with happy prospects and success you must take order that divine service be publicklie [held] and attentive hearkned unto and that you joine in devout prayers to God that the worship of him may not be neglected that pietie and charitie and sobrietie may dwell amongst us and all swearing and gamming abolished

" You must not forget to search whether there be any trees thereabouts that will afford timber to make caske and be serviceable for hoopes we have heard ,that pipes have been sometimes made of pine timber and for hoopes young beach will serve   The birch there being large and great as yt is yeeld ? for a neede ? stuffe for caske and seing it is most certaine that oakes are in some places of this country you may peradventure upon search light upon some place where it grow.

" To make experience of the nature of the country for sheep were not amis because there want not warme and firtill places and abundance of poules things most requisite for that kind of husbandrie

" The cherrie trees and peare trees and filberd trees by removing and graffing may prove as good and as large as ours and for the filberds though they are small yet they are good and being gathered when they are ripe may do you some pleasure we would have you send us home a few of them [for in] flanders they buy barkes lading with hazell nuts to make oyle for which [we] do [think that] these will serve as they.

" [We] require you to have a due regard [to the carrying out] of these our instructions and of all such [as you may in] your discretion judge may any kinde of way to [turn to the use] and benefit of this enterprize committed to your [care] "

These instructions and the letters of Guy, Colston, and Mason indicate a well-considered scheme of colonisation. In this letter of advice there is a curious blending of the practical trader and the enthusiastic theorist; the suggestions to buy cod oil at eight pound per ton and send late cargoes of fish to Spain, are the ideas of good business men, shrewdly intent on making money; whilst those about the manufacture of glass, soap, charcoal, &c. may have come from the experimental philosophy of Bacon. The last project to make oil out of the wild hazel nuts on Southern River can hardly come within the scope of practical projects, it resembles too much the extraction of sunbeams from cucumbers. It is clear, however, from this paper that these recommendations were prepared by keen traders, who knew all about Newfoundland and the business they were embarking in.

At first everything went well with the new Colony; they had a remarkably fine passage out, in twenty-three days they sighted their new home in the deep Bay de Grave (now Port de Grave), Conception

CUPIDS.

Bay. In the bottom of this estuary lies the beautiful little land-locked harbour of Cupids. It was so far embayed that the resident fishermen, who were then sparsely scattered about Harbour Grace, Carbonear, and the bottom of the bay, had passed by this little sequestered nook as unsuitable for the fishery. The selection of the site for the new Colony was a happy one. At the head of the inlet of Bay de Grave, now known as Clarke's Beach, two beautiful rivers dis-charge their waters into Conception Bay. There are many picturesque scenes in the peninsula of Avalon, but we know of no more charming

G

vista in all Newfoundland than these beautiful rivers with their lovely wooded banks and smiling fields.

At Cupids, Guy built three houses besides his wharves, stores, and fishing establishment A fort ninety feet wide by a hundred and twenty feet long was enclosed by a strong stockade, and a battery

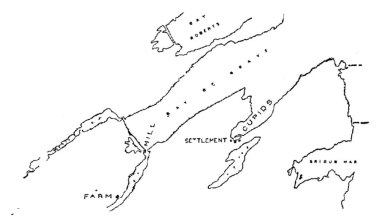

was mounted with three guns. On Southern River they erected mills, houses, and farm buildings, a considerable quantity of land was cleared and surrounded by stone walls Early in this century the remains of these buildings were found, together with mill stones, coins, &c [1] A paper was read on the subject by Admiral Robinson, brother of our late Judge Sir Bryan, before the Royal Geographical Society. There was much discussion on the subject, but no one identified the remains as Guy's Recently some of the old oak beams were used in the construction of a bridge Happily we can now have no longer any doubt about the identification of Guy's buildings, as in the Records we find an account in 1620 of damage to the Company's mills reported by Governor

[1] There has been considerable misapprehension regarding the site of Guy's settlement, in most Newfoundland histories Mosquito Cove is named as the locality, all doubts about the locality are set at rest by the English *Calendar of State Papers. Colonial Series* These volumes have been of inestimable value to me in preparing this work, it is a great misfortune that our own records have not been published in the admirable way General Lefroy has written the Chronicles of Bermuda The late Sir R J Pinsent, D C L, was for some time engaged on this work in Newfoundland I hope some one may eventually give the public the benefit of all the labour he has bestowed on our Colonial Calendar

Early in this century a party of settlers proceeding up Southern River observed at a distance of six or seven miles above the bay the appearance of stone walls rising above the surface, on removing the sard and alluvial earth they ascertained these to be the remains of ancient buildings, with oak beams and mill stones sunk in oaken beds, enclosures resembling gardens were also traced out, and plants of various kinds not indigenous to the island were growing around, among the ruins were found different European coins, some of Dutch gold, others of copper That these were the remains of Guy's buildings is proved by the fact that in 1621 Guy's saw mill and grist mill were partially destroyed by the West Country fishermen, and the damage is estimated at £40

Mason Guy and Colston's letters, which will be found appended, are interesting, as showing how little change has taken place in our climate The Alderman was not the first settler[1] or the first Englishman to discover that Newfoundland, on the whole, was a very pleasant country to live in The great advantage of Guy's plantation was the bringing of the valuable resources of the island under the immediate notice of the British public.

Soon after the formation of the Colony, hostilities were commenced against the permanent settlers, called planters, by the western adventurers,—the ship fishermen from Devonshire No doubt the proclamation of laws made by the Alderman Governor on the 30th August 1611 roused their indignation They had been accustomed to look on Newfoundland as peculiarly their own possession. A young upstart of a Governor building a fort and permanent residence, calling his new mansion, after the fashion of English gentlemen, "Sea Forest House"—all this assumption of authority, especially the making of laws, excited the ire of the belligerent West Countrymen They attempted to destroy the Colony by preparing a petition to the Crown

---

[1] The presence of other settlers is shown by Mason's letters about the carts hauling caplin for manure, the provision of salt for sale to fishermen, and later on, in Baltimore's charter, the reservation of St John's and Petty Harbours, Baltimore mentions numbers of families in Conception Bay which could not have been Guy's settlers
There are several other proofs in the Records of the settlement of the Colony anterior to Guy. Baudoin says, in Harbour Grace they told him of a man who had been born there about 1610 or 1611, this must have been the son of an early settler not belonging to the Alderman's colony There is no record of the official settlement of Bristol's Hope—Harbour Grace until about 1618

[2] Guy's Laws.
Certaine orders for the fishermen to observe and keepe in the Newfoundlande published the 30th daie of August 1611 by Mr John Guy the Gov'nor of the Colony ther
By authority of our Sov Lord James by grace of God of England Scotland Ffrance Ireland and Newfoundland Kinge A Plantation and Government is begun to be settled within this Country of Newfoundland and whereas among those persons that use the trade of fishing in these parts many disorders abuses and bad customs are crept in which are continued and yearly practised, more of a corrupt usage then of malicious designs, forasmuch as it concerns not only the fishing but also the public good, if all such grievances should be stopped to the end that all persons

should reform themselves in their proceedings, and not plead ignorance that any prohibicion was made, The Governor in the Kings name doth charge and command all persons of what nature soever that shall frequent those parts for flishing as well strangers as subjects that they offend not in any thing forbidden in the Proclamation, under penalty herein specified and as they will answer to the contrary at their peril
1 Ballast or anything hurtful to Harbours not to be throwne out but to be carried ashore—Penalty £5 for every offence
2 No person to destroy, deface, or spoile any stage cooke room flakes &c—Penalty £10
3 Every Admiral of each Harbour for time being reserve only so much beach and flake or both as is needful for number of boates—Penalty £10
4 No person to deface or alter, markes of any boates—Penalty £5
5 No person to convert to his own use, boates belonging to others without their consent except in case of necessity and then to give notice to Admiral—Penalty £5.
6 No person to set fire in woods—Penalty £10
7 No person, at end of voyage to destroy stage cooke room or flakes that he hath that year used—Penalty £10
8 No master of any ship to receive into his ship any person of the Colony, that are already planted by virtue of His Majesty's gracious Patent without speciall warrant under the handwriting of the Governor of the Colony or Colonies in the Newfoundlande aforesaide

'against it [1] Devon, in this and every succeeding reign, was strong in Court influence   They found out, however, that the Company, with Bacon at its back, was too strongly intrenched in King James's favour to be injured by this kind of attack.   Discovering by the King's answer to their petition that the settlers were not to be molested, they seem to have set some evil-doer to wreck the plantation, for according to Mason's account they partially destroyed the Company's grist mill and saw mill.

[1] PETITION AGAINST PLANTERS, &c
ARTICLES OF GRIEVANCES MENTIONED IN THE PETITION OF THE WESTERN PORTES TOUCHING THOSE OF PLANTERS OF NEWFOUNDLAND, DECR. 1618

1 That those of the Plantacions there have put sundrie of the Petitioners from the chiefest places of ffishinge there and disposed of the same to such as pleased them

2 That they have taken awaie great quantities of salt, casks, boates, stages and other provisions there lefte by the Petitioners and converted the same to their own use.

3 That they have denied and letted the Petitioners from taking birdes upon the Island of Bacculeau, the flesh of which birds the Petitioners have heretofore used for baite until the ordinarie bait come upon that Coaste

4 That in the chiefest tyme of ffishinge those in the said Plantacion have summoned a Courte of Admiraltie and exacted ffees of trayne and fishe for not apperinge

5 That those of the said Plantacion have harbored pirats there and dealt with them which hath beene the meanes to induce them to frequent that place to the great prejudice and hinderance of the Petitioners

ANSWER OF THE COMPANY OF PLANTERS OF NEWFOUNDLAND TO ARTICLES OF GRIEVANCES OF WESTERN PORTES—DECR 1618

To 1st Article That in regard of theire chargeable maintenance of a Colonie on land there all the yeare, it is conceivable to be lawful for them the Inhabitants to make choice of their fishing place, and not to leave the benefit thereof to the uncertayne commers thither, and have not put out anie shippes out of anie harbours being placed there to fishe accordinge to their ancient customs.

To 2nd Article They know of no such wrong done to fishermen and suppose none of the Colonie that do inhabit there will presume so to do neither do they approve thereof

To the 3d Art . If any of their Colonie have denied the taking of birds for fishermen's baites being a thing altogether unknown to them here — It shall be ordered to the contrary

To the 4th Art   That none of their Colonie have attempted any such acts but have

heard that some of the western partes have done such things to the hurt of the fishermen which they utterly disclaim.

To the 5th Art. That they have received very great damage by pirates almost to the overthrow of their Colonie as not being able to resist them they have come and possessed their houses and taken all their provisions at theire pleasure and carried away such men as pleased them and therefore very unlike that they should induce them to come thither, as is alleged But their coming is to be believed of their friends being some of the western men who are still willing to help them (as it seems to us) with provisions and will make no resistance, tho' they be able to surprize them if they were stronger than they be and therefore we shall humbly desire that some course may be taken for prevention of such mischiefes as by reason of their coming thither may be to further danger of our Colonies And we are desirous to join with the western menne in this business and also for keeping good order in the countrie in the contrarie whereof themselves are guilty for we have caused certain orders to be there published in His Majestys name which they have not obeyed

Signed
　JOHN SLANEY, Treasurer.
　HUMFREY HANDFORDE.
　HUMFREY SLANEY.
　ROBART GAIRARD
　WM PAYNE
　WM FREEMAN

REPLY OF THE PETITIONERS OF THE WESTERN PORTES TO THE ANSWER OF GOVERNORS

No privilege given by the Charter to Planters for fishing before others, if choice of places is admitted, contrary to common usage, the Petitioners contend that they ought rather to have it Desire that the liberties reserved to them by charter may be confirmed Disclaim committing any abuses in the country and request that the offender may be examined The Petitioners knowing better how to manage their fishing than the Planters can direct, declare that they are altogether unwilling to be ordered by the Planters, or to join with them as they desire.

Guy was ambitious of civic honours, his heart hankered after Bristol; he stayed in Newfoundland from 1610 to the end of 1611, as we learn from his letters. In the autumn of this year he returned to England. Next spring, 1612, he came again with more adventurers, "all of civil life"—artizans and farmers—horses, cattle, pigs, poultry, farming implements, &c.; being a sound Churchman, he brought with him, as

CLARKE'S BEACH, SOUTHERN RIVER.
From a photograph by S. H. Parsons.

chaplain of the forces, the afterwards celebrated Evangelical divine, the Rev. Erasmus Stourton.[1]

The Alderman had not only to contend with the opposition from Devonshire. This year, as duly recorded by Whitbourne, the arch-pirate Peter Easton robbed the fishermen, English and foreign, in

[1] Erasmus Stourton, the first Church of England clergyman permanently settled in Newfoundland, came out with Guy on his second voyage, 1612; he belonged to the ecclesiastical party in the English Church, which we now call Evangelical or Low Church as distinguished from the Ritualistic party, who in the days of Elizabeth and the Stuarts adhered to nearly all the doctrines of the Roman Catholic Church, except papal supremacy and the worship of the Virgin Mary; he appears to have been a narrow minded sectary, and a troublesome, meddlesome busy-body. In Conception Bay he ministered to a considerable congregation, between 150 and 200 permanent settlers, besides migratory fishermen. In 1628 the Reverend Erasmus came into collision with Lord Baltimore; all his militant Protestantism was stirred up by Calvert's Catholic worship, and the Seminary priests in the new settlement of Ferryland. Baltimore banished him from the Colony as an audacious man for his misdeeds. Stourton's offence that he speaks of must have been of a very aggravating character to excite such wrath in the mild and benevolent Calvert, whose character for liberality and enlightenment, rare in that age, is borne out by all contemporary historians. On his arrival in England, Stourton hastened to pour into the ears of his Puritan allies the frightful fact that Baltimore had actually had mass celebrated. No one apparently took the least notice of Stourton's complaint

Newfoundland. We are told that he took a hundred men from Conception Bay No doubt some of these would be Guy's men The Governor was a merchant, not a fighting man, and it is not surprising that next year we find him returning home to Bristol Five years later, 1618, he had the distinguished honour of being appointed Mayor of the ancient city. In this exalted position he greatly distinguished himself as a spirited and independent Chief Magistrate [1]

William Colston, his deputy governor, seems to have remained only one year, 1613 to 1614 About this time there appears to have been a good deal of disorder in the country. Guy, though nominally Governor, had no force to execute laws, and it was doubtless from Colston's report on the condition of the Colony that, in 1614, Whitbourne went home to obtain some definite authority to repress disorders The records of this period are full of information about pirates Raleigh's captains, on the last voyage before his death, turned privateers or pirates. The respected Sir Henry Manering, or Mainwaring, was a titled robber, judging by the account of his actions. The following notice of disorders and pirates only extends from 1612 to 1621 In the year 1625 the English fleet suffered still more serious loss from the attacks of sea rovers The Colony was practically without law or government; there was no civil or military force to maintain order amongst a floating population of fifteen to twenty thousand turbulent fishermen. No wonder there were disorders and crimes! The marvel is that there were not more But for the exercise of authority by the English ships no one could have lived here There must have been some violent scenes in St. John's in those days.

The following Records give us a partial list of the depredations of some of the "erring captains"—Whitbourne's euphonious name for the lawless privateers and pirates of the age :—

" 1621 —The names of certaine pirattes with the damage done by them in Newfoundland since the yeare 1612

" The pirate Eason brought 4 ships from Ile of May with captains and soldiers which he increased to 9 ships, all which he carried away with him besides 100 pieces of ordenance with all manner of victualles and munition to the value of ten thousand four hundred pounds of the goods of the English, besides 500 fishermen of His Majesty's subjects taken from their honest trade of fishing (many being volunteers) but the most enforced to serve them in their conrses of piracy. The hurt done by said pirates to subjects of French king by robbing and spoiling 25 ships fishing about coasts of Newfoundland amounts to £6,000. Damage done by them to States of the low countries by taking a great Flemish ship £1,000. By spoiling voyage of 12 Portugal ships £3,000 The total of damage done to all nations by the great Eason and his complices in and about Newfoundland— £20,400.

[1] During Guy's year of office ne resisted a requisition for £2,500 made upon the city to suppress piracy—contending that £1,000 was enough compared with amounts subscribed by London, &c

" Anno 1614. — Captain Maneringe with divers other captains arrived in Newfoundland the 4th June having 8 sails of warlike ships one whereof they took at the bank another upon the mayne of Newfoundland, from all the harbours whereof they commanded carpenters maryners victuals munitions and all necessaries from fishing fleet after this rate—of every six maryners they take one, and the one first part of all their victuals ; from the Portugal ships they took all their wine and other provisions save their bread , from a French ship in Harbour de Grace they took 10,000 fish , some of the company of many ships did run away unto them. ' They took a French ship fishing in Carboneir &c. and so after they had continued three months and an half in the country taking their pleasure of the fishing fleet, the 14th Sep. 1614 they departed having with them from the fishing fleet about 400 mariners and fishermen, many volunteers, many compelled.

" Anno 1616.—Captain Jacob a Flemish pirate with one Captain Ellis an English pirate took a French and Portugese ship—damage done to both being at least £1500 They took all the ordinance from a ship of Bristol and a ship of Gurnsey to the value of £200.

" Anno 1618 —Part of the fleet of Sir Walter Raleigh in their return from Orenoqe consisting of two ships and a cartell wherein was chief commander one Capt Wollaston with divers other captains who took from four French ships their lading of dry fish which they carried away and sold at Ligorne in Italy to value of £3000   More three ships they took and carried with them which they sold at Ligorne to value of £2400   One French ship they left in Newfoundland which was immediately sent home by the Governor of plantation, yet loss of her fishing voyage was £500. On first coming pillaged French fishers 500 pounds. Then taxing of fishermen in all the harbours of Newfoundland for powder shot &c amounted to £2000, besides one hundred and thirty men they took away.

" Some few instances of certane misdemeanors and injuries comitted by the fishers this last yeare in Newfoundland. 1620.

" Eight stages in several harbours worth at least in labour and cost £180 maliciously burned by certain English fishers, besides many more in the harbours of the country, greatly to prejudice of fishing trade, and not punishable but by good laws to be settled there by His Majestie.

" A man slaine in a controversy for ' halinge of a Scyne '

" Certain English fishermen entered aboard a Portugal ship in the night in St John's harbour with swords and axes wherewith they cut many of his ropes and would have cut his cables to the overthrow of the ship had they not been restrained by certain masters of English ships.

" A great combat betweene some insolent English and certain Portugals in Petyte Harbour, and one of the English dangerously hurt with a pike

" Great damage done by certain English fishers to a saw mill and a grist mill built by the plantacon not to be repaired for forty pounds.

" The woods daily spoiled by fishers in taking the rind and bark of the trees and 5000 acres of wood burned maliciously by the fishers in the bay of Conception anno 1619 with many more thousands of acres burned and destroyed by them within these 20 years

" Harbours frequented by English near 40 in number, almost spoiled by casting out their balast and presse stones into them

" Portugals, French and all other nations frequenting that trade are more conformable to good orders than the English fishers."

In 1615 the strongest and ablest ruler of all appeared on the scene—Captain John Mason.[1] The connection of this remarkable man—the future founder, with Sir Ferdinando Gorges, of the State of New Hampshire—with our Colony has been entirely ignored. Mason made himself well acquainted with his new Government, carried on the fish business in Cupids and Harbour Grace prosperously, surveyed part of the coast, and must have been specially energetic in defending the settlers' rights, as it was in his time that the petition was made to the king by the western adventurers.

One very interesting incident occurred during Mason's residence in the Colony, which brings out in a very clear and distinct manner the close connection between the early colonists in Newfoundland and the first settlers in New England, the similarity of the trade and fishery in both colonies. The romantic adventures of the Indian Squantum, his infamous capture by Hunt, and his subsequent slavery in Spain, his visit to Cupids, and his later services as friend and ally of the Pilgrim Fathers, reads more like a scene in a cheap novel than the true story of a poor Redskin.[2]

[1] John Mason was born at King's Lynn, Norfolk, England; he was an Oxford man, and a classical scholar, very early in life he entered the Royal Navy; in 1606 he went with Knox, Bishop of the Isles, to reclaim the islanders of the Hebrides. Says an English admiral "The Christian world could not show a more barbarous, more bloody, or more untamed generation." Mason had command of two ships of war and two pinnaces, and did his work well, but received no payment whatever from James, but probably to requite him in some way for his valuable services he was appointed Governor of the Newfoundland Plantation. Mason came out to Newfoundland with his wife in 1615, and remained six years; he explored the Island, made a map, the first English chart from actual survey which approaches to any degree of accuracy, he also wrote a short treatise *A Brief Discourse of the New-foundland*, published in 1620, and sent to his friend Sir John Scott, of Edinburgh. In 1621, just before Mason's departure from the Island on the petition of divers Scottish adventurers, application was made to the King to send two ships of war to Newfoundland, and to appoint John Mason King's Lieutenant in the Island. This appears to have been granted, and Mason also received at the same time a commission from the Lord High Admiral. Sir Ferdinando Gorges having been appointed one of the Commissioners in England to regulate the Newfoundland fisheries, Mason, on his return to England in 1621, became acquainted with him and, with Sir William Alexander and

his little book on Newfoundland, stirred up the latter, afterwards Earl of Stirling, to obtain a patent for Nova Scotia. In 1622, Mason and Gorges obtained a share of New England which seven years later was named New Hampshire. Mason became afterwards Treasurer of the Army, and Captain of South Sea Castle, and Governor of Portsmouth, England. He died in 1635 and was buried in Westminster Abbey; a monument was erected to his memory in the garrison church of Portsmouth in 1874. I am indebted for all these particulars to the excellent memoir of Mason by Charles Wesley Tuttle, Ph.D., published by the Prince Society of Boston, U.S.

[2] Squantum was seized by Thomas Hunt, one of John Smith's captains in the expedition to New England of 1614, and with nineteen more Indians taken to Malaga and sold as slaves. He was very intelligent, and, probably, being allowed his liberty, wandered about the quay at Malaga. After four years of slavery, he met a captain of a ship belonging to Guy's Colony. He was smuggled aboard, and taken to London, and then out to Cupids. Here he met Mason and Dermer. Dermer knowing of the great interest Sir Ferdinando took in New England, brought him home to Plymouth. From there he went out with Dermer on one of Gorges' expeditions to New England. He was left behind by Dermer in his native land.

When the Pilgrim Fathers arrived, they were astonished at being accosted by an Indian who spoke good English. Squantum was the lifelong friend and ally of the

Mason's tract on Newfoundland is a very quaint and valuable work, it was written between 1618 and 1619, and sent to his friend, Sir John Scott, of Scots Tarvet, Edinburgh, to whom he had also written in 1617

The map did not appear in print until 1625, in Vaughan's " Golden Fleece " It, however, was made in 1617. The letter is directed .—

"To the Right Worshipfull Mr John Scott of Scottisterbatt, in Scotland, Director to His Majesty's Court of Chancery there at his house on the Cawsy of Edenborough." [1]

After alluding to the various hindrances to his duty as Governor, he continued —

"I am now setting my foote into that path where I ended last to discover to the westward of this land, and for two months absence I have fitted myselfe with a small new galley of 15 Tonnes and to row with fourteen oares (having lost one former) we shall visit the naturalls [Indians] of the country with whom I propose to trade and thereafter shall give you a taste of the event, hoping that with all *Terra Nova* will produce *dona nova*, to manifest our gratificacion Untill which tyme I rest and shall remayne *Tuus, dum suus* John Mason.

The tract is entitled—

A

BRIEFE DISCOURSE

Of the New-found-land

with the situation, temperature,
and commodities thereof,
inciting our nation to goe
forward in that hop
-full plantation begunne.
care tuum nihil est, nisite scire noc sciat alter.

A H.
EDINBURGH.
Printed by Andro Hart. 1620.

Colonists. He taught them how to plant Indian corn, and to use fish manure to make it grow well He was their guide, philosopher, and friend, clothed in an old soldier's uniform, Squantum's heart swelled with importance, he made his fellow countrymen believe that, from close association with the white men, he had gained the control of disease and death, that he could bring them out of sickness, or bury them at will

This remarkable Indian spoke three languages, and had embraced four religions; first, his native heathenism, secondly, the genial friars in Malaga (in my experience, the kindliest Christians in the world) made him a good Catholic, Mistress Anne Mason converted him into a sound High Churchman; finally, the Brownists captured him; his last request was for Governor Bradford to pray for him that " he might goe to ye Englishman's God in heaven "

The early part of Bradford's history is full of Squantum and his services to the Pilgrims, with his death the Indian trade for the time ceased When he died, in 1622, he was most sincerely lamented Governor Bradford says his useful services to the infant settlement entitle him to grateful remembrance

I am indebted to my friend James Phinney Baxter, B A, for this note

[1] The full address —
" Deliver this,—
" I desire Moyses Slaney to repaire downe to Whitehall with this letter and to inquire for Sir William Alexander, Master of the Requests for Scotland, and to procure of him conveiance for this letter accordingly " It shows all the trouble that had to be taken to forward a letter in those days.

Mason begins by describing the geographical position of Newfoundland; next the climate.   He says:—

"It is fruitfull enough both of sommer and winter corne . . . . wheate, rye,
barlie, oates and pease, which have growen and ripened there as well and as timely
as in Yorkshire in England."

This is not in the least exaggerated.   Sir Terence O'Brien, K.C.M.G.,
our Governor, has lately imported some Russian wheat; the return crop,
grown by Mr. Ross, Grove Farm, showed splendid grain.   Barley, rye,
and oats are ripened every year in Newfoundland by our farmers.
Splendid wheat has been grown over and over again; the price of flour,
however, is so low that there is no inducement to grow it.   Garden
vegetables, peas, beans, cauliflower, &c., are grown to perfection.

MASON'S MAP.[1]

From Vaughan's Golden Fleece, 1645.

His description of the wild fruit is also correct.   Of the fishery he
says:—

"May hath herings one equall to 2 of ours, cants and cod in good quantity.
June hath Capline a fish much resembling smeltes in forme and eating and such
aboundance dry on shoare as to lade cartes, in some partes pretty store of Salmond,
and cods so thicke by the shoare that we nearlie have been able to rowe a boate
through them, I have killed of them with a pike; of these three men to sea in a
boat with some on shoare to dresse and dry them in 30 dayes will kill commonlie

---

[1] A close examination of this map shows
that it was not constructed by Mason, all its
features being traceable in much older maps,
the only contribution of Mason being "the
great Lake or Sea"—Fortune Bay, which he
probably saw from some hill in Placentia
Bay on one of his exploring expeditions.
The map belongs to the Anglo-Dutch group,
and is mainly of French origin.

betwixt 25 and 30,000, worth, with the oyle arising from them, 100 or 120 pound. And the fish and traine in one harbour called Sainct Johns is yearly in the summer worth 17 or 18 thousand pounds. Julie and so till November hath Macrill in aboundance one thereof as great as two of ours. August hath great large Cods, but not in such aboundance as the smaller, which continueth, with some little decreasing until December.

" I have heard some countries extolled for their two fowld Haruest which heare thou hast tho' in different kinde yet both as profitable. . . . that country say I which in one month's time with reasonable paines wil pay landlord's rent seruants wages and all household charges."

He notes the four advantages that Newfoundland possesses :—

" 1st. The nearenes to our owne home. In March April and May, which alwayes accommodate faire windes to pass thether in 14 or 20 days seldome in 30 days. Return in June to Novr. in 12, 16, 20 and now and then 30 days.

" 2nd. The great intercourse of trade with our nation these three score years and upwards in no small number frequenting the Newfoundland and daylie increasing imploying 3000 seamen also fraiting 300 ships. . . . Revenue to the King by the customes of French Spanish and Straights goods imported from the proceeds of this fish trade at least £10,000 yearly.

" 3. The conueniency of transporting planters at the old rate 10/– the man and 20'– for victuals . . likewise other commodities by shippes that goe sackes at ten shillings per tunne out and thirtie shillings home. Whereas Virginia and Birmooda fraightes are fiue pounds the man and three pound the tunne . . .

" 4. Securitie from Foreign and domesticke enemies. Few savages in the north. None in the south, by whom the planter as yet never suffered damage. Ice a bulwark in winter. In summer we have nine or 10,000 of our own nation with maney good and warlike shippes who must defend the fishing season for their living sake as they have formerly done in the warres with Spaine."

" In the midle of the Month of April many Ships arriue of the *English*, some *French*, and in the midest of May some *Portingalls*. All which as so many Reapers come to the Haruest, gathering in aboundance the wonderfull blessings of the Lord.

" I might heare further discourse of our discoueries, conference with the Saluages by Master *Iohn Gye*, their maner of life. Likewise of the managinge our businesse in our Plantations, with the descriptions of their situations in 2. places 16. miles distant from other, on the northside the bay of Conception ; of the manner charge and benefite of our fishings with the seuerall strange formes, and natures of Fishes. projects for making Yron, Salt, Pitch, Tarre, Tirpintine, Frank-Incense, Furres, Hope of Trade with Saluages and such like, with many accidents and occurrences in the time of my gouerment there, but these may suffice as *Verbum sapienti* ; being of sufficient trueth to remoue errours of conceiuing the Countrie more pleasant by reason of his naturall sight in the Spheare, then it is indeede, also to convince and take away malicious and scandelous speeches of maligne persons, who out of enuy to GOD and good Actions (instructed by their father the Deuill) haue sought to dispoile it of the dewe, and blamish the good name thereof.

" And lastlie to induce thee, gentle Reader, to the true consideration thereof as a thing of great consequence to our Nation not only at present, but like to bee much more beneficiall when the plaintations there shall increase, which God grant to his owne glorie and the good of our Common-Wealth."

GOVERNOR'S HOUSE, PORTSMOUTH.[1]
From a print in the B.M.

In May 1620 Mason received a commission from the Admiralty to suppress the pirates. We do not know how many he seized in Newfoundland, but we have his own account of the capture of a Sallee Rover, the *Good Fortune*, in Crookhaven in 1625.[2]

[1] Most probably the house where Mason spent his last days.

[2] COMMISSION TO MASON AND BUSHELL.

" Grant of a Commission from George, Duke of Buckingham, Lord Admiral &c &c. to the Treasurer & Company of the Colony of Newfoundland, to take up & press such ships with mariners, Soldiers, gunners, munitions of war, stores &c as may be necessary for the purpose of suppressing pirates and Sea Rovers, who interfere with the sea traffic, & plunder &c the merchant ships. That the s[d] Treasurer & Company are to set forth in a voyage to Newfoundland the good ship *Peter & Andrew* of London of 320 tons burthen, Capt. Iohn Mason, & W[m]. Bushell, master, with men, ordnance &c. for the purpose of taking such pirates or Sea Rovers & their ships, & to bring such ships into any of our ports, Creeks &c. And all Vice Admirals, Justices of the peace, Mayors, Sheriffs, Constables & Gaolers are to aid & assist the s[d] Capt. John Mason, & W[s] Bushell, & to carefully keep any pirates in prison as may be brought to them, until their trial to answer to Justice,

& suffer the pains of the law for their piracies, or be acquitted thereof. And the said Company is authorised to take possession of such ships as may be captured, a moiety of their proceeds to go to the Admiralty & the other moiety to the said Company.

"Given in the High Court of Admiralty 29 May 17 K. James. A.D. 1620."
—*Dom. Eliz.* 1590.
Admiralty. Eliz. James I. & Charles I. Vol. 237. ss. 30–32.

Mason gallantly captured a Sallee pirate called the *Harts Desire* or *Good Ffortune* at Crookhaven in Ireland. In the report of his claim to the Admiralty about the ship, which was 100 tons, " she was continuallie imployed in pyracyes these 3 or 4 yeares, and theirfore Mr. Wyen needs not make any scruple to proceed legallye to a condemnation." It appears the Admiralty case came before the great Sir John Eliot, Vice Admiral of Devon. Eliot distinguished himself by the capture of pirates, especially one Nutt ; this corsair had powerful friends at Court, and, at his suit, Eliot was imprisoned.

Mason, like Guy, was young, restless, and ambitious, his little book stirred up a Colonial fever amongst his Scotch friends. On his visit to England in 1621 he found his services in requisition, Buckingham wanted a capable, reliable man as Treasurer for the Navy,[1] and so poor Newfoundland lost a ruler under whose prudent and energetic sway her destinies might have been completely changed. Probably sweet Mistress Anne Mason, a High Churchwoman, influenced the gallant Governor, she found Cupids and the long preaching of Erasmus Stourton rather dull, and longed for a livelier existence in London[2] Even the pleasant trips and picnics up Southern River did not reconcile her to banishment from England.

Guy's Company appears to have existed up to 1628, at least. In that year we find negotiations going on between Slaney the treasurer, through a Dr. Meadus and Lord and Lady Conway, about a purchase of part of their grant. On June 27th, 1628, Dr. Meadus writes to Lady Conway.—

" Have conferred with Mr. Paine about the Newfoundland business; he will part with his Presidentship if John Slaney, the Governor of the whole land, consents Hopes of mines of iron and silver in Newfoundland; present profit by fishing, furs and sarsaparilla "

There is another letter on June 30th on the same subject In 1637 Hamilton and Kirke's grant recites that all the patentees had abandoned Newfoundland. This statement, however, is doubtful

All writers on Newfoundland history, except Chief Justice Reeves, seem to have gone entirely astray on the subject of the various colonisation companies in the reigns of James and Charles I. A study of the records and various writers would have shown them how these different projects were founded, and how long they existed. Bishop Howley speaks of the Alderman's Colony having been abandoned some ten or twelve years previous to Lord Baltimore's settlement in Ferryland, and the Rev. Dr. M Harvey says, " We have no authentic account of Guy's settlement " Evidently they were unaware of the existence of the books of Mason, Hayman, and Vaughan on this subject Reeves gives distinctly the boundaries of Baltimore's grant. The Rev Dr M Harvey says Lord Baltimore obtained a grant of the whole southern peninsula of Newfoundland between Trinity and Placentia Bays

---

[1] It was in Mason's house Buckingham was stabbed by Felton

[2] Robert Hayman, a poet of the Quigley and Swanborough type, in 1628 thus addressed her —
" To all those worthy women who have any desire to live in Newfoundland specially to the modest and discreet gentlewoman Mistress Mason wife to Captaine Mason who lived there divers years.

" Sweet creatures, did you truly understand

The pleasant life you'd live in Newfoundland,

You would with teares desire to be brought thither

I wish you, when you go, faire wind, faire weather."

Quodlibets (1628), II Bk. p. 31.

Bishop Howley, more cautious, quotes from Kirke, and says Baltimore's grant "applies to the whole peninsula of Avalon, and this is the common opinion of nearly all historians." Richardson, he quotes as contending that Baltimore obtained the whole Island. Then his Lordship goes on to prove that Baltimore established the Catholic religion in Newfoundland—a pure fiction. His further statements (p. 80), that Guy's Colony "failed through the incursions of the Indians," and that Baltimore bought out the Company in 1621 (p. 82), are entirely opposed to the evidence in the Records.

All the time there was extant and well known, Baltimore's grant and the exact boundaries of his province. Pedley attributes the large proportion of Irishmen and the influence of Roman Catholics in this country to Lord Falkland's Company, a bogus concern that fell flat on the market; its prospectus will be given later on.

Fortunately, we have at hand all the materials to correct these errors. No less than six colonies existed in Newfoundland during the reign of James I. Guy's, the parent Colony; "Bristol's Hope," an offshoot from Guy's at Harbour Grace; a distinct Colony of St. John's, extending south from Cape St. Francis to Petty Harbour, and to the present Holyrood; Vaughan's Colony, with head-quarters at Trepassey; Falkland's comprising part of Trinity Bay, called North Falkland and South Falkland, between Renews and Aquaforte; and lastly, Baltimore's Plantation. The exact division of Baltimore's grant is given, and it will be seen from these minute boundaries, how small a portion of Avalon he really possessed. Though Guy had a large nominal grant, the territory in his actual possession was very limited, and is described in Baltimore's bounds. The sale to Sir William Vaughan in 1616 by Guy's Company was part of the peninsula of Avalon between Petty Harbour and Cape Race, extending across to Placentia Bay.

SKETCH MAP OF THE SIX COLONIES.

Sir William Vaughan, D.C.L.—a brother of Lord Carberry, celebrated as the host of Jeremy Taylor, at Golden Grove, Carmarthenshire—

founded his Welsh colony in Trepassey Harbour, naming it "Cambriol Colchos," and "Golden Grove" after their ancient seat, and "Vaughan's Cove," as we may see it marked on Mason's map of 1617. Vaughan

FERRYLAND, SHOWING BALTIMORE'S HOUSE.
From Fitzburgh's map, 1693.

sent over his first batch of emigrants in this year, and in 1618 Whitbourne, it appears, came out with another detachment.

He informs us :—

"I sayled thither in a shippe of my own which was victualled by that gentleman myself and some others. We likewise did set forth another shippe for a fishing voyage which also carried some victuals for those people which had been formerly sent to inhabit there, but this ship was intercepted by an English erring captaine [a Pirate] that went forth with Sir Walter Rawleigh . . . . . . whereby the fishing voyage of both our shippes was overthrown and the Plantation hindered."

Poor Sir William Vaughan, after remaining out in Newfoundland some years and spending his time writing his remarkable works, through want of means was first compelled to sell a block of land to Lord Falkland; this piece was six miles wide, extending from Renews to a point between Fermeuse and Aquaforte, and thence extending in two parallel lines west to Placentia Bay. After making this sale, Vaughan disposed of the remaining northern portion of his big territory to Lord Baltimore. They had been friends and fellow students at Oxford, and quite in a natural way, as one pawns off a worthless horse on a friend, so Sir William sold a large portion of his grant at a very high price to Lord Baltimore.

Whitbourne gives a sorry description of Vaughan's colonists :—

"For certainly I have already seen and known by experience that the desired plantation can never be made beneficial by such idle fellows as I found there in 1618 when I was there with power by virtue of a graunte from the Patentees, which people had remained there a whole yeere before I came theare or knew any or them and never applied themselves to any commendable thing, no not so much as to make themselves a house to lodge in, but lay in such cold and simple rooms all the winter as the fishermen had formerly built there for their necessary occasions the yeere before those men arrived there."

These wretched emigrants appear to have ruined poor Vaughan : instead of looking after their work and superintending their labours the learned Sir William was busy preparing his fantastic works ; friends in England advised him that the best chance for selling his books was to give them curious titles, thus we have his "Newlander's Cure" and his "Golden Fleece," most extraordinary medleys about religion, medicine, and colonisation. King James appears to have been generous and kind to this remarkable exile, a great scholar and most absurd pedant, after the king's own heart. A grant was made to him in his extreme need, and partly at his instance, in 1623, two men of war were sent out to convoy the Newfoundland fleet home.

BALTIMORE ARMS.

From Winsor's N. & C. H. of America.

The names given by Vaughan and Lord Falkland to the southern shore have entirely disappeared ; all the other official colonisation schemes, from Bacon to Baltimore and Kirke, failed. They had elaborate charters prepared in the chambers of kings : princes and potentates lent the weight of their names and dignity to these great state documents ; they offered court barons, court leet, and territorial aggrandisement to their associates ; later on they had those remarkable dignitaries, the Nova Scotia Baronets ; all these fantastic titles and aristocratic forms, the devices of principalities and powers, faded and died away in the rude free air of the Colonies. None of the great patentees, from Gilbert to Baltimore, exercised the least permanent influence on the history of the Colony, least of all Baltimore ; he came and stayed an uneasy

discontented stay of two seasons; all his company of forty persons left
the colony together, and then his Lordship and his seminary priests[1]
and his noble retinue and his Welsh colonists vanish from our annals.

There has been much acrimonious discussion about Calvert's character; on one side he is lauded as a saint, whilst some extreme writers
have denounced him as a bigot. With his bastard son he can hardly
be set down as a saint, but he was far ahead of his age in enlightenment;
his religion was real and sincere; his zeal for the Catholic faith was
genuine and honest, it was opposed to all his worldly interests.

The truth is that, though an amiable, gentle and honest man in
private life, in public affairs Baltimore was a weak man; in Parliament he prostituted his talents for Court favour; he was undoubtedly
brave and an enthusiastic pioneer
in colonisation, but the rude life
and rough winds of Avalon were
morally and physically too strong
for him; he was neither an epoch
maker nor an empire founder,
simply an honest religious Cavalier.
The treatment of his son by the
Stuarts, whom the father had so
loyally and abjectly served, is one
of the most treacherous and dishonourable acts of Charles I.

FIRST LORD BALTIMORE.
From Winsor's N. & C. H. of America.

St. John's and the neighbourhood, from Petty Harbour on the
south around by Cape St. Francis
to Holyrood, Conception Bay, was
the first settled part of the Island;
from the very earliest times St.
John's was the capital, the metropolis and head-quarters of the great
fishery and exchange carried on in
Newfoundland; the rendezvous for
all the convoys, it was connected with the neighbouring settlements by
rude paths cut through the woods.

Newfoundland was colonised not by aristocratic and fantastic patentees, but by hard-working humble settlers from the West of England;
oppressed by the harsh laws of the Stuarts, and persecuted by the

---

[1] The Southampton Records show that
one of Baltimore's priests came home, under
an assumed name, in August 1629.—(See
Southampton Municipal Archives—Book of
Examinations, Informations, and Depositions.
No. 42, A.D. 1622 to 1643).

H

western adventurers, they clung with sturdy tenacity to the land they
had made their home   From the very earliest times they carried on a
rude kind of agriculture, raised vegetables, and reared cattle and swine.
They lived in the midst of a rude plenty, game and fish being simply in
unlimited supply.   The settlements were very much scattered, and these
hardy pioneers, most skilful in woodcraft, traversed the country in all
directions, made visits to each other—"cruizing" it is still called in
this country [1]

Baudoin says —

"The French deem the country impassable.   Not so the English, they know
it perfectly, even that part which belongs to France, for they guided us everywhere
through the woods and along the coasts, where for more than *one hundred and
ninety leagues* they have roads beaten fit for horseback " [2]

Many peculiarities of the Colony can be traced back to our
Devonshire forefathers   There are no lakes in the West of England,
only ponds, so all our lakes are all called ponds, they had no grouse,
so our willow grouse has always been most erroneously called a
partridge, our people possess remarkable skill as mechanics, mostly
self-taught   The first winter crews left in the Colony, who became
permanent settlers, were ship and house carpenters, blacksmiths, &c.
Our fishermen's manual dexterity is no doubt partly inherited skill,
and partly arises from necessity—the mother of invention

It was doubtless owing to harsh laws and the hostility of the
Devonshire ship-fishermen that the settlers planted their homes in
creeks and coves, where ships could not safely lie   In these open
roadsteads they were free from molestation   This explains the early
settlement of such places as Torbay, Pouch Cove, Grates, and Bonavista,
which soon became large settlements   Official returns about the population are misleading, the settlers purposely concealed their numbers from
the naval authorities   We notice a great discrepancy between the
numbers as given by the French Abbé Baudoin and the official census.

The year 1615 marks the first primitive attempt to create a formal
court of justice in Newfoundland, our old friend Sir Richard
Whitbourne was sent out to hold courts of Vice-Admiralty in the
Colony, it was all carried out at the poor old captain's own expense,
he had not so much as a bum-bailiff to serve process, or a room to
hold court in, or any power whatever to enforce his decrees.   Was
there ever such an absurd plan of governing a country, maintaining
order, and administering justice, as this cheap device of King James !

[1] A lady sent her servant—an out-
harbour man—to ask a friend to go calling
with her   The message delivered was —
"The Mistress wants to know, 'Mam,' if you
will go *cruizing* with her this afternoon."
[2] BAUDOIN's *MS Diary, Quebec MSS.*

Most extraordinary things have been done in modern times in the Colony; early in this century an ardent liberal medico started on a pan of ice to aid Ypsilanti, the Greek patriot. This project was hardly a wilder scheme than Whitbourne's Vice-Admiralty Court.

Of course it was the duty of the doughty Sir Richard to magnify his duties, and filled with all the dignity of office, and rejoicing in the confidence of his sovereign, he tells us, in his own inimitable way, the result of his judicial round of lectures to the wild rovers and daring

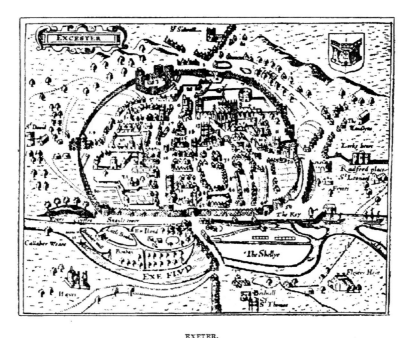

EXETER.

From Speed's Prospect, 1640.

adventurers that then carried on the Newfoundland trade; no doubt they listened to the old mariner with respect, and all promised to behave themselves. During the next two or three years disorders were worse than ever.

Whitbourne tells us :—

"I set forth from the Port of Exceter on the 11th May 1615 in a Bark victualled and manned with 11 men and boyes at my own charge; on the 4th June being Trinity Sunday, I anchored in Trinity Harbour and there in the name of the Holy and Indiuiduall Trinity I called together by virtue of my commission the masters of the English ships there lying, and so began to hold the first Court of Admiralty in your Majesty's name that ever was as I believe holden in that

Country to the use of any Christian Prince and proceeded therein according to course of law as the tenour of my commission did warrant me therein, also in other Harbours of the said Coast I did the like." [1]

Having carefully inquired into the disorders committed on the coast, the masters of one hundred and seventy English ships " delivered to the Court, under their hands and seals, their presentments," which in turn Whitbourne transferred to the High Court of Admiralty. These presentments are summarised under twelve heads, the most important were :—

" Non-observance of the Sabbath Day.
" Injury to the Harbours by casting into them large stones.
" Destroying fishing stages and huts
" Monopoly of convenient space.
" Entering the service of other countries.
" Burning woods.
" And lastly Idleness parent of all evils." [1]

The masters who put their presentments on record declared that these disorders should cease. Thus ended this legal farce. It is to be hoped old Whitbourne got through his cases in what an old bailiff used to call a "summinary" manner, so as to enable him and his crew to get a load of fish when he threw off the burthen of his judicial dignity.

Whitbourne is the Captain John Smith of our colonial history, like his great prototype—the most picturesque figure in the annals of Virginia—he was a devout High Churchman, an utter despiser of Brownists, Puritans, and all other new-fangled religions, a sound high-hearted Englishman, devoted to his country and her ancient Colony, like Smith he was everything by turns—sailor, traveller, author, judge, and colonial governor, in his last years we can fancy the fine old mariner sitting in his pleasant cottage at Exmouth, within sound of the sea he loved so well, writing with his crabbed old hand —

" A relation of the Newfoundland with a more ample discovery of that Country than euer was yet set foorth to the open viewe together with the Briefes or such Presentments as were there taken to use of your Majestie, by vertue of a commission vnder the Broad Scale of the Admiraltie directed to me Richard Whitbourne." [1]

He concludes his work with an eloquent appeal to the King :—

" And these excellent benefits distribute themselues, between your Maiestie and your Subiects: your Highnesse part will be the Honour of the Action ; the accesse of Territory, increase of strength and power, aduantage against other Princes, augmentation of Reuenew, and ease of your Maiesties Kingdomes, &c The Subiects part will be the bettering and securing of their Trade, inriching of themselues ; reliefe of other Trades, and a meanes of further Discoueries.

[1] WHITBOURNE's *Discourse*

But these two haue a relation and dependency, the one on the other, that neither can subsist without the other. I will not therefore diuide your Maiestie from your Subiects, your Highnesse prosperitie being their happinesse; and their wealth, your Maiesties riches

" The first thing which is to be hoped for, and which hath euer been your Maiesties principall care, is the propagation of the Christian faith · and by that meanes onely, the poore vnbeleeuing Inhabitants of that Countrey may be brought to the knowledge of God, and a ciuill kinde of gouernement: and it is not a thing impossible, but that from those slender beginnings which may bee made in New-found-land, all the regions adioyning (which betweene this place, and the countries actually possessed by the King of Spaine, and to the north of New-found-land, are so spacious as all Europe) may be conuerted to the true worship of God

" The next is, the vniting of a Countrey so beneficiall already, and so promising vnto your Maiesties Crowne, without bloodshed, charge, or vsurpation, which must needs be a perpetuall Honour to your Maiestie, in all succeeding ages; neither will it be an Honour onely to your Highnesse, but a benefit to the State, by a new accesse of Dominion. And what Prince can enlarge his Territories by a more easie and more iust meanes then this, seeing that of right it appertaineth to your Maiestie, and therefore deserues to · be imbraced?

" Now if it please your most excellent Maiestie not onely to lend your care to a Proiect of this nature, but also to approue the matter proiected, and vouchsafe the furtherance therein, the which out of my soules deuotion, and zealous affection to do seruice to your Maiestie and your Kingdomes, I tender on my knees; most humbly beseeching your Highnesse, both to accept of my honest and zealous intent, as also to pardon my boldnesse and presumption therein, for it is, and so hath euer been my resolution, rather to beare the burden of pouerty, than iustly to deserue, or giue cause of reproach, and to subiect all the dayes of my life, and the manifold dangers thereof, thereby to approue my selfe a profitable member, both to your Maiestie, and to my countrey that gaue mee my first breath; for which onely cause I haue adventured to publish this my simple and plaine Discourse, whereunto my very conscience hath a long time, and still doth not forbeare to sollicite me

" The prosecution and perfection of the worke, I leaue to the pleasure of God, and your Maiesties happy directions, in the discourse and discouery whereof, if I haue either been tedious, or any other way offensiue, it is to be imputed to my want of learning · and so, though perhaps I doe not satisfie some men's curiosities, yet I hope I haue sufficiently informed their iudgements; and beseech God to incline their affections to the furtherance of so pious and so profitable a businesse, as this appeareth to be.

" And so I rest, and euer will remaine, a faithfull and loyall Subiect to your Maiestie, an hearty and true louer of my Conntrey, and a zealous wellwisher to this intended plantation

" RICHARD WHITBOURNE." [1]

With a twinkle in his humorous old eye he tells us of the " mosquitos ".—

" Those flies seeme to have a greate power and authority upon all loytering people that come to the Newfoundland; for they have the property, that when they find any such lying lazily, or sleeping in the Woods, they will presently bee

---

[1] WHITBOURNE'S *Discourse.*

more nimble to seize on them, than any Sargeant will bee to arrest a man for debt, neither will they leave stinging or sucking out the blood of such sluggards, untill like a beadle they bring him to his Master, where hee should labour ; in which time of loytering those flies will so brand such idle persons in their faces, that they may be known from others as the Turks doe their slaves." [1]

Whitbourne's book, with its quaint conceits, took the fancy of King James, himself a " Royall and noble Author ", he gave him the sole right of printing and selling it for twenty-one years, and orders were sent to the archbishops for its distribution in every parish in the kingdom   Our author seems to have made some profit out of his work, as there were no less than seven editions of the book published between 1621 and 1623.

The last we hear of old Sir Richard is a petition to the Stuarts for a small post under the Crown as inspector of provisions for the merchant ships, he asks—

" To be allowed to superintend the orderly salting and preserving of victuals or the well baking of biskett bread, the tymelie and well breewing of beare, and also the filling of sweet casks for the same. In which kind of employment he has had long experience "

He also prays to be appointed superintendent of one of the western forts, or to get command of a ship, he proposes a method, at no charge to His Majesty or to His Majesty's subjects, for keeping two men of war and pinnaces for the protection of the Newfoundland fishery Whitbourne's relations belonged to Widdecome, in Devon, where many yeomen of his kith and kin lie buried   There is no monument to mark the last resting place of the poor old battered and decayed Elizabethan hero, our constant ally and friend, Sir Richard Whitbourne [2]

Lord Falkland, the nominal head of the Dublin Company for colonising Newfoundland, must not be confounded with his son, the

[1] WHITBOURNE's *Discourse*

[2] 1626, November 10, in a Petition to the Duke of Buckingham, in the reign of Charles I (contained in the Calendar of State Papers), Whitbourne states : " A traveller and adventurer into foreign countries at 15 years of age, he was captain of a good ship of his own in 1588, and rendered good service, has often been greatly wronged by pirates in Newfoundland, where he was subsequently employed, by commission, for the reformation of abuses yearly committed there, and other special affairs on that coast, wrote a large discourse, which was presented to King James, and ordered to be printed and distributed in every parish throughout England, to show the benefits of settling a plantation there. Has been twice to that country to help advance a plantation undertaken by Lord Falkland

encloses a certificate of his good services and losses "

Whitbourne was probably knighted for his " Large Discourse " and his services in the Armada fight, which he states "is to be seen recorded in the book at Whitehall " For this sturdy old sailor every Newfoundlander should feel a deep affection His love for our island was wonderful, through good report and evil report he always stood by us, his description of the Colony is in the main a true report, and agrees with contemporary accounts of Peckham, Mason, Vaughan, Hayes, &c, he threw in a few wonderful tales, such as the " Marmaide " and the " Mosquito,' to tickle the ears of the groundlings The Hon R Bond did suitable respect to the memory of the old " Worthy of Devon," by naming our first important railway junction " Whitbourne "

distinguished patriot and hero of the Civil War.   Falkland's colonisation scheme embraced a settlement between Baltimore's and Vaughan's colony : it extended six miles wide from a straight line drawn half-way between Aquaforte and Fermeuse to Placentia Bay, and a similar line drawn west on the southern boundary.

Henry Cary, the first Lord Falkland, was made Lord Deputy of Ireland by James I. ; he was a man of considerable literary ability, and took a deep interest in schemes for colonising America ; the organisation of his colony was carried out by his associates ; he appears to have taken very little active part in the company.   The colonists were like the uncivilized Welsh brought out by Wynne ; it was the custom of the age to capture men for all kinds of service, and in all probability Vaughan's settlers and Falkland's colonists were simply corralled like so many cattle, and sent out to the new settlement.   There was no practical farmer to teach them how to clear the land ; they were green hands, and no use at the fishery ; it is no marvel, therefore, to find, after reading Whitbourne's account of their idleness, and Hayman's description of their management, and the dishonesty of agents like Wynne and Powell, that they were failures ; these causes, combined with the want of a practical, energetic, experienced man at the head of affairs, fully explains why these aristocratic schemes to colonise Newfoundland did not succeed.

FIRST LORD FALKLAND.
From an engraving after Harding.

We can admire the enthusiasm that set them on foot, the eloquent language with which they were recommended to the public ; the colonies were settled by poor hardworking fearless men, not by these courtiers and enthusiastic writers or the poor slaves they sent out to people the New World.   Not a vestige of these colonies now remain ; all the fantastic names of New Falkland, Cambriol Colchos, Vaughan's Cove, Brittaniola, &c., with the one exception of Baltimore's Avalon, have disappeared from the maps, and there is not a Welsh family remaining on the whole southern shore of Newfoundland, except the honoured family of Williams of Bay Bulls.

Lord Falkland's proposals were printed in a book entitled :—

"A short discourse of the New-found-land contayning diverse reasons and inducements for the planting of that countrey.

"Published for the satisfaction of all such as shall be willing to be adventurers in the said Plantation.

"Dublin : Printed by the Societie of Stationer- MDC.XXIII.

" To the Right Hon. Henry Lo. Cary Viscount Falkland Lo. Deputie Generall of Ireland and one of His Majesties most honourable privie Councell in the Realme of England.

" My Lord,

" I present with the view of your judicious censure the short Discourse or rather an abstract of a discourse, intended only as a satisfaction unto such as may be willing to joyne with your Lordship in so noble a designe as is the plantation of the Newfoundland, wherein it is not to be doubted but that many will follow your Lordship's stepps in so honourable a worke especially in the Kingdome where the name of a *Plantation* is so farre from being a stranger as it hath been the originall cause from whence very many have derived their happinesse. I cannot deeme but that the weake handling of this discourse better beseemes the poor demonstration of my zeale to your Lordship's service than any possibility to comprehend the worthinesse of the action within the compasse of a bare relation.

" Reasons for planting—it is for the Honour of God and the King ; that Part of the Country is not inhabited ; His Majestys undoubted right to the Country ; that the London Plantation has been settled 13 years [Guys] ; the Bristol Plantation 5 years, and Lord Baltimore the two years last past ; the advantages of Trade from Ireland to Newfoundland.

" Conditions are, that any one paying £100 is to have half a Harbour on the north side of Trinity Bay and Stages Room in Fermeuse or Renews, and 1000 acres of land. For £200 a whole Harbour in Trinity Bay, 4000 acres north of Trinity Harbour, and stage room for 2 Rooms at Renews and Fermeuse. Other amounts paid, to obtain benefits proportionably."

The pamphlet is very well written. Sir Francis Tanfield, who figures in Guy's Company, was appointed governor ; it appears he never came out to his kingdom, and the whole scheme fell through.

JACOBSZ' MAP, 1621.

In the latter part of James I.'s reign a very important point about fishery rights in the plantations began to be agitated ; it raised the whole question as to the absolute authority of the Crown over the colonies, and had a dire effect on the Stuart dynasty.

The Plymouth Company claimed the right to charge the English ship-fishermen who frequented the coast a licence fee equal to eighty-three cents per ton, and to forbid vessels engaged in commerce to enter any port along the entire coast without liability to seizure and confiscation, and such punishment for

the captain and crew as the Council thought proper to inflict   Bradford
says —

'About ye later end of June came in a ship with Captaine Francis West who
had a Comission to be Admirall of New England to restraine interlopers and
such fishing ships as came to fish and trade without a licence from ye Counsell of
New England, for which they should pay a rounde sume of money   But he could
doe no good of them, for they were to stronge for him and he found ye fisher men
to be stuberne fellows "

The West Countrymen brought their grievance before Parliament.
A discussion arose, in which Calvert, the Secretary of State, defended
the patentees' right to this monstrous monopoly   He argued, "America
" is not annexed to the realm, it is a plantation solely governed by the
" Crown"   The great lawyer Coke[1] made Sir Ferdinando Gorges, the
principal patentee, come to the bar of the House   Coke argued —

"Your Patent contains many particulars contrary to law and the liberty of
the subject, it is a monopoly, and the ends of private gain are concealed under
color of planting a Colony, to prevent our Fishermen from visiting the Sea Coast
for fishing, is to make a monopoly upon the seas which are wont to be free, if you
alone are to pack and dry fish you attempt a monopoly of the wind and sun."

On the accession of Charles I., the Commons passed a Bill for the
maintenance and increase of shipping and navigation, and for liberty of
fishing in Newfoundland, Virginia, and New England   The Bill was
thrown out by the Court party in the Lords, on this the Commons
refused to grant the king a subsidy.   It was one of the first difficulties
between Charles and Parliament.

---

[1] Coke posed as a reformer in this matter,
the real motive was his bitter hatred of his
rival, Bacon.   All the same, he rendered great
service to England as adviser to those who
opposed the tyranny of the Crown   The
London Company, who led this attack on
Gorges, and the Plymouth patentees had a
similar monopoly.   For further information
on this interesting subject consult *Sir Ferd.-
nando Gorges*, by James Phinney Baxter,
B A

APPENDIX TO CHAPTER V.

I. London and Bristol Co.'s Charter.

(Harl 58ª, fol 8)

James by the Grace of god kinge of England Scottland ffrance and Irelande defender of the faith to all people to whome these presents shall come greeteing,

Knowe yee whereas divers our lovinge and well dispo ed subjectes are desirous to make plantacõn to inhabite and establishe a Colony or Colonies in the Southerne and easterne p'tes of the country and Islande commonlie called Newfoundland unto the coast and harbours whereof the subjects of this our Realme of England have for the space of fiftie yeares and upwards yearlie used to resorte in noe small numbers to fishe, intendinge by such plantacõn and inhabitinge both to secure and make safe the trade of fishinge to our subjectes for ever, and also to make some commendable bemfitt for the use of man inkinde by the land and profitt thereof which hitherto from the beginninge, (as it seemeth manifest) hath remained unprofittable

And for better performance of such their purpose and intencõns have humblie besoughte our royal authoritie and assistance, we beinge well assured that the same country adjoininge to the foresaid coastes, where our subjects use to fishe remaineth so destitute and so desolate of inhabitaunte that scarce any one salvage person hath in many yeares beene seene in the moste p'tes thereof. And well knowing that the same lyeing and being soo vacant is as well for the reasons aforesaid as for many other reasons very commodious for us and our dominions and that by the lawe of nature and nations we maie of our royall authoritie possesse ourselves, and make graunte thereof without doeinge wronge, to anie other prince or state, consideringe they cannot justely pretend anie soueraignitie or righte thereunto in respect that the same remaineth soo vacant and not actuallie possessed and inhabited by any Christian or any other whomesoever, and therefore thinckeinge it a matter and action well beseeming a Christian kinge to make use of that w'ch God from the beginning created for mankinde, and thereby intendinge not onlie to worke and pruve the benifitt and good of many of our subjectes, but principallie to ourselves to encrease the knowledge of the omnipotent God and the propagacõn of our Christian faith have graciouslie assented of their intention and suite

And therefore doe of our speciall grace, certaine knowledge and meere motion for us our heires and successors give graunte and confirme by these p'ts unto our right deare and right wellbeloved cossinne and fellow Henry Earle of Northampton, keeper of our privie seale and to our trustie and right welbeloved Sir Lawrence Tanffield knight cheife barron of our exchequer Sir John Doddridge knighte one of our serjaunts at Lawe Sir ffraunces Bacon knight our Sollicitor generall [here follow forty-two names including] John Slany, John Guy, Philip Guy and Robert Aldworth, theire heires and assignes and to soo many as they shall hereafter admitt to be joyned with them in forme hereafter expressed, whether they goe in their persons to be planters in the plantacõn or whether they goe not but doe adventure theire moneys goods and chattells

That they shalbe one bodie or communitie perpetuall and shall have perpetuall possession and oue common seale and that they and their successors shalbe knowne as the *Tresorer and company of adventurers and planters of the cittie of London and Bristoll for the colony or plantacõn in Newfoundland* and that they and theire successors shalbe from henceforth for ever enabled to purchase by that name (license from us first obtayned) lande and goods within our realme of England and Walles and that they shalbe likewise enabled by that name to pleade and to be impleaded before any our judges in any of our courtes and in any actions

And under the reservacõns limitacõns and declaracõns hereafter expressed *all that p'te and portion* of the country commonlie called Newfoundland *w'ch is situate, lying and being to the southward of the parallel lyne to be conceaved to passe by the cape commonlie called Bonuiste inclusive w'ch cape is to the Northward of Trinitie Bay and also w'ch is situate to the eastward of the meredian line to pass by the cape St Maries inclusive w'ch cape is to the eastward of the bay of Placentia* together with the shoare and *islands lying within tenne leagues* of any p'te of the sea coast of the country and *alsoe all those countryes lande and Islands* commonlie called Newfoundland w'ch are situate *betweene forty and sixe degrees of Northerlie latitude and two and fiftie degrees of the like latitude* and all the lande soile grounde havens, portes rivers mines aswell royall mines of gold and silver as other mineralls pearles and precious stones woods quarries marshes waters fishing hunnting hawkinge fowleinge commodities and hereditaments whatsoever together w'th all prerogatives jurisdictions royalties, priviledges franchizes and preheminites thereto or thereaboute both by sea and land belonging or appertaininge and w'ch we by our letters patiente canne graunte and in as ample manner as we or any of our noble progenitors have graunted to any adventurers or undertakers of any discoverie plantacon, or traffique into any forraigne p'tes and in as ample manner as if the same weere heerein p'ticularlie mentioned

Nevertheless that there be saved and reserved unto *all manner of persons of what nation soever and also to all our loving subjectes w'ch doe at this p'nt or hereafter shall trade or voyadge to the partes aforesaid for fishing* all liberties powers easements and all other benifitts *as well concerning their fishing as well all other circumstances and incidents thereunto* in as ample manner as they have heretofore used and enjoyed the same without any impedimente disturbance or oposition any thinge in these p'nts to the contrarie notwithstandinge

To have and hould all the lands Countryes and territories, with all the premises to the sole and proper use of them, &c to be holden of us our heires and successors as of our manor of East Greenewich in the county of Kente in free and common soccage ? and not in capito Yeeldinge to us the fifthe parte of all the stoire of gold and silver gotten and obtayned for all services duties and demands

And for as much as the good and prosperous successe of the plantacon cannot but cheifelie depend most under the blessing of god and the support of our royall authoritie upon the provident and good direction of the whole enterprize by a carefull and understanding counsell, and that it is not convenient, that all the adventurers shalbe soo often drawen to meete and assemble as shalbe requisite for them to have meetings and conference about their affaires

Therefore that these shalbe perpetuallie one counsell consistinge of twelve p'sons here resident in London w'ch shall governe the plantacon or any colonies to be established, w'ch counsell shall have a seale, besides the legall seale of the company, each of w'ch shall have our armes engraven on the one side and our portrature on the other and that the legall seale shall have round about on both sides these words *Sigillum thesaurarii et commimitatis terra nova* and that for the counsell *Sigilum Regis magnae Britanniae frauncie et hibernie* and on the other side. *Pro concilio terrae novae*

And further that Sir Percivall Willoughbie Knight John Weld Esquire

Raphe ffreman, Richard ffisheburne, John Stookely William Turner, William Jones, John Slany, Humfrey Slaney, John Weeld, Thomas Lupon and Thomas Jones shalbe the counsell and John Slany tresurer with authoritie for the warning of the counsell and summoning the companie and the counsell and tresurer shalbe chosen continued displaced changed and supplied as occasions shall require out of the adventurers by the voite of the greater p'te in their assembly for that purpose.

And that the companie maie cause to be made a coine to passe current betweene the people inhabitinge in these territories for the more ease traffique and bargaining between and amongst them of such nature mettle manner and forme as the counsell there shall lymitt and appointe

And that if the tresurer for the tyme being be sicke or absente from the cittie of London he may constitute one of the counsell to be deputie with power to doe all things which belong to the tresurer

And further to nominate by such names or styles as shall seeme good to them (and likewise to revoke) all governours, officers and ministers and to make lawes, formes and ceremonies of government and magistratie and revoke and change not onlie within the precincts of the colonie but also upon the seas in going and coming for the good of the adventurers and inhabitors there

And for divers reasons and considerations that immediatelie from and after such tyme as any governour soe to be nominated shall arive in Newfoundland and give notice of his commission in that behalfe, all officers governours and ministers formerly appointed shalbe discharged, straighthe commanding them and everie other p'son resident in the Colonie upon their alleageance that they forthwith be obedient to such government as the counsell heere resident shall have named and to all directions w'ch they shall receive from them as well in their p'nt resigneing their authoritie as in all other attendance as shall be by them required.

And that the counsell heere resident in London or any five of them the tresurer being one shall have full power to admitt any other person with their companie or freedome

And further in a generall assemblie of the adventurers with the consent of the greater p'te upon good cause to put any person out of the freedome

And by direction of the governour there to digg and to search for gould silver cooz-iron lead tynne and other minerells as well within the precincts as within *any p'te of the maineland not formerlie graunted to any*

other and to have the gould &c to the use of the company

Yeelding thearefrom yearlie unto us as aforesaid without any other manner of profitt or accounte to be given or yeelded

And to take into that voyage and for and towards the plantačon all of our loveing subjects or any other strangers that will become our subjects and live under our allegeance as shall willinglie accompanie them with sufficient shipping weepons vittailes and such marchandize or wares as maie be fitting to transport into those partes ; and clothing, implements, furniture cattle, horses and mares and all other things necessary and for the use and desoine and trade w'th the people there, yf any be inhabiting in that country or *shall come out of other p'tes*, there to trade with the plantačon and passing and returning to and froe all such comodities or marchandize as shalbe from thence brought without paying custome for *seaven years*.

Provided that none of the persons be such as shalbe hereafter by speciall name restrained and for their further incouragement that they shalbe free of all customes in Newfoundland for the space of *twenty one years*, and *from all taxes for ever* upon any merchardize at any tyme hereafter either upon importačon *thether* or exportačon *from thence* into our *Realme of England* or into any of our dominions (*except* onehe the five pounds per centum due for custome upon all such goods as shall be brought into our Realme of England according to the ancient trade of merchants), w'ch five pound per centum onehe being paid it shalbe thenceforth free for the said adventurers the same goods to exporte out of our said dominions into forraine p tes without any custome

Provided that the said goods be shipped out within thirteen months after the first landing.

And every governours maie for their defence and saftie repell by force and armes by sea and land and by all waies and meanes all persons as without the speciall licence of the tresurer shall attempt to inhabite within the severall precincts and also all persons as shall attempt distruction invasion hurte detriment or annoyance to the Colonie and to take all persons with their shipps and goods and other furniture trafficking in any harbour creeke or place within the limmitts of any colony to be made within any the limmitts aforesaid and not being allowed by the companie to bee adventurers or planters of the Colony untill such time being of any realme under our obedience shall paie or agree to pay to the officer deputed over and above such subsidie as the company is to paie five pounds per centum upon all goods so brought in thither *other than such as shalbe brought*

in for the necessarie use of fishing us hath beene heeretofore accustomed and also five pounds per centum upon all goods shipped out from thence *other than fishing and other necessaries requisite to fishing* and being straungers and not under our obedience until they have paid over and above such subsidie as the company is to pay tenne pound per centum and the same sommes of money during the space of *one and twentie years shalbe wholly* employed to the *benefitt of the companie* and the one and twenty years *ended* the same shall be taken *to the use of us* by such officers as by us shalbe thereunto appointed.

Alsoe that all persons being our subjects w'ch shall goe and inhabite within any Colony and everie of their children and posteritie that shall to be borne there shall enjoye all liberties of free denizons and naturall subjects within any of our other dominions to all intents and purposes as if they had beene abiding and borne within this our Realme of England &c

And for as much as it shalbe necessary for all our loving subjects as shall inhabite within any those territories to determine to live together in the feare and true worship of allmightie god Christian peace and civill quietness each with other whereby every one maie with more safetie pleasure and profitt, enjoy that whereunto they shall attaine with great paine and perrill

Wee graunte that governours officers and ministers according to the nature and limitts of their offices and places respectively shall in Newfoundland or in the waie thither and from thither have absolute power to punish, pardon and rule all subjects of us as shall adventure themselves in any voyage thither or that shall inhabite in the precincts of the land according to such orders as by the counsell shalbe established and in deserte thereof according to the good discretions of the governour as well in cases capitall and criminall as civill both marine and other, soe alwaies as the statutes as neere as convenienthe maie be agreable to the lawes of this our Realme of England

And that such principall governours shall have full power to axercise Marshall lawe in cases of rebellion or mutinye in as our lieutenaunts in our counties of England have by force of their commissions

And furthermore if any Adventurers or planters shall transport any moneys or marchandizes out of any of our kingdomes with a pretence to land sell or otherwise dispose them within the limitts of the territories and yet nevertheless being at sea or after he hath landed within the territories shall carry them into any forraigne country there to dispose thereof that the goods together with the shipp wherein such transportacon was made shalbe forfeited to us.

And further that in any difficultie of construction or interpretation of anything contayned in these our letters pattents the same shalbe taken and interpreted in most ample and beneficiall use of the company and every member thereof.

And finally our will is that all persons w'ch shall hereafter adventure any somme of money in and towards the plantacon and shall be admitted as adventurers in forme aforesaid and shall be inrolled in the booke or recorde be accounted and reputed adventurers and enjoye all priviledges as fully as if they had been named in these our letters pattents

And lastly because the principall effects which we can desire of this action is the conversion of the people in those p'tes if any be there inhabiting unto the true worshipp of god and Christian religion in which respecte we would be loathe that any p'son should be permitted to passe that be suspected to asserte the superstitions of the Church of Rome

Wee declare that none be permitted to pass in any voyage but such as shall first have taken the oath of supremacie tor which purpose we doe give full power to the tresurer and any three of the counsell and to any our Mayors Baylieffes or any other our cheife officers in any portes where any person shall take shipping to tender the oath to all persons as shall be sent to remaine and plant there

Provided and we doe hereby declare to all Christians kings princes and States that if any persons which shall be of any Colony or any other by their license or appointment shall robbe by sea or land or doe any acte of unlawfull hostilitie to any the subjectes of us or any kinge being in amitie with us that upon complainte of such prince or their subjects we shall make open proclamacon within the partes of our realme of England commodious for that purpose that the persons having committed any robberie shall within the tyme to be limitted by such proclamacon make full restitution so as the said princes and others soe complayning may hold themselves fullie sattisfied and that if the persons should not make satisfaction accordinglie within such tyme that then it shalbe lawfull to us to put them out of our protection And that it shalbe lawfull for all to pursue with hostilitie the offenders

In Witness whereof we have caused these our letters to be made pattente Witnes our selfe at WESTMINSTER the second day of MAIE in the eighth year of our Raigne of ENGLAND FFRANCE and IRELAND and of SCOTLAND the three and fortieth *Per breve de privato sigillo.*

II. Letters from Cupids.

(*a*) Master JOHN GUY, his letter to Master SLANEY, Treasurer, and to the Counsell of the New-found-land plantation.

RIGHT WORSHIPFULL,—It may please you to understand that it was the tenth day of this month of May before the barke of Northam, called the *Consent,* arriued here in New-found-land, notwithstanding that a ship of Bristoll, called the *Lionesse,* came to this countrey the second of May in a moneth's space and the *Trial of Dartmouth* arriued here before in sixteene days By reason of which stay of the aforesaid barke, nothing could be done to take any of the places desired all being possessed before So that the ship that commeth, whereof as yet there is no news, is to trust to the place here, which is reserved for her, which I hope will prove a good place Some yeares as great a voyage hath bin made here, as in any place in this land God send her hither in safetie I haue not yet seene any of the country to the southward, or northward of this Bay of Conception since this spring, because I expected daily the arriual of the barke and thought it not fit to be absent here hence until she were arriued, and dispatched but presently upon her departure, no time, God willing, shall be lost The care that was taken to require generally the fishermen to assist us, and to supply our wants, if any should be, was most joyfull and comfortable to us which was most willingly accomplished by the most part of those which I have yet seen. Yet, God be praised, such was the state of all things with us as we were in no want of victuals, but had a great remainder, as you shall after understand.

The state of the autumne and winter was in those parts of Newfoundland after this manner In both the moneths of October and November there were scarce six days wherein it either freezed or snowed, and that so little that presently it was thawed and melted with the strength of the sunne. All the residue of the aforesaid two months being both warmer and drier than in England In December we had sometimes faire weather, sometimes frost and snow and sometimes open weather and raine, for in the latter end it was rainie, and was open weather All these three moneths the winde was variable as it would euery fortnight visite all the points of the compasse The most part of January and February into the middle of March the frost continued. the winde being for the most part westerly, and now and then northerly, notwithstanding three or four times when the winde was at south it began to thaw and did raine That which fell in this season was for the most part snow, which with the heate of the sunne would be consumed in the open places within a few dayes. That which abode longest was in February.

During this time many dayes the sunne shone warme and bright from morning to night . notwithstanding the length of this frosty weather, small brookes that did run almost in cuell with a slow course, were not the whole winter three nights ouer frozen so thicke as that the ice could bare a dogge to goe ouer it, which I found by good proofe for euery morning I went to the brooke which runneth by our house to wash. The snow was neuer aboue eighteene inches thicke generally out of the drift, so that the feare of wanting wood or water neuer tooke hold of us for albeit we made no prouision for them, yet at a minute of an houres warning we were furnished where there were lakes of fresh water that stood still and did not run, there it remained frozen able to beare a man almost three moneths, and was not dissolued untill the middle of Aprile But where the ayre had entrance and issued out of them, there was no frost When the spring wind in the winter time in England is at the north-east one moneth together, the frost is greater, and the cold more sharpe, then it is here at all There was no moneth in all the winter that some of our company did not trauel in, either by land or by water, and lie abroad and drinke water, in places distant two, three, foure and fiue leagues from our habitation, and sometimes lay in the woods without fire, and receiued no harme When April came our spring began, and the first that did bud was the small keser or the corinth tree Our company was not letted in working abroad and in the woods and open ayre fifteen dayes the whole winter We neuer wanted the company of rauens and small birds So that the doubt that haue bin made of the extremity of the winter season in these parts of New-fonnd-land are found by our experience causelesse, and that not only men may safely inhabit here without any need of stoue, but nauigation may be made to and fro from England to these parts at any time of the yeare.

Concerning the healthfulnesse of these countries, we hauing bin now more than ten moneths upon this voyage, of nine and thirty persons, which was all our number which wintered here, there are wanting only foure, whereof one Thomas Percy, sawyer, died the eleuenth of December of thought, hauing slain a man in Rochester, which was the cause, being unknown unto mee until a day before he died, that he came this voyage And one other called John Morris Tyler, miscarried the first of February by reason of a bruse. The third, called Marmaduke Whittington, was neuer perfectly well after he had the small poxe, which he brought out of Bristoll with him, who died the fifteenth of February. And the fourth, called William Stone, having at the first only a stiffnesse in one of his knees,

kept his bed ten weekes, and would never stirre his body, which lasinesse brought him to his end, who died the thirteenth of April Of the rest foure or five haue bin sicke, some three moneths, and some four moneths ; who now are better than they were, except one. All of them, if they had had as good will to work, as they had good stomackes to their victuals, would long since haue bin recovered. One Richard Fletcher, that is master pilot here and a director of the fishing, reported unto me, that he was one of the company, consisting of forty persons, that went in a drumbler of Ipswich, called the *Amitie*, to the north part of Ireland about eleuen yeeres ago from London in the late Queen's seruice, under the charge of one Captaine Fleming, and continued there for the space of two yeares In which time two and thirty died of the Scuruie, and that only eight of them returned home, whereof the said Richard Fletcher was one So that the accident of death or sicknesse of any persons in these our parts of New-found-land is not to argue any unhealthfulnesse of this country, no more than Ireland is to be discredited by the loss of those two and thirty men , notwithstanding that there were to be had fresh uictuals and many other helpes, which this country as yet hath not, but in good time may haue

From the first of October until the sixteenth of May our company had bin imployed in making of a store-house to hold our prouisions, and a dwelling house for our habitation, which was finished about the first of December , with a square inclosure of one hundred and twenty feet long and ninetie foot broad, compassing these two houses, and a work house to work dry in, to make boats or any other work out of the raine; and three pieces of ordinance are planted there to command the harboroughs, upon a platform made of great posts, and railes, and great poles sixteene foot long set upright round about, with two plankers to scoure the quarters A boat, about twelue tons big, with a deck, is almost finished to saile and row about the headlands . six fishing boates and pinnesses a second saw-pit at the fresh lake of two miles in length and the sixth part of a mile broad standing within twelue score of our habitation, to saw the timber to be had out of the fresh lake, in keeping two pairs of sawyers to saw planks for the said buildings, in ridding of some ground to sow corn and garden seeds in cutting of wood for the colher, in coling of it in working at the smith's forge iron workers for all needful uses : in costing both by land and sea to many places within the Bay of Conception in making the frame of timber of a farre greater and fairer house, then that which as yet we dwell in which is almost finished, and diuors other things We haue sowed all sorts of graine this spring, which prosper well hitherto Our goats haue liued here all this winter ; and there is one lustie kiddie, which was yeaned in the dead of winter Our swine prosper Pidgens and cowies will endure exceedingly well

Our poultry haue not onely laid egges plentifully, but there are eighteen young chickens, that are a week old, besides other that are a hatching

The feare of wilde beasts we haue found to be almost needlesse. Our great ram-goat was missing fifteen days in October, and come home well againe, and is yet well with us. If the industry of men and presence of domesticall cattle were applied to the good of this country of New-found-land, there would shortly arise just cause of contentment to the inhabitants thereof. Many of our masters and sea-faring men seeing our safetie, and hearing what a milde winter we had, and that no ice had bin seen fleeting in any of the bayes of this country all this yeare (notwithstanding that they met one hundred and fifty leagues off in the sea, greate store of islands of ice) doe begin to be in lone with the countrey, and doe talke of comming to take land here to inhabit, falling in the reckoning as well of the commodities that they may make by the banke fishing, as by the husbandry of the land, besides the ordinary fishing At the Green Bay, where some of our companie where a-fishing in November, they report there is great store of good grounds without woods, and there is a thousand acres together which they say may be mowed this yere There is great store of deer, whereof they saw some divers times, and twice they came within shot of them, and the greyhound, who is lustie, had a course, but could not get upon them But nearer unto Cape Razo, Reneuse, and Trepasse there is a great quantitie of open ground and stagges It is most likely that all the sackes will be departed out of England before the returne of this, our barke, which shall not make any matter, because I am now of opinion that nothing should be sent hither before the returne of the ships from fishing For as concerning sending of cattle, it will be best that it be deferred untill the next spring And concerning vituals, in regard to the quantity, we haue of it remaining of old, together with that that it come now, as with the dry fish that here we may be stored with, I am in good hope there will not want any to last till this time twelue moneths. And according to the vituals which shall be found at the end of the fishing, the number of persons that shall remaine here all the next winter shall be fitted, that there shall not want, notwithstanding about Alhollantide, or the beginning of December, a ship may be sent, such a one as our Fleming was with salt from Rochel, for at any time of the winter ships may as well goe and come hither, as when they doe, especially before January This summer I purpose to see most places between Cape Rase, Placentia,

and Bona Vista, and at the returne of the fishing ships to entertaine a fit number of men to maintaine here the winter, and to set over them and to take the care of all things here, with your patience, one master William Colton, a discreete young man, and my brother, Philip Guy, who haue wintered with me, and haue promised me to undertake this charge untill my returne the next spring, or till it shall be otherwise disposed of by you, and then together with such of the company as are willing to goe home, and such others as are not fit longer to be entertained here, I intend to take passage in the fishing ships, and so return home, and then betweene that and the spring to bo present, to give you more ample satisfaction in all things, and to take such further resolution as the importance of the enterprise shall require, wherein you shall finde me alwayes as ready as euer I have bin to proceede and goe forward, God willing. And because at my comming home it will be time enough for mee to lay before you mine opinion touching what is to be undertaken the next yeare, I will forbeare now to write of it, because you should be the sooner aduertised of our welfare, and because such of the company as are sent home both for their owne good, and that the unprofitable expense of vituals and wages might cease I have laden little or nothing backe, that the said company might the better be at ease in the hold Onely there is sent three hogsheads of charcoels, where numers 1° is, they are of burch, No. 2° is, of pine and spruce, No. 3° is of firre, being the lightest wood, yet it maketh good coles, and is used by our smithe I send them because you shall see the goodnesse of each kinde of cole. Also I send you an hogshead of the skinnes and furres of such beasts as have been taken here, the particulers whereof appeare in the bill of lading

While I was writing I had newes of the *Vineyard*, the ship which you send to fishing, to haue bin in company with another ship that is arriued on this side of the Banke and that the master intended to goe to Farillon or Ferland God send her in safety So praying God for the prosperity of your Worships and the whole company, with hope that his diuine Maiestie, which hath giuen us so good a beginning, will alwayes bless our proceedings My dutie most humbly remembered, I take my leaue.

Dated in Cupers Cove, the 16th of May 1611.

(b) Guy's Letter of July 1612

RIGHT WORSHIPFULL, by my last of the 17th of June [not preserved] I wrote you of the estate then by the Holland ship, which I hope is long since safely arrived, together with Master Colston who hath (I doubt not) made by word of mouth full relations of all matters Because the proceedings of one Easton are most fit to be knowne who

remained in Harbour de Grace trimming and
repairing his shipping and taken munitions
&c together with about a hundred men out
of the Bay, he purposes to have five hundred
out of the land before he goeth   Two several
companies of 180 men each being discontented
have stolen away from him in two ships of
Barnstable and Plimmoth that they tooke

As I sailed from hence towards Renoose
in a small Barke, I fell into one of their hands
and one of my company was hurt with a
muskett   There was one of their crew that
wintered with me here the first year, by whose
means, and because I was in the Bark they
made shew, that they were sorry that they
had meddled with us   And so they departed
from us without coming aboard   That which
they sought after was men to increase their
number [5]   Then Guy mentions that Easton
had plundered all along the coast and was
then at Ferriland waiting to hear news of his
pardon [which was granted but never reached
him] which if he did not get he would seek
the protection of the Duke of Florence [which
he eventually did].

(c) Colston's Letter in 1613

We have not the actual text of this, but
Purchas printed it in substance on p. 930 of
the 1617 edition and also on p 1880 of the
1625 edition

William Colston describes the winter of
1612–13 as being more severe than that
1611–12   They had there Filberds, Fish,
Makerels, Foxes, in the Winter   Partridges
white in the Winter, in Summer somewhat like
ours, but greater, they are much afraid of
Rauens   they killed a Wolfe with a Mastiue
and a Grey-hound.   Nicolas Gure's wife was
delivered of a lusty boy March 27   Then he
described a voyage made by Guy and thirteen
others in the *Indeauour* and five in the
Shallop in October 1612 to Sauage Harbour,
Trinity Bay, where they found houses of
Sauages which were nothing but poles set
round and meeting in the top, ten foot broad,
the fire in the middest, couered with Deeres-
skins.   They are of reasonable stature, beard-
lesse, and in some conditions like those which
Sir M Frobisher discovered, broad-faced,
full-eyed, coloured on their faces and apparell
with red Oaker   Their Boates of barke, as
in Canada, twentie foote long, four and a
halfe broad, not weighing a 100 weight, made
in forme of a new Moone, which carry foure
men, and are by them carried to all places of
their remouings

A few days later they met with the Natiues,
Whittington, Tipton, Guy himself, and Master
Teage landed and bartered with them.   All
along the coast they carefully abstained from
taking any of the furs evidently left by the
natives for trade without leaving some
trinket in exchange, thus carrying out the
instructions given by the Company to Guy.
[See also p 133]

There wintered 1612 fiftie foure men,

six women and two children   They killed
there, Beares, Otters, Sables, sowed Wheat,
Rye, Turneps, Coleworts   Their Winter till
April 1613, was dry and cleere with some
frost and snow

Divers had the Scurvie, whereto their
Turneps, there sowne, were an excellent
remedie, no lesse then Cartiers Tree.   April
was worse then the middest of Winter by
reason of East windes which came from the
Islands of Ice, which the current bringeth at
that time from the north

Purchas continues   The same I have seene
confirmed by a letter of Thomas Dermer,
one of that Colonie dated at Cupers Cove,
the ninth of September last, 1616   In other
moneths, hee sayth, the Temperature is as
England   He mentions Muske-Cats and
Muske-Rats in those parts ; the fertilitie of
the soyle in producing Pease, Rye, Barly
and Oates, probabilities of Metals, with
promises of more full Relations hereafter

III. Letters from Ferryland.

(a) A letter from Captain Edward Wynne,
Governor of the Colony of Ferryland, within
the Province of Avalon, in Newfoundland,
unto the Right Honourable Sir George
Calvert, Knight, His Majesty's Principal
Secretary, July, 1622.

May it please your Honour,—

Upon the 17 day of May, I received &
have your letters of the 19 of February from
the hands of Robert Stoning   Upon the 26
of the same, a ship of Master Jennins with
your people and provision arrived here in
safety, and from the hands of Captain Powell
I received then your Honours Letters of 14th
March   And upon the last of June Master
James came hither, from Renouze and the
Salt-maker Master John Hickson, from
whose hands I received two Letters more,
that by Master James being of the 4th May,
& the other by Hickson of the 10th of the
same.

All these being received by me, with an
humble & a most thankful hand, first, unto
God for your Honours health, and next, to
your Honour for your continuall favour towards
me, beseeching the same Almighty God, long
and long to continue your health, to the
advancement of his glory, both here, at home
and elsewhere   I most humbly pray you to
build upon my dutiful care and diligence, in
the setting forwards and following of your
Honours businesse, even to your best advantage, and advancement of the worke, and also
that I shall bee a dutiful observer of your
pleasure & commandment

And so with the like humility, I doe
present your Honour with the good tydings
of all our healths, safety and good successe in
our proceedings (God's holy name be praised
for it)   It followeth now (as my duty
requireth) that I render unto your Honour a
due account of what hath been done by us

here this yeere, and of all things else, which appertaines unto me to doe

Therefore it may please your Honour, that as soone as I had delivered my last letters of the 5 of September, I immediately addressed my self onely to our businesse Notwithstanding our diligent labour & extraordinary paines-taking, it was All hallowtide before our first range of building was fitted for an habitable being The which being 44 foot of length, & 15 foot of breadth, containing a hall 18 foot long, an entry of 6 foot, & a cellar of 20 foot in length, and of the height betweene the ground floore and that over head about 8 foote, being devided above, that throughout into foure chambers, and four foot high to the roofe or a halfe storie The roofe over the hall, I covered with Deale boords, and the rest such thatch as I found growing here about the Harbour, as sedge, flagges and rushes, a farre better covering than boards, both for warmth & litenesse. When I had finished the frame, with onely one Chimney of stone worke in the hall, I went forward with our kitchin, of length 18 foot, 12 foot of breadth, and 8 foot high to the eves, and walled up with stone work, with a large Chimney in the frame. Over the kitchen I fitted another Chamber All which with a staire case and convenient passages both into the kitchin and the rooms over it, were finished by Christmas Eve. This is all the building with a hen house, that we have been able to accomplish before Christmass.

Many things else were done by us in the interim, as the getting home of timber trees, firewood, the raising up of a face of defence to the waterside ward, with the earth that we digged both for cellar & Kitchin roome (which we found a very laborious worke) also the sowing of some wheat for a triall, and many other businesses besides

After Christmas, we imployed our selves in the woods especially in hard weather, whence we got home as many boord-stocks, afforded us above two hundred boords and above two hundred timber trees besides We got home as much or as many trees as served us to palizado into the Plantation about foure Acres of ground, for the keeping off of both man & beast, with post and rayle seven foote high, sharpened in the toppe, the trees being pitched upright and fastened with spikes and nayles We got also together us much fire wood, as will serve us yet these two moneths Wee also fitted much garden ground for seede, I meane, Barley, Oates, Pease, and Beanes For addition of building, we have at this present a Parlour of fourteene foote besides the chimney, and twelve foot broad, of convenient height, and a lodging chamber over it, to each a chimney of stone worke with staires and a staire case, besides a tenement of two rooms, or a storie and a halfe, which serves for a store house till we are otherwise provided The Forge hath been finished this five weekes The Salt-worke is now

almost ready Notwithstanding this great taske for so few hands, we have both Wheat Barley, Oates, Pease, and Beanes about the quantity of two acres Of Garden roome about halfe an acre the corne though late sowne is now in earing, the Beanes and the goodliest Pease that I ever saw, have flourished in their bloomes this twenty dayes We have a plentiful kitchin garden of Lettice, Raddish, Carrets, Coleworts, Turneps and many other things We have also at this present a flourishing medow of at least three Acres, with many hay-cocks of exceeding good hay and hope to fit a great deale more against another yeere In the beginning of the last winter, sunke a well of sixteene foote deepe in the ground, the which affords us water in a sufficient measure The timber that wee have got home first and last, is above five hundred trees of good timber There have beene about three hundred boords besides the former, sawed since the arrival of Captaine Powell We have also broken much ground for a Brew-house roome and other Tenements We have a wharfe in good forwardnesse towards the Low-watermarke So that our indevour that way affoords a double benefit, the one of ridding and preparing the way to a further worke, the other of winning so much voyd or waste ground to so necessary a purpose as to enlarge this little roome, where on (with your Honours leave and liking) I hope to fortifie, so that within the same, for the comfort of neighbour-hood, another row of building may be so pitched that the whole may be made a prettie streete For the country and climate; it is better & not so cold England hitherto My comfort is, that the Lord is with your Honour, & your designes for wee have prospered to the admiration of all the beholders in what is done And thus with my humble dutie remembered, I rest,

Your Honour's most humble and faithfull
servant,

EDWARD WYNNE.

Ferryland 28 July, 1622.

Post ser—The ship with the rest of our provision arrived here this morning, and what is omitted by me, shall by Gods help shortly be performed. Your Honour hath greater hopes here, then here to fore I have been able to discerne. All things succeede beyond my expectation

(b) POWELL'S LETTER TO BALTIMORE

Right Honourable ·

May it please your Honour to understand, that on the 18 of April, my self, and all the company, whose names I sent you in the list, by my last from Plymmouth tooke shipping there and on the 26 of May (God's Holy Name be ever praised for it) wee all arrived safe & in good health in Newfoundland Our journey proved so long by reason of the contrary winds we continually had

I

For at the least three weeks to-gether, wee were forced to traverse the Seas to and againe, and got not forward to the west ward in all that time one hundred leagues The accidents which happened in our overbound passage were these The first weeke after our being at sea, three of our Ewe-Goats, by reason of their extreme leane-nesse when they were bought and brought aboord, died, so that now we have but onely one Ewe-Goate and a Buck Goate left the other Buck dying like wise within few dayes after our landing On the 16 of May the furnace in our ship tooke fire, and as God would have it, burst forth in the daytime otherwise it had endangered both ship and us On the 26 as aforesaid, early in the morning we deserved land in New-foundland, a little to the north ward of the Bay of Bulls, and before night came to anchor in Capeling Bay within one league of Ferry-land The next morning our ship came about to Ferryland Harbor and there landed all our people, where we found the Governour & all his company in good health, as we all continue in the same, praised be God for it.

The Coast and Harbours which we sailed by, are so bold & good, as I assure my self there can be no better in the world but the Woods along the Coasts, are so spoyled by the Fishermen, that it is a great pity to behold them, & without redresse, undoubtedly will be the ruine of this good land. For they wastfully barke, fell, and leave more wood behinde them to rot, then they use about their stages, although they imploy a world of wood upon them and by these their abuses doe so cumber the Woods every where near the shore, that it is not possible for any man to go a mile in a long houre. The Land where on our Governour hath planted, is so good and commodious, that for the quantity, I think there is no better in many parts of England His house which is strong & well contrived, standeth very warme, at the foote of an easie ascending hill, on the South-east, and defended with a hill, standing on the further side of the Haven on North-west The Beach on the North and South sides of the Land locke it, and the seas on both sides are so neere and indifferent to it, that one may shoot a Bird-bolt into either Sea No cold can offend it, although it bee accounted the coldest Harbor in the Land, and the Seas doe mak the Land behind it to the South-East, being neere 1000 Acres of good ground for hay, feeding of Cattell, and plenty of wood, almost an Island, safe to keepe any-thing from ravenous beasts. I have, since my comming, beene a little abroad, and finde much good ground for Medow, Pasture, and arable, about Aquafort, as well neere unto the head of the Harbor, as all the way betweene that & Ferryland. The neerenesse of the place, and the spacious-nesse of those grounds aforesaid, will give comfort and help to the present Plantation, and quickly ease your Honours charge, if a Plantation bee

there this next Spring settled. If therefore it will please your Honour to let me be fur-nished against that time, but with thirteen men, and give mee leave to settle my selfe there, I make no doubt (God blessing my endeavours) but to give your Honour, and the rest of the undertakers such content, that you shall have good incouragement to proceed further therein So for this time being loth to trouble your Honor any further until the returne of Master Wicot, I humbly take my leave, and ever rest ready to doe your Honour all possible service to the uttermost of my power

Your Honors humbly at command,
DANIEL POWELL.

Ferryland 28 July 1622.

(c) WINNE'S LETTER, 17TH AUGUST 1622.

The copy of another letter to Master Secretary Calvert, from Captaine Wynne, of the 17 of August 1622 May it please your Honour,

Upon the 17 day of May, your Honour's Letters of the 17 of February, I received here by the hands of Robert Stoning &c And so forward as in his former Letter of the 28 July, relating the manner and proportion of the building

We have Wheate Barly Oates and Beanes both eared and codded, and though the late sowing might occasion the contrary yet it ripens now so fast, that it carries the likeli-hood of an approaching harvest.

We have also a plentifull Kitchin-Garden and so ranke that I have not seene the like in England We have a medow of about three Acres.

At the Bristow Plantation, there is as goodly Rye now growing as can be in any part of England they are also well furnished with swine and a large breed of Goates, fairer by far than those that were sent over at first It may please your honour to under-stand, that our Saltmaker hath performed his part with a great deale of sufficiency by whom I have sent your honour a barrel of the best salt that ever my eyes beheld I shall humbly also desire you to remember my last years suite that our delicate Harbours and Woods may not be altogether destroyed For there hath been ruded this year not so few as 50,000 trees and they heave out ballast in the harbours though I looke on. Asks for men accustomed to labour, six Masons, foure Carpenters two or three Quarry Men, a Slater or two, a Lyme-burner and Lyme-stones, a good quantity of strong laths, a couple of strong maids, that (besides other work) can brew and bake and wheeles hemp and flax, and a convenient number of West-Countrey laborers to fit the ground for the Plough Asks for Guns and a gunner and many other things— A complete Magazine of requirements I went to Formose and

Renouze upon the fourth of this month and bought salt for the next yeares fishing amounting to 180 hogs-heads, because it is so deare in England

The last yeere I shewed your Honour of much courtesie receiued from sundry Masters Many this yeere haue done the like, though some like not our flourishing beginning

Your Honours &c

Ferryland 17   EDWARD WYNNE
August, 1622.

[Then follow, in Whitbourne's 1623 edition, 32 names of those that stay with Wynne that yeer.] He looked for a Mason and one more out of the Bay of Conception

(d) N H's LETTER, AUGUST 1622.

The coppy of a letter from N H (Nicholas Hoskins?) a gentleman living at Ferryland to a worthy friend W. P of the 18 of August 1622.

After describing the climate and country he says " in the Whitson-holy daies (I taking with me Master Stoning) did coast some ten miles into the Country, Westward from our Plantation to make some discovery and to kill a Deere and being some 5 miles into the Land where we lodged that night, we found much champion ground of good levels of one two three or four hundred acres together, and at the foot of each hill we alwaise met a faire fresh River which did quench my thirst as well as Beere. We travelled three days but found no Deere save their footings which came to passe by meanes of a great fire that had burned the Woods, a little before, ten miles compasse It began between Fermouse and Aquafort, it burned a week and then was quenched by a great raine

" I know not who or what he was that gave fire to it but I think he was a servant hired by the deuill who will pay him for his worke In the night the Woolues being neer did somewhat affright us but did not hurt us for we had dogs, fire and sword to welcome them " Then follows a further description of various sorts of game and fish . . . . " Manny faire Flowers I haue seene heere, which I cannot name, although I had learned Gerrard's Herbal by heart. . . . . I wrote in haste to satisfy myselfe, desiring you to looke throught it as thorow a prospective glasse, wherin you may discerne a farre off, what I have seene neere hand &c.

Your servant to be
commanded, N H "

IV. The Charter of Avalon to Lord Baltimore, 1623.

(*Sloane MSS., 170.*)

JAMES by the Grace of God King; Whereas our right trusty Counsellor Sir George Calvert being excited with a laudable

and pious zeale to enlarge the extent of the Christian world and therewith ot our Empire hath heretofore to his great coste purchased a certain region in a country of ours called Newfoundland not yet husbanded or planted though in some parts thereof inhabited by certain barbarous people , And intending now to transport thither a very great colony of the English Nation hath humbly besought us to confirm all the said region with certain priveledges requisite for good government

BOUNDARIES

And by the said Pattent of ye said Province contains all ye entere portion of land as aforesaid, beginning southerly from the middle part of a certain neck or promintary situate between the two harbours of Fermose and Aqnofort, and from thence following the shore towards ye north unto the middle part or half way over a little harbour called in that regard Petit Port or Petit Harbour, which boundeth upon the south part of the plantacion of St John's, including the one half of a certain fresh river that floweth into the said porte of Petit Harbour, and so extending along the south border of the said Collony of St John's, extendeth itself to a certain little bay called Salmon Cove lying on the south side of the Bay of Conceperon, including the one half of the river that falleth into the said cove as also ye one half of ye said cove itself from whence passing along ye shore towards the south, and reaching unto ye bottom thereof where it meets with the land of John Guy, Citizen of Bristolle named Sea Fforest is bounded with a certain river or brooke which there falleth into the Sea, and from the mouth of the said brooke aforesaid unto the furthest spring or head thereof from thence passeth towards the south for six miles together along the borders of the said John Guie's his plantation, and thence crossing over westward in a right line reacheth unto the Bay of Placentia, and the space ot one legue within the said Bay from the shoare thereof, thence turning again towards the south passeth along the harbour of Placentia with the like distance from the shoare, and descending unto New Falkland towards the north west part thereof it reacheth itself in a right line eastward, continuing the whole southerly length upon the bounds of the said New Falkland unto the middle part or point of the Promentary or neck of land aforementioned between the Ports of Ffermose and Aquofort, at which place is described and finished the perambulance of the whole precint, &c &c

All the islands within ten leagues of the Eastern shoare of the said region.

POWERS.

The patronage and advowsons of all Churches to be built there Civil Rights as full as the Bishop of Durham Region to be held in capite by Knights service, yielding a fifth part of all gold and silver That the region may be Eminent above all other parts of Newfoundland and graced with larger titles we have thought fitt to erect the same into a Province, to be called the Province of Avalon. Power to make laws, appoint judges, to Pardon, on an emergency to make special laws without the consent of the freeholder, to muster & train men and declare Martial law, to confer titles and incorporate towns To be free from all customs and power to import and export to England and foreign countries all goods for ten years, afterwards to pay such customs as our subjects are bound to pay and no more Power to constitute ports of entry at which all ships must unlade and lade, any custom to the contrary notwithstanding

Saving always and ever reserved unto all our subjects free liberty of fishing as well in the sea as in the ports of the province and the priveledge of drying and salting their fish as heretofore they have reasonably enjoyed which they shall enjoy without doing any injury to Sir George Calvert or to the dwellers and inhabitants and specially in the woodes and be liable for damages Power to enjoy all customs payable or accruing And We shall at no time hereafter make any tax upon land tenements or merchandize laden or unladen within the province and this declaration is to be a full discharge to all officers No interpretation bee admitted whereby Gods holy and true Christian Religion or the allegiance due to us suffer any prejudice— Signed at Westminster the 7 of April in the 21 years of our reign of England

V. Lord Baltimore.

The first letter relating to his colony is from Ferryland, dated Sep 5, 1621 Captain Wynne, his Agent, writes that he had arrived with 12 men In 1622 Captain Daniel Powell arrived with 22 more

Wynne says the first range of buildings erected about All Hallow Tide was 44 feet long by 15 feet wide containing hall, entry cellar, four chambers, kitchen, staircase, passage, &c This building was at the foot of the Downs facing the sea "He raised up a face of defence to the water side ward, sowed wheat for triall and many other businesses besides After Christmas he built a parlour fourteene foote long and twelve foot broade a lodging chamber, a forge, salt works, a well sixteen foote deepe, a brewe house, a wharfe and a fortification so that the whole may be made a prettie street."

Aug. 17th, 1622. He gives an account of his crops and sends home a barrel of salt as a sample.

Wynne was a Welch man and his emigrants as we learn from his contemporaries were also from Wales

July 28, 1622 We have a letter from Capn Daniel Powell evidently a West Country man He describes the death of "three ewe goats by reason of their extreme leanesse, one ewe and buck goat survived"

Both Powell and Wynne so plundered the unsuspecting Baltimore, that at last he had to visit the Colony to look after his interests He writes to Lord Stafford in 1627 that "it was necessary for him to go over and settle the Colony in better order or lose the fruit of all his exertions" (*Stafford Corres*, i 39) He originally intended to come out in 1625 (not suspecting the failure of his schemes, for according to Sir Wm Alexander, Wynne had contrived to make some appearance of profit) but was prevented.—"March 15 1625 George Calvert to Coke." I intend shortly God willing a journey to Newfoundland to visit a plantation I have begun there some years since I hired the ship called *Jonathan* now in the River for the transport of myself and such plants as I carry with me But I understand she is stayed for the King so I must give place But I am by that means utterly disappointed and you should do me the duty to clear her and her marriners and also the *Peter Bonaventure* for which I contracted for carrying cattle Whatever favour you do me herein my Lord Duke will not be displeased at it (*Cowper MSS*)

In 1627 he made his first visit to Newfoundland to see how bad matters really were but only stayed a few weeks In 1628 he took with him his wife and all his children, except his eldest son, to permanently reside in his Plantation, his sons-in-law, Sir R Talbot & William Peasely, accompanied him At Ferryland they lived in a large substantial stone house, the scene in later years of many an incident connected with the Kirkes, Downings, Treworgie, and others The house was standing in 1674, Sir Joseph Williamson mentions it as being only a "quoits throw" from the shoare, and it appears to be depicted upon Fitzhugh's map in 1693 ; a view of it is given The Baltimore's claim to have spent £30,000 on buildings and breaking up land at Ferryland. The Kirkes also spent some money, but either could not or would not say how much, perhaps it was very little

In 1625, the last year of James's reign, Calvert, for his services to the Court, had been made Baron Baltimore, Ireland

Bishop Howley says "If Lord Baltimore had had the good fortune to settle in St John's, Trepassey &c" but these were outside his grant and his best available Harbour was Ferryland, admirably situated for defence from sea.

Soon after his arrival at Ferryland, Baltimore, in a letter to the King, describes his attack on "a French man of warre one Monsieur De La Rade of Deepe who with three ships and 400 men well armed and appointed came into my harbour of Cape

Broile, where he surprized divers of the fishermen took two of their shippes in the harbour and kept possession of them till I sent two ships of mine with some hundred men being all the force we could make upon the suddayne in this place where I am planted Upon the approach of which ships near to the Harbour mouth of Cape Broyle one of them being 360 Tons with 24 pieces of ordnance, the French let slip their cables and made to sea as fast as they could leaving behind them both the English ships and 67 of their own crew which I made prisoners We followed the chase so long as we saw any possibility of coming upp with them but they were much better of saile and we were forced to give over"

De La Rade had done much damage to the northward, so Baltimore went after him, found he had been driven away by a ship of London before he could get there

"Hereupon being still vexed with these men (and both myselfe and my poore fisherie heere and many others of Your Majesty's subjects much injured this yeere by them) I directed my ship in consort with Captain Feime's Man of Warre, then in this country, to seek out some of that nation at Trepasse a harbour to the South, where they used to fish. There they found six shippes 5 of Bayonne and one of St Jean de Luz whom they took with their lading, being fish and trayne, and have sent them to England"

Wherefore Baltimore prays the King to send two Men of War to guard the coast One of his prize ships the *St Claude* was sent out under the command of Leonard Calvert Lord Baltimore's natural son Bishop Howley says two ships were sent, the records show only one — "Dec 13, 1628. Sir F. Cottington to Lord Treasurer Weston has granted *one* of the six Prize ships which Nicholas says are good and warlike." In December of the same year there is a Petition from Will Peasley, on behalf of Lord Baltimore, to the Lords Commissioners of the Admiralty that the *St. Claude* may be substituted for the *Esperance*, and in December a Warrant issued " to deliver *one* of the prize ships [*St Claude*] to Leonard Calvert, son of Lord Baltimore to be lent for Twelve months."

In 1628 there was a dispute between Lord Baltimore and the merchants about the French prizes taken in Newfoundland by their ships, the *Benediction* and the *Victory* Baltimore claims for his part according to the consort ship, and very cunningly asks to have his letter-of-marque *antedated* to enable him to receive his proportion We have only Baltimore's version, so we cannot decide the merits of the case.

From Ferryland on Aug 19, 1629, Baltimore thanks the King upon his knees for the loan of *a fair ship*, complains of the malice and calumny of those who seek to make him appear foul in His Majesty's eyes,

and of the slanderous reports raised at Plymouth last winter by an audacious man [Stourton] who was banished for his misdeeds ; complains of cold and loss of life by sickness, asks for grant of a precinct of land in Virginia, where he wishes to remove some forty persons with such privileges as King James granted to him in Newfoundland.

Baltimore died in 1632 before his charter of Maryland was completed, it was, however, granted to his distinguished son Cecil, the second Lord, a far more able and energetic man than his father. He showed great ability, courage, and decision in dealing with his opponents in Maryland, and faced and overcame difficulties before which his father would have quailed The questions between Kirke and Baltimore are fully set forth in the law proceedings between the contending parties, nominally the right to Ferryland was conceded to Baltimore by Charles II, but practically the result was of no benefit to him The warrant directed to Sir Louis Kirke, Sir David's widow and his sons was issued in the reign of Charles II [For more information on this subject read the note on Kirke]

In 1754 the Baltimores renewed their claim to Avalon, but the Government decided their rights had lapsed through want of actual occupation and possession

VI. Beothics.

Since the above was in print, I have examined a MS in Lambeth Library which contains a much fuller description of Guy's visit to Trinity Bay than is given in Purchas's condensed account (p 128) Doubling the Grates they came to Heart's Content, and from thence to Spread Eagle and Bay Bulls arm Guy describes their pleasant intercourse with the Red Indians They are, he says, of middle size, broad-chested, and very erect They go bareheaded, wearing their hair somewhat long, behind they have a great lock of hair plaited with feathers, like a hawk's lure, with a feather on it standing upright by the crown of the head, with a small lock plaited before They wore a short gown or cassock made of stag skins, the fur innermost, that came down to the middle of the leg, with sleeves to the middle of the arm, and a bearskin about the neck Their hair was diverse, some black, some brown, some yellow Some of their wigwams were covered with skins, they had other square-shaped houses covered with canvas obtained from some Christians, probably the Biscayans, who had also given them hooks, and a copper utensil which was kept very bright Besides paddles, they had some oars shaped like the Biscayan oars The canoe is also described, it exactly resembles the one at p 372 Several Indian families must have resided at the bottom of Trinity Bay about this period

CHAPTER VI.

REIGN OF CHARLES I.

1625-1649.

1625 —Capture of 27 Newfoundland ships and 200 persons by Turkish pirates   Vaughan's "Golden Fleece" published   Mason's capture of the *Good Fortune*, at Crookhaven   Baltimore prevented from visiting Avalon   Bill for maintenance, &c of shipping thrown out by the Lords

1626 —Three hundred and fifty families of English settled between Cape Race and Bonavista , 250 English vessels fishing in Newfoundland   Whitbourne's appeal for a Government post as inspector of provisions

1627 —Lord Baltimore visits Ferryland for a few weeks , brought two priests, found inhabitants and an English clergyman, Stourton, in Conception Bay.   Patent to Sir W Alexander, of Nova Scotia, in 1621, confirmed by the King

1628 —Baltimore returned to Ferryland with his wife and family   Dr. Meadus negotiating a purchase of part of the plantation from Slany for Lord and Lady Conway Hayman's " Quodlibets " published   Baltimore drives away a French pirate, named De la Rade , prays for a convoy, one ship granted , dispute between Baltimore and the merchants about French prizes   Baltimore banishes Stourton

1629 —Baltimore's priests come to England under assumed names , he again prays for a ship to protect his settlements, complains of Stourton, and asks for a grant in Virginia, and permission to move his family and dependants there   Baltimore abandoned Newfoundland ; founded Maryland in Virginia

1630 —Proclamation of Charles I prohibiting disorderly trading with the Red Indians. Hayman's proposition to the King

1632 —Death of Baltimore.   Quebec, Port Royal, &c. restored to France at the peace of St Germains

1633 —Charles I , through the Star Chamber, made his celebrated code of regulations for the government of the Newfoundland fishery, establishing fishing admirals , first skipper arriving from England to be judge or vice admiral for fishing season Proclamation for the observance of Sunday in Newfoundland.

1634 —Star Chamber issued a charter " to the merchants and traders to Newfoundland " Order in Council passed making the Bishop of London Ordinary of the Plantation

1635.—Charles I gave permission to the French to cure and dry fish in Newfoundland on payment of 5 per cent. on the produce , continued for 41 years.   This was the first commencement of our difficulties with the French   Death of Mason

1636 —Mayor of Weymouth visits the king at Woodstock to get a convoy for the Newfoundland fleet.

1637.—Cecil Lord Baltimore's petition against any alienation of his grant of Avalon Grant to the Duke of Hamilton, Kirke, and others, of all Newfoundland.

1638.— Arrival of Sir D. Kirke at Ferryland

1639.   Pomponde Bellievre complains of Kirke's collection of taxes from French subjects Bishop of Exeter and others petition against Kirke   Kirke's letter to Laud.

1640.—Further complaints against Kirke. Kirke dismissed, and John Downing, senior, appointed Governor by Patentees. Memorandum about Dutch trading in Newfoundland.

1641.—Cargo of dry fish shipped from Boston to Europe.

1642.—Civil war between Charles and the Parliamentary Party.

1643.—First cargo of fish sent from Boston to Bilbao in Spain.

1645.—First vessel sent from Boston to fish at Bay Bulls seized by a royal cruiser.

1646.—Treworgie married a Miss Spencer, of Newberry, Mass.

1647.—Governor Winthrop records a great storm in Newfoundland.

1649.—Letter from Charles to Kirke about asylum for Lady Hawkins. Kirke offers the king an asylum in Newfoundland. Trial and execution of the king. Commonwealth cruisers sent to defend the fishing ships against Prince Rupert. Kirke only allowed to take to Newfoundland sufficient men to man his ships.

The short and troubled reign of this unfortunate king is, and probably always will be, the battle-ground for a fierce political discussion between Monarchists and Republicans, Cavaliers and Roundheads. Our colonial records throw a vivid side-light on this disastrous period. The treatment of our unfortunate Island by Charles I. was uniformly cruel, tyrannical, and stupid. In every way the interest of the patentees—the courtiers—was preferred to the welfare of the planters. Charles, like his father James I., was influenced entirely by his personal feelings for his immediate adherents; whilst he defended and perpetuated the absurd monopoly of the Plymouth Company in New England against the rights and claims of English merchants and fishermen, he pursued an exactly opposite course in Newfoundland.

CHARLES I.
From an engraving after Vandyke.

The king carried out his policy towards this Colony deliberately. From good, honest men, well acquainted with the Island, settlers, who had lived there, he received the very best advice as to how the Colony should be governed and settlement encouraged. Sir William Vaughan, his intimate friend and a staunch supporter of Royalty, in his "Golden Fleece" says :—[1]

"Many ships from Newfoundland taken by Moorish Pirates. . . . More confusion amongst Fishermen of Newfoundland than any other for want of being sufficiently guarded. . . . King James did about three years past 1622 or 1623]

[1] Part II., p. 102, 1626.

see into the discomforts and directed a commission at the suit of the corporation [Guy's Company] for plan of Newfoundland to provide a couple of good ships in the charge of the fishermen to protect them from Pirates who a few years before had pillaged them the extent of £40,000 besides 100 pieces of ordnance and had taken away 1500 mariners to the hurt of Newfoundland and the Planters."

Vaughan urges that—

"The ships should be retained both in peace and war. That God had reserved Newfoundland for Britain as the next land beyond the sea and not above 9 or 10 days sail that it might be inhabited the sooner by Your Majesty's subjects . . . that the same God overlooks Newfoundland as Europe . . I am sorry to find so many hopeless in my country of Wales whereas close by us in Devonshire 150 ships go to Newfoundland transporting from thence those commodities without which Spain and Italy can hardly live. . . Experience of this fishery sheweth that it yearly maintains 8000 people for six months in Newfoundland . products of the colony, tar, pitch &c codfish, salmon, mackerel, herring &c. &c.

"The benefits of a colony would be to restrain our own fishermen [ship fishers] who seize on one anothers stages; it will serve to restrain their insolence who brag that they are there ' West and by law ' Organization of a colony would prevent the depredations of the ship fishermen, firing the woods, stealing salt, and fish, casting ballast into the Harbours, &c &c."

All these practical suggestions were addressed to royal ears that would not hear. The colonies under Charles were as much neglected and misgoverned as his Royal Navy, with its rotten ships and unpaid sailors

Vaughan says :—

"Capt Wynne and Welchmen settled Ferryland for Lord Baltimore One man near Renoos killed 700 Partridges, 3 men catch in 30 days 25,000 to 30,000 fish worth with oil £160; many sail to Newfoundland in 12 to 16 days about 600 leagues [1800 miles], 500 to 600 ships yearly resort there, freight 20/- per ton 10/- for a man passenger. Newfoundland a good security for Spain and other foreign enemies as there are constantly between 300 and 400 of our ships there [This includes fishing ships and cargo vessels.]

"1623 King James sent two ships of war as convoys

"1626 Discontinued by Charles I Wooden house best for cold weather. Exercise best to keep off scurvy. Strong liquor prejudicial in cold countries, barley water & spruce beer best Salt costs England £20,000 annually, may be made in Newfoundland for 3d per bushel. French salt costs 20d per bushel."

It is absolutely necessary for us to see the contemporary records before we can believe that any king or government should decree that this great Colony was not to be inhabited, that any chance settlers remaining should be persecuted, hampered, and impeded in all their labours and industry, that though they were fishermen and had to live by the sea, it was solemnly decreed that none of them should reside within six miles of its shores, all these barbarities were made law in order that West Country fishermen should catch fish on the coast, and a few courtiers make their fortune

Besides the good sensible advice contained in Vaughan's book, there is more of the same character in another work written at Harbour Grace, in 1630.

"A proposition of profitt and honour proposed to my dread and gratious sove, eigne Lord King Charles by Robert Hayman"

Hayman succeeded John Mason as Governor of Guy's Colony, one part of the Company seems to have separated from the Colony at "Sea Fforest," Cupids, and formed a plantation or colony at Harbour Grace, which they named "Bristolls Hope." We learn from Mason's letter that he had a fishing room or plantation there; and in 1697 the inhabitants told Abbé Baudoin that their harbour was the first place settled in the country by the English, that a man had died there in 1693 or 1694 aged 83. He might, possibly, be the son of one of Guy's settlers, but in all probability he was a descendant of one of the original planters long anterior to Guy's arrival—most likely a Davis, a Thistle, a Pike, a Pynn, a Crawley, or a Parsons—the oldest families in the Bay Metropolis.

Hayman proposes for the king —

"To build a citie where I have placed your Carolinopole [Harbour Grace] and to privilege that Towne with that fishing Your Majesty might likewise make it a Mart or free market for fish, has two Harbours three miles apart and would grow populous rich and strong I would humbly pray this Island may be called Brittaniola

"The French and Biscays do yearly in great number fish at the Mayne and dispossess us Proposals about salt, also proposes to take Cape de Verd Island, offers further explanation in person and asks the King to decide in twenty-four hours Many ship owners are forthcoming to aid the project." [It was an appeal to unwilling ears.]

"He presents a plat [map] of His Majesty's Dominions both possessed pretended and intended &c but among the several lands God made you Lord over I recommend to Your Majesty's special viewe, a work left for you to finish and furnish with millions of Your subjects viz. Newfoundland.

"In this Island at one time I lived fifteen months together and since I have spent almost every summer in it I had lots of time, being an overseer and no labour to do But seeing to my grief the poor support of divers treatises, read over by some, liked by some, derided by others, and neglected by almost all, and these few have either insufficiently begun, or have been deluded and wronged by those they employed or mistaken in good meaning, or have not been able to spread or out of heart with poore lowt, unsupported retournes, or demands of new supplies.

"That unless Your Majesty suddainly assist this costly business is like to vanishe lamentably . . . As to patents to certain noblemen . these noblemen were but only named, or adventured very little Those gents were soon made weary; those merchants acquainted with most speedy gain first falling out among themselves by reason whereof the principal undertaker [Guy] a man of their qualitie, wise yet inconstant, falling off they concluded to divide the land into severall parts since when some have done a little to no purpose and the most nothing

"I confess since that time divers noble gents have adventured somewhat, first Sir Percival Willoughbee, then Dr. Vaughan and have been annoyed by dishonest, idle, unfit men, those employed by them and my Lord Falkland, worse; only my Lord Baltimore after much injurie done him [evidently by Wynne & Powell] adventured happily thither himself, where seeing how to mend it and the goodness of the action resolved wisely to see his business done himself and Dr Vaughan intends to follow his example. But experience of former and these times makes me jealous of their success unless Your Majesty steps in." [1]

He then shows how, in Ireland,—

"No good was done until the King began to take the matter in hand, so Newfoundland Colonies will never flourish continuously unless undertaken by the King. If Newfoundland were peopled I dare prove that 1000 good ships only [may succeed]. But it may be thought how we stand with France and Spain if a large quantity of fish were sent will have small vent, and I know the Mallowyans [men of St. Malo] have promised their King and the Biskans theirs to furnish them with this commoditie whereupon they have not only proclaimed forfeiture of importation thereof taken by us, but I heare in Spain Hamburghers were this yeare denounced for doing, but Your Majesty might easily amend this, in preventing theirs and making them glad of ours, for without this [fish] they cannot conveniently subsist. Hunger will break down walls. In Queen Elizabeths time they had it from their enemies the Hollanders." [1]

DE LAET'S MAP, 1630.

Hayman then enumerates the products of the country—pitch, tar, timber, &c.

" Newfoundland is a land worth possessing. There is a rich fishing near this land called the Bank where yearly 400 French ships fish and from whence your subjects have never reaped any." [1]

In 1625 the Commons passed

CHAMPLAIN'S MAP, 1632.

"a Bill for the maintenance and " increase of shipping and naviga- " tion, and for liberty of fishing in " Newfoundland, Virginia, and New " England." The Bill was thrown out by Charles's party in the House of Lords. The Commons refused a subsidy, and Parliament was dissolved in anger. The question of free fishery was one of the causes which led to hostility between Charles and Parliament.

In Newfoundland he gave an exclusive monopoly of the Island fishery to the Western adventurers or ship fishermen from Devonshire against the settlers in the Island. Most tyrannical laws were enacted

[1] B.M MSS., Eg. 2541.

for their governance, from which the English fishermen by express enactment were to be at all times exempted. These laws will be found in the Appendix to this chapter under the head of Star Chamber Rules.[1]

The extraordinary provision in these regulations, making the first rude English skipper who entered the harbour admiral and judge over all for the fishing season, seems to us, in this age, a monstrous anomaly; but it was, as the Rules declare, *an Ancient Custom*, now for the first time legalised. The old arrangement that the first who entered harbour was the admiral, prevailed not only amongst the English but with all the foreign fishermen. The ancient practice, however, was to change about each week. The most curious part of this proceeding is that a highly civilized nation like the French, under France's most able minister

HARBOUR GRACE.

Colbert, adopted precisely the same regulation. By the ordinance of Louis XIV., after prescribing most minute regulations about nets, &c., he gives the following Rules for the Newfoundland fishery :—

" 1. The first who shall arrive at or send his boat to the Harbour called Le Havre du Petit Maitre,[2] shall have the choice, and take the space of ground necessary for his fishery; he shall then put up at the place called the ' Scaffold of the Grapple ' a Bill signed by him stating the day of his arrival and the Harbour which he has chosen.

" 2. All other Masters on their arrival shall go or send to the same place, and write down on the same bill, the day of their arrival, the number of their men, and the name of the Harbour and place, which they have chosen, in proportion to the burthen of their ships and the number of their mariners.

" 3. The captain that arrives first shall cause the Bill or placard to be guarded by one of his men, who shall remain upon the place till all the Masters shall have made their declaration, which afterwards shall be put into his hands.

" 4. No Master or Mariners may settle in any Harbour or station, till they have made their declaration in the form aforesaid; nor shall they disturb any other master in the choice that he may have made under the penalty of 500 livres."

This law applied to all the coasts of New France. The first captain was to keep a correct account of all offences committed against this ordinance, and on his return it was to be delivered to the judge of the Admiralty Court. Ships fishing on the banks were not allowed to set sail at night. *All* French subjects, of what quality or condition soever, might cause ships to be built or bought, and carry on a trade at sea, by themselves or agents, without its being considered derogatory to their quality, provided they sold nothing by retail. The first French Master who arrived in the harbour was constituted, like his English prototype, Admiral, supreme Ruler, and Judge over all the French fishermen in the port. The fishing admiral still survives in the French prud'homme of the N.E. and West Coast.

STAR CHAMBER.

The Star Chamber Rules were for the benefit of the Duke of Hamilton, Sir David Kirke, and other partisans. When this extraordinary patent was granted, the Newfoundland settlers had been in possession of their homes for a long period. They had built houses and stages and cleared small patches of ground. All this expenditure of money and labour all their lawful title to their hard-earned possessions, was ruthlessly swept away, in order to gratify the cupidity of a few courtiers As far as the king's grant could annul all the rights of former occupants and patentees under King James's charters, this new title to Hamilton and Kirke was intended to do so , there is no saving clause, no reservation , the whole Island is granted to the new patentees This charter to the Duke of Hamilton, Kirke, and others has such an important bearing on our history that it is set out fully

Nothing shows more clearly the treachery and ingratitude of Charles than his dealings with Lord Baltimore respecting this new grant The king was bound by every sentiment of personal feeling and gratitude to treat the Calverts with kindness and consideration The first Lord Baltimore had been the faithful, abject servant of his father, and his own great personal friend. The records show us how Charles acted in the matter. In February 1637 Cecil Lord Baltimore, in a petition, sets forth his grant and the large sum of money—£20,000—he had expended in the Colony ; and that he had left a governor in the Island up to the time of his father's death. He says :—

" It is reported that some persons of quality have a design to demand customs upon all fish taken or sold in Newfoundland, which must needs trench upon his rights , desires that nothing may be done to his prejudice before His Counsel is heard and satisfaction given If really for the King's service will lay his rights at His Majesty's feet, confident that his great charges will be taken into consideration "

In reply to this petition, in May of the same year, this answer was sent —

" The King to the Commissioners for Foreign Plantations and all other officers and Ministers ; is informed by Lord Baltimore that some grants concerning Foreign Plantations may pass the seals prejudicial to his letters patent for Newfoundland and Maryland. They are therefore commanded not to permit any patent commission or other warrant for plantation or discovery near the Provinces of Avalon and Maryland to pass which may in any way infringe upon the rights or privileges of Lord Baltimore and his heirs for whose better encouragement *the King engages his Royal word never to permit any ' quo warranto' or other proceeding for infringing or overthrowing either of his patents* "

To show the value of the royal word of Charles I, on the 13th November of the same year, 1637, the charter was granted to Hamilton, Kirke, and others of the whole Island of Newfoundland , and the reason for this grant is set out, that Lord Baltimore, Lord Bacon, and others, to whom grants have been made, have deserted the Island The contents of this remarkable patent afford a striking illustration of the high-handed tyranny of Charles I , without the slightest regard for the settlers in the Colony, or the interest of the former patentees, Baltimore, Guy, Falkland, &c. who had expended large sums of money in developing the resources of the Island, he gives away to strangers all their valuable possessions held under grants from his father, James I. The influence of Devonshire seems to have been all powerful at Court; all their policy is embodied in this deed. Settlers were not to dwell within six miles of the shores, and practically all their rights were given over to the ship fishermen from the West of England. Special power is given to the patentees to collect taxes from all strangers. Under this charter Sir David Kirke went out to Newfoundland and took possession of all Lord Baltimore's property. On this grant, obtained by fraud and Court influence, the Devonshire fishermen always based their claim to exclusive rights of fishing and their right to banish the settlers from the shore. About the 20th February 1634 a charter was issued out of the Star Chamber to the merchants and traders to Newfoundland. This grant has been lost, but it evidently embodied the Star Chamber Rules and the orders in Hamilton's grant. The Crown did all it could do to destroy settlements and to injure the settlers. Fortunately, the king had no force to carry out his tyrannical policy. The charter was a dead letter. The planters continued to live about the harbours, creeks, and coves on the east coast from Cape Race

DUKE OF HAMILTON.
From an engraving after Vandyke.

to Cape Bonavista. The densest population was in the neighbourhood of St. John's. None of the noble patentees exercised any special control in this neighbourhood, at least over the English settlers, or anywhere else, except in the neighbourhood of Ferryland. They owned two rooms in St. John's Harbour, and these remained their sole possession. One was about the present Queen's Wharf and Messrs. March and Harvey & Co.'s premises; the other room was directly east of Messrs. Mudge & Co.'s, on the south side, known as the "Naval Dock and Storehouse," and still owned by the Imperial authorities. The patentee's business and fishing and trading operations were all carried on at Lord Baltimore's premises in Ferryland.

After reciting that Lord Baltimore, Lord Bacon, and the London and
" divers " other companies to whom grants had been made had deserted
the Island, the king grants the whole Island to Hamilton, Kirke, and
others between 46° and 53°—

" All being divided from the Continent by an arm of the sea .   . and
all rivers, Harbours, stages, ports, and forts, land and woods, lakes and buildings
. . . . . and all and all manner of fish whatsoever in any of the seas or rivers
. . . . . gold, gems &c .   . Patronage and advowson of the churches
which are or shall hereafter be built and all Rights Jurisdiction &c   .   which
have at any time heretofore been held or enjoyed and they, the said Hamilton &c.
to be the true and absolute Lords and Proprietors of the said Continent, Island and
region of Newfoundland except only the allegiance due to His Majestye

" Neither Hamilton &c. nor any Planter or Inhabitant shall fell wood *nor build
within six miles of the sea* between Cape Race and Cape Bonavista save only that
the Planters shall have liberty to fish there and cut wood for fishing as other our
subjects have and enjoy . .   . And also shall have full power and liberty to
build any fort or forts for defence of said Country and fishing and shall have
timber where it may be spared to the least prejudice of the fishery .   .
Inhabitants shall not take up before the arrival of the fishermen all the best
beaches within the capes aforesaid . .   nor take away burn &c any stage or any
necessaries which they may leave there . nor shall commit any act or thing
to alter change or disturb hinder or interrupt the manner and use of fishing now or
at any time hereafter used or accustomed .   . . . . . and all our
subjects borne or to be borne within our Kingdom of England or in any of our
Kingdoms or Dominions may from time to time and at all times peaceably hold
use and enjoy ye freedom of fishing, in any of the seas, lakes, or rivers, of the said
Island or in or about or adjoining with full liberty to land, salt, and dry fish
Yielding the one fifth part of all gold &c. to the Crown

" Power to make laws with the assent of the freeholders or the major part of
them Freeholders to attend when summoned Power to put the laws in execution and exact the penalty . .   . But the *said laws are not to extend to any
fishermen who are to be for ever free from the jurisdiction of the Government of
Newfoundland* who are to be subject to and immediately under ye order rule and
government of us our heirs &c. as We shall from time to time appoint make and
direct and unto the laws made in the 9th year of our reign which laws shall be
inviolably kept and observed by the fishermen .   power to grantees to
appoint magistrates . . . to punish and pardon offenders . . . . to
execute justice and to see the said laws be observed if not contrary to the laws of
England or prejudicial to the fishery . .   . Proprietors to make laws in case
freeholders cannot be called . . to publish and make them known. Leave
to all to congregate there, and build forts, all the Inhabitants and children to be
free denizens and to enjoy all English priviledges, to transport their goods without
paying Customs provided they get leave in writing from the said Treasurer
Power to make warre and call to their standard all persons whatsoever and
wheresoever (except fishermen) and to appoint a General . . . . to declare
martial law . . . to confer honours   . to incorporate Towns
. only to pay customs on goods sent to England as natural born subjects
. . Power to build forts . .   . . saving alway and reserving to us &c.
free and ample liberty of fishing in any of ye sea lakes rivers &c

" Strangers to pay five per cent. after Christmas day next and the same by all
strangers who shall buy fish, and the same for all oyles made there . . . and
we will and require the said Proprietors to put this in execution . . Collectors
of Customs to receive the same before they load or depart. Proprietors to be
collectors and to account to His Majesty. For their trouble Proprietors to have
five per cent. from all strangers making use of any ground and the same five per
cent. from all strangers that come there in sack ships and the like out of the oyles
. . . These customs to last 51 years. The Crown to have ten per cent. thereof,
and giving account of all gold &c. . . . The Proprietors confirmed in all things
but the fishing and the sole trade of the country except the fishing. Power to
admit partners merchants and others who are to have the same privileges as the
others, not to pay any tax. Their ships not to be detained at any port except in
case of invasion of England. Every one over Twelve years old to take the oaths
upon the Holy Evangelists before Hamilton Kirke or his Deputy to establish the
orthodox religion . . . Power to transport necessaries thither . . . All his
subjects to aide and assist them."

No county in England contains so many small proprietors as
Devonshire; no other county produced so many courtiers during the

FOWEY.

Tudor and Stuart period as this fair southern shire. The influence of
this western aristocracy was bound up with the Devonshire adventurers
to Newfoundland, and it was entirely to suit their selfish monopoly and
greed that laws were enacted. Newfoundland, for more than a century,
had been pouring wealth into the western counties. The landed gentry
were directly or indirectly interested in this lucrative trade. Through
this business the landlord was often paid his rent. The hard riding,
hard drinking squires obtained their potent sherry, and port, and

aguardiente from the Newfoundland fleet; the housewives' preserves, marmalades, dried fruit, and oil, all came from exchange with the foreigners in Newfoundland. Manufacturers of Bridport cordage and West of England cloth made a large portion of their sales through the Transatlantic fishery and trade. Devonshire was largely interested in the fishery, the western courtiers, powerful at Court, used their influence with the king to carry out the selfish, grasping policy of Devon. For two hundred years following we shall always find the Courtenays, Carews, Northcotes, and other great county families, uniformly assisting to keep Newfoundland simply as a fishing place for their countrymen. The fatal effect of this influence really begins in this reign. It had been attempted before, as we have seen, against Guy, but had failed. Now, however, it burst forth in full vigour, and for two centuries it fell like a blight upon the unfortunate Colony. Paralysing all progress and advancement, it was a fatal barrier alike to agriculture and the peaceful development of the great resources of the island. A Devonian myself, I should be utterly recreant to my duty as a historian if I did not fully set forth the dire effects of West Country influence upon the progress of the Colony.

Whilst nothing can palliate the selfish and persistent attitude of Devonshire-traders towards the island, the only possible excuse for their conduct lies in the ignorance of the age, and the claim, or pretended claim, which the West Countrymen set up, that Newfoundland was their own possession, gained by their strong right arms, without aid from the Crown, and defended against all foreign foes by their own dauntless courage. The real blame attaches to the Government, who permitted such a destructive policy to be carried out. In all ages the rule of traders has been selfish and narrow. Bacon had the Devonshire men in his mind when, in his essay on plantations, he said: "Let not the Government of any " plantation depend upon too many counsellors and undertakers in the " country that planteth, but upon a temperate number, and let those be " rather noblemen and gentlemen than merchants, *for they look ever to* " *the present gain.*"

We have seen the constant danger to which both settlers and ship fishermen were exposed from pirates in the preceding period. In the first years of Charles's reign a new peril arose from the Turks. In many instances these so-called Sallee rovers were renegade Englishmen, Frenchmen, and Spaniards, who adopted the Turkish ensign simply as the most convenient flag under which to carry out their depredations on the peaceful commerce of Europe. The following letter from the Mayor of Poole to the Privy Council sets out in graphic terms the danger to

K

which the ship fishermen were exposed from this new enemy, and the disgraceful condition of the Navy under the degenerate rule of the Stuarts. With the exception of two vessels sent out by James I. to protect and convoy the Newfoundland fleet at the instance of Vaughan, and one man-of-war lent to Lord Baltimore, no Royal ships ever visited the Colony during the early part of this reign

"Letter from Mayor of Poole to Privy Council.   Aug. 8th, 1625.

" Right Honourable my very good Lords,

"I have thought it my bounden duty to advertize Your Lordships that the fouerth of this August ther was taken some eyght or nyne leagues off from Plymouth by the Turkish men of warr belonging to Sallye, the *Anne of Poole* The examination of her Mr. Nicholas Murray have sent Your Lordships here enclosed and with all ye great damage that ye Towne of Poole hath before this lately received having in captivitye, diverse men with two shippes of this town taken by this fleete and now we heare that unlesse Your Lordships shall be pleased to take it into your consideration that ye Newfoundland fleete being about two hundred and fiftye sayle of shippes and barques of noe defence haveing some fower or five thousand men belonging to ye Westerne ports expected homewards scattering within this moneth may be provided for by some such provision as shall seeme best to Your Lordships which are not onely threatened to be surprised by this fleet of Sallye but also menacing that within this two years they will not leave his most excellent Majesty Saylors to man his fleetes   Thus leaving the busyneese of soe great conseqnence unto Your Honourable consideration soe with all humble dutye take my leave." [1]

Also from Mayor of Plymouth, August 12th, 1625.—

"Says there are general fears for the ships from Virginia and Newfoundland. The Turkish pirates [2] had taken in ten dayes 27 ships and 200 persons" [3]

And in the Weymouth Records [4] again of September 1636.—

"The 300 English ships from Newfoundland will be in great peril from Turkish Pirates.   The Mayor of Weymouth followed the King to Woodstock to get help for the [fishing] fleet but was only told the [Royal] fleet should come down with the first fair wind.   The Mayor said this would only mitigate not cure the business.   The Archbishop [Laud] striking his hand upon his breast said while he had life, he would do his utmost to advance so consequential a business, that within this twelve months, not a Turkish ship should be able to putt out."

This extract gives a vivid picture of the times, a remarkable illustration of the character of Charles I   We can imagine the anxious mayor galloping for his life to save the great fleet of merchantmen on which four fair counties were dependent almost for their existence, on whose safety hung the lives and fortunes of half the seamen from Devon, Dorset, Cornwall, and Somerset   The answer of the king shows his utter incapacity to appreciate the vital interests of his subjects.   How

---

[1] *Records*
[2] Such names as "Turks Gut" and "Turks Cove" in Newfoundland record the memory of these terrible corsairs

[3] *Records.*
[4] H. J. MOULE, *Descriptive Catalogue of the Charters of Weymouth*

differently Elizabeth or Cromwell would have acted; all their pride and patriotism would have been roused by this daring attack on Englishmen by outlandish pirates.

' How imminent must have been the danger, how terrible the anxiety and fear of the chief magistrate, when it nerved his worship's poor diffident tongue to insist most strenuously, even in the august presence of majesty, on the necessity of sending off the Royal ships Perhaps the most striking part of the story is the arrogance of Laud—the swelling pride of this little Protestant Wolsey—with his vague threat to annihilate the Turkish pirates How much more practical it would have been had he used his influence with his Royal master to send immediate help to the endangered Newfoundland fleet

Besides the ocean pirates, the fishermen suffered grievously from the pressgang, not only were men pressed for the Royal Navy, but even girls were captured to be sent out to the plantations : " October 19, 1613 " —In Somerset it was reported that forty maidens had fled from their " homes to obscure places to escape the pressgang "

Sir David Kirke, the active manager of Hamilton's Company, was one of the most remarkable heroes of this age ; his gallant capture of Quebec and destruction of the French power in Canada, the most brilliant naval exploit in colonial history The pusillanimous king threw away, at one blow, all the immense advantages he had gained for the struggling English colonies, and, with true Stuart ingratitude, left Kirke and his associates to bear the enormous expense of the expedition, undertaken under a direct commission from his sovereign.

The policy of scuttle is supposed to be one of the products of modern English statesmanship, but a knowledge of the dealings of the Stuarts with the English dominions in America will convince us that they fairly rivalled the nineteenth century rulers of England in this line. Sir David Kirke and a few gallant adherents had won Nova Scotia for the Crown of England ; British sovereigns claimed the country by right of discovery ; James I. had made a grant of it to the eccentric Sir William Alexander ; Englishmen had it in possession, the young colonies of New England clamoured for its retention as a barrier against their ruthless foes, the French, yet, at the peace of St. Germains, 1632, notwithstanding England was then in possession of the principal French territories in North America—Quebec, Port Royal, St. Croix, and Pentagoet—by the thirteenth article of the treaty, all these places were restored to France

Cromwell felt the loss of Nova Scotia so keenly that, even though at peace with France, he re-occupied the Colony, and sent out a Governor,

Sir Thomas Temple.   In 1662 Charles II. intended to give it back to France, but New England sent such a spirited petition to the House of Commons, that the treacherous hand of the king was stayed for a time, by the treaty of Breda, however, Charles ceded Nova Scotia again to the French, the stout, old Governor Temple stood out; he and his adherents had spent large sums of money on the fortifications, and the country was not finally surrendered to our enemies until 1670   In the policy of scuttle, the Stuarts have a fair claim to pre-eminence.

Bishop Howley and Mr Henry Kirke's accounts of Sir David are not quite in accord with the testimony of the English records.   Kirke and his brothers, Louis and Thomas, were born in Dieppe; David was a member of Sir William Alexander's company, it was probably in some way to recompense him for his losses in the Quebec expedition that the king granted the patent, which was at first in his name alone   He came out to Newfoundland with one hundred men in 1638, accompanied by his wife and family. having taken possession of all Lord Baltimore's property at Ferryland he vigorously set to work to make money in the Colony, charged rent for stage rooms, sold tavern licences, and did a roaring trade in everything   The charter gave him authority to exact dues from foreigners, so he travelled all around the Island, and made every Frenchman and foreigner pay him a commission on their catch, so stringently did the old mariner wring these taxes from the French that on May 16, 1639, Pompone de Bellievre, Seigneur de Grignon, the French Ambassador, complained to King Charles, of Kirke's imposition on French subjects in Newfoundland, in the following letter :—

" L'on m'a aussi donné avis que les nommé Kerq avoient une patente du Roy de la G. B. pour lever quelque chose sur la pesche des morues, ce qu'ils se proposent de prendre non seulement sur les sujets du Roy de la G B mais general-ment sur tous ceux qui iront pour faire cette pesches, ce qui seroit contraire a tout droit et à la liberté avec laquelle on en a usé jusques icy, ce qui fait que je .m'imagine que le Roy de la G. B ne l'entend pas ainsy et que personne autre que ses sujets ne se resoudra à le souffrir."

" I have also been informed that the said Kerq[s] have a patent from the King of Great Britain to collect something on the cod fishery and that they propose to take this not only from British subjects but also from all who go there to fish This will be contrary to all justice and to the freedom which has been enjoyed there up to this time   I surmise that the King of Great Britain does not know what has been done and that no one but his own subjects will submit to this "

The king, in reply, referred the Ambassador to the Council Board, who reported :—

" The Lords having been acquainted by Mr Attorney with the Commission granted to Sir David Kirke the Lord Chamberlain and others, it was decided that a firm but fair answer should be given and the imposition laid by the French on English merchants considered in justification." [1]

For once Charles was firm and decided.

The following ludicrous incident, duly recorded in the Calendar of State Papers, illustrates the extraordinary mode in which merchant

ENGLISH MAN-OF-WAR.
From Dudley's Arcano del Mare, 1646.

vessels were transformed into men-of-war, and the wretched condition of the Royal Navy under Charles I. :—

"Petition of James Marquis of Hamilton and the rest of the Adventurers of Newfoundland To the King. John Kirke Manager of their business in London sold to Nathan Wright and Richard Craudley Merchants of London 6000 qtls. of Newfoundland fish at 10/- per qtl., far under the value, on condition of their setting out the *Confident* as a man of war to attend the Petitioners fleet; but Edward Mabb the Master discovering to the French that *he was no man of war* the French afterwards refused to pay any more ground leave, and Wright and Craudley will not pay for the 1000 qtls. of fish value £1346 previously delivered by the French. Pray that the business may be referred to some honourable persons to determine. Referred to Lord Keeper &c. . . . . . ." [1]

In dealing with both the Tudor and the Stuart period we must always remember that in our sense of the word there was neither organized government, army, nor royal navy then existing, no civil service, or great departments of State, home, foreign, or colonial; there were only the rudiments of such institutions. In many of the writers, even of the Stuart period, we have mention of a "man-of-war of Torbay," a "man of war of London" or "Bristol"; these were simply

[1] *Records.*

armed merchantmen, sometimes with a royal commission, sometimes without, in many cases simply piratical cruisers who made war on Frenchmen and Spaniards, occasionally when no better opportunity offered plundering their own countrymen

For one more year Kirke went on mulcting the foreigners and rolling up money, leasing out stages, selling liquor, and doing the general Newfoundland business · he acted as monarch of all he surveyed, and his rude strong hands fell heavily on the settlers, even the sturdy West of England fishermen had to submit to this tyrannical old sea captain   During the first year of his reign, as we learn from Kirke's letter to the Earl of Pembroke, 25th January 1639,[1] the West of England had risen in arms ; the Bishop of Exeter stood by his diocese and headed the petition against the new Governor, charges were made that Kirke had destroyed cook rooms and stages, had disposed of the principal places to aliens, and had set up taverns, and it is urgently requested, that some timely course may be taken for prevention of such abuses

Sir David manfully replied to these charges —

" Ffereland 12 September 1640—To the Privy Council he protests before God that all they have alleged against me is most false   Many of the fishermen this year, upon what grounds I know not, have driven in their stages and cooke-roomes so much that ye most civil and wisest men amongst them did complain to me of those outrages . .   . I confesse he that would interrupt the ffishinge of Newfoundland which is one of the most considerable Business for the Kingdom of His Majesty and benefit of His Subjects and navigation is worthy the name of Traitour, the least thought and imagination whereof I do abhor. .   . . .   Hopes by good proofs to clear himself from causeless clamours against him. Has sent warrants to all Planters and fishermen to see the clauses in the 9th of H M.'s reign [Star Chamber Rules] duly kept[1] . .   . ,

The king ordered a commission to investigate charges against Sir David   After a careful consideration of the facts contained in the records it appears that Kirke's real offence was against his associates, he was evidently unscrupulous, he appears to have followed the old Scotchman's advice to his sons " Make money honestly if you can, but make money "; he had no hesitation in appropriating Lord Baltimore's property, and he evidently was doing the same with his partners, so in 1640 they dismissed him and sent out John Downing, senior, as Governor, with the following letter of instructions :—[1]

' INSTRUCTIONS for JOHN DOWNING of London Merchant concerning the affairs of the Lords Proprietors Pattentees of Newfoundland and others interested and adventurers therein.

" Mr Downinge, when God shall send you safe arrivall in Newfoundland, we would have you to performe and doe so much as in you lieth for your parte, our joint instructions deliver'd unto you & Mr Rigby wherein we would have your to advise together, & assist one another all that you can, soe long as Mr. Rigby remaineth in the country.

"In regard Sr Dav'd Kirke he is to come over hither, we would have you to stay and remain in the house in Ferryland, wherein Sir David Kirke now dwelleth, untill you shall receive advice from us what to do

"We would have you inform yourself in the best manner you can conferring with Sir David Kirke & otherwise, what course is best to be taken for planting of people in ye countrey & for the reducing the Indians that live in Newfoundland into civility, that soe they may be brot in time to know God

"We doubt not but you shall find a sufficient quantity of provisions to maintain you, and the Colony all the winter   The next year there shall be further supply, with what further shall be necessary, as we shall receive advice . in case you should want any provision sooner Mr. Rigby will assist you in procuring same, from some ships in the Country or otherwise, but we presume there will be no cause, only thus wee write that you may know what to doe if the Worst should happen

"Wee would have you give us all needful advice from time to time by all conveyances.   And soe we rest

"Whitehall ye 20th June 1640   HAMILTON   PEMBROKE
                                                MONTGOMERY   HOLLAND "

All through the Colonial records in the first half of the seventeenth century there are constant proofs of the importance of this Island as a great centre of trade, nowhere else in America between 1620 and 1640 were so many Englishmen gathered together and employed in one occupation as in Newfoundland   To the poor, ill-treated colonist, who groaned under the tyranny of Argall in Virginia, or the white slavery of Bermuda, Newfoundland was the haven of refuge to which his longing eyes were turned, we have several instances in these early annals of the hair-breadth escapes of men in open boats fleeing to gain their freedom amongst the settlers and fishermen of the ancient Colony.

In 1623, when Virginia was in a terrible state of poverty and want, their hopes of succour from hunger and starvation lay in the timely arrival of a cargo of fish from Newfoundland   When the infant Colony of New York was struggling into existence, the Commissioner Mavericke thus writes home :—

"Tryalls have been made severall times this spring for codfish with very good success, a small ketch sent out by ye Governour hath founde severall good fishing bancks, amongst ye rest one not above two or three leagues from Sandy Hook, on which in a few houres four men took from 1100 to 1200 excellent good codd the last time they were out ; and most of ye vessels that goe to and from Virginia take good quantities. A vessel to goe to Newfoundland to get fishermen, lines hooks and other necessaryes for fishing   I doubt not but this coast will afford fish in abundance." [1]

The first authentic account of trade between New England and Newfoundland occurs in 1645 : by this time the commerce and shipping of the American Colonies had marvellously increased, everything was

[1] *Records*

NEW YORK IN 1673.

From Winsor's N. & C. H. of America.

done to promote the great fishing industry; in 1639 an act was passed by the local government exempting fishermen from military duty, and all fishing property from taxation; by 1641 Governor Winthrop records that three hundred thousand dry fish were sent to market, probably first to England. In 1643 the excellent Governor mentions the return of the *Trial.*

"Mr. Thomas Graves, an able and godly man, master from a voyage to Bilbao and Malaga, her outward cargo consisted of dry codfish which she sold at a good rate and she brought as a return wine, fruit, oil, iron and wool which was a great advantage to the country [and which probably the godly man smuggled] it gave great encouragement to trade."[1]

In 1644 a Bristol ship was captured by a cruiser of the Parliamentary party in Boston; the sympathies of the majority were with the Commonwealth, and after some wrangling the Cromwellian vessel carried off her prize. Even in distant Newfoundland the effects of this fierce civil war fell like a blight upon the fishing trade; Winthrop, in 1645, tells of a fishing expedition to Bay Bulls, Newfoundland, sent by merchants of Boston and Charlestown. When the vessels had nearly completed their loading the ship and most of the fish were seized by a Royal cruiser, and retained to the great loss of the merchants.

Newfoundland appears to have been Royalist, or at any rate neutral, and the Devonshire men were under the protection of the king's party. Charles, however, recognised rightly that New England's sympathies were

[1] *Records.*

with his opponents. He seems to have had grave doubts about their loyalty, so as an additional precaution passengers going out to the Colony were compelled to take the oath of allegiance

"Petition of Stephen Goodyeare Merchant. *John* of London about to proceed to Newfoundland and Spain Leave granted to carry goods and passengers to New England on taking the oath of allegiance at Gravesend. 1640 Jany 26.

"Similar order about *Charles* of Gloucester freighted for a voyage to the foreign Plantations and thence to Newfoundland Passage allowed for 100 to New England on taking the oath of allegiance May 27, 1640.

"Same date similar order for *Amity* 120 passengers to New England"[1]

The sack ships or freighters, now generally known in Newfoundland as "Foreigners," were constantly employed during these early years transporting freight and passengers to New England, many of the Newfoundland merchants were also concerned in the New England trade and fishery; their ships were sent from Maine and New England to fish about the Newfoundland coast before the New England traders made a regular business of the Newfoundland barter trade. By 1652 there was a steady commerce and connexion between New England and Newfoundland, traders came every year to the Island and bartered their corn and cattle for the Newfoundland fish and oil, even thus early in our history the New Englanders began the practice of stealing away the Devonshire fishermen's servants, in which afterwards they were so extensively engaged

Hubbard relates in 1652, concerning a petition to the Lords Commissioners of Trade and Plantations with respect to regulations about the fishery, fees for culling, &c, on which disputes had arisen between the Government and the fishing interest, that the petition was only signed by twenty-five —

"These were for the most part, either young men who came over as Servants and never had over much show of religion in them, or fishermen of Marblehead feared to be profane persons, divers of whom were brought from Newfoundland for the fishing season"[1]

The New Englanders of that age showed all the cuteness and unscrupulous cunning of the Yankee inventor of wooden nutmegs, Charles II was terribly wroth at the audacity of the colonists in coining shillings with a rude figure of a pine tree, the colonists roundly swore to His Majesty that it was not a pine but an oak, and was intended to show their loyalty and His Royal Majesty's providential escape in the oak tree. The merry monarch was a humorist, and he enjoyed the fine flavour of this impudent falsehood, to further conciliate His Majesty they sent him ten barrels of cranberries and three thousand dried codfish The earliest account of the New Englanders in the Colony from the Newfoundland records occurs in John Downing's narrative, 1676.[2]

[1] *Records*   [2] *See* p. 205

APPENDIX TO CHAPTER VI.

I. Star Chamber Rules of Charles I. and additions by Charles II.

Order of Star Chamber 24th Jan'y 1633—On 20th Feb'y foll'g Charter was granted according to tenor of this order unto ye Merchants and Traders of Newfoundland which was since on 24th Jan'y 1660 renewed and confirmed by his Majestie with an additional provision —(*B T Nfld, Vol 3, p 5*)

In renewal of Charter by Charles II the Patent of Chas I is recited—

"Whereas our late Royall Father of blessed Memorie by his Lettres Patent under his Greate Seale of Englande beareing date at Westminstre the tenth day of Ffebruary in the nynth yeare of his reigne hereby reciteing that the region or Countrey called Newfoundland had been acquired to the Dominion of his Progenitors, which he held &c &c"

His people had many years resorted to those parts—employed themselves in ffishing whereby great number of his people had been "sett on Worke" & the navigation and mariners of the realm much increased and his subjects resorting thither "one by the other and the natives of these parts were orderly and gently intreated" till of late some of his subjects of realm of England planting themselves in that Countrey "upon conceipt that for wrongs or injuries done there either on the shoares or in the sea adjoining they could not be here impeached" & the rather that he and his progenitors had not given laws to inhabitants—subjects resorting thither injured one another & "used all manner of excesse" to hindrance of voyage and common damage of realme—for preventing of such inconveniences for future he did declare in what manner people of Newfoundland and seas adjoining and Bays and Creeks and fresh rivers there sh'd be guided and governed & did make and order &c "We doe by these presents renew ratify and confirme the laws following in the things after specified"—

1st If any man kill another or steale to value of forty shillings to be brought to prison to England & the crime made known to Earl Marshall of Eng'd & if proved by two witnesses—delinquent to suffer death

2 No ballast to be thrown out to prejudice of harbor

3. That no person deface or spoyle any stage, Cookroome &c

4 That such ship as first entereth a harbour shall be admiral—wherein for time being he shall reserve only so much beach & flakes as is needful for number of boates as he shall use, with overplus only for one boat, as privilege for his first coming, after content themselves with what he shall have use for with keeping more to prejudice of others next coming—any that possess several places in several harbours with intent to keep all before they can resolve which to choose shall be bound to resolve and send advice to such aftercomers & within 48 howres if the weather so serve, said aftercomers may likewise choose —so none receive prejudice by others delayes.

5 That no person deface or alter the marks of any boats to defraud the owners of them

6 That no person steale any fish, trayne, or salt or any other provision belonging to fishing ships

7. That no person set fire to the woodes or rinde the trees except for Cookeroomes

8 That no man case anchor or ought else hurtful which may breed annoyance or hinder the "haleing of seines" for baytes in places accustomed thereto

9 That no person robb the nets of others out of any drift boate

10. That no person set up any taverne for selling wine, beere. strong waters, cider or tobacco —by such means fishermen neglect their labours, and spend wages upon which their wives and children depend they are likewise hurtful in many other ways—men make themselves hurtful by purloyning and stealing from owners.

11. On Sunday Divine service to be said by some of the Masters of ships, such prayers as are in Book of Common prayer.

And moreover and further then was ordayned by the laws of our said late ffather and for the encouragement of our subjects in said Newfoundland All owners of ships trading to Newfoundland forbidden to carry any persons not of ships Company or such as are to plant or do intend to settle there, & that speedy punishment may be inflicted on offenders—ordeyned as formerly that "Every of the Maiors of Southton Weymouth and Melcome Regis Lynne Plymouth Dartmouth Eastlowe ffoy and Barnstaple" for time being take cogni'ce of all complaints [on land] and by oath of witness examine, award, amend to parties specified and punish delinquent by fine and imprisonment &c and Vice-Admls in Counties of Southton Dorsett Devon and Cornwall proceed against offenders upon the sea—"Also wee will and ordeyne that these laws and ordinances shall stand in forse and be put in due execution untill wee shall otherwise provide and ordeine And we doe require the admirals in every harbour in this next season ensuing calling together such as shall be in that harbour publickly to proclayme these presents and they alsoe proclayme the same on the shoare in Witness &c Witness ourselfe at Westminster the six and twentieth day of January."

(Patent Roll, 12 *Chas. II ,* part 17, 30)

On the 23rd Decr 1670 a Pet'n for regulation of Fishery was presented to His Majestie by Westerne Merchants & Traders & Council of foreign Planters having made report of several rules necessary for support of trade His Majesty was pleased to order that they sh'd be added to the former Charter viz—

1. That H.M's Subjects may take bayte of fish in Newfoundland provided they submit to established orders.

2. That no alien take bait.

3. That no planter cut down any wood, or plant within six miles of sea shore.

4. That no inhabitant or planter take up best stages before arrival of fishermen

5. That no master or owner of ships transport seamen or fishermen to Nfld unless belonging to his ship's Company

6. That no person carry more than 60 persons to a hundred tonnes

7 That every fifth man be a green man [that is] not a seaman

8 That masters of ships provide victuals in England according to number of men, for whole voyage, salt only excepted.

9. That no fishing ship part hence for Newfoundland before the month of March

10. That Masters give bond of £100 to respective Mayors not to carry any persons to Newfoundland as aforesaid & to bring back such as they carry out, or shall employ with fish for market voyages.

11. That no master take up a stage with less than 25 men

12 That no fisherman or seaman remain behind after fishing is ended

13 That Adm'l, Vice Adm'l and Rear Adm'l do put these orders in execution and preserve the peace

14 And bring offenders for any crime into England

15. That they proclaim on 20th Septr yearly H.M 's orders.

16 And keep Journals.

17 That Recorders and Justices of the Peace be Joyned in Commission with Mayors.

18. That reasonable fines be imposed on offenders

19 That a Bill sh'd be prepared for the Greate Seale, for confirm'n of said Charter, with these additional powers.

20 That the clause touching the Marshall sh'd be reviewed by the Atty Gen'l &c who should present to board, someway of Judicature for determining of causes in Newfoundland.

(B T Nfld., Vol. 3, p 13.)

II. Sir David Kirke.

KIRKE TO ARCHBISHOP LAUD.

Oct 2, 1639

" Out of 100 persons they took over only one died of sickness. [The temperature and general state of the country is described] . . The air of Newfoundland agrees perfectly well with all God's creatures except Jesuits and Schismatics. A great mortality amongst the former tribe so affrighted my Lord of Baltimore that he utterly deserted the country . . . of the other sect [The Puritans] many frenzies are heard from their next neighbouring Plantation, the greatest His Maj'y hath in America Their chiefest safety is a strict observance of the rites and service of the Church of England Doubts not but the country will be numerously peopled in a short time." *(Endorsed by Laud rec Jan 1640)*

There is considerable difficulty in ascertaining the exact facts about the later history of this celebrated old sea captain When ordered home by Charles I, he appears to have remained in England some time , he was, however, returned to the Island before 1649 In this year there is a most pathetic letter from the unfortunate Charles to Kirke, written not long before his execution, praying him to find an asylum for his sister Lady Hawkins " in these troublous times "

Under the Commonwealth Kirke's property was taken possession of by the Commissioners, at least all that belonged to the company. Besides Baltimore's mansion at Ferryland, there appear to have been other houses in which George Kirke, Lady Kirke, and the family resided There was very long delay and putting off of Kirke's case. Sir James Kirke obtained a new Patent in conjunction with Claypole, Cromwell's son-in-law.

In 1651 Kirke is ordered to repair to England He went out to Newfoundland again in 1652, and was under bonds to return the same year Either in 1652 or in the following year he died in prison at the suit of Lord Baltimore Sikes, Pyle, and Treworgie speak of him as dead in 1654 ; he appears to have died about June 1653

Witnesses on both sides in the controversy between Kirke and Baltimore seem to give evidence only on behalf of their friends Amy Wrixon, William Wrixon, and Ann Low swear that " for 7 or 8 years before the arrival of Sir David Kirke Baltimore never had possession or person there upon the property " Cecil Lord Baltimore, on the other hand, testifies that " his father died in 1632, that he, Cecil, had sent out Captain William Hill as his deputy ; Captain Hill repaired thither, took possession and gave him a yearly account of his proceedings and the profit, and resided four or five years in Lord Baltimore's house in Ferryland Not long before the beginning of the late war, Duke Hamilton and others by their power at Court procured a Patent of all Newfoundland, including therein the Province of Avalon, whereupon in 1638 Sir D. Kirke went to Ferryland in Newfoundland, and by force of arms turned Captain Hill out of Lord Baltimore's chief Mansion house (where the said Lord Baltimore had at the time divers things of good value) and took possession of the whole Province and of divers cattle and horses belonging to Lord Baltimore "

Baltimore prays for redress through Parliament, " his property being now in possession of persons sent by the Council of State to dispossess Sir David Kirke "

These Commissioners were Captains Raynor and Pearce; their characters are given in a gossipping letter from Charles Hill, Ferryland, 12 Sep 1661, to Mr John Kirke, London —

HILL TO KIRKE

Ferryland 12 September 1661
MR JOHN KIRKE.

I was advised by Mr Geo Kirke of what you was pleased to write to mee at the end of his letter, and could wish I had more pleasing intelligence to write to you than the continuation of the calamity of this Country occasioned not only by the continuance of bad voyages, but to the Inhabitants in a more particular manner by the late Governors arrival here, who have sought themselves so much that I believe they will have but a few Tennants in ye Lord Baltimore's part of Avilon Upon their arrival here the Inhabitants, as also the masters of ships were summoned, when their patent granted them for ye space or term of 14 years from the now Lord Baltimore was read and then a letter from the Kings Majesty under his hand and privy seal, wherein it was signified that there had beene a tryell between your family and Baltimore about the patent and upon report of His Majestys two Justices of Common Pleas and other Counceell it was declared that ye Patent of ye old Lord Baltimore was a good patent and that it was surreptitiously taken away by Sir David Kirke and that therefore His Majesty did require Sir Lewis Kirke &c to surrender to Lord Baltimore all his houses lands goods &c, and that all Masters and Admirals of ships should be ayding and assisting Lord Baltimore if required

I pre-advised My Lady and Mr Geo Kirke what answer to make unto the Governours, they being absent at ye reading of the Proclamation, when they came with the masters of ships to put them in free possession, who having made a complaymentall demand was suddenly answered that since it was His Majestys pleasure to order ye same they should not in the least dispute but with all readiness surrender it to his use and service, and as for what could be approvedly visible to belong to Lord Baltimore But as for the houses built by Sir D Kirke at his own cost

My Lady would attornie tenant for the same and pay the acknowledge due to Lord Baltimore for the same.

My Lady and Mr George have been much threatened to be dispossessed but the fitt is now over for the two Governors do one so thwart the other that they dissent in their judgments Captain Raynor is a desperado and looks not for right, but Captain Pearce is more a braver soldier and I believe would quit his ingagement upon honourable termes, he hath had very many civil expressions and good affections to your family and said he was resolved for England again, and should be loth to act any thing in Newfoundland that he might not answer in England. He hath heretofore been Sir Davids Leeftenant in ye King's ships and howsoever he was trepaned into this employment, hath very large respects to your famiey They pretended to have a Commission from the King for full management of all his concerns in the whole Island, which was granted but three days before they came away I know not how true, you can advise yourself, but thereupon and pretending ye King's letter, Captain Raynor hath received rents and arrears out of the precincts of Avilonia, and hath beene so hard to some that I think few will trust them longer than the next yeare There hath beene but 150 qtls. [of fish] per bont for the generalitie. Many planters have not made soo much I know Mr George hath advised you at full 'Tis reported Captain Reynells is returned for England, he is of a good family, who may do something for him. His Bond is £180 [security for return to Lord Baltimore] If you advise next yeare shall send it if opportunity present to exportation [probably some fish]

I shall further advise you, in the interim shall pray for your welfare with the tender of my humble services remayne,

Your Servant to command,
CHARLES HILL

(B M MSS. Eg. 2395)

The ingratitude of the Stuarts to their devoted adherents is proverbial, all the Kirkes had fought gallantly for their King, all were deserted and abandoned in their sore hour of need. The curtain closes over the gallant Sir David Kirke's family in misfortune and poverty, all poor Lady Kirke's appeals to her sovereign were entirely unheeded

In 1673 a Dutch squadron of four ships of 40 guns each entered the Harbour of Ferryland where " they plundered, ruined, fired, and destroyed the commodities, cattle, household goods and other stores belonging to the inhabitants." The family of Sir David Kirke were then residing there as ordinary Planters, consisting of Lady Kirke, her son George and his wife and four children, David with his wife and one child, and Philip, unmarried—altogether they had 66 men servants, 14 boats, 3 staves, and 3 oil vats. We learn this from a letter of Dudley Lovelace, a prisoner aboard the Dutch fleet at the time, he says, Lady Kirke and her family were the greatest sufferers on this occasion (Public Records, quoted by Browne in his *History of C. Breton*)

The following accounts of Sir David Kirke's government may have been sworn to in 1667 to support the opposition to the Newfoundland settlers' petition (18th March 1667, B M. MSS., Eg 2395), that his son, George Kirke, should be appointed governor of the district from Petty Harbour to Ferryland These depositions probably were modelled after those of 1639 to support Exeter and other petitioners against Kirke

DEPOSITIONS TAKEN AT TOPSHAM, BY VIRTUE OF A COMMISSION DATED AUGUST 28, 1667

Thomas Cruse of Ashprinton deposes above fifty years last past he went to ye Newfoundland in a ship of Topsham on a ffishing voyage at which time there was noe Governour there, or above two or three poor people inhabited there, and such salt, boates, staiges and other materialls for ye ffishing trade left by ye shippes the fformer year they usually found in ye like condition without hurt or any diminution ye following year

And about thirty-two years past he went from London to ye Newfoundland and arrived there in ye Harbour of Bay Bulls, where he inhabited eighteen yeares, which was about four yeares before Sir David Kirke the ffirst Governour that came there after ye Lord Baltimore who was there only one winter and then left the countrey saying it was an unfitt place for man or beast to live in.

During all which time of this Deponents aboade there noe nation did ever in ye leaste attempt to molest or trouble ye English there or thare ffishery, neither were thare any ffortiffications erected untill the coming there of Sir David Kirke who planted some ffew gunns at Fferriland and two or three other places, and that before Sir David Kirke came there noe one paid any custome or tax concerning the said ffishery or otherwise, butt all was free

But after Sir David Kirke arrived there (who brought with him about thirty servants) he imposed taxes on all ye inhabitants to pay a great ffine and yearly rents for the houses and ground by ye water side in several Harbours

and ffishing places, as this Deponent did ffor a house and some ground graunted to him by ye said Sir David Kirke as by writing made in ye year 1640 ffor which he paid the yearlly rent of £3 6 8 and a *ffat hog* or 20/ in lew thereof.

And the said Sir David Kirke did summon ye Inhabitants of ye severall harbours to repair at Fferriland and compelled them to take estates in land in severall harbours for erecting of houses and ffishing places by ye water side, and to pay great ffines, tax and rents for the same and in case of reffusall thretned to expel them out of ye land; and alsoe entized them to take licenses off him ffor ye selling off wine and other liquors and made them pay great rents yearly ffor the same and made this Deponent take and pay for such a license £15 per annum

And ye said Sir David Kirke himselfe did keepe a Common Taverne in his own House which did drawe and keepe ship masters, ffishermen and others ffrom theire ffishing employments to the great prejudice and hinderance of their voyadges. And Sir David Kirke's constant practice was to engross salt and other necessary provisions brought thither for sale which he sold again to ye shippers at excessive rates And that during the abode of the Deponent, there was not any Church and if one should be built people too far away to come to Church through the woods, whereas in midst of the harbours there were not above two or three poore families [this means at Bay Bulls]

Similar depositions from Nicholas Luce of Dartmouth, Thomas Pitcher, Richard Parker, Christopher Selman, Thomas Fowler of St Mary Church, Gabriel Widdomas of Berry Pomeroy, all swear to the same effect, also to Kirke's coming with armed men and turning them out of their stages in June and putting his friends in possession.

(WORTH'S *Plymouth Municipal Records*.)

These Depositions, all of one tenour and purpose, are rather suspicious documents, the old West Countrymen swore as boldly, uniformly, and unblushingly as a corporal's guard in a brush with civilians. No doubt Sir David was a tyrant, a bold, determined ruler, who kept everybody—even the West Countrymen—in order It was not quite in keeping with his gubernatorial dignity for the gallant knight to keep a "grog shop" at Government House, in excuse for him it should be remembered that he had no salary

CHAPTER VII.

INTERREGNUM. 1649-1653

CROMWELL, PROTECTOR, 1653-1658.

RICHARD CROMWELL, Sept. 1658 to May 1659.

1659-1660, INTERREGNUM.

1649, July 24.—Notification to Colonies of change of Government

1650.—Warrant served by Matthews against N Redwood at St. Mary's Newfoundland at this time probably contained 350 families, or about 2,000 inhabitants, in fifteen settlements, between Cape Race and Cape Bonavista.

1651.—Commission to Treworgie, Sikes, &c to govern Newfoundland Kirke ordered to repair to England Council for the Plantations send for Holdsworth, and supply him with copies of Kirke's defence.

1652.—Kirke in Newfoundland again. Hubbard mentions Newfoundland fishermen being at Marblehead, Mass

1653.—Treworgie, sole Governor

1654.—Treworgie arrested by Kirke and imprisoned Death of Sir D Kirke in prison, at suit of Lord Baltimore

1655.—Petition from Plymouth for two men-of-war for convoy to Newfoundland. Charter granted to Claypole and Sir James Kirke Street's and Sikes' petitions for payment of salary.

1656.—Report of Committee on Newfoundland Trade —Twelve Articles to be turned (except 11th Article) into instruction to commanders of convoys going thither, and to the Governor there; encouragement of the Newfoundland trade to be respected in the pressing of seamen.

1657.—Convoy provided for several ships bound to Newfoundland.

1659.—Treworgie petitions for payment of six years' salary.

1660.—Mr. Povey's report upon Treworgie's petition

The stirring events of the great English revolution, the judicial murder of the king, the downfall of the monarchy, and the establishment of the Commonwealth, seem to have had marvellously small effect on the English colonies One plucky little island, Barbadoes, alone stood in arms for the fallen monarch; it is the proud boast of the Barbadoes negro of to-day —

" While Bados true to her
England nebber fear."

Nowhere else amongst the growing British dependencies was there any great commotion or armed resistance to the new government. The orderly course of law and administration in the Colonies went on unimpeded, but Rupert's piratical fleet and the Commonwealth's cruizers seriously interfered with trade; the Newfoundland fish business from the West of England shrank from two hundred and seventy vessels in the reign of James to about 100 sail; New England bullocks which had been worth £25 fell to £10, with a dull sale. The civil war fell like a blight on commerce and industry.

That aristocratic Mr. Facing-both-ways—Cecil, Lord Baltimore—boasted of his prompt conversion to the new republic. Cavalier Virginia made a show of resistance, but surrendered on the first appearance of the Commonwealth's armed force. The Puritans of the old country and New England embraced each other. The American rejoiced that his brethren in the motherland had followed his example in establishing a godly government out of which the shrewd New Englanders got worldly profit and advantage in the shape of various contracts for Jamaica, &c.

CROMWELL.

From an engraving after Houbraken.

The extortions and tyranny of Kirke as a representative of Charles's government had its influence on the western adventurers in Newfoundland; they welcomed the new power that had put an end to Kirke's reign; and though the Devonshire gentry were cavaliers to a man, the merchants and middle class who traded to Newfoundland seem to have all gone over to the Parliamentary party. We find in the records that the new government consulted Mr. Holdsworth,[1] of Dartmouth, a leading man amongst the western adventurers, in making their arrangements for the affairs of the Colony.

The policy of the Protector towards Newfoundland was in marked contrast to the tyrannical oppression of the monarchy. Even in our Island the sagacious statesmanship and firm, strong hand of Cromwell

[1] 1651, January 20. "The Council for the Plantations about Newfoundland affairs are directed to send for Mr. Oldsworth or any others who can speak to that business."

On February 11 orders were sent for Holdsworth to have copies of Kirke's defence; he was evidently one of the leading opponents of Kirke.

made itself felt. The rulers appointed for the Colony by the Parliamentary party were designated Commissioners; they were the first real Governors of the Island; all former administrators, although called in

DUDLEY'S MAP, 1647.

our histories Governors of Newfoundland—Gilbert, Guy, Mason, Hayman, Wynne, and Kirke—were in reality only the managers of colonisation companies, and had no direct commission from the Crown; the

English authorities at home had never given to either or any of these self-styled Governors either a naval or a military force to execute their decrees; under Cromwell's administration all this was changed The Commissioners, as will be seen from Governor Treworgie's letter of appointment and instruction, were real Governors.—

"You have hereby full power and authority to command such ships and vessels as are upon the coast, to keep together or otherwise to dispose of themselves as may bee most for the comon safety   . and all Captaynes of Convoys are hereby required to be assisting to you in the execution thereof and you are to consider in what manner any of the Harbours and Bayes belonging to the Country may bee fortified for preservation both of the Country and fishing

"You are by yor'selfe or such fit persons as you shall appoint to collect the imposition of fish due from and payd by strangers and likewise the imposition of oyle for the use of this Commonwealth " [1]

The first act of the Commonwealth regarding Newfoundland is contained in the records of February 23rd, 1649. Sir David Kirke, a staunch Royalist, evidently intended to send over a considerable force to sustain the royal cause in the Colony and to operate in conjunction with Prince Rupert, who was taking some of his ships to plunder the fishing fleet An order therefore is issued to the Comptrollers of Plymouth, Dartmouth, and Barnstaple —

"That 400 seamen taken up under pretence of being transported to Newfoundland by Sir David Kirke at great wages and other advantages offered are not to be allowed to go—only sufficient seamen necessary for the service of each ship be permitted to leave " [1]

And in May 27 of the same year, the following notice is sent to the generals at sea ·—

"Are informed that it is the intention of Prince Rupert to send some of his revolted ships to Newfoundland to disturb the fishing there · Desire that two ships may be sent thither if they can be spared to defend the fishing vessels " [1]

These wise precautions had the desired effect, Kirke was kept a prisoner under the control of the State, and Rupert's fleet, instead of ruining the Newfoundland fishermen, crippled the English trade in the Mediterranean and the West Indies

On the 24th of July of the same year there is an order from the Council of State —

"That letters be written to the English plantations to give them notice of the change of Government, to send the papers necessary for their information, and to require them to continue their obedience as they look for protection." [1]

The first Commissioners appointed (on April 8th, 1651) by the Commonwealth were John Littlebury, John Treworgie, Walter Sikes,

[1] *Records*

L

Captain Thomas Thoroughgood, Commander of the *Crescent*; Captain Thomas Jones, Commander of the *Ann and Joyce*; and Captain William Haddock, Commander of the *America*, who, together with other Commissioners—Redwood, Griggs, Pyle, Clotworthy, and Hendy—are to take examinations touching the miscarriages committed by Kirke. The first-named Commissioners are to take charge of the government, and particularly to collect the impositions on fish paid by strangers.

Our history does not concern itself with these various Commissioners.

TOAD'S COVE.
From a drawing by the Hon. and Rev. W. Gray.

Mr. Sikes appears to have been, like Sir David Kirke, troubled a good deal about his accounts with the Commonwealth. The charges against the Governor, after being put off from time to time, were at length finally dropped. His brother, Sir James, having managed to secure Cromwell's son-in-law, Claypole, on his side by the bribe of a share in Lord Baltimore's plantation at Ferryland, a charter seems to have been granted about 1655 to Sir James Kirke, Claypole, and others. It came utterly to naught.

Newfoundland does not appear to have suffered so much commercially from the Civil War as New England The Puritans of Boston and New Plymouth complained bitterly of the stagnation of trade during this period, when the seas were infested with hostile cruisers, Parliamentary and Royal pirates. The export of fish to the Mediterranean must have been a terribly risky business.

The Newfoundland ships, numerous (though terribly reduced from the grand fleet of the days of Elizabeth), well armed, and escorted by three men-of-war, ran the gauntlet to t'e Straits of Gibraltar each season, and there appears to be no complaint of captures The Dutch, from the time of the Armada, had become, like the English at the pres-nt day, the great carriers for the world.[1] They bought large quantities of dry cod in Newfoundland, and exported it to Europe and the West Indies.

The most distinguished name in the annals of Newfoundland during the Cromwellian period is John Treworgie, or Treworgay[2]. he was the first real Governor of the Colony. The best illustration we can gather of the character of this able, honest administrator is furnished by his opponents The West Countrymen found him a far more formidable ruler than Kirke. In the Parliamentary Report published in 1718 they complain of his having encouraged settlement in Newfoundland by transporting passengers and protecting planters. He had been living in Maine, carrying on business for his grandfather, Alexander Shapleigh of Dartmouth Trained and brought up in the Colonies, he had seen the good effects of orderly settlements and the division of the State into townships, and in Newfoundland he endeavoured to carry out the same enlightened ideas Even a virulent Tory like Downing admits that good order was maintained during his government, and the poor Newfoundland planters were protected in their possessions So high was his character that, during the interregnum between the end of the

---

[1] 1640. "Memorandum concerning 'The Bill' to be preferred by the West Countrymen about the Newfoundland fishery."

The paper shows the advantage to British navigation if the Dutch were prohibited from buying fish there, and aliens required to pay the same duties there that are paid in England. It also mentions complaints from Bahamas and Virginia about Dutch traders.

They were universal carriers, and had very fine ships — (*Calendar of State Papers, Colonial Series.*)

[2] John Treworgie, or Treworgay, appears to have been the son of James Treworgie, who married a daughter of Alexander Shapleigh, of Dartmouth, Devon, all my endeavours to elicit any information from Rev Baring Gould and others about the Treworgie family in Cornwall have failed The Shapleighs, how-

ever, are an old West Country stock Four monuments, with coats of arms of the family, are to be found in the Parish Church of Dartmouth, Devon From some law papers we find that John Treworgie went out to Maine in 1640, when a very young man, as agent for his grandfather Shapleigh. He lived several years at Sturgeon Creek, Kittery, Maine, and figured in law suits about his grandfather's property with John Heard in 1643 and 1646 He was married in January 1646 to a Miss Spenser, of Newberry, Mass Treworgie and several other merchants in Maine went to Newfoundland for trading and fishing Governor Treworgie did business with our Island, for on May 27th, 1653, when appointed sole Governor or Commissioner for Newfoundland, it is specially mentioned that he was then residing there.

Commonwealth and the restoration of Charles II, Treworgie was again appointed Governor of the Colony

The Lord Protector's Government treated Treworgie meanly; they seem to have been just as neglectful as the Stuarts in paying their servants   There is in the records a humble petition from the poor Colonial Governor, praying for the payment of six years' arrears of "sallery," which, as we gather from a similar petition in 1655 from Anne Mansfield, mother of Thomas Street (one of the Commissioners who had been appointed with Sikes in 1652), was only at the rate of £250 per annum, and £61 for disbursements

Another incident in Treworgie's tenure of office illustrates in a remarkable way the impartial and independent administration of justice under Cromwell's Government   In April 1654 Treworgie complains—

"That in this year Sir James Kirke had him arrested in an action for £600 and kept him close prisoner as a malefactor, thinking by a trick to gain money for his liberty; he prays that Kirke, Hill, and the bailiffs may be ordered to show cause why the Petitioner should not proceed in his Commission [as Governor of Newfoundland] without interruption or arrest, and that he may be secured against them." [1]

By order of Cromwell the petition is referred to Colonel Jones and others, "to consider of a way for the Petitioner's indemnity." Under the Stuarts, such an interference by the courts with a Colonial Governor would have been visited with summary punishment, under the orderly administration of Cromwell the courts of justice, even when they acted perversely against his own officers, were never interfered with. Royalists like Kirke and Baltimore could freely bring their differences before the Protector's courts of law without any fear of such Government action as was the rule under the Stuarts

Under the fostering care and able management of Treworgie, which extended from 1653 to 1660, the settlement, trade, and fisheries of the Colony were largely increased; no injustice to planters was permitted under his firm control, the cultivation of the land was encouraged; trade between the island and the continental colonies was promoted; the celebrated Trelawney of Richmond Island, Maine, sent ships to Newfoundland. Treworgie himself was connected with the trade of both colonies   New England prospered immensely under the Commonwealth, and so did our island Colony. Amidst the dreary record of wrong and oppression, Treworgie's seven years administration is the one bright spot in our history.

[1] *Records.*

The records show that there was a large amount of both ship-building [1] and boat-building going on in the Colony at this period. The English naval officers mention the great superiority of the English-built

SHIPS OF THE TIME OF CHARLES II.
From a drawing by C. W. Wyllie.

fishing boat as compared with the French, and very stringent orders were given to prevent our rivals obtaining Newfoundland boats from the settlers. Even at this early period there was a smuggling business

---

[1] In the Parliamentary Report of 1718 it is stated that nearly all the Poole vessels engaged in the Newfoundland trade were built in the Colony. Spurrier-built barques, brigs, and ships at Oderin, Burin, and St. Lawrence.

going on with the French; it continued after they were removed to Louisbourgh, Cape Breton, and is in full activity up to the present time. The New Englanders were so keen about trade that they actually sold to their enemies the very bricks and boards they afterwards battered down. By the end of the Commonwealth period the New England trade was firmly established in our Colony; it had a general agent in St. John's, with branch agencies in all the principal settlements

APPENDIX TO CHAPTER VII.

I. Treworgie's Instructions.

(*Domestic State Papers, Interregnum Council of State Order Book   April 29 to July 1, 1653. Vol 97*)

Friday 3d of June 1653, afternoone.

Majõ Gen^{ll} Desbrow the Lord Generall, M Gen^{ll} Lambert, Col Jones, M Gen^{ll} Harrison, Mr Strickland, Col Stapley, Col Tomlinson, Col Bennet, Mr Moyer, Sr Gilb Pickering

INSTRUCTIONS to JOHN TREWORGIE Gent appointed Commis^r for manageing and ordering the affaires and Interest of this Comonwealth in Newfoundland for this present yeare

WHEREAS upon consideration had of the present state and condition of affaires in Newfoundland relateing to this Comonwealth, The Councell have thought it expedient to continue you for this sumer upon the place as a Comissioner for manageing and ordering the affaires there   You are therefore to demeane yo'selfe in that trust and imploym^t according to the powers instructions and authority hereafter mentioned.

1st.—You are hereby required and authorized to take care for the Governm^t and well ordering of the said country of Newfoundland and the people there inhabiting, and likewise the fishery according to such lawes and ordinances as are hereto annexed

2nd   You are by yo'selfe or such fit persons as you shall appoint to collect the imposition of fish due from and payd by strangers, and likewise the imposition of Oyle for the use of this Comonwealth, and Adventur^{rs} aforesaid, until the Supreame authority shall declare their further pleasure therein.

3rd   You are to use yor best endeavo^{rs} to secure the fishery there against any that shall attempt to disturbe or interrupt it and to that end you have hereby full power and authority to comand such ships and vessells as are upon that coast or in any of the Harbo^{rs} to keepe together or otherwise to dispose of themselves in such manner as may bee most for the comon safety and to use such other meanes for the end aforesaid as you shall judge meet, And all Captaynes of Convoyes are hereby required to bee assisting to you in the execution thereof   And you are to consider in what manner any of the Harbo^{rs} and Bayes, belonging to the country may bee fortified for preservation both of the country and fishing

4.—Whereas securitie is given by Sr David Kirke such as the Councell doe approve of, for his appearance to the Councell and being responsible as to any matters to bee objected against him, Upon which the sequestration or former seisure upon his Estate is to bee taken off, You are therefore to deliver up unto such person or persons as he shall appoint all that remaines of his there that was formerly sequestred or seised, or that belongeth to him, onely of the Ordnance or any other things that doe properly belong to ye Comonwealth you are to take a particular notice and inventory, and unto the person or persons in whose charge you shall leave the same you are to give strict directions that they take care the same bee preserved and forthcoming to the use of the Comonwealth.   You are to receive and examine all such complaints as shall bee made unto you as well by strangers as others of any wrong or injury done unto them by any person or persons whatsoever and to certifie their particular cases unto the Councell.

You are upon the close of this sumers fishery to returne back into England and to repaire to the Councell or the Supreame authority of this Comonwealth and to give as well a just and true accompt of all such money and profitts as have come to yor hands due to the Comonwealth or Adventurers, as of all yor proceedings and in what condition you left all things there at yor coming away

Lawes, Rules, and Ordinances whereby the Affaires and fishery of Newfoundland are to be governed untill the Parlam^t shall take further order.

1 —That noe Ballast, Prest stones nor anything else hurtfull to the Harbours bee throwne out to the prejudice of said Harbours, but that it be carryed ashore and layd where it may not doe annoyance.

2.—That noe person whatsoever either fishermen or inhabitants doe destroy or deface or any way worke any spoyle or detriment to any stage, Cookeroome, Flakes, Spikes, Nayles or any thing else that belongeth to the stages whatsoever either at the end of the Voyage when he hath done, and is to depart the country   But that he or they content themselves with such stage or stages onely as shall bee needtul for them, and that for the repairing of such stages, as he or they take, they shall fetch timber out of the woods, and not to do it with ruining or teareing down of other stages

3 —That according to the ancient Custome, every ship or fisher that first entereth a

Harbour, in behalfe of the ship, be Admirall of the said Harbour, wherein for the time being he shall onely reseive soe much beach and flakes oi both as is needful for the number of boats he shall use with an overplus onely for one boate more than he needeth as a priviledge for his first cominge. And that every ship cominge after content himselfe with what he shall have necessarye use for without keepeinge or deteyneing any more to ye p'judice of others next cominge And that any yt are possessed of several places in several Harbo'' with intent to keepe them all before they cann resolve upon which to chuse, shalbe bound to resolve and send advice to such after comers in those places as expect his resolution and that within 48 houres if ye weather soe serve that ye said after Comers may likewise choose their place and soe none reaeive p'judice by others delayes

4 —That noe person cut out, deface or any way alter or change the marks of any boates or trayne fatts whereby to defraud ye right owners, and that no person convert to his own use ye said boates or trayne fatts soe belonging to others without their consents nor remove nor take them frō ye places where they be left by ye owners except in case of necessitye, and then to give notice thereof to ye Adm'' and others whereby ye owners may knowe what has become of them

5 —That noe person doe deminish take away perloyne or steale any of ye fish or trayne or salt which is putt in caske Trayne Fatts or Cookeroomes or other houses in any of ye Harbo'' or Fishinge places of ye countrye, or any other provisions belonginge to ye fishinge Trade or to ye ships

6 —That noe person sett fire in any of ye woods of ye countrye oi work any detrim' or destruction to ye same by ruding of ye trees either for ye seeling of ships houlds or for roomes on shoare or for any other uses except for ye coveringe of ye roofes for Cookeroomes to dresse their meate and these roomes not to extend above 30 foote in length at ye most

7 —That noe man cast anchor or ought else hurtfull which may breed annoyance or hinder ye haleing of Saynes for Bayte in places accustomed thereunto

8 —That noe person robb ye netts of others out of any drifts boate or drover for bayte by night, nor take away any bayte out of their fishing boates by their ships sides nor robb nor steale any of their netts or any part thereof.

9 —That noe person doe sett up any Tavernes for sellinge of wynes beere oi strong waters Syder or tobacco to entertyne ye fishermen because it is found that by such meanes they aie debauched, neglecting their labors and poore ill governed men not onely spend most part of their shares before they come home upon which ye life and maynten

ance of their wives and children dependeth but are likewise hurtfull in divers other ways as by neglecting and making themselves unfit for their labor by purloyneing and stealing frō their owners and by making unlawfull shifts to supply their disorders which disorders they frequently followe since these occasions have presented themselves

10 —That noe planter be permitted to keepe any more stage roome than he hath fishinge men in possōn for ye manageing of it and yt every planter in each Harbo' may take their stages and fishing roome together in one part of ye Harbour and not scattering as they now doe wasting as much roome for one oi two boates as may serve 6 or 8 boates

11 —That noe planter be permitted to build any dwelling house, store house, courtledge or garden oi keepe any Piggs oi other cattle upon or near ye ground where fish is saved or dryed

12 —That all provisions imported for sale necessarye for fishing be free for any person to buy for his own present occasion, soe it be demanded within six dayes after its arrivall, and not to be ingrossed by a few to make benefitt on others thereby

13 —That upon ye Lords day ye Accompanye assemble in meet place for divine worship

Signed
JOHN DISBROW Pst

Whitehall 3d.
  of June 1653

II. Petition of John Treworgie.

To the Right Honourable the Council of State

The humble Petition of John Treworgie Commander of the Colonie of this nation in Newfoundland,

SHEWETH,

That your Petitioner being in the year 1653 commissioned to ye Newfoundland by the Council of State for the managing of the affairs of that Country hath according to his instructions, yearly given them an account of his proceedings therein and for want of a due supply from heare hath been necessitated to return unto England and now takes on him the boldness to inform your Honour with the state of affairs in that Island and also to acquaint your Honour of six years sallary due to your Petitioner May it therefore please your power to take the matter into consideration and to grant unto your Petitioner a Commission for the advising the affairs there and to appoint two ,or three frigates (which vessels have been there to assist your Petitioner in collecting the impost surprizing of such Spanish ships as shall be found and to conduct English shipping from heare . . .
. . .

III. Mr. Povey's Report, May 11, 1660.

To the Right Hon the Committee of the Council for Foreign Plantations.

After reciting the various Patents. . .

. . . .

After the death of Duke Hamilton the Council of State did in 1650 give a Commission to John Treworgie merchant who was there upon the place to order affairs there for the best advantage of the State which Commission was also renewed in 1653 Sir David Kirke the only survivor of the former Patentees obtained in 1655 [prob. Sir James Kirke] a Commission from the late Protector Oliver wherein John Claypole Esq. and Col. John Coffin were joined with him but little or nothing was acted thereupon. Upon the whole matter it appeareth by reason of ye severall patents for the settlement . . . . . the disorders of the late time the interest of State suffers. . . . and it seems very expedient that some suitable person be employed and instructed to hasten thither to manage His Majesty's affaires therefor ye next season of fishing whereby many advantages and profits may arise to His Majesty which must else be wholly neglected and lost of which the person employed is to give an account here in England at ye end of the yeare. For the present it may be expedient that ye aforesaid John Treworgie hath a commission and fit instrument to goe to Newfoundland therefore forthwith he having been a person well used and experienced in those affaires. . . . . liberty to return to England and give an account of his Trust.

J. POVEY.

Endorsed ·—

By order of Committee of State sitting and taking care of Government in the intervall between ye suppression of ye Rump of ye Parliament and ye return of His Majesty which was not many days before the date of this Report.

CHAPTER VIII.

REIGN OF CHARLES II.

1660-1685.

1660.—Proclamation for stricter observance of Lent. Petition, on June 11th, of Sir L. Kirke and others for better protection of the fishing fleet. Petition, in June, of Lord Baltimore for a renewal of his patent, Sir O Bridgeman and Col Finch report, on June 17th, that the patent is good, and still in force; that they cannot calculate the money expended by the Kirkes on the plantation. Warrant granted to Baltimore to take possession from the Kirkes. Gargot probably received commission as Governor of Placentia.

1661.—Captains Raynor and Pearce at Ferryland as Baltimore's commissioners. Charter to Western merchants renewed on 26th January; no persons other than those going to fish or to settle to be permitted to sail, duty on salt remitted Petition of Lady Kirke that she and her children are starving Letter from Hill to Kirke in September.

1662.—Placentia founded by French Immediately after accession of Charles II., who was a vassal of France, Louis XIV. sent out 150 men, guns, and ammunition of war to Placentia Baltimore obtained renewal of his patent Mathews, sent by Pearse and Raynor to Placentia, arrested by the French, but escaped

1663.—Mayors, &c instructed to enforce an order prohibiting masters of vessels from carrying settlers to Newfoundland; fisheries exempted from tax or toll. The celebrated James Young in Newfoundland as surgeon on the *Reformation*

1664.—Deposition and complaint made to King Charles II of French proceedings in Grand Placentia in 1662, when, as sworn to by one Isaac Dethick, soldiers, women, and men landed there from a great French ship, sent to the king by the hands of Mr Robert Prowse. First agitation against French pretensions in Newfoundland

1665 —First edition of " Sir J Child's Discourse " Position of the Newfoundland fishery fully debated with reference to the Dutch war, only one ship of Dartmouth to go out. In June, De Ruyter, Dutch Admiral, plundered and destroyed St John's and several other harbours C. Martin endeavoured to defend St John's

1666.—H d'Almy's propositions about the fishery

1667.—William Hinton in Newfoundland hoping to be made Governor. Petition, on 18th March, to make George Kirke Governor Petition of Totnes, &c. on 28th August against a Governor. Depositions taken on 28th August, at Topsham, about Sir D Kirke's misrule, and on 20th November at Totnes Petition of Bristol and the Merchants Adventurers for a Governor and soldiers, on 6th December, referred to Lord Anglesey. C Martin again fortifying St John's. Proclamation of Louis granting bounty to Newfoundlanders settling at Placentia

1669 —Merchants petition the king against sending out a Governor to Newfoundland, as proposed by Captain Robert Robinson on 15th December; Robinson summoned to London

1670.—February 4, Order in Council that a chaplain should be sent with the annual convoy to Newfoundland "for keeping people living there in Christianity" Rules issued by the Lords of the Council to regulate fisheries, every fifth man to be a green man; captains to give bond for £100 to bring back every fisherman they took out, &c, &c. James Young, who kept a diary of his journeys, wrote about the fishery. On 23rd December a petition, presented by Western merchants, for the regulation of the fishery.

1671.—Deposition of Mathews sworn on 27th January Letter from Prowse to Gould on 14th March

1672.—Order enforcing bonds to prevent men going to New England, ships required to be better armed.

1673.—Dutch squadron of four ships plundered the Kirkes at Ferryland, but beaten off from St John's by Christopher Martin. The king appointed a Select Committee to take depositions in the West about the fishery.

1674.—Orders made by the Commissioners of Trade and Plantations forbidding planters to inhabit within six miles of the shore, from Cape Race to Cape Bonavista Sir J Williamson alludes to Lord Baltimore's house at Ferryland as being still habitable.

1675.—Charles II gave up duty of 5 per cent paid by French On the 12th February both sides were heard about the fishery, on 15th April the Council for Trade reported against a Governor and fortifications; and on 5th May they required the settlers to return to England, or go to other plantations. Letter on 12th September, from Berry to Southwell, about the planters Troate's report about a murder in St. John's not investigated, though known about by Captain Carter, &c.

1676.—27th January, old charter renewed with additional clauses Captain Russell compelling several ship fishermen to rebuild stages they had destroyed Order to Sir John Berry to burn houses, and root out population, owing to the exertions of John Downing, a resident merchant, an order from the king procured to annul it Mr John Alyrod's account of Placentia 24th October, Downing's narrative; first mention of New England traders Downing's petition of 7th November heard. T. Martin treated by the merchants in St John's as an alien, and forced to hire a stage Thompson's report on Placentia Dutch reported to have destroyed many French fishing vessels

1677.—Petitions of C and T Martin and Troate, of H M S *Swan*, and on 25th January and 23rd March further petitions of Downing. Order sent on March 28th, by the *St. John's Merchant*, directing ship fishermen not to molest the settlers, confirmed on 18th May by Captain Wheler Petition of St John's merchants on 10th December brought to England by Sir W Poole, H M.S. *Leopard*. T Oxford's petition reciting damage done to stages

1679.—Petitions of W Downing on 10th February and 2nd April; of Oxford on 2nd April, reciting that his family had a warehouse in St John's for seventy years; of Oxford and Downing, on April 29th, for a Governor, fortifications, and a minister; also petition of Oxford, about his negro servant, on 3rd July; and of Downing on 4th November T Weighmouth breaking into Downing's rooms. Captain Wright, H.M S. *Reverse*, keeping order in St. John's.

1680.—In May, Robinson asking leave to build a fort at St. John's Petitions of Hinton and Downing. W. Downing probably died on his way to Newfoundland. Account of Downing's family. Captain Robert Robinson and three merchants at Bay Bulls, on 29th September; condemn four fishermen to be ducked for damaging French room at Colinet, &c., and two merchants to pay the damages

1681.—Destrick and Molin's report of Placentia Fort in ruins. Twenty-two Basque vessels from Port of Passage fishing and whaling in Newfoundland French attempting to prevent Basque fishing in their neighbourhood Captains Talbot and Storys on the coast Bad fishery.

1682.—Captain D. Jones, H M S *Diamond*, reports about New Englanders, on 12th September, from Bay Bulls Captain Wren at Bay Bulls in the *Centurion*

1683.—Petition of Downing on the 11th October.

1684.—Captain Wheler, H M S *Tiger*, reports on French settlements and fishing, no wood to be had within two miles of St. John's; good fishery

The Commonwealth had only been maintained by the strong hand of Cromwell; soon after his death the English republic came to an end. The general voice of the country was in favour of a limited monarchy and a hereditary sovereign. Under the astute tactics of Monk the Restoration was brought about—unbridled licence, in place of Puritan severity.

From the records, reports of naval officers (which began in this reign), and private letters (now for the first time published), we are able to give a pretty accurate description of Newfoundland under the Restoration. It was an unfortunate change for our poor Colony. Charles

CHARLES II.
From an engraving after Lely.

the father had chastised the settlers with whips, the dissolute son chastised them with scorpions. Lest I should be accused of exaggeration in the matter of the expulsion of the settlers in this reign, I have given in all possible cases the official documents, or, when too long, a *résumé* of their contents. Information about the Colony is much fuller in this period. There was no regular post in England, but we have the rudiments of a newspaper, the short-lived *Publique Intelligencer*, and the still existing *London Gazette*.

The two most important events in this reign were the irruption of the French into the Colony, the foundation of their capital at Placentia in 1662, and the attempted expulsion of the settlers by an Order in Council from Charles II. in 1675.

On these subjects I have endeavoured to give all the information that can be gathered from the contemporary records. I have been obliged, from want of space, to omit the long discussion before the Council contained in Secretary Williamson's note-book, a very interesting paper from Sir R. Robinson in favour of a Governor, and numbers of naval reports. I have stated the main argument on both sides—all that space would permit; my endeavour has been to give my readers a general view of the actors performing on the Newfoundland scene—to bring to life the dead and forgotten Terra-novian heroes of those days.

One of the first acts of Charles II. in 1660 was the issuing of a long proclamation for the stricter observance of Lent, assigning as one reason " the good it produces in the employment of fishermen." The Puritans of the day refused to fast in Lent or to eat fish; it savoured of prelacy and superstition; they would have none of it. New England's plan of giving a remission of taxation to the citizen who could prove his consumption of fish for one-third of the year, was a more workable way of encouraging the sale of fish.

SMALL CRAFT.

From De Veer's Waerachtighe, 1605.

West Country interest was all-prevailing with the king, so in the same year, 1660, an Act was passed remitting the duty on salt used in the fishery, and exempting other materials required in this industry from all duties. In 1663 the Newfoundland fishery was to be for ever relieved from all taxes and tolls, and the same Act imposed stringent duties on all fish and products of the seas imported into the kingdom by foreigners and aliens. It was a wise and beneficial measure, made entirely for the interest of the West Country adventurers.

There were no court-houses, jails, or regular administration of justice in the Colony in those days. Sir David Kirke, in a patriarchal way, had been wont to administer quarter-deck law from the parlour of his old house in Ferryland. The captain of the convoy, for the first time in our history, assumes this authority, and we have a very full account of the trial of four prisoners for the destruction of the "cabbin" of a Frenchman called Ducarrow, at Colinet Island, where he was the admiral, and of the robbery and destruction of his shalloways and shallops. The case was clearly proved on the admission of the delinquents.

From the evidence it appears to have been a common practice amongst the fishermen to steal French boats in the winter Both the depredators and the planters who supplied them and shared their plunder richly deserved punishment Captain Robert Robinson, R N. (afterwards knighted, and an applicant for the Governorship of Newfoundland), tried them on board the man-of-war. Three merchants sat as nautical assessors, after the Admiralty practice, or as a primitive jury the whole proceeding was illegal, but it was eminently just, summary, and effective.

The judgment of the Court was ·—

" Ducarrow v Knap and ors.

" Whereas Francis Knapman, John Wallis, William Couch, Samuel Wood, four of the six persons who did the damage at Colinet last winter to the Frenchmen haven been taken and confined aboard this ship :

" We the undersigned have seriously considered to have ye above duck[1] at ye maine yarde of this ship for a public example to all this Island , and they shall be liable for the said damage legally proved and the damage shall be made good by Pollard and Rolson who fitted them out for that fishing voyage. The damage is said to be no more than £50 or £60

> H.M S. Assistance, Bay Bulls, Sep. 29, 1680.
> Robert Robinson, Captain, R N
> Stephen Akarman of Bay Bulls.
> John Beverley   do.
> Aaron Browning   do   and at Trepassey."

We have to recount about this period the ignominous failure of the English Navy in North America and elsewhere , the men, however, were just as brave as ever , the English merchant sailors showed a gallant front to the enemy, whilst Charles's Royal Navy was being thrashed by the Dutch.

An old West Country captain, Christopher Martin, master mariner of Cockington, in Devon, in 1673, the closing year of our war with Holland, beat off the Dutch from St John's, and defeated four noted pirates, Captain Everson and his comrades

No doubt there were many such encounters as Martin describes, many mute inglorious Nelsons amongst these Devonian skippers, who fished and traded in Newfoundland , the records give us an account of a still more gallant action fought by Captain Holman, which will be described later on

Martin was not only a brave mariner, but a sensible, shrewd old fellow , his practical suggestions about a Governor and increase of inhabitants were opposed to the views of all his Devonshire associates

---

[1] Ducking from the yard-arm, like keel-hauling, was an ancient naval punishment in use probably up to the last century The culprit was hoisted to the yard-arm, suddenly dropped and hauled up again from one to seven times In keel-hauling, the sailor was run from yard arm to yard-arm right under the keel of the ship They were both most barbarous punishments.

I will let this gallant old merchant captain tell his own tale in his own way :—

"Report of Christopher Martin, of Cockington, Devon.

"Has been 17 years Vice-Admiral of St. John's, was once Admiral. If French took Newfoundland and St. John's very hard to get it back again and there would be great danger to ships passing so near the coast to and from America

"In 1665 and 1667 he landed his guns and built small forts with earth and with his own ammunition defended the harbour In October 1673, with 6 guns out of the *Elias Andrews* defended St. Johns against Hollanders on their way from New York, he was there with provisions: defended St Johns against Captain Everson and three other men of warr and with less than 30 men forced them from the Harbour's mouth.

"Considers a Governor and increase of inhabitants absolutely necessary to keep off the French who have three quarters of the Island and Placentia strongly fortified"[1]

In view of the constant danger to which our infant Colony was exposed from pirates, and the still more formidable encounters with the fleets of our enemies, it seems very strange that there were no military or naval preparations to resist this constant, ever menacing danger. Beyond the odd ship or two for convoy of our fishing fleet to the Mediterranean in August and September, England gave us no protection, and no ruler or governor virtually until 1728, and then only a floating ruler for about two months in the year

Many strenuous efforts were made to obtain a commander-in-chief for the Colony the attempt was always fiercely resisted by the West Countrymen. In this struggle about the Governorship we catch glimpses of the social condition of the Colony, and of the wealth and position of the leaders of society in the four principal settlements, St John's, Ferryland, Harbour Grace, and Quidi Vidi

One of the claimants for the office of Governor appears to have been Captain Robert Robinson, R N, who made interest with James II, then Duke of York

Another was William Hinton, an old hanger-on of the Stuart family His father had been Gentleman of the Chamber, and had spent great sums of money for the king, £700 in Sir George Booth's business raising a troop of horse. The son was several years abroad with His Majesty Charles II when in exile, and says in his petitions—

"That he never asked the King for anything but the Governorship of Newfoundland which His Majesty had promised to him several times.

"He hath all sorts of household stuff in the country—£2,500 worth—which have layen there a great while and the Inhabitants being sensible of his large expense and endeavours for their welfare, that if the King gives it to any one else he will be ruined, that he hath for a long time studied the advancement of the Colony, and no one His Majesty can send will pretend to know more about the country than he does"[1]

[1] *Board of Trade, Newfoundland*

This application from an old and faithful retainer received no response ; Charles's ministers were bribed and controlled by Child and the West Countrymen

The only other rival for the Governorship, which was worth £400 per annum, was William Downing. He proposes—

"The just and readiest way the tax upon the boats may be collected is through
    George Kirke Esquire at Fermouze,
    Mr. John Downing at Qua de Vide,
    Mr Thomas Oxford at St. Johns,
    Mr John Pinn at Havre de Grace , [1]
all these persons having correspondence through the whole country would collect the money at no trouble to the Governour " [2]

The Downings were the sons of the former Governor under Hamilton's charter Mr Thomas Oxford appears to have been, like Hinton, a man of some position He kept a negro house-servant— a most aristocratic appendage in those days—whom the West Country-men forcibly took away [3]

Many of the Devonians, more sensible and patriotic than their fellows, strongly urged the appointment of a Governor and the fortifi-cation of the principal harbours Weymouth, Bristol, and London were strongly in favour of the appointment Their efforts were in vain

The population of Newfoundland during this reign is variously estimated The various rough calculations are given in the statistics ; they appear to understate the number of the resident planters.

By far the most important event in this reign is the occupation of the Island by the French

It may be argued that the assumption as to the turpitude of Charles in this transaction is based on very slender grounds. I do not think so , the character of Charles is so vile that, to use a New-foundland expression, we would not " put it past him " He gave up Dunkirk at the very same time.

To fitly describe the epoch in English annals known in our histories as "The happy restoration of Our Sovereign Lord King Charles," one has to borrow the epithet which an American authoress applied to the administration of Indian affairs in the United States—"A century of dishonour ," and truly the sovereignty of Charles II was a veritable reign of infamy

Fire and plague decimated the land. To these terrible calamities were added the horrors of war We were defeated by the Dutch, the

---

[1] The Pynns are one of the oldest Eng-lish families in this country , the principal branch left about 1842, and emigrated to Wisconsin, where they have helped to build up that rising State.
Sir Henry Pynn, a brave officer, knighted for his gallant conduct on the field of battle, is a descendant of this John Pynn.

[2] *Board of Trade, Newfoundland*

[3] " Also had his covenant negro servant valued worth €60 taken from him last fishing season, all which he is ready to make out by bill of sale and oath " (*B. T., Nfld*)

enemy's guns were heard in London destroying Sheerness and the shipping in the river.   Never since the Norman Conquest had England suffered such humiliation.   The crowning disgrace of the reign, however, was the secret treaty between Charles and Louis XIV., by which England became the vassal of France, English policy, foreign and domestic, being virtually governed by the French king.   Out of this arose the war with our ancient allies, the Dutch.

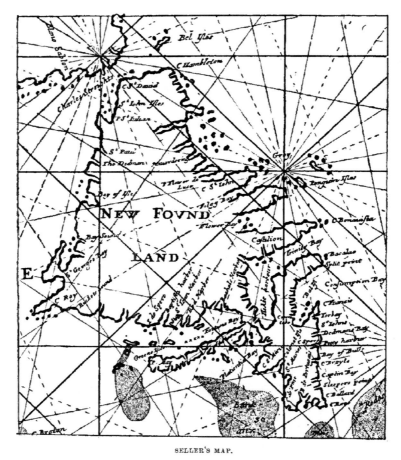

SELLER'S MAP.

From the English Pilot, 1671.

The details of this arrangement are now published, but there were many other questions agreed upon known only to the two conspirators and their immediate confidants; amongst these was, doubtless, the

M

agreement by which all the southern and western portion of Newfoundland, from Cape Race to Cape Ray, was passed over to France

No positive evidence, no State documents, can now be produced to prove this surrender of English territory, but the circumstances under which it took place, and the evidence of the contemporary records, leave little doubt that the occupation of Placentia by the French in 1662 was made with the connivance and consent of the English king

During both the administration of Cromwell and the reign of Charles I. no foreigner had attempted to make any permanent settlement in Newfoundland. Up to 1662 no Frenchman had ever lived a winter on the Island.[1]

I will describe, as well as it can be gathered from the records, the surrounding circumstances of the base surrender by which France, without firing a shot, obtained the largest and fairest portion of our Island colony. By this betrayal of English territory and English rights Charles planted in our midst our most bitter rival, he exposed our infant settlements to those murderous raids afterwards made on the English planters Not only did the king endanger the safety of this Island, but all the North American Colonies suffered in aftertime from this augmentation of French naval power in America.

The most important evidence on the subject is the testimony of Isaac Dethick, an English resident at Placentia. By this time the British inhabitants had spread themselves not only around the eastern coast, but some small parties had gone beyond Bonavista, fishing and furring as far as Notre Dame Bay, and some, like Dethick, had been attracted by the splendid position of Placentia, and had made it their residence —

"Deposition of John Raynor late deputy Governor in Newfoundland

"In 1662 a great French ship full of men and women put into Grand Placentia, where she landed a great number of soldiers and passengers who fortified the Harbour with 18 pieces of ordnance as one Isaac Dethick who was there affirmed

"Dethick saw the Governor's Commission under the great seal of France for the command of the whole country of Newfoundland, and the following year was forced to remove from his Plantation and settle at the Bay of Ards [Bay de Verds]

---

[1] Answer, in 1614, to the complaints presented to King James I by the Sieur de Busseanx, French Ambassador at the Court of His Majesty
The reply to the first point (which concerned Newfoundland) sets forth the title of England "to the fishery there, which is carried on every year with at least two hundred vessels and more than six thousand persons in the English Colony, who have always treated the French well, and protected them

in their fishing, and allowed them to leave their vessels until they return to fish the next year
"The French do not inhabit any part of Newfoundland, but are much further away, in a place called Canada, which they call New France, therefore the accusation against the English is most unjust and far from the truth, seeing they have never been near New France, neither hindered or disturbed the French fishery, nor done any injury

where deponent found him and took from him an account of the French proceedings which he sent for England by Mr. Robert Prowse to be presented to the King"[1]

Besides this testimony we have the further evidence of John Matthews of Ferryland, who appears to have been a sort of sheriff's officer or bailiff in the employ of the governors of the Ferryland plantation. Raynor and Captain Pearce were deputy-governors and also agents for Lord Baltimore when his patent was revived in 1660 Having to take proceedings against a Mr. Russell, in St Mary's, about a claim for rent, they heard at the same time that some Canadian Indians, who were allies of the French, were shooting and trapping in the same neighbourhood (then and now the finest game preserve in the Island) They despatched John Matthews to arrest Russell and the leader or chief of the Indians, and bring them to Ferryland to explain their proceedings to the Deputy-Governor. Matthews gives a graphic account of his adventures —

"These are to certify to whom it may concerne that I John Matthews in ye yeare 1662 being in ye Newfoundland was sent by Captain Pearce and Mr. Raynor the Honble Deputy-Governors with their warrants to St. Marys to bring one Mr. Russell ye Inhabitant there and ye master of ye Indians (who came to kill beavers and other beasts for ffurres) before them to Ffeiryland, but instead of having the warrant obeyed, a French Captain seized on me demanding what I came for. I replyed for ye said Mr Russell and ye Master of ye Indians to go before ye Governours to answer and give an account of their actions for making an attempt upon ye Islande without any authority from His Majesty of Great Brittaine , which he scornfully answered, saying we had no power there nor in any other of ye Southern parts of ye Lande but all did belong to ye Ffrench Kinge whereupon I averring that our King was King thereof and of all for about 30 or 40 leagues around about it, was taken prisoner and so kept tor about 2 dayes when ye French carryed me aboard and sett forward untill we came nigh Plaisance Fort which was furnished with 28 gunns from whence a shallop came out from ye Governour with command for our returne to St Maries in pursuite for ye Indians where by Gods providence I made my escape.

"I also further humbly testify that in the year (50) or (51) I having then a lawe-suit depending there against one Nicholas Redhood did procure a Commission out of ye High Court of Admiraltie directed to Sir David Kirke the then Governour to examine witnesses in that cause which said Commission was speeded and returned hither to ye Admiraltie in due forme of lawe.

"And whensover any differences arose between ye Planters and Inhabitants these ye said Sir David Kirke did always judge and determine the same , whereby ye said lande was peaceably and quietly governed to ye generall benefitt of ye population and no persons were suffered to carry wood away in shipps, only to cut what was necessary for fishing and all this I do testify upon my certaine knowledge to be true witness my hand this 27th day of January 1670.

"Jo Matthews"[2]

Lady Hopkings also states, "That the French declared that "King Louis had a grant from the King of England to take as his

[1] *Records*   [2] *B M MSS , Eg.* 2395.

" proper right from Cape Race round by the southward and westward
" to Cape Bonavista." [1]

I think we may fairly gather from these statements and from the
formal action of the French, their taking possession of a part of the
Colony in such an official manner, that King Charles had really
surrendered the best part of the Island to the French, leaving only from
Cape Race to Bonavista for the English. In further proof of this, in one
of his Orders in Council, the English boundary is given as between
Cape Race and Cape Bonavista.

Of course such a transaction was kept a profound secret from his
subjects both in England and America Poor dupes like Raynor, Lady
Hopkings, and Robert Prowse busied themselves with remonstrances
and petitions to the king about the monstrous aggression of the French

The petitioners presented their addresses and affidavits. In the Court
language still in use, " They were laid at the foot of the throne, and his
" Majesty was graciously pleased to receive the same." I have heard
a Hibernian orator and colonial official expatiate at great length on
this expression, as showing the peculiar interest the sovereign takes in
the Colony. This stereotyped answer, written by an under-clerk, was
the only reply the anxious settlers received from the king

The French showed excellent judgment in the selection of their
colonial capital. The situation of Placentia is extremely beautiful and
picturesque, the railway from Whitbourne, instead of descending the
north-east valley into the ancient French metropolis, by a curious freak
of engineering ascends, and from a lofty height the traveller sees the
whole panorama of Plaisance spread out before him, below is the
beautiful north-east arm dotted with islands, cottages, and farms,

---

[1] 1660 [? 1670.]

" The information and relation of the
Lady Hopkings who came purposely ffrom
Newfoundland to make knowne to His Royall
Majesty as ffollowes

" That the lat Sir David Knke being sent
for over by the late usurper and all his estate
taken away ffor his faithful service to His
late Majesty in Newfoundland and since
deceased.

" That Island hath been without a Governour and the Ffrench takeing notice thereof
have settled a garrison about eight or nine
years since at Plesentia and about two years
since another at *Chapian Rouge* 25 leagues
distance ffrom the other (which in Sir David
Kirke's lifetime they never durst attempt)
and by their yeerly intriguing and threatning
of ye English gives them just cause of appre-
hention of their own saffety and the losse of
the Island to ye great prejudice of His

Majesty's affaires, if not timely prevented,
and the rather the Governour for ye Ffrench
keeps ten vessels all ye winter there which
cairye 30 or 40 men a pece and are very well
fitted to coast, which vessels are sufficient to
destroy the English plantation as now it
stands And by sad experience the rutter [?]
coming . there without controlle took gounes
[guns] shippes cattle, goods and what he
pleased, to ye runing of His Majesty's subjects in Newfoundland for want of Government

" The Ffrench this year have given out
that the French King hasse a grant ffrom the
King of England to take as his proper writ
from Cape D race all to the Westward and
from Bonavista to ye Norward "

(*B M MSS, Eg.* 2395)

The date 1660 is evidently wrong; it
has been added by some Board of Trade
official

beyond is the shining sea, the beach, and the town, with its beautiful
Catholic chapel and houses.   As the traveller descends a very steep
grade to the Jersey side, the other part of the grand panorama unfolds
itself; the beautiful south-east arms sweeping past tall fir-crowned
bluffs in a winding circuit for eight miles.

It was not, however, for its romantic beauty, but for the sterner
reason of defence against the enemy, and for its practical advantage as
a trading and fishing port, that the French selected Placentia as their
capital and chief port in Newfoundland.

BURIN PLACENTIA BAY.

Whilst French colonisation has been a failure, her military organisation, and especially her skill in works of defence and military
engineering, have always been specially prominent.   The selection of
Placentia was fully justified——it was never captured by the English.

The first fort erected in 1662 was at the entrance of the gut on
the Placentia side;[1] the defence was afterwards strengthened by another
battery on the Jersey side.   The large battery on Castle Hill, Fort
Louis, is mistakenly placed by Bishop Howley and Dr. Mullock at
the entrance of the gut; the small batteries at Crevecour and Point
Verd are of later date.   Placentia was the Gibraltar of North America.

---

[1] This fort Le Hontan describes :—" It
stood upon a point of land so close to the
narrow entrance of the Harbour [the gut]
that ships going in graze so to speak upon
the angle of the bastion."

This first fort on the Placentia side of
the gut must not be confused with Fort Louis
on the hill, built afterwards, or with the
second fort erected on the Jersey side, which
made Placentia so strong.

Le Hontan was on duty at Placentia for
several years; he did not bear a very good
character.

It successfully resisted Commodore Williams' attack in 1692, and the still more formidable squadron of Hovenden Walker in 1711. The site was not only admirably situated for military purposes, it was equally well chosen as a metropolis of their fish trade It was a great oversight on the part of the English not to have secured this desirable harbour, its freedom from field ice in the spring makes it earlier than the eastern bays for fishing operations, its proximity to Cape St Mary's and its abundant supply of spring herring for bait renders it one of the very best places for the cod fishery.

The gut was then larger and much deeper than it is at present; the beach, with an extension at Little Placentia, an admirable ship harbour in Placentia arm, provided safety for their fleet and drying room for the large French catch.

Strategically, politically, and piscatorially, Placentia was admirably chosen as a capital place of defence and fishing centre. At a later period it became prominent as the only settlement in Newfoundland where there was an important resident French population, chapel, substantial fortress, and garrison

Our enemies did all in their power to entice the English to settle there. By a proclamation of Louis, about 1667, masters of ships were allowed five livres for every man and three for every woman they carried to Placentia Newfoundlanders were offered one year free subsistence—afterwards increased to three

The Colony did not flourish The first royal governor was an adventurer named Gargot; he had no salary, but was not left without remuneration He set up a royal store, and obliged all the fishermen to buy from him; one of his occupations was measuring out the beach room for the ships As she arrived, each vessel took as much water frontage as her foreyard measured, for a consideration Gargot would throw in a few more feet

All the French fishing admirals were under the Placentia governor; they had to report and be governed by his instructions Naturally the French are much more subservient to their superiors than the English. Garneau tells us the French Newfoundlanders were a free and hardy race They chafed under the tyranny of Gargot and his successor De La Poype, and petitioned the king against their harsh rule [1]

Five times before 1685 English buccaneers raided Placentia, and stripped the inhabitants of all their moveables The French Government, like the English, soon began to grudge the expense of the

[1] Baron Le Hontan says —"The French Governor look upon their places as a gold mine given them in order to enrich themselves, so that the public good must always march behind private interest"

garrison and fortifications at Placentia   Captain Wheler, Commander of the English convoy in 1684, says :—

"The French leave Placentia in July   They have large ships of 36 guns, about 30 vessels altogether   The French inhabitants are much fewer than ours, they have but one old ruined fort and little ammunition; the Inhabitants are as negligent as ours in the matter of strength.

"Our ships are not denied liberty to fish in the French districts   No forainers fish up the Eastern Coast, but upon the Banks the French frequent much.

"They have a Governor at Placentia   The first Master at each port is Admiral but receives his orders from the French Governor who is of great use to measure out rooms [and thus put an end to the constant fighting that went on about the debateable subject of fishing premises, known in Newfoundland as *rooms*].

"Seldom any convoy for the French Merchant vessels   At Trepasse but two or three French families where our nation and theirs fish without disagreeing.   The French begin to fish about 18 leagues north of Bonavista for 40 leagues [along the N E. coast] and are at utter variance with the Indians [Red Indians—Beothics, I presume, on account of the terrible massacre mentioned by Kirke] who are numerous and so the French never reside in winter and always have their arms by them   Six years since their trade was great—60 great ships   Any ship of another nation bearing proportion of expense of defence [in those days the attacks were from pirates] might fish.   They catch about 200 qtls per boat with five men and give high wages, the French come in June and stay sometimes until October. Trade decaying extremely   About 52° N. some Biscayners used to fish with no improvement.

"French have advantage of us, as there are plenty of fish at Placentia, and going sooner to market, their fishing ships gain considerably "[1]

This is a plain narration of facts, and agrees with the history of the times

To understand this weakness of both French and English in Newfoundland, we must bear in mind that from 1665 both countries were at war with the Dutch, then the greatest naval power in Europe They made two successful attacks on the English in Newfoundland—in 1665 on St John's, and in 1673 on Ferryland   In 1676, from the *English News Letter* of October 3, we have an account of a successful Dutch raid on the French :—

"The Merchants hear that six Dutch capers have quite destroyed the French fishing fleet in Newfoundland having taken 90 out of 100 sail that were there— They had afterwards landed and taken the Castle of Canida "[2]

It is probable this refers to Placentia, and may be exaggerated, but we may readily believe if the Dutch attacked the English settlements they would not spare their inveterate enemies the French, who had commenced a most unprovoked war against them.

Curiously enough, in studying the early history of the French colonies in America, we find the same causes at work which retarded

---

[1] *Records.*   [2] *Historical MS Comn Report*

Newfoundland. The first French settlers in Canada were under the control of "The company of one hundred associates"—they were greedy monopolists; like the West Country adventurers in Newfoundland, fishing and furring were their only occupations, and they did all in their power to prevent colonisation.

PLAN OF PLACENTIA.
From La Hontan's Nouveaux Voyages, 1703.

The fortifications were neglected, and agriculture so little attended to that, except under the walls of the forts, there was absolutely no cleared land; the country was to be kept for furring and fishing only

All this was changed, however, by the arrival of Frontenac, twice viceroy, the ablest ruler that ever guided the destiny of New France. It was under this gallant Frenchman and his distinguished subordinate, D'Iberville, that the subsequent successful attacks were made on Newfoundland in 1696 and 1697.

In 1676 the French fished at St. Maries, Coroneat (Colinet Island), St. Peter's, Great and Little St. Lawrence, Three Islands, Petit Nord, and several places west, besides Placentia, their chief place. As far as we can learn, the French had really only one permanent settlement — (Placentia), and this was begun in 1662 ; all the other places mentioned are merely resorted to by the ship fishermen from France for the fishing season, and were abandoned in the autumn.

We have clear proof of this in the evidence given on the inquiry about the damage to Johannis Ducarrow's fishing cabin and premises at Admiral's Beach and Colinet Island.[1] We find from testimony of the servants who confessed to the destruction of the cabin at Colinet Island, and their shelter in the vat at St. Mary's, that all these places were at that date, 1680, uninhabited. Thomson says, in 1676 —

"Placentia had two Forts thirteen guns fifteen families of which four are English That there were only two French families at Trepassey."[1]

There were probably guns and some small fortifications at St. Pierre, but at present it seems to me doubtful if there were any winter residents before 1670 Downing says, in 1670 the French had Placentia and St. Peter's fortified Mr. John Aylrod's description of two hundred and fifty families and 2,000 people, besides the 400 soldiers, is clearly exaggerated, after the treaty of Utrecht in 1713 only one hundred and eighty persons from all the French settlements in Newfoundland left the Island (in war time they would be within the forts), all had to go by the terms of the treaty. The only inhabited places then mentioned as belonging to the French were Placentia and St. Pierre Baudoin says that the French settlements were small compared with the English In 1702, when Sir John Leake destroyed St. Peter's, there was only one small fort with six guns. There were French residents in Fortune Bay in 1680. but few in number compared to the Jersey and English settlers

We get the following description of Placentia in 1681 from two Englishmen residing there, Stephen Destrick and one Molins. They say —

' The payment of French Fishermen is made by boat [bounty]
" The Fort of 12 guns is in ruins, not above 3 guns now mounted.

[1] *Board of Trade, Newfoundland*

" The Governor has no allowance from the King nor anything allowed for arms and ammunition but he fishes as other planters do and keeps 8 boats.

" The French have caught this year 300 to 400 qtls. per boat.

" Fish came in sooner upon that coast than on the Eastern shore.

" There are ships of 200 to 400 tons from Bordeaux and St. Jean de Luz, and 15 to 16 Biscainers of 20 and 24 guns.

" Ships of St. Malloes fish at St. Peters. There are 100 ships from St. Mary's to St. Peters and the trade is increasing.

" They let no English live among them except they turn Roman Catholics; and there is a Priest in every ship and they leave some behind to keep the people steadfast in their religion.

" The French have few plantations more than for herbs and roots and a few cattle and do so as we do in winter.

" French generally have a better catch and live cheaper, consequently make more gain.

" A fort at St. Peters is reported.

" There is no trade between the English and French planters.

" The *Biscainers* with ships of great force do fish to the northward of Bonavista and Salvage, and frequently with the French but not with us." [1]

PLACENTIA FARM AND FISHING STAGE.
From Potherie's Histoire, 1722.

The last of the great Spanish fleet now came only by stealth and under the protection of the French. They were up to this date, 1680, still the great whalers and seal killers on this coast. A shore seal fishery was carried on from the very first settlement by the English, on a small scale, with nets and boats. The product fluctuated very much.

In reading the histories of England and America about this period, the fisheries are almost completely ignored; the truth is that writers love the heroics and despise the economics; the personal, the picturesque, is always attractive, whilst the plain, prosaic aspect of human life, the

[1] *Board of Trade, Newfoundland.*

adventures of commerce, the increase of human food, are unnoticed by historians.

Religion and economics are the greatest influences in the world, the two most potent factors in the progress or retardation of the human race. Nothing comes out clearer in our North American history than the preponderating effect of the fishery.

The relative influence and strength of France and England in the New World was entirely controlled by this business. Towards the close of the Stuart period, at the end of the seventeenth century, the French fishery in Newfoundland and the Gulf of St. Lawrence rose to abnormal dimensions; it is variously estimated as employing from sixteen thousand to twenty thousand men; it extended to Nova Scotia, Cape Breton, St. John's Island, now Prince Edward Island, Gaspé, and Newfoundland. The naval power of France rose in proportion: all the

SALMONIER, ST. MARY'S BAY.

English expeditions against New France and Acadié were miserable failures, whilst under Frontenac and D'Iberville the English possessions were raided from Newfoundland to Hudson's Bay. Until the last fall of Louisbourgh and Quebec, France threatened the very existence of the American colonies. She had then undoubtedly the preponderance of sea power in America.

The fishery is the recognised nursery for her navy; the only alleged excuse for the extravagant bounties given to her fishermen at St. Pierre and Iceland is to secure a supply of men for the Marine.

At the profligate Court at St. James's, the Devonshire gentry still held a foremost place; their influence for evil against the Newfoundland settlers was immensely increased by the support of Sir Josiah Child, author of a pamphlet, first published in 1665, "A New Discourse on Trade." He issued a second edition, very much enlarged (from which these extracts are taken) on December 24th, 1694.

His character has been powerfully drawn by Macaulay. An exceedingly able merchant, a vigorous writer, with immense wealth, which he used most unscrupulously to bribe and corrupt. This great monopolist, head of the East India Company, was the evil genius of Newfoundland. He begins his discourse on the various trades by enumerating .—

" Amongst the Trades not yet lost is the Newfoundland fish trade [1] In the year 1605 the English employed 250 sail of ships great and small in fishing upon that coast and it is now too apparent that we do not so employ from all parts above 80 ships. So that the price of fish has increased from seventeen rials—eight shillings and sixpence—to twenty-four rials or twelve shillings as it now sells in this country.

" This being the case of England in relation to this trade it is certainly worth the enquiry—

" 1st How we came to decay in it? 2ndly. What means may be used to recover our ancient greatness or at least to prevent our further diminution therein?

" The decay I attribute, First and principally to the growing liberty which is every year more and more used in Romish countries, as well as others, of eating flesh in Lent and on Fish days.

" 2 To a late abuse crept in that trade of sending over private boat keepers which hath much diminished the number of fishing ships

" 3 To the great increase of the French fishery of Placentia and other ports on the back side of Newfoundland.

" 4 To the several wars within these twenty years which have much impoverished the Western Merchants, and reduced them to carry on a great part of that trade at Bottomry taken upon adventure of the ship at 20 % per annum.

" What means may be used to recover it. For this two contrary ways have been propounded.

" Firstly to send a Governour to reside there, as well for the defence of the country against invasion, as to manage the fishery there by Inhabitants upon the place, this hath often been propounded by the Planters and some merchants in London.

" The second way propounded and which is directly contrary to the former is by West Country Merchants and owners of the fishing ships, and that is to have *no Governour nor Inhabitants permitted to reside at Newfoundland nor any passengers or private boat keepers suffered to fish at Newfoundland This latter way is most agreeable to my proposition and if it could be effected I am persuaded would revive the decayed English fishing trade at Newfoundland and be otherwise greatly for the advantage of this Kingdom* and that for the following reasons —

" Because most of the provisions the Planters do make use of viz Bread, Beef, Pork, Butter, Cheese, Clothes, and Irish Bandel Cloth, Linen and Woollen, Irish Stockings, as also nets, hooks, lines &c. they are supplied with from New England and Ireland and with wine oyle and linnen by the salt ships from France

[1] Preface

and Spain, in consequence the labour as well as the clothing and feeding of so many men is lost to England . . .

"If it be the interest of all trading nations principally to encourage navigation especially those trades which employ most shipping . .   . . . . then certainly it is the interest of England to discountenance and abate the number of Planters at Newfoundland for if they should increase it will happen to us as it hath to the fishery of New England which many years since was managed by English ships from the Western Ports but as Plantations there increased fell to the sole employment of the people settled there and nothing of the trade is left the poor old Englishmen but the liberty of carrying now and then by courtesie or purchase a ship-loading of fish to Bilboa when their own New England ships are better employed or not at leasure to do it . . .

"It is manifest before there were boat keepers fish was sold cheaper than it is now by 40 % Reason because boat keepers being able fishermen and earlier on the ground beat the ship fishermen but after driving away English ship fishermen from New England and Newfoundland they became lazy"

Then follow the usual West County arguments against a governor. Speaking of the fishing admirals he says :—

"A Government there is already of ancient custom amongst the masters of the ships to which the fishermen are inured and that free from oppression and adapted to the trade insomuch *that though a better might be wished,* I never hope to see it.

"New England is the most prejudicial plantation to this kingdom because of all the American plantations His Majesty has none so apt for building of shipping as New England, nor comparably so qualified for the breeding of seamen not only by reason of the natural industry of that people but principally by reason of their cod and mackerel fisheries and in my poor opinion there is nothing more prejudicial and in prospect more dangerous to any Mother Country than the increase of shipping in her colonies plantations or Provinces"[1]

Well might Bacon expatiate on the narrow selfishness of traders. This shrewd business man could not see that prosperous colonies were England's best customers In order to rightly appreciate the enormous influence of a monopolist like Child in the corrupt age of Charles II, we must try and picture to ourselves the president of one of the gigantic American trusts of our own time owning all the ministers of State, and the Courts, with unlimited money and unlimited power to bribe, and no questions asked about funds

Child never rendered an account of the thousands he spent in bribery—£10,000 to Charles, £10,000 to his brother, the Duke of York, diamonds and thousands to the king's mistresses and ministers Imagine all this if you can, and then you can faintly realise the enormous power of this gigantic bully, this Restoration Jay Gould, on the destinies of Newfoundland

The main object of Child was to defend the East India Company It shows how great was his ability and the power of his corrupting

[1] SIR JOSIAH CHILD, *A New Discourse on Trade*, 1694, pp. 205-215

influence, that he maintained himself to the last against all his opponents. The Newfoundland matter was only a trifle to amuse his leisure and help his brother monopolists, the West Countrymen.

This plan, so speciously sketched out to exterminate the Newfoundland Colonists, although determined upon, was not immediately carried into effect, even the king and his advisers shrunk from such cold-blooded cruelty. In 1665, when this pamphlet was first published, we were at war with the Dutch, and it was thought advisable that some permanent settlers should be left to defend the Colony.

Various minor attempts, however, were made to carry out this policy piecemeal; a very valuable series of parliamentary papers[1] on Newfoundland affairs set forth the various measures that were taken to destroy the colonial population

SIR JOSIAH CHILD.
From an engraving after Riley.

Neither the Commissioners for Foreign Trade and Plantation, nor the Western Adventurers, nor least of all Sir Josiah Child, saw anything extraordinary or improper in this decision to destroy a whole population of Englishmen, to condemn them to ruin, extermination, and exile from their cherished homes and all the accumulated wealth of several generations. This paper, which is too long to quote in full, begins by setting forth the state of the fishery in 1644, when, as the Western Adventurers allege :—

" There were 270 ships annually employed in the Newfoundland fishery besides those who brought salt and carried the fish to market computing the ships at 80 tons each and for every 100 tons 50 men and 10 boats. There were in all 21,600 tons 10,800 seamen 2,160 boats. To each boat is allowed 5 men. Usual catch 200 to 300 qtls., which was then sold at from 14 to 16 rials—7s. to 8s. per qtl. They attribute the subsequent decline to the civil war and to the settlements encouraged by Treworgie.

" By letters patent 26 Jany. 1660 this additional clause was inserted in the new charter: that no person was to be carried or transported in any of the ships except those of the ships company or such as are to plant and do intend to settle there. In 1663 circular letters were written to the mayors and magistrates of West Country Towns to enforce this order.

[1] I am indebted to George H. Emerson, Q.C., for this work, which formerly belonged to John Hatt Noble, Deputy Naval Officer in Newfoundland.

" In 1669 an order was made to obtain the return of the names of offenders against this rule and in the meantime to stop them proceeding on the voyage to Newfoundland Then followed a long dispute about the appointment of a Governor which after a protracted debate in the Council was finally rejected in 1670

" The Western adventurers proposed that the inhabitants should transport themselves to Jamaica, St Kitts, or some other of His Majesty's plantations. This suggestion the Council refused to adopt.

" In 1674 solicitation was again made for the appointment of a Governor.

" On the 15th April 1675 their Lordships the Committee of the Council for Trade reported That the French had considerably advanced their fishery in Newfoundland, that the people of New England annually took 60,000 qtls of fish on their own coast, that the adventurers had lost many of their ships in the late war, that the inhabitants destroyed the woods and whatsoever the adventurers left behind, that they occupied the best places, sold brandy and seduced many to stay behind, that a Governor could not cure any part of these evils because the Planters were scattered in 25 harbours 80 leagues apart; that the Trade could not support the charge of forts and a Governor, and that in winter the colony was defended by ice and in summer by the ship fishermen.

" So that unless there was proper reasons for a colony they could see none for a Governor; and against a Colony there are not only the rigours of the climate and the infertility of the soil but that they, the inhabitants, chiefly consumed the products of New England and other foreign parts. . . . So that on the whole their Lordships having recourse unto the Rules of 1670 found them all so proper and effectual for the advantage of the Trade as to need only the following additions to make their trade revive and flourish.—

"That all Plantations and inhabiting in that Country be discouraged, and in order thereupon that the Commander of His Majestys Convoy should have a Commission to declare at his going this year His Majestys will and pleasure to all planters *that they come voluntarily away* and in case of disobedience that the charter be put in execution next year, for in this single point consists the validity and good effect of the whole Regulation. That the Convoy help and assist those in their transportation who desire to return home, and do declare that if they choose to betake themselves to any other of His Majesty's Plantations, that the Governors are wrote unto to receive them with all favour

' On the 5th May following His Majesty in Council thought fit for the several considerations in the said Report mentioned to order the Commander of His Convoy bound to Newfoundland *to admonish the Inhabitants either to return home to England, or to betake themselves to others of his Plantations,* and to direct that letters be prepared unto the severall Governors of the said Plantations, that in case any of the said Inhabitants of Newfoundland should arrive within their respective Governments, that they be received with favour And that all convenient help and assistance towards their settlement be afforded unto them

" And on the 27 Jany 1675 His Majesty after due consideration had of the best ways and means of regulating, securing, and improving the fishing Trade in Newfoundland passed the New Charter which recited and confirmed all the Old Laws, and several others were added for the better Government of the Fishery. which if they had been as steadily supported and executed, as they were carefully concerted, in all probability, the subjects of France and the people of New England had reaped very little benefit by their fisheries, and this valuable branch of the British Trade had been firmly re-established and secured.

" The Additional Regulations to the Charter were as follows —

" 1st That His Majestys subjects may take bait and fish in Newfoundland, and cut wood for stages &c. provided they submit unto and observe the Rules and Orders that are or shall be established.

"2nd. *That no alien take bait* or fish between Cape Race and Cape Bonavista.

"3rd. *That no Planter cut down any wood or inhabit within six miles of the shore*

"4th. That no Planter shall take up any of the stages &c. before arrival of the fishermen and that they be all provided for.

"5th That no Master of a fishing vessel transport any seamen or others to Newfoundland unless they belong to the ships company

"6th That no more than 60 persons to the 100 Tons be allowed to sail

"7th That every fifth Man carried out of England be a green man and not a seaman, and that the Masters provide in England Victuals and other necessaries for the whole voyage, salt only excepted.

"8th That no vessel do depart directly for Newfoundland in any year before the 1st of March.

"9th That the Masters give Bonds in £100 to return all persons to England except those employed in carrying fish to market

"10th No Master to take up any stage already built with less than twenty-five men No fishermen to remain in the country at the end of the voyage.

"11th Admirals, Rear-Admirals and Vice-Admirals are authorised and required to preserve the peace in the Harbours as well as on shore and to see the rules of the fishery put in execution

"12th To secure and bring home offenders to England

"13th. That they yearly publish on the 20th of Sepr these orders.

"14th That they keep journals and deliver Copies to the Council

"And lastly because there is no Court Martial in Newfoundland at present, that if any man there shall kill another, or steal goods to the value of 40s. he shall be brought a prisoner to England, and his crime made known to one of H M Principal Secretaries of State to the end order may be given to punish such offenders according to Law.

"Under these encouragements [says the report] the Western Adventurers immediately returned to the fishery."

The report goes on to say —

"However the adventurers being encouraged by the Lords of the Committee *to put the laws of the charter in execution, they began in 1676 to restrain the disorders of the Planters* and to prevent the transportation of their servants; but they were restrained upon the Petition of the said Planters in November following and the solicitation of those who were either excited by the hopes of procuring advantage for themselves or influenced by the French whose fishery must have been soon rendered precarious if the Charter had been observed"

This is part of "The Report of the Lords Commissioners for Trade " and Plantations to His Majesty relating to the Newfoundland Trade " and Fishery dated 19 Decr 1718."

The Western Adventurers, having obtained this most inhuman order to extirpate the inhabitants, went over to Newfoundland flushed with success,[1] and immediately on their arrival began the work of destruction

---

[1] PETITION OF THOMAS MARTIN, 29 Jany 1677

"I have been in the trade from a boy and now command a shipp The Fishermen by their late Patent call all that part where the English cure their fish in St John's their own.

Coming from the West Indies in 1676 I asked the then admiral for roome for my sailing crew to fish and cure. He answered I was *an alien* and not concerned in the Patent and therefore I was forced to hire a stage

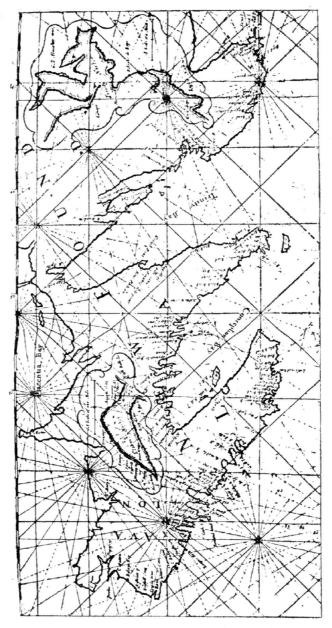

THORNTON'S TRADING PART OF NEWFOUNDLAND, WITH INSET PLANS OF ST. JOHN'S AND TRINITY.

From the English Pilot, 1689.

The king had delivered their enemies the planters into their hands, so they considered they had full liberty to wreak their vengeance. The poor settlers at first were frightened and dismayed, there was terrible havoc and damage; Oxford says "fifteen hundred men would not in three weeks repair the wanton injury and destruction" committed in the first few days by these brutal adventurers.[1]

However, the planters, though taken at first by surprise, banded themselves together under the leadership of the four most prominent settlers in the Colony, Pynn, John Downing,[2] Oxford, and Geo Kirke. The Pynns, a gallant race, long settled in Harbour Grace, stuck to their rights, and sharply attacked their assailants, Oxford and John Downing headed the defence in St John's, and George Kirke took command on the southern shore. Immediately Sir John Berry,[3] commander of the convoy, and Captain Davis[4] arrived, they put a stop to further attacks. John Downing, the son of a former governor, was elected by all the

[1] THOMAS OXFORD'S PETITION.

"The humble Petition of Thomas Oxford Merchant and late Inhabitant of St John's.

"That he and his predecessors have been possessed of houses stages &c in the said Harbour of St John's for about seventy years but of late they not able to call anything their own by reason of West Country men, who pretend as priveledge not only to take away houses &c, but threatened their persons both by blows and imprisonment which hath caused your Petitioner and family to quit that Country almost to his utter ruine. Such damage was done last year in severall Harbours, that fifteen hundred men in the Harbour of St John's will hardly make good the damage done there in three weeks, besides the loss of their goods which they violently take away. Petitioner prays for redress Petitions for a Governor with great guns and ammunition and an Orthodox Minister, who they will maintain at their own cost, so that those removed may be invited to return &c" (*Board of Trade*)

[2] EXTRACTS from Reports in which John Downing is mentioned

"Acc't of ye Inhabitants in St John's Harbour & Quitevide thereunto belonging with their names and what wives and children they have as also their men and women servants and boats they employ.

In St John's Harbour	Wives.	Sons	Dau'trs.	Women Servt.	MenServants Winter	Sumr	Boats
John Downing	01	00	03	02	15	12	05

Rec'd the 11th Oct. 1860.

An Acc't of ye Planters belonging to St John's Harbour 1682

Planters' Names	Men	Women	Children	Boats	Stage.	flats.
Jno Downing -	1	03	00	02	01	01

[3] Sir John Berry, whose humane exertions and firmness mainly prevented the expulsion of the settlers, began life as a West Country fisherman in Newfoundland, his brother was also in the fish trade His career was a very remarkable one He joined the Royal Navy first as a boatswain in the *Swallow* ketch; for his gallantry under the following circumstances, the Governor of Jamaica made him a lieutenant —The *Swallow*, Captain Insam, was sent to capture a pirate They found the enemy at anchor off Hispaniola Insam had only 40 men and eight guns, whilst the pirate had 20 guns and 60 men Insam did not want to fight Berry ordered him into his cabin, took command, and gallantly captured the pirate, but was tried by court martial for coercing his commander, but honourably acquitted. Sir John is described in the *Biographia Nautica* as a great, gallant and good man, who had received the honour of knighthood for his bravery against the Dutch at the battle of Solebay; he had a pension from the king.

[4] Captain Davis, R N, had been engaged in the Newfoundland trade as a West Country skipper before he was promoted to the Royal Navy

inhabitants as their representative and delegate to proceed to England and defend their rights.

To appreciate the full measure of this iniquitous order to destroy the property of the Newfoundland planters and to force them out of the country, we must pause for a moment to consider their position. Merchants and planters had been settled in St. John's and around the coast for many years anterior even to Gilbert's arrival. The tilt and the log hut had long disappeared; they lived in substantial, comfortable wooden houses. Everyone acquainted with the Newfoundland trade is aware of the number of buildings that are required, and how large is the expense of a great fishing establishment. Baudoin speaks of the great wealth of the settlers at Carbonear and Harbour Grace. Captain Davis, R N, a good authority, speaks of one thousand two hundred settlers. A great many of these planters were substantial men, who not only had their houses, stages, &c, and all the paraphernalia of the Newfoundland business; they also possessed cleared land, horses, cattle, sheep, &c. Downing himself was conspicuous as a farmer; he had a small plantation near the present Virginia Lake, known to the old settlers, and called on the old maps "Downing's Pond." By this peremptory order of January 27, 1676, all the Newfoundland settlers were called upon immediately to relinquish their property, to surrender at a moment's notice the patient labour of a lifetime.

Englishmen accustomed to their own highly cultivated land, the labour of many generations, can hardly understand the strong ties of affection which bound the Newfoundlanders to their rugged homes. Their little gardens and fields were rude and rough compared with English culture, but they were the work of their own hands; the apple trees and small bushes brought from the old country, tended with loving care, had developed and blossomed and borne fruit, the admiration and wonder of the little settlement. To be driven from home and the smiling fields and gardens, carved, or as Downing puts it, "cleansed from the wildernesse," was a terrible wrench at their heart strings, a separation that seemed like death.

The poet has sung to us of the sorrows of Evangeline and of the evictions from Grand Pré. The Acadians were not in a more miserable plight than the poor Newfoundland settlers during that long period from 1675 to 1677, whilst the terrible edict hung over their heads. With what anxiety in their lonely homes they awaited during the weary winter months the result of Downing's mission!

The ministry, gagged and bound by the bribes of Child and his colleagues, were for a time deaf to the urgent demands from the colonists for protection against these barbarous attacks. Bye-and-bye, however, the eloquent appeal of Downing and his counsel began to stir public opinion.   There were many West Country towns that gave the settlers strong support   John Carter, Mayor of Poole, sent—

"A set of reasons why the Inhabitants should not be removed signed by several Merchants and Masters of Ships which for many years have used the trade of fishing there." [They declare] "the Inhabitants are faithful subjects and that the most eminent of them now resident there, were forced over in the time of the late civil war for their loyalty to His Majesty"[1]

Besides the assistance the settlers received from Poole and Weymouth, there seems to have been a strong party on their side both in Bideford and Barnstaple.   All the man-of-war officers were with the settlers. A careful examination of the lengthy documents put forward by both sides shows how well Downing worked up his case   There was a most protracted debate;[2] the decision, long hung in the balance, was at last given in favour of the planters.

Sir John Berry and Captain Davis and several other enlightened West Country men came forward with such arguments on behalf of the planters, that even the Court had to give way.   A peremptory order first went forth by the ship *St. John's Merchant*, leaving Dartmouth in March 1677, directing the masters and seamen to forbear all violence to the planters, and in May came the following order.—

"That the Planters in Newfoundland be continued in possession of their Houses and stages according to the usage of the last years, until further orders."[3]

As the reader will see from the petition of Oxford,[4] they asked for protection for the future.   Their children were growing up without

---

[1] *Records*

[2] The following letter is in the *Plymouth Records*, Prowse was very active on the settlers' side —

R. PROWSE TO WM. GOULD.
14 March 1670

"We heare of your bad success at the choice of Mr Reynell that your boone companion were too hard a party for you. I suppose you hardly return before the terme because tis supposed the House may not sit above 14 days longer therefore I advise you that your Newfoundland business is passed the King in Councill and the Duke of York is by one order to be attended, the Attorney Generall by another, and there is another order that is to come down to strengthen ye business before it passes into a Patent. I am out of purse already &c &c and am taken sick

"Yours,—R. Prows"

There is also a letter to Wm. Gould about R Prowse, from which it appears he

was trying in a small way, by presents, to counteract the bribes of the other side.

[3] *Records*

[4] PROPOSALS OF WM. DOWNING AND THOMAS OXFORD ON BEHALF OF THE INHABITANTS.

(Recd. 29 April 1679)

"To fortify St John's, naturally very strong, with twenty five guns and two hundred small arms and some small arms to defend the creek Que de Vide to prevent surprise. This Que de Vide is a place where a few skiffs fish, cleared through the rocks by some Inhabitants of St John's, as well as other conveniences about that harbour to the value of some of thousands of pounds

"To fortify Carbonere with fifteen great guns and eighty small arms. Salvadge forty leagues from St. John's being about seven years since cleared and possessed only by Inhabitants, never before used by any to fortify it, ten guns and eighty small arms Ferryland seventeen guns and a hundred

the ordinances of religion, there was no one to command or organize in case of defence, and there were no fortifications.

They were not allowed, however, to have the Governor, established minister, or forts they prayed for. The residents offered to group themselves in any towns or harbours selected by the Government, to assist about fortifications, and to bear their share of all expenses.

It is only on the assumption of bribery that we can explain the minister's obstinacy in refusing to organize the defences of the Colony. France, their ancient enemy, was at their gate; twice the Dutch had successfully attacked St. John's and Ferryland. De Ruyter declared when he captured St. John's on the 6th of June 1665, that if there had been six guns mounted he would not have ventured in.

ADMIRAL DE RUYTER.

The commerce between Newfoundland and the North American Colonies, generally referred to in our Records as " New England," but which at this period embraced New York and Philadelphia, had risen from its modest commencement in 1645 to considerable dimensions; it was largely increased during the time of the Commonwealth.

The New Englanders, it has been noticed,[1] were mostly traders, not fishermen. They found a lucrative market for inferior fish, first in the English West India Islands, and afterwards amongst the French,

---

small arms. Fformous eighteen guns and sixty small arms. In what other Harbours besides St. John's it shall be thought fitt for them to settle, it is not desired to give any hindrance to the Fishing ships but they may fish in any of these places, the Inhabitants enjoying such convenient houses and stages as they have formerly built and now enjoy and no more, but as their children grow up they may accordingly enlarge.

"That a Government may be settled to defend them and the Country especially against the French, who are very powerfull there, and against some West Country Merchants whom they have long groaned under.

"For the preservation of navigation they desire to pass their men back and forward by freight or hyer. . . . . Inhabitants will be always willing to protect boats left by fishing ships. . . . .

"The Inhabitants desire (to prevent malicious pretence) that an equal number of Masters be with them to decide all differences.

"Queen Elizabeth was proclaimed Queen of the Whole Country but now the French enjoy two thirds and so far from complaints of them by West Country men that they would not owne any settled there although too much apparent, as appears by the oathes of Oxford T. C. Martin and N. Tront and Masters of Convoys. They humbly beg the Governor may have power over both Inhabitants and fishermen equally, and that they may have a Minister and fforrifications and what also Your Honourable Board think fit."
—(Board of Trade, Newfoundland.)

[1] See p. 153.

Dutch, and Spanish possessions, they were not allowed by the French or Spaniards to trade with their Islands, except to barter fish for molasses, they came first to Newfoundland with cattle, corn, lumber, lime, salted beef, pork, pitch, &c In the course of fifty years the English planters, who had previously obtained all their provisions from England by 1680, received nearly all their supplies from New England.

The planters' best fish, known already in the trade as " prime merchantable codfish," was sold to the English merchants or to traders, who came in the sack ships ; the payment was always made by bills on England at 60 or 90 days, these drafts were the usual currency of the Colony. Except for occasional payments in these bills or in gold the trade between British North America and our Island was essentially a barter trade.

The New Englanders, the steadfast friends of the Newfoundlanders, and zealous for their own rights and liberties, gave material aid in the fierce struggle with the West Countrymen Child and his colleagues were fiercer against them even than against the Newfoundland planters ; one witness declares the New Englanders spoke infamously about His Sacred Majesty King Charles II

There was a constant intercourse between the two countries West Country servants smuggled away came back in a few seasons as genuine New England men, they cursed, and drank, and swore, in a way to horrify the Puritan divines, but being good sailors and good fishermen their blasphemies were forgiven ; " ungodly men and swearers, fishermen chiefly from Newfoundland," is Hubbard's description of them.

Besides their trade in produce and West India fish for the negroes, and the Weatherfield onion business, the Americans soon drove a big trade in rum [1] Artemus Ward speaks of the New England rum and the measles as equally disagreeable No doubt the compound was villainous, it was probably worse than the Spanish aguardiente, or the worst French brandy. It had, however, two distinct merits for the fishermen, it was very strong and very cheap. Probably the planter bought it wholesale for not more than 25 cents a gallon, by 1789 it was retailed out to fishermen at $1·20 a gallon, more than double the old-fashioned price

---

[1] It is said that previous to the commencement of this trade, molasses was thrown away by the planters, and that this article, now so extensively used in commerce, was first saved and put into casks to be brought to New England and distilled into rum — (SABINE)

The American colonists at this period did a·trade, mostly contraband, all over the world; besides sending fish to market, they were running negroes from Africa, whaling, smuggling, and frequently selling their fine ships in England. One great business in Newfoundland was stealing servants from the West Countrymen. For his passage the kidnapped fisherman had to serve a long period, as a kind of white bond slave. Probably Massachusett's gave a premium on the introduction of desirable emigrants; but, however that may be, there can be no doubt that the servants were smuggled away. The colonial records are full of statements to that effect, of which the following is an example:—

> " REPORT of Captain DANIEL JONES, R N , H.M S. *Diamond*
>
> " Bay Bulls 12th Sepr 1682.
>
> " Did not arrive until Aug. 23d Admiralty instructions to sail 1st Sepr. with convoy weather permitting I have sent to your Honour four Bonds for I find none that violate your rules so much as ye Traders from New England spiriting away men. I was an eye witness of one at St. John's coming in with 11 hands and sailing with 20 in addition had not my pinnace brought him to anchor. So I took bonds of the New England men and acquainted Captain Wren of H.M S. *Centurion.* Bad fishery only 150 qtls. per boat, not as good as reported the French have made Nothing but confusion and disorder here they require a Governour.
>
> " Bonds of John Sawley of Salem, Mass., of Geo. Snell of Portsmouth or Piscadawery New Hampshire of Thomas Harvey of Portsmouth N H. and of William Pepperill of Portsmouth N.H , not to take away men from Newfoundland "[1]

Treworgie had combined in his person the anomalous positions of chief factor to the New England merchants in Newfoundland and the governorship of the Colony, he was a perfectly honest man, and seems to have performed both duties to the satisfaction of his employers At his death the position of chief factor of the American colonies fell to Mr. Gould, who appears on all occasions during this reign as representing New England, and advocating their interests in opposition to the English fishermen.

It is impossible now to give any exact figures about the colonial trade with Newfoundland, it was carried on in an underhand way, its operations were carefully concealed from the captains of the Royal Navy. In their annual reports the only notices to be found of the Americans are accounts of their " spiriting away " the West Countrymen's servants When Downing writes of eight New England vessels coming to the Island he must have meant St John's, he had no means of knowing how many other vessels visited the distant outposts, and traded off their goods for fish and furs, berries, cod's-tongues and fish-sounds, taking their balances in merchants' bills on England Early in the eighteenth

[1] *Board of Trade, Newfoundland*

century at least forty[1] vessels came from the American colonies to Newfoundland, Palliser estimated the trade in 1765 at half a million dollars annually, and by the commencement of the Revolution it had risen to one and a half millions of dollars

　　By the end of Charles II.'s reign New England had so marvellously increased and extended her agricultural and commercial operations that she was pretty well able to supply our Island planters with nearly everything they required.[2]　The two countries on which the wrath of the West Countryman and Child was poured out are singularly enough Ireland and New England.　The monopolists treat both these great English dependencies as foreign countries, and decidedly hostile and opposed to the interests of England

　　The fault of poor Erin, her glaring offence in the eyes of the Devonshire men, was her woollen manufactures, which were absurdly cheap and remarkably good ; in the plantations they were, like Irish

[1] AMERICAN VESSELS COMING TO NEWFOUNDLAND IN 1698

[Many of these vessels made several voyages to the Island in each year]

Where from	Master's Name	Tons	Port of Call in Newfoundland.	Fish bought	Inward Cargo	Destination outwards.
				Quintals		
Carolina	Wm Clay	30	Renowse	350	Provisions	Barbadoes.
New York	Thos Glave	75	Bay Bulls	1,200	Do	Bilboa
Carolina	T Phelps	50	Carbonear	400	Provisions and rum	Barbadoes.
Bermoodes	S Perley	30	Bay Verds	200	Salt and rum	Do.
Boston	T Barrington	60	St John's	—	Provisions	New England.
Montserrat	N Hawker	30	Do	100	Rum and sugar	Montserrat
Lime (Lima)	Thos Thomas	80	Brigus	800	Provisions and salt	Lime (Lima).
Antigoe (Antigua)	William Wood	54	Port de Grave	500	Salt, rum, and molasses	Oporto.
New England	Michl Gill	40	St John's	—	Pork and cyder	New England.
Boston	Jno Watkins	30	Do	—	Rum and cyder	Boston.
Do	N Easter	50	Do	—	Rum and molasses	Do
New England	Samuel Mould	80	Do	1,800	Rum and sugar	Jamaica
Barbadoes	Christopher Munke	200	Do.	2,000	Do	Oporto.
Boston	T Pry	41	Do	500	Rum, sugar, and bread.	Do.
New England	Wm. Law	50	Do	—	Provisions	New England.
Boston	John Pitts	30	Do.	—	Salt and molasses.	Boston.
St John's, New England.	R. Holdsworth	25	Do	—	Do	Piscattaway
Piscattaway	John Card	45	Do	—	Boards	Do.
New England	William Follett	126	Do	—	Deals	New England.
Bermoodes	Terence Smith	80	Harbour Grace	450	Salt	Virginia, in ballast.
Boston	John Thacker	40	Ferriland	600	Rum and sugar	Barbadoes.

(*Board of Trade, Newfoundland.*)

　　By about 1690 New England was exporting boots and shoes to Newfoundland. In the manifest of a cargo sent for the use of the St John's garrison in 1697 are 200 pairs of shoes, 200 pairs of stockings, 26 boxes of medicine, and some garden seeds, "liv hoggs and fowles," 19 bushels of turnpe 3 bushels of carrots, 10 hhds. of molasses, and 1 hhd of "Yorke Tobacco" (*Board of Trade*).

pork and Irish beef and Irish "youngsters,'[1] half the price of the English article, and somehow they got to be the leading staples in the Newfoundland trade. The cheapest goods have always been the ones selected for the planters' and fishermen's use

It was to buy these Irish woollens, "Frises, Bandel-cloths," "stockins,' pork, beef, butter, and to engage Irish servants, that the West Country-men first touched at Waterford and Cork on their way out to New-foundland, and thus commenced the Irish Newfoundland trade in "youngsters" and provisions.

The first Irishmen in the Colony were these youngsters, shipped for two summers and a winter; as Baudoin tells us, they were servants to the English, who treated them ill During the troubled times of 1690, the period of the wars in Ireland and the battle of the Boyne, the peasants were only too glad to flee from the country, so the bye-boat keepers took them out in the West Country vessels in still larger numbers By this time it had become an established practice for the Devonshire vessels to call at Waterford, Cork, and other harbours on the south coast of Ireland, principally Waterford, to take in a supply of provisions, manufactures and youngsters. I notice a request of the merchants in 1690 for the convoy to call at Cork for forty-eight hours.

Gradually these brave Irish boys amalgamated with the English settlers, married the planters' daughters, and became an important part of the resident population; compared however with the English, their numbers at first were small The large Irish population now resident about St. John's and the southern portion of the Island is chiefly the result of the emigration to this country which took place at the end of the eighteenth and the early part of the nineteenth century

Lest I should be accused of putting the case against the ship fishermen too strongly, the last of their proposals in the reign of Charles II., on the much disputed question of settling the Colony " with a governor, a minister, forts, and great guns," is given. In 1680 the Commissioners for Foreign Plantations, who were merely the mouth-pieces of Devonshire, declared :—

"That to entrust the regulating of the fishery in a Governor will tend greatly to the prejudice of the Newfoundland fishery . . But if His Majesty should think fit to fortify the Harbor of St John's and to make a Governor of the Fort and to arm the Governor with a military power to command the people of that country (*on occasion*) for their defence, and with civil power for punishing vice and keeping good order—*without having any power over the Fishery* or infringing the

---

[1] In the ordinary way a youngster in Newfoundland meant an unmarried servant, just as a boy in Ireland is an unmarried man and remains a boy even when he is eighty.

charter—they thought the same might be of good use, and no prejudice to the Trade and His Majesty's Customs." [1]

· The same able statesmen a few years later modified their opinion about planters France had just invaded the Island, and laid all the fishing establishments in ruins. The Commissioners then expressed their opinion, after referring to the necessity for forts and soldiers :—

"That Planters in moderate numbers were at all times convenient for the preparation and preservation of boats, stages, and other things necessary for the fishery *but they should not exceed one thousand.*" [1]

· There is one further suggestion, somewhat later, from a military Solomon,—the lieutenant-governor of the Island, Major Elford ·—

"That they allow no women to land in the Island and that means should be adopted to remove those that were there" [1]

We can hardly credit rational human beings with the production of these barbarous ordinances for the extirpation of British colonists, and their still more absurd restrictions, they read more like the production of some mischievous demon—the grotesque laws for some Gargantuan island or the territory of the Yahoos—than the sober production of English statesmen.

The eight years succeeding the defeat of the project to expel the settlers are not very eventful ones in the history of Newfoundland; the agitation for a governor was still kept up By far the ablest argument on this subject is from the pen of Sir Robert Robinson, for many years captain-of-convoy on the coast. He points out very forcibly that, owing to the terrorism of the West Countrymen, many of the planters had gone to live with the French, and—

' the chiefest have gone to New England [2] That by a settled Government and harbours fortified they will avoid the abuses of the ungoverned seamen, who deal with them as they please They will be preserved from sea rovers and enemies, have a Minister to christen, instruct, marry, and bury them; and they will have equal justice which will greatly encourage all except those who desire to live under no Government, but in all things to be their own carvers"

But the strongest argument of all was the danger of a French invasion One per cent. on the fish caught would have borne all the

---

[1] *Records*

[2] PETITION OF WILLIAM DOWNING

"That whereas on 11th Oct last the Lords of Trade made an order about settlement Newfoundland under Government and fortifications

"That there is now an account given to your petition that (the inhabitants having no security and utterly disparing of redress) the greater part have bought vessels whereby (upon the first alaram of wars) they may remove to other Plantations and the rest are already retireing nearer the French and declare they will put themselves under their protection All which on oath if required And that the season again draweth nigh for the ships to go thither. Your petitioner therefore most humbly prays for a speedy conclusion of the settlement &c"

Not endorsed, prob 1683]

(*Board of Trade, Newfoundland*)

moderate expense required for an established government, forts,[1] artillery, and a minister :—

"If the French [says Robinson] should take it, whereas they now employ about four hundred sail and eighteen thousand seamen and the English three hundred sail and fifteen thousand seamen, they would employ seven hundred ships and thirty thousand seamen, and the English be shut out of £700,000 yearly; besides which the French would make double that sum. The Newfoundland fishery is the great nursery for seamen. If the French should add, what the English have planted there, to what they possess already in Canada, Nova Scotia and other places thereabouts, they would be bad neighbours to His Majesty's flourishing Plantations of New England, New York, and Virginia."

THORNTON'S MAP, 1689.

From the English Pilot.

Robinson grossly exaggerated numbers, but his argument is unanswerable as regards the danger to all North America from the French encroachments in Newfoundland. West Country obstinacy,

[1] PROPOSED BUILDING OF A FORT AT ST. JOHN'S IN 1680.

On April 5, Sir Robt. Robinson asks leave to be allowed to use his crew and such Planters as are willing to raise fortifications, which shall be done with no expense except a little brandy to the crew for labouring [This was probably the commencement of a fort on the site of Fort William; it is referred to in 1696 and 1697 in the Invasion by D'Iberville and Brouillon.]

however, still opposed all reasonable proposals to defend the Colony from such an obvious danger. A few years later they suffered terribly for their refusal to listen to reason. There was a strong party on Robinson's side; he tried to bring over the Duke of York (afterwards James II.) to his views, but, like his brother, he was the recipient of large bribes from Child and his associates—the Parliament also of that day was utterly corrupt—and so his efforts had no result.

The Colony was left to drift along, a prey to every enemy. Each year the naval officers on the station made reports on the wanton aggression of the ship fishermen,[1] the disorders in the Island, and the need for a settled government; but it was all to no purpose. During the latter

PLAN OF ST. JOHN'S IN 1689.
From Thornton's Map.

years of Charles II.'s reign there were no attacks from the French; both nations quietly fished without disturbing each other. Like ourselves, the French had no military or naval power, their fortresses were in ruins, and there was not a single royal soldier or sailor in any of their settlements.[2] The parent Government was busily employed in Europe; and after the first outburst of energy in 1662, the soldiers were withdrawn, and their defences were entirely neglected; they seldom had even a convoy for their merchant ships.

[1] CAPTAIN OF CONVOY'S REPORT, 1684.
Fishermen now using casks instead of ffats for their oil.
Hardly a house but sells drink.
If the people do assemble it is not for divine service.
Order 23 March 1677 allows them to live near the shore.
Order 18 May 1677 allows planters to keep their own house, &c.
Order 16 Jany 1677 Masters allowed to bring over passengers.
Order 16 Jany 1677 Bonds not required.
He has had a hundred complaints and Admiral would do nothing at all to redress wrongs.
Charge of fitting out 10 boats and a ship of 80 tons for the West Adventurers service Receive £1350 pay £984—profit £365.
Planters 2 boats take £216 cost £268 loss £52.
[Very full details of both estimates given in the Records.]
(*Records.*)
[2] The Naval Report of 1684 says: "Seldom any convoy for French vessels." —"Forts in ruins."

APPENDIX TO CHAPTER VIII.

I. Downing's Narrative.

A Brief Narrative concerning New-foundland, by John Downing

Recd 24th October 1676

" Recites various patents given—in all which ample privileges were granted for encourag' of all, that w'd inhabit, that the Children there born should be free denizens of England with many other freedoms &c , my father in 1640 was sent over by H M 's Commissioners, Duke Hamilton, Earl of Pembroke & Earl of Holland's Instructions to take charge of the Colony, Sir David Kirke being by His Matie's Letter by him sent, called home ; my father found under the command of Sir David Kirke, their Gov'r fifty six guns mounted in several forts, as Ferryland, St. John's, Bay Bull, &c, the forts fitted with small arms &c, & manned by inhabitants The proprietors had given them, even to Duke Hambleton, and the rest six admiralls places for fishing, accounted the the best, even St John's and the rest alsoe five fishes in six score caught or bought by any shipp having more strangers aboard than free denizens of England , all nations in amity with his Matie might freely buy and catch fish build houses &c as freely as English, provided if demanded he paid his impost.

" By Patent the inhabitants were not within six miles to destroy woods, nor convert rooms for drying fish to other uses, as to plant, plow same, and the rest Even in Crom-well's time, in the worst of times the in-habitants being accused for traitors to his Government, yett by an order then, wee had liberty to enjoy our houses wee had built &c Cromwell's Governor Treworgie and his men of war took impost, as proprietors aforementioned had done, even as far as Trespasse.

" There hath been a generat" of men ever since any people settled in Newfoundland, practiceing the ruin of inhabit'. First that no merchants have any fish but from themselves and at their rates and pleasures, next that all men employed in fishing affairs work for and serve for such victualls and pay as they choose to give them. Inhabitants distance from Supreme Rulers Seats, render them liable to false calumnies—that inhabitants burn their train ffats of £60 value which one with other were not worth first year they were built £6 if they were soe wronged they might and would have Reparat" from those that wronged yearly . But I never c'd hear of any man there that c'd complain of any such wrong I having

lived there and been every summer these thirty odd yeares

" The inhabitants burne their stages they complain themselves, as the fishing sailes burne for dressing their victualls & brewing their beare, wood their shipps carry home some to their owners yards give leave to the shipps that take in their fish to take aboard what they will, other shipps wanting wood take leave, some give some to some inhabitants, others howse all their stages and flake stuff for another yeare, by this meanes before all the shipps depart some yeares in St. John's where it is said three hundred boats have been kept, is left of all their stages two or three pieces standing. In 1674 . at the goeing out of the last ships was left standing but the Bedd of one of the Admirals Stages which at Spring following the Admiral enjoyed In 1675 by the care of Sir John Berry their Stages and Roomes were for the most part well left & as well found at their returne as themselves have there & must if called here acknowledge. In 1676, before my coming out, Capt Russell Command'r of H M 's shipp "Reserve " forced several Masters of shipps, even their admiral for one to build up again their trayne houses, themselves had cut down contrary to their order Trees are rinded, the shipps doing it most, and the comers out of England—done not only for 18 foot Cooke Roomes but to cover whole stages and lodging houses, even last summer it was done Inhab'ts stages and houses are most covered with New England and the country's boards, so have little occasion of rinding. Woods fired by foreigners and English Shipps Com-panys going into woods for timber in warme weather & throwing carelessly the fire they light tobacco with.

" From New Eng'd one y'r with other come commonly 8 sail of vessels burthen'd from 16 tons to 60 tons with commodities the produce of which they invest here in Brandy, Cloath'g, apparel for their vessels, pieces of eight, if they can get them some ffrench & Spanish wines, some redd stinking fish for the Negroes of Barbadoes As for men Inhabi-tants have out of fishing ships we have Masters good will to have them soe have New Eng'd men it sav'g the owners victuals they eat homew'ds & often they carry passengers in their places who pay own'rs for passages.

" Practiceers of ruin of Inhabits (if obtained) will produce to themselves this profit of their Labour as formerly the ffrench found before any Governor was sent to Newfoundland by K Chas Ist—Some English inhabitants w'd burn frenchmen's boats, carry away some, carry away salt, break open their houses and rifle them they being sure to find nothing left nor they who had done it   The English fishing ships leave always either salt or fish or goods for fishing and all their boats, which if their boats be spoiled the voyage is ruined utterly before they can there saw boards or build boats—no merchants will send salt or any other goods to supply any that want or waste salt & provis'ns in his passage over for if it be to be housed no house but Cook rooms allowed of 18 feet & they but for the winter, yet houses unfit for salt neither any man to take charge of it   Some years fishing ships have beene lost forty, sixty leagues from shore being rackt by ice yet in boats some of their men have come to land and been cured of their hurts by cold and hunger, by inhabitants   Almost every year, some of their men sent for possess'n might with cold and hunger starve if not relieved by Inhab'ts; yearly their men are received when sick with scurvy and other sickness into Inhabitants houses and there most times got their cures & become able to do service

" In case according to some mens desires the inhabitants be forced to quit their houses and employments, they and their man and families and come home they will fall to extreme poverty and want and if they get relief it must come from the landed gentlemen to whom the exteme poverty of distressed families will be neither pleasant nor profitable.

" Of french promiting their interest more and more in Newfoundl'd complainers agst inhabitants take no notice   In yr 1670 French had Placentia fortified with ordnance a Garrison of Soldires and Chaine also St Peters fortified with great guns garris'n of Soldrs at both places many inhabitants great stores of Cattle and sheepe   Since this time K of France hath pub'd in Seaports of France that he will pay passage of any that go and inhabit in Newfld give a gratuity to Masr that passeth them other, by Governor they shall be supplied with clothes & necessaries from three years & then pay King in fish fur or board, by these encouragements inhabitants grow more and more numerous, some English live amongst them & are courteously treated, lately more of English Inhabts have been as formerly by French Captains invited to dwell amongst them promising them kindness and protection.

" A Merch't of Waterford in Ireland Mr John Aylrod being in Newfoundland in June 1676 gave foll'g relation concerning Placentia—French inhabitants were there now 250 families which according to our famil's may be more than 2000 men, their garrison of soldiers 400 men paid by King   300 kintalls for each boat one yeai with another accounted with them an ordinary voyage; their fishes from Trepass round the Isl'd near to Bona vista many French and Biskenners, the

Biskenners subject to King of Spain—French ships supposed to be not less than 200 sail of ships of good force from 30 guns to 12, they have 2 men of war about 50 guns each, to that part of the land where the French forts are as Placentia, St Peters & the rest, no Indians come but some Canida Indians from forts of Canida in french shallowayes with french fowling pieces all spared them by french of Canida so for them need no chaine, soldiers nor ordinance

" It is said Newfoundland is guarded after fish'g ships go suffic'tly by foggs & ice till arrival of English fishermen therefore need no other guard to prevent invasion that it is theirs who are strongest at sea.   St John's & Fferryland and other harbours are deemed by some men accustomed to war so strongly fortified by nature that some of them having one fort and necessaries for defence its hard for any ship though never so bravely furnished to enter and if they sh'd pass without burning or sinking or being cast ashore when entered they may stay there perhaps 14 days for a wind to go out the meantime fight rocks and fort   Two or three of these harbours fortified are enough after the manner of french fishing to make use of all the English have for fishing in their pattent from Cape de Race to Cape de Bouavista; except the fortified harbours they may spoyle the rest for ships rideing in the tortified harb'rs their own ships may ride even in war and fish as the French do and go in their boats after the fish from three to eighteen leagues each side their harbours mouth there salt their fish in tilts on shore, after carry and dry it where their shipps ride in guard of forts, when they have taken in their fish a strong westerly wind with night in hand frees them from danger of enemies lying off the shore.

" English fishing ships commonly all gone in September or quickly in October— not to sail out of England till 1st March

" From England Ireland France & Spain & Portugal & New Eng'd have vessels come to Newfoundland in November & Dec'r & have loaden oyle summer fish & winter fish out of the houses & gone out some of them three days before Christmas & have gone well to their ports desired

" In beginning of March Ships have arrived from England, French fishing ships have been off St John's and Ferryland the 2nd Feby and might have come in if they pleased, some of the french harbour, in Feby some in March, their best fish'g being in May. Ice comes on coast commonly in middle of Feb'y, some years in March, some years in April some years none to be seen it is not made here even the ice but breaks up the summer before in some cold straits & so winds and current bring it on this Coast.

Jo Downing.

(Col Papers, Newfoundland, 56)

II. Downing's Petitions.

(a) To the King's Most Excellent Matie

" The Humble Petition of John Downing, Gentleman, Inhabitant of Newfoundland. Sheweth .

" That your Petitioner's Father was sent to Newfoundland, armed with your Royal Father's Commission and authority and instructions from the then Lords Proprietors to plant people there, and reduce the Indians to civility and religion   That to that purpose severall lawes and orders were then made and sent over by your Royal Father to be observed there . . That after some yeares service there, having secured the forts and fishings and brought into some regularity and security the place and imposts payable to your Majesty, Your Petitioner's Father there died, and since his death your Petitioner amongst several others of your subjects hath settled there and lived for many years under the said lawes and orders given them and by their industry built houses for their habitation and cleansed the wildernesses of the place, whereby to keep some cattle for their sustenance and the support of such of your Majesty's subjects as come to trade there and have by leave of the former Governors and Proprietors erected severall stages and Roomes for their winter and summer fisheries and support

" They have hitherto lived your Majestys obedient subjects maintaining by their own industry, themselves their wives and their children in peace and comfort   But now some of Your Subjects, pretending Your Majesty's patent and orders for the same, coming over thither, have not only taken the houses goode stages and roomes built and enjoyed by Your Petitioner and his father for many yeares last past, but spoile the boats, keeping, and breake open the houses of the said Inhabitants at their wills and pleasures contrary to the antient lawes and orders of the said place, and also to those of common humanity and the freedome which all other nations which have settled in these parts enjoy

" For that the said Inhahitants can neither enjoy the effects of their own industry nor have any security from the invasion or spoiles of their neighbours

May it therefore please Your Majesty that out of Your Royal Favour, you will be pleased to command that for the future no such outrages be committed, but that Your Petitioner may enjoy such houses stages &c. as have been built and enjoyed by his Father and himself according to the said antient lawes and orders of the place and find security for himself, his wife and family from such outrages from time to come

And Your Petitioner shall ever pray.

At the Court at Whitehall,
November 7, 1676

" His Majesty is graciously pleased to refer this Petition to the Rt Honble. The Committee of the Council for Foraigne Plantacions to consider the contents thereof and take such orders therein as to their Honours shall seeme meete for the reliefe of the Petr

Thos Povey.

(b) Downing's Petition.

" To the Rt Honble ye Lords of his Ma't's most Honble Privy Councell appointed a Committee for Trade and Plantations

" The Humble Petition of John Downing Gent Inhabitant of Newfoundland Sheweth

" That your Pet'r did on the 6th day of Nov'r last give in a Peticon to his Matie humbly imploring his protection to secure himself and family from ye outrages under which they had suffered, as by ye said Peticon reference being had thereunto doth more at large appeare

" That his Matie was thereupon graciously pleased on ye 7th Nov'r to refer your Petr to this Honourable Committee to take such order for his releife as they should think fitt. and that your Petr hath ever since attended for what redresse this Honble Board shall judge meet for him

" That ye season of ye year is now instant wherein shipps bound for Newfld doe set forth and, if he omit ye takeing of his passage now, it may tend to ye utter ruine and undoing of himselfs, his wife and family who are still remaining there

" Wherefore he most humbly prayes, this Honble Commee would be pleased to commiserate his condicon and take into their serious consideracon his Mat's said reference, that your Peti may speedily obtain some relief what in your Honor's great wisdom shall be deem'd fitting, and soe may prosecute his voyage, and take care for ye support of his ruinous familly.

And he shall ever pray &c

Endorsed

Peticon of John Downing Gent of Newfoundland

Recd 25th January 1676 [o s]

(Colonial Papers, No. 56, p 104)

(c) Downing's Further Petition

To the King's Most Excellent Matie

" The further Peticon of John Downing Inhabitant of Newfoundland Sheweth

" That the said Inhabitants till your Maties happy restauracon had a Governor there and fifty-six guns allowed them and fforts for their securities And that the same were maintained by the six admiralties and imposts of the said place

" That since the practices of the last Patentees, all the same have been neglected and decayed and the said Inhabitants not only oppressed by the Patentees (who now engross the whole trade and profitt and admiralties to themselves) But alsoe are left naked and defenceless to the Invasion of others especially the ffrench their too Potent neighbours To redresse which the said Inhabitants doe humbly offer, that your Matie may be pleased to appoint them a Governor and a minister to live amongst them, and to whom the said inhabitants enjoying their former immunities and Estates will allow a competent maintenance fitt for the support of such employments and having allowed them the said Competent number of guns will erect and maintain fforts necessary for the defence and safety of the s'd place and security of the people, And further to pay and secure to your Matie such imposts and further customes as have been accustomed to be received by such Governour .

Therefore may it please Your Matie to consider the deplorable condicon of the said inhabitants and to take such order herein as to you seeme most meete.

And your Petr shall pray &c

Endorsed Petn of John Downing

Newfoundland

read in Councill March 23rd 1676 [o. s]

(Col Papers, No. 56)

III. Report concerning the Fishery & Colony of Newfoundland.

Read in Councill March 28th 1677.

"In obedience to H. Matie's order in Council of 23rd inst &c &c have called before them the Petn of John Downing appearing on behalf of himself and rest of Colony, as also several Gentlemen of W. Country, & Merchts concerned in the Fishery, but it was alleged by said Gentlemen and Merchants, that by reason of the short warning given them for their appearance, they were in noe manner prepared to make out their pretensions in the validity of their Charter, which they did not doubt to satisfy them in, if space of fifteen days were given them to acquaint their correspondents in the Country and provide themselves with those evidences & demonstrations of right by wh their patent is supported Did allow of soe reasonable a request, and did assign them the 10th of April next, at which time propose to enter into further examination of whole matter for final settlement But in meanwhile least Planters at present residing in Newfoundland should be molested by Msrs of Fisg Ships upon pretence of their Charter, offer unto H Matie that orders bee forthwith sent by a Ship called St. John's Merchant, now at Dartmouh, unto admirals in Newfoundland, whereby Masters and Seamen may be directed to forbear any violence to Planters, upon pretence of said Western Charter and suffer them to inhabit and fish according to usage , provided they do conform to the rules of Charter—and inhabitants do likewise continue good correspondences with Fish'men, until, H Matie shall proceed to a further resolution."

DANBY, ANGLESEY,
ORMONDE, CARLISLE,
CRAVEN, BRIDGWATER,
FFAUCONBERG

Council Chamber
26 March 1677.

"Which being read in Councill—H M was pleased to order, that Council for Trade and Plant'ns cause orders to be sent to admirals according to their Lordships advice in said report."

JOHN NICHOLAS.

(Col. Papers, No. 56.)

CHAPTER IX.

REIGN OF JAMES II
1685–1688.

THE REVOLUTION

REIGN OF WILLIAM AND MARY.
1688–1694

1688.—War between France and England.

1689.—Bill of Rights passed. Frontenac Viceroy of New France

1690.—Battle of the Boyne. Capture of Port Royal. Failure to take Quebec. Garrison of Chedabuctou sent to Placentia

1692.—De Brouillon appointed Governor of Placentia. Commodore Williams's unsuccessful attack on Placentia.

1694.—Death of Queen Mary.

REIGN OF WILLIAM III ALONE
1694–1702.

1694.—Holman's defeat of the French at Ferryland

1695.—Considerable damage done by eight French privateers to the English settlements.

1696.—Unsuccessful attack on St John's by Chevalier Nesmond. Capture of St John's by D'Iberville and De Brouillon in November; destruction of all the settlements except Carbonear and Bonavista

1697.—Sir John Norris, with fleet and two thousand soldiers, sent out to recover Newfoundland, found it abandoned by the French, he built forts, &c. Treaty of Ryswick left the French in possession of Placentia. Colonel Handyside and three hundred men left to garrison the forts; two hundred and fourteen died. Board of Trade recommended that one thousand persons only might be permitted to remain on the Island to construct boats and stages for drying fish. Rev J Jackson, with the sanction of the Bishop of London, settled in St John's

1698.—Act of William III appointing fishing admirals, vice-admirals, and rear-admirals; no alien to fish or take bait, rooms built since 1685 that did not belong to fishing ships made property of residents; colonial produce relieved of duty. Order on 31st March, establishing a permanent garrison in St John's; Lieutenant Lilburne and sixty soldiers and gunners winter in St. John's. Cock of Bonavista's letter to Colonel Norris about English settlements to the northward.

1699.—Captain Andrews, an engineer, in command at St. John's

O

1700.—Captain A Holdsworth, Admiral of St John's.

1701 —Large increase of trade with New England ; continued complaints against New England transporting fishermen   S P G incorporated   Report of Mr George Larkin on the affairs of the Colony

The short period of three years during which James II. reigned over England is only memorable for the treaty made in 1686 between Louis XIV. and the English king for the settlement of their respective territories in America. . It was not recognised by James' successor. Like his brother, the new English monarch was the humble dependant and vassal of France. It shows how insecure was the tenure by which our enemies claimed to hold their portion of Newfoundland, that, at the commencement of this reign, Louis XIV. requested permission from James II. to hold Placentia and the other portions of Newfoundland occupied by the French

I cannot gather from the records that there was any great excitement amongst the fishing folk in our Island over the accession of the Duke of York, and there was certainly no lamentation over his downfall   The Colony was then really more distant from England than the far-off islands of the Pacific · News was conveyed slowly and fitfully   A few of the leading planters, who were Royalists, and some who were Puritans, may have been moved about the great events in the mother country, but to the great bulk of the settlers and the ship fishermen it was of infinitely less importance to them than the price of fish or a good " caplin school," that came early and lasted long   All the old chroniclers declare that on this movement of the bait fishes mainly depended the success of the year's fishing voyage   Though the cod was most abundant, there were then, as now, good and bad seasons—some years abundance to overflowing, in others the fisherman's occupation was almost a complete failure.

The following letter is one out of many illustrations on this subject —

' Rennouse 29 July 1680

" At Trepassie first ships have 220 qtls. per boat and 3 h'ds. of Traine, later ships 180 to 190 qtls and 2½ h'ds of Traine   The French men that is there have done 250 to 300 from St Shott's. The Admirals of St Maries and Collinet were at Trepassie last week, who did inform us, that at Placentia of 36 saile not ten ships would be loaden and St Mary's fishing doth fail also   . I do judge there are severall of our neighbours that will sell their fish, if they can attaine, at a considerable price " [1]

Prior to the accession of William III. in 1688 and the declaration of war there had been a long interval of repose   There were raids by

[1] *Records.*

English and French privateers, but, with one short interval, no open conflict. On neither side were there soldiers or men-of-war to fight, and the defences both of St. John's and Placentia had fallen into complete ruin. With the return of the warlike Marquis de Frontenac to the Government of New France in 1689 this peaceful state of affairs quickly came to an end. The defences of Placentia were thoroughly repaired, Fort Louis (now Castle Hill) was built, the trading governor, with his fishing boats and Government store, was replaced by a smart young officer who had served under the great Luxembourg and campaigned in Flanders; everywhere in North America the old order was changed.

WILLIAM III.
From an engraving by Gole.

The Marquis was an admirable organiser, a brave soldier; he realised that either France had to destroy the English colonies, or soon New England would rout him out of Canada. He vainly imagined, with his nine thousand Canadians, that he could annihilate the two hundred thousand hardy and prosperous English colonists. At first he had no regular troops nor supplies, so he trained militia. In Newfoundland he contented himself with sending French privateers to harry our settlements. In 1690 the garrison of Chedabucton, in Acadie, which had made a glorious defence against Sir William Phipps, was sent to Placentia with their gallant commander, De Montorgueil. In 1692 De Brouillon, afterwards the successful invader of the English settlements, was made Governor of Placentia.

Owing to the continued attacks of French privateers[1] on the English settlers, England determined to send a powerful fleet to destroy Placentia. The command was given to Commodore Williams, with three sixty-gun ships and two smaller vessels. Brown, in his "History of Cape Breton," says :—

"The only defences of the place were Fort Louis, with a garrison of fifty men, situated upon a rock a hundred feet in height on the eastern side of the narrow

[1] "The French [in 1695] did considerable damage in Newfoundland, where most of the English settlements were destroyed by eight large privateers, and the *Saphire*, a fifth rate, was burnt to prevent her falling into their hands."—S. COLLIBER, *Columna Rostata*, 1728, p 268.

entrance of the Harbour, and a battery hastily constructed by the Governor, M. de Brouillon, and manned by Sailors from the Privateers and Merchant ships in the Harbour. The Commodore in 1692 after six hours bombardment ignominiously retired having only partially destroyed a portion of the works."

The admiral of the powerful French squadron, Chevalier de Palais, seemed to have been the counterpart of the English commodore; whilst De Brouillon was defending his beleaguered little town, the noble chevalier remained snugly harboured in Sydney.

It is pleasant to turn from these contemptible naval commanders to the exploits of our heroic merchant seamen, who on several occasions gallantly defended Newfoundland from the French. The story of Holman's action at Ferryland in 1694, for which the Lords of the Admiralty gave him a "meddall and chayne," and the defeat of two powerful French frigates of forty and fifty guns, is recounted in the English records. This smart naval action would have been "unhonoured and unsung," but for a very prosaic reason. The following petition

NAVAL FIGHT BETWEEN AN ENGLISH AND A FRENCH SHIP.

From La Hontan's Nouveaux Voyages, 1703.

and affidavit for payment of powder expended in defending the Colony alone have preserved it from oblivion.[1]

[1] Holman's claim was for £495; £150 for spoiled fish, £12 for brandy given to encourage his men in time of fight, &c. On the 24th June 1697, the Board of Trade recommended the payment of £345, and left the £150 for spoiled fish to be paid if the Treasury thought fit. Holman was probably recompensed by the Government giving him a contract for freighting victuals, &c. for the garrison in Newfoundland this year.

"Account of an action that happened at the Harbour of Ferryland in Newfoundland on August 31st 1694

"There being eight or nine English ships in the said harbour catching fish, some English Prisoners made their escape from Placentia, came to Ferryland and acquainted Captain William Holman Commander of ye *William and Mary* galley having letters of marque and sixteen guns and the rest of the Masters of ships, that the French had a design to come with five ships of war, one fireship and a Bomb-ketch to destroy the English fishery all along the coast, upon which Captain Holman proposed to build fortifications for defence of the harbour which had been twice before taken by the French   He built four Forts or Fortifications in less than a month and placed in them his and other guns to the number of thirty in all "

Commander Charles Desborow, R N, who arrived at Ferryland in October 1694, in H.M S *Virgin Prize*, tells us —

" Holman's greatest difficulty was to keep the inhabitants to his assistance, who had got their arms and were making their flight to the mountains; Holman sent after them and let them know that if they at such time did desert him he would certainly make division of their fish amongst the seamen to encourage them to stand by him, and not only so but he would burn and destroy all their houses; upon which seeing the defence Captain Holman was ready to make, they did return, and with his bravery and prudent management, they so battered the French men of war, that they, after five hours fight, ran off leaving their anchors and cables behind them and ye French lost eighty or ninety men as we are informed by some English prisoners who were on board the French, which so discouraged them that they gave over their intended spoile, which might have ruined the whole country there being then no more men of war to defend it." [Affidavits sworn to by Jno. Cleer, Val Carter and Richard Christian][1]

The Devonshire men, who had been the staunchest adherents of Charles II. and James—patrons and defenders of their monopolies—now became the equally devoted admirers of the Prince of Orange. They hoisted his flag and drank his health in New England rum, with as much noise and enthusiasm as Ulster men of to-day commemorate the same "pious and immortal memory"

Amidst wars and rumours of wars all contentions between planter and ship fishermen were for the time laid aside, they had now to fight for their lives. — Many an attack was made on them and repelled with gallantry.

Early in the summer of 1696 the Chevalier Nesmond, Commander of a large French fleet, attacked St. John's. Two small hastily constructed forts, one about Chain Rock, and the other opposite on the south side (Fort Frederick, as it is now called), defended the entrance. The newly erected battlements of Fort William then crowned the hill on the site of the present railway terminus; West Country mariners handled the guns and manned the forts. Nesmond's powerful fleet and his disciplined sailors and soldiers were completely routed by the inhabitants and the undisciplined West Country crews. Wooden ships in those days had no chance against well-manned forts, especially in the narrow entrance to our harbour

This first battle of 1696 happened in the early summer. All through the season, news came from Placentia about French preparations, the gathering of stores, the arrival of Canadian Indians, under French officers, still no precautions were taken to put St. John's in a thorough state of defence.

When the Devonshire ships left the coast in August and September, there appear to have been no men-of-war stationed in Newfoundland. The only guard were the people and their Governor Miners—a planter like themselves—a brave, sensible, determined man, elected to the highly honourable and dangerous position for his well-recognised valour.

It never entered their mind that the French would attack by land, preparations were only made to resist shipping. We may infer from the French narrative of Baudoin that De Brouillon had made an attack on St John's about the end of September 1696, and had been ignominiously repulsed. Doubtless the deluded English settlers thought that two defeats in the same summer would have checked the French. They little knew the daring enemies with whom they had to contend.

To fully understand all the horrors of this war we must revert a little to the early operations of De Frontenac. These desultory attacks of the French privateers on Newfoundland were only preliminary skirmishes in advance of his great design to destroy the English in America. From the date of his second arrival in October 1689, until the Peace of Ryswick in 1697, New England was kept in perpetual terror by the midnight attacks of French and Indians. Shenectady, Haverill, Salmon Falls, are amongst the most memorable scenes of these barbarous massacres.

In the pages of Charlevoix, all the incidents of these affrays are minutely related and gloried in, even to the presentment of the English scalps to the aristocratic Marquis de Frontenac. The horrible cruelties and cowardly attacks on helpless women and children are described by the French historian as if they were so many glorious deeds—splendid and honourable actions. The French Governor boasted of his design to destroy New England, but he prudently avoided a conflict with the powerful colony. The gallantry of France was displayed in minor attacks on fishing villages and unarmed settlers.

Newfoundland soon experienced all the horrors and barbarities of an Indian and French invasion. The leader was the most distinguished Canadian naval officer of his age - the Nelson of the New World—

Captain de Fragate, Pierre Le Moyne D'Iberville.[1] In the spring of 1696 he had received command from De Frontenac to destroy the English settlements in Newfoundland.

The two French men-of-war under his command were the *L'Envieux* and the *Profond*, the latter commanded by M. de Bonaventure. When they arrived in Placentia, on the 12th of September 1696, they found

LE MOYNE D'IBERVILLE.
From Winsor's N. & C. H. of America.

that the Governor, De Brouillon, with his men from St. Malo, had made an attempt on St. John's, but had failed.

D'Iberville, a Canadian, well acquainted with the stealthy Indian warfare, proposed to attack the unguarded English settlements by land.

---

[1] Le Moine D'Iberville and his brother Bienville, two of the most remarkable Canadians, distinguished themselves in French expeditions to Hudson's Bay and the Mississippi. Le Moine died at Havannah a few years later of fever.

De Brouillon contended for an attack by sea. There were bitter quarrels between the two leaders. Baudoin, the Recollet Father, who was chaplain, tried to reconcile them. The Canadians and Indians would only follow D'Iberville, and he now threatened to go to France. As a final compromise D'Iberville with his Canadians and Indians agreed to proceed against St John's by land, whilst De Brouillon's Malovians were to make the attack by sea.

From French sources we learn that the Governor had nine privateers belonging to St. Malo, three corvettes and two fireships, and that they all—Canadians and Malovians—embarked for St. John's. Owing to head winds the expedition was a partial failure, they had to return to Placentia for want of provisions, having captured thirty-one vessels (probably boats), and destroyed some fishing establishments. Baudoin does not mention this adventure, and it probably refers to De Brouillon's attempt alone.

On the 1st of November 1696 D'Iberville, with his Frenchmen and Canadian Indians, started to walk on the ice up the south-east arm of Placentia. Amongst the hybrid population, half English, half French, then living there, no doubt they had obtained a guide for the interior. To carry provisions, arms, and ammunition across such a country was a great exploit; white men alone could not have done it.

On the 10th November they arrived in Ferryland, having been for two days short of provisions. The *Profond* was anchored in Renews. All the Ferryland men had run away to Bay Bulls. On the 21st they started for Bay Bulls in boats; there was no defence, and the French captured a vessel of a hundred tons. On the 26th, according to Baudoin's narrative, there was a fight in Petty Harbour with the English settlers, and thirty-six of the inhabitants were slain. On the 28th the French encountered a body of the English from St John's, numbering eighty-eight, who were posted in a burnt wood, full of rocks, behind which they lay in ambush.

The English account of this battle is that they went out to help the Petty Harbour men, and that about a mile from St John's they encountered the French on the south side hill. There were four hundred French disciplined troops, and it speaks well for the courage of the planters that they fought against this overwhelming majority for half an hour, and it was only when nearly half their number—thirty-four men—were killed that they retired in good order and reached the fort. The French say nothing about their men-of-war, but they were doubtless brought round to St John's.

The unfortunate settlers, without ammunition or supplies, with no military force, no military or naval officers to direct the defence, were in a desperate strait   They held out for three days,[1] and it was only after the brutal threats to scalp all their prisoners, in the same manner as they had fiendishly tortured William Drew, that they capitulated on articles of surrender, which the French commanders dishonourably evaded.

Baudoin[2] says that after the skirmish outside the town the French advanced and captured the two small forts.

"Seeing [he continued] the inhabitants were about to defend themselves [in Fort William] we sent to Bay Boulle for the mortars and bumbs and powder   On the night of the 29th and 30th MM. de Mins and de Montigny went with sixty Canadians to burn the houses near the fort   The 30th, the day of St Andrew, a man came from the fort with a white flag, to speak of surrender   Afterwards the Governour with four of the principal citizens came for an interview.   They would not allow us to enter the fort, lest we should see the miserable plight to which they were reduced.   It was agreed they should surrender on condition of being allowed to depart for England.   The capitulation was brought in writing to the fort, and approved of by the principal citizens and signed by the Governour and M de Brouillon." [3]

The barbarous treatment of Drew will not surprise anyone who has read the heartrending stories of Haverhill, Seneca Falls, or Shenectady, where the French, after joining in the solemn rites of the church the night before, crept into the villages, murdered the inhabitants, and calmly looked on whilst their Indian allies brained infants and slaughtered children, the French, in fact, encouraged the Indians in their cruelties A letter was intercepted from Costabelle, Governor of Placentia, to the Minister, dated July 4th, 1711 :—

"Had despatched more officers and people, who knew all the savages, to incite them to defend and take part of a feast which they would have of English flesh at Quebec." [4]

---

[1] "Upon the approach of the French the inhabitants of St John's fled, but Mr. Miners and Mr. Roberts, with some other stout men, retired to the greatest fortification and kept their ground for 48 hours without any provisions." (*The Post Man*, Jan 12, 1697.)

[2] BAUDOIN'S *MS Diary*, *Quebec MSS.*

[3] ARTICLES OF SURRENDER OF ST JOHN'S HARBOUR TO DE BROUILLON, 1696.

"These are to certify you who are Inhabitants of the Harbour of St. John's that upon the quiet surrender, that you shall have good quarter and those that will have boats to go in the Bay shall have them to-morrow and those that will go for England shall have two ships to carry them home and they shall have one pound of bread per day for each person for a month and all necessaries convenient for the passage and all those that will stay here and take the oath of allegiance to the King of France shall live as they doe and go oft with them and so depart the Fort immediately and every one to go to his own home and no man shall molest them and carry what they have with them given under my hand "

BURALEET

And those that will go to the Northward to take passage in what ship they can shall have a Passport

St Johns the 20th (30) November 1696."
(*Records*)

[4] Quoted in BROWN'S *History of C. Breton.*

Baudoin gives a very depreciatory account of the settlers, who, he said, were good shots but great cowards, so that one hundred of them would fly before one Frenchman.

"They have not [he says] a single minister of religion in these establishments, though more than twenty of them are larger settlements than Placentia They do not know what religion they belong to The greater part of them, born in this country, have never received any instruction, and never make any act of religion, no more than mere savages Drunkenness and impurity are common and public among them, even among the women. It is impossible to imagine anything more abominable than the life led by the English on these coasts ; they are left altogether without the succour of religion and are degenerated into a race almost worst than savages. Crime of the most loathsome nature is quite public among them ; they *endeavoured even to entice our men to evil.*"

To anyone acquainted with the morals—especially the military morals—of that age, the idea of French soldiers, the most dissolute set

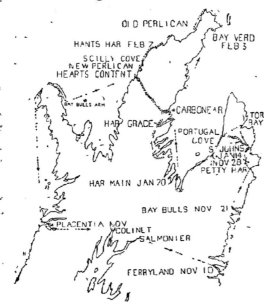

of ruffians in Europe, being led from the path of innocence by our poor honest settlers' wives and daughters is simply incredible

This bloodthirsty little Recollet Father cursing his enemies and exulting over the slaughter, ruin, and spoliation of the unfortunate Newfoundland settlers is quite in the spirit— the cruel barbarous temper—of the age, which made the New England divines hang Quakers and witnessed the Reverend Cotton Mather on horseback superintending with fiery religious zeal the judicial murder of witches.

PLAN OF THE CAMPAIGNS OF 1698

The victims of a hundred years of calumny, our self-reliant settlers, constantly petitioning for a settled government and a minister, stand out in contrast to the rough ship fishermen , they constantly succoured[1]

---

[1] See Downing's narrative, p 205 Downing's statement is confirmed by nearly all the English naval officers

shipwrecked sailors, and nursed them through sicknesses. There was a baser element among them, as in all communities, subject as they were for many months to the incursion of ten to twenty thousand fishermen, many of them steeped in the wickedness of the great ports of the Old World; in the hurry to be rich during the short season by supplying rum to those unruly crowds, some in the larger settlements, like St. John's, were occasionally wild and lawless.[1]

The long and very interesting diary of Baudoin is an important contribution to our local history;[2] he gives a graphic account of the expedition, a description of all the various English settlements around Conception Bay and on the east coast; he tells us of the comfortable homes of the settlers, their stocks of cattle, horses, &c., the large mercantile establishments in St. John's, Carbonear, and Harbour Grace. Several extracts from this diary will be found in the Notes, it is much too long to quote in full.

FRENCH SOLDIER IN 1705.
From Winsor's N. & C. H. of America.

A critical examination shows that many of the chaplain's statements are incorrect. We must remember that, in accordance with French usage—of which many amusing instances are given by Parkman—Baudoin was a spy on his superior officers—De Brouillon and D'Iberville. Every official was encouraged to make these kind of reports, so the chaplain recounts, with avidity, to "Sa Grandeur"—evidently the head of his order—the misdeeds of De Brouillon, his quarrels, and his avarice, whilst everything good is said of his own captain—D'Iberville.

What makes one doubt the truthfulness of this diary is, first, it is the story of a spy; secondly, the absence of a list of the French killed and wounded. Our settlers were splendid shots; if so many English were killed in these first encounters, the French must have equally suffered, yet all their loss is put down at one man killed. Baudoin's

---

[1] Captain Tavenor, a Newfoundland skipper, reported in 1714 that the English freighters and skippers from Spain and Portugal refused to sell salt to the planters unless they took also a certain quantity of wine and spirits.

[2] The manuscript in French was lent to me by Bishop Howley, and has been carefully translated by my friend, Madame Ribaillier des Isles. Charlevoix used it, almost word for word, for his description of this campaign.

explanation about the inferiority of the English guns, and the superior skill of the Canadian Indians in bush fighting, admitting it all to be true, would not account for the tremendous disparity between the losses on both sides   Mr Christopher Pollard petitioned in 1697 that the planters from Newfoundland should be sent back to take part in the war, because they were such good shots, and accustomed to camping out in the winter.   He said the regular soldiers would not be able to fight successfully against the Canadians and Indians.

As to the accusation of cowardice he makes against the Newfoundlanders, his own account of the sally of the brave eighty-eight men to defend their brothers in Petty Harbour is an eloquent reply to this charge   Every movement of the French was watched by our people, the little garrison knew all about the large force of disciplined soldiers they had to contend with, yet these gallant civilians threw themselves into the breach—like the immortal three hundred Greeks—to die in defence of their country.   Talk about cowardice !   Colonial history has seldom recorded a more heroic action than the battle of this dauntless handful of fishermen against their four hundred foes.

After all, the gasconading chaplain admits that his brave French never made any serious attempt to attack a real fortification like Carbonear.   All their heroic exploits were assaults on poor fishermen, helpless women, and children—the burning of their houses, and the plunder and pillage of their goods   One regrets, for the honour of such a distinguished Canadian as D'Iberville, that he acted in bad faith, both at the surrender of St. John's and in the attempted exchange of prisoners at Carbonear Island.   The march through the country in winter was a great military feat ; but after the capture of St. John's their exploits during the rest of the campaign were simply acts of barbarity, worthy of the savage Abenaquis, certainly they added no fresh laurels to the great military glories of France.

The French, after their various raids between 1696 and 1713, never remained in possession of any part of the English settlements They simply swooped down on the peaceful English settlements like birds of prey, harried them, and then flew away to their nests in Placentia.

Their officers and troops were paid out of the booty taken   These expeditions partook more of the nature of a freebooting expedition than a definite scheme of conquest   The rich English settlements, of which, Charlevoix said, the meanest was better than Placentia,[1] offered a tempting bait—a suitable opportunity of employing restless Canadians

---

[1] SUFA's Char'croix.

and Indian braves during the winter; they always retired before the advent of the English fishing fleet.[1]

During the wars of this reign, especially in the French expedition under D'Iberville, tremendous losses were inflicted on the English in Newfoundland. In a petition to King William the damage to the little Devonshire town of Bideford alone is estimated at £24,700; the planters' loss at Ferryland is put down at £12,000. The greatest sufferers of all were the unfortunate inhabitants of St. John's. Accounts in the reign of Charles II. show the substantial character of the settlers' houses, their wealth, their large stores, shops, and extensive fishing establishments. In this generation we have twice seen our fair city reduced to a heap of ashes. Some of us can remember all the horrors and miseries of that terrible night of June 1846, when thousands of poor forlorn families were huddled together without shelter, food, or clothing. The night of the fire of '46 was a terrible time of calamity, but its miseries were as nothing compared to the sufferings of the inhabi-

BIDEFORD.

tants of St. John's in the bitter winter weather of 1696. By the invasion and destruction of St. John's they were not only made homeless

[1] PENHALLOW says: "Newfoundland has given a melancholy account of the many ravages that have been committed there by the powerful assistance of those savages."

and beggars, they were banished from the land they loved so dearly; many of them had seen their brothers, sons, husbands, and lovers, who had sallied out so boldly on that frosty November morning to assist the men of Petty Harbour, brought back to them dead and mutilated by the savage allies of the French, to crown all the anguish of this terrible time, they were crowded together in one small vessel, two hundred and twenty-four men, women, and children The horrors of that awful winter passage no pen can describe.[1]

This total destruction of the Newfoundland settlements by the French in 1697 caused great excitement and alarm in New England[2] and Virginia King William's Government was at length aroused to action. There was tremendous indignation in England against the Ministry for the loss of Newfoundland, and their neglect to send a naval and military force to defend the Island. When it was too late, and the whole English Colony and their possessions had been swept away from the face of the earth, a large squadron, under Admiral Norris, and no less than fifteen hundred soldiers — two regiments, one from Ireland, under Colonel Gibson—were sent out (1697) to recapture Newfoundland[3] They found St John's completely abandoned The French had burnt, pillaged, and destroyed everything movable and immovable in the once flourishing settlement. There was not a solitary building left standing, all the forts were razed to the ground, literally, there was not one stone left upon another.[4]

[1] The following entry on the cover of the parish register of the old church of Coffinswell describes these events in simple, but pathetic, language It was extracted for me by the late Hon S Rendell.—

"The 12th November 1696 St John's in the Newfoundland was taken by the French and ye Indians, and many men were killed They in the Fort yielded upon articles, and had of the French a ship to bring them home to England They came out of the ship 224 souls Elias Bickford came home the 10th of January the ship came to Dartmouth
John Bickford, Parish Clerk "

[2] ROYAL LETTER SENT TO THE GOVERNOUR OF MASSACHUSETTS BAY.

24 March 1697.

Relative to the capture of St. John's by the French, the Governour is required to send ships and land forces as may be spared and provisions to join the Royal ships between Cape Race and Cape Bonavista. The letter says more particularly that the Colony of New England is concerned in recovering what has been lost in Newfoundland

[3] The "Life of Captain Stephen Martin," by Clements R Markham, contains a full account of this expedition.

[4] There is a very interesting account of the defence of Little Belle Isle in 1696-97

The first resident on this small island in Conception Bay was John Earle, a West Countryman. He was a very smart, well educated young man, just of age in 1698, when he married in Harbour Grace Fanny Garland, sister of the well-known Justice Garland, a Mr Pinsent and a Mr Lilly married other sisters of Mr. Garland The French attacked Little Belle Isle with two barges full of soldiers. John Earle had cannon upon the cliff; he sank one barge with a shot, and the other then rowed off; he had scarecrows dressed up as men on the top of the cliff to make the enemy believe he had a large force. Earle used to tell of the high prices in those days, Garland, of Trinity, as a favour to a relation, sold him one spring one cwt and a half of flour for £5 st'g, and one hh'd. of salt for £2. John Earle lived and died and was buried on Little Belle Isle. One of his sons, William, lived in Juggler's Cove, Bay Roberts, and died there of small pox in 1777. The other son, John, lived in Portugal Cove, and is mentioned in the census of 1794-5 There are numerous descendants of both branches. The family bible of the first John Earle's wife is in the St John's Museum

The soldiers were set to work at once, and a new Fort William was erected upon the old site under the direction of a Mr. Richards, an engineer. Not much was done the first year beyond erecting the palisade, but between 1698 and 1708 the ramparts were faced with brick and bomb-proof parapets, and powder-magazines and substantial barracks erected. An additional fort—Fort George—was made below for the townspeople, and connected by a subway with Fort William. All the work about Fort William is the labour of English hands, commenced anew in 1697, with considerable additions made from time to time by English engineers. The French were never in possession of the present fort except from June to September 1762. It appears to have been only partially destroyed in 1708 by St. Ovide, as we find Governor Collins mentioning the fort in 1709 as still in existence. Two substantial batteries were also built between 1697 and 1704 on the site of the earthworks of Captain Martin—the Chain Rock and Fort Frederick batteries of our days.

ADMIRAL NORRIS.

From an engraving after Burford.

So strong were the sea defences of St. John's that it resisted all the attacks of the French ships. D'Iberville, with true military genius, was the first to discover that our capital —well-nigh impregnable by sea— could be easily captured in the winter by land.

The movements of the naval and military forces were very much hampered by being under separate commands, and required to call councils of war. Admiral Norris next year had supreme control as Governor for the time being. As a result, there was much indecision. When Nesmond's fleet was reported, in August, to be outside the harbour, instead of going out to engage it, an extra cable was put across the harbour, so that the two imposing expeditions sent out by France and England returned home without having exchanged a blow. Norris's conduct of the war is severely censured by Burnet.

Lieutenant-Colonel Handyside and three hundred men were left at St. John's for the winter, but the buildings were so badly built, the winter so severe, and provisions so scarce (a ship from

New England having failed to reach them), that two hundred and fourteen died.

On the 31st of March the Privy Council had decided to station a permanent garrison at St. John's, to improve the fortifications, and erect a boom across the harbour. The Board of Ordnance did not carry out this last order; in fact, they objected to do anything for the Colony, claiming that the expense should be borne by the settlers, like the other plantations. Lieutenant Lilburne, with sixty soldiers and gunners, remained through the winter, and in 1699 a Captain Andrews seems to have been in command. Ten recruits sent out from England this year were returned as not being required, so we may conclude that the fortifications were complete, and were considered to be practically impregnable.

ENGLISH SOLDIERS IN 1710.
From Winsor's N. & C. H. of America.

The reign of William III., the first real constitutional sovereign of England, has been drawn for us by Macaulay in a history which, despite all its faults and its grievous misstatements, ever will remain an imperishable monument to the character of this illustrious warrior and statesman—the noblest history in the world. William was the hereditary enemy of France. Under his firm rule England threw off the galling yoke of subserviency to the arrogant Louis, which had been borne by Charles and James.

All the pretensions of the French in the Colony were sternly ignored. The king declared that no alien or stranger shall fish or take bait in Newfoundland, and in his first declaration of war against the French he sets forth :—

"It was not long since the French took license from the Governor of Newfoundland to fish upon the coast and paid a tribute for such licenses as an acknowledgement of the sole right of the Crown of England to that Island; but of late the encroachments of the French on his Majesty's subjects trading and fishing there had been more like the invasions of an enemy than becoming friends, who enjoyed the advantages of that trade only by permission."

This is a plain and clear statement of the English dominion over the island. Unfortunately, William was too much occupied defending Holland to give his brave words effect until the terrible disaster of 1696-7. After the Peace of Ryswick, which left France in possession of all her territory in America, including part of Newfoundland, no great effort was made to drive the French out of Newfoundland.

On the 9th December 1698, in his speech from the throne, King William recommended Parliament "to employ their thoughts about some good Bills for the advancement of trade, they were enjoyned to take the state of the Newfoundland fishery into their consideration"; and in order to restore good government and to prevent contentions and disorders for the future, an Act was passed entitled "*An Act to encourage the Trade to Newfoundland.*" At this distance of time we cannot understand how any intelligent Minister could have propounded such a Bill, but William's Government was notoriously corrupt. It is only through the strong influence of Devonshire and bribery that we can explain the passage of such a measure.

In the first section of the Act the right of England to the Colony was clearly set forth. No alien or stranger whatsoever was to take bait or fish there. It was a re-assertion of our claim to the whole island, but King William's Government never gave it any practical effect.

The only reasonable provision in the Act was the seventh clause, which gave a title "to all persons who have built houses stages &c since 1685 that did not belong to fishing ships they to occupy and enjoy the same"

The absurdity and monstrosity of the scheme which was arranged for the interest of the West Countrymen lay in the surrender of the entire control of the Colony, including the administration of justice, into the rude hands of a set of ignorant skippers, who were so illiterate, that out of the whole body of these marine justiciaries, only four could be found able to sign their names.

There is one very singular feature about the Act of William III The statute is entirely declaratory and directory; there is not a single penal clause in it from beginning to end, nor is any compulsory jurisdiction given to any authority acting under it. The framers of the Act had evidently very little confidence in fishing admirals, vice-admirals, and rear-admirals, for they virtually gave them no power to compel anyone to obey their edicts, all the technical words used to constitute a court have been very carefully omitted from this remarkable statute. Charles' Star Chamber Rules contained penalties for certain offences here there were none—every punishment inflicted by a fishing admiral was, therefore, wholly illegal.

Besides the admirals, there were other functionaries with still more high-sounding titles. We read in the records of the violent acts of Ford, the " Governor of Petty Harbour," and the truculent humours of the " King of Quiddy Vitty " [1]

I will try and describe the fishing admiral, as he appeared to our ancestors, clothed, not in the dignity of office, not in the flowing judicial robes, not in the simple and sober black of the police magistrate, but in his ordinary blue flushing jacket and trousers, economically besmeared with pitch, tar, and fish slime, his head adorned with an old sealskin cap, robbed from an Indian, or bartered for a glass of rum and a stick of tobacco. The sacred temple of law and equity was a fish store, the judicial seat an inverted butter firkin. Justice was freely dispensed to the suitor who paid the most for it. In the absence of a higher bribe, his worship's decision was often favourably affected by the judicious presentation of a few New England apples

The litigant who commenced his case with the production of a flowing bowl of calabogus [2] captivated the judicial mind most effectually. Sometimes, alas ' the dignity of the Bench was diminished by the sudden fall of the Court prostrate on the floor, overcome by the too potent effects of new rum and spruce beer

The fishing admirals were not satisfied with the powers conferred upon them. The Western adventurers petitioned to allow them to appoint *deputies* to exercise their duties , this was sternly refused Time would fail to recount all the enormities and barbarities of these ignorant vulgar tyrants They displaced the rightful owners of room, seizing them either for themselves or their friends ; they fined, triangled,[3] and whipped at their pleasure every unfortunate wretch who earned their displeasure, and against whom some trumped-up charge could be made out

They always put off hearing any cases until August. Invariably they tried their own causes first. Chief Justice Brady, on his first visit to a Western outport, found, to his astonishment, that the agent of the great English house in the place had sat on the Bench and given a number of judgments in favour of his own firm. " How dare you, sir, commit such a perversion of justice ? " said the indignant

---

[1] The oldest ship fisherman in each harbour was called the " king "

[2] Calabogus was a favourite drink with the Admirals It was composed of rum, molasses, and spruce beer Their principal toast " The Pope and ten dollars " (meaning ten dollars a quintal for fish).

[3] Mr. Pearce, of Twillingate, who died not long ago, remembered as a boy seeing a man triangled—tied by the outstretched arms— and whipped by order of a fishing admiral.

Chief. "Well," said the agent, quite unabashed, "I must be a pretty sort of a vule of a judge if I could not do justice to myself." This remarkable Justice rejoiced in the name of "the Lord High Hadmiral."

The most celebrated of the fishing admirals—Commander-in-Chief and Generalissimo of the West Country adventurers in 1700—was Captain Arthur Holdsworth, Admiral of the Harbour of St. John's. The old Devonshire family of the Holdsworths of Dartmouth are closely connected with our history. Cromwell consulted a Mr. Holdsworth (or Oldsworth)—probably this Captain Arthur's father—about the affairs of the Colony. A later descendant—also Arthur Holdsworth—was Governor of Dartmouth Castle, probably a grandson of Admiral

AQUAFORTE.

From a drawing by the Hon. and Rev. W. Gray.

Holdsworth. He was the last member of the old family who took any personal share in our trade. He built the large stone house still existing in Ferryland, occupied by Mr. Morey. The late Mr. White

Castle—a very tall, powerful man   The family is still in existence, and own large property in St John's (Holdsworth Street, &c). Both the Brookings and the Studdys are connected with the Holdsworth family. Mr. Brooking, who managed their firm's affairs in Newfoundland in our own time, was called Thomas Holdsworth.

In 1701 the English Government sent out Mr. Larkin, a barrister, to draw up a confidential report on all the English North American colonies.   In his report on Newfoundland he shows how the West Country men worked this Act of William III. to their own advantage In 1701 he says, writing from St John's :—

" The then admiral of this Harbour, Captain Arthur Holdsworth, brought over from England this fishing season 236 passengers all or great part of which were bye boat keepers and they were brought, under a pretence of being freighters aboard his ship, though it was only for some few provisions for their necessary use.   These persons he had put and continued in the most convenient stages in the Harbour which all along since the year 1685 had belonged to fishing ships, insomuch that several masters of fishing vessels had been obliged to hire rooms of the Planters.

"These bye boat keepers," says Mr Larkin, "were most of them able fishermen and there was not one fresh man or green man amongst them as the Act requires."

Mr. Larkin goes on to state :—

"That Captain Arthur Holdsworth and one or two more who constantly used the fishery, made it their business in the beginning of the year to ride from one market town to another in the West of England on purpose to get passengers, with whom they made an agreement, that in case they should happen to be Admirals of any of the Harbours [The first, second, or third to arrive in the Harbour] they would put and continue Mr. Holdsworth and such persons as he approved of in fishing ships rooms

"This," says Mr Larkin, "was very great abuse and discouragement to the other Adventurers ; besides, these bye boat keepers could afford to sell their fish cheaper than the Adventurers, which must lessen the number of fishing ships."

In the last year of King William's reign the great English Missionary Society, which has done and is still doing so much to sustain the Church of England in this Colony, was founded and incorporated as " The Society for the Propagation of the Gospel in Foreign Parts," under a Royal Charter, dated the 16th June 1701. There had been previously several abortive attempts to establish a similar scheme.   Laud had proposed one to Charles   Cromwell planned an institution for all Protestant churches that was to rival the great Propaganda of Rome, but up to the beginning of the eighteenth century the Church of England had not properly fulfilled the Divine command to go forth and preach the gospel to all nations.   Since then she has nobly redeemed her early neglect of missions.   Rome had her enthusiastic missionaries, especially a devoted band of Jesuits, braving all dangers and bearing the message of the Cross to many lands long before the English Church had a single labourer in the field.   There is, however, no record of any Roman Catholic priest living in the English settlements during this or the two succeeding reigns, unless Cowling, mentioned by Roope, was a resident of St. John's

To the venerable English society, Newfoundland is indebted for the first resident clergyman, the Rev John Jackson.   He had been chaplain of one of the men-of-war that came with Sir John Norris' expedition in 1697, and had resided in St. John's and ministered to a congregation, and a small church had been built close to Fort William, several years before the first grant was made by the S P G   In 1703 we find the following entry in the records of the Society.—

' In Newfoundland no public exercise of religion except at St John's where there is a congregation but unable to subsist a minister   To Mr. Jackson £50 per annum and a benefaction of £30 "

Probably this was given to enable him to bring out his wife and family.   Jackson seems to have been a good, earnest man.   He had a difficult part to play ; to many of the lawless residents the restraints of religious observances of decency and morality were irksome in the extreme   What rendered the poor chaplain's position still more difficult was the direct opposition and bad example of the Commandant and resident Governor.

APPENDIX TO CHAPTER IX.

I. The Campaign of 1696-7.

(a) ENGLISH ACCOUNT OF THE FRENCH ATTACK ON ST JOHN'S, 1696

Philip Roberts, Richard Gelman and Samuel May late Inhabitants and fishermen of St John's in the North part of Newfoundland came this present 10th day of January 1696-7 before me Thomas Hood Esquire Mayor of the Borough of Clifton, Dartmouth Hardness and John Palmer Esquire the last preceeding Mayor, two of His Majesty's Justices of the Peace within the same, to swear that on the 16th November last the Inhabitants of St John's had information that the French to the number of sixteen men had taken Petty Harbour a small fishing place about nine miles distant from St. John's,

Upon which the Inhabitants aforesaid sent out thirty four men, armed to their releife   But the weather proving full of snow they returned the next day, being the 17th November, without effecting anything   On the 18th they sent out another party of men to the number of eighty four armed to the aid and assistance of the Inhabitants of Petty Harbour who had not marched above a mile from St John's up the South Hill until they met a body of French and Soldier- and Canada Indians, to the number of Four hundred or thereabouts, with whom they engaged half an hour , in which action were killed of the Inhabitants thirty four men and several others wounded, the rest retreating back to the Harbour of St John's, the French pursuing.

About one hundred and eighty men of the Inhabitants besides women and children entered into a fortification called King William's Ffort, which they kept and defended for three days, the French in the meantime burning and destroying all houses boats stages and provisions.

And these Deponents further say that the French took one William Drew, an Inhabitant a Prisoner and cutt all around his scalp and then by the strength of hand stript his skin from the forehead to the crowne and so sent him into the fortification, assuring the Inhabitants that they would serve them all in like manner if they did not surrender, who wanting ammunition and provisions and receiving articles of surrender from the French (of which the annexed is a true copy) were accordingly obliged to doe and with about eighty men of the said Inhabitants went off to the Southward with the French, most of them being forced so to doe contrary to the articles of capitulation.

And Samuell May saith that being present with the Governor of Placentia [De Brouillon] after the said articles of surrender were signed, he heard the said Governor declare by an interpreter, that the English were asleep and fools to suffer their plantation to be thus taken from them ; That the French did not doubt of taking all New England next summer except Boston ; and that they now intended to inhabit Renews having already fortified that place.

The body of the French and Indians, who attacked them, were commanded by the Governor of Placentia and Canada, who came with the said forces from Placentia in ships and boats to Bay Bulls, and from thence to Petty Harbour and St John's aforesaid by land and that after the destruction of St. John's a party of the aforesaid forces were detached to march through the woods to commit the like spoyle on all the harbours to the northward

That on 16th December last these Deponents with about two hundred and twenty men women and children Inhabitants came from St John's in a small vessel given them by the French to carry them for England, and that at the same time about eighty men more of the Inhabitants were sent in another vessel to France, contrary to the capitulation, and that at the time of these Deponents leaving the Country a party of French were then in possession of St John's.

(b) BALDOIN'S DIARY

THE CAPTURE OF ST. JOHN'S BY THE FRENCH, NOVEMBER 1696

On the morning of the 28th of November M de Montigny, a brave Canadian [Montigny was at the taking of Schenectady and Pemaquid and served in after years under Subercase and Ovide in Newfoundland], M D'Iberville's lieutenant, was keeping the advanced guard with thirty Canadians marching about one hundred yards in advance M De Brouillon and M D'Iberville followed with the main body of the troops M De Brouillon had orders to allow the Canadians to take the lead in case of a sudden attack.

After two hours' march our advance guard came upon the enemy and at about a pistol shot from them, they numbered eighty-eight. They occupied an advantageous position on a rocky hill amongst burnt woods These hills [South Side Hills] served to protect them Our advanced guard opened fire upon the enemy who thinking we numbered but twenty four returned fire These gentlemen [D'Iberville and De Brouillon] soon joined us, and after having received absolution, every man threw aside the load he had been carrying and rushed upon the enemy M De Brouillon attacked them first, then M D'Iberville chose the left flank and discovering the enemy amongst the rocks and bushes, he killed a great number; after half an hour's engagement they gave in. The real number

of French in this fight was about 400 men] M D'Iberville pursued them sword in hand right into St. John's, which was a distance of about three-quarters of a league He entered St John's fully a quarter of an hour before the arrival of M De Brouillon with the main body of our troops M D'Iberville got into St John's at the same time as the enemy, and immediately took possession of two of the first forts which the enemy had abandoned , he also took thirty-three prisoners, amongst the number some entire families The others retreated, some into the large Fort and some into a vessel which was then in the Harbour Fear was so general amongst the enemy [the English] that had M D'Iberville had one hundred men with him he would have taken the larger Fort also, for there were in it but about two hundred men according to the accounts given us by the prisoners, and these but poorly prepared for war

M De Brouillon having arrived with our main army, M De Muis encamped in the Fort nearest to the enemy with his sixty men, and within cannon shot of them This Fort was palisaded The remainder of our troops encamped in the houses. The wind being favourable the Vessel which lay in the Harbour set sail laden with all that was best in St John's and eighty or a hundred men The enemy lost fifty men, M De Brouillon's trumpeter was killed whilst standing beside him, three of his men were wounded and two of M D'Iberville's M De Brouillon acted all through like a brave man, I was quite near him most of the time, and so can judge of his doings

These people would require one or two campaigns with the Iroquois to learn how to defend themselves against the enemy Verily the Canadians had much the advantage, having learned how to fight in all then terrible wars with the Iroquois In these wars, as in this one, it is far better to be killed outright than to be wounded, for there are no remedies to be had, no help, no refreshment for the sick, each man having only just what he can carry on his back, the march being so difficult through this barren island

We sent a prisoner immediately to the fort, but he was retained there 29th November, it is snowing heavily, some of our Canadians going into the woods took eight prisoners, and some others came and gave themselves up These gentlemen [the French commanders] seeing that our enemies are determined to defend themselves, sent to Bay Bulls for the mortars, the bombs, and the powder which M D'Iberville had left there On the night of the 29th-30th MM De Muis and De Montigny went with sixty Canadians to burn the houses which were near and beyond the fort , M D'Iberville stationed himself with thirty of his men to support them, and M De Brouillon remained at the advanced posts with his men.

The 30th November, St. Andrew's day, a man came out of the fort carrying a white flag and asking for terms. Our commanders agree to an interview The Governor of the fort came out with forty of the chief inhabitants, they would not allow even one of our people to go within the fort, lest we might see in what a miserable state it was, and to what straits they were reduced. They insisted upon deferring their surrender until the morrow, hoping that the two large vessels [these may have been H M S Dreadnought and Oxford, sent out to rch eve them] which they had seen for two days off their Harbour might find a favourable wind to bring them into it But the commanders would not consent to make any delay They then decided to surrender, on condition that two ships should be given them to return to England, that those who wished might go to Bonavista, and leave for England from there, and that they should not be searched, which was granted

The written capitulation was taken to the fort and approved of by the principal inhabitants, it was afterwards brought back to our camp where it was signed by the English Governor [probably Miuers or Roberts] and after by M De Brouillon; this latter did not even offer it M D'Iberville for his signature, though he had had at least as much to do with the taking of the place as had M De Brouillon

I confess, my Lord, that this act shocked me greatly The Governor then re-entered his fort, from whence he soon afterwards came out accompanied by the whole garrison composed of one hundred and fifty men, some master mariners and some sailors engaged for the fishery, besides women and children Our enemies had but one man wounded during the time we were reconnoitring the fort This fort was situated on the hill to the north-west, commanded on one side by two heights both within gunshot of it, it was square in shape, with four bastions, a palisade eight feet high, a covered trench now full of snow, also a drawbridge, with a small tower upon which there were four cannons, the balls for which weighed four pounds, under the tower there was a cellar for keeping gunpowder There was, however, very little powder in it, and only a couple of dozen of cannon balls. The English not having had time to carry anything to their fort, they only took refuge there when they saw us coming

They depended solely upon the eighty-eight men whom they had chosen from their entire force to defend them, but these latter were provided with very inferior guns, only suited for fishermen and for those who never had the slightest idea what war really was. The Governor of this fort was simply an inhabitant of the place, and not a captain of one of the English ships, he was without soldiers, and had no commission from the King of England

Thus one cannot feel surprised at M D'Iberville's venturing an attack upon this place, falling upon St John's during the night, and taking the inhabitants entirely by surprise Their forts being without men and their houses quite far one from the other, we should actually have run much less risk than had our advance been discovered

St John's has a very fine harbour, which can hold two hundred ships. The entrance lies between two very high mountains, distant one from the other about a gunshot They are surmounted by a battery of eight guns. The inhabitants of St John's are very well settled along the north side of the harbour to a distance of about half a league. There were three forts, one on the side towards the roads westward, another in the centre having a native as Governor with sixty men, and a third which gave us a good deal of trouble before capitulating This latter fort protects the entrance to the harbour, although at a distance from it, it commands the harbour, and a number of the houses—the best part of St John's—was around this fort and the best houses were built there Unfortunately these latter were burnt on the night before the capitulation

On the 2nd of December we took Portugal Cove, which contained three families, also Torbay, which had likewise three families, and Kenvidi [Quidi Vidi], which had nine families. We burnt every house in St John's, and the boats in the harbour On the 14th of January 1697, we started for Portugal Cove, and arrived there on the 19th Thence we travelled along the shore of Conception Bay to the bottom, where we found some men sawing wood, who had come from Carbonniere On the 20th we took Harbor Men [Maine], where there was one house. On the 23rd we left in three boats for Carbonniere We passed by Brigue, where there were about sixty men, and arrived at Port Grave, which we took There were one hundred and ten men and seventeen houses there, well armed.

On the 24th we set out for Carbonniere, Le Sr de Montigny was sent with a detachment to take Musquito In passing from Harbor Grace to Carbonniere in boats we discovered that the inhabitants of this latter place had entrenched themselves on the Island, and they fired some cannon shots at us. There were about two hundred on the Island, having fled there from Harbor Grace, Musquito, and even St John's They had erected barracks and strong forts Having arrived at Carbonniere, the commander sent to summon the people on the Island, but were met with defiance We found it impossible to attack it, as it was steep on all sides, with the exception of two places of landing, which were well guarded On the 29th we received prisoners from Brigue, among whom were eight Irishmen, whom the English treat as slaves.

Several attempts were made by M D'Iberville to land on the Island, but in vain.

On the night of the 31st we went all round the Island in boats. The sentry challenged us and fired. We had ninety men in nine boats, and M. Montigny, when challenged by the sentinel at pistol shot distance off, could almost touch the Island with his hand, he was going to leap ashore first.

On the 3rd we took Bay Ver, where there were some fourteen houses and about ninety men. From there we went to Old Perlican, there were there nineteen houses, several stores, more than thirty head of horned cattle, and a number of sheep and pigs. On the 7th we went to Ance Havre [Hants Harbor]. There were four houses, but the people had all fled. On the morning of the 8th we started for Cehcove [Silly Cove], where there were four houses and a great quantity of fish and cattle. Thence we came to New Perlican, there were there nine houses and stores. We left immediately for Harbor Content [Havre Content], where there was a sort of fort or barricade, made of boards, with portholes above and below. This temporary fortress was commanded by an Irishman. They surrendered on being summoned. There were thirty men, besides women and children.

Having left the place in charge of M. Deschaufours with ten men, M. D'Iberville started the following day for Carbonniere. When arrived there he found that the English had taken prisoners one Frenchman and three Irishmen, who had taken part with the French. A detachment under Boisbriand was sent to burn Brigne, Port Grave, &c. Harbor Grace had fourteen houses, Carbonniere, twenty-two,—the best built in all Newfoundland. Some of the merchants were men of £100,000 worth of property.

On the 17th we entered into negotiations with the people on the Island for an exchange of prisoners. The English demanded one Englishman in lieu of their French prisoner, and three for each Irishman. The place of exchange was agreed upon, namely, out of gunshot of the Island, about half-way between it and the shore. The English came without their prisoners, and some words ensued. Our officer accused them of breaking their word, and casting ridicule upon the orders of the King. The Commander seized the English officers, and took them prisoners.

On the 28th we burned Carbonniere, and left again for Havre Content. On the 1st of March M. D'Iberville sent MM. de Montigny and de la Perriere to go with all the prisoners (about two hundred) to Bay Boulle [Bay Bulls Arm], in the bottom of Trinity Bay. He left M. de Boisbriand with a detachment at Havre Content, with orders to keep a strict watch on Carbonniere, and he himself, with nine men, set out across the woods for Plaisance. The road is not quite as good as between Paris and Versailles.

[The list in the Statistical Chapter gives the number of the settlers, fishing establishments, number of fishing boats, and quintals of fish caught as noted by Baudoin.]

II. Act of William III.

10 & 11 Wm III, Cap xxv

An Act
to encourage the trade to Newfoundland

WHEREAS the trade of and fishing at Newfoundland is a beneficial trade to this kingdom, not only in the employing great numbers of seamen and ships, and exporting and consuming great quantities of provisions and manufactures of this realm, but also in the bringing into this nation by returns of the effects of the said fishery from other countries great quantities of wine, oil, plate, iron, wool, &c., to the increase of revenue, and the encouragement of trade and navigation.

Be it enacted that from henceforth it shall be lawful for all his Majesty's subjects, residing within this realm of England, or its dominions, trading to Newfoundland, to enjoy the free trade of merchandize and fishing to and from Newfoundland, peaceably to take bait and liberty to go on shore on any part of Newfoundland for the curing, salting, drying, and husbanding of their fish and for making oil, and to cut down trees for building stages, shiprooms, train-fats, hurdles, ships, boats and other necessaries for themselves &c. and all other things which may be useful for their fishing trade, as fully as at any time heretofore, and that no alien shall take bait or use any sort of trade or fishing there.

2. And to preserve the harbours . . that from the 1st March 1700 no ballast &c. shall be cast out but carried on shore.

3. And . . . . that at their departing no person shall destroy flakes and at their arrival they shall content themselves with such stages as are needful for them, and they shall not repair them by rinding trees or demolishing other stages.

4. And . . . . . that (according to the ancient custom there used) the master of such ship as shall first enter a harbour shall be Admiral, the second Vice-Admiral, and the third Rear-Admiral and that the master of every ship content himself with such beach as he shall have necessary use for, and if possessed of places in other harbours, shall make his election in forty-eight hours of such place as he shall chuse to abide in, and the Admirals shall settle differences and proportion the places to the several ships according to the number of boats which each ship shall keep.

5. And whereas several inhabitants in Newfoundland and other persons have since the year 1685 detained in their own hands, and for their private benefit stages, cookrooms &c. and other places (which before that time belonged to fishing ships) for taking of bait and fishing and curing their fish to

the great prejudice of the fishing ships and sometimes to the overthrow of their voyage and to the great discouragement of traders there,

.   .   .   that all persons as since the year 1685 have taken stages &c shall on the 25th of March next relinquish them to the use of the fishing ships

6   And to prevent ingrossing in future, that no fisherman or inhabitant of Newfoundland shall take any stage &c which at any time since 1685 belonged to any fishing ship until all such ships shall be provided with stages

7   Provided always that *all such persons as since the 25th of March 1685 have built houses and stages that did not belong to fishing ships since 1685 shall peaceably enjoy the same without any disturbance from any person whatever*

8   And   .   .   .   That all by-boat keepers shall not pretend to meddle with any stage &c that did belong to the fishing ships since 1685

9   And   .   .   .   that every master of a by-boat shall carry out two fresh men in six and that every inhabitant shall be obliged to hire two fresh men like by-boat keepers, and masters of ships one fresh man in five and the masters of by-boats and ships shall take oath before the collector, &c that they have such fresh men, and the officers are required to give a certificate thereof without any fee.

10   And   .   .   .   .   that masters of ships take every fifth man a green man

11   And   .   .   .   that no person shall deface masts of boats &c

12   And   .   .   .   that no person shall rind trees nor set fire to the woods, nor cut timber except for repairing and no person shall cast anchor or do anything to hinder the hailing of sayns in the accustomed baiting places, nor steal nets or cut adrift boats.

13   And whereas several persons that have been guilty of thefts, murders and other felonies, have escaped unpunished because the trial of such offenders hath been ordered before no other court but the Lord High Constable and Earl Marshall of England   .   .   that all robberies and murders &c committed there may be tried in any shire of England by virtue of the King's commission of oyer and terminer and gaol delivery according to the laws of this realm

14   And   .   .   .   that admirals are required (in the harbours and on shore) to see the rules of this present act duly put in execution and that each shall keep a journal of the ships, boats, stages, transports and of all the seamen imployed in their respective harbours and deliver a true copy to the Privy Council

15   And   .   .   .   in case of dispute between the fishing ships and the inhabitants the Admirals shall determine them and if any

party shall think themselves aggrieved they can appeal to the commanders of His Majesty's ships of war appointed as convoys

16   And to the end all may join their solemn prayers and addresses to Almighty God for his blessing on their persons and endeavours   .   .   .   that all the inhabitants shall strictly keep every Lords Day and that none keeping taverns shall sell wine &c on that day.

17   And whereas by an act to grant his Majesty a further subsidy of five per cent on all merchandize imported (all manner of fish English taken excepted) and whereas some doubt has arisen whether oil, blubber and fins are not liable to the said duty   .   .   that all oils &c of English fishing taken in the seas of Newfoundland and imported in English shipping are hereby declared to be free of the said duties.

III. Baron de Lahontan

Louis Armand de lom d'Arce Baron de Lahontan was born at the village of Lahontan in the department of the Basses Pyrénées, on the 9th of June 1666   He went out to Canada as a young officer in the French Army in 1683, at the age of 17 years, and arrived in Quebec on the 8th of November   In 1684 he went up the river to Montreal with his detachment to fight against the Iroquois   He continued there until 1687, when he was appointed commander of Fort St. Joseph on the Lakes   In 1689 he returned to Quebec   Frontenac was called this year for the second time to the post of Governor of New France   On July 27th Lahontan embarked at Quebec aboard the frigate *La Sainte Anne*   The *La Sainte Anne* called at Placentia on August 18th, and remained one month for the fleet of Basque fishing boats which she was to convoy home   On September 14th, fifty fishing vessels were assembled at the foot of Bastin of Placentia waiting a favourable wind   Two soldiers returned from Cape St Mary's where they had been in search of some deserters   They reported a squadron of five English vessels moored at the cove of Pourchet, probably Distress Cove, a rock off the cove is called Perure rock, five leagues (about twelve miles) from Placentia   This fleet anchored in the road the following day, 15th September.   De Brouillan had only fifty men in the fort at this time, commanded by Lieutenants Pastour, Costebelle, and St Ovide.   He pressed into his service the fishing captains and crews   The Gut was barred by four cables attached to anchors on each side, La Hontan with sixty Basque sailors was detached to Lafontaine (Freshwater)   The enemy was occupied taking soundings and observations with their telescopes   On the 17th, eight hundred soldiers in boats approached the place where La Hontan lay in ambush (Fresh Water Cove)   The Basques in their impatience could not be restrained, they rushed out before the English landed, and the latter seeing them, retired to a point a half league away (Point Latimé), and setting fire to it, retired. De Brouillan profiting by this first repulse of the enemy fortified the place; he built a stone redoubt on the height of the mountain, from whence he could put out the fire of their batteries. The fishing ships ranged themselves in line to defend the entrance (the Gut), he also placed four new guns opposite to the forts (i e, on the Jersey side)

On the 18th, a Chaloupe with a white banner floating approached the fort from the Admiral's ship. The Governor sent a serjeant to meet him. His eyes were bandaged and he was conducted to the Commandant. It was a Mr Williams, General of the besieging fleet, who said he had several French prisoners whom he would exchange. M De Brouillan sent La Hontan and Costebelle aboard to hold a colloquy, and also to try and find out the strength of the enemy. The Admiral received them with the greatest courtesy, gave them the latest news of Europe, &c. Mr Williams had been kept as a hostage, was released on returning of the French envoys. He then informed De Brouillan that he was charged to call upon him to surrender. This De Brouillan refused, of course, to do. On the 19th the English vessels were towed by their Chaloupes within range and placed themselves in line of battle. The Admiral sent to De Brouillan, saying, if during the attack he wished to speak to him he should hoist a *red* flag. De Brouillan thought this showed some sign of weakness or faint-heartedness on the part of the English. He thought it probable that the English seeing the number of the masts behind the fort might have thought it a fleet of warships. De Brouillan fired a broadside from all his batteries to the cry of "Vive le Roi," the English ships replied, for six hours the fire was kept up pretty lively. Then Brouillan found his powder coming short, and ceased firing, and allowed the English to continue. The fire from the French redoubts (Castle Hill) was so well directed that the admiral had to retire his line of attack. The vessels were all very much smashed up, both in the hulls and rigging. This unexpected retreat saved Brouillan, who was reduced to his last . . (gargousse) of powder, and for balls he used only those of the enemy, which he had collected from among the houses which were all riddled. Two thousand shots were fired against the place. De Brouillan, profiting by the retreat of the English, set to work to repair the breaches. He had only five men injured. On the 20th, a French prisoner jumped overboard from the English fleet, and swam ashore, near where La Hontan lay in ambuscade. He reported the English discouraged. They did not think Placentia

such a strong place, and so well fortified. The English abandoned the attack altogether, and went and burnt the houses on Point Verde. The French were in great rejoicement, all had worked well. The fishing captains pointing the cannons. De Brouillan in his report gave great praise to the officers, Costebelle, Pastour, St Ovide, and especially La Hontan. On October 6th, La Hontan left for France, and arrived at St. Nazare on the 23rd (17 days). For full history of this attack, *see* La Hontan Lettre XXIIIe. He was appointed lieutenant du Roi for Placentia.

La Hontan arrived at Placentia in June 1693, he was very coldly received by De Brouillan, who intended the post for his brother, quarrels soon became very bitter between the Governor and La Hontan. De Brouillan, though a very brave officer, and an experienced soldier, was grasping and tyrannical, he employed the soldiers in the fishery and took all the proceeds of their labour; like most colonial officials of that day his pay was small, and he made it up by plundering the military of both pay and provisions. La Hontan as the Indendant put a check on these proceedings. Reckless and insubordinate, La Hontan ventured his wit on the old martinet, lampooned him, made poems about him, which were sung in the Placentia taverns. Stung to madness, De Brouillan, with his servants, all masked, forcibly entered La Hontan's house, where he was entertaining a few Placentia friends, broke all his windows, furniture, and crockery. A reconciliation was effected between the bitter rivals by the good office of the Recollet Fathers, but it was a hollow truce. La Hontan in despair left the Colony by the last vessel, 11th December 1693. By this mad act he severed his allegiance with France. An officer who deserts his post in time of war deserves condign punishment, and despite all La Hontan's prayers, and the intercession of powerful friends, his grave offence would neither be overlooked or pardoned, finding all appeals were made in vain, he abandoned his country, his religion, and his King. His book is a fierce attack on the French colonial administration and the Catholic Priests. In a very clever dialogue he puts into the mouth of the savage Adario all the stock arguments of that day against Christianity. It is believed that a renegade priest helped La Hontan in this part of his work. The book which anticipated Voltaire in its attacks on religion made a great stir in the early part of the 18th Century. A large portion of the account of discoveries is untrue, the particulars relating to the savages is obscene, and from a renegade one could not expect honour, truth, or decency. La Hontan was first a protégée of the King of Denmark, his first English edition is dedicated to the Duke of Devonshire.

CHAPTER X.

REIGN OF ANNE

1702-1714

1702 —Captain Leake destroyed French fishing stages at Trepassey, St Mary's, Colinet, St. Lawrence, and dismantled the fort at St Peter's. French attack on Sillycove and Bonavista

1703 —Lieutenant Lloyd succeeded Captain Richards in command at Fort William, St John's Admiral Graydon's unsuccessful expedition against Placentia Grant from S P G to Reverend J Jackson John Roope sent out to superintend the placing of a boom at St John's. Further French attacks on Bonavista by way of Trinity and Placentia Bay porterage

1704 —La Grange repulsed from Bonavista by Captain Gill Battle of Blenheim. Captain Lloyd suspended by Captain Bridge on petition of the soldiers; Lieutenant Moody succeeded to the command Reverend J Jackson returned to England to support his complaints against Lloyd

1705 —Attack on St John's by Subercase, Governor of Placentia, and about five hundred troops, successful defence of the forts by Moody and Latham, town destroyed, many inhabitants taken prisoners to Placentia, Montigny and the Abenaquis plundered, during the summer, all the settlements in the northern bays except Carbonear Island, and spoilt the fishing In November, Captain Moody and the old company replaced by Major Lloyd and ninety-one fresh soldiers Fishery very much curtailed, only twenty ships from England and seventy-two thousand qtls of fish exported

1706 —Attack on the French fishing stations on the northern part of the Island by Captains Underdown and Carleton and Major Lloyd

1707 —Union of England and Scotland. House of Commons' petition to the Queen about the Newfoundland Trade.

1708 —Destruction of St John's by St Ovide de Broullon, Major Lloyd and the garrison taken prisoners and sent to Placentia, Quebec, and thence to France Unsuccessful attack on Buoy's Island by a French man-of-war Militia formed in St John's.

1709 —Captain Moody again in command at St John's during the summer Captains Aldred, Pudner, and Purvis destroyed French fishing stations in the North Commodore Taylour partially rebuilt Fort William and gave Governor's commissions to Collins for St John's and the coast as far as Carbonear, to Pynn for Carbonear Island, &c.

1711.—Admiral Hovenden Walker with fifteen ships, nine hundred guns, and four thousand men, decided he was not able to attack Placentia. Preliminaries of peace between France and England. Voluntary assembly made laws, Captain Crowe, R.A., presiding.

1712.—Armistice signed.

1713.—Treaty of Utrecht. The Island was declared to belong of right wholly to Great Britain; French allowed to fish between Bonavista and Point Riche. Survey of the Island ordered to be made by Captain Taverner, R.N., but not carried out for want of funds. One hundred French settlers arrived at Louisburgh from Placentia and St. Pierre.

During the whole of this reign our unfortunate Colony was devastated by war; besides minor attacks from French privateers, twice within this short period of twelve years St. John's and the outlying English settlements were destroyed by the French. Belgium has been designated " the cock-pit of Europe"; we were certainly the cock-pit of America.

QUEEN ANNE.
From an engraving after Kneller.

Whilst the British army in Europe was covering itself with glory at Blenheim, Malplaquet, and Ramilies under Marlborough, and the British Navy winning victories under the gallant Rooke and Teake, Benbow and Sir Cloudesley Shovel, North America witnessed the most contemptible British cowardice and inefficiency; anything more ludicrous than the abortive expeditions of Admiral Graydon and Admiral Hovenden Walker against Placentia cannot be conceived.

Amongst the voluminous reports of the Board of Trade at this period is one which brings our history directly in contact with the wits and poets of the classic age of Queen Anne. It purports to be a report of Lord Dartmouth, but it was really written by the genial poet and hard-working official Matthew Prior, whose signature is appended to it.

This interesting document, which is too long to quote in full, is very well written. It denounces the conduct of the fishing admirals, their injustice and incapacity. As one might anticipate from Prior's well-known ability, it is far more moderate, well-reasoned, and sensible than any previous paper on the Colony. It points out very distinctly that Newfoundland can never prosper whilst the French hold Placentia.

In 1703 Graydon was sent out to protect the West Indies after the death of Benbow; he was ordered to attack Placentia; he had a large fleet and a considerable land force. When off Placentia he held a council of war, consisting of Rear-Admiral Whetstone, thirteen captains in the Royal Navy, Colonel Rivers, commander-in-chief of the land forces, six captains, and an engineer. They decided that an attack on Placentia was impracticable, *and might tend to the dishonour of Her Majesty's arms.* For his cowardice Graydon was dismissed from the service. The failure of this expedition no doubt encouraged our enemies to attack the Colony.

MATTHEW PRIOR.
From a print in the B.M.

Admiral Hovenden Walker's great expedition to capture Quebec and Placentia, in 1711, was a still more ludicrous failure. This nautical Falstaff complained bitterly that "frivolous pamphleteers" had laughed him to scorn as an idiot and a coward; he was terribly indignant because they had held him up to ridicule for not taking Placentia. The frivolous writers declared :—

"The taking of the French Newfoundland Capital would have been as easy a task for the admiral as a citizen riding home in his chaise from Hampstead calling at a cake house to regale himself and his wife with a glass of cyder and a cheesecake."

And well they might scout and ridicule a British admiral with fifteen ships of war, nine hundred guns, and a land force of four thousand men, actually declaring that it was not practicable to make an attempt on Placentia, whilst they knew from an intercepted despatch of Costabelle's, the French Governor, that the little garrison was in want of supplies of all kinds, that the promised reinforcement of two companies of soldiers had not arrived, and that *La Valeur*, their only armed ship on the station, had been lost.

Anyone who studies the topography of Placentia will see at once
that it could have been captured by a flank movement similar to the

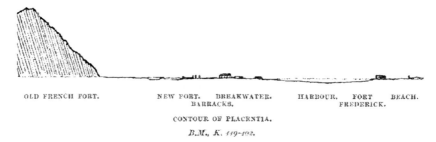

OLD FRENCH FORT.   NEW FORT.   BREAKWATER.   HARBOUR.   FORT   BEACH.
                                     BARRACKS.   FREDERICK.

CONTOUR OF PLACENTIA.

B.M., K. 119-102.

one adopted against Louisbourg; the attacking force could easily land
under cover of night at Little Placentia, and seize the heights commanding Castle Hill. All the defences were seaward; it was open to
any vigorous attack on the land side, especially to such overwhelming
forces as Graydon and Hovenden Walker commanded. With Castle
Hill taken, Placentia was at the mercy of the attacking force.

Between 1697 and 1705 the French directed their whole attention to
the unprotected outlying settlements in Conception and Trinity Bays;

TOPSAIL HILL, CONCEPTION BAY.

From a photograph by S. H. Parsons.

detachments of Canadians and Indians came from Placentia either by
land or in small boats by the porterage in Trinity Bay. We have an

account of an attack on one settlement, and Mr Campbell mentions losses sustained by him at Bonavista in 1702 and 1703 .—

"To Mr Samuel Merrett.   Sept 21, 1702 from Pool.

"This serves to advice you that yesterday Mr. Thos. Wadham in the *Hopewell* of this place arrived here in three weeks from Trinity Harbour, he brings the bad news that about a week before he left 40 or 50 armed Frenchmen came over by land from Placentia to Silheove, surprised the inhabitants killing 3 or 4 and took Mr. John Masters out of his bed rifled his house, and carried him and his goods aboard a Jersey ship laden with fish and sailed northward with the ship and 1,000 qtls of fish but took no fish from the rocks ; they much doubt their being gone to Bonavista where is only Captain Weston. A French man of war hath been off St. John's all the summer and hath taken seven ships in sight of that harbour The Convoys were not arrived when he came away."

Charlevoix mentions a further attack on Bonavista in 1704 made by La Grange, who had served in Hudson's Bay under d'Ibberville :—

"Equipping two barks with a hundred Canadians, he came to Bonavista in the hope of surprising the ships there. On arriving within twelve leagues of that port, he left his bark to escape observation and kept on in two gigs entered the port at night, boarded a 24 gun frigate loaded with codfish captured it, burned two store-ships of two or three hundred tons each, sank another small frigate and sailed off with his prize and a great number of prisoners. There were six hundred English in Fort Bonavista, who appeared under arms next morning but it was too late, our gallant fellows were already under sail "

The following very graphic letter, which agrees with Penhallow's description, exposes the skilful evasions of the French writer :—

"*The Flying Post.*—March 10th, 1705

"St John's in Newfoundland, Sep. 21
"On the 18th of August last, about 144 French and Canada Indians came about two o'clock in the morning in two sloops and canoes to Bonavista Harbour, about 30 leagues to the Northward of this place and surprised the *Pembroke* galley of London of 250 tuns, 44 men and 20 guns, John Noll, Commander laden with dry fish   And the *Society* of Pool of 140 tons, 14 guns and 24 men, Captain Auten, Commander. And also the *William* of about 115 tuns, 10 men but no guns, having ·30 tuns of lamp oil on board. They also attempted to surprize Captain Michael Gill of Charles-Town in New England, of 14 guns and 24 men, who discovering their boat to be French, fired briskly upon them, killed and wounded some of them so that they returned to the Prizes they had taken and brought the great guns of both ships to bear upon Captain Gill and continued firing upon him with both great and small arms for the space of 6 hours, till his ship was much shattered   He, on the other hand, playing his great guns and small arms all the time on them.

"During the action, he veered his ship somewhat to the shoar. About 8 o'clock, when they found he could not be taken, they set fire to the *Society* and cut her loose in a flame to drive upon him, but by the great diligence of Captain

Gill, he got clear of her and she burnt to the keel. Finding that would not do, they set fire to the ship *William* and set her before the wind, furiously burning to that degree, that the lamp oil burning in a flame on the water, was like to have set him on fire, but that both he and his men laboured in the fire, and turned her clear of them. [The buoy-rope of the *William's* anchor got between the rudder and the stern and kept her clear of them.—*Penhallow.*] And when the inhabitants who had fled into the woods and rocks, saw Captain Gill's courage, they came down and appeared in a body in arms, which when the French saw, they immediately weighed and set sail and carried the Masters and men with them. And about forty leagues off [on the N.E. coast], they gave the Masters and some of the men a boat, who soon after returned, to whom the French declared, that had they taken Captain Gill they would not have left house stage or goods in the harbour; all which is owing under God to the courage and conduct of Captain Gill. He had but one man killed and three wounded; but the enemy had several killed and wounded."

To understand rightly Gill's success we must remember that New England, from the very first, had a trained militia. The American soldiers were the admiration of the British officers who came to America. They were fine marksmen and scientific artilleryists; we need not then wonder at Gill being such a splendid gunner. It requires no effort of the imagination to picture to ourselves the scene on that memorable morning of the 18th of August, 1704; the fish vessels lying at anchor in calm placid waters of Bonavista; the stealthy approach of the French

BONAVISTA.

From a photograph by S. H. Parsons.

with the war-vessels, and the Indians in their canoes; the sudden attack, surprise, and surrender of the West Country vessels; the fright of the inhabitants. Newfoundlanders dreaded the murderous savages—the Abenaquis—more than the foreign foe. Above all this panic and din and craven fear rises the master spirit of the bold New England skipper, Michael Gill; in a moment he is on the alert, the deck is cleared for action, his guns are loaded, his men at their post ready to give the French a warm reception.

Capt. Michael Gill, of Charles Town, in New England, first appears in our history in the list of shipping for 1698. Capt Michael's vessel was a very small one at this time, only 40 tons, and she brought rather a-mixed cargo salt, pork, and New England cider.

By the year 1704 our old friend Capt Michael, a shrewd trader—brave as a lion—had profited by the Newfoundland business. His little hooker of 1698 had been exchanged for a fine ship of 150 tons, carrying 24 men, and armed with 14 guns There had been considerable trade between New England and Newfoundland from 1698 to 1704. Fort William was being rebuilt in St. John's, there was a garrison, and large supplies were required The English commandant complains bitterly of the way he was fleeced by provincials. Gill's name does not appear as one of the army suppliers, but there is mention of a shrewd Bostonian, Captain Gladstane. Gill found more profit in the out-ports, and he appears to have traded chiefly with Bonavista.

Gill's[1] gallant conduct saved Bonavista, but when Montigny appeared there next spring, George Seiffington, who was in command, being a Quaker and "the spirit not moving him," capitulated at once and paid a ransom. But more serious attempts were soon to be made upon the English settlements. On the 7th of September Lieutenant Lloyd was suspended by Commodore Bridge upon a petition of his own soldiers, and when the fleet departed Lieutenant Moody was left in command at St John's. Moody, though a remarkably brave man, had not sufficient control over his subordinates, his authority was soon disputed by Roope, an engineer, and by the next in command, Lieutenant Latham, a master mason

Latham disliked the position assigned to him as commander of the "south side castle," a substantial stone fort with a wooden block-house; besides, his commission as lieutenant does not appear to have been quite in order, and no doubt at the south side he had not as full scope to trade on his own account as he had had under Captain Lloyd.

Roope, who was engaged at "Maggott's Cove, near Mr Latham's house," in constructing the boom, wishing to have a little authority, advised the planters not to keep watch in the north battery, a terribly trying duty, or obey Mr Moody's regulations The planters, not having been paid for former services of this kind or for scouting, though the

---

[1] Michael Gill seems to have resided in New England; about 1748 or 1750 his son Michael came to this colony He soon rose to an eminent position, was the first colonel of militia. His brother Nicholas was naval officer and afterwards chief magistrate in St John's The son of this Nicholas Gill, also called Nicholas, and whom some of us can remember as a very old man, carried on a large West India business. The only survivor of his children is old Mr Frederick Gill (Torbay Road), great grandson of the hero of Bonavista, 1704 His sister, Miss Gill, died recently, leaving $7,000 to the Church of England, and $500 to the Belvidere Orphanage.

money had been sent from England, were easily persuaded. Another
actor on the scene was Colin Campbell, the prize agent.

Campbell and Roope were accused of treachery in furnishing the
French with information; the charges and countercharges do not seem
to have been at all justified. Most certainly the French had spies in
St. John's at this time, in consequence, nearly everyone except Moody
and Latham were accused; it was a time of painful suspicion, every
man mistrusted his neighbour. The truth seems to have been, that when
in the power of the French and exposed to the strong arguments of
the Indians, Roope, Campbell, and others turned cowards and time-
servers, and became subservient to the crafty French tactics. The
fishing admirals took the side of Roope and afterwards of Major Lloyd.

PETTY HARBOUR.
From a photograph by S. H. Parsons.

In November three men were murdered at Renewse by the Indians,
but it was not till the middle of January that Subercase, with about two
hundred and fifty inhabitants of Placentia and Canada, ninety regulars,
and a hundred Indians, passed through Bay Bulls and Petty Harbour
and camped a short distance from St. John's. The snow was falling
heavily. Rising before daybreak, benumbed, and doubtless without
food, the French, in their cruel rage, attacked the slumbering inhabitants near the fort, and killed many in cold blood. With a strange
lack of generalship they failed to promptly attack the fort, which it
appears might easily have been taken. The garrison once aroused,
their opportunity was lost. Securing the men as prisoners in the church,
they sent the women and children into the fort in the hope of starving
the garrison out. These brave women were afterwards of great help to

Lieutenant Moody in strengthening the defences. At first the French were sheltered by houses built dangerously near the fort, but they were gradually driven from these by the heavy firing and burning them. They retreated under cover of the smoke to a safer position.

The garrison were taken at a great disadvantage. On Friday there had been a very heavy fall of snow, and on Sunday, the morning of the attack, the guns were still buried deep in snow. The soldiers, wretchedly clothed, and many without boots or stockings, set to work with a will to clear them. They suffered also in another way; the guns were mounted on the ramparts without any shields to protect the gunners from the galling fire of the enemy, directed from various points of vantage near the fort; working night and day with the help of the women, and even, in defiance of military custom, during the four days' armistice, this was partially remedied. Fortunately they had no lack of provisions and ammunition.

CANADIAN SOLDIER ON RACQUETS.
From Potherie's Histoire, 1722.

The French had no heart to take the fort by storm, so they tried to effect it by intimidation, by flattery, by bribery, by playing Moody against Latham. Moody says :—

"About eight o'clock on the morning of the attack the French sent one of the inhabitants with a flag of truce with a young child in his arms with its throat cut, threatening if I killed one of their men they would put all persons (without distinction of age or sex) to the sword— and hang me at the Fort Gate."

Perceiving after a fortnight's siege that he could neither force nor bribe the English commanders to surrender, Subercase sent them the following letters :—

"M. SUBERCASE to LIEUT. MOODY.

"SIR,

"I would not until now let you know my business here (it was not convenient) I now say it is my intention to possess myself of all ye English settlements which by God's help I have done with an intention to intirely ruin the trade, hoping in a little time to become master of ye Forts that you command and I believe you yourself see the impossibility that you can long defend yourself against the attacks that I can make, I do not at all doubt of it; but to save blood am willing to grant a reasonable capitulation provided it be done in a few days otherwise I shall not be able to hinder the fury of ye Indians which with the rest of our

troops do importune me vigorously to prosecute my design; its your business to
consider ye fate of ye number of prisoners I have in my hands and also ye
plantations and settlements.

"I will send you one of ye prisoners that you shall think fit if you think of
entering into a treaty [Prisoners sent in because Moody could not understand
French]

"If I can do you any particular service as to your owne affairs you may
command me who am

"Your most humble servant,

"February 1705.   SUBERCASS."

"MR. JOHN ROOPE to MR ROBERT LATHAM [written under SUBERCASE's dictation]

"Feby. 4, 1705

"My misfortune hath made me a prisoner but I hope in good hands, ye
Governor having hitherto been very kind. He was much enraged against you
because there were three musketts fired at his flag of truce but I told him it must
be done without your knowledge in which he seemed satisfied He declared he
knew nothing of the burning of your house but to the contrary he is for making
anything good to an officer. There is a treaty on foot between Mr. Moody and
him I think it is about a surrender, he would not at first hear that you should be
concerned in ye treaty but now is satisfied, so desire you to take ye best measures
that you can think of for ye good of all and the preservation of whole country
which is threatened with fire and sword, ye properest measures you know better
than I can inform you so commit you to ye protection and direction of Allmighty
God

"Your humble servant,
"JOHN ROOPE."

Moody procrastinated, and asked for four days' truce, employing
the time in strengthening the fort. After several conferences with
Campbell and Pemberton, two of the principal inhabitants, Moody
refused to surrender Subercase sent him a brace of partridges, and
proposed a personal interview, but Moody said it would be of no use.

The French, after burning nearly all the houses on the north side,
directed all their attention to the castle. They first tried to induce
Lieutenant Latham, by means of a letter from Moody, taken by
Campbell, to cross over to consult with Moody, intending to kill him
on the way, but Latham stubbornly refused to quit his post, and the
Indians could scarcely be restrained from murdering Campbell in their
rage at his failure. They then bombarded the castle with two guns,
found on the south side, which they loaded with powder they had
accidentally discovered in the "Queen's warehouse at the waterside."
They had spoilt most of their powder in fording rivers on their march
The guns having no effect they tried fire-arrows, but they were badly
made, and fell harmless.

Their provisions and powder exhausted, the planters from Placentia
more anxious to carry off their spoil than to risk their lives. and their
expected supplies of ammunition not arriving, the French retired to
Ferryland after a five weeks' siege. They took to Placentia, where

Subercase now returned, the best of the fishermen to carry their plunder and assist in their fishery. Some eventually were sent to Canada and France, some escaped to St. John's, and the rest, chiefly Irish, entered the French Service. The coolness, judgment, and bravery shown by Moody and Latham in the face of overwhelming numbers and French diplomacy is worthy of the highest praise. On the other hand, the French showed great want of courage, and again availed themselves of the barbarities committed upon the helpless planters by Montigny and the Abenaquis. In the words of their own chronicler, "The very name of Montigny made the arms fall from the hands of the most resolute." The English loss in the forts was very small, but the French suffered very heavily, though probably the English estimate of two hundred is exaggerated.

From Ferryland, Montigny and the Indians marched through Holyrood to Harbour Grace, murdering and destroying as they went. Carbonear Island, gallantly defended by Davis and Pynne, again resisted their attack, much to Montigny's mortification.

CANADIAN SOLDIER.
From Winsor's N. & C. H. America.

" LETTER from CARBONERE, 29 March 1705.

"Montigny £500 out of pocket on his Indians and resolved to have it of us and have our lives, and will wait all the summer to take vengeance on us for keeping the Island, for which he says he will lose his Commission."

Montigny then proceeded to Bonavista, where the inhabitants had retired to Green Island, under command of Geo. Sciffington, but he surrendered at once upon terms of ransom.

Moody says in his narrative :—

" The French surprised Bonavista but about 80 or 90 of the inhabitants got on Green Island where they fortified themselves and might have made good their defence but their courage failing and unwarily admitting the enemy to come among them, they heaved their guns (being nine in number) over the cliffs into the sea and afterwards the inhabitants capitulated and ransomed their houses for 450 pounds payable to Montigny."

In July 1706, Montigny was reinforced by more Indians from Placentia. Lurking in the woods, they kept the whole of Trinity and Conception Bay in terror, and spoilt the year's fishing. They carried their spoil away by the porterage at Bay Bulls arm, in Trinity Bay, to Placentia.

Captain Moody and his company, who appear to have been resident in St. John's since 1698, were in November succeeded by Major Lloyd and ninety-one new soldiers, volunteers from various English regiments. Major Lloyd, who was in England, had skilfully used Moody's disgrace to secure his own re-appointment; he came out armed with a power of holding court-martial. During the winter of 1705-6 Lloyd behaved with great vigour, personally leading out detachments of troops to protect Ferryland, Harbour Grace, and other points threatened by the French and Indians.

Captain Moody, upon his return to England, explained his conduct to the satisfaction of the Board of Trade, who strongly recommended him for promotion. In a few years Nemesis overtook the tyrant Lloyd, and his rival Moody was again in command at St. John's.

The loss incurred by the planters in 1705 was very great; it shows the recuperative power of the people that they were able to survive it :—

" Sworn value of destruction made to Captain Moody.

St. John's and Quidividi -	-	-	-	45,000
Ferryland and Bay Bulls -	-	-	-	25,000
Harbour Grace &c.	-	-	-	38,000
Carbonere, Bay de Verds &c.	-	-	-	46,000
Parlican, Trinity &c.	-	-	-	34,000

£188,000 Stg."

Beyond the destruction of the French fishing stages at Trepassey, St. Mary's, Colonet, St. Lawrence, and the dismantling of the fort at

ADMIRAL LEAKE.
From an engraving by Cook.

St. Peter's, by Captain Leake in 1702, and the abortive attempt of Graydon on Placentia, all the English operations had been directed to the capture of the French fishing fleets on their way out from France and back, and in this they had been very successful;[1] we have noticed the presence of a special prize agent at St. John's. Now, however, acting upon the suggestion of Roope and others, the Government determined to destroy the French fishery in the Petit Nord. Anspach thus describes these operations :—

" In the following year, viz. on the 25th July, 1706, a report was brought to

---

[1] " For about the same time '703 Captain John Leake (afterwards Sir John), sailing with a small squadron to Newfoundland, took or destroyed no less than fifty-one ships and ruined all the French settlements on the islands." S. COLLIBER, *Columna Rostrata,* 1727, p 292.

St. John's, that the enemy had a considerable number of ships employed in the fishery in several harbours to the northward, and other parts of the island Captain John Underdown, commander of the Queen's ship the *Falkland*, was then in St John's harbour with the *Nonsuch*, commanded by Captain Carleton Having been petitioned by the merchants, masters of vessels, and inhabitants of that place, to protect the British trade in those parts, he accordingly set sail from St. John's, on the 26th of July, accompanied by Major Lloyd, who desired to be employed in this expedition with twenty of his company, on board the *Falkland*, and as many on board the *Nonsuch*. The next day they came before Bonavista, and finding there no appearance of an enemy, the Commodore ordered Captain Hughes, commander of the *Medway* on that station, to join him with a French ship of war, which the latter had taken a few days before

"On the 2nd of August they stood into Blanche Bay till they arrived off Fleur-de-Lys Harbour, when Major Lloyd in the Commodore's pinnace, and the first lieutenant of the *Falkland* in the pinnace belonging to the *Nonsuch*, were immediately sent into the harbour   They found there several stages and other necessaries for the fishery, which they destroyed, and afterwards returned to their ships.   At six o'clock next morning they doubled the Cape, and saw a ship which struck upon the brisk exchange of a few shot, this was found to be *Le Duc d'Orleans*, from Saint Maloes, of about three hundred and sixty tons, thirty guns, and one hundred and ten men

"In another arm of the same bay, called Eguillete, they saw another large ship, but the place being rocky, and the water so shallow that none of the English men of war could come near her, the *Medway's* prize was ordered to go in as close as she could with safety, whilst Captain Carleton, Major Lloyd, and the first lieutenant of the *Falkland*, in boats well manned and armed, were directed to land upon the island under which that ship lay.   This was executed so promptly and ably that the French ship struck, after having fired several broadsides, her crew being no longer able to keep the deck against the small shot from the shore.   This ship also belonged to Saint Maloes, carrying twenty guns and eighty men

"Having here received information that about three leagues farther north, in a place called La Conche, or Conche Harbour, there were two ships of thirty-two and twenty-six guns, both of Saint Maloes, the commodore directed Captain Hughes to burn the last prize, and afterwards to join him at that place, whither he proceeded himself with the *Falkland* and the *Nonsuch*   On the afternoon of the fifth, they arrived at Conche Harbour where they found two ships ready for sailing.   After exchanging several broadsides, the French set their ships on fire, and went over to the next harbour, called Carouge.   The commodore being informed that there were four French ships in that place, immediately stood for it, meeting in his way, at about eight o'clock in the evening, the *Medway's* prize; but there being very little wind, and that at south-west, it was near six o'clock the next morning before he could get off the harbour's mouth   He then sent in his boat, and found that the French ships had escaped, taking advantage of their great number of men and boats by cutting and towing out.

"The English ships then proceeded to the northward, and about five o'clock in the afternoon came off the harbour of Saint Julian where they discovered a large French ship; standing in for that harbour, they came to an anchor in twenty-six fathom water   The place where that ship had been hauled in being very narrow and shoaly, the *Medway's* prize was ordered to go as near her as possible   The French ship then fired two guns, but it being late in the evening, and the enemy appearing determined to make a spirited resistance, it was not thought advisable to commence the attack before the following morning.

"On the sixth of August, at four o'clock in the forenoon, Captain Carleton, Major Lloyd, and Lieut Eagle went towards her with all their boats, well manned and armed ; and having effected their landing, attacked, and at last drove the enemy from a strong post which they occupied on the shore. They then boarded the French ship, where they found several trains of powder laid for the purpose of blowing her up. By this timely discovery the ship was preserved, and, by noon, towed out to sea

"The British pilots being unacquainted with the coast, the commodore resolved not to proceed any farther north, but to sail back to Carouge and there await the arrival of the *Duke of Orleans* prize, which had been left at Grand Canarie with a lieutenant and sixty men They looked into Petit Maitre, where they destroyed a considerable number of stages and boats, and found vast quantities of fish and oil , and at about seven o'clock in the afternoon they came to an anchor, and moored in Carouge Harbour On the 12th and 13th it blew a hard gale at south-west; on the 14th, having been joined by the *Duke of Orleans* prize, they weighed at four o'clock in the morning, stood out to sea with her, and came into Saint John's Harbour, where the *Falkland* and the *Nonsuch* arrived with the two prizes on the 17th, the *Medway's* prize having before been ordered to proceed to Trinity

"From this expedition, which deserves to be recorded on account of the activity and judgment displayed by Captain Underdown and his associates, equal to the good fortune that attended their operations, it appears that, while the English had on that station only the *Falkland* and *Nonsuch* in St John's, and the *Medway* at Bonavista, the French had in the northern parts of the island no less than ten armed ships, mounting from twenty to thirty-two guns. The loss which the latter suffered by the capture or destruction of six of them and the ruin of their fisheries, must have been a severe blow to their trade. So large a force shows the degree of importance which they then attached to the Newfoundland trade "[1]

The French, after a period of inactivity, caused doubtless by the better organisation for defence of the different settlements, again attacked St John's in 1708, and this time with success They must have been acquainted through their spies in St John's of the want of vigilance shown by the once energetic Major Lloyd The first exaggerated reports brought to England accused him of treachery, but there appears to have been no real foundation whatever for this charge, it would seem more likely, from the account of Keen and the serjeant, that he had become quite incapable, perhaps through intemperance.

The French guides, either through design or mistake, brought St. Ovide de Brouillon and his troops too late to St. John's to effect a complete surprise they were seen advancing in the clear moonlight by

' ANSPACH's *H of Newfoundland*, pp 124 129

the sentry on the new fort, but, in spite of his alarm, the French were soon in possession of Fort William, and, through a blunder, the Colonial Militia were unable to enter the fort by the subterranean passage specially provided for such a contingency   The capture of Fort William was effected in half an hour   The new fort, which was overlooked by Fort William, surrendered upon terms of quarter which were not fully kept   The "south side" castle surrendered next day.

St Ovide, anxious to secure all the advantage to himself of his fortunate adventure, sent word direct to France, and immediately two hundred soldiers were dispatched with a commission appointing him Governor of St John's; but they arrived too late. Costabelle, partly jealous of St Ovide's success, and presuming that the home Government were too much occupied in Europe to spare troops for the retention of St. John's, had ordered St Ovide to destroy the fortifications and return immediately to Placentia, which he was reluctantly obliged to do, leaving St John's on March 31st

During his stay in St. John's, St Ovide sent Captain Larond to take Ferryland, but the inhabitants were too strongly fortified, it is significant to note they even refused to admit a flag of truce

Major Lloyd was first taken to Placentia and Quebec, and afterwards to France   Captain Moody succeeded him in command, but returned to England for the winter to report upon the condition of affairs. One of his proposals was to remove the garrison to Ferryland, and not rebuild the fortifications at St John's, but it met with no favour

The only other French movement during this year was an unsuccessful attack on Buoy's Island, Ferryland, by a French man-of-war. The settlers were by this time too well organised to be surprised Commodore Taylour employed his men in 1709 in rebuilding Fort William,[1] which had been entirely demolished except the earthworks, upon an improved plan, mounted eight guns, and erected huts in the fort for the inhabitants for the winter. The fort and the coast from Ferryland to Carbonear were placed under John Collins, Pynn was in command at Carbonear, and others at Trinity and Bonavista, with local commissioned officers under them   The French claimed a ransom for St John's and neighbourhood of over £7,000 which appears to have been promptly paid to the Placentia Governor Costabelle   This was one of the last episodes in the dreary guerilla warfare carried on by the

[1] There is a rough plan of the new fort in the Record Office, *Bd of Trade*, *Newfoundland*, No. 6, K 21

French from Placentia against our settlements; from 1708 the land had rest for over fifty years.

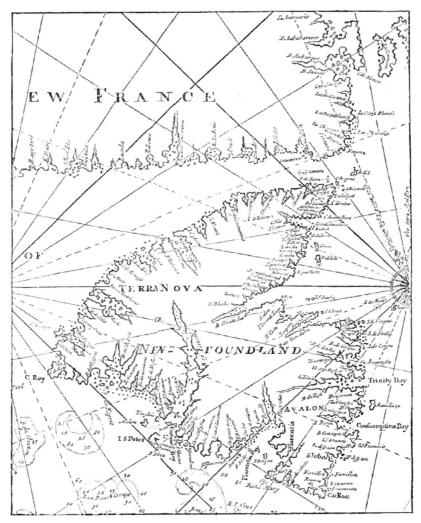

FRIEND'S MAP OF 1713.

B. M.—S. 9(8)36.

Turning from these stirring scenes of fights and pillage to the more peaceful subject of the fishery, we realise in the terribly shrunken state of the trade the immense destruction loss and waste produced by the incessant warfare waged by the two countries in this unfortunate Colony.

These poor meagre figures in the war times of 1705 are in striking contrast to the great results of former affluent seasons of peace :—

" An account of the trade and fishery of Newfoundland for the year 1705 —

Number of fishing ships · · · ·	20
Number of sack ships · · · ·	20
Number of ships from America · · ·	20
	—— 60
Burthen of fishing ships · · · ·	2,400 tuns
Number of fishing ships' boats · · ·	60
Number of by-boats · · · · ·	40
Number of inhabitants' boats · · ·	160
	—— 260
Quantity of fish made by ships · · ·	18,000
Quantity of fish made by boats · · ·	12,000
Quantity of fish made by inhabitants' boats ·	4,800
	—— 78,000 qtls.
Quantity of fish carreyed to market · ·	72,000 qtls.
Quantity of train-oil made by ships - · ·	105
Quantity of train-oil made by boats - · ·	70
Quantity of train-oil made by inhabitants ·	280
	—— 455 tuns
Number of stages · · · · ·	80
" Number of inhabitants —	
Men · · · · · · ·	800
Women · · · · · ·	130
Children · · · · · ·	200
	—— 1,130

Besides 6,000 Qtls. of fish left on land, A further quantity was spoyld by bad weather computed at 2 000 Qtls

STATISTICS OF THE NEWFOUNDLAND FISHERY.

1700 to 1713

From the Reports of the Naval Officers.

Years			Fishing Ships	Boats	Inhabitants' Boats.
1700	-	-	171	800	764
1701	-	-	75	338	—
1702	-	-	16	35	380
1703	-	-	23	44	214
1704	-	-	23	—	—
1705	-	-	20	60	200
1706	-	-	46	136	232
1707	-	-	70	196	257
1708 - -	-	-	49	170	356
1709	-	-	35	130	258
1710	-	-	49	153	365
1711	-	-	62	168	439
1712	-	-	66	198	370
1713	-	-	46	162	483

In the former reign mention was made of the Reverend John Jackson, the first resident clergyman appointed by the Society for the Propagation of the Gospel in Newfoundland, and his difficulties with the military commandant and governor of the Colony, Major Lloyd. The records give us a very full account of these proceedings

Major Lloyd was appointed commandant of the forces in Newfoundland in 1703, succeeding Major Richards, as being the "eldest lieutenant", he came to Newfoundland in 1700 as paymaster. It is hard to imagine anything more scandalous than the conduct of this unprincipled and tyrannical officer. He seems to have taken a mischievous delight in annoying and insulting Parson Jackson. The naval chaplain, however, was not one to fear the face of man. Lloyd's character is typical of the military roué of that day— unprincipled, reckless, dissipated, yet withal as valiant a soldier as ever sought " the bubble reputation at the cannon's mouth." Anspach has given us some account of his exploits in 1706. The condensed account of the charges made against him by the Reverend John Jackson, all of which are substantiated by the evidence of the various witnesses, is graphic and grotesque.

Mr Jackson spent many weary months in London, tormented with sickness, petitioning the Government and the Church He and his large family were recommended to the attention of charitable people, eventually he was appointed to a living in England by Queen Anne Lloyd was killed in France, probably in a duel with some fire-eating Frenchman whom he had insulted. Thackeray's immortal Irish hero, Barry Lyndon, strongly resembles this brave, unprincipled swashbuckler.

"1705.—Complaints against the then Lt Thomas Lloyd In letter from Mr John Jackson Minister at St John's to the Lords Commissioners for trade and plantations.—

1st.—Lt Thos Lloyd came to command in chief at Fort William in St John's harbour, Sept 24th 1703 He put in practice all sinister ways and base means he could devise to get money. £660 of Queen's money to pay soldiers he converted into trade Supplanted inhabitants by falling price of fish, buying liquors at low rates &c

2ndly.—Ruined families by his tyranny, beat one Adams a planter, so that poor man is incapable of getting bread for his numerous family

3rdly.—Caused Mr James Benger to be imprisoned for not paying debt of £50 another man owed him, and though Benger paid it, got him kept in prison till season was past in order to ruin him Benger dealt that year for about 2000 qtls. of fish and said Lloyd worsted him £300 that year

4thly.—His debtors would run from their flakes and business in fishing season as from an Indian when they saw him coming, which he often did with his sword and came in his hand and threatening, if not beating, those he lighted on When ships arrived in harbour he would forestall inhabitants in choosing goods and when Masters of ships demanded pay cavilled with and beat them as Capt Hatch, Capt Davy, Capt Pickering, &c for demanding reasonable rates

5thly —In taking farewell demanded hands of inhabitants to testimony of good behaviour &c, refusers he threatens to murther and beat, drew his sword upon some and pulled them out of their beds

6thly —His return to the country amasing to most; old traders left the country fearing he should treat them as formerly

7thly —If speedy care be not taken, trade of country must fall to ruin. He has declared as it cost him dear to reassume command, is resolved to repay himself by trade.

8thly —So greedy of getting money he neglected seriously the garrison and soldiers

9thly —Took to live with him a woman of disreputable character, who caused the soldiers to be whipped and abused at her pleasure

10thly.—A constant breaker of the Sabbath, threatening and cursing those who would attend service, going about the harbour with his fiddle to divert the people and spending remainder of the day in most disgraceful rioting &c

11thly —Took care no account should reach home and intercepted letters relating to his conduct

12thly.—Suspended by Commodore, command devolved on Lieut John Moody "

The following complaints were made against Major Lloyd during his second term of office, from 1705 to 1708, and may be appropriately mentioned here   He told the planters it had cost him a large sum to obtain his re-appointment, and he meant to have it out of them   Many settlers left the country on his account :—

" Mr Minshew's Affidavit.

1707-8.

" (a) His tyranny in generall; (b) his dispossessing Mr Benger, for not signing a paper against Moody, (c) his wounding an inhabitant; (d) his barbarity to the surgeon, (e) his cruelty to his maid servant; (f) his small allowance to the soldiers letting them out to hire and taking three parts in four of their wages, (g.) his plundering in the north; (h) his feasting Monsr Bellater, (i) his extorting three qtls out of every fishing boat, (k.) his oppression causing the inhabitants to remove, (l) his contriving certificates and compelling them to subscribe them, (m) his agent's cruelty to Adams, (n) his barbarity to Burt, (o.) his injustice to Minshew's wife, (p.) his menacing Minshew for asking his money, (q) his abuse to Commodore Underdowne, (r.) Minshew durst not return to his family

" Seven affidavits with other papers to prove the allegations in Mr. Campbel's memorial relating to the unwarrantable proceedings of Major Lloyd in Newfoundland "

One most beneficial effect flowed from these extraordinary proceedings of Major Lloyd. As the result of the inquiry into these scandals, the position of Governor was taken from the Commander of Fort William and conferred upon the commodore, and remained vested in the superior naval officer on the Newfoundland station from 1708 until 1825   It appears from the records that from 1697 to 1703 the commodore had been governor, in the latter year the appointment was conferred on Lloyd as commandant

The command in Newfoundland became afterwards one of the great prizes of the service, it was held by some of the most distinguished officers in the navy. Sir John Leake, Rodney, Duckworth, Graves, Lord Radstock, &c., are amongst the honoured names of Newfoundland's floating governors.

Much abuse has been bestowed on our naval rulers; never was censure less deserved. No doubt they were often severe, sometimes narrow in their views. We must remember they were always hampered by instructions to repress settlement. On the whole, I think they filled their very difficult positions admirably. In order to protect the settlers, they encroached on the prerogatives of the fishing admirals, and after a few years virtually superseded them. Of course, quarter-deck law was their sole guide; in the rude state of society then existing amongst the fishermen it was probably the best. As the Colony became more populous and civilised, naval government became simply intolerable: it was, however, decidedly a great improvement on the fishing admirals' law.

"In the year 1711, I find," says Mr Reeves, in his history of New-foundland, "a record of several laws and orders made at St John's " It is worth while considering whether such a local legislature which " the people seem in this instance to have created for themselves might " not be legally lodged somewhere for making bye-laws and regulations " as occasion should require." The Commander, Captain Crowe, pre-sided at this voluntary assembly. His successor, it seems, followed his example, and held a meeting of the same sort. These assemblies were somewhat anomalous, a kind of legislative, judicial, and executive all blended together

It is very easy to discover the original idea from whence Captain Crowe and Sir Nicholas Trevanion's voluntary assemblies were taken. These gatherings of the inhabitants were literal copies of the New England town meetings. All the citizens of the township assemble in general meeting once a year or oftener, levy taxes, decide on improve-ments, and appoint the necessary executive officers to carry out their arrangements during the ensuing twelve months. All men meet on an equality, every citizen is entitled to free speech and free vote. As the New England towns become more populous they pass out of the stage of town meetings into representative government.

Unfortunately for the development of home rule in this Colony, we stopped short at the callow stage of the town meeting. What one admires most in this assembly is the political ability of the New Englander who engineered the proceedings; we have had clever wire-pullers in the Colony, but we doubt if any of our party managers were ever skilful enough to blend together into one harmonious meeting such antagonistic elements as the fishing admirals, the Devonshire adventurers, and the planters. The great principle of politics is compromise; these laws show us how adroitly the American satisfied the Devonshire party by declaring certain rooms used by the bye-boat keepers were ship's rooms, and turned out the all-grasping Holdsworth. The inhabitants were gratified by the arrangements for their defence and the support of their minister.

Under this astute settlement, everything seems to have worked harmoniously; doubtless the war and their common danger from the French made the discordant elements for the time at least united. We notice the poor pay received by the Rev. Jacob Rice; it was, perhaps, the insufficient salary which had driven away his predecessor, J. Jackson.

HARLEY, EARL OF OXFORD.[1]
From an engraving after Reveant.

From the re-appointment of our old friend Governor Collins, it appears that the Home Government had again withdrawn the military, otherwise a civilian would not have been left in charge of the forts.

At this time preliminaries for peace began; for two years the negotiations dragged their slow length along. From 1710 the merchants kept making representations to the Board of Trade that in any treaty of peace with the French, Newfoundland might be reserved wholly to the English. This idea was adopted by the Board, who pressed it strongly on the Ministry. The treacherous way in which the peace of Utrecht was concluded is well known, how England abandoned her allies. The literature of the day is full of the subject; one of Dick Steele's most trenchant articles is an attack on

---

[1] Harley was impeached for his conduct in negotiating the Treaty of Utrecht.

this peace. No condition was more disgraceful than the surrender of the Newfoundland fishery to the French.

English statesmen in Queen Anne's reign were violent partisans,[1] many of them corrupt and venal, but the most prejudiced and ignorant amongst them understood that in the struggle with France victory rested with the nation that possessed the strongest sea power; they were also well aware that France was almost solely dependent on her great North American fishery for the manning of her navy; they knew also that her restless aggressive policy was a constant menace to English power, both in Europe and America.

In 1713 France was at England's feet; never since Crecy and Agincourt had the French armies received such overwhelming defeats.

FRENCH FISHING STAGES AT ST. JULIAN.

France has always valued her trans-Atlantic fishery not for the sake of peaceful commerce, but as an engine of war. The enormous bounties paid to her fishermen in Newfoundland are not to sustain the paltry trade of St. Pierre, but, as it has been declared over and over again by French Ministers, to recruit her navy.

It may be argued that, compared with the European interests involved in the Utrecht negotiations, the North American fishery was of quite minor importance. But this is not the case. For England, the

[1] Contemporary writers quoted by Hallam say that "The desire for French wine and the demands of its alienated many from the Duke of Marlborough. The hard drinkers complained that they were poisoned by port all the boon companions, many physicians, a great many of the lawyers, the inferior clergy, and the loose women, were united in a faction against the Duke."

North American fishery was of paramount importance, it involved the question of British supremacy at sea, and the English dominion in North America

The vast naval force of France had grown up and was sustained by her fishery in Newfoundland and the St. Lawrence, yet with the full knowledge of all that happened in the past, England, with her enemy at her mercy, gave back to her rival both Cape Breton and the fishery in Newfoundland.

In the negotiations about the treaty of Utrecht the French knew that they must lose Newfoundland English public feeling at the time was indignant at the frequent French raids made on the Island, and insisted on its entire possession. France offered to surrender our Island and the fisheries and St Martin and St Bartholomew in the West Indies for Acadie (Nova Scotia) The English Government were firm in their refusal to give up Nova Scotia, and insisted on fishing rights in Cape Breton, and that it should not be fortified. But in all these demands, except the retention of Nova Scotia and Newfoundland, they were outwitted by their opponents

The French argument about Cape Breton was that the English and French could-not-fish together there—that it would be impossible to preserve peace amongst them Yet in the face of this unanswerable argument, England consented that there should be a concurrent fishery in Newfoundland, involving perpetual quarrels between the subjects of both nations - The surrender of the Newfoundland fishery was a wilful blunder on the part of the English Ministry

The entire exclusion-of the French from Newfoundland and from all participation in the fishery was strongly urged on the Government by the Board of Trade, by the whole body of British merchants, by the united voice of the North American colonies, and by the urgent entreaty of the Newfoundland settlers The appeal was made to unwilling ears. Prior, one of the chief negotiators, had expressed in his report in 170 ; the absolute necessity of excluding the French from the Island, every naval commander had reiterated the same opinion, but it was all to no purpose—there has hardly ever been a more senseless surrender, the consequences have been lasting and widespread—for the English Colonies an exhausting war Unfortunately to-day we suffer for the base treachery of Queen Anne's Ministry

This great treaty, over which the fierce intellectual giant, Swift, and the well-beloved Joseph Addison fought their great literary battles, is to-day the rule under which the French fisherman builds his temporary hut and erects his stage on the treaty shore of Newfoundland

R

It remains a dangerous cause of quarrel between two great nations a perpetual irritating sore, a bar to the progress and prosperity of the Colony.

By Article XIII. of the Treaty of Utrecht, 1713, it was agreed that—

"The island called Newfoundland, with the adjacent islands, shall, from this time forward, *belong of right wholly to Britain,* and to that end the town and fortress of Placentia, and whatever other places in the said Island are in the possession of the French, shall be yielded and given up within seven months from the exchange of the ratifications of this treaty, or sooner, if possible, by the Most Christian King to those who have a commission from the Queen of Great Britain for that purpose. Nor shall the Most Christian King, his heirs and successors, or any of their subjects, at any time hereafter *lay claim to any right to the said island* and islands, or to any part of it or them. *Moreover, it shall not be lawful for the subjects of France to fortify any place in the said island of Newfoundland, or to erect any buildings there, besides stages made of boards, and huts necessary and useful for drying of fish, or to resort to the said island beyond the time necessary for fishing and drying of fish. But it shall be allowed to the subjects of France to catch fish and to*

FRENCH FISHING ROOMS AT CAPE ROUGE HARBOUR.

From Black and White.

dry them on land in that part only, and in no other besides that, of the said Island of Newfoundland, which stretches from the place called Cape Bonavista to the northern point of the said island, and from thence running down by the western side, reaches as far as the place called Point Riche. But the island called Cape Breton, as also all others, both in the mouth of the River St. Lawrence and in the gulf of the same name, shall hereafter belong of right to the French, and the Most Christian King shall have all manner of liberty to fortify any place or places there."

The language of this treaty is very clear and explicit, the sovereignty of Great Britain over the Island of Newfoundland is made absolute

The French are confined to a temporary user of the shore for one purpose only, the *fishing and drying of fish*, no other rights are granted to them It will be seen that their preposterous claim to build factories and tin lobsters is entirely opposed to the plain language of this treaty, which is still in force No other fishery but the cod fishery was in existence at that time, and no other fishery was contemplated by the treaty, which view is further confirmed by the Treaty of Versailles, 1783 :—

"The XIII. Article of the Treaty of Utrecht and the method of carrying on the fishery, which has at all times been acknowledged [a ship cod fishery], shall be the plan upon which the fishery shall be carried on there, it shall not be deviated from by either party, the French fishermen building only their scaffolds, confining themselves to the repair of their fishing vessels, and not wintering there, the subjects of His Britannic Majesty on their part not molesting in any manner the French fishermen during their fishing nor injuring their scaffolds during their absence"

In the original draft proposal of the French the word used was *codfish*, not fish, but the purists who drew the treaty considered codfish too vulgar a word, and inserted in place of it *fish* The meaning, however, is exactly the same, as the codfishery was the only fishery then carried on as a ship-fishery by both nations, the only fishery in which stages and *flakes* (scaffolds) are used

By the terms of the Treaty of Utrecht, Placentia was to be given up to the English immediately. Brown writes —

"M De Costabelle, the Governor, therefore lost no time in sending off the garrison and inhabitants to Cape Breton so that the latter might not lose their summer's fishing. Some of the people objected to leaving Plaisance [probably the English and Irish] and would willingly have remained under English domination, but Costabelle urged all to go except idlers and vagabonds, whom he discreetly left as a legacy to his successor.

"In the first instance the garrison and inhabitants went to Havre à L'Anglois (Louisbourg), which was known to be favourably situated for carrying on the fishery In the course of the summer about one hundred and eighty persons, chiefly fishermen and their families, arrived from Plaisance and the Isle of St. Pierre. Some of these settled at Baleine, Scatari and the out harbours, but the majority took up their abode at Havre à L'Anglois All were supplied with provisions by the French Government for some time after their arrival"[1]

This is the last episode in the history of the French Colony in Newfoundland. The settlement existed there over half a century, but during all that time it never increased, it was essentially military, after fifty years of occupation the whole permanent French population of Newfoundland numbered less than two hundred souls. As colonisers the

[1] Brown's *History of Cape Breton*

R 2

French have been failures, always and everywhere. In one respect they were superior to their English rivals. "No other Europeans," says Merivale, in his lecture on colonies and colonisation, "have ever " displayed equal talents for conciliating savages, and, it must be added, " for approximating to their usages and modes of life as the French"

The French in Cape Breton were just as bad neighbours to Nova Scotia as they had been to Newfoundland; they secretly encouraged the Indians · to make raids on the English settlers; they were always planning the re-conquest of Acadie.

French writers differ somewhat in their views of the Treaty of Utrecht. Charlevoix says:—

"France was amply compensated for the loss of Newfoundland by the acquisition of Cape Breton, where the inhabitants of Plaisance found themselves more agreeably and more advantageously situated than they had ever been in Newfoundland, whilst the English were now absolute masters of the country, where before they could not assure themselves of anything so long as they had us for their neighbours."

Abbé Raynal laments bitterly over the loss of Newfoundland and Acadie. Garneau says :—

"The Treaty of Utrecht snatched from the feeble hands of Louis the portals of Canada, Acadie, and Newfoundland. From this treaty dates the decline of the monarchy and the coming of the revolution."

APPENDIX TO CHAPTER X.

I. Campaign of 1704-5.

[No event in the whole of our history is so fully recorded as this siege of Fort William, we can trace the course of events from day to day, after a lapse of almost two hundred years]

(a) CHARLEVOIX'S ACCOUNT.

M. de Subercase set out on the 15th of January with 450 well armed men, soldiers, Canadians, privateersmen and Indians, all determined men accustomed to walk in snow shoes Each man had provisions for twenty days, his arms, his blanket and a tent to each mess in turn

The severest part of the march was caused by four of the rivers not being frozen over Arriving at Rebou [Bay Bulls] on the 26th at noon the people begged for quarter Here the army found considerable provisions. They proceeded after 48 hours rest three leagues to Petty Harbour. They entered it the next day and leaving forty men to guard the prisoners taken at Rebou, marched forward. The English at St John's were ignorant of the proximity of the French and perhaps of their departure from Placentia, but the want of order preserved in leaving Petty Harbour and the neglect to reconnoitre St John's well, deprived the army of all advantage of surprising it

There were then at St John's two forts, one much larger than the other. They began at the former, which was well defended, the English keeping upon the besiegers a constant fire of bombs and cannon balls which the French stood with all possible intrepidity. Nevertheless we had only fifteen killed or wounded, the Chevalier de Lo, ensign among them. Want of ammunition at last forced our men to raise the siege, a part of the powder brought from Placentia having been wet in crossing the rivers but they did not draw off till they had laid in ashes every house around the harbour.

On the 5th of March the army decamped and marched to Forillon, where the inhabitants at first made a show of defence but soon surrendered The town was burned, after which Martigny, who had brought his faithful Nescambiouit, was detached with the Indians and a part of the Canadians to Carbonniere and Bonavista with orders to burn and destroy all the coast, which he executed without losing a single man, so great was the terror among the English

His very name made the arms fall from the hands of the most resolute and gave him a number of prisoners whom he had only the trouble of binding But he had to reserve Carbonniere Island for another time It held three hundred, and was, as I have said, inaccessible in winter

Every other place was carried or submitted, MM. de Linctot, de Villedonné and de Beletre thoroughly supported Montigny, and Nescambiouit, as usual, distinguished himself. In fine, this campaign completely ruined the English trade in Newfoundland (SHEA's *Charlevoix*)

(b) PENHALLOW'S DESCRIPTION

The descent that the enemy again made on Newfoundland was more terrible and surprising than the former, for on January 21st, at break of day, M Supercass fell on St John's, where in the space of two hours all were become prisoners of war except those in the castle and fort The night before the enterprise, they were obliged to lie on a bed of snow, six feet deep, for fear of being discovered, which caused such numbness in the joints of several, that the General vowed revenge, and accordingly executed his resentment, for that he destroyed all before him, and gave no quarter for some time, till M. Boocore, who was a gentleman of more humanity, did interpose and abate his fury The number that they took alive was one hundred and forty, whom they sent into the garrison, not out of pity to the prisoners but with a design to starve the whole [confirmed by Lieut Moody] After that they laid siege to the garrison and fort, which continued thirty days without relief; (excepting three who made their escape to the former and seventeen to the latter) In the fort were only forty men under the command of Captain Moody and twelve in the castle under Captain Latham, who behaved themselves with such bravery that they slighted all manner of tenders or made them of surrender, with the highest contempt imaginable. Upon this, the enemy committed many barbarities and sent several threatenings; but they had no influence on either officers or soldiers, for they plied their bombs and mortar pieces to so good effect, that they killed several, and lost but three in the whole engagement

After this the French steered to Consumption Bay, having first demolished all the English settlements in Trinity and Bonavista, where they burnt their stages and boats and laid a contribution besides upon the inhabitants From thence they went to Carboneer, where they met with some repulse, and finding their provisions fell short, they sent a further number [of the inhabitants] into the fort [William], reserving the most skilful and able fishermen for themselves until the succeeding spring [The latter part of the account is slightly confused] [S. Penhallow, *Indian Wars*, 1723]

(c.) Campbell's Account

Account on June 15th 1705 of Colin Campbell merchant of the attack on St John's written from memory—the despatches from Lt Moody &c having been thrown overboard to prevent their falling into the hands of a French privateer ·—

That on the 21st Jany 1705 the French forces under M Subercass to the number of 600 men (Indians and Canadians about 150 included) marched from Placentia to Bay Bulls and Petty Harbour, reaching St John's at 3 o'clock in the morning, took it by surprise and after having barbarously murdered many of the inhabitants and made the best prisoners, they laid siege to the fort and castle commanded in chief by Lt. John Moody and Mr Robert Latham with seventy men, whereof about twenty inhabitants , they continued in the harbour till the 23 February in which time the French had many men killed and wounded amongst whom were severall officers of note particularly the Governour's own nephew ; the fort and castle were bravely defended without the loss of any more than one serjeant and two or three private men , during the time the French burnt and distroyed all the houses storehouses goods &c whatsoever in St John's and marched South as far as Fair Ellen's [Ferryland] carrying away as prisoners all the inhabitants and myself (a few sick men excepted) and left behind the Canadians and Indians to make good their retreat, who joined them soon after committing the like barbarity as they had done at St John's all along as they went as Kitty Vitty, Petty Harbour, Bay of Bulls, and Fair Ellen &c , where I obtained my liberty by humble solicitations At Fair Ellen M Subercass ordered the Canadians and Indians [about one hundred and fifty men] under M Montigny to march Northward which next day they did by Holyrood burning and destroying in like manner the harbours of Harbourmaine, Breckhouse [Brigus] Portegrave, Island Cove, Harbour Grace, Carbineer, Bay of Vardes &c and when I came away on the 4th May they were not gone away from Trinity Bay, M Subercass with the rest of the forces returned to Placentia by Trepasse and St. Mary's with 200 English prisoners and is there safely arrived

He says further . The packet also contained depositions from Lt. Moody against one Mr John Roop of St. John's importing that the said Roop had indeavoured to persuade the inhabitants during the winter from contributing any assistance by watching at the forts and harbour and while the French

were there discovered to them whatever he knew of the weakness of the Fort and Castle and that the enemy acknowledged to have received considerable services from him and after three or four days he was at perfect liberty during all the time the French continued at St John's I believe the fortifications require to be repaired especially Fort William and the outworks

(Records)

(d.) Campbell's Further Account

Collen Campbell maketh oath that M Supercass' men during the time they were at St John's, they in a most barbarous manner did murder in and about St John's to the number of thirty and failing to reduce the forts burnt all the houses, 2 or 3 excepted, and when they departed the Governor said in his hearing : That at another time they would destroy what they now left, and carried away as prisoners the greater part of the harbour , as far as he can remember the losses sustained by them from the French on this occasion did amount according to the oaths of the principal inhabitants taken by Lt Moody to between one hundred and forty and one hundred and fifty thousand pounds stg

COLN CAMPBELL.

(Records)

(e) Richard Sampson's Account

He says two companies of French soldiers each between 40 and 50 commanded by M Supercass, 90 Indians and between two and three hundred inhabitants of Placentia arrived at St John's on the 21st January half an hour before day and surprised the harbour (they not having kept this winter any guards and killed nine of ye inhabitants viz. · [names given] and some of the soldiers who were permitted to lie in the harbour

There being no guard kept in ye North Battery they took ye Cannon there being 13 with which they annoyed ye South Battery having found two barrells of powder which belonged to ye fort or ye *Queens storehouse by the water side* The first day they attacked the South Battery which was commanded by Lt Robert Latham who had 12 soldiers and 15 inhabitants ; ye French fired on them out of ye woods very much with two great guns which they found on ye South point

In ye main garrison we had two men killed J Bargery a serjt and John Tieldad inhabitant The French sent very often small parties between 10 and 20 to amuse the garrison which were generally commanded by a Serjt but to the south side they always sent a commissioned officer. They allowed the people at Kitty Vitty having a hundred men fit to bear arms to live in their own houses but they never offered to go to the help of the garrison and told the enemy of one Richard King proposing going to ye fort and they had him presently killed   Several inhabitants were suspected of being in correspondence with the French

They destroyed all the town except four houses and took all the inhabitants with them to Petty Harbour four men being killed on the road from whence the inhabitants were at liberty except 60 or 70 whom they carried to Placentia several of which have since escaped

The said Campbell and one Pemberton was sent from ye French several times with a flag of truce and that the French having found some papers with John Roope have taken him to Placentia and intend to send him to France and the sd Roope is afraid they will never release him.

                                    RICHARD SAMPSON
18 June 1705.

(Records)

(f) ROOPE'S ACCOUNT.

M Supercass surprized the town all but ye garrison and neare ye fort for some little time gave no quarter but soone contradicted that order, all ye men which were about 222 were put in ye Church for a prison which is an open place and itt being bitter sharp frost and much snow often falling severall died of ye cold and several had their feet frozen Some days after he sent some Indians to Torbay who killed two men several hours after they had given them quarter; and after those in ye Church had been there a month he sent 80 of them under guard of a French party without Indians (each prisoner having a burden of 80 lbs on his back) to carry to Petit harbour their plunder but five being faint and not able to carry their burdens and for no other reason were barbarously murdered

The Indians for some months after went in parties and everywhere disturbed ye fishery and in Trinity Bay and Bonavista committed several barbarous murders as 'tis said 10 men and 2 little children after quarter.

M Supercass when departed burned and destroyed all ye boates, houses &c and carried with him 150 of the ablest men and forced them by ill usage to work on their fishery, some officers did pay them others did not and ye inhabitants gave them nothing, and att ye end of the season he sent severall to Canada, some to France and some still at Placentia who are said to have entered the French service all ye Irish are certainly entred

(Records)

(g) ROOPE'S FURTHER ACCOUNT

About daybreak M Subercass came and in two bodies fell in uppon ye harbour viz one of them by ye fort who killed and tooke all ye people yt were in ye houses under ye glacis neare an hour before it was known in ye fort and it was known by means of one Archebald Taylour a soldier about suns ryseing lowered ye little drawbridge and went out with a bottle of rum to drink with some of his consorts but when he came to ye uttmost part of ye glacis he saw ye enemy who fyered on him which made him turne and runn to ye bridge and pull it up and allarmed ye garrisons who came some cloathed and some not and then about five or six of the enemy crep up to the top of the glacis and fired and killed one of our people, one of them was killed, ye rest retireed to their body which was under shelter of some houses about 80 paces from there and then our people went to clear away ye snow from ye gunns which there was all ye times ye enemy was neare ye forts. And immediately after they sate fire to one of ye houses and retired in ye smoake thereof, about 14 days after M Subercass sent a truce with a letter, a copy of which I herewith offer [see p. 243] ye purport whereof was to have a parlee, which was held for four days and then broke off, on ye 2d day M Subercass forced me to write the letter to Mr Latham then commanded ye Southside Castle and that is the letter yr Lordships were informed was treasonable which letter I herewith present [see p. 244]. M. Subercass not gaining his point, having found two barrels of powder gott two sacre guns on a hill about 300 yards from ye Southside Castle began to cannonade ye woodwork thereof and fired on ye first day about 50 shot but seeing he did little or no damage, he fired but now and then and seeing ye sloope he had ordered to come with 200 shells and an 11 inch mortar did not appear nor their fire-arrows that they threw into ye Southside Castle did not take (for they were not well made) he prepared to go off.

I have before described how they burnt ye houses and treated ye prisoners, I only forgot that one Goning a missionary Jesuit allways kept close to ye Indians until they came to Ferriland In eight days he arrived at Ferriland where they destroyed all, for on going forth they had burned none and whilst in St John's they declared that if they could take the fort they would destroy nothing, that M. Costabelle ye Leut du Roy was to be Governour and a Capucian Friar come to be chaplain, that which friar came from Quebec and is still at Placentia and tis said there that there was an order from ye Court of France for ye expedition; 'tis agreed by all there that as soon as ye *Charente* which is a Kings ship arrived att Placentia, *La Vespe* was with all speed fitted out for Quebec and brought back about 100 Indians and Canadians of ye race of ye French.

Three days after they came to Ferriland they departed and then sent away M Montigny and most of the Canadians who went first to Conception Bay and plundered and destroyed all there (Carbonear Island excepted), from thence to Trinity Bay, from thence to Buena Vista where Lt Moody (as 'tis said) had constituted one George Sciffinton Chiefe who is a Quaker and ye spirit not moving him, he capitulated as soon as summoned and agreed to pay a certain sum, 250 li of wch was to be paid by bill of exchange in Boston to M Montigny but when he capitulated he was on an Island and had 120 men with 8 guns and severall stores and arms of ye Queens which he had had from Lt Moody, had notice of ye enemy and well on ye watch as 'tis said

They carried all ye plunder of Conception and Trinity Bay over ye isthmus of Bay Bulls in Trinity Bay where ye land carriage is butt 2 little miles on plaine ground and where they launch over boats of three or four tun and it is that way they infest our northern parts

About ye beginning of July there came to Placentia about 150 Indians of another nation and brought their wives and children and went immediately to disturb our fishery and ye Governor did declare that our fishery should always be disturbed and that he expected a greater force and then would again attempt St Johns

JOHN ROOPE.

(Records)

(h) ANOTHER FRENCH ACCOUNT

[Bishop Howley, who translated this MS and published it in the *Evening Telegram* of December 13, 1893, says — "This account is taken from the *Collection de Documents Relatifs à l'Histoire de la Nouvelle France*, published under the auspices of the Legislature of Quebec in 1883 The original of the present MS is in French The name of the author is unknown, but it is supposed to be either *Chausseyros de Lery* or *Gedeon de Catalogne*"]

Monsieur de Subercasse was named Governor of Placentia in 1702 In 1704, M Subercasse sent to Quebec to M the Marquess of Vaudreuil, Governor-General and Commander-in-Chief of Canada, the King's ship *Le Vespe*, commanded by Monsieur Delepiney, to demand a detachment of troops to go and destroy the colonies (or settlements) of the English on the coasts of Newfoundland * * * We left Quebec on the 2nd of November (*le lendemain de la Toussaint*) to the number of 40 French, and 40 Abenaquis (Indians), and arrived at Placentia the 15th Preparations were at once made, rackets and slides got ready to go direct to St John s But as the winter was very mild and it did not freeze up to the 13th of January, we began to despair of carrying out the project, although everything was ready

On the 14th it froze hard, and on the 15th we began the march Each one carried his outfit and grub (*vivres*) on his back, as there was no snow down to enable us to use the slides, which were left behind, and the

greater part also threw away their rackets, but when we were at a short distance from Beboulle, an English settlement, snow fell to a depth of two feet So we were delayed for two days Among 400 men we had only 60 pairs of rackets It was pitiable to see those who had none sinking to the thighs in the snow

At length we arrived at Beboulle, where we surprised the inhabitants, and we refreshed ourselves for two days and left a garrison there We then scaled the mountain, which is very steep, high, and wooded, then follow a sort of marshes or barrens (*plaines*) for four leagues, with little drokes of woods here and there. The snow was very deep, and the men without rackets were very much fatigued M de Costabelle was of this number, and, not being able to reach the camp, he remained in a small wood, where he had spread a sail to serve as a tent, and, being seated beneath it, one of his men, in cutting a tree to make a fire, let it fall upon the tent, so that M de Costabelle was caught like a marten-cat in a trap ! It was necessary to cut the tree in order to get him out, during which time he was very much inconvenienced We did not know anything of this accident until the following day M Subercasse sent me with four strong Canadians to his assistance I found him lying down, and unable to walk I made a litter and had him carried by two men, and in many places we had to cut a road through the bushes to get him along That evening we made a tilt for him (*cabane*), the troops took Petty Harbour without any resistance The following day we left him in charge of 8 Abenaquis, to whom we promised eight dollars (*huict escus*) So we left him there with a good escort

The following day, 31st March, we gained the depth of the wood to round the bottom of the bay of the harbour of St John's, where we arrived before sunset Altho' it was intensely cold we were not allowed to make a fire Each one sought a bed beneath the firs, which are very thick, and we placed our moccasins under us, to thaw them, so that we would be able to put them on next day. Before nightfall we ascended with M Subercasse a height from which one could see all the harbour without being able to distinguish the fort Having returned, M de Subercasse told me that M De Costabelle and the other Messieurs (*qu officers*) were not for attacking the fort until after all the merchants and inhabitants should have been taken I said that that was a sure way not to succeed They relied upon the fact that they had despatched, from Placentia, a brigantine, with orders to join us at St John's She was armed with a mortar and a number of bombs However, he gave orders to M De Beaucourt to go straight to the fort, to surprise and enter it, saying to him that appetite comes with eating M de Montigny commanded another detachment of Canadians and Indians, and M L'Hermitte marched at the head of the Placentia men, who, for want of rackets, could not follow the racketers, who waited for them till broad daylight

He (L'Hermitte) had taken the beaten path by which the English bring their wood, so that it was necessary to run at full speed to invest all the houses, and the inhabitants were taken in their night shirts (*tous nuds en chemise*, the MS is not very clear here — M F. H)

At the fort —M de Beancourt contented himself with walking along the glacis of the fort, without a soul stirring ; and the Indians took three or four families outside, or beyond the fort. For all that the garrison did not wake up, and it was about 8 o'clock when I arrived at the foot of the glacis, where I found M L'Hermitte, who was awaiting orders I proposed to him to go direct to the fort The ditches were filled with snow, he said he had not orders to do that At last an Englishman appeared on the parapet, who admired us running on rackets upon the snow, and when we aimed at him he ran to give word to the guard, who, with shovels, cleared the cannons of snow and commenced to cannonade us, and forced us to retire, and killed two or our men

All the inhabitants and merchants, to the number of 317, were placed in the *temple* (*sic*), and four merchants who were left on parole among our people. As there were about 60 women, who would have caused disorder, I advised M Subercasse to send them to the fort, which was done The fort was enclosed with stakes to a certain height in form of a terrace, which gave it the depth of a ditch, which palisade was also terraced behind, and almost bristling with cannon. Over the fosse (or ditch) there is a drawbridge, and the glacis on the water side and towards the houses is sloping at a moderate incline (*en pente entre la donce et la rapid*) Vis-à-vis on the other side of the harbour was the castle, enclosed by good and strong walls, partly wet at high tide, to attack vessels either entering or going out (*qu Cham Rock Battery — M. F H*) There were two other batteries, one above the other, the first well vaulted and ranging at water level (*battant a fleur de l'eau*), with cannon of 36 (*qu lbs*) The one above of 12, the batteries made in form of horse-shoe (*qu Waldegrave and Queen's batteries*)

As the stores and houses of the inhabitants were situated all along the harbour for about half a league, the French troops took up their lodgings as they chose, but out of range of the cannon, and they established a service of guards at the foot of the glacis

Some days passed without any action being taken, although the garrison made several discharges of cannon every morning upon the houses from which they saw smoke issuing. One ball carried away the pillow from under the heads of MM Monsengs and

Davigrand, who were sleeping together. without wounding them.

At about a league from the fort there is a small harbour, called Quidimity, where there were 72 English fishing M. De Montigny, with some Canadians and Indians, went to take them, and there was there a Reformer of the Tremblers, a Quaker (*un Religionnaire de la Tremblade un Quakie*), who was their commander They asked to be allowed their parole. It was granted on condition that if anyone deserted to go to the fort, all the rest would be put to the sword, to which they consented Some of our Indians went there occasionally to count them As soon as the Indian came they all put themselves in a row It happened that one day one of them wished to desert, the others followed and arrested him, and gave notice of it to the French, and without further trial or procedure he had his head broken on the spot where he was taken

After three or four days of refreshment M Subercasse sent M de Beaucourt and an interpreter to summon the governor, whose name was John Maudy, to surrender the fort He replied that first he would like to consult with Mr Cambell, the Commissary, and two of the principal merchants, who were prisoners He asked M Subercasse to send them to him under parole, an irreparable mistake, for, instead of intimidating him they only reassured him, and in reply he requested M Subercasse to send and find out the sentiments of the commander of the castle, which he did , but at the approach of the flag, the commander fired upon them and would not enter into any discussion

As this castle is at the foot of the mountain which commands it, almost perpendicularly (*meme en plongeant*), we hoisted up with capstans four pieces of cannon, of those which we had taken from the detached platforms We fired a few shots with but little effect However, we formed a guard to harass them night and day They kept themselves always on guard for the 33 days that we besieged them. The steep brow of the hill prevented the cannon from the fort from doing much harm, as they could not reach the houses So they erected a scaffolding in the fort and placed cannon on it, by which means they could command the houses. One shot struck a chimney, and some of the bricks or stones flying from it broke the leg of a Spaniard whom they (the French) had as a prisoner ; also of M Delean, nephew of M de Subercasse. The former died the next day, the latter the third day after

Seeing that the brigantine did not come, and as the season was advancing, they determined to decamp They took three loads (*charrors*) of goods from the stores and houses, estimated at the value of about 40,000 pounds *livres, en francs*) M de Montigny escorted them by night time past the castle

The night before the departure it froze hard, and the whole harbour was ca strong enough to bear a horse, which them to burn the boats and alm ᵈ merchandise, not being able to b· by land In the meantime the n ·, · of Quimidity, who had twelve shal· ·eady, offered to carry our loads to Bebo Their offer was accepted, but we only gave them provisions to carry And we left on the 5th of March, after having set fire to all the vessels, and broken up a ship, and a great number of boats.

Note that M Montigny had been to Conception Bay, where he found all the inhabitants retired to the Isle of Carbonniere, which is inaccessible. When we got to Petit Harbour, where we had left M. de Costabelle, as we had made almost all our prisoners follow, we resolved to send on some of them, so we fitted out three shaloupes. M de Costabelle embarked on one of them; M Durant, commissary, on another, and we coasted along, destroying all the English settlements.

When we arrived at Forillon the enemy were entrenched with cannon M Subercasse sent to summon them to surrender, which they refused to do, so he determined to give battle. As soon as the enemy saw this movement, they abandoned their posts, opened the door to us, and surrendered at discretion.

As we had no further enemies to fear, M de Montigny demanded a detachment of Canadians and Indians to go and try to take the island of Carbonniere. They made some prisoners there, and some plunder, and returned to Placentia, where we had arrived about a month previously. M de Montigny was scarcely arrived, when he asked for a party to go along the English coasts, which was granted He left, and took the route of the Bay of Carmel, made the portage of Trinity Bay, where he captured the inhabitants, and took their effects in his little boat, which he sent back to Placentia, and he himself continued his course to *Bonneviste*, where he found the inhabitants entrenched on the island. He attacked them and, without much resistance, they surrendered to about 50 men. The commander of the English, who was a merchant, asked to ransom himself for 4,000 pounds sterling, which he paid by a draught on Mr. Nelson, of Boston De Montigny, on receipt of the money, retired to Placentia, promising the people that they should not be further molested by the French, and that they might pursue their fishery in peace

After that another Canadian went to Bonavista and seized more prisoners, who also had to offer round sums to secure their ransom

In the month of June, M Levire, commander of a vessel, captured a prize which was going from Boston to St John's,

and brought her to Placentia The two citizens in charge of her, Geffry and Quinn, asked to be allowed free on parole, which was granted, but a few days afterwards Quinn managed to get a shaloupe and escape to St John's Geffry was afterwards exchanged for a Basque named Melle Roup, whom the St John's people had taken.

(1) GENERAL NOTE

These narratives do not by any means exhaust the matter preserved about this troubled year, but have been chosen as illustrating the period best Lieut. Moody kept a diary recording the events of each day; it is very interesting but too long to print, and not easy to condense The evidence of Campbell and Sampson must be received with discrimination Sampson, who was Campbell's servant, made a further affidavit that he had been made drunk by Major Lloyd and compelled to sign his first and afterwards signed a third, reciting that the second had been obtained by Campbell placing a pistol at his head

II Lord Dartmouth's Report, 1706.

(Abstract)
[Written by MATTHEW PRIOR, January 16, 1706]

The English have at all times used this Fishery on the Eastern coast and in Harbours and Fishing places on that side, wherein they are protected against the French in the Summer Season by yearly convoys and men of war sent thither A Fort was erected some years past in Bay St. John's for the defence of the inhabitants and retreat of others that may come for protection from other harbours during the winter

The French who usually fish from Placentia on the south to westward, and Northward of the Island, have their fortifications in Placentia Bay for defence of their Trade and Protection of their fishery

Since the beginning of the last war, the Convoys and men of war sent to Newfoundland have at times very much molested the French in their trade and fishery, taken considerable number of ships and destroyed their fishing Materials on the South Coast, so the French have taken all advantage to annoy her Majesty's subjects by their shipping, but chiefly by land, with assistance of Canadians as well French as Indians.

Mons Subercase, Governor of Placentia came in January last with about 430 men, surprised the fishing places to the Southward of St John's and possessed himself of that Harbour, Forts excepted, where garrisons maintained themselves against the enemy abt. thirty days when they retired

They marched from St John's to Ferryland and then Northward to Bonavista and committed barbarities and destroyed boats and flakes in the harbours

Mons. de Subercasse took away with him a hundred and fifty of our ablest men, forcing them to work in the French Fishery, at the end of the season sent several of the young men to Canada and to France, the rest are still at Placentia, they are said to have entered French service particularly the Irish

Placentia is the only place fortified by the French in Newfoundland, Two Forts there In lower Fort thirty-six Guns and in the Castle on the Hill eleven Guns and two Mortars. Three company's of soldiers, in whole one hundred and twenty men. Inhabitants—two hundred fighting men and can draw further supply's from Settlements in Canada, besides Indians

Our chief Fishery is on the East of Newfoundland from Cape Race to Cape Bonavista and French employ craft around rest of Island Fish coming from the Southward reach the French in the beginning of April, whereas they do not come to our most southern Harbours before the end of the month and not to St John's till the middle of May, the French having beach on the coast side, to dry and cure fish can be ready to Fish in four or five days after their arrival and on the E and N side of the Island, having not met with molestation from us in these desolate harbours, find their stages and flakes in condition they left them, whereas we have suffered much in destruction of houses flakes and stages by incursions of French of Placentia assisted by their neighbours of Canada

We have upon the petition of Merchants reported our opinion that two or more men of war might be appointed early in the year to convoy the Fishing Ships and two others to convoy sack ships, which have been accordingly ordered

Salt for fishery chiefly supplied from Portugal, ordered convoy's for salt ships from Lisbon to Newfoundland

Has been our care, to prevent Irregularities committed by inhabitants and Fishermen, to give Instruction to Commodore, with regard to the late Act of Parliament

We further offer; That the English that continue yearly in Newfoundland are dispersed into about thirty greater harbours besides coves and other Fishing places above Eighty leagues distant from N to S according to following scheme — [Omitted]

That the English live there the whole year without civil or Military Government except St John's where are fortifications with a Captain who commands only his own officers and soldiers, By reason of the distances of the habitations from each other and the inhabitants being under no discipline they will be exposed to incursions of the enemy, who are under strict rules of Government

For better security of the harbours of St John's a boom and chain has been placed at the entrance of the harbour on representation to Her Majesty. And for benefit of Merchants and Planters, we represented to Her Majesty that the officers of the Garrison of St John's be strictly prohibited from trading for thereby they have opportunity of engrossing trade and forestalling the Market

And that the Prize officer settled there be for the same reasons forbidden to trade except for disposal of ships and goods brought as prizes into Newfoundland Orders in this behalf have in like manner been given

Our Fishery has not of late years been so considerable as formerly, imputed chiefly to the interruptions occasioned by war as well in winter as Fishing Seasons and in the passage of our ships to and from Europe as also by want of a vent for our Fish in the dominions of Spain and other parts of the Mediterranean.

This trade was first supported by an Act of Parliament in the second year of King Edward the Sixth, a commission was sent in 1615 for enquiring into abuses, several regulations having been thereupon agreed in the Star Chamber the same were framed into a charter in 1633 known as the western charter—this continued in 'force till 1699 when an Act of Parliament was past to Encourage Trade to Newfoundland by which the same is at present regulated—and we, having carefully observed the management of the Fishery in pursuance of the said Act, do find by Information, of divers matters prejudical to this Trade

That in general the inhabitants have not due regard to the Regulations of the Act of Parliament it being found that N. of St John's as far as Carbonier and S. as far as Ferryland, the trees have been rinded and woods destroyed as much as before the Act

Fishing Admirals and masters of ships do not exactly observe the Rules of the Act There are few Admirals capable of keeping Journals and Accounts as the Act directs. Fishing Admirals before the 20th of August will hear complaints, but none received after; they being generally the greatest offenders themselves

Vessels from New England supply Newfoundland with provisions viz Bread, Beef, Pork, Flour, Pease, Butter, Boards, and great Quantitys of Tobacco European commodities carried to Newfoundland by masters of ships as follows from France in time of peace, Brandy, Wine, Salt linnen canvas paper, Hats and Silks, from Spain, Wine, Brandy, Iron, from Portugal Wine, Brandy, Salt, Oyle and Linnen, all which goods sold or truckt with traders from New England for Tobacco Sugar &c which they carry to Foreign Parts so at the end of the year masters are wholy taken up in Management of that illegal trade.

New England Traders seldom depart till men of war are sailed and then carry away handy-crafts-Men, Seamen and fishermen whom they entice in expectation of great wages.

Masters of ships negligent in bringing their men home, whereby they save the charge of their passage, men so left are inticed and carried away to New England.

The Reason why the New England men fish upon the coast of Newfoundland besides carrying on illegal trade is that they may get those men, they having otherwise a most advantageous fishery on their own coast

The preventing of which Irregularities we humbly offer to this Honble House our opinion, that a power be given by a clause in an Act that shall be passed to commanders of Her Majesty's Ships of war, and to admirals of each Harbour in Newfoundland, to lay fines and penalties upon offenders against the said Act, such fine not exceeding the sum of £5 stg and power likewise given them of confining such offenders in case of non-payment, such confinement not exceeding the space of ten days

That the commanders of Her Majestys Ships may have the power of a custom house officer to search New England Ships upon their coming, and to take account of the number of their crew and Passengers and to take bond from each of the masters that they shall not carry away a greater number of men than they brought, which we hope would in a great measure prevent irregularities committed by New England Traders

As early as the year 1615 the fish killed by English ammounted to 300,000 Quintals, and we have been well informed, that in several years after ye year 1650, we have taken (season favourable) above 400,000 Quintals, but that about ye year 1651, (until which year and some time afterwards, we furnished France itself with fish) the French entered upon that Trade, and have possession of a large part of the Island, and have by degrees advanced their fishing so as to be superiour to ours, by which means our trade has decreased, they having since furnished the Dominion of France and even other nations before solely supplied by us

Upon all which foregoing considerations, we cannot but conclude that whilst Placentia does remain in the hands of the French, our Fishery will be under continual discouragement all which is most humbly submitted.

III. Capture of St. John's in 1708.

(a) Charlevoix's Account

I have already observed that the centre and stores of all the English settlements on that island were on St John's Bay   De St Ovide proposed to M de Costebelle to reduce St John's at his own expense . .
He arrived on the last day of the year [with one hundred and sixty-four men including Indians] about five leagues from St John's without being observed   Two hours before day, they pushed on in a clear moon light to the head of St John's Harbour, whence he reconnoitred the whole place securely   He

then marched on, led by bad guides, whom he should have distrusted

As soon as he detected their treachery, he moved from the centre where he was, to the van, where the volunteers were and put himself at their head   He was discovered three hundred paces from the fort he designed attacking, so that some musketry fire opened on him as he approached the first pallisade   Some of his volunteers abandoned him, but this did not prevent his pushing on to the covered way, the entrance to which they had fortunately neglected to close   He entered shouting *Vive le Roy*, a cry that raised the courage of his men and made the English lose all heart   Leaving fifteen or sixteen men to guard the covered way, he crossed the ditch under the fire of two other forts, which wounded ten of his men, planted two ladders against the rampart, which was twenty foot high, and scaled in with six men, three of whom were dangerously wounded

At that moment Despenseus arrived with his detachment and planted his ladders   He was the first to ascend, entering the fort with two or three others.   Renou, Johannis, du Plessis, la Chesnaye, d'Argenteuil and d'Aillebout his brother followed close on this brave man, some seized the barracks, others the Governor's quarters, some others ran to the drawbridge connecting this fort called Fort William with that of the colonists and the Governor, who was hastening to throw in three hundred settlers, was struck down with three wounds   Despenseus immediately lowered the drawbridge and opened the gate   Then all the rest of the army entered and the English cried quarter

Thus in less than half an hour the French took two forts, either of which might have resisted a whole army, one had eighteen guns mounted, four mortars for bombshells, twenty for grenades and a garrison of over a hundred men, commanded by a very brave officer. The other had six hundred colonists well entrenched, ready to come to the succour of the first fort, but a subterranean door by which they expected to pass when occasion required, was found so well closed that it could not be forced open in time   A small fort still remained at the entrance of the port. De St Ovide sent to summon it, and the commander asked twenty-four hours to reply, and although he had eighty men in a strong-work, provisions for several months, quite a good supply of artillery, large cannon and a bomb mortar, as well as a bomb-proof vault, he surrendered

Ovide dispatched a messenger to inform Costabelle of his success   Learning that some English had escaped to Belle Isle and had embarked from there to England, he sent word at once by a small ship to France, that the Court there might learn what had been achieved as early as that of London   This step offended M de Costabelle, who considering it useless to expect troops from

France and not having men enough to defend both places, ordered De St Ovide to demolish the forts and return to Placentia by the end of March at least They brought away large stores, as three hundred English were on the point of marching to surprise Placentia

(b) First English Account

Letter from H E Harbargrace Island 4 Jany 1709 On the 21st December, the French from Placentia to the number of one hundred and sixty came to the fort of St John's and there with scaling ladders got over the work without any assistance, only two small guns the sentry fired; Major Lloyd then asleep in his bed and after the French got into the fort, the inhabitants in the New Fort rose in arms and would have taken the fort again from the French but the soldiers could not get the keys out of the Major's house, but when the French came he could find them, so from some of those men that made their escape to those respective islands Harbargrace and Carbonere Islands, the fort was actually sold to the French or else that number could never have taken it They surrendered the Castle next day being never an officer in it to command it

(c.) The Post Boy, Feby. 8.

On Tuesday last an express arrived from Lisbon that the French have made themselves masters of Fort St Johns by treachery, the wooden palisadoes that defended the same having been cut down upon notice of the enemy's advancing that way under pretence of putting iron spikes in their stead

(d) John Collins' Account

About four in the morning the sentinel of the S W corner of the New Fort discovered the enemy but his gun would not go off so he called to the sentinel of the N W corner who fired his piece which allarmed the place; this deponent being one of the Captains of Militia for the New Fort went to his appointed quarters which was the guard house of the fort where two other companies besides his were appointed their quarters. He then heard firing at the N W corner between the enemy and our men The deponent saith to the best of his remembrance at the time of the firing he heard quarter called in the old fort and presently after the French there cried *Vive le Roy* three times upon which this deponent and others in the old fort gave three *Huzaas* and the enemy immediately fired at them and they at them and eight of our men were killed and seven wounded They of the new fort called to those in the old fort to have the sally port opened and the bridge let down but could have no answer, some of the soldiers of the old fort got into the new fort and said there were five hundred French and that they gave no quarter (upon which we accepted the offer of quarter on the 26th, ?j)

This deponent heard Sarjeant Steel say at Mr. Winchen's house, that when the French entered the old fort but one man was beside himself on the works and that Major Lloyd came as far as the ramparts and said "Fight boys," and went away and he never saw him afterwards, until the garrison was taken which was within half an hour of the alarm and that he believed it was lost by neglect [and not by treachery]

(e) Mr Wm Keen's Journal

Decr 21 1708. About 4 this morning we were allarmed by the firing of small musketts and were within half an hour's time surprized to hear the fort was taken without meting resistance; some small time after the Fort surrendered, the Castle took the alarm and fired two guns, all the inhabitants of that side being about sixty men were retired into the Castle; about 7 this morning two French officers came to assure the inhabitants of good quarters and took with them the Most Master Inhabitants and Merchants into the Fort where I saw Major Lloyd very heavy eyd'd and little notice taken of him, in entering the fort the French lost three killed by the inhabitants, about five in the evening the inhabitants and servants were imprisoned in storehouses, excepting some few that were kept in their own houses.

A fire happened and burnt two streets of houses; Mr Russell was committed to the guard house, Mr. Wm Keen was confined in his own house, Captain Dennis was sent to have the castle surrender, which was at first refused but next day the 22nd the people gave it up, the French hoisted a white flag and fired three guns; the people were to have their clothes and provisions and be reinstated in their houses which was not complied with, on the 24 the Comissr St Ovide de Brouillon sent four hundred and seventy-seven men prisoners to the church and the house of Mr Collins allowing them one pound of bread four ozs of pork and four ozs of pease per diem—the prisoners were set in ranks and counted by the Indians who threatened if any escaped they would kill an equal number in their room; on the 25th an account was taken of the goods in the town, on the 26 an express was sent to Placentia which returned in nineteen days—the French did not resort with the English during this time With the express arrived two hundred more soldiers from Placentia The French sent Major Lloyd, Lieut Philips, Engineer Vane and his wife by ship to Placentia on Jany 8.

M. St. Ovide gave the inhabitants 24 hours to consider his proposals of ransom which if rejected he would send them all prisoners to Canada; he said it was His Master's intention to keep the country. The inhabitants under threat of burning the town were forced to agree to terms of ransom A party of men were sent to Ferryland under M. Larond but failed to take it, the inhabitants refusing to admit a flag of truce The French retreat was hindered for a month by ice After the destruction of the fort M St Ovide retired to the castle where he was nearly blown up by powder, one officer was killed

March 27 M St Ovide sailed for Placentia taking R Cole, Allyn Southmayd, Wm Keen, Thomas Russell, Wm Nicholls, John Collins, and Squarry and arrived at Placentia the 5th of April

On the 13th May Mr Lloyd and Mr. Phillips sailed for Canada On the 26th of May arrived the Fiddell man-of-war from France with two hundred soldiers for reinforcing St John's and St Ovide received news of his being created Knight of St Lewis and Governor of St John's On the 26th of June, the principal merchants arrived back in St John's having been kept several months longer than they had been told they would be upon St Ovide's word of honour

(f) Terms of Surrender

The inhabitants of St John's, Petty Harbour, Bay Bulls, Quidi Vidi, Tur Bay, Portugal Cove and Parlican have this day (2nd Feby 1709) desired M St Ovide to grant us liberty to ransom or buy our goods as specified in the 9 following articles —

First We promise to pay M St Ovide or his order, a hundred quintals for each shallop and fifty for each half-shallop sent fishing of the fish first cured or if the English take this port, to St Ovide's order in London seventy and thirty-five pounds sterling respectively in August or October

Second That our houses and clothes be preserved

Third That no damage be done to our stages, boats, &c

Fourth That the said St Ovide is to furnish us twenty hogsheads of salt per shallop ransomed

Fifth That the French do not waste our victuals

Sixth That our boats be allowed to go fishing

Seventh That any French plundering us shall make restitution and be punished by M. St Ovide

Eighth We promise to be neuter until our ransom be paid

Ninth If the French retain Newfoundland, to have liberty to go to New or Old England or remain in the country and retain our houses.

	St John's	Petty Harbour	Bay Bulls	Quidi Vidi	Tur Bay and Portugal Cove
Signed -	19	14	15	12	4

The whole ransom was computed at £7,280.

(g) Governor Collins' Petition

By Captain JOSEPH TAYLOUR Commander of her Maj ship Litchfield and Commander-in-chief of her Majesties forces in Newfoundland to JOHN COLLINS Esqre hereby appointed Governour and Commander in Chief of the Fort and Harbour of St John's and all the sea coasts between Ferryland and Carbonear Island

By virtue of the power given me by Her Maj I do hereby Constitute and appoint you, until further order Governour and Commander in chief of the Fort and Harbour of St. John's and all the sea coasts between Ferryland and Carbonear Island, Willing and requiring you forthwith to take upon you the said charge and command, Requiring all officers inhabitants and others to be obedient to you as their Governour and you are to take care to secure and defend the said fort against the enemy and to keep good order and disciple amongst those under your command and to order all the inhabitants into the said fort and to compel them to bring their provision there and for your better security and guard of the said Fort and Harbour of St John's, you are hereby empowerd to make as many Captains, Lieuts, Ensigns, and inferior officers as you find necessary and to do what is further for Her Majesties service

Given under my hand and seal H M S Litchfield in St Johns Harbour 6 Oct 1709

JOSEPH TAYLOUR

To the Queen's Most Excellent Majesty

The humble petn of JOHN COLLINS Esqr your Maj present gov of St John's Fort

Sheweth

That about Decm 1708 the said fort was surprized by the French and the then governour Capt Loyd taken therein, at which time yr petr being Commander of the Militia raised the best force he could and attempted the Relief of the said garrison with great hazard of his life, the two nearest persons to him being, the one killed and the other wounded But the town being altogether defenceless and under the garrison, yr petr was forced (after all possible resistance) to submit with the rest of the inhabitants and to pay a considerable ransom after which he was treacherously carryd away to Placentia and detained there to his great prejudice several months before he was permitted to return

That in Oct 1709 Capt Taylour yr Maj Commodore being there, and impowered and authorized to grant a commission to whomsoever he should find most deserving upon the place (The former Governour Captain Loyd being carried into France and since killed there) your petitioner was appointed govr and

Com^r in chief of the Fort of St. John's which he accepted at the request of the s^d Commodore the several Merchants and Traders and all other the inhabitants of the Place and y^r pet^r has ever since held the same at his own great charge and to the satisfaction of all concerned in the Trade there. Wherefore y^r pet^r having supplanted no other pretension (coming in upon an entire vacancy) pet^s for Governour's pay and continuance in Govt and not to be removed without just Reason and your pet^r &c &c

To the Queen's Most Excellent Majesty

The humble address of the inhabitants in Newfoundland

Dread Sovereign

We your most dutiful subjects inhabiting yr province of Newfoundland do humbly beg leave to tender our unfeigned gratitude for favours   which with God's assistance have in a great measure contributed to our being protected against the violent outrages of our barbarous neighbours the French, whose bold attempt upon our coast have rendered the adjacent unfortified harbours most dangerous as they would our residing at St John's had not yr Maj Royal Wisdom thought proper to order our being regulated into a Militia and to be put under command of John Collins whose extraordinary vigilance and prudent conduct in guarding and repairing yr Maj Fort in St. John's and regulating and ordering us for its defence have been manifested to our entire satisfaction

We therefore beg leave to recommend him for the care he has taken and the great and necessary expence he has been at to the prejudice of his private affairs

Subscribed by all the best inhabitants that are masters of families

Concurring petⁿ from a number of principal Merchants and Masters of ships in London (and more are ready to do it if needful).

IV. Captain Crowe's Laws

By Captain Jos Crowe, Commander-in-Chief of HM ships, forts, and garrison in Newfoundland

A record of several laws and orders debated at several courts Present, commanders of merchant ships, chief inhabitants, and witnesses being examined, it was brought to following conclusion, between 23rd August and 23rd October 1711 —.

1st. That a sum of money should be collected by voluntary gift from commanders of ships, merchants, masters of families, and others, for repairing churc) which was demolished, and subsistence of minister.

2nd That orders be put up at public-houses and other places for suppressing drunkenness, cursing, and swearing Fines and punishment according to annexed copy [omitted].

3rd A body of seamen or others should keep guard in the night to prevent mischiefs by spyes of the enemy and others to be raised as follows, viz., from the complements of the ship in the harbour, one man for every fifteen, and one man for every three boats of inhabitants and by boat keepers, a commander of a ship and a merchant to command them each night

4th The tenements, store-houses, and stages which are now in possession of persons under-mentioned (to wit), Richard Colesworthy, upper stage-house and room at ffort at Bursthart Ihll, Captain Stafford, in behalf of Henry Perden, one store-house on vice-admiral's room, Thomas and John Squary, one store-house on admiral's room, Mrs. Turf's, in behalf of Mrs Anne Earll, the upper stage adjoining to his own two boats room, Governor Collins, in behalf of Mrs Holeman, one store-house on the vice admiral's room, Hugh Tucker, in behalf of John Harris, Esq, of Exon, one store house on the admiral's room, Captain Holsworth in behalf of Michael Martin, one store house on the admiral's room Being proved formerly belonging to fishing ships and ingrossed since the year 1685 contrary to Act of Parliament to prejudice of said ships, &c. I do therefore hereby dispossess them of same in right of ffishing ships

5th Inhabitants, ffishermen, and servants to repair to winter quarters allotted them by 1st of October, and be under command of several governors for better security against the enemy in small bodies to particular places (to wit) —

| St John's Quitty Vitty Torbay Petty Harbour | Into Fort William, under Governor Collins |

| Conception Bay upon | Carbonear Island, Little Bell Isle, and Harbergrass Island | Under their respective governors |

Trinity Bay, on Foxe's Island and Dildo Island

| Bay of Bull, Witt-less Bay, and Toad's Cove | On Gull Island, under Governor Colesworthy. |

From Isle of Speer, Southerly, into fort at Ferryland.

6th Houses in ffort William not to be sold or let, but in case the person who built it does not inhabit it themselves, said houses to be at the disposal of Governor Collins, to put in persons destitute of habitation in said fort

7th. Owners of such houses not having proportion of people to said house, at discretion of Governor Collins to put in others

8th. If not sufficient ground in fort to build habitations, Governor Collins to give leave for building proper habitations under the guns within outwork of fort

9th. To prevent servants hiring themselves to one, two, or three masters at once, governor to oblige them to pay for such offence £2 10s, or otherwise cause them to be whipt three times forward and backward along some public place

10th. Five men for each ship in harbour shall go into the woods and cut twenty stockades and pallasadoes to repair works of fort of St John's, and boat keepers for every boat to fetch as many

11th Plantation of John Drue, of St John's, proved to be ship's room, yet, in regard to his age, and thereby past labour, may enjoy same during life, but after his decease to return to right of ships

12th Mr Turf's confirmed at second application to loose upper stage adjoining his own two boats room that he now holds in behalf of Mrs Anne Earl, mentioned in 4th Article.

13th Whosoever shall demolish, deface, or break down any stage, cooke room, house, or flakes by removing raffters, rinds, floorings, shoars, stakes, or layers, except to employ them on same room next year, shall forfeit £10 for repairing same to possessor of said stage and room

14th. House in possession of Captain Arthur Holdsworth that formerly belonged to Mr. Lint, confirmed to said Captain Holdsworth, right being assigned to him by Mr Richard Colesworthy

15th Minister to have subscription for ensuing year from shollups, three, the two men boats, two, and the ship one quintol of dry merchandable fish to be levied as followeth —One from owner of stage, one from boat keeper, and one from servants

16th. A plantation of three boats rooms in possession of Abraham Barrot and Richard Sutton in Torbay. Being ships rooms, they are dispossessed in right of ships that have occasion for them next year

Jos Crowe

V. Sir N. Trevanion's Orders and Fishery Scheme.

(a) By Sir Nicholas Trevanion, Knight, Commander of H M Ships and Garrisons, and Governor-in-Chief at Newfoundland

(Decr 10, 1712)

A Record of several Courts held at St John's for better discipline and good order of people, &c Debated at Courts held Present Admiral and Vice-Admiral, Merchants, and Chief Inhabitants , and witnesses being examined, it was brought to the following conclusions —

1st That orders be put up at public houses and other places for suppressing drunkenness, &c

2nd. Confirmed last year by Captain J Crow, that Mr Jacob Rice, minister of St. John's, should have as follows —

From shallops - three ⎫ quintals of dry
From two-men boat two ⎬ merchandable
From the skiffs - one ⎭ fish.

And planters very backward in paying, he got only one hundred quintals of fish this season.

Confirms what Commander Crow and Court agreed to for minister's subsistence, and to encourage him to remain

3rd Confirms John Collyns, Esq , Governor of Fort William, and it is appointed, during cessation, that twenty men lie in fort every night

4th Warrant granted to call Mr Benger before him [the Governor] relating to Sir William Hopkins' place at Ferryland, now in possession of Widow Clapp, and tenement formerly in possession of Sir David Kirk; but Mr Benger did not appear

5th. Mrs Benger, wife of James Benger, appeared relating to a tenement formerly in possession of William Bennet, deceased. Mrs Benger willing to allow to heirs of William Bennet, deceased, to one Tomson Reeve £10 per annum till further decided.

6th. Other matters between masters of ships and planters and boat-keepers relate to debts not mentioned, parties being satisfied

---

(b) Fishery Scheme for 1712

1st. Referred to annexed scheme for number of English planters [always given on a separate sheet].

2nd. Planters receive little sustenance from the countries, and kill few beavers and other wild beasts.

3rd Inhabitants have most salt provisions from Ireland , fresh provisions, as bread, pease, &c , from New England and Pensilvania , salt from Lisbon and Isle of May, and in war time from prizes brought in.

4th Strict orders that no trees be cut down or rinded, nor woods set on fire, except for building, nor trees cut down on account of making oyle.

5th Has taken all care to settle matters between fishing ships and planters, to give each their rights

6th No complaints of fishing ships

7th Care taken that bye boat keepers and fishing ships do carry such number of fresh men and green men as Act directs

8th No complaints of marks of any boats or train vats being altered

9th No complaints of any person leaving the country, do not destroy or injure stages, &c

10th No complaints that any admiral, vice-admiral, and rear-admiral do ingross more beach or flakes than they patch upon at their arrival.

11th Orders sent to admirals and chief planters of every little cove, to give account of boats and fish and of inhabitants, which is hereunto annexed

12th General court held twice a week with admiral and vice-admiral to assist, and endeavoured to settle differences relating to planters and boat keepers, servants, &c.

13th Orders to captains of men-of-war and admirals of harbours, that no ballast be thrown out of ships in harbours

14th Care taken that offals have not been offensive, stages so near water, when thrown in it is washed away.

15th Care that Lord's Day duly observed Corrections to all so offending

16th None but Her Majesty's subjects fish or take bait in ports inhabited by English

17th Care taken that fish be preserved with good salt and sent to market in good condition.

18th. No wine nor brandy brought from New England, only rum and molasses, which is the liquor drunk by servants Bad year of fishing. Planters in debt to masters of ships and merchants to pay ensuing year if able.

19th 17th of September when governour arrived, so could not get master's names, most of them gone before his arrival, but by scheme it is found there were twenty sail belonging to America, brought bread, pease, rice, rum, tobacco, mollasses, and cattle, &c, &c

20th. Provisions from England, Ireland, and New England New England men return home in their ballast

21st Account in former article of provisions brought hither, there is sugar and tobacco, but cannot find any cotton wooll, indico, ginger, fustick, or any dying wood, nor any put on board ships to Spain, Portugal, or any foreign part

22nd Refers for information to scheme for number of boats and men employed by inhabitants

23rd As to 27th Article, refers to scheme for number of fishing ships and boats, with burthens, &c Men's food is beef, fish, pease, &c Beer brewed with molasses and spruce. Go out of harbours in shallops, seven men and five men in a boat, catch fish with hook and line, first part of year their bait is muscles and lances, about middle of June bait is capeling, squid, and fresh herring, and end of year they fish with herring only—nets purposely for taking the sort of bait

24th Price of fish this year from thirty to thirty-six ryalls per quintal good merchandable fish Broken fish which they call refuse fish sold for twenty ryalls per quintal, and carried to Spain and Portugal and oyl made of livers carried to England; value of oyl 16l. per tun.

25th Refers to scheme for number of sack ships They load with dry fish bound to several ports as Spain and Portugal But eight ships this year could not get loading and forced to go in ballast to Virginia to seek freight.

26th Staat charge to carry back men brought from England

27th Best enquiries made to know what inhabitants at Placentia, five hundred men, two hundred women, and children Great quantities of fish catched there this year and sold for twenty-two ryalls a quintal

28th Fort and platform of sixty guns, ammunition, and victuals from France and Canada Quantities of ammunition not informed of and provisions no want of.

29th Thirty sail from Placentia this year—most came to make fishing voyage, and some to buy fish to carry to market—ships that fish upon banks taking cod and salting and carrying them in bulk to France, and in bay they fish upon coast of Canada, and salt fish after same manner

30th No other nation besides England and France, except Spaniards, come by stealth into harbours where they are not discovered.

31st Care taken to see all New England men out of port, so that they do not carry away any of Her Majesty's subjects

CHAPTER XI.

REIGN OF GEORGE I.

1714–1727.

1714.—Difficulties about fishing rooms in Placentia sold by French to planters and officers

1715.—Spaniards not allowed to fish, by order of Governor of Placentia

1718.—Difficulties with the French about English settlers' fishing establishments near Cape Bonavista.

1719.—Claim again made by Biscayans to fish in Newfoundland disallowed

1723.—Grant of salmon fishery to Skiffington between Cape Bonavista and Cape John.

Under the sovereignty of the first Hanoverian King there were few stirring events in the Colony; the history of our Island in this reign is a chronicle of the piping times of peace. English trade flourished, settlements increased, the poor Newfoundland planter no longer listened for the dreaded war-whoop of the Abenaquis, or the tramp of the invading French soldiers.[1]

The immediate result of the peace is best shown by the enormous increase of the English fishery. Whilst in 1713 there were only forty-six fishing ships, with one hundred and sixty-two boats, one hundred and ninety-five bye-boats, and two hundred and eighty-eight inhabitants' boats, in the following years the figures were:—

			Fishing Ships.	Boats	Bye boats	Inhabitants' Boats	Fish caught by Ship Fishermen	Fish caught by Inhabitants and Bye boats
							Quintals.	Quintals.
1714	.	.	106	441	133	362	115,000	45,000
1715	.	.	108	376	197	468	89,622	35,531
1716	.	.	86	319	184	408	88,469	33,830

[1] In 1717 the "Second Somersetshire Regiment," now the First Battalion Prince of Wales' Volunteers, the "Fighting Fortieth "—a corps familiarly known by the sobriquet of "Excellers" (XL-ers)—was formed of eight independent companies raised in Nova Scotia and Newfoundland. The field officers carried half-pikes, the company-officers, spontoons, the serjeants, halberds, and the rank-and-file, flint-lock muskets and short swords. Having served in the Colonies for nearly fifty years, the regiment was transferred to Ireland in 1764, where it remained throughout a decade, having six years previously to its recall from Canada won the first "honour" inscribed on its colours at the memorable siege of Louisburg.

The Regimental Records have been edited by Captain Raymond Smythies.

In 1711 and 1712 the common danger had united the ship fisher-men and the planters in arrangements for orderly government. Their town meetings lasted, however, only for the two years. When once the stern pressure of war was removed by the peace of 1713 all the old quarrels revived, the fishing admirals and the merchant adventurers returned to their normal habits of disorder tyranny, and persecution.

GEORGE I.

From an engraving after Kneller.

The Commodore and his officers were gradually curtailing the fishing admirals' powers. If we are to judge by Mr. Larkin's report, in some instances this was going from bad to worse. The lieutenants in Captain Poulton and Captain Fairbourne's time all took bribes of fish. "The present Commander, Captain Graydon," he says, "had taken much pains to do the country justice and to settle religion amongst them." Larkin gives a doleful picture of the disorders prevalent in the Colony.

This unfortunate condition of affairs was due to the extraordinary imbecility of the British Government. They endeavoured to rule the Colony without a Governor, to defend it from invasion without adequate military or naval force, to distribute justice without duly constituted courts or laws made by the authority of the Imperial Parliament; in fine, they went on administering the affairs of the Island in the most blundering manner, and then stupidly wondered because the inevitable result was chronic disorder and chaotic confusion.

After the Treaty of Utrecht, by a very singular and ill-conceived arrangement, Placentia was placed under the government of Nova Scotia, whilst the rest of the island was ruled by the admiral or commodore. A very troublesome question arose out of the Queen's sympathy with the sufferings of the French Protestants undergoing the hardships and cruelties of the galleys by order of Louis XIV. In order to get these poor slaves released, she made the following liberal arrangement.

s 2

The Treaty of Utrecht was signed on the 31st of March 1713; on the 23rd of June of the same year Queen Anne wrote to Nicholson, Governor of Nova Scotia:—

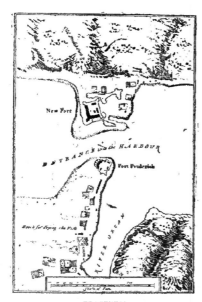

PLACENTIA.

B.M. MSS., 22,875.

"Whereas our good brother the most Christian King hath at our desire released from imprisonment aboard his galleys such of his subjects as were detained there on account of their professing the Protestant religion, we being willing to shew by some mark of our favour towards his subjects how kind we take his compliance therein, have therefore thought fit hereby to signify our will and pleasure to you; that you permit such of them as have any lands or tenements in places under your Government in Acadia and Newfound Land, that have been, or are to be yielded to Us by virtue of the late Treaty of Peace, and are willing to continue our subjects, to retain and enjoy their said lands and tenements, without molestation, as fully and freely as others of our subjects do or may possess their lands or estates, or to sell the same, if they shall choose to remove elsewhere. And for so doing this shall be your warrant."

Legal questions arose out of this transaction. Most of the Frenchmen, before leaving Placentia, sold their places; Governor Moody and the English officers bought several pieces of land; some of these at the gut were required for fortifications, and, after some delay, Moody was paid for his land by order of the Board of Trade. The ship fishermen complained bitterly of this transaction, which deprived them of free ships' rooms, and as Placentia was renowned for fishing, they could not benefit by the new acquisition without paying high rents to officers and the Governor.

It appears, notwithstanding Costabelle's urgent appeal, many French remained behind in Placentia, and secretly encouraged Biscayans and French Basques to fish there. The poor Biscayans were misled by the Spanish authorities; they believed that, under Article XV. of the Treaty of Utrecht, they had fishing rights in Newfoundland.

This Article declares:—

"And because it is contended on behalf of Spain, that the Biscayans and other subjects of His Catholic Majesty have a certain right of fishing in Newfoundland His Britannic Majesty agrees that to the Biscayans and other Inhabitants of Spain be reserved *all the privileges to which they can with right pretend.*"

The English declared the Biscayans had no fishery rights in New-foundland, and under no circumstances would they tolerate the Spanish pretensions. In the year 1715, according to the Spanish records, some Biscayan vessels arrived at Placentia and, as they had expected, the English Governor of Placentia ordered them off. He said —

"He had no orders from the king to consent that the Spaniards should enjoy any fishing privileges under the Treaty of Utrecht."

The unfortunate ship masters had to return empty to Spain, losing their voyage and the large expense of outfit, however, notwithstanding this order, many Biscayan ships fished out of Placentia, and when the English Government became very strict, they transferred their vessels nominally to English owners, and sailed under the English flag. A case is mentioned as late as 1765, in which two ships were found to be owned by Spaniards.

It has been contended by the French that the English never settled or fished north of Cape Bonavista prior to 1765. This statement is contradicted by many facts recorded in contemporary history. There can be no doubt that in the sixteenth and in the early part of the seventeenth century the French fished about Notre Dame Bay, and it was in this locality that they came in collision with the Red Indians, but afterwards we find all their fishing establishments were further north, only an occasional ship locating east of Fleur-de-Lys, in Notre Dame Bay[1] In proof of this we have the expedition of Captains Underdown and Lloyd in 1706, all the French places mentioned are on the line of coast extending from White Bay to Quirpon, none were found elsewhere

The reason why our opponents selected this portion of the coast is very obvious, it contained a number of excellent harbours, it was removed from their dreaded enemies the Red Indians and the English, and for fishing vessels it afforded the very best field for operations. We know from the records that the French moved about a good deal, shifting their quarters oftener than the English, here, at Petit Nord, they had the best part of the north-east coast and the Straits of Belle Isle, then as now, the very best fishing ground in the Colony.

Subsequent to the French attack of 1696-7, from about 1700, the English settlements were gradually extended north from Bonavista;

---

[1] "Thomas Mitchell captured and taken to White Island 7th June 1697. This island lies half a mile from the shoare and is fourteen leagues N. of Cape Frills. No more ships there, *but there were thirty or forty further along the coast.*" (*B of T., Nfld*)

STARVE HARBOUR, ON THE OLD FRENCH SHORE.

From a drawing by the Hon. and Rev. W. Gray.

some of the first "liviers," in Old Newfoundland parlance, had by this
time built their huts and fishing stages as far north as Twillingate,
Exploits, and Fogo.

T. COUR LOTTER'S MAP OF 1720.

B.M., 70620 (5).

There can be no surer guide to the nationality of the occupiers of
the Newfoundland coast than the names of the various harbours. Placentia Bay, St. Mary's Bay, Fortune Bay, and the western shore towards
Cape Ray, all testify by their nomenclature to French occupation;
similarly such vulgar English names as Bett's Cove, Tilt Cove, Seldom-
Come-By, Nippers Harbour, Joe Batts Arm, Leading Tickles, undoubtedly
prove the presence of English fishermen as the occupiers and first settlers
in these localities. Turning Partridge Point we find from the bottom

of White Bay to Quirpon mainly French names, showing that these harbours were used by our opponents. The following historical evidence bears out the same conclusion :—

"LETTER from Wm COCH of Bonavista to Col. NORRIS 7 Sep 1698

" I think it my duty to acquaint your Honour that to the North side of this bay are many extraordinary harbours and better fishing, one William Wyng has fished there some years (it being 14 leagues N Wc N° from this place) who has still increased the inhabitants of this place very considerably, and this year one Nowill has been that way who has more fish for his two boats than they have for shallops, so that next summer severall of the inhabitants of this harbour design to remove thither and their masters of ships that have fished there this year intend to be likewise, for it is certain the fewer boats are kept in a place the better the fishing

" I write this that those sent to settle affairs may have power as far as Cape Frills. I think a draught [chart] ought to be drawn of that place There is room for five hundred sail." [1]

The English settlements north of Bonavista grew so rapidly that in 1732 the commodore was instructed to include in his "scheme" an account of Fogo, Twillingate, and any other places he thought fit, but none appears to have been furnished until that of Captain Vanbrugh in 1738.

The most important particulars then were —

	Fishing Ships.	Sack Ships.	Passengers.	Boats of Fishing Ships	Boats of Inhabitants	Bye-boat men	Fish	Seal Oil Value.	Furs Value.	Families.	Farmers	Inhabitants.	Remained last Winter.
							Qntls	£	£				
Fogo	7	4	70	14	24	135	19,000	770	300	21	None	215	143
Twillingate	2	3	50	8	16	130	12,000	440	100	16	None	184	152

In 1739, 386 persons remained during the winter In 1742 Fogo and Twillingate were credited with making £2,550 from seal oil.[1]

These official returns prove conclusively the English occupation prior to 1763; and there can be no doubt that there were a number of smaller settlements which never made any returns.

Palliser, in his report of 1768, says Twillingate was never formerly used by the French, and the master of the *Bon Ami* admitted that he received an extra bounty from the French Government to fish there, in order to annoy and drive away the English settlers.

There are entries in the books of Messrs. Gundry, Bridport, showing purchases of nets, lines, and cordage by the Nobles as far back as 1760, and thirty years later (1790) Rowsell's accounts with this most ancient firm showed very large dealings and very extensive fishery operations, amounting in some cases to £1,000 for the year. John Slade of Poole, who carried on business in Twillingate early in the eighteenth century, died in 1792, leaving a fortune computed at £70,000 sterling, all made out of the Newfoundland trade.

All these facts form a complete answer to the French contention that the English never occupied any place north of Cape Bonavista prior to 1763. It is well known that during the celebrated Seven Years' War which commenced in 1756 the French virtually abandoned Newfoundland; they were chased from the North American seas by British cruisers during the ten years prior to 1763, and English fishermen occupied all the deserted French establishments as far north as Quirpon. There is abundant evidence on this point from the records. Many years, however, prior to 1763 there were British settlements sparsely scattered all around Green Bay and along the Newfoundland coast from Cape Bonavista to Cape John.

By the treaty of Utrecht the boundaries of the New-foundland coast on which the French were permitted to fish extended from the well-known point Cape Bonavista to Point Riche. The French claimed that Point Riche was Cape Ray, citing in proof of their contention a map of Hermann Moll. The merchants and planters of Newfoundland, in a petition presented to Parliament in 1716, declared the Point should be fixed at fifty and one-half degrees of North latitude. A letter was found from Prior, settling the limits, and was admitted by the French as conclusive, in 1764.

MOLL'S MAP.

B.M., K. 118-38.

Later on our opponents alleged that they had found a map drawn by Jean Denys, to which reference had been made in the negotiation of 1713, which placed Point Riche at 49°, upon the borders and to the north of the Bay of Three Islands (Bay of Islands), now called North

[1] Moll was led astray by La Hontan, who was then in London. Moll's knowledge of the interior of Canada was also mainly derived from La Hontan.

Head. "This," said the Abbé Reynal, "was a reasonable and just
" demand, and yet the French, who ventured to frequent the contested
" space, experienced the loss and disgrace of having their boats
" confiscated." This dispute continued between the two nations until
.1778. As a matter of fact, both nations showed a marvellous ignorance
of geography, Point Riche is really situated a little to the north of
Ingornachois Bay.

There were other difficulties with the French besides the question of
Point Riche Many English settlers had fishing establishments and
dwelling-houses north of Cape Bonavista; the French claimed that
they interfered with their fishery rights under the treaty, and that they
should be removed. The English Government, as usual, did nothing

This question arose again in a still more troublesome and complicated form in 1763, at the Treaty of Paris, when there was a still larger
English settlement, extending from Bonavista to Cape John, some stray
English fishermen having fixed establishments as far north even as
Quirpon. An Irishman—a Mr Dunien—was so obstreperous in his
altercations with the French at St. Julian's, that Admiral Palliser ordered
him to be banished from the Colony.

Whilst the French had occupied Placentia, all the best places on the
beach, and the most convenient positions for fishing stations, had been
appropriated by the Governor and his officers; a regular part of the
business of the soldiers, marines, and sailors was to catch fish for their
masters, a small share was allowed them, but, of course, the lion's portion
went to the officers. The Frenchmen complained bitterly that they had
not so much beach room and conveniences for the fishery at Louisbourg
as they had enjoyed for many years at Placentia.

When the English took possession, Governor Moody and his successor, Governor Gledhill, followed the same practice as their predecessors. Moody, and some of his subordinates, bought out the French
officers, and, as we have seen before, their rights were confirmed. This
military dominion and military trading was too much for the West
Countrymen, and a peremptory order was sent to the lieutenant-
governor of Placentia, Colonel Gledhill, putting an end to their trading
and fishing. In defence of the officers, it should be remembered that
they were always very badly paid, often not paid at all, and frequently
in arrear. They had no alternative but to eke out a living in some
way.

Other peculiarities were copied from the French in Placentia disputes
were decided according to French rules and it was some considerable
time before Plaisance became a thoroughly English settlement and

settled down to English ways. It remained under the government of Nova Scotia until 1729.

In the records we find an account of a large salmon fishery carried on by Mr. Skeffington, from Bonavista, between Cape Bonavista and Cape John, which it is expressly stated was never used by fishing ships. After considerable delay and a reference to the law officers of the Crown, Skeffington obtained a grant in 1723 for twenty-one years in a sole fishery for salmon in Freshwater Bay, Ragged Harbour, Gander Bay, and Dog Creek. About this time the salmon fishery was also extended to Exploits and various other rivers in Notre Dame Bay, and with this new enterprise there was a corresponding increase of the resident English population in this portion of the Colony.

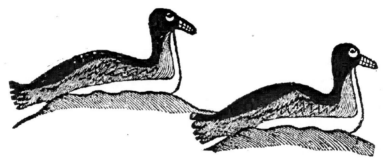

GREAT AUK.
From the English Pilot, 1753.

The whole of this period, 1714 to 1727, was like the heavy prosaic Hanoverian monarch—dull, uneventful, peaceful, and prosperous. Population and the fishery increased considerably; the trade with England for provisions almost entirely ceased; salt beef, pork, butter, bacon, all came from Ireland; fresh meat, live stock, corn, flour, lumber, lime, and bricks were all imported from the North American colonies; woollen cloths were largely shipped from Ireland; linen, &c. from France and Spain, and from the latter country iron, for which the Basque provinces have always been famous.

The tyranny of the fishing admirals still prevailed, but it was very much tempered by the interference of the naval officers, who assumed their functions, and in a rough-and-ready sort of way administered justice. The want of a ruler and a settled government was felt acutely at this period : representation after representation was made to the home Government on the subject, and, at last, after many delays, in 1729, a Governor and Commander-in-Chief was appointed.

CHAPTER XII.

REIGN OF GEORGE II

1727-1760.

1729 —Lord Vere Beauclerc recommended for first Governor, but Captain Osborne, R N, eventually appointed Governor and Commander-in-Chief; Placentia placed under him, Island divided into six districts; J P's appointed; contests between fishing admirals and justices, Osborne's letter to the Duke of Newcastle, J P Taylor, of St John's, allowed to open a shop in Boston.

1730 —Court House and Prison at St John's completed in September   St John's magistrates threaten to resign on account of indignities and obstructions expected during the winter.

1731.—Captain Cluton, R N, appointed Governor.

1732 —Captain Falkinham, R N, of H M S *Duiseley Galley*, Governor, Governors requested to furnish account of inhabitants, &c at Fogo and Twillingate.

1733.—Lord Muskerry, Governor.

1735 —Great complaints of French competition in European fish markets

1737.—Court of Oyer and Terminer appointed, owing to inconvenience of trying two cases of murder in 1736   Captain Vanbrugh, R N, Governor

1738.—Captain Vanbrugh's account of inhabitants at Fogo and Twillingate.

1740 —Lord George Graham, Captain, R.N., Governor

1741.—Hon Jno Byng, R N, Governor.   Mr William Keen appointed Naval Officer to collect returns about the fishery, also to be Health Officer and Judge of the Vice-Admiralty Court.

1742.—War between France and England, Captain Welch prosecuted at Boston for bringing passengers from Newfoundland without reporting them

1743 —Captain Byng appointed Naval Officer to prevent smuggling.

1745.—Louisbourg, Cape Breton, captured by Pepperell and Admiral Warren; great rejoicings in England over the victory, won principally by New England troops; Admiral Watson, Governor.

1747 —British-American officers recruiting in Newfoundland

1748 —Peace of Aix-la-Chapelle between England and France; Louisbourg restored to France, great indignation in New England; Col Bradstreet, Lieut.-Governor.

1749.—Captain George Brydges Rodney, R.N., Governor (celebrated as Lord Rodney).

1750.—Captain Francis W. Drake, Governor.   Commission of Oyer and Terminer to try felons in Newfoundland.   R Carter, Esq, J P. for Ferryland; Murder of William Keen, the magistrate.

1753.—Confederation of British North American Colonies for mutual defence against the French   Governor Bonfoy   Grant of Isle aux Bois to R Carter.

1754.—Lord Baltimore renewed his claim upon part of Avalon; ruled that his title had lapsed.

1755.—Richard Dorril, Governor. Roman Catholics prosecuted for celebrating Mass Bradley reports from Fogo, presence of forty French armed ships surveying and fishing; also capture of French spies; complaint by Harbour Grace fishing admiral of destruction of property by loose characters living in huts at the end of the harbour.

1756.—Commencement of the Seven Years' War.

1757.—Local Militia appointed; Michael Gill, J.P., honorary colonel. Governor Edwards. Small-pox epidemic. Number of French prizes captured; a captured Waterford vessel recaptured by her own crew.

1759.—Quebec captured by Wolfe; great power of France in America destroyed. New English church built at St. John's; Rev. Edward Langman, minister. The Molasses Act.

1760.—Governor Webb; Gundry's of Bridport supplying lines and seines to Noble at Fogo.

The period covered by the reign of the second Hanoverian king is distinguished by two of the most stirring events in the history of North America, the capture of Louisbourg and the fall of Quebec. For Newfoundland there was the dawn of a brighter day : England at last determined to confer the blessings of government on the unfortunate Colony.

During the preceding years of peace the trade and fisheries of the Island had wonderfully increased. The average catch for the years 1749, 1750, and 1751 was about four hundred and thirty thousand quintals of fish and two thousand five hundred tons of cod oil; the population had become about six thousand permanent inhabitants.

Whilst no rude alarms of war disturbed the Newfoundland colonists, the mother country all through this reign experienced the perils and dangers of '45—the Jacobite rebellion. The air was full of war and

GEORGE II.
From an engraving by Faber.

warlike preparations. To the alarm caused by Prince Charles Edward we owe the efficient fortification of St. John's, Trinity, Carbonear, Ferryland, and the maintenance of garrisons and artillery; it was all allowed to fall into decay just before the French again made another successful attack on St. John's.

Acting on the most urgent representations of the naval commanders the Ministry determined to appoint a Governor. The Committee of Council had recommended that Lord Vere Beauclerc, who had been Commodore on the Newfoundland station, should be appointed—

"Governor and Commander-in-chief in and over the Island of Newfoundland, our fort and garrison at Placentia, and all forts and garrisons erected and to be erected in the Island, with authority to appoint Justices of the Peace and to erect Court Houses and Prisons, that a person skilled in the laws should be sent annually to the Island with His Majesty's Commission of Oyer and Terminer, and that Placentia should be separated from the Government of Nova Scotia and placed under the control of Newfoundland."

As usual with the Home Government, this wise and practical measure was frustrated and marred in its execution; instead of the learned counsel skilled in the law being sent out, it was thought quite sufficient to forward copies of the Acts of Parliament and eleven sets of "Shaw's Practical Justice of the Peace," impressed on the covers in gold letters—Placentia, St John's, Carbonear, Bay of Bulls, St. Mary's, Trepassey, Ferryland, Bay de Verd, Trinity Bay, Bonavista, and Old Parlekin, in Newfoundland This ancient treatise—as dull and pedantic as were all law books before Blackstone wrote in the language of a scholar, and with the style of a gentleman—were to guide the Governor in all matters of justice, in place of a lawyer to advise him, he was to have unintelligible law books.

Instead of the able and energetic Lord Vere,[1] who had experience of the Colony, and was both a politician and a naval officer, a subordinate, Captain Henry Osborne, Commander H M S. *Squirrel*, was appointed the first Governor of Newfoundland.

Osborne proved himself a painstaking, honest, and conscientious ruler, but he had neither the weight nor the strength of will to contend successfully with the great difficulties that surrounded him; he was both badly advised and badly supported by the Home Government.

The Governor, in all his ways and works, was vigorously attacked by the West Country adventurers. They argued, with a show of reason, that their fishing admirals had authority under an Act of Parliament, whilst Osborne's justices derived their authority only from one estate of the realm, the king; of course, the great mistake made was in not passing an Act of Parliament for the government of Newfoundland and the establishment of courts of justice.

Subservient Crown lawyers in the Georgian era might hold that the king had absolute power over the plantations, and could, by his mere motion, create governments and constitutions and courts of law for the Colony. Intelligent public opinion took a different view; independent lawyers advised that an Act of Parliament was necessary for the constitution, law, and government of the Island, but from this date until

---

[1] Lord Vere would have had to vacate his seat in Parliament on accepting an office of emolument under the Crown the Ministry wanted his vote, so this arrangement fell through

1791 the necessary measure was not passed; in consequence there was nothing but contention, confusion, and uncertainty. The following letter explains the new Governor's proceedings:—

" GOVERNOR OSBORNE to the DUKE OF NEWCASTLE.

" St. John's Newfoundland, 14th October 1729.

" Transmits to His Grace particulars of his proceedings since his arrival in Newfoundland; as the principal powers he had to execute were establishing Justices of the Peace and other Ministers of Justice, has divided the Island into convenient Districts and has appointed over each—of those the little time I have been here would admit me to visit—out of the Inhabitants and Planters of the best characters—such a number of justices of the Peace and Constables according to the bigness of the fishery they preside over, as he judged necessary, in case they did their duty, to preserve peace and quietness in the Island. Further particulars of which he has enclosed for His Grace's approbation, as likewise a copy of the Commission given to justices drawn up in the best manner he was capable of doing not being well acquainted with forms of such Commissions nor with powers granted him not having time enough to prepare himself with them before he received His Majesty's commands to be gone. In consideration of which he begs His Grace to look favourably upon it. Could set apart no house proper for a prison and in regard many delinquents escape with impunity for want of places to secure them, has ordered a rate presented to him by justices of the Peace of little burthen to the people, to be raised in Districts of St. John's and Ferryland for building a prison in each of these places—rate half a quintal of Merchantable fish per boat, and half a quintal for every boat's room, including the ships rooms of those fishing on the Banks that have no boats, with like proportionable rate upon persons in trade and not concerned in the fishery and only for one fishing season.

" For punishing of petty crimes has erected several pairs of stocks. Makes no doubt but all these measures will be sufficient to suppress great disorders in the Island. But what is yet to be feared is that as the best of these magistrates are but mean people and not used to be subject to any Government, that no longer than they have a superior amongst them will they be obedient to any orders that are given. Besides these measures my Lord Vere and he have done many acts of justice to inhabitants and planters and particularly at Placentia where they had restored several Planters which Col. Gledhill had unjustly dispossessed for several years and apprehend would have taken from him many more which he holds by very unjust ' Tenners,' had the proper proprietors been on the spot to have sued.'

By September 1730 the Governor had the satisfaction of completing his new court house and prison in St. John's; he hoped his stocks and his jails would be a sufficient terror to evil doers and to all his opponents. The opposition, however, to the Governor's authority increased rather than diminished. The admirals declared the justices were only *Winter Justices*, and accordingly they had licensed public-houses, seized, fined, and whipped at their pleasure, and entirely set aside his new-fledged magistrates. Their worships were not the men to resist these bullying old ship-fishermen. In September 1730, just before the

Governor sailed, the St. John's magistrates, Wm Keen, William Weston, and A Southmayd, wrote :—

"They have reason to think that they are like to meet with some obstructions in the execution of their office from Admirals whose authority is limited to disputes relating to the fishery, but who oppose all authority but their own Rather than suffer any indignities as justices shall resign their authority "

The Attorney-General very properly advised that Osborne's taxes were illegal, he suggested there should be a grand jury to fix the rates, and that they should be assessed, not on property, but on persons,—a nice distinction which the Newfoundlanders do not seem to have appreciated. No doubt the Crown could appoint justices, it is part of the prerogative When, however, it came to the creation of a superior court of record and taxation, it was clear that the authority of an Act of Parliament was required After a time this fact dawned upon the authorities at home The contest between the Western Adventurers and the fishing admirals on one side, and the Governors and the justices on the other, continued for more than half a century.

The merchants declared that some of the justices were New England men—probably referring to M Gill, who was a provincial, and that they supplied the fishermen with intoxicating liquors at higher rates than the merchants. Their great offence, however, was that they summoned masters and merchants to pay wages—an unknown thing in the Colony—the merchants having been specially exempted from the jurisdiction of the fishing admirals.

Owing to an affray in Torbay, in which one of the ancient family of Gosse was killed by a man called Blackmore, and another case of murder by one Steele, with the expense and delay of sending home the accused and the witnesses for trial, generally at Exeter. In 1737 in Governor Vanbrugh's Commission a clause was inserted giving him authority to hold one Court of Oyer and Terminer whilst he was resident in the Colony, but not to suffer any sentence to be executed " till report thereof be made to His Majesty "

When the Commission went before the Privy Council, the clause was struck out, it was ultimately granted in Governor Drake's Commission in 1750. All these difficulties about creating an efficient court of justice were really prompted by West Country influence, and by narrow commercial jealously, they lasted until about the year 1828. The story of the fight against the Courts and Government was as bitter a controversy as the design to extirpate the settlers.

In following the course of our history through this period we find amongst our naval Governors such distinguished names as Lord George

Graham in 1740, and the Hon. John Byng in 1741. In this year Mr. William Keen, a merchant of St. John's, one of the first justices, was appointed Naval Officer, Health Officer for the port, and Judge of the Vice-Admiralty Court—another attempt to create a court of justice, which subsequently led to a curious conflict between this tribunal and the rival civil court.

In 1742 war was declared between France and England, and in 1745 that most brilliant victory—the capture of Louisbourg—was achieved by the American colonists under the gallant Pepperell and Admiral Warren. The siege was being carried on under great difficulties, until the timely arrival of the English squadron from Newfoundland gave the besiegers the necessary additional force and supplies to capture the great French fortress.

When the French retired from Placentia in 1713, Cape Breton became the head-quarters of their fishery.[1] Always bent on aggression, they spent millions of dollars in raising a great fortress at Louisbourg. The fishery carried on by the French in Cape Breton, St. John's Island (Prince Edward's Island), Gaspé, and Newfoundland employed at this time sixteen thousand men. France was at the height of her power in North America. Her constant raids and insidious attacks on the neighbouring colonies raised such a spirit

HON. JOHN BYNG.
From an engraving after Houston.

of resentment in New England that, immediately the war broke out in 1742, preparations were commenced for an attack on the great Island fortress.

Both in England and British America the fall of Louisbourg was

[1] Besides the fishery the French carried on a large smuggling business in Cape Breton; French brandy, silks, &c., and West India produce were clandestinely exchanged with New England traders for fish, fur, lumber, flour, &c. Whole cargoes of English Newfoundland fish were exchanged with the French traders. All North America joined in this extensive smuggling trade, and in cheating the French and English governments. The very fortifications of Louisbourg, in defiance of laws which prohibited trading with the enemy, were built with Yankee bricks, boards, lime, and stone.

hailed with a far wilder excitement and enthusiasm than the fall of Sebastopol in our own days. In 1747, when a French attack to recover the fortress was expected, Shirley and Pepperell's officers were busy recruiting all over the provinces; many soldiers for the service were obtained from Newfoundland. At the Peace of Aix-la-Chapelle in 1748, Cape Breton was restored to France. New England was naturally indignant over this base surrender of a conquest achieved at the cost of so many valuable lives, which they looked on with just pride, not only as a proof of their own prowess, but also as a material guarantee for the security of their fisheries and commerce. They were furious that this great fortress should be given up in exchange for "a petty factory (Madras) in the East Indies." The Colonies, after a time, received £235,200 sterling to recompense them for their expenditure incurred in the capture of Louisbourg. Colonel John Bradstreet of Massachusetts, who had distinguished himself in the siege, was made Lieutenant Governor of St. John's our second colonial ruler [1]

In 1749 arrived the most distinguished of our early naval governors —Captain George Brydges Rodney [2] — the heroic admiral who broke

[1] Bradstreet, whose name appears in our records as Lieutenant-Governor of St. John's in 1749, was a very distinguished American officer. Besides his brilliant services at Louisbourg, he was conspicuous for his gallantry in several other encounters with the French. In the absence of the Commodore he was the real Governor of the Colony for nine months of the year.

John Bradstreet, soldier, born in Horbling, England, in 1711; died in New York city, 25th September 1774. When a young officer he was sent to join the British forces in America, where he remained for the rest of his life. In 1745 he served with the expedition against Louisbourg, as lieutenant-colonel of Pepperell's (York, Me.) regiment, and contributed largely to its success by his zeal, activity, and judgment, and by his particular knowledge of the circumstances of the place. On the 5th of September 1745, he was made a captain, and on 16th September 1746, was appointed to the lieutenant-governorship of St. John's, Newfoundland, a sinecure. In 1755 he was ordered by General Braddock to Oswego, and became the adjutant-general to Governor Shirley. During the following summer he conveyed from Albany a great quantity of stores, with six months' provisions, to Oswego, and on his return from the fort was attacked by a strong party of French whom he defeated. In March 1757 he was appointed to a company in the 60th Regiment, Royal

American, and in December was made lieutenant-colonel and deputy quartermaster-general with the rank of colonel. On 27th August 1758, he captured Fort Frontenac, which he razed to the ground, and destroyed such stores as could not be removed. He served under Amherst in his expedition against Ticonderoga and Crown Point in 1759, received his coloneley in February 1762, and was advanced to the rank of major-general on 25th May 1772. During Pontiac's war he commanded an expedition against the western Indians, with whom he negotiated a treaty of peace in Detroit 7th September 1764.

[2] Rodney, next to Nelson the most renowned British naval hero, when appointed Commodore, Governor, and Commander-in-Chief in Newfoundland, in 1749, was only thirty-one; he was a post captain at twenty-four, and two years before coming to the Colony had distinguished himself in Hawke's great victory off Ushant. As Governor of the Island Rodney showed shrewd common sense, firmness, a great regard for justice and fair play, and, what is most remarkable in that age, a kindly benevolent feeling for our hardy toilers of the sea; he carefully protected them from their grasping employers. As Wellington has been immortalized in a boot, so Rodney is for ever remembered in the name of a small boat. One remarkable event in Rodney's life shows the character of the age. Disappointed at not obtaining the

the line, and achieved the great victory over the French in the West Indies. In Rodney's time the Newfoundland appointment was one of the coveted prizes of the service. Though a very young man, Rodney showed marked ability. In giving instructions to his surrogate, Lieutenant Frankland, R.N., lieutenant of H.M.S. *Rainbow*, he says :—

"In case any other complaints shall appear before you of crimes and misdemeanours committed upon the land you have full power and authority to adjudge and determine the same according to the custom of the country *and the best of your judgment.*"

LORD RODNEY.
From an engraving after Reynolds.

Governor Rodney figures largely in our colonial records. Two letters of his are characteristic; one is in reply to George Garland, and the magistrates in Harbour Grace, who asked leave to reduce the servants' wages on account of a bad fishery :—

"In regard to what you have laid before me concerning the merchants' request that the servants may bear an equal proportion with them in their losses— I can by no means approve of it, as both law and equity declare the labourer to be worthy of his hire.

"Mr. Drake and myself would be glad to ease the merchants in all that lay in our power, but we are by no means capable of committing so flagrant a piece of injustice as desired to serve any people whatever. I have only one question to ask namely : had the season been good, in proportion as it has proved bad, would the merchants or boat keepers have *raised* the men's wages ?

"I am Sir
"Your most obedient humble servant
G. B. R.

"To
"George Garland Esq."

Governorship at Jamaica, Rodney was living in Paris ; by election expenses and high play he was in terrible money difficulties. On the breaking out of the war he was in great straits ; from this he was relieved by his noble French friend Maréchal Biron, and enabled to take command and destroy the prestige of the French Navy. When the French Prince Philippe Égalité asked Rodney what would happen if he, the Duke, met the English at sea off Brest : "That your Highness will have an opportunity of learning English," was the Admiral's ready answer. Within two years he had taken two Spanish, one French, and one Dutch admiral, and on the 9th of April 1782 came his crowning victory over De Grasse at Dominica, when he broke the line. Rodney was remarkable for decision, boldness in attack, and confident self-reliance; these qualities were conspicuous in his character both as a young commodore and as an experienced and victorious admiral.

The other letter is to the same Harbour Grace magistrates, about their neglect to summon John Pike, who was charged with cruelly whipping David Careen and Michael Moreen. Pike, after a sharp reprimand from Rodney to the magistrates, appeared before the court on the 25th of September. He was fined £25 sterling and costs in Careen and Moreen's cases, and ordered to pay £100 to Amos Vincent, whose fish he had seized illegally. The Governor was not a man to be trifled with.

FREDERICK LORD BALTIMORE.
From the London Magazine, 1768.

Rodney was succeeded, in 1750, by Commodore Francis William Drake, R.N. He appears to have been Rodney's senior officer, for whilst in the Colony, Rodney acted as his surrogate. Drake remained in command until 1752, when Captain Hugh Bonfoy, R.N., succeeded him.

Several horrible murders were committed about this time, the most notable being the killing of the magistrate, William Keen. Nine persons were involved in it.

Four were hung, two the day after the conviction, and two the next day; the other five were respited on condition of their leaving the Colony. Keen was murdered partly out of revenge for the punishment of a man charged with larceny, and partly for the sake of money he had hid under his bed. The details, which are given at length in the records, are most revolting. A woman, dressed in man's clothes, was one of the prime instigators of this horrible crime; three of the murderers were soldiers. The principal culprits were hung on a gallows erected at the end of Keen's Wharf, west of Hunter's Cove.

Another case about the same time illustrates the curious way in which justice was dispensed. A man named Martin Doyle was charged with causing the death of his servant at Bay Bulls in a drunken fray. The jury acquitted him " by reason no man saw him lift hand against " the deceased, so we all give in our opinion for the man to be not

" guilty " Whereupon Doyle was set at liberty *on payment of the charges of the court*

In 1753 the North American Colonies confederated for mutual defence against the French In the next year a descendant of Lord Baltimore's attempted to renew his claim to the exclusive possession of part of Avalon. The Council decided unanimously that the title had lapsed

We find from the records that the defences of the Colony were considerable compared with former times There was one company of infantry and a train of artillery in St. John's, sixty-six foot and nineteen artillerymen at Placentia. Fort William mounted in 1753 seven twenty-four-pounders, six eighteen-pounders, and ten six-pounders ; Fort George—the lower gun battery—thirteen twenty-four-pounders and ten guns on the platform, and the south side battery—Fort Frederick—four eighteen-pounders

In this year a grant was made to Robert Carter, of Ferryland, of Isle aux Bois, described in the application as Little Bog Island. In 1755 Christopher Bradley, residing at Fogo, reports the arrival of forty French ships on the north-east coast, engaged in the fishery, well armed, and surveying the harbours He also mentions the capture of French spies at Fogo In the next year, 1756, the Seven Years' War commenced, and the French virtually abandoned the Newfoundland fishery, English fishermen during this period taking possession of the French fishing establishments at Petit Nord

Governor Dorrill's administration of the Government in 1755 and 1756 is distinguished by intolerant bigotry and the persecution of Roman Catholics for exercising their religion The Governor and other officials naively lament that these poor Irish—hunted down like wild beasts—were disloyal What else could anyone expect them to be?

In 1755 Governor Dorrell wrote to the magistrates of Harbour Grace —

"Whereas I am informed that a Roman Catholic priest is at this time at Harbour Grace, and that he publicly read mass, which is contrary to law, and against the peace of our sovereign lord the king You are hereby required and directed on the receipt of this, to cause the said priest to be taken into custody and sent round to this place. In this you are not to fail "

The magistrate replied —

"As concerning the Roman priest of whom you were informed that he read public mass at Harbour Grace, it was misrepresented, it was at a place called Caplin Cove, somewhat below the Harbour ; for if he read it in the Harbour I should have known it and would have secured him. After he was informed that I had intelligence of him, immediately [he] left the place, and yesterday [I] was informed he was gone to Harbour Main "

The matter was, however, not allowed to drop, as the following record shows :—

"By Thomas Burnett, Esq , deputy or surrogate,
to Richard Dorrell, Esq., governor, &c.

"At a court held before me at Harbour Main the 20th of September, at which you, Charles Garland, was present, at which time Michael Katem did appear before us, and by his own confession did admit a Roman priest to celebrate public mass according to the Church of Rome, in one of his fish-rooms or store-houses, and he, being present himself, which is contrary to law, and against our sovereign lord the king, we think proper to fine him the sum of fifty pounds, and to *demolish the said fish-room or store-room where mass was said*, and I do likewise order the said Michael Katem to sell all the possessions he has or holds in this harbour, on or before the 25th day of November ensuing   At the same day appeared before us Michael Landrican, who was guilty of the same crimes, for which we think proper to fine him the sum of twenty pounds, *to burn his house and stage down to the ground*, and he to quit the said harbour by the 25th of November ensuing   At the same time appeared before us, Darby Costley, Robert Finn, Michael Mooring, and Ronold McDonald, all which by their own confession are Roman Catholics and inhabitants of this place, which is contrary to law that they should hold any property in this island   We therefore think proper to fine the said Darby Costley ten pounds, Robert Finn ten pounds, Michael Mooring the sum of eight pounds, and Ronold McDonald the sum of two pounds ten shillings, all the said fines in sterling money of Great Britain, and all the said persons to quit the said island by 25th of November ensuing.

"T Burnett

" To Charles Garland, Esq., one of His Majesty's
" Justices of the Peace at Harbour Main "

These were not the only sufferers, sixteen others in Harbour Main and many at Harbour Grace and Carbonier were convicted, and in every case the building where the service had been held was destroyed.

In 1757, owing to the breaking out of the great Seven Years' War in the previous year, a local militia was formed in St John's. Mr Michael Gill, judge of the Vice-Admiralty Court, was appointed colonel, Wm. Thommasley captain of the first company, John Stripling of the second, Wm Baird of the third, Robert Hutchings of the fourth, Messrs Green, Robert Hutchings, junr, Cocking, Morley, Stokes, Fly, Chafe, Tucker, and George Hutchings, lieutenants   Every officer had to take the oath of allegiance, supremacy, and abjuration

In 1755 there is a complaint from the fishing admiral of Harbour Grace, signed by Webber, Parsons, Snow, Martin, Sheppard, &c, " com-" plaining of the destruction of their sheep and cattle by people living " in huts at the upper end of the harbour [River Head], loose and bad " characters, harbouring numbers of idle persons "

In 1757, under the active and spirited Governor Edwards, a number of French prizes are brought into St John's   Judge Gill and his officials reaped a rich harvest of fees and commissions   in one case a vessel from Waterford was captured by a French privateer, and afterwards gallantly recaptured by her own crew   An unfortunate epidemic of small-pox broke out this year   The magistrate was ordered to take steps to prevent its spreading

In 1759 it appears that four hundred pounds had been collected towards the building of a new English church, near the site of the present Anglican cathedral.   The building committee and trustees were Michael Gill, treasurer, the Rev Edward Langman, B A , of Balliol College, Oxford, incumbent, John Monier, William Bevill, and William Thomas :—

" Decided at a meeting of the Treasurer, Trustees. Subscribers &c 29 Oct 1759.— That the pulpit, Communion Table, clerk's desk &c be as in the old church   The West Gallery for the boat keepers as in the old Church ; the North Gallery to be divided into three pews, the middle one for the Governor, one for the officers of the garrison and the other for the officers of the Navy.   Bells to be put up in the belfry at the west end

" That William Keen should have the first pew on the right coming in at the west door and Michael Gill the first on the south door

That the Parson should have a pew built for himself and family under the pulpit next the clerk's desk

" First choice of pews to subscribers from £25 to £15 to be settled by lot

" That those of £10 should have one square pew setled in the same manner

" £5 to £10 subscribers to have single pews setled in the same manner.

" That the Gallows should be removed and put on Gallows Hill

" That the bodys which is buried in the old church should be left at the election of their friends whether they would remove them or no "

Governor Edwards' method of completing the new church was eminently practical. he did not beat the drum ecclesiastic, or hold a bazaar, or appeal to anyone's religious feelings, but following the naval practice in vogue, he simply made prisoners of all the leading persons of the town who had not paid their subscriptions like " the well disposed inhabitants "   He satisfied his own conscience by putting down his name for £25 , there is no reference to its payment.   The thirty-four substantial residents mentioned in the margin, who were apparently. judging from their names, chiefly Roman Catholics, Presbyterians, and Nonconformists, all had to work on the church or pay a carpenter, or else go to jail   The whole proceeding was illegal.   The Governor's proclamation reads thus —

" By Richard Edwards, Esquire, Governor, &c

" Whereas the Church of this place, St John's, has been carried on by the subscription of well disposed persons and it being highly necessary that the same should be covered as soon as possible, you are therefore hereby required and directed, to cause the men mentioned in the margin to repair to work on the said church from the date hereof to the 4th day of November next, as it appears that they are livers in this place and have not subscribed towards the building of the same; or to cause each of them that shall neglect complying herewith to pay the usual price given to carpenters daily in this place [till that time].

"For which this shall be your order.

"R. EDWARDS.
By command of the Governor,

"To His Majesty's Justices of the Peace
"for the District of St. John's.

B. PAYNE."

The end of George II.'s reign was signalized by Wolfe's victory at Quebec, and the complete destruction of the great French empire in America.

Lieutenant Griffith Williams, R.A., who was stationed at Carbonear Island in 1745 (afterwards promoted to St. John's, where he lived for some twelve or fourteen years), was a very active, enterprising young officer. He cleared the present Grove Farm, Quidi Vidi, and obtained a grant of two hundred acres. Subsequently he served in the American war and attained the rank of general. He was connected with the old family of Williams in this Colony; the late Sir Robert Pinsent, D.C.L., and the distinguished Sir Monier-Williams are his collateral descendants. In 1765 he published an account of the Colony. Commenting on the very irregular and unsatisfactory manner in which the fishery returns were made up at the time, he says:—

GENERAL WOLFE.

From an engraving after Schaak.

"I remember one of the above kind of Returns being sent to the Governor with an account of the number of boats kept, the quantity of fish, the oil caught &c. Having a boat and men of my own I had the curiosity to know how near they came to the truth, and therefore began at Bay de Verds in Conception Bay and went into every creek and cove quite round to Portugal Cove and found they had not got within a third part in any one account.

"I found in Conception Bay 496 boats kept, and computed on an average each boat caught 500 qtls. of fish (though many caught 750 and several at Trinity Harbour 990). These made 248,000 qtls.; I allow for the shipping about 10,000, which I make 258,000 and allow for men, women and children employed in catching and curing the fish of each boat (as they all equally work) ten, which will make 4,960 and for the shipping 300 making in all 5,260 people.

"It is not so easy to come at the exact quantity of oil as some years the livers of the fish yield so much more than in others; and some years the Cape Cod men meet with great success in the whale fishery and at other times little or none, either in that or the seal fishery. Some years from the shore fish you have three hhds. of oil to 100 qtls. of fish and from the bank fish you have but a small quantity, however I shall allow one hhd. to the 100 qtls. which will be 645 tuns of train oil.

I have known that oil sell at Newfoundland from £8 to £16 per tun and in England from £14 to £36 per tun.

"As the fishery of Conception Bay was reckoned equal to one quarter part of the whole fishery of Newfoundland from the year 1745 to 1752 i.e. Trinity, Bonavista, Catalina with the creeks thereunto belonging one quarter ; Bay de Verd, Carboneire Harbour Grace and the several creeks and coves thereunto belonging one quarter ; Torbay, Kidivide, St. John's and Petty Harbour a quarter ; Bay of Bulls, Firiland, Firmoves, Trepassey and Placentia Bay another quarter part; so that the whole produce of fish and oil for one of the aforesaid years will be (exclusive of the whale and seal oil) of fish 1,032,000 qtls. and oil 5,160 tuns.

"Fish upon an average sell at foreign markets from eighteen to thirty shillings per quintal but suppose it at 20/- it will then amount to £1,032,000. Oil is often sent to Spain which upon an average sells at £18 per tun, it will then amount to £92,880 sterling.

"I shall make no calculation on the fur trade, which was very considerable before the French had such vast possessions to the northward. The salmon fishery is of no great consequence, though before the French were so powerful many a hundred tierces were sent to the Italian markets."

Referring to the forts, he says :—

"St. John's from 1745 to 1750 was very well garrisoned by four companies of Foot, a captain of artillery with about 50 men. It was also well supplied with all manner of stores and about 40 pieces of cannon. Feriland, Carboniere and Trinity Harbours had each an officer of artillery with about 18 or 20 men and an officer of Foot and 30 men. There were 200 small arms at each place for the use of the Inhabitants. If those defences had been kept up the French would not have succeeded in capturing these places in 1762."

The gallant major is very bitter against Irishmen, says they are not half so good as Newfoundlanders and English to catch fish. He gives us a life-like description of the fishery at this period, its wonderful productiveness. Nine hundred and ninety quintals a boat seems to us an enormous catch, but on the Labrador, even within my recollection, some of Hunt & Henley's men have equalled this. We must remember there were five men in a boat, or rather a large skiff.

Williams complains of the large expense of olive oil, owing to its having to be brought to England. The fishermen could not do without it to cook their salt fish ; butter was scarce and dear. Olive oil is universally used for cooking in Spain, and, when good, it is the best to fry fish with. The native Spaniard does not care for the mild Lucca liquid, he likes his oil with a flavour—"que huele."

We still hear a good deal in these records about the bye-boat men[1]— the planters who brought out West Country servants. The late Hon. Stephen Rendell has often told me that even when he came to the Colony in 1834, hundreds of sturdy Devonshire lads came out every spring to Rowell's, Boden's, Bulley's, Mudge's, Job's, and many others on

---

[1] Bye - boat keepers were what we should now call planters or middlemen. They were not possessed of fishing ships, but they generally either had fishing establishments or hired them ; they fitted out a number of men and boats ; all who were independent sold their fish for the best price to sack-ships, traders, &c.

the South Side and in Hoyle's Town (Magotty Cove), and to Torbay, Bay Bulls, Petty Harbour, &c. All these "youngsters" were shipped for two summers and a winter.

Mr Rendell said nearly every labouring man about Coffinswell had been a servant in Newfoundland The regular place for shipping was at Newton Abbott, in the still existing hostelry, "The Dartmouth Inn and Newfoundland Tavern" Here the engagement was "wetted" with cyder, strong beer, and the still more potent Jamaica There were the same scenes enacted every spring. The coming and going of the Newfoundland men was an event in Devonshire. The rurals reckoned the time by the old Church of England lectionary "Jan! the Parson be in Proverbs, the Newfanlan men will soon be a coming whome"

Dartmouth, Teignmouth, Exmouth, and "the seven strong firms" of Poole, every year sent out their contingent of West Countrymen to fish and work in Newfoundland. Jersey men and Newman's crew, even in our day, all had their passenger vessels sailing spring and autumn.

What helped to keep more Devonshire men in the country later on in the eighteenth century was the development of the ship seal fishery. Most writers on Newfoundland have described the seal fishery as only commencing about 1790, but this is a mistake. Ever since Newfoundland had permanent settlers there was more or less of a seal fishery, carried on at first simply as a shore fishery, with nets, afterwards in punts, and gradually in larger boats, until schooners came into play The statistics show how it fluctuated, rising from £1,016 worth of seal oil in 1749 to £12,664 in 1768, at the price of oil ruling then, this latter figure shows quite a respectable "haul," even in those early days Every " Room " and every merchant's establishment at that time had its vats, both for seal and cod oil, the latter always called "Train" But besides the seal fishery there was more or less of a whale fishery. New Englanders from Cape Cod were expert whale men, and with their splendid Hampton boats killed the cetaceans around our southern coast, particularly about Fortune Bay [1]

---

[1] Of the whale fishery in Fortune Bay the Rev P Toque says —

"It appears from evidence given by Henry Butler, before a committee of the House of Assembly, in 1840, that the whale fishery was carried on by the Americans to a great extent in Hermitage Bay, Bay of Despair, and Fortune Bay, during the years 1796, 1797, 1798, and 1799, that during the three first years, twelve vessels were employed by them, manned by fifteen men each, that all of the vessels returned nearly loaded, that they carried on the whale fishery in this part of the country until about the year 1807, when it was discontinued, owing to some dispute arising between Great Britain and the United States, that three years after this a schooner was fitted out by the Americans, which arrived at Burin, but on account of a man-of-war being stationed there, the schooner proceeded to St Mary's Bay, where she remained until the month of August, and had nearly completed her load when she was taken by a British sloop-of-war, and ordered to St John's, but the crew being too strong for the prize-master, the schooner shaped her course for America, and arrived in safety at Cape Cod. With this ended the American whale fishery on the western shores of Newfoundland Mr Butler stated that a whale fishery commenced in Hermitage Bay, under the firm of Peter

Considering the large intercourse between Newfoundland and New England at this period, American records contain very little information on the subject. In 1729, in the Boston Records, there is an entry about the admission of James Pulman Taylor, of St. John's, and "liberty " granted to him to open a shop on giving Bond in £100 to indemnifie " the Town." In 1742 Captain Nathaniel Welch was to be prosecuted for bringing passengers from Newfoundland without reporting them at the impost office. In 1735 there are great complaints about French competition in the European fish markets.

England, in 1759, imposed a duty of sixpence per gallon on molasses, rum, and sugar imported from the West India Islands other than British. It caused great excitement in Massachusetts and New England; the colonists declared they were ruined to appease the clamours of the British West India planters; all the same, the Americans

A VIEW OF LOUISBOURG, IN THE POSSESSION OF THE PEPERELL FAMILY.
From Winsor's N. & C. H. of America.

never paid any duty. In 1764 the Act was renewed, and larger powers given to the Admiralty courts to try smuggling cases without a jury,

Le Messurier & Co., which continued for four years only, when the partnership dissolved; that the natives of Hermitage Bay, having some idea of the fishery, began a whale fishery on a very small scale; that a person of the name of McDonald had made a large property by it; that the house of Newman & Co. being aware of these proceedings, purchased the premises that had been Peter Le Messurier & Co.'s, and began the whale fishery on a large scale."

On Messrs. Newman's establishment at Gaulton, Hermitage Bay, there are still the buildings and machinery for carrying on an extensive whaling business. The premises are situated on an Island in that beautiful land-locked harbour; they have not, however, been used for some years past.

besides arming the Custom House officers with formidable power under
writs of assistance. The Yankees evaded this law by lading their vessels
in the French islands and purchasing clearances signed with the name,
if not in the handwriting, of the Governor of Anguilla, who acted as
collector. Anguilla—a British island—was so small as not to afford a
cargo for a single vessel, yet the collectors in New England allowed all
vessels with these clearances to pass without inquiry. Suddenly this was
all changed; a vessel putting into Bermuda was seized and sold, the
Governor getting one-third, the Colony one-third, and the informer
one-third of the forfeiture.

Most American writers admit that this molasses difficulty was one of
the primary causes of the Revolution. England was absolutely within

CANNON FOUND AT LOUISBOURG.
From Bourinot's History of Cape Breton.

her right in protecting her sugar islands, but Americans, in their
ignorant impatience of taxation, thought they had good cause to be
angry. Both Burke and Josiah Quincy declared these Acts were amongst
the causes which led to separation. The result of the Molasses Act was
to increase the direct trade between Newfoundland and the British
West Indies, from whence rum, sugar, and molasses could be imported
free, and to decrease the imports from New England.

APPENDIX TO CHAPTER XII.

Persons appointed to administer Justice in the several Districts of Newfoundland in 1732.

Each particular District.	Limits of the same.	Places within ye same.	No. of Justices.	Names of Justices.	No. of Constables.	Names of Constables.
Bonavista	From Cape Bonavista to the No'ward.	Bonavista, Bavaeys Cove	Three.	Mr. John Clerk, the Rev. Mr. Henry Jones, Mr. John Hemming.	Three.	Mich. Reed, Will. Tully, Will. Trusler.
Trinity	From Cape Bonavista all within Trinity Bay to ye Bay de Verds.	English Harbour, New Parilikin, Trinity—Old Parilikin, Bay de Verds.	Three.	Mr. Jacob Taverner, Mr. Thos. Floyd, Mr. Richard Waterman.	Five.	Richard Archer, Wm. Martin, David Langer, Tho. Williams, Tho. Stone.
Carbonier	From the Bay de Verds as far So'ward as Cape St. Francis.	Musketo, Carbonier, Harbour Grace, Bay Roberts.	Two.	Mr. Will. Pynn, George Garland.	Seven.	Mr. Fred Ash, Hugh Perry, Robt. D. G. Greaves, Jno. Sheppard, Tho. Thistle, Wm. Bulfcock, Richd. Porter.
St. John's	From Cape St. Francis to So'ward as far as the Bay of Bulls.	Torbay, Quidi Vidi, St. John's, Petty Harbour, Bay of Bulls.	Four.	Mr. Will Keen, Mr. Will Weston, Mr. Alex. Southmayde, Mr. Nathl. Brooks.	Four.	Jno. Huddle, Jno. Curtis, Adam Lendon, Jno. Clenick.
Ferryland	From the Bay of Bulls to the So'ward as far as Cape Race and to the We'ward as far as Cape Pine.	Tools Cove, Ferryland, Fermouse, Renowse, Trepassey.	Five.	Mr. Jno. Ludwig, Mr. John Kates, Mr. Saml. Hutchins, Mr. Jno. Jenkins, Mr. Will. Jackson.	Nine.	Mr. Henry Rex, Mr. Wm. Pidgron, Mr. Dalton and Packer, Mr. Rouse and Stevens, Mr. John Rose, Mr. Thos. Cary, Andrew Armstrong.
Placentia	From Cape Pine to Placentia and the western side of that Bay.	St. Marys, Placentia, Petty Placentia.	Three.	Mr. Peter Sigmat—deoul, Mr. Tho. Saltous, Mr. Tho. Buchanan.	Three.	Lawrence Harden, Mr. Henry Huxford, Mr. Jno. Brand.

This list was enclosed in Capt. Falkingham's Report, Oct. 4, 1732. Another list of Districts of the same description is enclosed in Governor Osborne's letter Sep. 25, 1730, without the names of the Justices, the only change being in St. John's.

CHAPTER XIII

REIGN OF GEORGE III

1760–1820

1760   Captain Webb Governor

1761.—Captain (afterwards Lord) Graves Governor.

1762.—St John's, Carbonear, and Trinity captured by the French; re-captured same year, in September, by Colonel Amherst; battle of Quidi Vidi

1763.—War with Spain; importation of fish from Newfoundland prohibited   Treaty of Paris; St Pierre and Miquelon confirmed to France; all the rest of North America given up to England   Survey of the Island by Cook   Labrador re-annexed to Newfoundland

1764.—Sir Hugh Palliser Governor   Collector of customs appointed in St John's   Court of Vice-Admiralty, St John's

1765.—Rev Laurence Coughlan introduced Wesleyanism

1766.—Riots in St John's and Harbour Grace   Lieut Cartwright made an unsuccessful attempt to effect friendly intercourse with Beothies   Repeal of the American Stamp Act.

1772.—Lord Shuldham, Governor, issued Proclamation 24th June, regulating river salmon fishery; French not mentioned

1774.—Continental Congress in America, all exportation to Newfoundland from North American States prohibited   Quebec Act, 14 Geo III c. 83; Labrador annexed to Canada

1775.—Rev John Jones first Congregational minister in St John's   Heaviest storm ever known in Newfoundland; 300 persons drowned   Palliser's Act, 15 Geo III.; Commodore Duff issues Proclamation about salmon fisheries at Exploits, Gander Bay, &c

1776.—Declaration of Independence, United States

1777.—Admiral Montague fitted out armed vessels to cruise against American privateers

1782.—Independence of United States acknowledged by England

1783.—Treaty of Versailles; French allowed to fish from Cape John to Cape Ray; Declaration of King George III that English were not to interrupt French fishery by their competition

1784.—Religious freedom established in the Colony; Dr O'Donel, first Roman Catholic Prefect Apostolic, arrived

1786.—Act 26 Geo III. c. 26, continuing bounty to Bank fishery for ten years   Jurisdiction of Courts of Vice-Admiralty to try fishery cases transferred to Sessions Courts   Prince William Henry arrived in Newfoundland

1787.—Bishop Inglis appointed as Anglican Bishop of Canada, New Brunswick, Nova Scotia, and Newfoundland.

1788.—Bermudian vessels fishing in Newfoundland.

1789.—French Revolution. Court of Common Pleas established for the Colony.

1791.—Reeves appointed Judge of " the Court of Civil Jurisdiction of Our Lord the King at St. John's, in the Island of Newfoundland."

1792.—" Supreme Court of Judicature of the Island of Newfoundland " created.

1793.—Chief Justice D'Ewes Coke.

1794.—Murder of Lieut. Lawrie, R.N. France declares war against England.

1795.—Royal Newfoundland regiment embodied; Commander, Colonel Skinner.

1796.—French destroyed Bay Bulls. England and Spain at war. Dr. O'Donel consecrated Bishop of Thyatira *in partibus*, and Vicar Apostolic of Newfoundland; first Roman Catholic Bishop.

1797.—Battle of Cape St. Vincent. Mutiny of the Nore.

1799.—First grammar school opened.

1800.—Mutiny in the garrison at St. John's.

1802.—Treaty of Amiens, signed by England, France, Spain, and Holland.

1803.—" The Newfoundland Light Infantry " formed.

1805.—The first Post Office established in the Colony.

1806.—Benevolent Irish Society formed. Dr. Lambert, Roman Catholic Bishop of Chitra *in partibus*, arrived. Volunteer Corps, Newfoundland Rangers, embodied.

1807.—The " Royal Gazette and Newfoundland Advertizer " first published.

1808.—Formation of Volunteer Corps for defence of the Capital and Island. Lieut. Spratt, R.N., sent with paintings to the Beothies.

1809.—Labrador and Anticosti re-annexed to the Government of Newfoundland by Act 49 Geo. III., which also established permanent Courts of Judicature in Newfoundland.

1810.—Proclamation to protect Red Indians. Sir John Thos. Duckworth, Governor.

1811.—Lieut. Buchan's expedition to Beothies. Waterside in St. John's cleared of ships' rooms; leased by auction to the public. Permission first granted to erect permanent houses.

1812.—Second American war. Harbour of St. John's full of prizes. Volunteer force reorganised.

1813.—Capture of the *Chesapeake* by H.M.S. *Shannon*. Sir Richard Godwin Keats, Governor. First grants of land. Publication of Dr. William Carson's pamphlet; agitation for Colonial Parliament.

1814.—First Treaty of Paris.

1815.—Second Treaty of Paris; last Treaty made between England and France about the Newfoundland fishery; confirms Treaty of Versailles, 1783. Numerous failures caused by the peace and the depreciation of fish in foreign markets.

1816.—St. John's nearly destroyed by fire; cargo of provisions sent in winter by benevolent people of Boston, U.S. Francis Forbes, Esq., afterwards Sir Francis, Chief Justice, arrived. First visit of an Anglican Bishop to Newfoundland. Dr. Scallan, Roman Catholic Bishop of Drago *in partibus*, and Vicar Apostolic of Newfoundland.

1817.—St. John's again visited by fires, November 7th and 21st; 200 houses destroyed. " The winter of the Rals."

1818.—Convention with the United States respecting the fisheries. Admiral Pickmore, first resident Governor, died in St. John's. Captain Bowker, Administrator. Sir C. Hamilton, Governor.

1819.—Case of Butler and Lundrigan. Great fire in St. John's.

The reign of our sovereign lord King George, "the good King George" of our forefathers, is the longest and most eventful in English history. It begins in an age which appears to us remote; it ends in a period in which many of us have lived, and with which we are all familiar.

GEORGE III.

From an engraving after Ramsay.

It witnessed great disasters and great victories—the loss of the American colonies, the overthrow of France in three great wars. It commenced when the British navy was neither well organised nor in uniform; it ends with making England the greatest sea power the world has ever seen, and the British fleet a real invincible armada, which had beaten every nation in fair fight, a fleet from which Spanish and gallant French officers were carefully instructed by their respective Governments to flee away on the wings of the wind.

It begins with the bungling appliances of the eighteenth century; it ends with steam, macadamised roads, the electric telegraph, the railway, and the steamboat.

Our own history also advances with this age of progress. We pass away from the fishing admirals into the modern epoch, with roads, education, responsible government, and courts of justice. This later Georgian era is the transition period in our history between the bad old days of tyranny, corruption, and violence, and the dawning of the brighter days of civilisation and progress.

In the first year of this reign the Governor and Commander-in-Chief was Webb.[1] All the captains appointed on this station were given the honorary rank of commodore whilst in this commission. The new Governor was active and vigilant. He captured a large number of French vessels; one of these, the *Tavignor*, realised at the Admiralty sale, by order of Michael Gill, Judge of the Vice-Admiralty Court, the handsome sum of £2,570 sterling for three thousand five hundred quintals of fish, the price being fairly good, with a brisk demand in the Mediterranean markets. The French merchant navy was almost

[1] Captain James Webb became a commander in 1745. In 1746-7-8, he distinguished himself very greatly by the capture of a large number of French privateers. He took command of the *Sunderland* (60), on the recommencement of the war with France in 1756. He died on the 14th May 1761 on board the *Antelope*, which was then prepared to sail to Newfoundland.

annihilated by English privateers and men-of-war The merchant fleet convoyed from Newfoundland in 1761 consisted of seventy sail of vessels, armed with two hundred guns, and manned by six hundred and eighty hardy West Country sailors They all arrived safely, and sold their fish well.

Governor Webb seems to have given most of his time to capturing stray French vessels The civil business of the Government was of a very petty character—writing threatening letters to some of the merchants' debtors, and settling the titles to land.

Newman's land at the foot of McBride's Hill, Keen's property at the foot of Prescott Street, extending to Hunter's Cove (then called Hudson's Cove), the property of Peter Weston, Esquire, J.P , at Ferryland (ancestor of Sir F. B T. Carter, K C M G.), and, amongst others, the titles of the Gosses and Codners in Torbay, were thus disposed of by his Excellency. There is a curious report about a murder at St. Pierre, then in possession of the Grandys of Belloram and other English families, which will be found in the chapter on the French colony of St. Pierre and Miquelon

Though war was raging with France, the Colony seems to have been very peaceful and orderly and fairly prosperous up to the end of 1761 After their numerous defeats the French were anxious for peace. To secure favourable terms, and especially a share of the fishery, it was most desirable that they should capture some English possession. Their well-served Intelligence Department informed them of the defenceless state of St John's, its neglected military condition and weakened garrison. On our capital, therefore, they made their successful attempt.

Whilst England had been spending millions of dollars on the colonisation and defence of Nova Scotia, St John's was left with less than a single company of soldiers—sixty-three men—and all the forts in a state of decay.

The French Government, in the spring of 1762, sent out four ships of war, thirty-two officers, and nearly seven hundred troops, under the command of Count D'Haussonville They managed to elude the British cruisers by sailing from Brest in a thick fog Sir Edward Hawke was sent in pursuit of them, but they escaped, and the squadron under Admiral De Ternay, with the troops and transports, took Bay Bulls on the 24th June, and marched towards the capital.

On the 27th they arrived before St. John's Against such an over-whelming force no resistance could be made by a handful of men and one English sloop-of-war the *Grammont*, of twenty-two guns After this easy capture, the French general set to work to repair the ruined fortifications and erect fresh defences on Signal Hill, where the remains of the old French barracks are now crumbling into decay.

When the intelligence of the capture of St. John's, Carbonear, and Trinity, and the devastation of the trade and fishery reached England, the English Ministry were loudly and universally blamed for their neglect of the great Chatham's advice about the defence of the Colony.

FORT AMHERST, ST. JOHN'S.
From a photograph by S. H. Parsons.

Preparations were at once made on an extensive scale to retrieve their negligence. Fortunately for our Island the governorship of Newfoundland had been entrusted to one of the bravest and most skilful naval officers of the period—the distinguished Captain Graves, afterwards Lord Graves.

Captain Douglas, R.N., of H.M.S. *Syren*, happened at the time of the French invasion to be on a cruise off Cape Race. As soon as he heard of their arrival in Bay Bulls he pressed into the service two English merchant vessels in St. Mary's Harbour—the brig *William* and the sloop *Bonetta*. The master of the *Syren*, Peter Burne, was given charge of the sloop, and a petty officer was placed in charge of the brig, with orders to cruise on the banks and endeavour to intercept Captain Graves[1] in H.M.S. *Antelope*, with the English convoy.

[1] Thomas Lord Graves entered the navy at an early age, and was present at the unsuccessful attack on Carthagena in 1741. He was a lieutenant in the *Romney* at the notorious action off Toulon on 11th February 1744; was on the *Monmouth* in Anson's action off Finisterre, and Hawke's action in the Bay of Biscay in 1747. He was tried by court-martial in 1757 for not endeavouring to discover whether a French ship he met was

The *William* missed the fleet, and proceeded with her intelligence to Halifax, U.S. Burne, however, met Graves at the outer edge of the Grand Bank with his large convoy. The Governor ordered him to land a party of marines at Ferryland, and then to proceed at once with despatches to Halifax. Graves in the meantime put the defences of Placentia in order, and Captain Douglas looked after Ferryland.

QUIDI VIDI, LOOKING TOWARDS THE SCENE OF THE ACTION.

Colonel William Amherst,[1] who commanded the troops, was in New York at the time. He at once proceeded to embark with part of the Royal Americans—a fine regiment, mostly composed of Swiss and

a man-of-war or an East Indiaman, and was reprimanded. In 1759 he was at the bombardment of Havre de Grace; he was appointed to the *Antelope* immediately on the death of Webb, in May 1761. In 1778 he went with Byron to North America and the West Indies, and in 1781 became commander-in-chief on the North American station. He was unsuccessful in an action with De Grasse at the mouth of the Chesapeake, for which he was much blamed. In 1787 he was vice-admiral, and next year commander in-chief at Plymouth. He became admiral in 1794, and had an important share in Lord Howe's victory; for his gallant conduct he was created an Irish peer, and received a pension. He was wounded in this engagement, so he resigned his command; he died in February 1802. (STEPHEN'S *Dict. of Nat. Biography.*)

[1] General Amherst was an ensign 3rd Foot Guards, 1753; lieutenant and captain, 1757; colonel, 1766; colonel 32nd Regiment,

1775; major-general, 1777; and lieutenant-general, 1779. During his distinguished career he held the appointment of Lieutenant-Governor of Portsmouth, adjutant-general at head-quarters, and aide-de-camp to the King. He died 13th May 1781. He married a Miss Patterson, a celebrated beauty at George III.'s Court. The portrait of him is from a painting by Sir J. Reynolds at Montreal, Sevenoaks, in the possession of the Right Hon. Earl Amherst; it is reproduced from a photograph by Mr. E. Essenhigh Corke, Sevenoaks. Amherst's pen was as sharp as his sword; he tells D'Haussonville, in answer to his gasconading: "If any injury is done to the fort, he will put every man to the sword." In pith and point the gallant Colonel's despatches remind one of the Duke of Wellington's. General Amherst's son, William Pitt, who succeeded his uncle as second Baron, served as Ambassador to China, and as Governor-General of India, he was created Earl Amherst.

Germans; troops were also despatched from Louisbourg.[1] On the 11th of September the fleet, under the command of Lord Colville,[2] and the transports with the troops, were off the narrows of St. John's.

The French, besides the strong, almost impregnable position which they occupied in St. John's with seven hundred soldiers, had a squadron consisting of the *Robuste* (74), *L'Eveille* (64), *La Garonne* (44), *La Sicorne* (30), and a bomb ketch. The whole English force was less than seven hundred.

Amherst had distinguished himself at Louisbourg and Quebec, and right gallantly he led his troops. The French attempted to stop his landing at Torbay but the light infantry, under Captain McDonnell, soon drove them back. The English then advanced rapidly on Quidi Vidi, where there was a sharp fight. The French retreated up Signal Hill with such precipitation that they left several prisoners in our hands.

Before daylight the next morning an assault was made on Signal Hill; the heroic McDonnell actually passed the sentries, and was not discovered by the enemy until they saw him

FRENCH SOLDIER, 1755.
From Winsor's N. & C. H. of America.

[1] The British troops were composed of companies of the —

Royals, now the Royal Scots (Lothian Regiment).
77th, or Montgomery's Highlanders; disbanded in 1763 [1775?].
78th, or Fraser's Highlanders; disbanded in 1763.
Royal Americans, afterwards 60th Rifles.

Montgomery's was raised in 1757 by A. Montgomery, afterwards Earl of Eglinton; Frazer's by Sir Simon Fraser, son of the celebrated Lord Lovat; the Royal Scots is the most ancient and one of the most distinguished of the British regiments. The French were very much afraid of these kilted warriors; no better troops could have been chosen for the work they were thoroughly at home in the difficult country around Quidi Vidi.

[2] Alexander Lord Colville, the fourth Baron, served in the Mediterranean in 1744 as captain of the *Dursley galley*. He distinguished himself by capturing a French vessel, and destroying eight others off Genoa. In 1755 he was sent to North America; and in 1757 was present at the unsuccessful attack on Louisbourg, by Admiral Holburne, and at the taking of the same place next year. He was left on the station with temporary commodore's rank during the winter. He served under Sir C. Saunders in the expedition against Quebec in 1759. He wintered at Halifax, and was engaged in 1760 trying to intercept supplies to the French army then besieging Quebec. He continued to serve in North America during 1761 and 1762. On returning to England after the recapture of St. John's in 1762, he was made Rear-Admiral of the White. He subsequently served as commander in chief on the North American station. He returned to England in 1768, and died in 1770. (CHARNOCK's *Biographia Navalis*.)

at the top of the hill. Against such determined bravery the French could not stand. The gallant McDonnell was badly wounded in the moment of victory,[1] and Lieutenant Schuyler of the Royal Americans and about thirty men were killed. Under cover of a thick fog, the French admiral slipped his cables, and left the troops to their fate. On the 20th the whole French garrison surrendered.

The retaking of St. John's in 1762 is represented as one of the best conducted, most splendid, and most important of all the successes of the glorious war which resulted in the capture of Havanna and Manilla.

QUIDI VIDI FROM SIGNAL HILL.

From a drawing by Col. Skinner about 1795. B.M. MSS., 33,233.

The fleet and the army co-operated with singular harmony and success; both the whole plan and the subordinate parts of the expedition were conducted with consummate wisdom and heroic bravery.[2]

In order to understand the surroundings of the Treaty of Paris,[3] which concluded the war in the next year, it is necessary to explain shortly the preceding events.

[1] Captain McDonnell, the hero of this gallant attack, though severely wounded, was not killed; he finally recovered and returned to England. During his illness he was most carefully nursed by Mrs. Horwood, of Quidi Vidi, great grandmother of Mr. John Horwood, best known amongst us as "Protestant John, of Quidi Vidi."

[2] A very full account of these gallant actions will be found in the Appendix to this chapter taken from the "Gentleman's Magazine" of October 1762, kindly lent to me by Dr. Pilot.

[3] TREATY OF PARIS.

Article V.—It is agreed that the subjects of France shall have the liberty of fishing and drying fish on a part of the coast of the Island of Newfoundland such as is specified in Article XIII. of the Treaty of Utrecht, which article is renewed and confirmed by the

When George III. came to the throne the Seven Years' War was still in progress; Frederick the Great was gallantly fighting France and Austria—the alliance "des trois cotillons"—three petticoats—Maria Theresa Empress of Austria, Madame de Pompadour, and the Empress of Russia. The English had beaten the French at sea, in the East and West Indies, and in America; there had been one fatal miscarriage at Minorca, for which Admiral Byng was shot, according to Voltaire, "killing one admiral to encourage the others." Pitt, in order to balance the loss of Minorca, captured Belle Isle in the Bay of Biscay.

LORD CHATHAM.

From an engraving by Brampton.

Whilst negotiations for peace were being carried on throughout 1761, Pitt suddenly found the French growing bolder in their demands; they insisted that the Spaniards, as well as themselves, should have the right of fishing in Newfoundland. He declared he would not consent to this, even if the Spaniards captured the Tower of London. Pitt found out through his agents that there was a secret treaty between France and Spain — the family compact — and that Spain was only awaiting the arrival of her treasure ships to declare war.

The genius of Chatham saw through their designs, and to counteract them he resolved to immediately begin the fight with Spain. George III. opposed him, his colleagues were timid, and as he could not carry out what he believed to be the true policy for England, he resigned on the 5th October 1761.

present Treaty (except what relates to the Island of Cape Breton as well as to the other islands and coasts in the month and in the Gulf St. Lawrence),and His Britannic Majesty consents to leave to the subjects of the most Christian King the liberty of fishing in the Gulf of St. Lawrence on condition that the subjects of France do not exercise the same fishery, but at the distance of three leagues from all the coasts belonging to Great Britain as well those of the continent as those of the islands situated in the Gulf of St. Lawrence. And as to what relates to the fishery on the coast of the Island of Cape Breton, out of the said Gulf the subjects of the most Christian King shall not be permitted to exercise the said fishery but at a distance of fifteen leagues from the coast of the Island of Cape Breton, and the fishery on the coasts of Nova Scotia or Acadie, and everywhere else out of the said Gulf shall remain on the foot of former treaties.

Article VI.—The King of Great Britain cedes the Islands of St. Pierre and Miquelon,

On the 2nd of January 1762, his feeble and corrupt successor, Bute, had to declare the very war against Spain which he had foreseen was inevitable. In one short year the unfortunate Spaniards saw their armies beaten in Portugal, Cuba and Manilla torn from their grasp, their commerce destroyed, and their fleets annihilated.

Both our antagonists were now clamorous for peace. Pitt had declared to Choiseul, the French minister, that he would make no second Treaty of Utrecht. On the 10th of February 1763, the Treaty of Paris was signed. It excited even more indignation in England than the former one of 1713.

LORD BUTE.
From an engraving in the B.M.

The great Chatham, so ill that he had to be allowed to sit in the House, denounced, in one of his most magnificent speeches, the terms of this infamous treaty. Almost in the language of prophecy he predicted what the cession of St. Pierre and Miquelon would be to this Colony; he vehemently attacked the surrender of the right of fishery in Newfoundland to the French, and the restoration of Cuba—the pearl of the West Indies—to the Spaniards.

Bute was openly charged in the House of Commons with bribery; the very sum, £300,000, was named, that had been paid to him by the French.[1] There can be no other explanation of this shameless surrender of territory actually in our possession.

The folly of the English Ministry in ceding the fishery and St. Pierre and Miquelon to France had nearly been eclipsed by a still more

in full right, to His most Christian Majesty, to serve as a shelter to the French fishermen; and his said most Christian Majesty engages not to fortify the said Islands, to erect no buildings upon them, but merely for the convenience of the fishery, and to keep upon them a guard of fifty men only, for the police.

[1] Junius, in his celebrated letter to the Duke of Bedford, does not scruple to charge his Grace, who was one of Bute's colleagues, with bribery:—" Belle Isle, Goree, Guadaloupe, St. Lucia, Martinique, The Fishery, and the Havana, are glorious monuments of your Grace's talents for negotiation. My Lord, we are too well acquainted with your pecuniary character to think it possible that so many public sacrifices should have been made without some private compensation. Your conduct carries with it an internal evidence, beyond all the legal proofs of a Court of Justice."

outrageous proposition A strong party in the Ministry were in favour of restoring Canada to France ; it was mainly due to the strong protests of the American Colonies, through their most able diplomatist, Benjamin Franklin, that this was prevented.

The secret history of the treaty, which is now laid bare, shows the ministry in their very worst light. They voluntarily offered to restore the fishing privileges given under the Utrecht Treaty In the commencement of the negotiations, France agreed to surrender Canada, provided she was allowed to keep Cape Breton, and to enjoy the fishery in the St Lawrence and on the banks and Island of Newfoundland. The fortifications of Louisbourg were to be destroyed, and the harbour laid out for common use.

The English Ministry flatly refused all concession of Cape Breton, Nova Scotia, or Canada. They would give the right of fishing in Newfoundland, if the stipulations about the dismantling of the French fortifications at Dunkirk were agreed to They might have St Pierre on four conditions :—

" 1. That the Island should not be fortified or troops be stationed there

" 2. That no other vessels should be admitted there even for shelter, that the harbour should be used for her own fishermen alone. [This was meant to keep out Basques and to prevent smuggling, an utterly unworkable condition]

" 3. That the possession of St. Pierre should not be deemed to extend in any way the stipulations of the Treaty of Utrecht that is to say—

" A loco Cap Bonavista non cupato, usque ad extremitatem ejusdem insulæ septentrionalem, indique at latus occidentale recuriendo usque ad locum Pointe Riche appellatum "

" From the place called Cape Bonavista to the northern extremity of the said Island and thence running westerly to the place denominated Point Riche "

" 4 That an English Commissary should be allowed to reside at St. Pierre, and the Commander of the British Man of War on the Newfoundland station should have liberty to visit the Island and see that these four conditions were complied with "

The French were dissatisfied They did not want St Pierre They said it was too small, that it was so near Placentia, that it would not serve as a shelter, and that it would create disputes between the two nations. They would prefer Prince Edward Island or Cape Breton ; finally they agreed to accept Canseau.

The British Ministry would not consent to give up Canseau. Of course New England and Nova Scotia had strong influence, and they did all in their power to prevent the French getting any settlement on the continent Finally, when the English Ministry threw in Miquelon, they then accepted the terms offered.

The French agreed to keep up no military establishment, only a guard of fifty men to support police regulations, *and 'that as much as possible with so weak a force they would prevent all foreign vessels from sheltering as required.*

How childlike and bland were these French diplomatists. By the light of the present day, when St Pierre is the common resort of all the smugglers in North America, and when on no consideration will France allow England to have a consul in their Colony, this paragraph reads very humorously

The French agreed that their fishery in Newfoundland should be regulated by the terms of the Treaty of Utrecht ; they made no objections whatever to the residence of the commissary.

As usual, the whole commercial world of England was opposed to any concession of the Newfoundland fishery to France. The commerce of England had suffered very much from the French navy and the privateers of Dunkirk. They knew that the fishery was a great source of wealth to their enemy, and the chief nursery for her seamen, on strong national, as well as commercial grounds, they sternly opposed the concession. The Common Council of London, as representing the whole mercantile interest of Great Britain, transmitted to the House of Commons peremptory instructions to the city members The Newfoundland fishery, it was said, was worth more than all Canada. They declared " that the sole and exclusive right of fishing in the American seas should be reserved to the subjects of the British Crown" All the ablest and most patriotic Englishmen of the day were opposed to the fishery clauses of the treaty ; the pamphlets and periodicals of the time are full of denunciations of Bute. The literature on the subject is fuller and far more fierce than the famous opposition to the Treaty of Utrecht , the scurrilous Wilkes, and the unscrupulous Churchill, abused and caricatured the authors of the treaty in every mood and tense of objurgation

Notwithstanding all these attacks and all the intelligent opposition, the treaty was carried by the immense majority of three hundred and nineteen against sixty-five in the corrupt House of Commons. All Pitt's splendid eloquence was wasted on members that were bribed and bought by the ministry Chatham said in his great philippic against Lord Bute that England's exclusive right to the fishery and to the possession of St. Pierre and Miquelon was an object worthy to be contested by the extremity of war.

Under the governorship of Lord Rodney, 1749, begin a series of records preserved in the Colonial Secretary's Office. Through the courtesy of the Hon. Robert Bond, I have been allowed to peruse them; they make reference to other record books, which are either mislaid or were removed to England, or destroyed in the French invasion. They are not quite complete, but for the period over which they extend are an excellent guide to our local history.

Amongst the names in these books, distinguished amongst many celebrities, is that of Thomas Graves, R.N., Captain of H.M.S. *Antelope*. One cannot peruse these musty old papers without forming pictures in the mind's eye of the various worthies whose acts are recorded in these gubernatorial diaries. I must confess to a strange liking for this worthy hero; as I read his crabbed old writing I fancy him presiding with dignity in the Placentia court house, then held in a dingy room in Thomas Kennedy's house.

LORD GRAVES.
From an engraving after Northcote.

The cool, methodical way in which he sets to work to defend the Colony, his admirable arrangements, his lucid judgments, his entire freedom from the bigotry of the age, mark the high qualities of one who, in an age of naval heroes, was distinguished for his undaunted courage and skill. His fight with the French admiral largely contributed to Lord Howe's victory on the memorable first of June 1794. This terrible duel is one of the most stirring passages in English naval history. For his gallantry he was created Lord Graves.

Both before and after the peace he had difficult and arduous work, settling claims arising out of the war—restoring property plundered from the inhabitants. Many had taken advantage of the war to rob their merchants; Graves disposed of all these various questions promptly and fairly. I gather from these records that whilst the French held St. John's from the 27th of June until the 20th of September following, the English remained in possession of the other fortified places. Carbonear Island, however, for the only time in our history, was captured and the fortifications destroyed. Placentia, Ferryland, Carbonear, and Bay Bulls were peaceably occupied by part of Colonel Amherst's forces. Mr. Nathaniel Brooks of Bay Bulls, Mr. Robert Carter of Ferryland, and Mr Charles Garland, the Harbour Grace magistrate, furnished supplies to Carbonear, Ferryland, and Bay Bulls. These fine old merchants not only supplied the garrisons, but were most energetic in getting men, providing boats, and fitting out small vessels to aid in the defence of the Colony.

Besides the St. John's records, books were kept at Placentia, Ferryland, Harbour Grace, &c, containing the judgments of the surrogate courts. The most amusing are the papers from Placentia, under Robert Edgecumbe and Haddock, justices of the peace. Their worships were not contented with administering the law after an erratic fashion of their own, taxation even did not satisfy their lust for power—they determined the prices at which goods should be sold to the fishermen. In these records is a copy of an agreement made by their orders between Simon Honeyburn, on behalf of William Turner, Little Placentia, and his planters —

"Bread and flour at 20/- per cwt except when bought in Little Placentia then to be 22/-, Pork £3. 10/- per brl., Spanish Salt 16/- per hhd , Soap and Candles 8d. per lb , Rum 4/6 per gall., boots 25/- per pair, Leather 3/- per lb., Powder 2/- per lb , Tobacco 9d per lb., Molasses 4/- per gall. 15 °/o to be allowed on all slops supplied to their men , one third of balance to be paid in Bills of Exchange Little Placentia 8th Oct. 1761 !"

After settling the prices the court further ordered that no fisherman was to deliver his fish to the supplying merchant until he received his winter's supplies.

Honeyburn was evidently litigious and obstinate; he figures largely in the courts. He had a dispute with a spirited Irishman named Lawrence Reilly, who had struck him. Reilly charged Honeyburn with keeping his wages back and charging him twenty-four shillings for neglect of duty. The magistrates ordered Reilly to ask Honeyburn's pardon before the public court, he refused in a very emphatic manner, whereupon he was sentenced "to be confined for twenty-four hours in the black hole of the guard-house." William Collins was charged by John Green, his servant, with having beaten and turned him away , Collins was ordered to pay his servant's passage home "in order that the place may not be troubled with vagabonds." Collins evidently had the ear of the court. The reign of these burlesque justices came to an untimely end in 1764. They were summarily dismissed by Sir Hugh Palliser with a stinging reprimand, and Jervis Grossard, Richard Braithwaite, and William Bennett reigned in their stead.

In 1762 the first custom house came into existence, and the first collector, Mr. Hamilton, was appointed; he was under the control of the department in Boston, Mass., then the capital of the British North American Colonies. The West Country merchants were so reluctant to pay him any fees that, after trying to live there for one season, he threw up the post in disgust. He was succeeded the next year by a Scotchman, Alexander Dunn, who appears to have been made of sterner stuff; either his ominous name, steady perseverance, or better defined legal rights, enabled him to get in the fees.

In 1763 the survey of the Island was commenced by the immortal navigator, Cook. He had been employed as master in the navy at the siege of Louisbourg; with great gallantry, in face of the enemy's shot and shell, he had sounded and surveyed the St. Lawrence, and piloted the fleet in Wolfe's last fight. Cook was master of the *Northumberland* in Lord Colville's squadron in 1762, and had also been in Newfoundland under Governor Graves. He returned in 1764 with Sir Hugh Palliser, who highly appreciated his scientific ability and sterling qualities. Cook was engaged in the arduous work of surveying for four years, until 1767.

CAPTAIN COOK.
From an engraving by Hogg.

His account of an eclipse of the sun, seen at Burgeo, was published in the "Philosophical Transactions," and added greatly to his reputation as a skilled scientist; at Burgeo Islands, and several other places on the Newfoundland coast, his survey marks are still pointed out.

The great navigator, unlike his superior officer, Palliser, took a most hopeful view, both of the resources and the future of Newfoundland. He told his friends of the great mineral wealth of the Island, especially of the supply of coal; on what grounds he based this latter statement we are not informed; however, he declared that he had personally seen the coal, probably on the west coast, where it has been long known to exist.

To this day Cook's chart of our island is noted for its minute accuracy; it shows the indomitable perseverance and genius of the man

VIEWS ON THE HUMBER RIVER

who, from the very lowest origin, a poor cabin boy, solely by his own exertions, rose to the rank of captain in the Navy, and the highest

COOK'S MAP.[1]

position in his age as a navigator, nautical astronomer, and scientific observer.

[1] For convenience of reproduction the small copy of Cook's map given by Major Holland has been used. This map shows what was known of the interior prior to 1800.

In 1764 Admiral Graves was succeeded by Sir Hugh Palliser,[1] who was afterwards brought into notoriety by his charge against Admiral Keppel, and the subsequent court-martials held upon both accuser and accused. Public feeling was undoubtedly in favour of the gallant Keppel, and deservedly so.

One of the first duties of the new Governor was in connexion with the treaty of the previous year. He was instructed by the home government to issue the following proclamation. It begins with reciting the Treaty of Utrecht, enjoining :—

"1 That there should be no distinction or interruption given to the subjects of France in injoyment of the Fishery allowed them by the stipulations of the Treaties

"2. The Harbor Admirals and all officers were to take care that the said subjects of France be permitted and allowed in common with the king's subjects to choose their stations during the Fishery season according as they shall respectively arrive in the Harbors, and occupy such a space of Beach as shall be proportioned to their number of boats, as long as the said subjects of France shall be actually employed in fishing and drying of fish In case of dispute the Captains of H M 's ships and Harbor Admirals were to proceed with the strictest justice and report their proceedings; the subject matter to be taken in writing and transmitted by the admirals duly authenticated to the Commander in Chief or to the Governor, to be confirmed or annulled as justice may require

"3 The officers were not upon any pretence whatever to interfere in disputes which might arise between French subjects.

"4. The French were not to be disturbed in their persons, properties and effects, carrying or fishing within the limits aforesaid according to the treaties.

[1] Palliser was born in Yorkshire in 1722 ; he was sent at an early age to sea, under the care of a relation, became a lieutenant in 1742, and was at the action off Toulon in 1744. He commanded the *Weazle* sloop in 1746, and was promoted for capturing four French privateers off Beachy Head He was wounded by an accidental discharge of fire-arms at Dominica, and became ever after lame in the left leg, having a perpetual and sometimes very excruciating pain, this wound eventually caused his death While serving in Scotland he made many enemies, and being enticed on shore, was arrested and imprisoned in the Tolbooth for some days, until he was released by the Lords of Session He went with Keppel to Virginia in 1755. By taking a more southerly course his men arrived in good health, while Keppel's were all invalided. He was at the capture of Quebec in 1759; he arrived too late to take part in the recapture of St. John's in 1762. On account of his spirited policy while Governor of Newfoundland, the French ambassador presented many memorials against him, but he was fully supported by the English ministry. In 1770 he was Controller of the Navy, and 1773 was created a baronet In 1774 he represented Scarborough in Parliament, and in 1775 received his flag In 1775 he was lieutenant-general of marines, and Vice-Admiral of the Blue in 1778 The dispute between Keppel and Palliser (who had been great personal friends), owing to the indecisive action of the 27th July 1778, was connected partly with differences of opinion on the political aspect of the American war During the events succeeding the court-martial which he demanded on Keppel and himself, he resigned his appointments, but was subsequently made Governor of Greenwich Hospital He again entered Parliament, and sat for Huntingdon. He died Admiral of the White in 1796 There is a monument to him in Chalfont St Giles Church, Bucks, where he was interred His life was written by R M Hunt in 1844 (CHARNOCK'S *Biographia Navalis*.)

" 5. His Majesty having been informed that boats left in the harbors the winter before by the French were burnt or destroyed; H.M.'s subjects are enjoined to desist from such practices.

" 6. These Rules to be put up in some conspicuous place in every harbor."

Palliser has been highly praised in our histories; in some respects he is entitled to our gratitude; the bounty for the fishery in the Act 15 Geo. III. cap. xxxi.—Palliser's Act—is undoubtedly due to his exertions. He defined the French rights under the Treaty of Paris honestly and clearly. According to his lights, he was an excellent Governor—in labours incessant, the very spirit of unrest, remarkably clear-headed, but very dictatorial.

The Governor had only one great fault—beyond his own circumscribed vision he could see no horizon; he had no faith, no hope, no future for the Colony; the one narrow insular idea of the age pervaded his official mind, that it should be a fishing colony, used for one great purpose only in his eyes, supplying men for the Navy. With this aim every other consideration, every attempt to promote settlement, cultivation, and civilisation. must be ruthlessly swept aside. On all who opposed his views he poured out the vials of his wrath. He could see clearly enough that settlement could not be prevented, so he abused the Colony and the colonist. No ruler since the days of Charles II. hated the country he was set over more bitterly than Sir Hugh Palliser.

SIR H. PALLISER.
From an engraving by Orme.

The statement that he gave the servant by this Act a first claim on the fish for his wages, is altogether erroneous. It was an ancient custom of the fishery, proved over and over again; it is really founded on the principle of lien, which dates back to the very foundation of English law.

Much of Palliser's usefulness as a Governor was undoubtedly due to his able secretary, Jno. Horsenaill, whose beautiful writing and well-expressed letters are contained in our records during four years. Horsenaill must have been either an original genius, or else have been well trained; all the documents in his writing are distinguished for precision, clearness, and conciseness.

The Treaty of Paris, which Palliser was to put in force, extinguished the last hopes of the Basques to participate in the Newfoundland fishery, by Article XVIII. Spain "for ever relinquished all claims and pretensions to a right of fishing on the Island." In the brief war of 1763 the Spaniards had procured from His Holiness full liberty to eat meat instead of Newfoundland fish, the order, however, seems to have had small effect, the export of our staple commodity for that year being as large as in former years. Dried cod is one of the most convenient, portable, and, when nicely cooked, one of the most succulent articles of food for a warm country, it always has been, and always will be, a favourite dish in Spain, Italy, Portugal, Brazil, and the West Indies. In 1765 an ingenious attempt was made to get over the English law by sending out Basque vessels with English names, such as the *Bilbao Merchant*, with an English master and an Anglo-Spanish crew. The Governor allowed them to proceed to the banks.

Palliser's interpretation of the treaties is very clear and distinct. Whilst it was a concurrent fishery between the two nations, the control and regulation remained entirely in the hands of the English authorities. Great Britain, owning the territory and being the sovereign power, alone had authority to exercise coercive jurisdiction; under no circumstances were the French allowed to take the law into their own hands.

Palliser had no scruple or hesitation in vigorously enforcing the English view of the treaty[1] Some Frenchmen captured a whale at

1 "By His Excellency Hugh Palliser, &c., &c

"Whereas by the proceedings had before the Judge of the Vice-Admiralty Court here relating to a French snow, named *Le Montaran*, of Sables D'Olonne, arrested for being employed on a trading voyage upon that part of the coast of Newfoundland where by treaties the French are allowed to fish but not to trade, it appears by evidence on oath, as follows

"That so soon as the said snow arrived on the coast, which was not till the 13th July, the person named Andrew Colenet, who has charge of the cargo and the management of the voyage, went on shore at Engelee, and offered to sell to the inhabitants sundry merchandize (prohibited in this country) for fish, and this is in this part owned by . . .
. . . the said Colenet, on his examination, pleading in excuse that he did not know it was contrary to the laws of the country.

"It also appears by the ship's papers and the examination that she had aboard

(exclusive of the provisions, necessaries, and fishing utensils for the voyage) merchandize prohibited in this country, and which was offered as above for sale by the said Colenet, though the said merchandize is pretended to be consigned to South America

"It also appears by a written agreement between the said Colenet and the owners of the said snow (which writing the said Colenet acknowledged to be his hand), that he was authorised by them to trade on the coast of Newfoundland on their account, for fish and other merchandize.

"After duly considering all the proofs and circumstances attending this case, and finding that this vessel was actually employed trading as well as on a fishing voyage, I have examined the several laws relating to the trade of His Majesty's plantations, and considered the treaties subsisting between the two Crowns, and find that by the several laws no fore go ship or vessel can, on any pretence whatever, resort to or carry on any commerce to, from, or in any of His Majesty's plantations,

Great Orange Harbour, but it was taken from them and sold Others who remained behind after the 20th of September to cut wood and build boats, were seized and sent to France His ships captured English and American smugglers in St Peter's Roads, confiscated their vessels and cargoes, and banished them He made one Frenchman, who had put a deck on his fishing boat, take it out, and another, who had built a small vessel, was compelled to pull her to pieces Frenchmen and their vessels caught off the Newfoundland shore were promptly seized, the ship confiscated, and the owners landed at St Pierre On the other hand, English subjects who improperly interfered with Frenchmen were dealt with severely

John Duneen, evidently an Irishman, had opposed Forterie, a Frenchman, in the possession of a room at Great St Julien's The Frenchman's vessel having been the first to arrive, he was therefore entitled to first choice of fishing places. Duneen and all concerned were to be arrested and brought before the Governor, then to be put on board a man-of-war and sent home, and if they ever returned to Newfoundland they were to be arrested again, whipped, and banished. I think the bold Duneen was never caught, and this cruel sentence was only so much *brutum fulmen.*

In the time of the vigorous Sir Hugh there was no truckling to France, an English naval officer had no fear then of offending a Gallic admiral. We have a description, in 1762, of the treaty and its interpretation from a popular French point of view in a pamphlet freely circulated from Paris, and copied into the " Scots Magazine " of December of that year, when the terms of peace were known :—

" When we consider the vile concessions made of our territories, rights and possessions, which shall we most wonder at—the ambition and arrogance of the British ministry, or the pusillanimity, or perhaps open treachery, of our own Let us begin with what relates to the very valuable fishery in the North American seas. In the first place, then, we have given up Isle Royale, or Cape Breton, to regain which, at the last peace, we relinquished all Flanders and every conquest in Europe.

" In the next place, we have abandoned all the most valuable coasts from whence the dry cod was usually got

" By the second article of the Preliminaries, France cedes to Great Britain, besides Cape Breton, all the other Islands in the Gulf and River of St Lawrence without restriction; and by the third article we are excluded from fishing within three leagues of any of their coasts. The consequences of these cessions are obvious. We have nothing left us but a *precarious right*, subject to cavil and insult, to the '*morue verte*,' [literally green fish], a commodity not marketable in

but by the treaties the subjects of France are allowed to resort to a certain part of the coast of Newfoundland to fish, and to land and dry their fish during the fishing season; therefore, whilst they employ themselves in the business of fishing only, they are *under His Majesty's protection* from any molestation or hindrance therein "

X

Portugal, Spain or Italy, but only fit for our own home consumption. Ever since the happy Treaty of Utrecht France has enjoyed great advantages in the dry cod fishery. At the breaking out of this war we had in the Bay of Fundy, in Acadie, in Cape Breton, in St. John's [P. E. Island], Great Gaspé, and other places in the Gulf, above 16,000 fishermen, who carried on most successfully in shoal water the *pêche sedentaire*—[shore fishery]. Now all this is in the hands of the British; all our settlements are unpeopled. From the single island of St. John's [P. E. I.] Admiral Boscawen removed 5,000 inhabitants. ' What, then, is left to France? Nothing but the North coast from Cape Riche to Cape Bonavista, with liberty to land and erect stages for a short season, so that we must carry and recarry both our fish and fishermen; whilst the British settled on the spot, and carrying on the *pêche sedentaire*, will forestall us and undersell us in every market in the Mediterranean. Miquelon and St. Peters, two barren rocks indeed, are to be ours yet; even for them we have pledged the Royal Word, engaging not to erect in them any fortifications, so that even they, with their guard of fifty men for the police, will always lie at the mercy of the British."

DEOTHICS OF THE EXPLOITS.

From an engraving after a drawing by Cartwright.

Palliser's interpretation admits of no doubt. It was held to be a concurrent fishery in which all disputes were to be decided by English authorities alone. It only included a cod fishery, and gave no right whatever to the French to catch salmon, to trade or traffic; they were only to fish for codfish, and dry them on land; they were not even permitted to cut spars or to build boats.

This same treaty is still in operation; it controls to-day the French fishery on the treaty shore of Newfoundland. Beyond the alteration of coast-line from Cape St. John to Cape Ray, in place of Bonavista and Point Riche, and the declaration of King George in 1783 that the English should not interrupt the French by their competition, this old international difficulty stands precisely on the same ground as it did in 1763.

The Governor was directed by the authorities at home to give his special attention to the prevention of smuggling. In 1764, the Act had been passed which caused such disturbance in New England; it armed the Custom House authorities with new powers of seizure, arrest, &c., and directly gave a bounty to the Governor and informer in all such cases, His Excellency getting one-third of the plunder; this accounts for Palliser's abnormal activity in searching out illicit traders.[1]

JOHN CARTWRIGHT.
From an engraving after Hoppner.

The Newfoundland Government, in addition, had special instructions to look after the New Englanders, well known for their smuggling proclivities. No doubt Sir Hugh gave them a great deal of trouble, but they beat him, as they had beaten all the Custom House officers in America; they had an invincible prejudice and objection to the payment of duties of any kind to King George, and they lied like

---

[1] By His Excellency Hugh Palliser, &c., Governor.

"Mr. Thos. Stout, master of the *Good Intent* brigg, being convicted before me of having carryd in the said brigg sixty fishermen and seamen from this countrey to the continent of America, contrary to the king's express commands published the last year :

"For this disobediance and contempt of His Maj's. commands, I hereby order and direct the said Thomas Stout to pay into the hands of His Majesty's Justices of the Peace at St. John's the sum of sixty pounds, which sum of sixty pounds to be laid out in payment for the passages of such poor needy people to Britain or Ireland as shall be ordered by me or the said justices, and till the said sum of sixty pounds is paid the said brigantine is not to be permitted to go out of the harbour. And whereas William Cocking hath complained that two of the men carried away by the said Stout were in his debt, one of them in the sum of £6 6s. 0d., the other £6 7s. 9d. I hereby order and direct the said Stout to pay to William Cocking the said sums of £6 6s. 0d. and £6 7s. 9d. when Cocking swears to the said debts, over and above the afore-mentioned fine of sixty pounds. Given at St. John's, 16th Sept. 1765.

By command of HUGH PALLISER.
His Excellency,
Jno Horsnaill."

troopers   The following letter is the only one that I can find about this time relating to American smugglers ·—

> " Sir,   Great St Lawrence Harbr 8 July 1765
>
>   I have sent to St John's three New England schooners seized by Lieut A. Dickson, Commander of Her Majestys snow *Egmont* in St Pierres Road   I desire you will proceed against them in Court according to law, and immediately on receipt of this to cause the proper notice to be put up of the time allowed for claims to be put in, in order to their being sold as soon as possible and most for the benefit of the seizures.
>   " Such vessels are wanted for the fishery . . . . The vessels are the *Industrious Pretence* [good name for a smuggler] belonging to Cape Ann, the *Robin Hood* belonging to the same place, and the *Industry* of Marblehead."

There must have been some flaw in the proceedings, as they never came to anything.   The New Englanders found some way to get their vessels out of the rapacious clutches of the Admiralty Court and the Governor   There is not even a suggestion in this letter that the traders were either selling or purchasing anything, they declared they had gone in to water, which was a transparent fiction.

Governor Palliser took a great interest in Labrador and Anticosti, which had been annexed to his Government in 1763, he encouraged the salmon fishery, and laid down rules for the regulation of the cod fishery in Labrador as a ship fishery.   His Excellency was the first to establish friendly relations with the Eskimos and Mountaineer Indians; one of his proclamations threatens the most severe punishments against the French, whom he declares did last year—

> " Invite over to Quirpont the savages named Carahts and Esquemeaux's and had a considerable trade with them, and used many infamous, wicked, savage arts to prejudice those ignorant barbarous people against the English nation "

Sir Hugh made a treaty with the Labrador Indians.   In his dealings with the savages[1][2] and in looking after the interests of the fishermen he

---

[1] Amongst the various attempts to open up friendly intercourse with the Red Indians, perhaps the most remarkable is the story told by Anspach of the adventures of a ship-master, Scott   In 1762 he landed with another master and a strong crew at Exploits, and built a kind of fort   Some days after, a party of Indians appeared, they made a full stop, and would not come nearer, Scott then proposed to go and meet them, they proceeded with part of the crew unarmed   Scott went up to them, mixed with them, and shook hands, suddenly an old Indian, in pretended friendship, put his arm around Scott's neck, at the same instant another Indian stabbed him in the back; a shower of arrows fired at the party killed the other master and four of the crew, the remainder fled to their vessel, and brought one dead man to St John's, with the arrows sticking in his body.   Exactly the same conduct was shown to Buchan's expedition later   Whatever may be said about the Beothics, there can be no doubt they were a most bloodthirsty, treacherous race

[2] Lieutenant John Cartwright, R.N, is mentioned several times as Sir Hugh Palliser's surrogate for Trinity and Conception Bays   He was sent in 1768 to the Exploits with a proclamation to protect the Red Indians, whom, however, he did not succeed in meeting, though they had only recently deserted some of the camps which he passed   On his return he wrote an interesting account of the Indian remains which he had inspected;

was kind, humane, and considerate ; for French aggressors, for smuggling New Englanders, and for the riotous Irishmen, he seems to have been full of all the narrow prejudice of the age.   He was specially distinguished for his barbarous treatment of Roman Catholic Irishmen ; he would not allow any two of them to live in one dwelling, and none were permitted to keep public-houses.

During Palliser's reign of four years, Newfoundland increased rapidly in trade and population.   In his report of 1765 he gives the resident population as follows :—

" Men - - - - -	9,976
Women - - - -	1,645
Children - - - -	3,863
	15,484
Fishermen employed exclusive of Inhabitants -	9,152
Total - -	24,636 "

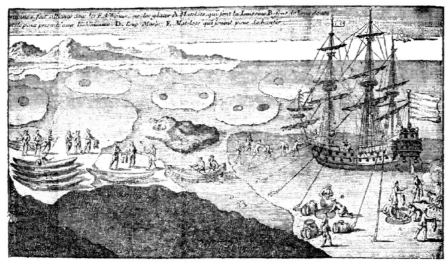

FRENCH TRADING WITH ESQUIMAUX.

From Potherie's Histoire, 1722.

this has been printed by his niece, as an appendix to the biography.   Cartwright was very strenuous in his efforts to protect the poor Irish in Conception Bay, and was generous in relieving their distress.   He has often been confused with his cousin Major George Cartwright (who accompanied him on his expedition to the Exploits), the founder of Cartwright, Labrador, and the author of a long and most peculiar d'ary of his sixteen years' experience on the coast.

John Cartwright afterwards rose to great distinction ; he took a prominent part in the discussion of all the great questions of the day, American independence, the supply of timber for the navy, the threatened French invasion, &c., and, as a Member of Parliament, supported the Reform Bill.   A statue was erected to his memory in Burton Crescent, London.   Cartwright was the first European who visited Red Indian Lake.

The catches of the English fishermen during the four years of his government were ·——

		1764		1765		1766		1767
Quintals	-	561,310	...	532,512	...	559,985	...	553,310

In 1765 he estimates the French resident population of St. Pierre and Miquelon at nearly sixteen hundred, the whole number of men employed in the French Newfoundland fishery at nearly fifteen thousand, and their catch at half a million quintals.

In reading our local records it is remarkable that whilst there was not a single lawyer in the Colony, the legal jargon was as copious, complicated, and absurd as anything to be found in the pages of " Chitty on Pleadings " Out of many examples I select one, the case against William Kitchen, a drunken soldier, for stealing a lamb of Mr. John Stripling's " grazing on the *Barons* of St John's."

" The Jurors of our Sovereign Lord the King upon oath present William Kitchen for that he did feloniously kill and bear off a certain lamb being the property of Mr John Stripling and that the said William Kitchen of St John's, a soldier, not having God before his eyes but moved and seduced by the instigation of the devil on   .   .   .   .   did feloniously of his forethought and mallice seize and kill a lamb the property of Mr. John Stripling grazing on the Barons of St. John's, and the said William Kitchen did with a knife skin and bear away the said lamb .   .   .   The sentence of the Court is as follows ·

" That you William Kitchen be returned to the gaol from whence you came and there remain till tomorrow at ten o'clock in the forenoon, when, before the Court House of St John's, you receive punishment of being burnt in your right hand with a hott iron marked with the letter R, your goods and chattels forfeited, and *after paying the charge of the Court* be set at liberty Then the Court was adjourned during the Governor's stay in the Island.

" Michael Gill.
" Edward Langman, &c."

This mild sentence is probably due to the influence of Parson Langman, as sheep stealing was punishable by hanging in those days.

It is only fair to the character of Sir Hugh to give the reverse of the shield, an example of his humanity and care in the protection of a poor fisherman from extortion and bad treatment I therefore append his short judgment in the case of Fling *v.* Cochran, an action for assault in which Fling injured Cochran in the hand, the amusing part of these proceedings is the high-handed way in which His Excellency takes the case out of the hands of Gill and Langman, and deals with it himself ——

" On a case of quarrel between James Cochran and James Fling it apearing James Fling was the first agresser, I therefore hereby order and direct that he shall be alowed nothing for his loss of wages and time The two doctors for their

exorbitant charge on account of a poor man shall have nothing, and Joseph
Cochran to pay £6. 10. 0. for Fling's maintenance during the cure of his hand, also
£3. 10. 0. for his passage home.

"Given at St. John's 27th September 1765.

"By command of His Excellency.   "HUGH PALLISER.

"Jno Horsenaill."

Commodore Palliser's administration lasted for the unusual period
of four years; his records are the longest and by far the most complete; he was an admirable man of business—orderly, methodical,
and industrious. He had set his heart on making his newly-
acquired territory of Labrador,
Anticosti, and the Magdalen
Islands, into a great fishery,
governed by the Rules of
William's Act. His first object
was to build a fort at Port
Pitt, Chateau Bay; this he
carried out with his accustomed
energy. Visiting all the places
within his territory both in
Newfoundland and Labrador,
he encountered obstacles and
difficulties from the resident
population, from the French,
the French Canadians, but
most of all from the American whalers. In a letter to
Governor Bernard of Massachusetts, 7th August 1776, he states:—

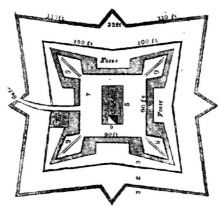

FORT YORK, LABRADOR.

"The great trouble and difficulty I meet with in keeping good order amongst
the fishers in a part of this government [Labrador] is occasioned chiefly by a
number of disorderly people from your Province. You will I hope excuse me for
giving you this trouble, to beg you will permit [the enclosed advertisement] to be
put up in the Towns within your Government where the vessels employed in the
whale fishery mostly belong; which I apprehend will greatly facilitate my proceedings in the execution of the King's orders for the benefit of H.M. subjects
carrying on the fishery within this Government.

"The last year whilst a tribe of four to five hundred of the Esquemeaux's savages
were with me at Pitt's Harbour (and by means of interpreters) I made a peace with
them and sent them away extremely well satisfied, without the least offensive thing
happening.

"I am well informed some New England vessels contrary to the orders I have
published went to the Northward, and robbed, plundered, and murdered some of

their old men, women and children, who they left at home, so I expect some mischief will happen this year, revenge being their declared principle

"I am Your Excellencies
"Most obt & humble servant
"Hugh Palliser

"P S —If you think proper to take any other method properer than what is above proposed for the reformation of those concerned I shall be extreamly obliged to you, for the complaints I have of the mischiefs committed by them are many great and barbarous"

The result of Sir Hugh's abnormal activity, and the rules he promulgated for his successors, was to stir up a determined hostility on the part of many Canadians and Englishmen who had fixed posts and settled property at Labrador, which were all to be destroyed under the Fishing Admiral rules, with the aid of the New Englanders they persistently resisted the Newfoundland Government, until at last the Home authorities restored Labrador to Canada, and reversed all Palliser's regulations in 1774 by the Quebec Act, 14 Geo. III. Cap lxxxiii

Coming nearer home Palliser found trouble in the garrisons of St John's and Placentia, Captain McDonald and his officers were at open war, half the soldiers at Placentia had deserted, they were short of beds, bedding, and clothing, both garrisons seem to have been badly paid, and worse provided. Palliser put an end to many abuses, and he pulled down a number of houses that had been built around Fort William which were looked upon by officers and soldiers as their private property On the 3rd of September 1766 he makes this order —

"The house owned by Mr William Newman standing under the Fort having been built by a soldier of the former garrison by sufference of his commanding officer and pretended to be sold by the soldier in payment of debts contracted for liquor and other unjustifiable dealings—Notice is given to Mr Wm Newman to take down the said house or he may dispose of the materials thereof. . Michael Gill's house built also by sufference may remain only during Gill's lifetime, no liquor to be sold there. . . . . Wood's house also built by sufference may remain, no liquor to be sold there; to remain only during Wood's lifetime, at his death to be pulled down"

These records show there was much grumbling against Alexander Dunn, the collector, about his fees, which were certainly heavy. There were several New England vessels seized for having rum on board without certificates or cockets, they mostly gave bonds from their agents in St John's, and always appear to have got off without penalty, they evidently knew how to manage the collectors of the Georgian era, as in nearly every case of theirs the Custom House officials reported favourable and mitigating circumstances

The whole New England trade with the Colony was one vast smuggle. Palliser estimates it in 1765 at "£102,304 stg., carried in one hundred and forty-two vessels, nine-tenths of which is paid for in Bills of Exchange on England." The real amount was at least two hundred thousand pounds, the year before the Revolution it was three hundred thousand pounds, or probably nearer four hundred thousand. During Palliser's and Byron's administrations a commercial war had begun between England and America, the Molasses Act commenced the fray in New England, the narrow commercial policy of England kept fanning the flame, until it culminated in the Stamp Act Some regulations of the English Government indicate the absurd lengths to which they carried their trade laws, they stopped coal-mining in Nova Scotia, fearing that it would interfere with English coal and encourage provincial manufactures, they were always jealous of colonial home-spun woollen and coarse linen cloths Palliser's letters show the strong prejudice that existed against New England long before the revolutionary war

THE LORD'S PRAYER, WRITTEN BY NEWFOUNDLAND MIC MACS
B M , Add MSS , 11,038

Nothing appeals more to the higher sentiments, the poetic feeling that is implanted in us, than the self-sacrificing devotion of a religious community to its worship and its ministers, typified amongst us by the warm attachment of the Irish to the poor hunted and silenced priests who ministered to their spiritual needs in Newfoundland The following official correspondence shows how the English colonial rulers appreciated the religious sentiments of the poor French exiles and the Indians of Acadia Sober history, it must be admitted, takes some of the beautiful bloom off Grand Pré and Evangeline [1]

"LIEUT.-GOVERNOR OF NOVA SCOTIA TO GOVERNOR PALLISER.

"SIR,   Halifax, Nova Scotia, 11 Sep. 1766.

"I have the honour to forward to Your Excellency a packet from the Secretary of State's office which came to me enclosed the 9th inst

"I think it necessary to acquaint Your Excellency that last summer the greatest part of the Indians of this Province assembled on the Isle of Breton, and by the flying reports which were spread by them, together with an unusual deportment to some of the neighbouring settlements, the people were much alarmed, however by

[1] See "The true story of Evangeline," by Rev T B Stephenson, D D , in the *Sunday Magazine*, November 189..

sending some gentlemen amongst the savages they were prevailed on to disperse—this summer they have also assembled again, although they behaved very peaceable, but as I find that Holy Water, Relicts, Books and other articles that relate to the superstition of the Romish religion are furnished to them, it is an evident proof they find means to hold communication with the Islands of St. Peter's and Miquelon, if they do not even receive from thence priests to officiate amongst them, which may in time prove of very ill consequence to this young province, as our settlements are very straggling and defenceless   I must therefore entreat your Excellency to give directions to the several cruisers under your command which may be stationed near these Islands to prevent as much as possible all communication between the savages and Acadians [or neutral French] of this Province with the French at St. Peter's or even with the Island of Newfoundland and that if any extraordinary occurrence should happen I may be informed of it

"MICHAEL FRANCKLIN."

To the fly thus cast by the Nova Scotian Governor, the Ultra-Protestant Palliser rose at once   In one respect, no doubt, they were right, the French have ever been inflated with the idea of recovering their lost empire in America, and St. Pierre has always been a thorn in our side, but to accomplish their great design France would need better and stronger allies than the Mic Macs and the poor simple Acadians. Neither Palliser nor Francklin seemed to realise their attachment to the clergy, which was signally manifested later on, when the whole body of Acadians left Miquelon, with their good curé, for the Magdalen Islands, sooner than subscribe to the hated doctrines of the Revolution   Palliser's reply is a smart reprimand to his fellow governor —

"GOVERNOR PALLISER to the HON MICHAEL FRANCKLIN Lieut -Governor of Nova Scotia

"SIR,   St Johns 16 Oct. 1766.

"Two days ago I had the honour to receive your letter of the 11th Sepr. and with it a packet from the Secretary of State's office which you was pleased to forward to me.

"The information you give me of the motives and behaviour of the Nova Scotia Indians is somewhat alarming and seem to require attention, but I confess it is nothing more than I have expected from the banefull effects of a communication with the French.

"As soon as I came to this Government I perceived the extensive views of France in contending for these two insignificant Islands (as they were called) St Pierre and Miquelon and that the uses for which they demanded them was the least part of their view, that of communicating with and preserving their influence over the bigoted savages and the rebellious and more dangerous Acadians was a more important part of their object.

"I did not fail to inform H M Ministers of my apprehensions of this, and that this part of H.M Dominions would thereby be endangered and the fishery and trade of his subjects here be greatly prejudiced as well as the New Colonies on the Continent be disturbed. The occurrences since that time have proved those apprehensions to be well founded . . . The intercourse you complain of between these people and the French is carried on by *your* clandestine traders with these Islands from the Island Breton and especially Miganich, likewise by passports granted to the Indians Last year the Chief, John Peqidawa-Oalaut, with two hundred men returned with passes from the Secretary's office in Halifax

" Miquelon is full of Acadians, who have come there with passes from different officers in your Government .   I shall leave two ships all the winter to drive away the Indians and keep the French off."

Two important events in the religious history of the Colony occurred during Sir Hugh's government—the commencement of the Moravian Mission at Labrador, and the first introduction of Wesleyanism into the island by the Rev. Lawrence Coughlan, a Church of England clergyman sent out by the S P G. in 1765 Coughlan was a devoted follower of John Wesley, whose method he followed, and in whose footsteps he endeavoured to tread The great founder of Methodism lived and died a member of the Church of England, and there is nothing at all incongruous in the first Wesleyan in the Colony being an Episcopalian, the new body was practically driven out of the Church and compelled to form themselves into a separate society.

The Rev. Lawrence Coughlan, an Irishman, a most earnest man like most enthusiasts in a good cause, was persecuted, but worse still, was not paid his legal salary; it is recorded that, in November 1765, a bond was signed by "the principal inhabitants of Harbour Grace, " Musquito, and Carbonier, in Conception Bay, for the rest of the " inhabitants of the Bay, by which they agreed to cheerfully contribute " annually the full sum of £100." Governor Byron, on the 18th July 1770, thus adjudicated upon this bond :—

" Whereas I am informed that the Revd Mr Coughlan is the Minister so procured and residing amongst you, and that, so far from your paying him cheerfully the stipend aforesaid, great numbers of you have refused to contribute towards it, insomuch that he is annually much in arrear to the disgrace of religion and dishonor of yourselves : I do therefore desire and command you and every one of you as aforesaid to pay him what sums are in arrear, and that you also comply with your said agreement in paying him annually his sallary of £100, every one of you according to your abilities "

Commodore Byron appointed Coughlan a justice of the peace for Harbour Grace, and was his firm friend and supporter until the last year of his government. The Harbour Grace merchants, finding that they were obliged to pay the salary, petitioned the Governor against him as a justice. Evidently Coughlan had made himself obnoxious by upholding the rights of the servants. To please the merchants, the stout old commodore bowed the knee to Baal, and dismissed Coughlan from the Bench, who thereupon left the Colony. Coughlan's memory, as a just and good man, was long held in pious reverence in Conception Bay.

A recent writer on the ecclesiastical history of the Colony has thought fit to take exception to the founders of the Newfoundland

Methodists and the Moravian missionaries. The results of the Brethren's one hundred and thirty years of work and labour of love in the Arctic Labrador are visible to all men ; out of the most hopeless savages they have brought up a Christian, educated, church-going, moral, and respectable population.   It is a mistake to state that the mission is self-supporting ; Captain Linklater informs me it is not so, the expenses are paid out of voluntary contributions, the two vessels employed alone costing £2,500 a year each. The character of the missions of the humble Moravian Brethren in Africa and America needs no defence. From the records it appears that Jans Haven, one of their first missionaries, had been sent by Palliser, in 1764, to conciliate the Eskimos and Mountaineer Indians.   Next year the Brethren received the following passport :—

ESQUIMAUX.

From Potherie's Histoire, 1722.

" By His Excellency Sir HUGH PALLISER Governor &c.

" Whereas the Society of the Unitas Fratrum under the protection of His Majesty have from a pious zeal of promoting the knowledge of the true God and of the religion of our blessed Lord and Saviour Jesus Christ amongst the heathen, formed a resolution of establishing a mission of their brethren upon the Coast of Labrador,

and for that purpose have appointed John Hill, Christian Drachart, Jans Haven, and Christian Andrew Schlozer to effect this pious purpose. And whereas the Lords Commissioners of the Admiralty and the Lords Commissioners of Trade and Plantations have signified to me their entire approbation of an undertaking so commendable in itself and that promises so great benefit to the publick and are desirous of giving all reasonable encouragement and assistance thereto. These are therefore to certify all persons whom it may concern that the said Brothers are under His Majesty's protection and all officers Civil and Military and all others His Majesty's subjects within my Government are hereby strictly charged and required not to give any interruption or hinderance to them but to afford them every aid and friendly assistance for the success of their pious undertaking for

the benefit of mankind in general and His Majesty's subjects in particular
13 April 1765

    " By command of His Excellency.   " JNO HORSENAILL "

On the eve of his final departure from the Colony in 1768 the
Governor cancelled the commission for the trial of murder, and the
High Sheriff's appointment. Sir Hugh had lavished every kind of office
on the Gills and the Keens, and now, at the last, he seems to have been
dissatisfied with the close ring of officials that surrounded him
The Gills seem to have held most of the Government offices, Michael
was Judge of the Vice-Admiralty Court, Keeper of the Rolls, J.P.,
public auctioneer, sole sworn broker, and sole notary public, and, later
on, lieutenant-colonel of militia, his brother Nicholas seems to have
had all the other posts   What caused Palliser to alter his mind about his
subordinates is not known; he states, "My reasons will be laid before
the King." Perhaps he did not get enough share of the prize money
He finds great fault with the resident naval officers, probably he found
the clique around him too greedy.

    Everything went on peaceably during his administration, there was,
indeed, a war scare in 1764 owing to alarming news brought home by a
man-of-war to England, that the French had a fleet at St. Pierre,
and were fortifying it; Palliser sent a frigate, and soon found out that
the whole story was a mere canard   During the last years of his
administration there was a growing spirit of disaffection all through the
North American Colonies, owing to the new taxes and the increased
severity of the Custom House officials; a very mild outbreak in
Newfoundland, in New England the precursor of the civil war.

    A French vessel, *Chere Marie*, Jacques Quenal, master, having
taken a parcel of furs on board at Port-au-Choix, was seized by
Lieutenant Stanford, and brought into the Vice-Admiralty Court for
adjudication and condemnation as contrary to the treaty. The following
plain-spoken letter shows the Governor's view of the French rights ·—

    " To M GEO LE NOUVEE Master of the French ship *La Rada*,
      M FRANCOIS JAHAN Master of the French ship *L'Etoile*

" GENTLEMEN,   14 Aug 1767.

    " The Governor directs me to acquaint you that your audacious attempts to
encroach on the fisheries on this Coast are in violation of the Treaties and in
disobedience to the strict orders you have received from Your King.   . .
He directs me to acquaint you that you need not give yourselves the trouble to
make any further application or enquiry about either your boats or people; that in
future, not only the boats that come on the Coasts, but the ships to which they
belong will be seized and confiscated + or encroaching and violating the Treaties.

                                     " JNO HORSENAILL."

On the 8th of July 1769 the Honourable John Byron,[1] Sir Hugh Palliser's successor, was sworn in with the usual oaths and honours as Governor of Newfoundland, Labrador, Magdalen Islands, and Anticosti. He made no alterations whatever in the rules and regulations established by his predecessor; he commanded the officers not to fire on ships leaving the harbour, and then claim the cost of the powder and shot from them, as had been the former practice; he was a martinet, and there is quite a long correspondence about the disposal of the old pickets when a new fence was put up at Fort William. Michael Gill,

AMERICAN BANKER AND FISHING BOAT IN 1741.

Parson Langman, and the other magistrates still presided in the courts of justice at St. John's, Mr. Weston and Mr. Carter at Ferryland, and Mr. Garland with Parson Coughlan at Harbour Grace.

In 1771 Byron sent special orders to Captain Gower, of H.M.S. *Pearl*, to put a stop to the disorderly proceedings of New England men in the Magdalen Islands, and not to permit them to carry on the seacow fishery without a licence from him. Frenchmen were also vigorously prosecuted for venturing to fish outside the treaty limits; several were arrested, brought to St. John's, and sent home to France.

The Honourable John Byron is best remembered as the grandfather of the great poet, who refers to him in "Don Juan" as "my grand dad." The marvellous description of the shipwreck in that poem is partly taken from the Commodore's adventures in H.M.S. *Wager*, as well as from his celebrated voyage to the South Pacific. Governor Byron

[1] Byron was born in 1723; was the second son of the fourth Lord Byron; was wrecked in the *Wager* on the Chili coast in 1741; after great hardships, he reached Valparaiso. In 1757, in the *America*, he was at the futile attack on Rochefort. In 1760 he was sent, with a small squadron, to superintend the destruction of the fortifications of Louisbourg. In 1764 Byron was Commander-in-Chief in the East Indies, flying his pennant on the *Dolphin* (the first vessel in the English Navy to be copper-sheathed). At Rio he met Lord Clive, who wanted to go in the *Dolphin* to India; but Byron refused, for his real instructions were to explore the Southern Seas. It was on this voyage that the Patagonian giants were said to have been seen. As a voyage of discovery it was a failure; Byron had no genius for such work. He was appointed Governor of Newfoundland in January 1769; Rear-Admiral in 1775; Vice-Admiral in 1778. His expedition in this year to intercept the Count d'Estaing was a failure. Byron, though brave, had not enough originality or ability to distinguish himself. He died, Vice-Admiral of the White, in 1786. There is a portrait by Reynolds, painted in 1759.—(STEPHEN'S *Nat. Dict. of Biography*.)

was made a commodore for his gallantry at the second siege of Louisbourg. He was a very plain, straightforward old sailor; like all the family, rather eccentric. He was known throughout the navy as "Foul-weather Jack." In the American War he did not distinguish himself.

Byron's administration was marked by the same humane treatment of the Eskimos that had characterised Palliser's dealings with them. An endeavour was again made to open up friendly intercourse with the Beothics, but without effect.

LORD SHULDHAM.
From an engraving after Dance.

The Governorship from this time forward appears to have been a regular three years' commission. Commodore Molineux Shuldham, R.N., afterwards Lord Shuldham,[1] was appointed in 1772; during his command, which extended to 1774, the commercial war between England and America culminated in the Continental Congress of September 1774. One of the first acts of this assembly was to prohibit all exportations to England or the British Colonies. War, however, did not actually begin until the 18th of April the following year, in the skirmish at Lexington, dignified by American historians into a battle.

[1] Molineux Shuldham was the second son of the Rev. S. Shuldham, of the diocese of Ossory, Ireland. He went to sea at ten years old; was Captain of the *Sheerness* in 1746. He saw very little fighting till, in 1756, he had the misfortune to be captured by three French men-of-war, which he had mistaken for merchantmen. He was honourably acquitted before a court-martial. He distinguished himself at the capture of Guadaloupe, but was unfortunate in losing his ship when again in the West Indies with Rodney; when attacking some coast batteries in Martinique, his ship struck and was wrecked. In 1772, on his return from Newfoundland, he brought an Esquimaux chief, who was presented to George III. Was Rear-Admiral of the White in 1775, and became Member for Fowey; Vice-Admiral of the Blue in 1776, when he was appointed to command on the American station. He convoyed Howe's army to Halifax from Boston in 1776, and thence to Station Island; in June of this year he was created an Irish peer. Nothing remarkable occurred during the remainder of his stay on the American station. In 1778 he successfully convoyed the outward-bound West Indian and American fleets, and on his return became Port-Admiral at Plymouth, which post he held till 1783. Made Admiral of the White, 1779; Admiral of the Blue, 1787; and Admiral of the White, 1793.—(CHARNOCK's *Biographia Navalis.*)

The year before the outbreak of the American War was remarkable for a terrific storm at sea, which destroyed a vast amount of fishing property. The water rose suddenly twenty feet above its usual level; this great tidal wave caused immense destruction, both by land and sea, and three hundred persons along our coast lost their lives. It is known in Newfoundland annals as the "Year of the Great Storm"

With the exception of this event, and the passing of Palliser's Act (15 Geo III), nothing remarkable occurred during Shuldham's tenure of office; the same questions, the same routine, prevail all through this period The New Englanders still gave trouble on the Labrador. The officer in command at Fort Pitt is complained of for having engaged in the seal fishery. A small "Behring Sea difficulty" arose at the Magdalen Islands, owing to the reckless and barbarous way in which the New Englanders were killing the sea-cows, driving them away from their quiet haunts, and preventing them from breeding, there is a long correspondence on this subject.

During this period the great Michael Gill died, and Edward White, Ordnance Storekeeper, became Judge of the Vice-Admiralty Court and Master of the Rolls, Edward Langman,[1] Charles Garland, Robert Gray, Nicholas Gill, and James Brooks, were the remaining justices of the quorum for St. John's, Robert Carter, J.P, was Keeper of the Rolls for Ferryland, William Keen for Bonavista, and D'Ewes Coke (afterwards Chief Justice) for Trinity, Nicholas Gill was Notary Public and Vendue Master, and John Philips, High Sheriff.[2] A proclamation was issued

[1] Langman, however, succeeded White as Keeper of the Rolls in 1773. The Gills seem to have soon recovered their old prestige Nicholas Gill in 1774 became Master of the Rolls and Judge of the Vice-Admiralty Court, which posts he held until his death in 1787.

[2] The following local events in 1773 are noticeable —

We notice in these records how property was acquired; for instance, the collector Alexander Dunn received a grant of Friendly Hall, Engineer Pringle the property now owned by Sir James Winter (Pringle's Dale), the hill now called Robinson's Hill was originally Dover's Hill

William Spurrier, of the great firm of Spurrier's of Poole, was made Naval Officer for St Mary's, Oderin, Burin, and Mortier, where his firm carried on their extensive business Mr John Slade, of the great firm of Slade's of Poole, was made Naval Officer for Twillingate In Spurrier's bill for expenses of a proceeding out of the Vice-Admiralty Court against a servant, 2s is

charged for the Whipper In 1773 Fort Townshend was commenced and the road to it from the Queen's Wharf, also the King's Road, the Military Road between Fort William and Fort Townshend, and the Signal Hill Road The way in which titles to property were acquired in St John's is curiously illustrative of the corruption and favouritism which prevailed in the days of our naval Governors, all around Fort William officers and soldiers had been allowed to take in land as far as the margin of Quidi Vidi Lake; on removal, soldiers and officers sold these to civilians in the town; valuable properties, both on the south and north side of Water Street, were purchased sometimes for a winter's provisions; a good building lot on the north side of Water Street, east of McBride's Hill, was given to one large firm for their cook's passage to England.

Ann Ellis acquired Ellis's estate in a curious way her brother had left it all to a woman not his wife; the sister produced to Governor Shuldham an opinion in her favour from the celebrated English lawyer, Dunning, embodying an admirable' set of regulations for the government of the salmon fishery on the coasts of Newfoundland and Labrador; the French are not mentioned, and it was evidently the practice at this time to completely exclude them from all occupations outside the cod fishery

Commodore Duff's[1] appointment lasted during 1775 The following proclamation, issued in July by him, is of so much importance, and in such striking contrast to the manner of dealing with obstreperous French naval officers at the present day, that it is given in full. The stout old commodore took the strictly correct legal view of the treaties and the rules of international law, would that the same spirit were infused into the British Governments of to-day, which calmly permit French officers to put up proclamations on British territory, ordering British subjects to sell their herrings only to Frenchmen, and allow them to enforce such arbitrary decrees The proclamation reads :—

" Whereas I have received authentick accounts that in the month of July 1763 a French ship of war named the 'Unicorn' visited several Ports within my Government, particularly 'Cremellaire,' where the Captain of the said ship interfered in matters relating to the laws and government of the Country In case you should meet with any French ships of war within the limits of your station you are in the most civil and friendly manner to enquire of the Captain the occasion of his coming, and should he be driven there by necessity or distress you are to offer him assistance, and every other friendly office in your power, but should he pretend to come there for the protection and defence of French fishers or any other pretence whatsoever, other than distress, you are to signify to him that the subjects of France resorting to any port of H. Britannick Majesty's dominions to follow any business or trade by virtue of the Treaties subsisting between the two nations are, whilst in H M. Dominions, *under the protection of H Britannick Majesty only*, and that in conformity to H. Majestys sentiments and firm resolution

and on this *ex parte* opinion she obtained her grant

Stripling, a stout Protestant and a publican, through the interest of the officers and soldiers, obtained a piece of land at Quidi Vidi, and afterwards, when he became a justice and sheriff, though utterly ignorant and illiterate, a grant of the land on the east side of King's Bridge Road, and all Stripling's plantation, were given to him

The title of the Thomas's dates back to the reign of Charles II, and was continued through the Bevils, and William Thomas, a justice in Palliser's time, down to the William and Henry Thomas of our own time.

The Keens, Gills, Williams, and others of the clique that surrounded Governor Palliser, all gained their properties through Court influence. Hutchings' estate was acquired by George Hutchings for his valuable services in

keeping a watch on Admiral de Ternaye's fleet in 1762

[1] Duff, a cousin of the first Earl of Fife, became a commander in 1744. In 1758 he was with Commodore Howe in the squadron convoying the expeditions against St Malo, Cherbourg, and St. Cas, and in 1759 was senior officer of a small squadron covering the Brittany coast while Hawke blockaded Brest. He was not present at Lord Hawke's victory over the French, but it was in chasing Duff's ships that the French came in sight of the main English fleet. He was with Rodney, in 1762, at the reduction of Martinique He endeavoured to relieve Gibraltar in 1779, but the Government were not able to strengthen his command, so he was recalled He became Vice-Admiral in 1778, and died in 1787. There is a portrait of him at the Royal United Service Institute.—(STEPHEN's *Nat. Dict. of Biography*)

Y

of maintaining with the utmost exactness probity and good faith the Treaties relating to the fishery I shall with an unbiassed and impartial justice to the subjects of both Crowns in my station inviolably observe H. Majesty's commands upon that head; but that I cannot permit any officer with a commission from His Most Christian Majesty and *with an armed force to resort to or exercise any authority within any part of* H. Majesty's dominions under my Government, their doing so being directly contrary to the spirit and words of the 13th section of the **Treaty of Utrecht,** by which the sovereignty, property, and full possession of this country is ceded to the Crown of Great Britain and the French expressly excluded from having forts or forces in any part of it and the tenor of the whole article is to provide against the French encroaching on H.M. Territories and on H.M. rights and privileges. That therefore I will not allow any Foreign officer with an armed force to resort to this country without first applying for and obtaining the King's leave for that purpose. In case you should meet with any French officer within the limits of your station you are to appoint a reasonable time for him to depart; beyond which time you are not to allow him to stay and for your justification herein you are to deliver to him a copy of this my order to you.

" ROBERT DUFF."

Several writers on Newfoundland history, in their anxiety to make out a case against the American colonists in their struggle with England, have magnified a street row—an ordinary Irish faction fight—in Harbour Grace, in 1766, into a serious battle, and the merchants' opposition to the new custom house as treason; they have exaggerated and perverted these small affairs into a sinister plan and preconcerted scheme of rebellion. There is not the slightest foundation for such a statement; at the time of the Declaration of Independence there was, no doubt, a good deal of lawlessness in the Colony, and some disaffection, but there was some little common sense amongst our islanders; the republicans were few and scattered, the loyalists were in an overwhelming majority; there were four or five men-of-war always on the coast, a strong garrison, and at least ten thousand sturdy West Countrymen. A rebellion in Newfoundland would not have stood for an hour against such overwhelming odds.

Underhand attempts, no doubt, were made to seduce all the colonies from their allegiance. They met with no favour in Newfoundland; against none were the new republicans more vindictive than against us; they knew that we were largely dependent on them for food, yet one of the first acts of the Congress of 1774 was to decree non-intercourse; this was not fully carried out, with all its dire effects on our population, until the following year; but in 1775—a terrible year of storm and suffering—our late colonial brethren, who had been on such friendly terms, did their utmost to starve us and to destroy our trade with their privateersmen, who knew every creek and cove along the Newfoundland coast. The extreme animosity of the Americans against us seems to be a very clear indication that in the great struggle our population were loyal to the core.[1]

It is not necessary to repeat again the oft-told story of the American revolution; how the obstinacy and stupidity of George III. and his ministers drove the colonists into rebellion; how the greatest statesmen in England—Chatham, Fox, and Burke—Franklin, Washington, and others, in America, tried to prevent war; how the gallant colonists at last achieved their liberty through the powerful assistance of France and a combination of nearly all Europe against England; this great history has been written in every form, from the "Spread-Eagle" one-sided view of some American historians, to the newest and fairest description of the events by Goldwin Smith. The

GRAND BANK, FORTUNE BAY.
From a photograph by J. Vey.

greatest blot on the character of the first American republicans is their treatment of the loyalists; in the words of Goldwin Smith:—

> "The first civil war was followed not by amnesty, but by an outpouring of the vengeance of the victors upon the fallen. Some royalists were put to death, many others were despoiled of all they had and driven from their country. . . . . . Massachusetts banished by name three hundred and eight of her people, making death the penalty for a second return."

These loyalist exiles peopled Nova Scotia, New Brunswick, and Upper Canada; some few of them came to this Colony; to one of these

[1] The following local events in 1775–6 are noticeable :—

Rev. Edward Langman, who appears to have been a very spirited and decided character, accused his brother justices of being partial and perjured; whereupon Edward White, Michael Gill, T. Dodd, John Stripling, and John Swingston complained of him to Governor Duff, and he was struck off the Commission of the Peace; he was restored by Governor Montague. There was a grant to A. Dunn, collector, of a site for the Custom House in its present situation, to the east of King's Road (a path leading to the New Fortification), on a hillock at the top of the Admiral's Beach, bounded on the north by a garden belonging to the late W. Delgrave. In 1776 General Howe removed the 65th Regiment, which was replaced by a company of the Royal Highland Emigrants.

banished Tories—Dr. Gardner of Boston, U.S.—we are indebted for a very interesting account of our Island.[1]

Rear-Admiral Montague,[2] who succeeded Duff, was sworn in, May 1776; one of his first acts was to graciously permit the French to cut wood in the Bay Despair and other places, and to build houses, &c. On war breaking out between France and England in 1778 he nevertheless promptly took possession of St. Pierre and Miquelon, destroyed all the buildings, and sent away all the inhabitants, thirteen hundred and ninety-two persons, prisoners to France.

In 1776 Montague, who had been specially selected for Newfoundland on account of his activity and daring, picked out a number of

CAPTURE OF A CONTINENTAL BRIG BY AN ENGLISH CUTTER.
From a drawing in the B.M.

the best fast sailing vessels in the trade and fitted them as armed cruisers, putting young lieutenants, masters, mates, midshipmen, and petty officers in charge of them. With the men-of-war under his command and these improvised sloops and cutters, he most effectually protected our coasts from the American privateers, who had done considerable damage the year before. The petition given below throws a flood of light on our social history in 1775; it shows clearly that the

[1] The fierce attacks of the Republicans on their Tory brother colonists, who had done them no wrong, and their treatment of the loyalists are some of the most serious blots and scandals of American history.

[2] John Montague was Commander of the *Hinchinbroke* in 1745; in 1747 he represented Huntingdon in Parliament. He held various commands, but saw very little service during the wars except off Toulon, where he helped to destroy the French fleet which endeavoured to effect a junction with De la Clue at Carthagena. Became Rear-Admiral of the Blue in 1770, and Commander-in-Chief at Halifax. After his return from Newfoundland in 1778 he never accepted any active command; he was Port-Admiral at Portsmouth, and a member of the Keppel court-martial. He died in 1795 at Fareham, Hants.—(CHARNOCK's *Biographia Navalis.*)

old West Country ideas were still prevalent, also that St. John's had become quite a town, and that there was (in spite of the stern edicts of the naval Governors) considerable cultivation of land going on near the city; foremost in this innovation were the officers of the garrison. There are many names around St. John's to remind us of these old soldiers who took to farming. The well-known Major's Path is named after Major Brady, R.A., 1787. Pringle's Bridge, Pringle's Dale (Sir James Winter's residence), after Chief Engineer Col. Pringle, R.E, who built Fort Townshend; Bally Haly after Col Haly. I recommend to my readers the perusal of this remarkable letter; it is copied from an admirable lecture on the fisheries by the late M. H. Warren in 1853, which is quite out of print, and was kindly lent to me by Mr. J. H. Noonan, of H.M. Customs, St. John's.[1]

[1] "To the Honourable the Commons of Great Britain in Parliament assembled —

"The Petition of the Merchants, Boat-keepers, and Principal Inhabitants of St. John's Petty Harbour, and Tor Bay, in the Island of Newfoundland, 1775

"Most Humbly Sheweth

"That your petitioners having Maturely Considered a Bill for amending and rendering more Effectually an Act made in the Fifteenth year of His present Majesty (George 3rd, 1776,) entitled 'An Act for the encouragement of the Fisheries carried on from Great Britain, Ireland, and the British Dominions in Europe, and for securing the return of the fishermen, sailors, and others Employed in the said fisheries to the ports thereof at the end of the fishing season,' and for repealing certain provisions in the said Act relative to the said fisheries, are of opinion that its General tendency is well calculated for the Benefit of this Island, at the same time beg leave to lay before you some amendments and additions, which we apprehend will also be of public utility.

"Relative to Bounties granted ships or vessels employed in the British fishery, on the Banks of Newfoundland, having been found inadequate to its intention (as to obtain it the adventurers were obliged to be at a considerable expense in outfitting their Vessels, carrying extra men, to entitle them to receive the same) that the said Bounties may be appropriated and allowed to such ships or vessels employed in the said fishery, navigated with ten men each, at the rate of six shillings per Ton, agreeable to their registers, subject to all the rules and restrictions as reserved in former Acts.

"That all the Plantations, Houses, Gardens, and so forth, in this Island, on being established property, to be nevertheless liable to the payment of debts, otherwise

those merchants and *others* who supply the Boat-keepers and Inhabitants will be deprived of that resource, for the discharge of their just debts

"That all Oil, Blubber, and Seal Skins, exported from this Island, caught by British subjects, may be imported into Great Britain free of Duty, oath being made by the Master or person having the charge of the said ship, that it was caught and cured as aforesaid

"If a Master or the person acting under him, should at any time see it necessary to correct any servant under them with moderation, (free from harshness or cruelty) for not doing his duty in a proper manner, that the said servant may not be allowed, for every frivolous disagreement or complaint to have his Master summon'd before a Justice of the Peace, which in the height of the fishery has been very detrimental and often known to be the case without a just cause of complaint

"Fishing Admirals being authorized to hear and determine matters relative to the fishery, the Trading People are often deprived of an immediate resource to them, they being employed fishing on the Banks

"That such fishing Admirals may be allowed to appoint deputy or deputies to act under them to hear or determine, on such matters as may come before them relative to the fishery aforesaid, with liberty to preside at any Court of Justice held in their different districts as a Justice, and also for their deputations to remain in force until the Twentieth of November, before which time the transactions, relative to the said fisheries, are not adjusted, as frequently, the fishing Admirals are obliged to sail from this Island, early in October

"As Lumber is at present a scarce commodity, and the intercourse of supply from Quebec, and Port Roseway, not yet warranted, from whence no doubt large quantities will be sent to this Island, in the intermediate space, Regard should be paid to

As a further illustration of the state of society, and of the manner in which the administration of justice was carried out at

the Timber Trees growing in this Island, which if not wantonly cut down would in a few years, become large spars, for Masts of Ships and other uses, as well as to saw into boards

" To prevent the said Trees from being unnecessary cut down the principal person of each crew (of which there are a great many who prosecute the Business of making Shingles for covering houses, stores, &c ; also hoops in the winter season) should be competent to judge such Timber as would suit his purpose, and not wantonly cut down any Trees but for their immediate use under certain restrictions

" Rinding Trees is also of a pernicious tendency, altho' that article is very necessary in the fishery, yet should be subject to Regulations, not for more *Trees* to be rinded than is necessary for curing and preserving the fish and for the covering temporary houses and huts, where boards are not to be obtained

' Codd Seans we deem a great nuizance as by them we destroy a great quantity of small fish, which after being inclosed in the sean (and not worth the attention of the person who hauls them) are left to rot, by which means a multitude of fish that would grow to maturity, perish

" Contiguous to the Northern Part of this Island are a great many Islands where Birds breed in vast abundance which were of great service to the inhabitants residing near them, for food in the winter, and also for bait in catching of fish during the summer, of which valuable resource they are now almost entirely deprived, as great part of the birds are destroyed within a few years by the crews of men who make it their business to kill them in their breeding season, for their feathers (of which they make a Traffic) and burning the carcasses, we have applied to get this with many other grievances redressed but have yet only retained a partial relief, therefore pray that an entire stop may be put to destroying the birds otherwise than for food or bait as before excepted

" Olive Oil and Cork, both articles very necessary for the fishery if allowed to be imported here duty free, we apprehend would not be detrimental to the revenue, and at the same time of public utility, as at present we are not allowed to import either, except its being first sent to England, which is attended with additional expense

" When Bread and Flour is to be purchased in Great Britain Ireland and Quebec at Twelve Shillings per cwt it can be supplied the inhabitant of this Island at such moderate prices as not to be a burthen or tax on the fishery, but when it exceeds the price before quoted, a bounty to be granted on what is

exported from Great Britain and Ireland, to reduce it to the said price of twelve shillings per cwt (in British vessels)

" Every Ship or Vessel that brings Passengers to Newfoundland not provided with Masters (which is often the case) the Master of such Vessel on his arrival should be obliged to enter into Bond, that such men as do not get employed during the summer (by which means they become very burthensome here, and frequently through Idleness and want commit Outrages, Breaking open Stores and Shops for plunder) and are not provided with a Master in the fall, either to carry them back from where they came or give proper security for their passages so that they may not be burthensome here, which would prevent a number of Idle Men remaining here the winter, all of that description being a great nuizance

" It has been a Custom lately with several Masters of Vessels on their arrival, to land many Passengers (great part thereof unprovided for) and then go off with most of their Cargoes (chiefly provisions) supposed for some part of the United States, leaving the said Passengers and others without even the resource of their Cargoes, for supplying them as also the Inhabitants, and by this means doubly distressing the Trade This we pray may be prevented in future by a clause, that every Vessel bringing provisions to this Island, should not be suffered to carry away more than sufficient Stock for said Vessel's intended Voyage, by suffering the Exportation, the Price here is consequently enhanced and the Inhabitants much distressed thereby.

" As our Season for prosecuting the Fish is of a short continuance the utmost industry during that period is very requisite, and therefore the fewer innovations or incentives to draw the Servants off from their duty the strictest their attention will be in the discharge of it

" Some few years back when the Fishery was prosecuted in the Harbour of St John's, with great vigour, three to four Houses Public by Licence for vending Spirituous and Malt Liquors were found sufficient, then the servant was obliged to apply to his Employer for Liquor when, if he made bad use of it getting intoxicated and thereby neglecting his duty, it was in the said Master's Power to prevent the like happening in future, but within a few years the number of Licenced Houses in the said Harbour are amounted to more than Eighty in number, many of which are houses of Ill-fame, where the fishermen and seamen resort, and get drunk, neglecting their duty to the great detriment of their Employers, it often happening through one

this period, I give in the notes an account of a few of the cases tried in 1777 [1]

servant's neglect of a few hours a considerable loss ensues, as fish is a perishing commodity too much care and attention can't be paid it To prevent the like in future we pray that the number may be reduced (of Houses Licenced for Selling Liquors) to twelve, which we deem full sufficient for the Entertainment both of the Inhabitants, as well as Strangers resorting to the Harbour, and that each person so authorized to Vend Liquors should be obliged to keep a Fishing Shallop and cure all the Fish said Shallop may catch

"The number of Shopkeepers and Retailers of Goods have increased lately in St John's to the great detriment of the Fish Catchers, as formerly every Employer had the supplying his own Servants, which we apprehend in Equity they are entitled to, from the very great wages given to them for the short season of prosecuting the Fishery, the profits arising from such supply was a small emolument to reduce the enormous wages given, but at present the Masters are deprived of this, by their Servants being supplied at those Retail Shops before alluded to, who in the fall of the year collect their Bills, in consequence of which the servants are often reduced to great distress during the winter, to prevent which we pray that each Shopkeeper of Goods may in future be obliged to keep a Shallop on the Fishery otherwise to have six months liberty to sell off his Goods and leave this Island, as we deem every person not immediately concerned in the Fishery (except his Majesty's Servants) is a burthen to the Island, and that every Tavern-keeper, or other person, known to supply a Servant belonging to or Employed by Merchants or Boat-keepers in the Fishery, on Proof to be fined Fifty Pounds.

"His Majesty's Officers having lately inclosed large Spots of Ground contiguous to this Harbour for erecting Houses, Planting Gardens, Farms, &c, by which means many of the public pathways leading to the woods are stopped, to the prejudice of the residents here, we therefore request that no more ground may be inclosed for farms, or otherwise, except as Gardens for the use of the said Officers families, which, when they may be recalled should go to the next that arrives according to their rank

"We therefore request you will deign to take the preceding matters into your serious consideration and grant us such redress as your Honourable House shall seem meet and as in duty bound your Petitioners shall ever pray, &c" — (WARREN's Lecture, Apps pp x–xv)

[1] CRIMINAL CASES TRIED IN 1777.

The jurors for our Lord the King, upon their oath, present that Richard Power, a native

of the kingdom of Ireland, labourer, not having God before his eyes, but being moved and seduced by the instigation of the Devil on the first day of October in the 15th year of our sovereign Lord, George the Third, of Great Britain, France, and Ireland, &c, &c At the hour of about 9 o'clock in the evening of the same day, with force and arms at St John's, &c, in and upon one John Cahill, of St John's, aforesaid, merchant, in the peace of God and our sovereign Lord the King, then and there being, the aforesaid John Cahill not having any weapon then drawn, nor the aforesaid John Cahill having first stricken, the said Richard Power feloniously did make an assault, and that he the aforesaid Richard Power, with a stone of no value which he the said Richard Power in his right hand then and there had and held, hit the said John Cahill in and upon the side of the head of him the said John Cahill, the aforesaid John Cahill as is aforesaid then and there not having any weapon drawn nor the aforesaid John Cahill then and there having first stricken, the said Richard Power then and there feloniously did strike, giving unto him the said John Cahill then and there with the stone aforesaid, in form aforesaid, in and upon the left side of the head of him the said John Cahill one mortal stroke or blow, of which he the said John Cahill languished until the evening of the 24th November and then died, &c, &c

This is an abbreviated form of the indictment against Power, there was no evidence to sustain it It appears that Cahill, a shop keeper or merchant, was having a drunken spree in his house, some boys looked in through the window, so he and other guests rushed out and struck the spectators with sticks, the accused, an Irish "youngster," was passing, and was struck violent blows on the head by Cahill and Lawrence Power, who were too drunk to distinguish anyone, after being struck, Richard Power immediately went home, and next day had his wounds dressed by Dr Delaney The jury found the prisoner not guilty, and he was discharged on payment of the fees of the court

Lawrence Hallahan, found guilty of forging a bill of £8, was sentenced as follows. "That you be carried back to the place from whence you came and thence be led to the place of execution and there to be hanged by the neck until you are Dead, Dead, Dead, and the Lord have mercy on your soul."

Next Lawrence Dalton, for forging two orders for 20s and 17s, received the same sentence Patrick Knowlan, for stealing a counterpane, value 10d, from Peter Prim, sentence· "That you P. Knowlan be whipped by the common whipper with a halter about

In the year 1776 came into operation the statute known in the Colony as "Palliser's Act" 15 Geo III c xxxi. This important measure was very ably drawn, and, although somewhat encumbered with the involved and redundant verbosity of the period, it was remarkably clear and definite; Sir Hugh's hand can be traced in every line. The distinct purpose of the measure was to make the Newfoundland business a British fishery, carried on by fishermen from England and the King's dominions in Europe; American colonists were rigidly excluded from any participation in the bounties and other benefits granted by it. The preamble clearly explains this object:—

" Whereas the fisheries carried on by H. M. subjects of G Britain and of the British dominions in Europe have been found to be the best nurseries for able and experienced seamen, always ready to man the Royal Navy when occasions require, and it is therefore of the highest national importance to give all due encouragement to the said fisheries, and to endeavour to secure the *annual return* of the fishermen, sailors, and others employed therein to the Ports of Great Britain &c. at the end of every fishing season

" Now in order to promote these great and important purposes and with a view in the first place to induce H. M. subjects to proceed early from the ports of G. Britain to the Banks of Newfoundland, and thereby to prosecute the fishery on the said banks to the greatest advantage it is enacted &c

" That from and after 1st Jany 1776 the bounties hereinafter mentioned shall be paid and allowed annually for 11 years   .   such vessels must be British built and owned by British subjects residing in England &c., not less than 50 tons burthen, not less than 15 men (three fourths of whom must be H M. subjects), to be fitted and cleared out from an English Port on the 1st January each year; they must catch on the Banks not less than 10,000 fish to be landed on the E coast of Newfoundland before the 15th July each year.

" Bounty of £40 per ship to the first 25 vessels making two trips to the Banks— next 100 vessels £20 each   Bounty for whale fishery £500 to the first vessel arriving with the largest quantity of oil

" No person allowed to fish in Newfoundland except those arriving from H. M. Dominions in Europe [intended to exclude the Americans] Provisions to be brought from England, Ireland, &c free   Fishing vessels to be free from restraint and only pay a Custom House fee of 2s 6d. Seal skins and oil to be free of duty.

" No fishing vessels to carry passengers to Newfoundland without permission Agreement in writing with fishermen obligatory No advance to fishermen to be more than half their wages—other half on return home Master must produce Shipping paper. Fish and oil liable preferentially for payment of servants wages.

your neck, that is to say you are to receive on your bare back twenty lashes at the common whipping post, then to be led by the halter to the Publick Path just opposite Mr Peter Prims door and there receive twenty lashes as before, and then led as before to the Vice-Admiral's Beach and there to receive twenty lashes as before, to forfeit all your goods and chattels, to pay the charges of the Court, and to depart this Island by the first vessel bound for Ireland never to return on pain of having the same punishment repeated every Monday morning; to be kept in prison till you go aboard "

Thus ended the assizes.

MCHL. GILL.
JOHN STRIPLING
EDWD. WHITE
THOS. DODD
EDWARD LANGMAN.
ROBT. BULLEY

Hallahan was hung 10th May 1777

Penalties for misconduct of fishermen. All disputes to be determined by Sessions Courts in Newfoundland or by Vice Admiralty Court [this was repealed as regards Admiralty Courts by 26 Geo. III. cap. xxvi. sec. 25].

" Fishermen to be free from press gang. Duty of 1/- per gallon on rum from America, &c. . . . ."

Palliser's Act was one of the results of the troubles with America. The bounty was given to encourage the loyal Colony of Newfoundland; by a provision in the Act, Americans, as well as all Colonists outside Newfoundland, were excluded from all participation in the colonial fishery. The bank fishery was specially reserved for the subjects of His Majesty's dominions in Europe. Hanoverians, Jersey men, &c. might fish; but Canadians, Nova Scotians, and Bermudians were rigidly excluded by this extraordinary narrow policy. As Ireland was at the time in strong sympathy with the American insurgents, it was thought desirable to win over the Celts by granting them the much-desired boon of free trade with the Colonies, and a bounty for their fishery. The Irish were so much concerned with Newfoundland at this time that historians speak of the bounty on our bank fishery as given to the *Irish Newfoundland fishery.* The trade between the two countries at this period was large; Arthur Young speaks of the farmers around Waterford fattening pigs for our markets; legal or illegal, the trade was carried on.

The West Countrymen always made a provision that the convoy out to Newfoundland should remain forty-eight hours in Cork. The effect of Palliser's Act was to increase the bank fishery, it had no other result. The provisions about servants' wages were bitterly disliked by the West Country merchants, and in every way they tried to evade the new law.

BERMUDIAN SLOOP OF THE EIGHTEENTH CENTURY.

In the years 1787 and 1788 a new trade question arose. The Devonshire men found a formidable competitor in a most unlooked-for quarter, Bermuda. The whole story of this sudden irruption into our island of the Somers Islanders and their lusty negroes is so graphically described by Jeremiah Coghlan, that I give his report in full; it is dated 25th October 1788, St. John's:—

" This new and alarming undertaking consisted this year of thirty four sloops of 30 to 60 tons burthen, from 8 to 12 men each, three parts of whom consist of robust able black men, natives of Bermuda, and slaves to owners of said vessels, other part were old country men, hired for splitting, salting, and conducting things abroad said vessels on the Banks, and the large vessels had each one of our expert fishermen to instruct the crew in managing their lines and disengaging the hooks with quickness when swallowed by the cod.

" These vessels came early in the spring from Bermuda, laden with salt which was brought from Turks Island. Part of them paid Masters of our fishing rooms 2/- per quintal for curing the fish they should take. The other part, particularly large size sloops, took possession of vacant ship's or admiral's rooms at different parts to the southward of St John's and hired one experienced Master of voyages to manage and inspect the curing of fish, occupying the said fishing rooms in the same manner as British ships are entitled to do.

" The first trips these our rivals made to the Grand Bank, they appeared as if they could not undergo the hardships of such a business, and as natives of a more southern climate could not endure fatigues, but they soon convinced the English fishers that they were equal to any young beginners who came before them, and to aid their endeavours they were greatly favoured by a most uncommon mild moderate season which was a great encouragement to their exertions, and which men, to the surprise of our fishermen, exceeded them in despatch, which appears by the following account.

" The smallest of these vessels, in July and August seldom exceed eight days in making fishing trips to the Grand Bank and in returning loaded from thence. For being not only remarkably fast sailors, but also, when it became calm, frequently the case in those months, these blacks (shewing example of attention for good of their Masters' interest worthy notice of our people) rowed their sloops from 2½ to 3 miles per hour and in working in and out of narrow harbours excelled the best of our fishing lugger shallops. No wind prevented them from getting on the Banks. Have been told that the Master of one of our banking ships being stopped in the Narrows of St John's by a strong wind blowing from the sea when bound on the Grand Bank, two of these Bermudian sloops passed him and worked out under low sail, the next evening the former got his vessel out of Harbour also and meeting a contrary time was five days after before he got on the fishing ground, at which time he fell in with one of the sloops before mentioned returning with her full take of fish which her crew were but four days in catching.

" Also learned from Masters of our Bankers who have been in company with Bermudians on Banks fishing in August, that the black men aboard of them became as expert in catching fish as old country men and as eager and attentive to catch as any of ours who are paid £4 10s per 1000 fish for catching only—some of which men have earned this year £45 stg for their separate share of a Banker's voyage.

" This information discovers to you the very great take of fish there has been on the Grand Bank this past season, which to a great degree exceeds any single year's take of that article within the memory of the oldest trader to this Country; a circumstance that (with many encouraging advantages these new Adventurers have in view superior to fishers from England) must terminate to the latter's prejudice if not speedily taken under the consideration of the Lords of Committee of Trade and Plantations and must cause great decline to this valuable nursery of British seamen.

" These Bermudian fishing vessels are to sanction the subtle views of Americans, who to evade the late restrictions laid on their exports, the wise check given their navigation, a wound their boasted liberty cannot readily heal, are now become concerned with their second selves, the Bermudians, in imposing this new and unexpected undertaking on Great Britain.

" The said fishing vessels, the alarming rivals of British European fishers, being manned with proprietors' own slaves and fitted out in much cheaper manner than English Bankers will have great superiority over the latter in case of a bad fishery happening, the former having no claim on owners for wages, which will enable them to undersell the English taken fish and also introduce a new mode of smuggling New England fish at all our West India Islands, where they can afford to supply them with fish of first quality as cheap as we can, what the Spanish market will not consume being such as we call refuse at this market

"Under colour of the said Banking vessels taking their fish from hence when cured to be reshipped on board larger size vessels at Bermudas and transported from thence to the Mediterranean markets, protected by our passes, said vessels will proceed to America and there receive New England fish to the amount of two thirds their cargoe, and proceed with such to the former markets which will be rivalling us at the same The Americans not daring to face the Mediterranean or get within reach of being made slaves by the Algerines, which also burdens their voyages made to the Straights with an additional premium for insurance that no markets can support and which markets we command at present

"The fishing crews, being slaves, the property of people of Bermuda and many American blacks, not being within reach of our men of war in case of rupture with European powers are only for the service of America [for manning ships of war]. The major part of these vessels will be supplied with cordage, canvas, iron work, &c from America and, being a great field for smuggling produce of that country into bays and creeks of Newfoundland, these vessels, under sanction of taking fish, will set aside the restrictions on importation of provisions &c from the Continent, which the greatest attention of the King's ships on this station cannot prevent, and they will be enabled thereby to undersell us at this market, and maintain their crews much cheaper than we English fishers

"The chief agent who came with our rival codfishers from Bermuda, whose name is Harvey, is a shrewd American He openly declares there will be 100 sail of Bermudian sloops fishing on the Grand Bank next season, and is now going to London, having all the bluster of the American party to support him in case of need, to make good their establishment at this Island The other agents are rank Americans, also Nathaniel Philips of St. John's who discovered himself so implacable a stickler for the Bostonians during the late troubles, is the person who undertakes to defray all matters and costs these mock Bermudians are subject to, and, though notwithstanding the Act of Parliament, these Bermudians, as they call themselves, have been permitted by the Government to all rights of British Europeans' ships to the surprize of every Englishman, who lay this evil at the door of the former's secretary [Aaron Graham] a much greater man than his master and governs this Island as he thinks fit, of which all the surrogates complain loudly To set aside any right of claim those mock Mudians can have to disinherit English fishers, I am solicited by a body of English fishers to lay those threatening *national grievances* before you, praying representation to Lord Hawkesbury (as owing to your judicious measures when our Governor, the rise and consequence of this Island is become *the envy of all nations*) that a better check to New England fishers [be arranged]"

The Bermudians were allowed to dry their fish this year, but they were afterwards rigidly tabooed [1]

This letter, addressed to Sir Hugh Palliser—the most virulent opponent of our native resident fishermen—gives a very clear statement of the case from the West Country standpoint. There can be very

---

[1] The Bermudians had fished in Newfoundland before this date, and after they were prohibited from landing and curing their fish, they carried it home green to Bermuda The damp climate of their Island was found, however, unsuitable for fish curing, and the enterprise had to be abandoned I have received valuable information on this subject from T. Reid, Esq, Bermuda Further information will be found in the Appendix

little doubt that the shrewd Yankees had a hand in this new dodge. The Nathaniel Philips referred to was a well-known merchant in St. John's, he had been the general agent for the New England trade in Newfoundland, a close-fisted, penurious old fellow, who had become very rich "by saving of candle ends and sich", he died in 1790, and was buried in the cathedral burying ground, at the corner near St. Andrew's Kirk[1] Three of his clerks were Henry Shea (father of Sir Ambrose, and the Hon Edward D'Alton Shea), Geo Lilly (afterwards Judge Lilly, father of the late R R W. Lilly, Q C), and William Lilly, of Harbour Grace Philips was navy agent all through the first American war, Hunt Stabb & Preston during the war of 1812 Philips' name figures largely in the judicial records, he had very large dealings, and appears frequently as a harsh creditor, screwing and selling up some unfortunate out-harbour planter.

Under the administration of the admiral-governors, there was a curious blending of judicial and executive functions, their excellencies wanted to have a hand in everything We find, for instance, Governor Montague issuing an order to the sheriff, John Philips, to hang Hallahan, and fixing the time for his execution On many occasions he not only manufactured a law to suit the special exigencies of the case, but also invented a punishment He fined publicans for a first or second offence, deciding that for a third they are to be banished to Ireland For fishermen disobeying the commands of their skippers he ordered first a forfeiture of all their wages, and secondly that they should be imprisoned and then sent on board a man-of-war, never to return to the Colony.

At this period of our history there had grown up a considerable trade with Greenock, Glasgow, and Belfast, besides the long standing commercial intercourse with Waterford Representations were made by the chief magistrates of these towns about the state of the civil government in the Colony, or rather the want of any efficient and orderly administration of law or government[2] Being anxious to increase

---

[1] In Philips' time clerks had a very hard life, they were treated almost like menial servants One day Michael, Philips' faithful old Irish servant, told his master the appalling news that the young gentlemen wanted a change in their dinner—all three had declared they would eat pork no longer "Not eat pork," said the old man in a furious rage, "I'll make 'em eat pork until the bristles grow on 'em"

[2] WRECK OF THE "TROIS FRERES"

" As every part of the conduct of the people at and about St Marie's concerned in this transaction appears to me the most inhuman and barbarous proceeding I ever heard of in a Christian country I rely on your doing that justice to the injured parties their unhappy case requires, and doubt not there may be some well disposed people there who will be happy to render you every assistance towards this discovery, and am gentlemen,

"Your very humble servant,
"J MONTAGUE

"To John Follett &
Jas Jackson, J P's,
Trepassey."

[This letter relates to the wreck and plundering of the French schooner *Trois Freres*, of Guadaloupe, Pierre Barthelemy Bloum, master, in April 1777]

their profitable business with the Island, they represented the deplorable state of affairs to the Ministry, but all to no purpose. Grievous complaints were made, especially about the administration of justice—Governor after Governor represented the matter to the Crown, but without effect.

Rear-Admiral Montague remained until 1778. In July of that year France recognised the independence of the United States, and declared war against England. This step had been in contemplation for some time; in the autumn of 1777 all the French fleet in Newfoundland, both men-of war and merchantmen, had been suddenly ordered to return to France. On the Governor's departure from the Colony at the usual time, in both the autumn of 1776 and 1777, he had left two frigates and two armed vessels at St. John's and Placentia, and at the earnest request of the merchants in 1777 a frigate remained on the coast up to the 25th of November to convoy the fish vessels to the Mediterranean.

GOVERNOR RICHARD EDWARDS.
From an engraving after Dance.

There is very little interesting matter in the records during Governor Edwards' tenure of office.[1] He was a very careful and attentive administrator. All available means were used to strengthen the defences of the Colony; nine men-of-war, between three and four hundred volunteers, and about four hundred and fifty regular troops were under his command; batteries were established at Quidi Vidi, Cuckold's Cove, Amherst Tower, Frederick's Battery, Chain Rock Battery, Fort William, Fort Townshend, and at Petty Harbour, and in the Torbay and Bay Bulls Roads; a ship was moored at River Head to defend the path leading into the town from Bay Bulls; the volunteers when under arms were allowed rations, pay, and each half a pint of rum per diem. About £5,000 in specie to pay troops and volunteers, and eight hundred stand of arms, were sent out from England. Edwards acknowledges in grateful terms the loyalty of the Newfoundland population; their active exertions to defend the Colony, their cheerful submission to

[1] Richard Edwards must not be confused with the Governor of the same name in George II.'s reign. He was appointed a Commander in 1747, and in 1777 was Captain of H.M.S. *Sandwich* (90) at Ushant, under Admiral Keppel, where his ship suffered very severely. He was a witness at the subsequent court-martial. On 19th March 1779, he became Rear-Admiral of the Blue, and soon after was sent to the Newfoundland station; he resigned this post in April 1782 on the change of administration. Edwards saw very little active service; he died, at an advanced age, in 1794. — (CHARNOCK'S *Biographia Navalis.*)

military rule and discipline, and their valuable aid in perfecting
the defences, both of the capital and the outports. Beyond tampering
with the guns at Renews, there is not a single complaint of disloyalty
or disaffection.

All through 1780 St. John's was kept in a state of vigilant watch-
fulness about the great French fleet, with a hundred transports, that
had sailed from Brest on May 2nd; its destiny, however, was the
United States, not Newfoundland. During all the first American contest no foreign men-of-war—either French, Spanish, or American—made
any serious attack on the Island. Newfoundland suffered much from

ST. JOHN'S IN 1770.

the scarcity and dearness of provisions, which had all to be imported
from England, as well as coal. On the other hand she enjoyed all the
fishery—bank and shore—without a rival; prices were good and the
harvest of the sea abundant. On the whole, the war time was a
prosperous period in Newfoundland history.

There were, however, many American privateers hovering about the
coast. They did most damage to the planters at Fogo and Twillingate.
In August 1780 Edwards writes that "already he has captured five
American privateers, but they are in force on the coast." With the
strong naval armament then cruising about Newfoundland they did
not venture on our shores, except in the early spring, when they might

do mischief to the northward, or late in the autumn, when the fleet had sailed for England. Beyond destroying a few fishing boats and stages they did not do much serious injury on the south coast. Some of the small outlying settlements were plundered by skippers who had been traders to the Island. They boldly sailed their vessels right into the wharves, and then requisitioned the inhabitants and carried off all the sailors they required. Several attempts were made to attack Carbonear and Harbour Grace, but they were successfully defended by the well-manned batteries on the islands. They seldom ventured near St John's; one privateer—a brig of twelve guns—is mentioned in a letter from Renews, but she did not dare to enter the harbour, which was fortified with six guns.

Many of their ships were captured. A silent witness to the smartness of the Royal Navy in these days lay for a long time sunk at River Head—the American privateer *George*. In 1781, in the early spring, H M S *Pluto* was lying in St John's Harbour dismantled; news was brought in by a fisherman at daybreak that two American privateers were cruising off Bay Bulls, and had captured several fishing vessels; before eight o'clock that morning the *Pluto* was made ready for sea, and before sundown she returned to St John's with the two captured Americans. One of these, the *George*, was found in 1882, when the dock was being built. In the second American war of 1812 there were far more Yankee vessels captured than in the revolutionary conflict.

In 1780, one of the English squadron, H M S *Antelope*, Captain Keppel, R N., cruising on the banks, fell in with and captured the American armed packet *Mercury*, with Mr Lawrence on board. As the vessels approached each other a packet was thrown by Henry Laurence, the American envoy to Europe, from the American vessel; a sailor from the English frigate dived overboard, and brought up the package, which contained the secret negotiations then being carried on by the Americans with France and Holland; by the smartness of this plucky tar, England was put in possession of all the designs of her enemies.

In 1781 the memorable capture of York Town and the surrender of Lord Cornwallis demonstrated, even to the obstinate old king, that the Americans were not to be brought back to their allegiance; next year (1782) preliminaries of peace were signed between England and America, although the United States had solemnly bound themselves with France to make no separate treaty.

During the American war England had been gallantly fighting the three greatest naval powers of Europe and their colonies, as well as her own rebellious provinces. The British lion was a little torn and ragged after these desperate encounters with French, Spanish, Dutch, and Americans but everywhere he had held his own Incapable generals, timid admirals, and divided counsellors had blundered and quarrelled over their stupid mistakes, yet England, in 1783, was more than a match for her four antagonists France, Spain, and Holland were utterly beggared and routed, America was at her wits' end, the old country was full of pluck and vigour, the national spirit was aroused, ships and regiments were being offered to the Government. Our old Governor Rodney's crowning victory at Domenica showed the world what English sailors could do when properly led.

In 1783 came the Treaty of Versailles, in which the Imperial Government had once more an opportunity of settling her North American fisheries on a permanent and satisfactory basis. The United States—always the spoiled child of diplomacy—though she had separated from England, claimed a right to the coast fishery in the English provinces. One of her first modest demands from England was Canada—she had previously divided Newfoundland provisionally with France However, as Mr Oswald, the first English diplomatist, an English merchant well acquainted with American affairs, would not listen to any of these proposals, they dropped Canada after their first interview, but they actually gained the right, in a modified form, to the coast fishery about Newfoundland and the maritime provinces. In brazen effrontery and diplomatic roguery the simple Quaker printer, Benjamin Franklin, taught European diplomatists a lesson which they have never forgotten.[1]

With respect to Newfoundland, we were again sacrificed by Mr. Alleyne Fitzherbert, afterwards Lord St Helen's Every detail of this important treaty had been agreed on after protracted discussion, only the fisheries remained The French claimed the exclusive right to the Newfoundland fishery from Cape John to Cape Ray. Fitzherbert told them the English Ministry dared not give away British territory on the Island, and he could put no such terms in the treaty There was a dead-lock, the French would not give way, both nations were anxious for peace. The diplomatists wanted to show their ability by finding some way out of the difficulty. At last, says Fitzherbert, "I ventured to propose as " a mezzo-termine (taking care, however, to add that the proposition " came from myself) that the exclusive right should not be mentioned " in the treaty, but that we should promise *ministerially* to secure " it to the French fishermen by means of proper instructions to that " effect to the government of Newfoundland." To this the Count de Vergennes assented. The whole transaction was dishonest; there was

[1] Read Wedderburn's attack on Franklin about the stolen Whateley correspondence

to be a sham treaty, signed and set before the English House of Commons; the real treaty was to depend on the word of the minister, and afterwards on the declaration of the king. The *treaty* says :—

"Article IV.—That His Majesty the King of Great Britain is maintained in his right to the Island of Newfoundland and to the adjacent Islands, as the whole were assured to him by the 13th article of the Treaty of Utrecht, except the Islands of St. Pierre and Miquelon, which are ceded in full right by the present Treaty to His Most Christian Majesty.

"Article V.—That the King of France, in order to prevent the quarrels which have hitherto arisen between the two nations of England and France, consents to renounce the right of fishing which belongs to him in virtue of the aforesaid article of the Treaty of Utrecht from Cape Bonavista to Cape John. . . . . . And His Majesty the King of Great Britain consents on his part that in the fishery assigned to the subjects of His Most Christian Majesty, beginning at the said Cape John, passing to the north and descending by the West Coast of Newfoundland to Cape Ray, the French fishermen shall enjoy the fishery as they had the right to enjoy that which was assigned to them by the Treaty of Utrecht."

LORD ST. HELEN'S.
From an engraving in the B.M.

The *declaration* 3rd Sept. 1783 states :—

"The King having entirely agreed with the French King upon the articles of the definite treaty, will seek every means which shall not only insure the execution thereof, with his accustomed good faith and punctuality; but will besides give, on his part, all possible efficacy to the principles which shall prevent even the least foundation of dispute for the future.

"To this end, and in order that the fishermen of the two nations may not give cause for daily quarrels, His Britannic Majesty will take the most positive measures for preventing his subjects from interfering in any manner *by their competition*, with the fishery of the French during the *temporary* exercise of it, which is granted to them upon the Coasts of Newfoundland; and he will for this purpose cause *the fixed settlements which shall be formed there to be removed.* His Britannic Majesty will give orders that the French fishermen be not incommoded in cutting the wood necessary for the repairs of their scaffolds, huts and fishing vessels."

It is perfectly clear that the English envoy virtually promised to give France exclusive rights from Cape John to Cape Ray, but the Ministry dare not put it in the Treaty—the clauses about Newfoundland were most unpopular. Fox and Burke tore away every vestige of credit from the Peace of Versailles, and the Ministry were turned out. This is the secret of the dubious character of the declaration; nowhere does it

Z

mention exclusive rights, neither in the proclamation issued by the Governors, nor in the Act 28 George III c. xxv , Lord Palmerston might well say —

" In no similar instrument which has ever come under the notice of the British Government, is so important a concession as an exclusive privilege of this description, announced in terms so loose and indefinite.

" Exclusive rights are privileges which from the very nature of things, are likely to be injurious to parties who are thereby debarred from some exercise of industry in which they would otherwise engage. Such rights are therefore certain to be at some time or other disputed, if there is any maintainable ground for contesting them, and for these reasons when negotiations have intended to grant exclusive rights, it has been their invariable practice to convey such rights in direct, unqualified, and comprehensive terms, so as to prevent the possibility of future dispute or doubt.

" In the present case, however, such forms of expression are entirely wanting, and the claim put forward on the part of France, is founded simply upon inference and upon an assumed interpretation of words."

This is a very ably written despatch. It appears to me, however, after having carefully read the immense correspondence on the subject, that, notwithstanding all the hair-splitting letters; the French argument that they have a prior claim to the fishing on the Treaty Shore had great force, and if they had been able to occupy every inch of the ground with their fishing operations, from Cape John to Cape Ray, they could maintain their position , but, unfortunately for them, they never could do so, and the inexorable logic of events—the failing shore fishery and the permanent settlement of so many British subjects on the shore (which was originally *encouraged* by the French), and the settlers' persistence in fishing—has, at present, reduced the French treaty rights to mere barren privileges. They can have no permanent buildings of any kind, they cannot remain behind to look after their property, and the codfish—their chief end and aim—has forsaken the coast, except in the early spring, when the western shore men snatch a voyage before the French arrive, and in the autumn take another good trip or two after they have left The assertion of French right has, in our days, become a mere dog-in-the-manger policy. Add to this the fact that they have virtually abandoned the treaty shore, and that about a dozen old brigs and two hundred French fishermen now represent the whole commercial status of France on this much-disputed territory.[1]

		Vessels	Tons	Men
[1] The exact figures for 1888 and 1889 are the following Since then they have much decreased - - -	St Juliens -	1	204	11
	Port au Choix -	1	204	11
	Ile St. Jean -	3	407	51
	Cap Rouge -	2	235	33
	Le Croc -	2	598	36
	Ile Rouge -	1	112	7
	West Coast	4	614	85
		14	2,874	234

Whilst the French have diminished, the English population has increased, and now numbers over *thirteen thousand permanent settlers*

The whole French case at the present day rests on the declaration of George III., a secret, fraudulent proceeding, foreign diplomatists would at once have found a way out of such a promise—England did not do so The strongest assurance the Emperor Nicholas could give was "on the honour of an English gentleman" Whatever one may think, therefore, either of the legality or of the morality of the Royal declaration, it was clearly binding on the English Government until abrogated by war, the original Treaty of Utrecht had a clear meaning it gave the French a *concurrent* fishery, regulated and controlled *exclusively* by English authorities, our history shows that this was the uniform system on which it was carried on up to 1783. It is an elementary rule of international law that the sovereign power alone exercises authority within its own territory Whatever rights France may have on the Newfoundland treaty shore, they must be carried out under English supervision and control; neither France nor any other foreign power can exercise coercive jurisdiction on English territory It will appear strange to many English readers, but it is nevertheless true, that England has never maintained this principle until the last few years Lord Salisbury was the first English minister to put his foot down firmly and declare that no French officer would be permitted to seize English boats, cut English nets, or to drive English fishermen out of their own harbours [1]

We have seen in the foregoing pages some of the outrageous proceedings of the courts of justice in their criminal proceedings, mainly directed against poor Irish Roman Catholics, subsequently these absurd tribunals went further and filled up the measure of their iniquity A more incongruous caricature of law and justice can hardly be imagined than the so-called Court of Oyer and Terminer The chief justice at one time was the Church of England minister, the Rev Edward Langman; at another time the ordnance storekeeper, White (later on the naval officer, sworn broker, sole notary public and sole auctioneer) The most cruel proceedings were under his tenure of the chief justiceship In 1785 he had grown so arrogant that he refused to serve as a justice unless he was made keeper of the Rolls, on the 6th of October of that year Governor Campbell therefore struck his name off the Commission of the Peace. The two cases I am about to

[1] The House of Commons in October 1890, was much amused at a note given by the Commander of H.M.S. *Pelican* to the English inhabitants of St George's Bay, prohibiting them from selling herring except to French vessels and, it follows as a consequence, at by prices the French chose to give for them

2 B

refer to are set forth fully in the parliamentary report on the courts of justice in Newfoundland. and also in the manuscript history of Dr. Gardner of Boston U S¹ In the summer of 1784 a French brig was lost at Greenspond

Dr Gardner says :—

" Finding that the vessel must be lost altogether, some of the Planters at Greenspond made free with some of the property on board which occasioned the French Captain to go to St John's and complain to the judge of the Vice-Admiralty Court, who immediately issued out a summons against sixteen of the principal planters, who he pretends had plundered his ship, and in the height of the fishing season they were sent prisoners to St John's to be tried for their lives and for that purpose detained there in custody until October, at the same time, previous to the trial, their effects were attached, the consequence was that upwards of £1500 is said to have been lost by this unlawful act

" The men were all acquitted except one who, being found guilty of having endeavoured to secrete some goods from on board the wreck, was condemned to die, but so shocking was this decree for a fault or crime which in this country [America] would be deemed petit larceny that the French Captain and the prosecutors petitioned the Governor to pardon him, who humanely complied with the request. The poor man, by name George Clarke, was so shocked at the treatment he sustained together with the loss of his property which was all sold by order of the Judge of the Vice-Admiralty Court (and the amount is now in his hands), that he came to England and soon died of grief

" It is melancholy to relate that some of these poor men were tried for their lives merely for having a dozen spike nails found upon them, which they delivered up to the first person who appeared to receive them The cruelty of these proceedings needs no comment Had a Court been instituted directly, and a person acquainted with the laws appointed to try them on the spot, the injured would have been redressed, and the guilty, if any, punished, and these industrious men by being employed in the fishery during the season enabled to make good their payments to their employers, or bail might have been taken for their appearance after the fishing season was over But that would not have suited the purpose of the Admiralty Court at St John's, the fees of which are most enormous .   ."²

The following statement is taken from the sworn evidence of Richard Routh, Collector of the Customs—afterwards appointed Chief Justice by the British Government :—

" For the sole purpose of fees the Magistrates licensed 108 Public Houses in St. John's alone at 4½ guineas each, one-half of this went to the three Justices, the other half to the Public funds.

¹ Dr Gardner was a leading physician in Boston, the first to introduce vaccination into New England, besides his practice he carried on a large wholesale drug business, supplying all the Eastern States with his medicines ; by this means, which was a great innovation on established practices, he made a large fortune, with which he founded the town of " Gardner," in Maine ; he was an ardent Royalist, and when the British troops left Boston he followed them, and came down to Newfoundland, after the Revolution, he returned to Boston where he died at a very advanced age He was a man distinguished for high character, for active benevolence, and stern unbending loyalty His history is in manuscript (B M MS 15493), I regret I have only space to make a few extracts from it

² This story is not a bit exaggerated The case is reported shortly in the Records, 23 Oct 17** — The French brig was called L' Actif, the master's name Y. le Pomelle, Louis Gouillon was second master, and Frans Gouillon surgeon.

"There were other means of increasing their incomes by fines the most oppressive. . . . A poor inoffensive taylor [Foreham] had for several days [in the summer of 1783] been intoxicated and was by that means rendered insane, in this situation he affronted his neighbour, a widow woman, with improper language, accusing everyone of robbing him She being unacquainted with the state of his mind applied to the magistrates. The taylor was summoned but regardless of every event [in his insane condition] he did not appear He was fined for contempt of Court *one hundred and fifty pounds* and his property attached for the amount . . " [1]

The three magistrates divided the fines, this would not be a bad day's work. Routh says there was not a single instance of a poor man recovering against a merchant before these justices except one. A judgment was given against a man named O'Driscoll of Bay Bulls, in the matter of Brook's estate, as he was passing along the street, down-hearted about his case, which spelled ruin for him, a friend pointed out Prince William Henry (afterwards William IV.), "get him to plead your case agen," said the Irish friend, " and bedad you will win before ould judge'; so O'Driscoll accosted the Prince, told him his miserable story, and the Prince, a jolly good-natured sailor, went off with him hot foot to the justice, and pleaded his cause so ably that judgment was given in his favour, the first case, it is alleged, old Mr Gill ever gave against a merchant

The following account of the Newfoundland courts of law was written in 1784 by Dr Gardner.—

"The present Government of Newfoundland such as it is, is in the Admiralty, they send out an Admiral annually for the Governor, who resides at St. John's the capital of the Island during the fishing season, which generally lasts near or quite four months. His Commission authorizes him to appoint Courts of Oyer and Terminer and Justices of the Peace in any Harbour in the Island, there are like-wise Justice Courts appointed by him to be held at St John's once every week [they were held twice a week—on Tuesdays and Fridays] These, with the Court of Vice-Admiralty, are the only Courts instituted in the Island

"The present Judge of the Admiralty, who the Governor seems to make the head of the Law Department, was obliged to leave this country about thirty years ago, and went to the Bay of Bulls at Newfoundland, where he lived as a Clerk to a gentleman concerned in the fishery. After some time he went to St. John's and kept a small school which he did not find answer his expectations, he therefore became a retailer of spirituous liquors However he may be found qualified for the business of a gin shop, those who are best acquainted with him declare with one voice that he is unworthy of holding the posts he now sustains

"The Judges who compose the Court of Oyer and Terminer are usually, the Judge of the Admiralty who presides, two or three justices, one or two Merchant men not the least acquainted with law or the form of it Their Commission is during the session and renewed every year They have no salaries and therefore

Gardner says the magistrates were well aware of Foreham's condition of mind He was a man of means, and therefore a good subject to be mulcted

we may suppose make the most of their places. The expense of the most trifling cause is commonly £20 and the poor wretches by paying it feel much misery and distress. The six persons usually on the Bench on these occasions with the sheriff have each two guineas for every trial. The clerks, gaolers, and constables' fees make up the rest; so that rather than be at so heavy an expense to prosecute, the culprit often goes without punishment."

The final result of all this cruelty and injustice was to create a terrible feeling of indignation against the courts. I have mentioned before that their constitution was illegal. Governor Edwards, after his return from Newfoundland, was sued at Exeter. The presiding judge, unwilling to have his Excellency's judgment exposed and his illegal proceedings published to the world, suggested a compromise. This case made the governors more cautious; they never took part again in open court. The final change came about in rather a curious way.

JOHN REEVES.
From an engraving after Drummond.

Admiral Mark Milbanke,[1] who entered on the government of Newfoundland in 1789, was advised by his admirable secretary, Aaron Graham, to create a court of common pleas, with regular judges, instead of justices of the peace. It was a fortunate mistake, as it led to a more careful investigation and inspection of our judicial system by the House of Commons. Grievous complaints were made by the merchants against Sir Mark's new tribunal. Finally, in 1791, the House of Commons passed an Act—31 Geo. III. c. xxix.—creating a court designated "The Court of Civil Jurisdiction of our Lord the King at St. John's, in the Island of Newfoundland." This was presided

[1] Mark Milbanke, the third son of Sir Ralph Milbanke, of Halnaby, Yorkshire, entered the Navy in 1736 as a scholar at Portsmouth. After serving in various ships without seeing much service, he was sent in 1759, in the *Guernsey*, on a mission to the Emperor of Morocco. He sat on the Keppel court-martial; was made rear-admiral of the White in 1779. During the following years he occasionally acted in place of Admiral Shuldham as commander-in-chief at Plymouth. In 1782 he held a command in the grand fleet under Lord Howe, with whom he took part in the demonstration in the North Sea, the relief of Gibraltar, and the action off Cape Spartel. From 1783 to 1786 he was port admiral at Plymouth, and 1790–1–2 Governor of Newfoundland. He was commander-in-chief at Portsmouth, 1799 to 1803, but had no active command during the war. He died in 1805.—(STEPHEN'S *Nat. Dict. of Biography.*)

over by Chief Justice Reeves,[1] and was only to continue for one year next year it was properly set forth by 32 Geo III c xlvi., as "The Supreme Court of Judicature of the Island of Newfoundland." It was also only for one year, but was continued annually until 1809. John Reeves, again made Chief Justice, had been law adviser to the Board of Trade; he was an admirable official—industrious, painstaking, firm, and resolutely impartial, the whole reformation in our judicial system is due to him, Aaron Graham,[2] and Admiral Mark Milbanke [3]

It was a terribly up-hill struggle, the West Country merchants fought as resolutely against the courts as they had formerly done against the

---

[1] Chief Justice Reeves, to whose high qualities I have endeavoured to do justice, shows in one of his judgments that, even under his able administration, the quality of mercy was not strained. He tried some fishermen for taking eggs at the Funk Islands, which was forbidden by Proclamation, it was proved that one of the culprits, Clarke, lived at Greenspond, he was in want of food for his family, and the eggs were taken solely to obtain some for his wife and children Whilst sentencing the other prisoners to be *publicly* whipped, he solemnly ordered that, out of regard to these mitigating circumstances in Clarke's case, he was only to be *privately* flogged We do not think this unfortunate victim of a cruel law appreciated the distinction.

[2] Aaron Graham had been secretary to the two former governors, to his advocacy we are largely indebted for our courts of justice, and every improvement in their administration. He was a most able and enlightened official, and, as Coghlan truly says, was the virtual governor of the Colony He afterwards filled the important position of police magistrate in London

THE FORMATION OF THE SUPREME COURT

Whitehall, 22nd March, 1794

MY LORDS,

I am to inform your Lordships that in the sessions of Parliament of 1791, 1792 and 1793, there were passed the annual Acts for instituting Courts of Judicature in Newfoundland (Stat 31 Geo III cap xxix., 32 Geo III c xlvi and 33 Geo III c. lxxvi.).

Under the first of these Acts, His Majesty was pleased by the authority thereby vested in him, to appoint Mr Reeves Chief Judge of the said island, and the Governor of the said island, in conjunction with Mr Reeves, under the authority vested in them by the said Act, appointed Mr. Aaron Graham, the Governor's secretary, and Mr D'Lws Coke, a magistrate resident in the said island to be assessors in the said Court

Mr Reeves accordingly proceeded to Newfoundland, and there, with the assistance of those two gentlemen, discharged the duties of his office and returned back to England.

In the year 1792 His Majesty was pleased by virtue of the power vested in him by the second of the said Acts to appoint Mr. Reeves Chief Justice, and that gentleman did accordingly a second time proceed to Newfoundland, and return back to this kingdom In this second Act there was no direction as to appointing any assessors

In the last session of Parliament, His Majesty was in like manner again authorized to appoint a Chief Justice and he was pleased to appoint the before mentioned D'Ewes Coke to be Chief Justice in the court established by the third of the said Acts For the trouble these gentlemen have had in discharging the duties of their respective offices, I am of opinion they should be paid the following sums, viz —

For the first year, Mr Reeves, £500, Mr. Graham, £200, Mr Coke, £200.

For the second year, Mr Reeves, £500

For the third year, Mr Coke, £300

By the first of the before-mentioned Acts of Parliament, the Governor and the Chief Justice are authorized to settle the allowance to be made to the assessors, and they have recommended the above sums as reasonable compensation The Governor and Chief Justice have also authority under all the acts to settle what should be paid to the clerks for their trouble, and it has been agreed by them as follows —

For the first year, to the first clerk, £40, to the second clerk, £25

For the second year to the clerk, £40.

For the third year, £40

It has been found since the first year that one clerk is sufficient to conduct the business These salaries were to be allowed in lieu of all fees or emoluments whatsoever.

I am, &c

HENRY DUNDAS

Lords Commissioners of the Treasury

settlers The two most determined antagonists were Mr Peter Ougier, a Devonshire merchant in Bay Bulls, and Mr William Newman of Dartmouth As a sample of their reasonable proposals, I will quote one case only. Judgment was given against a merchant on a bill of exchange for £12 for a servant's wages ; the defendant would not pay, on the ground that the bill was endorsed by a marksman The court, holding the endorsement good, gave judgment accordingly, and, as the merchant's agent would not pay, execution had to issue The defendant considered himself most cruelly ill-treated because the Privy Council, on his urgent appeal, refused to send home, as prisoners to England, the judges, the sheriff, and all officers of the court concerned in the transaction Reeves, by his firmness, courtesy, and resolute impartiality, finally triumphed over all opposition ; it was, however, a very long time before things quieted down

The records of the first courts, in the beautiful handwriting of the Chief Justice, are still preserved Besides his well-known " History of Newfoundland " we have his voluminous evidence given before the House of Commons Committee, and a treatise on the new court. Reeves was succeeded in 1792 by D'Ewes Coke. He had settled in Trinity as a surgeon , to eke out his small income as a doctor he had acted as a scrivener, justice of the peace, and keeper of rolls. From Trinity he migrated to St John's, became chief judge, and, later on, assessor with Aaron Graham in the first court of 1791. D'Ewes Coke continued to preside in the Supreme Court as Lord Chief Justice until 1797, when he was succeeded by Richard Routh, Collector of the Customs—a man of considerable ability, and firm, determined character.

The Governors required the Chief Justices to reside in the Colony. Routh prayed the Governor very earnestly that this rule might be relaxed on his behalf for one season (1800), which was granted , the vessel on her passage home was lost with all hands His widow was allowed a pension for several years afterwards. D'Ewes Coke had only £300 a year, but I think his successors had £500 During 1801 no Chief Justice was appointed, but in 1802 Jonathan Ogden was made Acting Chief Justice. He had been Supreme Surrogate and Deputy Naval Officer under Richard Hatt Noble, Naval Officer, who was allowed to remain in England and execute the office by deputy, a common practice in the Georgian era Jonathan Ogden had been sent out as a surgeon's mate to the St John's Hospital ; he seems only to have occupied the position for a short time, and appears to have been a man of sound judgment, on whom the Governor placed great reliance. After two doctors and a collector, the next Chief Justice was a merchant, Thomas Tremlett, or

Tremlett His firm had been very large Newfoundland merchants, they came to grief through some outside speculation, and, in accordance with the custom of the country, he received a Government office There never was a more independent, upright judge than Tremlett, his decisions gave great offence to his quondam friends in the trade They made constant complaints against him, finally they embodied their grievances in a long, elaborate petition containing three specific charges of injustice. The Governor, Admiral Duckworth, furnished the old chief with the complaints against him. His reply was unique.[1] I give it in full.—

"To the first charge Your Excellency I answer that it is a lie, to the second charge I say that it is a d——d lie, and to the third charge that it is a d——d infernal lie, and Your Excellency I have no more to say. Your Excellency's obt. Servant

"THOMAS TREMLETT"

Tremlett was sustained in his position both by the Governor and the authorities in England[2] It was, however, considered desirable that a man of more legal knowledge, of more popular manners, and unconnected with local interests, should be appointed. His Lordship was therefore transferred to Prince Edward's Island. The choice next fell upon an eccentric Irish gentleman of good family, Cæsar Colclough, who was Chief Justice of that Island. Tremlett was the last of the unlearned,

---

[1] Of course, besides this letter, there was a formal official one from Tremlett.

[2] DESPATCH OF GOVERNOR SIR J T DUCKWORTH ON THE CHARGES AGAINST CHIEF JUSTICE TREMLETT

" The chief justice of Newfoundland, as far as my intercourse with him has enabled me to judge, is a person who will not be influenced in the discharge of his duty by the approbation or disapprobation of any man. Of his legal knowledge I can form no opinion, but of his abilities I am far from thinking poorly, and a salary of seven hundred pounds a year is not likely to induce a more competent person to accept the office He is certainly a man of great diligence and application, but he has by an irritability of temper, and a certain rudeness of manner which are natural to him, and by separating himself entirely from the society of the people of the town, rendered himself in the last degree unpopular, and however circumspect his future conduct may be in the discharge of his public duties, he will never be approved by them. How far, in the cases now under discussion, he may have been to blame, it is extremely difficult for me to know. They occurred chiefly before I came to the Government and there is scarcely any person

capable of giving information relative to them who is not influenced in some measure by a feeling of party. The complainants are urgent for a *public examination* of evidence upon the spot, alleging that they are not equal to a discussion with the chief justice on *paper*; that his representations are filled with falsehood, and that there is no other method of proceeding effectually than that of a public enquiry at which they may be able to bring forward their witnesses upon oath. Your lordship will perceive from my correspondence with the complainants that they reserve to themselves to transmit additional statements. I have shown to them the defence of the chief justice which is enclosed herewith, and they aver that it is filled with misrepresentation If your lordship or the Lords of the Committee of Council should be pleased to require from me more minute information in this matter, I beg to be honoured with your commands, but it is my duty to state distinctly in this report that in whatever instances his judgement may have erred, I have not found in any part of the chief justice's conduct the most remote appearance of corruption, nor when I have called upon the complainants, have they ventured to charge him with it in any instance As your lordship will perceive that the accompanying statements are not of

subsequently the head of the Supreme Court was a barrister of not less
than seven years' standing.

Vice-Admiral John Campbell was Governor from 1782 to 1785,
he appears to have been an able and enlightened ruler [1] John Jones,
a dissenting preacher, who founded Congregationalism in the Colony
in 1782, gives a pleasing picture of his Excellency, "as beyond all
expression gentle, mild, and good-natured" In 1784 he issued the

a nature to admit of my sending duplicates to
the Lords of the Committee of Privy Council
for Trade, I take the liberty of requesting
that they may be forwarded when your lordship has done with them.

"I have the honour to be very respectfully
"My Lord,
"Your Lordship's
"Most obedient humble servant,
"J T. DUCKWORTH.
"To the Earl of Liverpool."

REPORT BY THE LORDS OF THE COM-
MITTEE OF COUNCIL FOR TRADE AND
FOREIGN PLANTATIONS

Downing Street, 13 June, 1812

"Referring to papers sent on 28 October
1811 of complaints preferred by the Merchants of St John's against the Chief Justice
of Newfoundland   .   .   .

"Their Lordships have averted in the
first instance to the charge made against
John Reeves Esq , late Chief Justice 'that he
had for several years together participated
in the salary of the Chief Justice after he
had ceased to fill that situation   ,

"Their Lordships say that they have no
reason to doubt the truth of Mr. Reeves'
declaration that he has never received any
money or money's worth in consideration of
the office of Chief Justice of Newfoundland
or any office place or thing relating to
Newfoundland

"After a full enquiry and deliberation it
does not appear that any act of wilful injustice has been sanctioned by Chief Justice
Tremlett nor is there any well attested proof
of partiality or oppression or of any un-
accountable delay or unwarrantable decision

"Under these circumstances their Lordships have not recommended His Royal
Highness to dismiss the Chief Justice from
the high and important situation which he
fills and H R.H is therefore pleased to
continue to confide to him the charge of
administering justice in the Island of
Newfoundland

"BATHURST

[In a separate paper]

"Their Lordships attribute the un-
popularity of the Chief Justice not to any
actual misconduct in his judicial capacity but
in some degree to the invidious nature of the
duties which he is called upon to execute
as well as to the peculiar nature of

which they may be occasionally performed
Although there may have existed no ground
for serious complaint and still less for any
charge of partiality or corruption there can
however be little doubt that whilst the Chief
Justice is continued in his present situation
there will not be that general satisfaction
and confidence which ought in all cases to
accompany the administration of justice ,
and although H R.H will on no account
consent to the dismissal of the Chief Justice
or to any act which might imply the least
suspicion of his integrity or even any disapprobation of his past conduct H R H
would nevertheless be desirous that some
arrangement should be made by which
Mr Tremlett might be employed with less
embarrassment and inconvenience to himself
and with greater prospect of advantage to
the public service   .   .   .

"Should an opportunity offer of placing
Mr Tremlett in a judicial situation of equal
emolument in some other settlement he will
not object to transfer his services from that
which he now fills "

Witnesses to be sworn against the Chief
Justice—

JOHN BLAND, High Sheriff	JOHN BURKE, cooper
GEO. LILLY, auctioneer	CHRISTOPHER BROOM
PATK. BRAZILL, cooper	

[1] John Campbell, the son of a minister of
Kirkbean, in Kirkcudbrightshire, was born in
that parish about, but probably before, the
year 1720 At an early age he was bound
apprentice to the master of a coasting vessel,
and is said to have entered the Navy by
offering himself in exchange for the mate of
this vessel, who had been pressed After
serving three years in the *Blenheim, Torbay,*
and *Russell*, he was, in 1740, appointed to
the *Centurion,* and sailed in her round the
world with Commodore Anson, as midshipman, master's mate, and master On his
return home he passed the examination for
lieutenant, and his certificate, dated 8th
January 1744-5, says that he appears to be
more than 24 years of age Through Anson's
interest he was very shortly afterwards
made a lieutenant, then commander, and
was advanced to post rank on the 23rd of
November 1747, and appointed to the
Bellona which he commanded with

following order, which stands in pleasing contrast to the proclamations
of his predecessors :—

"Pursuant to the King's instructions to me you are to allow all persons
inhabiting this Island to have full liberty of conscience and the free exercise of all
such modes of religious worship as are not prohibited by law, provided they be
contented with a quiet and peaceable enjoyment of the same, not giving offence or
scandal to Government

"Jno Campbell"

Under the benign sway of this excellent Governor the first
Roman Catholic chapel was built in this year, on the site known in
St. John's as the "old chapel," then called " Parson Langman's garden."
Bishop O'Donel came to the Colony first as Prefect-Apostolic, with
power to administer confirmation, on the 5th of January 1796 he was
appointed Vicar Apostolic of Newfoundland, and Bishop of Thyatira
in partibus. Bishop O'Donel's name is one of the most honoured in
this Colony; his deeply religious character, his polished manners, and
his inherent gentleness and goodness won all hearts. He had to overcome terrible obstacles—the prejudice and opposition of the strait-laced
old admiral, Milbanke, and the rampant Protestantism of his surrogate

Bishop O'Donel's career deserves every attention at the hands of
the local historian His arrival and his sojourn in the Colony are
of far more importance to us than the advent of half-a-dozen admiral-
governors He brought peace, quiet, and good order, instead of
silenced priests there was an authorised ecclesiastical organisation, an
open administration of the rites of the church The fugitive priests,
by their example and teaching, were not conducive to harmony In
fulfilment of the divine injunction to render to Cæsar the things that
are Cæsar's, Dr. O'Donel taught his people to be good Christians and
good citizens. I quote from Bishop Howley an extract from the body of

some success till the peace. He afterwards
commanded the *Mermaid,* in 1755, the
Prince, of 90 guns, and in 1757 the *Essex,*
of 64 guns, and was flag captain to Sir
Edward Hawke in 1759 in the *Royal George,*
and served in that capacity in the decisive
battle of Quiberon Bay, 20th November 1759.
Campbell was sent home with the despatches,
and was taken by Anson to be presented to
the king According to the received story,
Anson told him, on the way, that the king
would knight him if he wished. "Troth, my
lord," answered Campbell, "I ken nae use
that will be to me" "But," said Anson,
"your lady may like it" "Aweel," replied
Campbell, "His Majesty may knight her if
he pleases" He was, in fact, not knighted.
He afterwards commanded the *Dorsetshire,*
of 70 guns, till the peace, and in 1776 he was
in the *Royal Charlotte,* in which he remained

till promoted to his flag in 1778. In the
following spring he was chosen by Admiral
Keppel as first captain of the *Victory,* and
had thus an important share in the conduct
of the fleet in the indecisive action with the
French fleet under D'Orvilliers, on the 27th of
July, as well as on the previous days His
loyalty to Keppel, and the rancour which the
subsequent courts-martial excited, prevented
his having any further employment as long
as Lord Sandwich was in office, though he
attained, in course of seniority, the rank of
vice-admiral in 1779 In April 1782, when
his friend Keppel was installed as First Lord
of the Admiralty, Campbell was appointed
Governor of Newfoundland and commander-
in-chief on that station He held this office
for four years, and ended his service in 1786
He died in London on the 16th of December,
1790

the Diocesan Statutes of 1801 for the guidance of priests in the Colony, prepared by Bishop O'Donel. He directed :—

"That public prayers be offered up every Sunday and holiday (though but few of the latter can be observed in this Mission, and the Superior will hereafter, by a private notice, designate such as can be observed) for our Most Sovereign King George III and his Royal family ; that the priests should use every means to turn aside their flocks from the vortex of modern anarchy ; that they should inculcate a willing obedience to the salutary laws of England, and to the commands of the Governor and magistrates of this Island.   .   . We most earnestly entreat, and by all the spiritual authority we hold, ordain that all missioners oppose with all the means in their power all plotters, conspirators, and favorers of the infidel French, and use every endeavour to withdraw their people from the plausible cajolery of French deceit, for the aim of this conspiracy is to dissolve all bonds, all laws, by which society is held together, and more especially the laws of England, which are to be preferred to those of any other country in Europe "

The patriotic services of Bishop O'Donel at the particular crisis of the French Revolution, when rebellion and anarchy were rampant, his especial service in putting an end to the conspiracy amongst the soldiers and United Irishmen to murder the whole population of St John's,[1] the dangers he voluntarily encountered, the secret influence his deep religious fervour exercised over these poor ignorant dupes, are only known to the Omnipotent   Under such obligations, can we wonder that Protestant vied with Catholic to do him honour, and to show their love for one who, with Colonel Skerret, under Providence had been the saviour of their lives ?[2]

In recognition of his loyal conduct he had a pension from the Crown of £50 a year, it was only obtained after much petitioning and persistent application by the Governors, especially Waldegrave ; everyone must agree with Bishop Mullock, that he was very poorly rewarded. A friendship existed not only amongst the Catholic and the Protestant laity, but also between Father Yore and the Church of England minister, Parson Dingle.   The following letter shows, however, that all the priests were not of the same amicable disposition as their gentle chief pastor —

" Sir,   St. Johns 19 Oct. 1785
    " Mr. WILLIAM SAUNDERS having represented to me that there is a Romish Priest named Landergan at Placentia of a very violent and turbulent spirit, who

---

[1] See the letter on this subject from Chief Justice Ogden to Governor Waldegrave, in the Appendix, p 418

[2] In a petition to the King from Bishop O'Donel, praying for a continuation of his pension after his retirement from the Island, he declares " that his own loyalty and services have been acknowledged and fully approved of by every Governor and particularly by General Skerret who found himself under great embarrassment in 1799 as having no force either by sea or land to oppose a most dangerous conspiracy formed against all the people of property in the Island Petitioner was fortunate enough to bring the maddened scum of the people to cool reflection and dispersed the dangerous cloud that was ready to burst on the heads of the principal Inhabitants of this Town and even of the whole Island for which he often received the thanks of the very deluded people who were led into this dark design of robbery and assassination

has given great interruption to Mr. Burk, a regular and sober man of the Catholick persuasion, and that unless the former is sent out of the Country the peace of the place is in imminent danger of being disturbed—I desire that you will cause the said Landergan to be put aboard the first vessel that may sail from Placentia for England or Ireland.

" JNO. CAMPBELL.

" H.M. Justices of the Peace at Placentia."

The toleration shown to the Roman Catholic Church had great influence on the permanent settlement of the Colony. The country boys who came out from Ireland were full of the earth hunger which distinguishes their race; they cherished the little spots of land they cleared and cultivated; the best farms around the capital are the work of either West Countrymen or Irishmen; to these two classes of settlers we owe the good cultivation and picturesque homesteads around St. John's and Conception Bay.

It is impossible, in a history of this character, to give details about the various administrations of the twenty-three governors who ruled the Island during the long reign of George III.[1] Two events, however, require more than a passing notice—the arrival of Prince William Henry (afterwards William IV.) as captain of H.M.S. *Pegasus*, in 1786, and the last attack of the French, in 1796.

His Royal Highness, in accordance with the naval rule of the day, was appointed surrogate by his commanding officer, Governor Elliott.

PRINCE WILLIAM.
From an engraving after Holmes.

In his letters to the Governor, the Prince appears as an attentive, careful subordinate, most respectful towards his superior officer. Later on we have a very animated and lengthy correspondence between his younger brother, the Duke of Kent (father of Her Majesty), and Governor Waldegrave, who sternly refused to recognise the Duke's authority, as lieutenant-general of the forces in Nova Scotia, over the military in Newfoundland. " Your Royal Highness has no more control over me

---

[1] The appointment of each governor, and the principal events during his tenure of office, will be found in orderly sequence in the chronology in Chapter xxiii.

than you have over the Emperor of China," said the Governor of New-foundland.   The Duke was right, but still, all through the discussion His Royal Highness is most respectful in his language to our haughty ruler.

Our naval Royal Highness—the Duke of Clarence—was not a model prince, but he was very good natured, and a good friend to the Colony ; he ordered the building of the English church in Placentia (1787), contributed handsomely to its erection, and furnished the massive communion service, long in the custody of Dr. Bradshaw's family at Placentia.   He gave a commission to one of the Collins family, who afterwards became a lieutenant.[1]

FLAKES OVER THE ROAD AT QUIDI VIDI.
From a photograph by S. H. Parsons.

On the 20th of July 1786 a great event happened in Placentia ; on that memorable day His Royal Highness presided as surrogate in the noble court house of the ancient capital ; the justices showed their respect for the Protestant succession by issuing an order, " That no more Catholics should be buried in the graveyard."

One of his judicial decisions is given in the Records :—

" A riot happening on shore at 4 o'clock, the Magistrate attending to suppress it, was insulted.   The Prince came on shore with a guard of marines, arrested the ringleader, called a Court, and sentenced him to receive 100 lashes—he was only able to receive 80.   *Next day inquired into the facts of the case ;* (and report has it that they had whipped the *wrong man*)."

[1] The story goes that, in order to test the courage of . . . . occasions, the Prince made . . . . them a . . . . view with a stick.   Young Collins, a stolid strong fellow, never budged, and was accordingly chosen for His Majesty's service.

Many tales are told of his stay in Newfoundland. Mr. Warren, afterwards a partner in Stuart and Rennie, was going home under the flakes which covered the streets in those days ; he carried a lantern ; suddenly he had it seized from him by the Prince who walked before him until they arrived opposite to where his ship lay at anchor. His Royal Highness wished him good night and returned the lantern. A lieutenant's wife got her husband's company for him by presenting a Newfoundland wild goose. But the best is about an old gentleman, who had known the Prince well in Newfoundland, calling at Kensington Palace. His Majesty was delighted to see him, gave him a glass of calabogus, and talked pleasantly over a pipe. The Newfoundlander considered it the right thing to ask after the Queen's health. His Majesty said Queen Adelaide was quite well, and would have had much pleasure in seeing him, but unfortunately it was *washing day.*

Many other anecdotes are current in the Colony about our Royal visitor. One told by Bishop Howley, about his being fired at, is, apparently, a perversion of the well-known story of Sir John Harvey's son being shot by Mitchell, the butcher, for robbing his garden on Circular Road, and I cannot believe his account of the insults to Bishop O'Donel.

ADMIRAL SIR R. KING, BART.
From an engraving after Saunders.

The great and ominous events of the year 1789—the outbreak of the French Revolution, followed by the murder of Louis XVI. and Marie Antoinette in 1793—again brought on war between England and France. On the 14th of May, our Governor, Vice-Admiral King, took possession of St. Pierre.[1] A far more memorable event even than the arrival of His Royal Highness, is the last attack of the French on the Colony, under Admiral Richery in 1796 ; the story is told in the Colonial Records, but is more graphically described by

[1] An account of this capture will be found in the chapter devoted to the history of the French Newfoundland Colonies of St. Pierre and Miquelon.

Sir R. King, born in 1730, entered the service in 1738 on the *Berwick*, of which his father was master, but was soon moved to the *Dragon*, in command of his uncle, Curtis Barrett, whom he accompanied to the Mediterranean and the East Indies ; he became a lieutenant in 1746, and commanded the boats at the capture of Calcutta in 1757.

an eye-witness, quoted by the Rev P. Tocque   Mr. George Hutchings, grandfather of the present Mr George A Hutchings, rendered valuable service to the Colony by reconnoitring the movements of the invading fleet, he was specially distinguished by the Governor for his patriotic conduct.

In the mute testimony of the Records we can see the gallant old Admiral, Sir Richard Wallace, superintending, ruling, and managing everybody, the young merchants and gentlemen of the town vying with each other who should get guns and stores first up the long steep hill to the Block House, the careful watch and reports of the various parties sent along the coast from Cape Spear to Cape Race   No country has produced more gallant soldiers and sailors than fair France; Citizen Richery was not one of them, with his big fleet he never dared to come in contact with Wallace[1] and his hastily improvised levies.   I quote the Rev. P Tocque's account of the attack —

"1794. Estimates had been prepared and approved of for repairing and improving the existing defences, and plans had also been submitted to the Board of Ordnance for fortifying Signal Hill, which having met the approbation of the Honourable Board, preparations were entered into for that object proportionate to the magnitude of the undertaking   Early this summer, Colonel Skinner, Commanding Royal Engineer, received a letter of service directing him to raise a Regiment of Fencible Infantry, to be called the Royal Newfoundland Fencibles, of which he was appointed Colonel; and having the appointment of his officers, selections were made here and at the out-ports, of such gentlemen as were likely, from their loyalty, responsibility and influence, soon to raise the quotas of men required for their respective commissions.   The recruiting service commenced with great spirit about the latter end of September, at the close of the fishery, and in two months more than half the number were enlisted   An Adjutant, late a non-commissioned officer of the Royal Artillery, a Quartermaster, and Sergeant-major, arrived from England.

"1795 It has been stated that the Nova Scotia Regiment was chiefly formed of old refugee soldiers from the American Army, many of whom were well disciplined non commissioned officers, and were of great service in drilling and forming the young recruits of the Royal Newfoundland Regiment, and it was

He saw some service on the home station in 1760, and in 1762 went with General Draper to the East Indies again, took part in the Manila expedition, and assisted Captain Parker in the capture of a rich Spanish galleon, his personal share of prize money amounting to £30,000.   After various services he was again in the East Indies in 1779 in the *Exeter*, and was made an established commodore and second-in-command to Sir E. Hughes   In the action off Sadras in February 1782, the *Exeter* received the whole brunt of the French attack, King's flag captain being killed by his side, and his ship dismasted, asked what was to be done, he replied, "Nothing but to fight her till she

sinks"   King took part in the four actions between Hughes and Suffren, and the *Exeter* became so unseaworthy that she was condemned at the Cape   King was knighted on his return to England, and became rear-admiral in 1787, he was made a baronet in 1792, and after his return from Newfoundland was elected M P for Rochester   He became a full admiral in 1795, and died in 1806.— (Stephen's *Nat. Dict of Biog*)

[1] The existing memorial of Sir James Wallace is the pointed rock often called Crow's Nest but properly named Wallace's Battery, it is being gradually destroyed— being used by speculators as a stone quarry

astonishing how soon the latter became fit for duty; when this service was performed the Nova Scotia Regiment were ordered to return to Halifax.

"In the meantime some buildings were erected at Signal Hill, and the first block-house commenced . . . . There being no carriage road to Signal Hill, all the guns required for the Hill were taken by men of the garrison, and parbuckled up the face of the rock at Crow's Nest, and thence to the respective batteries—a most laborious and dangerous service.

"Preparations for the more effectual defence of the Narrows were also going on, in the formation of three furnaces for heating shot, viz.: At Fort Frederick, Chain Rock, and Fort William. A large naval force from different stations met here that summer, consisting of the *Monarch* (74), the Governor's ship the *Ramilies* (74), the *Adamant*, and another 50; four frigates, and three sloops of war, all in the harbour at the same time.

"1796. The levy of the Royal Newfoundland Regiment had been completed the preceding fall; and it was found that the barracks at Forts Townsend and William were insufficient to contain so many men; it was therefore ordered that

PART OF ST. JOHN'S HARBOUR NEWFOUNDLAND FROM ABOVE THE LONG BRIDGE, AT RIVER HEAD. WITH SIGNAL HILL AND THE CROWS NEST.

London, Published by H Colburn C.t Marlborough Street 1842

the garrison should go under canvas for a few months while the old barracks were being repaired and cleansed, and some of the new barracks at Signal Hill finished, and also for the greater facility of practising the officers and men of that young regiment in the indispensable tactics and operations of the field. A camp was accordingly formed on the general parade ground with a small park of artillery, of which the troops took possession about the middle of June. The improved defences of the Narrows being finished, some experiments were tried with heated shot before His Excellency Admiral Sir James Wallace, the Governor, which gave general satisfaction. A large platform of wood was built on South Point called the Duke of York's Battery, on which were mounted eight 24-pounder guns, three or four 18-pounder carronades, and two 10-inch mortars. The Block-house was so forward as to admit six guns to be mounted on the second floor. The regiment by this time—the latter part of August—was approaching fast to systematic regularity and discipline, and of approved internal economy.

A A

" Such being the state of the garrison and fortifications, together with the efficiency of the volunteer companies—a fine set of men particularly the company of volunteer artillery selected from among the flower of the Inhabitants of St. John's—as well as the undoubted loyalty of the Inhabitants, a wish seemed to be inspired that something might happen to test the fidelity of the whole. If such was the case it was not long before that wish was realised, for early in the morning of the first day of September the signal was made for an enemy's fleet to the Southward, which proved to be the French Admiral with seven sail of the line, two frigates and some other small vessels of war. The signal of alarm in the town was instantly made at Signal Hill and all the forts. There was only the Governor's ship and one frigate in Port [The Governor's own report says there was one fifty-gun ship, two frigates, and a sloop of war.] His Excellency Admiral Sir James Wallace,[1] a Governor of warlike celebrity, immediately proclaimed martial law and ordered all the men in the town fit for service—merchants with their domestic and wharf establishments, Captains of vessels with their crews, planters with their fishermen and sharemen—to muster in front of the camp where they were enrolled and told off to the forts and batteries and they were not to be dismissed until the Governor's pleasure was known.

" The enemy stood off and on near Cape Spear all that day and during the night the road was open from Magotty Cove Bridge through the enclosures leading to Signal Hill, by direction of the Governor, in order to expedite the transport of ammunition, stores, and provisions to Signal Hill, as well as the camp equipage, which had been struck in the evening, and by daylight in the morning of the 2nd the tents were all pitched on the summit of the Hill—from the Duke of York's battery to Cuckold Head and also on the south side Hills over Fort Amherst. This warlike demonstration with the display of three or four thousand men on the Hill must have had a very intimidating effect on Monsieur when viewed from the sea.

" This day passed off under something like a passive hesitation on the part of the enemy a great deal of telegraphing and boat communication took place with the flagship and towards the evening the fleet stood a little further off to sea, reconnoitring parties were out along the shore day and night in anticipation of a landing being effected. A great many seamen were employed that day in raising the chain across the Narrows, the great capstan at the south side being assisted by three schooners placed at equal distances from Chain Rock and by grappling the chain with their anchors and heaving all together they raised it to the surface of the water. These vessels were also charged with combustibles and were intended

[1] The first notice of Wallace is his command of the *Trial* sloop in 1763, on the Newfoundland station; in 1774 he was again on this station, in the *Rose* (20). He was sent by Admiral Shuldham from St John's to Boston, with a detachment of the 65th Regiment. An armed mob having seized cannon and ammunition in Fort George, Newport, and carried them to Providence, he demanded to know why the Governor had allowed the fort to be dismantled. The reply was "To prevent them falling into the hands of the King's servant, and to make use of them against any Power that shall molest us." Wallace was in many of the engagements in 1775-6-7-8 at Rhode Island and New York. He very gallantly repulsed the French squadron sent to take the Channel Islands in 1779, and went with Admiral Darby to the relief of Gibraltar in 1781. His attack upon a French 74 in this same year is one of the most brilliant examples of British valour and perseverance. He was soon appointed to the *Warrior* (74), in 1793 became colonel of marines; in 1794 Rear-Admiral of the White, and to command at Newfoundland; and in 1795 Vice-Admiral of the White. For his exertions to repel Admiral Richery, he was voted the sincere and heartfelt thanks of the merchants of St John's. He undertook no further service after retiring from the Newfoundland command, and died in 1803. He was knighted in 1777. His services during the American War were very brilliant, but, in spite of his abilities and worth, he did not receive the degree of attention and reward he was entitled to.—(From ROLFE's *Naval Biography*, vol 1, p. 413.)

to be used as fire ships on the enemy coming in contact with the chain. The flag ship and the frigate were also placed in enfilading distances in the Harbour to give them a warm reception on entering the Narrows. On the first appearance of the enemy the shot furnaces were kindled, it was found difficult however to preserve the proper degree of heat and to prevent fusion which happened to some of the shot.

"On the 3d. the enemy formed a line and stood in for the Narrows, when it was expected their intention was to attempt a landing; they stood on until the van ships came within the extreme range of the guns of Fort Amherst, when she and all of them put about and stood out to sea. They remained in sight for several days and at last bore away to the southward and arrived at Bay Bulls where they landed and to consummate their dastardly conduct, they drove the poor defenceless inhabitants to the woods."

In the words of the local poet of the southern shore—

> " Burnt their stores and houses,
>   Took their fish and oil,
>   The hard-earned produce
>   Of their yearly toil."

Thus terminated the great excitement occasioned by the appearance of this formidable armament. The detachments at the respective posts were all continued until the French fleet had entirely left the coast. Only one man and a boy were allowed on each merchant's establishment, all the rest were stationed at the forts and batteries. The enemy remained in Bay Bulls from the 4th to the 8th. On the 5th they set the town on fire; on the 6th a gale of wind came and prevented their further progress; on the 8th they unmoored and left. Their further exploits were to destroy what remained of St. Pierre— then in possession of the English; they also burnt some fishing rooms in the straits of Belle Isle. In Bay Bulls the French captured a couple of merchant vessels, and Mr. Dingle,

MILITARY COSTUME.
From B.M. MS., 33,321.

the magistrate. One captain was brought on board of Admiral Richery's flag ship, the *Jupiter*. When asked about the strength of St. John's, he lied "like an ambassador for the good of his country"; he said there were five thousand troops; that they could not enter St. John's on account of the boom and chain, and that two hundred guns would play on them if they came in. The French seemed to doubt the number of troops, but on his boldly repeating his statement the Admiral gave up the idea of attacking the town.

The French Republican newspapers gave a flaming account of Richery's great warlike exploit; that he had landed fifteen hundred men at Bay Bulls, two thousand at Portugal Cove, and had captured a large number of ships and fishing vessels and a thousand sailors, which had been sent to St. Domingo.

The Honourable William Waldegrave [1]—the last naval Governor in the eighteenth century, 1797-8-9—was a son of the Earl of Waldegrave. No administrator of the Colony, with the exception of Palliser, did more for the island. He had greatly distinguished himself as a dashing captain of a frigate and as admiral. The period of his government was a very troubled one, the mutiny of the Nore extending even to Newfoundland. A rebellion broke out on board H.M.S. *Latona*, and was only quelled by the officers drawing their swords and the marines presenting their bayonets — they actually had to prick the mutineers before they would give in. In his address to the ship's crew on the following Sunday the Admiral told them : —

LORD RADSTOCK.
From an engraving after Hayter.

" You are all eager for news and newspapers. I thank God I have the satisfaction to inform you that your great delegate Parker is hanged, with many other of his atrocious companions. You looked up to him as an example whilst he was

---

[1] William Waldegrave, first Lord Radstock, G.C.B., born 9th July 1753, was second son of John, third Earl of Waldegrave (by Elizabeth Gower, sister of Granville, first Marquess of Stafford, K.G.); entered the Navy about 1766. As early as 1775 he obtained command of the *Zephyr* sloop, and was shortly afterwards—May 30th, 1766—posted into the *Ripon*, 60, bearing the broad pennant of Sir Edward Vernon, in the East Indies. He afterwards commanded the *Pomone*, 28, in which ship he captured the *Cumberland*, a notorious American

privateer of 20 guns and 170 men ; and in the *Prudente*, 38 — aided to some extent by the *Licorne*, 32—he succeeded in capturing —4th July 1780—the French frigate *La Capricieuse* of 32 guns and 308 men, more than 100 of whom, in the course of an obstinate engagement of four hours, were either killed or wounded, with a loss to the *Prudente* of 17 killed and 28 wounded ; he afterwards, in the same ship, took *L'Américaine* privateer of 32 guns and 245 men. He accompanied Admiral Darby to the relief of Gibraltar, and assisted under Admiral

in his glory, I recommend you to look to his end as an example also. . . . .
. . . . I have now to tell you that I have given orders to all your officers, that
in case of any further signs of mutiny they are not to think of confining the ringleaders, but to put them to death instantly, and what is still more, I have given
orders to the batteries to burn the *Latona* with red-hot shot in case you drive me
by your mutinous conduct to that extremity   I know in this case the officers must
perish with you, but there is not one of them but is ready to sacrifice himself for the
good of his country in any mode whatever . . . . And now go to
church and pray God to inspire you with such sentiments as may acquire you the
respect and love of your Countrymen in this World and eternal happiness in the
next."

The fire-eating old sailor who made this address was most sincerely
religious, and, in private life, the kindest and most benevolent of men ;
he looked carefully after the food and comfort of the soldiers and
sailors organised a society for the relief of the poor in St. John's, and
was all his life a permanent subscriber of £20 annually to this fund
It was mainly through his exertions that the old Anglican church in
St John's was thoroughly repaired and improved : it had fallen into such
a dilapidated condition that it could not be used, and divine service had
to be held every Sunday in the court house   Through Waldegrave's
active exertions over £1,500 was obtained from the king, the Society
for the Propagation of the Gospel, and private friends.—His Excellency
being the most liberal subscriber of all.   He exerted himself also to
increase the miserable salaries of the clergymen in the Colony.   Bishop
O'Donel, and all who came in contact with the Admiral, pay a warm
tribute to his fine character .   It was very fortunate for our island that
in such troublous times as the Irish rebellion, the conspiracy in
St. John's, and the mutiny of the *Latona*, the Government was in the
hands of a ruler at once so benevolent, so just, and above all so
courageous.

Kempenfeldt in capturing part of a French
convoy under M. De Guichen, and obtained
possession of another privateer, the *Boulogne*,
of 16 guns   During the subsequent peace,
Captain Waldegrave, with the exception of a
short period in command of the *Majestic*, 74,
was on half-pay. In 1793, on the commencement of the French revolutionary war, he
was appointed to the command of the
Courageux, 74, when he served under Lord
Hood in the Mediterranean   He was
nominated a colonel of marines on 11th of
April 1794, and was advanced the 4th of
July following to the rank of rear-admiral,
and on the 1st June 1795 was made a vice-
admiral.   In the spring of 1796 he was sent
with five ships of the line to conduct a
negotiation of great delicacy with the Bey
of Tunis. Subsequently he fought as third

in command in Sir John Jervis' victory over
the Spanish fleet off Cape St Vincent,
February 14th, 1797   For his cool, steady,
and meritorious conduct on that memorable
occasion, he was offered a baronetcy, which
he declined, as being inferior to the rank of
an earl's son. He was shortly afterwards
appointed Governor of Newfoundland, where
he remained for three years, and on the 29th
of December 1800 was raised to the peerage
of Ireland as Baron Radstock of Castle Town,
Queen's County   In April 1802 he became a
full admiral   About the same period he was
nominated commander-in-chief in the East
Indies, but in consequence of the cessation of
hostilities he did not accept the appointment
He was created a G C B. in 1815, and died
on the 20th August 1825

The opening years of the present century were peaceful and uneventful in our island Colony; the fisheries were successful, the country prosperous. After the dangerous conspiracy of the United Irishmen had been put down with a strong hand, and the mutiny on board the *Latona* quelled by the firmness and severity of Waldegrave, the magistrates report to the new Governor for 1800—Vice-Admiral Charles Morice Pole [1]—"that peace and good order prevail both in the city and the Colony." Next year there was neither Governor nor

ADMIRAL SIR C. M. POLE, BART.
From an engraving after Northcote.

Chief Justice. Admiral Pole never returned to the Colony, and poor Routh was drowned on the passage home in November; Newfoundland, however, does not appear to have felt their loss. Later on, at the end of the summer, Doctor J. Ogden [2] was made Acting Chief Justice, and Captain Robert Barton, of H.M.S. *La Concorde*, Lieut.-Governor. Barton gave himself more airs and assumed more authority than a duly commissioned administrator. His presumption caused a little friction with Brigadier-General Skerrett, an old campaigner, with six hundred troops under his command, who could not brook being ordered about by a young captain in the Navy. The magistrates for St. John's—Ogden, Rev. J. Harris, and George Williams,

---

[1] Sir C. M. Pole, born in 1757, entered the Royal Naval Academy, Portsmouth, in 1770; was a lieutenant in the commodore's ship in the action with the French off Tranjolly, and commanded a body of seamen and marines at the siege of Pondicherry; on the surrender of that place he was made master of the *Cormorant* sloop; he became post-captain in 1779. He gallantly captured a large Spanish frigate, the *Santa Catalina*, in 1782, for which he was praised by Nelson, who wrote: "In seamanship he showed himself as superior to the Don as in gallantry"; "never was a young man who bore his own merits with so much modesty." In 1788 he he was made a groom of the bedchamber to the Duke of Clarence. He served with Lord Hood at Toulon, and in 1795 became Rear-

Admiral of the Blue. He was in command at the unsuccessful attack on the Spanish fleet at the Isle of Aix in 1799, and next year was appointed to the Newfoundland station; he only held the post for one year, as he was appointed to succeed Nelson, who was indisposed, in the Baltic. He was made a baronet in 1801 and vice-admiral; in 1802 he sat for Newark. In 1803 he was president of the Board of Naval Commissioners to investigate abuses, and 1806 became one of the Lords of the Admiralty. In 1805 he was made Admiral of the Blue, and in 1818 G.C.B. (From RALFE'S *Naval Biography*, vol. ii., p. 129.)

[2] Chief Justice Ogden received his formal commission and was actually sworn in May 1802.

chief magistrate—appealed strenuously to Barton to allow the licences to remain at thirty-six instead of being reduced to twenty-four, they urged that the publicans were paying high rents, that they had laid in a choice stock of liquor, and that they would be ruined; His Honour's reply was very curt and peremptory—his order must be obeyed[1]. There were strict instructions from England about the change in the flag—the Union Jack—consequent upon the union of England and Ireland, consummated on July 2nd, 1800.

All this time war was raging, but its effects never reached Newfoundland, Englishmen had the whole island and banks to themselves, including St. Pierre and Miquelon, our only competitors were a few American fishermen. We had large well-armed convoys with resolute naval officers to protect our fishing fleets, and men-of-war permanently stationed on the coast[2] American vessels going to the Mediterranean were always in danger from the Algerine pirates, and they therefore smuggled a good deal of their cod abroad in English bottoms This year, and each succeeding year, licences were issued to import provisions strictly in British vessels manned by British crews, but it appears very evident from the Governor's proclamation that these rules were evaded; American traders came disguised as fishing vessels, sold and bartered their goods in the outports, and stole away the men just as usual. Admiral Gambier strongly recommended support being given to the seal fishery, as a powerful incentive to keep the men in the Colony during the winter, and thus prevent the constant emigration to America

James Gambier,[3] Vice-Admiral of the White, who was Governor from 1802 to the end of 1803, was not only a very gallant naval officer, but

[1] LIST of Persons who have obtained LICENSES to keep PUBLIC HOUSES from Michelmas, 1797, to Michelmas, 1798

Michael Little.
John Cox
John Bolan
Sarah Martin.
John Cahill
Wm Power
Patk. Flannery
AugustusMcNamara.
Wm. McCarthy.
Wm. Welsh
Patrick McDonald.
Andrew S St. John.
Peter Lyons.
Michael Mara
James Maher
John Flood
John Brophy

John Widdicomb
Edmond Doyle
Michael Hanlon
Patrick Redmond.
John Power.
Thomas Murphy
Wm Prendergast
Dominic King
George Shepherd
David Power
Michael Welsh.
John Nevean
Phil Harrahan.
Daniel Delaney
Mark Codey
Michael Welsh

[2] Captain Edgell, H.M S Pluto, had a house and farm near St John's, and resided here many years The Pluto, a sloop, appears to have remained in Newfoundland for about twenty years, off and on

[3] James Gambier, born in 1756 at New Providence, was placed on the books of the Yarmouth, guardship at Chatham, when eleven years old, under the care of his uncle Became lieutenant in 1777 while serving on the North American station, was captured in 1778 by the French, but was soon exchanged, he took part in the relief of Jersey in 1779, and the capture of Charlestown in 1780 He had no further appointment afloat till 1793, when he commissioned the Defence (74), for the Channel fleet Gambier's notions of religion and morality were much stricter than those in vogue at that time; his ship was known as "a praying ship," but she proved

was far in advance of his age, both in regard to his views on the future prospects and government of the Colony, and in the furthering of all humane and benevolent ideas for educating the settlers' children, and civilizing the poor Beothics. The naval ruler has been much abused in our histories; it will therefore probably astonish many of my readers to find a naval governor strongly urging on the British

Ministry the necessity of granting responsible government to New-foundland in 1802. This communi-cation of Gambier's shows that he was a Liberal far in advance of his time; he had seen the benefits of local government in America and Nova Scotia, and knew that it was necessary for the progressive ad-vancement of the Colony. He wrote to Lord Hobart on December 12th, 1803, as follows :—

LORD GAMBIER.
From an engraving after Beechey.

"I am led to apprehend that the present system of policy observed towards this Island is defective, being insufficient for effecting the happiness and good order of the community which is the chief end of all government. This I attribute to the want of *a power in the Island for framing laws for its internal regulation*, and for raising the sums necessary to promote any measure of public utility by which expense must be incurred. . . . No money can be raised here except by voluntary contribution, and that mode must be always inadequate for the many useful purposes for which it is required. . . . . . I therefore feel it incumbent on me to propose to your Lordship's consideration *the establishment of*

she was also "a fighting ship" by being the first to break the line on 1st June 1794. His ship suffered severely; the story is told that Captain Pakenham passing within hail said to Gambier, "I see you've been knocked about a good deal: never mind, Jimmy, whom the Lord loveth He chasteneth." Gambier's conduct was noticed by Howe, and he received a gold medal. In 1795 he was an Admiralty Lord, and though made rear-admiral and vice-admiral in 1799, he remained at the Admiralty till 1801, when he became third in command in the Channel. In 1802 he was Governor of Newfoundland, and in 1804 again went to the Admiralty. He was mainly responsible for the omission of the order from the "King's Regulations" requiring foreign ships within the Narrow Seas to salute the flag, an order maintained since King John's time, if not from the days of William the Conqueror. In 1807 he was made a peer for his conduct at Copenhagen, and again went to the Admiralty. Gambier was strongly opposed to Lord Cochrane's attempt to use fire-ships against the French in Basque Roads in 1809. Hearing that Cochrane would oppose a vote of thanks, Gambier applied for a court-martial, and was acquitted by one expressly selected as friendly to him. In 1814 he was a commissioner for negotiating a treaty with the United States. Was made a G.C.B. in 1815, and Admiral of the Fleet in 1830; he died in 1833. He was only at sea five and a half years between his promotions to lieutenant and rear-admiral; his naval experience was thus extremely limited.—(STEPHEN's *Nat. Dict. of Biography.*)

a Legislative power in Newfoundland, similar to that which *has been found necessary to the prosperity and good government* of other parts of H.M foreign dominions.''

The British Government would not listen to his proposal, they had given Nova Scotia Home Rule years before, but poor Newfoundland had still to struggle thirty years more for this great boon Even when the privilege of a proper court of justice was granted after a long fight—though an able lawyer like Reeves was sent out for the first two years —the salary of the chief justice on the second appointment was reduced to £300 a year, resulting in cheap and inefficient judges—an out-port doctor, a worn-out poor old navy surgeon, a broken-down merchant, and an impecunious Irish squireen.

One important event occurred during Gambier's administration, the peace of Amiens in 1802 All the conquered territory was to be given back, so St. Pierre and Miquelon were again returned to the French,[1] and the right of fishery restored to them " in the manner they were " entitled to enjoy the same under the Treaty of Utrecht ", so runs the Governor's proclamation

The utmost harmony seems to have prevailed between the Governor, Bishop O'Donel, and the Protestant clergyman Two schools, known as the St. John's Charity Schools, were established, mainly through Gambier's influence, one for Roman Catholics and the other for Protestants. The Grammar School, established in 1799, with the Rev. Louis Amadeus Anspach as master, lasted only a few years, as in 1802 we find the author of the " History of Newfoundland "[2] a justice of the peace in Harbour Grace, and Church of England missionary there. Besides his efforts to promote education and to increase the clergy in the island, Gambier took a deep interest in the unfortunate Beothics, An Indian woman was brought to St. John's by the notorious William Cull, for which he received a reward of £50 Cull evidently did not take kindly to His Excellency's ideas about the savages, in his opinion the only decent Indian was a dead Indian ; he writes to the Governor : "The people do not hold with civilizing the Indians, as they " think that they will kill more than they did before" All thoughtful care and attention was shown to the poor Beothic woman, and she was to be sent back to her kindred loaded with presents. With the views held by Cull and his companions, it is very doubtful if she ever reached the wigwams of her tribe.

---

[1] An account of the surrender will be found in the chapter on St. Pierre

[2] Anspach's *History of Newfoundland* is a valuable addition to our knowledge of the Colony ; it is rather too full of his own affairs, his own importance, and his narrow religious views. It is also, unfortunately, very inaccurate and unreliable.

Sir Erasmus Gower [1] succeeded Gambier in 1804 ; he is principally remembered for the street, thirty feet wide, bearing his name, which he laid out. The population at this time was increasing rapidly ; six

SIR ERASMUS GOWER.
From an engraving after Livesey.

hundred and seventy Irish emigrants landed in St. John's in one year. In 1804 the population is returned as more than twenty thousand, the quantity of fish caught as over six hundred thousand quintals; for the same year the returns of the seal fishery show a net result of thirty-four thousand seals, and boat or schooner fishery of seventy-three thousand.[2] The records show great activity in ship-building, thirty vessels of two thousand three hundred tons having been built this year on the island. One important fishery seems to have been entirely neglected ; the whole pack of herrings is given as about a hundred barrels. The imports are very large: 221,162 gallons of rum ; bread and flour, 83,389 cwt. ; pork and beef, 10,522 cwt., not allowing for all the smuggled provisions brought in by Americans. One of these Yankee vessels was nearly caught at Tilton Harbour, but all that the naval captain could actually find out that she had on board were *garden seeds.*

We find in the annals of this time, and all through the history of the Colony, bitter complaints of the tyranny of the merchants towards

---

[1] Sir E. Gower, eldest son of Abel Gower, of Glandoven, Pembrokeshire, entered the Navy in 1755 under the care of his uncle, Captain Donkley. He served through the war on the American and home stations, passed for lieutenant 1762, and was lent to Portugal for service against the Bourbons. Served under Commodore Byron, and in 1769 under Sir George Rodney in Jamaica. In 1779 was first lieutenant in the *Sandwich*, Rodney's flagship, at the capture of the Spanish convoy off Cape Finisterre, and took command of the *Guipuscoa* prize. He gallantly captured the *Vryherd*, a Dutch ship of 50 guns, under the batteries at Cuddalore, and soon after the *Chasseur* sloop with important despatches to Suffren. From 1786 to 1789, Gower was Commodore Elliot's flag captain on the Newfoundland station, and in 1792

took Lord Macartney and his embassy to China in the *Lion*, for which service he was knighted. In 1794 he commanded the *Triumph*, one of the ships with Cornwallis in his celebrated retreat. During the mutiny at the Nore he hoisted a broad pennant on the *Neptune* for the defence of the Thames, which ship he continued to command till he became rear-admiral in 1799: he was made vice-admiral in 1704, and admiral in 1809. He died at Hambledon, in Hampshire, in 1814. —(STEPHEN's *Nat. Dict. of Biography.*)

[2] In the Appendix will be found a long and very interesting account of the early seal fishery, written by Mr. John Bland to Governor Gambier. 1817 was another year like 1862; a continuation of N.E. gales drove twenty-five vessels ashore, but no lives were lost.

then dealers. They never gave out the prices of the articles sold on credit to the fishermen, and they "broke the price of fish in August," just at the amount they liked[1] In good years some relief was obtained from the competition of the sack ships, who bought fish from the independent planters and gave good cash prices The labouring men complained to Governor Gower that the merchants "price their own " goods and ours also as they think most convenient to them"[2] To remedy this intolerable state of affairs His Excellency adopted the following drastic remedy —

"Whereas I am informed that a practice has prevailed in some of the outports of this island among the merchants of not informing their dealers of the prices of the supplies advanced for the season, or the prices they will allow for the produce, until they are in possession of the planter's voyage, whereby

[1] There were numerous complaints from outports about merchants' prices and their dealings with the fishermen. The one from Fogo says "For a number of years back we have been struggling with the world, as we suppose, through the impositions of the merchants and their agents by their exorbitant prices on shop goods and provisions, by which means we are from year to year held in debt so as not daring to find fault fearing we may starve at the approach of every winter We being at the distance of seventy leagues from the Capital, where we suppose they arrogate to themselves a power not warranted by any law, in selling to us every article of theirs at any price they think fit, and taking from us the produce of a whole year at whatever price they think fit to give They take it on themselves to price their own goods and ours also as they think most convenient to them"· The petition is signed by many Irishmen—Patrick Murray, Peter Fowler, Toby McGrath, Michael Burke, James Meehan, John Geary, Wm Broders, and Wm Keefe

[2] Prices of Provisions and other Commodities in Newfoundland during the Summer of 1805, in Barter for Fish

	At St John's		In Conception Bay.	At Trinity, Bonavista, Fogo	In Placentia Bay
	For Fish	For Bill			
Bread, per cwt.	40s to 45s	32s to 42s	45s	40s	11s to 47s.
Flour, per barrel	60s to 70s	50s to 68s	65s to 72s.	77s	7s.
Pork, per barrel	10s to 120s	95s to 100s.	126s	130s	130s
Butter, per lb	11d to 1s 2d	10d	1s 3d	1s 3d to 1s 6d	1s 4d to 1s 6d
Rum, per gallon	5s to 5s 6d	3s 3d to 3s 9d	6s 6d.	7s	6s to 7s
Molasses, do	6s to 6s 6d	4s to 4s 6d.	7s 6d	6s. 6d to 7s	7s
Salt, English, per bushel	11s 6d to 18s	11s 6d to 15s.	18s	20s	20s to 22s
Do Foreign, per bushel	18s to 25s	18s to 20s	24s	25s	22s to 26s
Cordage, new, per cwt	100s	100s	—	112s	112s
Do , twice laid, per cwt	50s to 56s	50s	—	75s	70s to 80s.
Grapnels and anchors, per lb	8d	7d	—	9d	—
Pitch, per barrel	60s to 63s	55s to 60s	—	6d per lb	70s
Tar, per barrel	42s to 50s	35s to 42s	—	{ 2s 6d to 2s 9d per gallon }	60s.
Tea (common), per lb	3s 6d to 4s 6d	2s 11d to 3s	—	5s to 5s 6d	6s
Tobacco, per lb	1s to 1s 3d	8d to 9d	—	1s 6d	1s 6d
Peas, per bushel	—	—	—	11s to 13s	12s.
Oatmeal, per cwt	—	—	—	25s to 32s.	26s
Canvas, per piece	81s.	—	—	95s	90s to 105s.

Of course it must be remembered that it was war time, and wheat was from 9s to 12s. per bushel, and pork and beef relatively high. The prices of molasses and salt are exorbitant

·"An old fisherman informs me that in the "spring of the Wadhams," he was wrecked at Greenspond, and lived part of the winter there, some of the people, he says, had never seen money from their birth to their grave, they were in debt to the merchant all their lives long.

the latter are exposed to great impositions, the merchants are hereby required to make known to their dealers before the 15th day of August in every year, or at the time of delivery, the prices of provisions and other commodities sold by them, and the prices they will give for fish and oil, and to fix a schedule thereof in some conspicuous part of their respective stores, and in case any merchant shall neglect to comply with this useful injunction, and a dispute shall arise between him and any dealer respecting the prices charged on such merchant's account, and each dispute shall be brought into a court of justice, the same shall be determined according to the *lowest* price charged for such goods, and the *highest* price given for fish and oil by any other merchant in that district. And the judge of the Supreme Court the surrogates and the magistrates, are hereby strictly enjoined in all such cases to govern themselves by this regulation.

> " Given under my hand, September 12, 1805
>
> " E Gower."

The evils of the truck system have been exposed by many able writers on political economy, a parliamentary commission showed its workings amongst the Shetland fisher folk, how men lived and died without even once getting their necks free from the yoke of the shop. In Newfoundland this terrible evil is almost coeval with the fishery. To this very day there are places in the Colony where neither the wages of the labourers on the merchants' wharves nor Government roads, nor even the widow's poor relief, are paid in cash Truck had to be killed by a stringent Act of Parliament in the United Kingdom, but no Government in Newfoundland has yet had the courage to declare that the labourer is really worthy of his hire—that payments in truck are illegal, and all such paymasters liable to a penalty Truck is not a crying evil in St John's; it is " the dark places of the earth that are full of wickedness," and it is in the distant out-ports, and amongst petty traders and old-fashioned houses, that it still flourishes in full vigour.

It is not necessary, for a clear view of our history, to dwell much on minute details From this period onwards the Colony began steadily to improve, a primitive post office was instituted in 1805, under Simon Solomon (father of our first postmaster-general, William Solomon),[1] a newspaper, the *Royal Gazette*, which still flourishes, was instituted by Mr John Ryan, an American loyalist, in 1806, it was published as a possible evil thing, under the most severe restrictions, security in £200 sterling had to be given, and the magistrates were to have the perusal

---

[1] The postage rates in 1815 were as follows —

From Canada On a ½ oz letter the postage from—		s	d	From Nova Scotia: On a ½-oz letter the postage from—		s	d
Quebec	- -	1	8	Winsor	- -	0	4½
Montreal	-	2	1	Digby	- -	0	9
Three Rivers	-	1	10½	Horton	-	0	7
Butler	-	2	1	Yarmouth	-	1	1½
York (Toronto)	-	2	9	Pictou	-	0	7
Niagara	-	2	9	Parrsboro	- -	0	7

of the contents of the paper before publication.[1] I am thankful that duty is not incumbent on us now, especially during the elections, when each party organ is full of audacity, mendacity, and scurrilous personal

VIEW ON THE NEWFOUNDLAND COAST.
From a drawing in the B.M.

abuse. Nothing better indicates the pleasant social relations of St. John's at this time than the founding of the Benevolent Irish Society; this

[1] PERSONS LICENSED 21ST SEPTEMBER 1807 TO KEEP TAVERNS IN THE TOWN OF ST. JOHN'S FOR THE ENSUING YEAR.

From the "Royal Gazette," *December* 24, 1807.

Persons licensed.	Sign of Tavern.
Robert Parsons	West India Coffee House, High Constable.

UPPER DIVISION.—From River Head to Mr. Boucher's, Bulley's Farm.

William Best	Bunch of Grapes.
John Widdicombe	Rose and Crown.
James Hayse	Ship.
Edward Angell	Britannia.
John Williams	Nelson.
John Cahill	Tavern for all Weathers.
Patrick Murine	Flower Pot.
William McCarthy	Hope.
Richard Heaney	Struggler.
Michael Murphy	Dove.
Mary Hennessey	Royal Standard.

MIDDLE DIVISION. — From Boucher's to Hudson Cove, Mr. Hunter's now Job's Cove].

Patrick Redmond	Ship Assistance.
William Power	Angel.

Angus Macnamara	Agincourt.
William Welsh	Swan.
Robert Dooling	Red Cow.
John Fitzgerald	Jolly Fisherman.
Edmond Doyle	Blue Ball.
Michael Hanlen	Shoulder of Mutton.
Dominick King	White Hart.
Graham Little	
Richard Perchard	Royal Oak.
Margaret Walsh	Sailor.

LOWER DIVISION.—From Hudson's Cove to the easternmost part of St. John's.

Cornelius Quirk	London Tavern.
Dennis Murphy	Wheatsheaf.
Daniel Driscoll	Bird-in-Hand.
Patrick Walsh	Union Flag.
Robert Brine	Butchery and at Pringle's Farm.
William Welsh	
Michael Mara	Sun.
John Murphy	Duke of York.
Thomas Murphy	Three Crowns.
Charles Power	Plough at Brine's Bridge.

All persons licensed to keep publichouses are constables for the district of St. John's.

institution, which still flourishes in full vigour, was instituted under the happiest circumstances James McBraire was the most active amongst the founders, and president from 1809 to 1821, when he left the Colony   I quote from Bishop Howley :—

" The preliminary meeting ' of a number of Irish gentlemen, desirous of re-
' lieving the wants and distresses of their countrymen and fellow-creatures at
' large, was held at the London Tavern, in St John's, on Wednesday, the
' 5th February, 1806. It was unanimously agreed ' That a society, formed upon
' true principles of benevolence and philanthropy, would be the most effectual mode
' of establishing a permanent relief to the wretched and distressed " Under this
' conviction, it was proposed to elect a committee from the gentlemen present to
' form a code of rules and regulations for the government of the society, the
' extension and regulations of the charity, and to consult with the Rt. Rev. Doctor
' O'Donel and others, whose local knowledge of this country could best inform
' them as to the most effectual and beneficial mode of establishing a CHARITABLE
' IRISH SOCIETY upon firm principles of loyalty, true benevolence, and philanthropy,
' when the following gentlemen were nominated and unanimously chosen:
' Lieut -Col John Murray, James McBraire, Esq , John McKellop, Esq ,
' Mr Joseph Church, Captain Winckworth Tonge.'

" From this it will be seen that the society was purely unsectarian in its origin, and all denominations of Christians were admissible to its ranks, the only quali-fications required being that one should be either an Irishman or a descendant of an Irishman "

James McBraire, who figures prominently in the social and political life of the Colony at this period, was a very remarkable character Originally a sergeant in the Army, he came out to Newfoundland a poor man he soon acquired the reputation of being one of the shrewdest and most prosperous business men of the place On the constitution of a volunteer corps he was appointed captain , he drilled his companies admirably, if severely ; some of the gentlemen, like Magill, complained of his being a martinet, and terribly overbearing , finally he rose to be major-commandant of the St John's Volunteer Rangers.[1] McBraire was of a very fine, commanding presence, and never looked better than when at the head of his table, dispensing hospitality In all riots the major was a terror to the mob In the year 1816 a transport, with troops for England, put into St. John's for water, with Dr Leslie on board. He

[1] In 1806 the Royal Newfoundland Rangers were embodied under Major McBraire, Commandant , Captains Parker, I Williams, Boucher, T Williams, and Batten , Lieutenants Henry Shea, Solomon, Lilly, Stevenson, Haire , Ensigns Parker, Gill, Thomas, Melledge, Parsons , Surgeon Coughlan , Quarter-Master Beenlen

In 1812 the corps had fallen into a disorganised state, and was reconstructed, on the breaking out of the American war, with the following officers - Major McBraire, Commandant , Captains Boucher, T Williams, Lilly, McAllister, G. R Robinson, Crawford, Haynes, 'Ryan, Trimingham, Thomas ; Lieutenants Melledge, Broom, Stewart, McLea, Simpson, Livingston, Grieve, Arnott, Clift, Shannon ; Ensigns Morris, McCalman, Rendell, Scott, Willis, N Gill, Niven Lang, Adjutant Hughes , Quarter-Master Barnes , Surgeon Dr Duggan

Major-General Campbell commanded the troops, which at this time numbered seven hundred and fifty

mentions dining in state at Major McBraire's with the principal merchants and officers of the garrison. After an excellent dinner, as the gentlemen were smoking, there was a great noise heard outside ; McBraire immediately put on his hat and rushed out with a long staff. The Doctor describes with delight the prompt way in which the redoubtable Major quelled the disturbance ; everyone went down before his terrible wand, and in five minutes the mob dispersed. McBraire left this Colony about 1822,[1] and settled with his only son at Berwick-on-Tweed ; he carried off a fortune of about £80,000 sterling. He was reputed to have made a great deal of money in the American war ; one of the prizes had a load of grind-stones, some twelve hundred ; of course these went for a song.

ADMIRAL HOLLOWAY.[2]
From an engraving by Cook.

Someone asked McBraire, who had purchased them, what he was going to do with such a lot ? "You will see," said he, and they did see. In the winter the town was short of biscuit, McBraire had his stores full ; every man who bought a bag of bread had also to buy a grind-stone for two dollars.

Sir Erasmus Gower not only distinguished himself by his benevolence, his promotion of religion and education, he was equally remarkable for his zeal in reforming the courts of justice ; he raised the salary of the Chief Justice from £300 to £500 per annum, and the stipendiary magistrates were under his administration first given permanent pay ; he significantly hints to all these officials that, for the future, they must not be concerned in any private or professional business in the town.[3] In his recommendations to the Home Government he endeavoured to impress upon them that St. John's was no longer a mere fishing station, but a large commercial seaport ; that the promotion of agriculture and a secure tenure of lands was absolutely necessary for its future welfare and progress. He said :—

"It is eighteen years since I was first on this station, and the great improvements and changes that have taken place in that time, render it now absolutely

---

[1] The story is told that as McBraire was going out of the Harbour he waved his hand and said : " Good-bye, Newfoundlanders ; good-bye, you poor fools."

[2] Admiral Holloway was Governor from 1807 to 1810. His name does not appear in any of the usual biographical works, nor in Stephen's *Nat. Dict. of Biography.*

[3] From the Census of 1794 it appears that at that date Chief Justice D'Ewes Coke owned and operated a fishing room at Quidi Vidi.

necessary that the capital of this Colony should no longer be cramped, cabined, and confined by laws and restrictions, which at present are entirely unsuited to its condition and progress "

He had to use at all times great pressure upon the Imperial Government to obtain their consent to the free importation of American provisions There was evidently a bitter dislike and jealousy of the United States, and it was only the absolute requirement of food for the Island that made the British Government reluctantly give way on this point In accordance with a strong petition from the merchants, he tried to obtain for Newfoundland the exclusive privilege of supplying the West Indies with salt codfish, and the British Army and Navy with regular rations twice a week of our great staple, but failed In 1809, Labrador and Anticosti were again re-united to the Newfoundland Government, and the courts made permanent under an Act of Parliament

In 1810 the celebrated Admiral, Sir John Thomas Duckworth,[1] became Governor. He made another and more serious attempt to conciliate the Red Indians Lieutenant Buchan, R.N., of H M S Pike, was sent to Exploits with a party of seamen and marines. It was in the winter, and after undergoing unparalleled hardships they at last came up with the Beothics. The gallant Buchan did all in his power to promote friendship with the savages ; he left two of his marines with them, and some Indians accompanied him The blood-thirsty character of these aborigines and their treachery is most forcibly exhibited by the terrible tragedy with which this promising effort to conciliate their savage nature ended. The two marines left by Buchan with the Indians were found lying about two hundred yards apart, that of the corporal, being first, was pierced by one arrow in the back, three had entered that of Bouthland ; they were laid out straight, with their feet towards the river, and back upwards, their heads were off, and had been carried

---

[1] Sir J. T Duckworth, born in 1748, was the son of Rev. A. Duckworth, afterwards Vicar of Stoke Pogis and Canon of Windsor, entered the Navy at eleven, and was present at the destruction of M de la Clue's squadron in Lagos Bay and the Battle of Queberon Bay Duckworth served in Byron's ship in the action off Grenada in 1779, and was immediately promoted to be commander of the Rover He was praised specially by Lord Howe for his behaviour in the Orion (74), at the action off Ushant, and received a gold medal He was present at the capitulation of Minorca in 1798, and expected to receive a baronetcy In 1799 he became Rear-Admiral of the White ; was with Lord St. Vincent in his unsuccessful pursuit of Admiral Bruix In 1800, when blockading Cadiz, he captured a rich Spanish convoy; his share of the prize-money has been said to have amounted to £75,000 Was made a K B for his services in the West Indies in 1801; he directed, in 1803, the operations which resulted in the surrender of General Rochambeau at San Domingo The operations conducted by him during 1805-6-7 were not at all successful He was Governor of Newfoundland from 1810 to 1813 ; on his return he was made a baronet, he became a full admiral in 1810. Of all the men who have attained distinction in the English Navy, there is none whose character has been more discussed.— (STEPHEN's Nat Dict. of Biography)

away. No blame can attach to Buchan for this melancholy disaster; the whole object of the expedition was to gain the friendship of the Indians by exhibiting confidence in them, and trusting white men unarmed amongst them.

Whatever our sentimental feelings may be for these primitive inhabitants, all their history shows that the one ineradicable feature in

SIR J. T. DUCKWORTH.
From an engraving after Beechey.

their character was an insatiable hatred of the pale faces. They must have known, if we give them credit for any intelligence, that this was a mission of peace, and that there was no intention of injuring them. Every other motive in them seems to have been overpowered by their instinct to kill the white man. There can be no doubt that the settlers hunted them like wolves, and shot them in cold blood whenever they encountered them. The captured Indian woman, Shandithit, declared that the hatred of the white man was so strong amongst her people that she would not be again tolerated by her tribe after speaking with Englishmen. With such feelings against Europeans all attempts at reconciliation were fruitless. There are many conjectures about the ultimate fate of the Red Indians. Bonnycastle thinks they may have emigrated in a body to the Canadian Labrador, and he mentions, in confirmation of this view, the arrival at the Bay of Seven Islands of a body of Indians who were neither Mountaineers nor Mic Macs, whom he therefore conjectures were the remnant of our Beothics. This may be so, but the general opinion of those who have studied the subject most closely is that the Red Indians were exterminated partly by the settlers, and the Mic Macs, partly by famine and disease.[1]

[1] Mr. James Howley tells me that the whole trouble was caused by the chief of the tribe. He understood Buchan had the presents on the river at the outlet from the lake He went thither with the English, and when he found they were a long way further down, he turned back, and created a suspicion amongst the Indians that Buchan's force was to capture them. On his return he took them all off into the woods.

B B

To the energy of Sir John Duckworth St. John's is indebted for many improvements; it was through his exertions that the Act 51 Geo. III. was passed in 1811. In September of that year His Excellency issued the following notice :—

" Whereas by an Act passed in the fifty-first year of His Majesty's reign, entitled ' An Act for taking away the public use of certain ships' rooms in the town of St. John's in the Island of Newfoundland, &c.,' it is enacted that the several ships' rooms therein mentioned, shall and may be granted, let and possessed as private property. Notice is, therefore, hereby given, that His Excellency the Governor will by virtue of the authority in him vested by the said recited Act, proceed to let or lease the said several fishing rooms in lots, for the accommodation of those who may be inclined to build thereon, conformably to a plan which may be seen by application at this office, on or before the 7th day of October next."

In a very short space of time the whole of this area was let on leases for thirty years, renewable at a rental amounting to £1,000 sterling per annum. A considerable space, both in the east and west end of the town, was reserved for ships' rooms and flakes ; it is within the memory of most of us when all the frontage below Brooking's and near Newman's was covered with flakes.

Anspach says of this leasing of the ships' rooms :—

" They were divided into a certain number of lots, and put up to public auction, in leases for thirty years, renewable at the expiration of that time upon payment in way of a fine of a sum equal to *three* years' rent of the lot so purchased if built with timber, and of a sum equal to *one* year's rent if built of stone or brick. The purchaser of a lot might at his option take the next lot adjoining backward at the same price that he paid for the first. Party walls between adjoining lots were to be built of brick or stone of twenty inches thick, to stand equally on each lot. The buildings were to be of the height of two stories, or not less than eighteen feet from sill to wall-plate, and no encroachments were to be made on the space alloted for the streets by bow-windows, porches, or other erections."

MR. EWEN STABB.

The merchants petitioned the Crown that this money might be retained in the Colony, for the purposes of providing police, lighting, and sewering of the town, and to afford protection from fire. This reasonable request was not complied with ; however, through Sir Thomas' representations, a few permanent police were established, but in order to protect themselves from fire, the Merchants' Society had to organise an association which was both a fire brigade and a vigilance committee; it was managed and controlled by the astute and ubiquitous McBraire.

In 1812 began the second American War. The ostensible cause was the right of search claimed by England, and the impressment of seamen. The real reason, as is now admitted by all candid American historians, was Madison's re-election as President. He did not want war, but felt that his chance of being elected again depended upon his taking that course. All the blood that was shed, and the English and American property destroyed in this terrible conflict, was simply to gratify the inordinate political ambition of this unscrupulous man. For once, the British Government were ready and prepared for the struggle; in St. John's alone there were three sail of the line and twenty-one frigates, with thirty-seven sloops, brigs, and schooners of war. Mr. Ewen Stabb told of thirty American prizes being brought into the harbour. I have heard a gentleman describe his walking across from Bennett's (now Duder's) to Alsop's, on the south side, on American prizes chained together.[1]

During the whole of the conflict Newfoundland was in a great state of prosperity; wages were high, provisions were very dear, having all to be brought from England and the British provinces, but fish and oil and all our produce was also abnormally high. On board the captured vessels were all sorts of valuable freights—Lyons silks and whole cargoes of champagne. The clerks at Hunt, Stabb, Preston & Co., prize agents,[2] spent their Sunday afternoons firing at champagne bottles on

ADMIRAL KEATS.

From an engraving after Jackson.

---

[1] Licences were granted in September 1815 to seventeen vessels from St. John's to proceed to the United States for provisions and live stock; out of these eleven were American prizes. They included the *Mercury*, brig, 156 tons, owned by Lang, Baine, & Co. (Baine, Johnston, & Co.); *Aid*, schooner, 60 tons; *John Dunscombe*, Dunscombe & Harvey, now Harvey & Co.; *Morell*, 61, schooner, Brown, Hoyles, & Co.; and the *Express*, 131, W. & H. Thomas & Co.

[2] Thomas Stabb, the resident partner in this firm, was the father of the late Ewen,

Nicholas, and Dr. Henry Stabb—of the Lunatic Asylum. The clerks in the firm who shot for champagne were Ewen Stabb, Thomas Brooking, and Samuel Prowse (afterwards collector at Twillingate). During this period, William Carter, Esquire, held the lucrative position of judge of the Admiralty Court; a most impartial and efficient judge. P. W. Carter was naval officer (afterwards the well known senior magistrate of St. John's): he was the son of Judge Carter, and father of our esteemed Chief Justice, Sir F. B. T. Carter, K.C.M.G.

a gumphead at the end of the wharf; the man who knocked the head off the bottle won a case, the one who missed had to pay for one

In the autumn of 1812, after the breaking out of the second American War, Newfoundland lost the valuable services of Sir John Thomas Duckworth; he was invited by the electors of New Romney to stand for Parliament, and had to resign his commission; he was succeeded by a still more distinguished admiral, Sir Richard Godwin Keats, K.B.[1] The naval career of this gallant officer ranks with the most brilliant in the heroic annals of that age Nothing could exceed his activity and zeal for the protection of the island from the attacks of the French and Americans.

Our American cousins pride themselves on their naval exploits in their two great wars with England; the Newfoundland records contain ample evidence of their losses and defeats by English cruisers, and very few instances of their success Occasionally they made a raid on some

---

[1] Sir R. G Keats was born on the 16th of January 1757. He served at the commencement of the American War, at the burning of Norfolk, in an attack upon Hampton, Virginia, and at the capture of New York, Fort Washington, and Rhode Island As a lieutenant he was on board the *Ramillies* in the action between Keppel and D Orvilliers, the 27th July 1778; also at the defeat of Don Juan de Lomgena by Rodney on 16th January 1780, and at the ensuing relief of Gibraltar, was promoted Commander into the *Rhinoceros* sloop of war, in September 1783, as a reward for the skilful manner in which he had conducted the naval part of an expedition against the enemy's small craft at New Brunswick Captain Keats also bore a distinguished part at the capture of the French 40-gun frigate *L'Aigle* In 1789 he attained post rank In the ensuing war, in command of the *Galatea*, he attended the expedition to Quiberon, and participated in the capture and destruction of several of the enemy's frigates and other vessels He was a long time employed in the *Boadicea* in watching the port of Brest, and, on the 2nd July 1799, commanded part of the force under Rear-Admiral Charles Morice Pole in an attack on a Spanish squadron in Aix Roads; and, in the *Superb*, distinguished himself in the defeat of the Franco-Spanish squadron by Sir James Saumarez in the Gut of Gibraltar, 12th July 1801 Keats ran his ship alongside two Spanish three-deckers, and engaged them both at the same time; then making sail, he passed out from between them unnoticed, and overtaking another of their fleet, whose force was more proportionate to that of the *Superb*, he soon compelled her to a surrender The two three-deckers, not perceiving his escape, continued, in the darkness of the night, to engage each other, until they both caught fire and were consumed together; thus giving to Captain Keats the honour of having, by a masterly manœuvre, occasioned the destruction of two first-rate line-of-battle ships belonging to the enemy, and capturing another of equal force, with a comparatively trifling loss on his own part He accompanied Lord Nelson to the West Indies in 1805 in pursuit of the combined fleets, and fought as flag-captain to Sir John Duckworth in the action off San Domingo 6th February 1806, and was in consequence presented with a sword valued at 100 guineas In October 1807 he became a rear-admiral, and shortly afterwards, on the outbreak of war with Russia, was appointed third in command to the fleet destined for the Baltic, under the command of Sir James Saumarez; and, in August 1808, being detached by the Commander-in-Chief, he was the instrument, with his flag on board his old ship, the *Superb*, of emancipating from French thraldom the Spanish troops stationed in the Danish provinces under the Marquis de Romana For the able management displayed by him on this occasion he was created a K B He afterwards served, in 1809, under Sir Richard Strachan during the operations against Walcheren, and assumed charge in 1810 of the squadron employed at the defence of Cadiz, and in 1811 was second in command in the Mediterranean From 1813 to 1816 he was Governor and Commander-in-Chief at Newfoundland In 1818 he was nominated a major-general of Marines, and made a full admiral in 1825; and from 1821 till his death, in 1834, he held the Governorship of Greenwich Hospital He died an Admiral of the White.

remote outpost of the Colony,[1] Major George Cartwright, in his long diary, gives a graphic account of the way his fine business at Labrador was spoiled and plundered by an enterprising New England privateer in the American war, there is also an account of the capture of three of our sealing schooners in 1817, given in the statistics of the Seal Fishery.[2] The destruction of American commerce and the capture of American vessels by British cruisers in our waters exceeded by ten to one the gains on the Republican side ; the English fleet on our shores far outnumbered their enemies. Under two such distinguished naval officers as Duckworth and Keats, the Governors of Newfoundland from 1812 to 1814, captains vied with each other in their activity, vigilance, and smartness. The Admiral Governor had no hours, he was always on duty.

I am indebted to my friend, Mr Robert Pike of St. Lawrence, for the two stories given below[3] about privateering on our coast

---

[1] Mr. Robert L. Newman furnishes me with the following information about the capture of their vessels by American and French privateers in the war of 1812, taken from the letter-books of their firm —

"1812 The *Duck* sailed from Little Bay, Fortune Bay, 5 Decr for Oporto On the 22 Decr was taken by two French frigates, Lon 16 04 Lat 42 35, who let her proceed after heaving overboard about 900 qtls of fish in order to put aboard 100 prisoners, recaptured by an English frigate and taken to Halifax

" On Jany 23 1812 The *Gosport* was taken by a French privateer *La Gavotte*, of 16 guns, who let her proceed after plundering her of 150 qtls. fish.

" In 1813 The *St Lawrence* boarded by an American privateer, who plundered, destroyed, and disabled the vessel in every way possible, flinging overboard the cargo She bore up for Dartmouth arriving 10 April.

" Dec 1813 The *Syren* captured and scuttled on her voyage from Oporto to Newfoundland by an American privateer

" 12 March 1814 The *Duck* was captured and given up, to bring upward of 100 Prisoners to England, after throwing all the fish that was between decks overboard to make room for the men

" 14 April 1814 The *Selby* captured on her voyage from Little Bay to Portugal on the Newfoundland coast, but given up

" 13 Aug 1814 The *St. Lawrence* on her passage to Bilbao with a cargo of fish was captured by an American privateer, recaptured by a British frigate, and again captured by another American privateer, the *Wig*, and sent to America, recaptured again by the English and sent to Portsmouth "

[2] *See* statistical chapter

[3] In 1813 an Irish youngster ran away from his master, Mr Bonnell, in St Lawrence, and went to Lann, found an American privateer there, went on board of her and joined the crew. He came down to Great St Lawrence with the Americans, and captured a Jersey brig belonging to a firm of three brothers, then carrying on a trade there The privateer was commanded by a little Irishman named Conolly She was afterwards captured in the passage between Columbier and St. Pierre—known as Hell's Mouth—by H M cutter *Lictor*, under command of Lieut. McKillop, R N The privateer got in the Doldrums (becalmed there), and surrendered without a fight

In the last French war, before the battle of Waterloo, Mr Henry Beck, an old Englishman, ancestor of the Becks of St Lawrence, had his fishing skiff armed. In the spring of 1814 he captured a large French banker, by boarding her and driving the crew off the deck He was taking his prize into Harbour Breton It was a fine day The French cook was in the galley getting dinner for all hands An altercation took place between one of Beck's fishermen and the cook, as the vessel was passing Little Cape the cook threw the contents of the frying pan into the Englishman's face, blinding him This was a preconcerted signal agreed on among the French crew, they seized Beck's men, and threw Beck into the hold, breaking his bones, he died soon after The Frenchmen took the banker to Boston, U S, where the St. Lawrence men were kept prisoners until the autumn, when they returned home.

The following ships were captured in 1808 —

The *Alfred*, Park, Master, from Newfoundland to Poole, and *Duke of Kent* from

One of the most striking events of this war was the capture of the American frigate *Chesapeake*, by Broke, in the *Shannon*, the boarders were led by their heroic captain, and the ship struck in eleven minutes. Mr Emerson, grandfather of the Honourable the Speaker, had a brother a midshipman in the *Shannon*, and he has often described the excitement in Halifax when young Lieut Provo Wallis brought the prize into the harbour. In connexion with this immortal combat there was one very curious circumstance. A number of Irish labourers were on board the brig *Duck*, belonging to Newman & Co., going out to Newfoundland, their vessel was captured by the American privateer *Governor Plumer*; she was in turn captured by the English privateer brig *Sir John Sherbrooke*, and as the *Shannon* was short of men the Irishmen were put on board of her, one of these labourers, Darby Murphy, used often to relate to his friends how he captured the Yankee frigate.

Cæsar Colclough,[1] Tremlett's successor on the Supreme Court bench, arrived in St John's in September 1813, from Prince Edward's Island, in place of Tremlett, who was sent there in a king's ship[2] He writes to his friend Reynolds, who was Postmaster-General at Lisbon, in the closing year of the great Peninsular War —

"St John's Newfoundland,
Sep. 29, 1813

" My dear Reynolds,

" Fate has removed me for my sins to this cursed spot as Chief Justice and I have by chance just heard that you are Postmaster-General at Lisbon. I write this in the counting house of a fish merchant, whose ship is bound to Lisbon. I have been here but a few days . . ."

Colclough remained in St John's for three years, he was not much of a lawyer, and a very sorry administrator, he had, however, shrewd mother wit, and the true Hibernian faculty of "gammoging the Saxon," and paid particular court to old Sir Richard Keats, impressing on His Excellency the great and patriotic services of Cæsar Colclough

Newfoundland captured, recaptured by H M S *Melpomene* Sent for Oporto, captured again 1st November

Union of Poole from Newfoundland captured, recaptured by H M S *Plover*

Nancy captured by French privateer, retaken by H M S *Dragon*.

Live Oak, Wimboro, Master, from Newfoundland to Oporto, captured by three Spanish rowboats, carried into Vigo after an engagement in which one man was killed and three wounded

Acorn from Newfoundland to Portugal captured and taken into Coruña

Margery and Mary from Newfoundland to Demerara captured, recaptured and taken to Dominica

[1] Chief Justice Colclough lived in the house near Mr Eden's shop, Rawlin's Cross He had a Royal coat-of-arms over his door, and compelled every one to take off his hat when passing the house When one of the Daltons was a trifle vociferous in court his Honour appealed to him, "If you can't be civil, Mr Dalton, be as civil as you can"

[2] On the 28th October 1811 charges of partiality and corruption were made by the Society of Merchants in St John's against

The result was eminently satisfactory, he had practically the dormant commission in the Governor's absence, and had his salary raised from £500 to £1,000 a year. I regret the inexorable requirements of space prevent me from quoting more from this humorous and fantastic Irishman's letters, but it is quite clear that in a difficulty he was little better than an old woman, he got out of all troubles by simply relying on the strong common sense, personal influence, and energy of McBraire, who was now magistrate, major-commandant, and president of the Commercial Society. The quondam serjeant, with his long staff, and humorously forcible way of knocking down all opposition, had a thousand times more power and influence over the people than this absurd Don Pomposo

Colclough reminds us forcibly of Thackeray's Malloney of Bally Malloney, who invites him to " come over to O'Dowd's town, my boy, we " are all English there, with a brogue as broad as from here to the Cove " of Cork " The Chief Justice was always running down his countrymen ; he exaggerated a " combine " to raise wages in the fishery into a terrible political conspiracy. he hints at murder—the only evidence he could produce was one soldier, whose evidence was worthless When all this blew over, then he begins again about the Irish faction fights on the Barrens, when General Finn stripped to fight General Muldowney for the honour of Waterford against the " yellow bellies " of Wexford These

the Chief Justice, Thomas Tremlett The Society at the same time charged the former Chief Justice, John Reeves, Esq , Law Clerk to the Council for Trade, with peculation and having received a portion of the salary of each of his successors The accusations against both Tremlett and Reeves were proved to be wholly malicious and unfounded In his report on the case (p 361) Sir J T Duckworth declared that Tremlett was a most independent Judge, that he had good ability and great industry, that in all his conduct there was not the most remote appearance of corruption, and that when the complainants were called upon they did not venture to charge him with corruption in any instance There is no doubt Tremlett was an irritable old bachelor, his manner was rude, and he swore terribly He exchanged in 1813 with Cæsar Colclough, Chief Justice of Prince Edward's Island Both these legal luminaries were at the time under a cloud, and it was considered a good arrangement to give each a new sphere, so a man-of-war carried Chief Justice Tremlett to the Island, and on her return voyage in October brought back the illustrious Cæsar I am indebted to Lieut -Governor Howland and Judge Alley for the following notes on

the careers of both these Judges in Prince Edward's Island — Colclough, an Irish barrister belonging to an old family in Wexford, was appointed Chief Justice of the Island on the 1st May 1807 For the first few years he gave great satisfaction, afterwards he got into trouble with Governor Des Barres, and was suspended in September 1812 Colclough claimed the right to appoint the sheriffs, he showed himself a partisan on the side of the proprietors against the settlers' society, known as the " loyal electors " Des Barres was recalled through the influence of the proprietors, and Colclough was reinstated , but as he was greatly disliked in Prince Edward's Island, and Tremlett was unpopular in Newfoundland, they exchanged offices. Tremlett as a Chief Justice in Prince Edward's Island was a complete failure Complaints were made against him, but the Tory Governor shielded him At last, in 1824, both Governor and Chief Justice were removed on an appeal to the king, supported by resolutions from an influential county meeting Tremlett died at Truro, Nova Scotia His ignorance of law and practice was a great bar to his success in his last situation He was surly and unpopular everywhere fights were simply for " divarsion " ; the town was dull after the fishery was finished, there were no politics or House of Assembly, no police office, no theatres, not even a bazaar ; what could an Irish boy do in those times without a bit of lively fun ? McBraire, who knew the Irish well, laughed at the whole thing.

The Chief Justice's description of the great riot is very good in its way. The constables came in to say that if he did not go out the town would be in ruins. This message, he writes, " was delivered without " any alleviation by a beast of an Irish maid servant, whilst I was " sitting in Mrs Colclough's sick room with all her children down in " the measles, with the addition, ' Madam, don't let him out, he will " ' probably be killed, and what will become of us ? ' " We picture the scene of Mrs Colclough weeping on his neck. He said he was not to be stigmatized as a coward, so out he must go. Guns were fired from the Hill, Fort Townshend, and Fort William—a signal that the troops were coming When the gallant Chief Justice arrived on the Barrens " lo ! behold ' there was nobody there," he says, " McBraire had driven them off." Whatever may have happened, it is clear the riot did not disturb old Coote, Mr. Blaikie, P. W. Carter, and the other magistrates, who were having a good dinner at the hospitable board of David Tasker. The fun of the whole thing was that the crowd followed Colclough, and hurrahed him, trying to make him believe that they were his assistants. In his letter, he seems to have had a lurking suspicion that the mob were mocking him McBraire would have invited them all in to drink at the store Neither priests, bishops, Colcloughs, nor justices, could have put down the faction fights ; they died out in time, and were succeeded by the more legitimate " divarsion " of politics

I judge Cæsar Colclough was no lawyer from a correspondence with the very able Attorney-General of Nova Scotia, Uniacke The Act provided for a sole judge, the Chief Justice wanted the Governor to appoint an associate judge, as he was afraid he could not get through the term ; Uniacke pointed out that an acting Chief Justice could be appointed in case Colclough was sick or absent, but when the law provided for one judge, the court would be illegally constituted with two on the bench Colclough was a mere tool of the Governor's, a striking contrast to Tremlett, who possessed the highest qualities of a judge— independence and impartiality. Tremlett's manners were, unfortunately, against him ; a crusty, ill-tempered, old bachelor, he did not make friends.

There was a merchants' society in St John's in these days which had been constituted about 1800, its object was to afford a medium of official communication and consultation between the Governor and the mercantile body about convoys, &c.[1]

The two leading men on whom Colclough, during the absence of the Governor in England, relied to guide him in his difficulties were McBraire and young Mr. James Stewart,[2] a very able, intelligent, gentlemanly man.

It is very doubtful if the conspiracy referred to by Colclough really ever existed, except in his own imagination; there was, however, a good deal of excitement amongst the people,[3] especially the Irish, who formed the great bulk of the "shipped" servants in St. John's, concerning the change in wages; the rumour had gone abroad that "wages were to be cut." Some of the merchants were very shrewd business men, they knew that the war was drawing to a close; France and America were exhausted, Napoleon's star was on the wane, Trafalgar and Wellington's Peninsular campaign had delivered Europe from his thraldom, they fully realized that if men were shipped on the old terms, should peace be suddenly proclaimed, the war prices for fish they were then getting would come down with a crash, with the high prices they had to pay for provisions and outfit, and with large sums for wages falling due in the autumn, they would all go under. McBraire forcibly impressed this on his brother merchants, but they had all been making money, the war had lasted with the French almost continuously since 1789, most of them believed it would still continue, they did not, therefore, take the wise precaution of preparing for a sudden fall in the markets.

Not only Newfoundland, but all British North America had prospered by the war. Compared with the United States, the British Provinces were very small and very thinly populated, during hostilities, however, all the trade with Newfoundland, hitherto monopolized by the Americans, had fallen into their hands. They supplied all the lumber, cattle, butter, oats, corn, hay, and other produce that had always been

---

[1] The Chamber of Commerce of St John's was founded on the 26th December 1823. First President, N W Hoyles (father of Sir Hugh Hoyles), secretary, John Boyd (father of Mrs James Baird).

[2] I have heard several persons speak in rather disparaging terms of this gentleman (who founded the firm of J & W Stewart), so I consulted the late Mr Brown, who knew him well. He says Stewart was a fine man of very superior parts, a perfect gentleman. In contradistinction to the old firm of Rennie Stuart & Co, in which he had been resident partner, his establishment was afterwards generally known as "Foxy Stewart's."

[3] In 1813 a very large Commission of the Peace was issued, under which the following gentlemen were appointed Justices —Coote, Broom, Rev Mr Roland, and Blaikie magistrates for St John's; Rev F. Carrington and Lilly for Harbour Grace, Rev J Clinch, M.D., and Burrell, Trinity, Egar, Greenspond, Ford, Bonavista, McKie and Angell, Bay Bulls; W Carter, Ferryland, Bradshaw and Blackburn, Placentia, Gosse, Carbonear, Anthoine, Fortune Bay, Bryant, Ferryland, Phippard, St Mary's, Pinson and S Prowse for Labrador. For the Island generally, the following naval officers —Captain Elliott, Cooksley, Skekel, Campbell, Holbrook, Buchan, also the Rev F. Carrington, and P C Le Geyt, the Governor's Secretary.

procured from America; of course, they could not furnish all the flour
that was required, but it shows what progress they were making that
out of eighty-five thousand cwt. of bread and flour, British America
supplied Newfoundland in 1813 with nearly twelve thousand cwt., also
with fourteen hundred oxen, fourteen hundred sheep, and two and a
quarter million feet of board. As an illustration that it was war time
and high wages, we have the enormous quantity of four hundred and
twenty-six thousand gallons of rum and spirits imported, besides all the
French brandy captured in the French and American prizes. There
were nearly seventeen thousand men employed in the fishery and trade;
this would give about twenty-six gallons per man; but the amount
imported was only a small portion of the liquor brought into the Colony,
there were prizes with whole ship loads of champagne and large cargoes
of French brandy and wines; all were sold by the prize agents in
St. John's. It has always been told as a tradition that the head of the
firm of prize agents never asked anyone to his table under a first
lieutenant; as there were from thirty-five to forty vessels of war on the
coast, it was about as much as he could be expected to do.

Whatever were the intentions of the merchants about wages, no
reduction was attempted. In 1814, £60 and even £70 was paid to a
common hand at
the fishery, whilst
a splitter obtained
from £90 to £140
for the season. No
doubt the merchants
were either en-
couraged to give
these high wages by
the results of 1813,
or else they were
compelled to do so
against their will: I
think most probably
they acted on com-

FARMER AND GIRL SPLITTING FISH.
From a drawing in the B.M.

pulsion; certainly no prudent men would run such fearful risks if they
could help it.[1]

[1] In Lieut. Chappell's book, "The Cruize
of the *Rosamund*," we have an account of
the social life of the Colony written in a very
superficial manner. He describes the trial
of an Irish fisherman for getting drunk at
the latter end of the fishing season. The
jury in the Surrogate Court having found

the prisoner guilty, Captain Campbell, R.N.,
the surrogate, passed the following sentence
on the culprit: "Prisoner, you have been
found guilty, after the most mature
deliberation, of unruly and disorderly
conduct; the law in such a case warrants
the court to cancel all your claim for

The greatest event occurring under the governorship of Sir Richard Keats was the order from the Home Government to grant titles to lands in the Colony   This change was brought about by various causes, by the suggestions and recommendations of Gower and Duckworth, but at the last chiefly by an organized determination on the part of the Merchants' Society to build houses without His Excellency's consent   A fund was provided to test the legality of the prohibitory orders against the erection of · buildings;[1] this movement, which was peaceable and constitutional, is stigmatized by Pedley as refractory, no doubt it was thought so by the Governor.   The author and instigator of this opposition

wages, but in consideration of your former industrious character, of your large family, and of your master having himself supplied the means of intoxication, you are hereby sentenced to be mulcted of *only one half of your wages* as a penalty for your drunkenness and misconduct"   "The effect," says Chappell, "produced by this righteous judgment was instantaneous, the countenances of the fishermen brightened, whilst those of the masters fell   . Our good Captain maintained the same impartiality and lenity throughout the whole line of his judicial career   . "

The prices of fish mentioned by Chappell are very high, 20s per quintal in outports, 32s. in St John's, and 42s sterling in Portugal   No wonder the merchants made fortunes   Glorious times when $30,000 in gold was obtained for an ordinary 3,000 quintal cargo   The fish was smuggled into Spain from Portugal, and the Newfoundland merchants had the whole Peninsular markets and Italy without a rival   Their immense success in these days led to reckless trading, and the final crash at the peace in 1818

Under Sir Richard G Keats in 1813 three men of war wintered in the Island, H M S. *Crescent* in St John's, H M S *Pheasant* at Ferryland, H M S *Prometheus* at Placentia   Chappell mentions the public reading room in St John's supplied with all the English daily papers, the "St John's Gazette," and most of the British monthly publications. He says "The President of the committee of merchants was an Irishman of low origin who had been a serjeant in the rebel army at the battle of Vinegar Hill." Evidently McBraire had not invited the lieutenant to dinner   There were over a dozen men-of-war in port   The convoy did not sail from St John's until 14th December 1813, and the fishing fleet joined the convoy again at Queenstown in the February following. Chappel mentions the LONDON TAVERN, this was kept by Cornelius Quirk; it was in Gower Street and Duckworth Street   On 25th August 1806, Quirk was allowed to extend his large public room, to widen his kitchen, and to

enlarge his store   This is the tavern mentioned by Dr, Chappell as being the best in St John's, it had a good billiard room Quirk was ancestor to Quirk who used to live at Bally Haly.

Ross's Valley was called after Captain Ross, R E., commanding the Royal Engineers in 1806

[1] LETTER from the Governor, M. K MILBANKE, to GEORGE HUTCHINS, Esq, dated Government House, St John's, Newfoundland, 15th October 1790

"SIR,—I have considered your request respecting the alteration which you wish to make in your Storehouse, near the waterside, and as it appears that the alteration will not be any ways injurious to the Fishery, you have hereby permission to make it   As to Alexander Long's house which has been built contrary to His Majesty's express commands, made known to the inhabitants of this place by my Proclamation of the 13th of last October, it must and shall come down. The pretence now set up of its being intended as a craft-house serves rather to aggravate than extenuate the offence, for by the confession of your tenant to the Magistrate who forbade him to go on with the work after it was begun, as well as to me when I viewed the house on Saturday last, no such use was to be made of it   as he said it was intended only as a covering to his potato cellar, though there is a complete chimney, if not two in it, and lodging for at least six or eight dieters   I shall embrace this opportunity of warning you against making an improper use of any other part of (what you are pleased to call) your ground, for you may rest assured that every house or other building erected upon it hereafter, without the permission (in writing) of the Governor for the time being (except such building and erection as shall be actually on purpose for the curing, salting, drying, and husbanding of Fish, which the fishermen from any part of His Majesty's European dominions, qualified agreeable to the Act of the 10th and 11th of William the

to English tyranny was Dr. William Carson,[1] the real founder of agriculture and constitutional government in the Colony. Governor Duckworth wrote to the Home Government asking leave to confiscate a number of pamphlets "coming from Scotland, which are of a " very libellous character " concerning the authorities " and the system of govern- " ment in the Colony"; he also understood "that another " is being prepared by the " same pen, of a still more " infamous character, and he " thought these monstrous " proceedings should be " stopped." The pamphleteer was Dr. Carson. After reading the whole correspon- dence, there can be very little doubt that the doctor was largely influenced by personal rancour in making these attacks; both Governors— Duckworth and Keats— treated him with unpardonable rudeness. They declined to let him peruse the records, and what stung more than any-

DR. CARSON.

From a silhouette in the possession of his daughter, Mrs. Job.

thing else, refused to pay his legal salary as surgeon to the volunteer of the house above mentioned, which you will no doubt assist him in executing.

" I am, &c.,

" To George Hutchings, Esq."

—WARREN's *Lecture*, App., pp. xv.-xvi.

[1] Dr. William Carson came to St. John's in 1808. He had practised for four- teen years in Birmingham, England; he ob- tained the highest medical honours from the University of Edinburgh; his character and standing is certified by the eight principal physicians of Birmingham. He was appointed surgeon to the Loyal Volunteers of St. John's in 1809, but when the corps was augmented to ten companies, denominated "The Loyal Volunteer Rangers," Carson was dismissed from the position of surgeon. In an indig- nant letter to Governor Duckworth occurs the following high-flown passage:—"The dark and secret machinations of the malignant may tease but cannot irritate me, the arm of power may humble my mind but cannot subdue it."

Third, and the 15th of George the Third, have a right to erect without asking permis- sion) must unavoidably be taken down and removed to obedience to his Majesty's said commands. And it may not be amiss at the same time to inform you, I am also directed not to allow any *possession as private pro- perty to be taken of, or any right of property whatever to be acknowledged in any land whatever* which is not actually employed in the Fishery, in terms of the aforementioned Act, whether possessed by pretended grants from former Governors or from any other (no matter what) unwarrantable pretences—there- fore it behoves you, with all possible dispatch, to employ the whole of the ground which you now lay claim to in the Fishery, lest others should profit by your neglect, and make that use of it which the Legislature of Great Britain intended should be made of all the land in this Country, and without which no one has a right to claim it as his own. The Sheriff will have directions about the removal

brigade.[1] Carson, a determined, pertinacious character, was not to be put down by any number of old admirals or hangers-on, like Colclough and the Government House clique; he stuck to his point, and ultimately got his pay.

Carson was an old Whig, of the same school as Sydney Smith and the Edinburgh Reviewers; there were many abuses in his time, and he exposed them. Douglas Jerrold says of the Conservatives of his day, "they would not allow a rat hole to be a rat hole, but a healthy ventilator." In the same spirit, Dr. Carson was attacked and persecuted by the Governors and their minions; the profound learning of Cæsar Colclough was invoked by His Excellency as to what should be done to this daring pamphleteer; but Colclough, though he breathed anathemas on the head of the doctor, gave forth but a very uncertain sound on the subject of prosecuting him. The authorities at home gave the Governor also but little satisfaction; there were plenty of libels at the time on the Prince Regent, and very little satisfaction had been got out of prosecuting the libellers. The fat Adonis of forty had not raised his reputation by libel information, so the English Ministry recommended their Excellencies, Duckworth and Keats, to possess their souls in peace, and to let Dr. Carson alone. The following extracts show the character of these slanders. They appear very logical, moderate, and well expressed. The statement of facts is unanswerable, and the conclusions on the subject of the government of the Colony are the only ones that a reasonable man could arrive at. The first, published in 1811, contains "the libellous and scurrilous attack" complained of by Governor Duckworth :—

"A naval commander accustomed to receive obedience, whether his orders are dictated by justice or injustice, by reason or false prejudice, cannot be expected to brook with temper any opposition to his will. The man whose duty calls upon him to defend his rights, and the just interest of his family, in opposition to the opinion and passions of such a Governor, will have but a small chance of success. An act of independence would be arraigned as an act of mutiny. All the influence of his office, all the arts of his satellites would be marshalled to effect his overthrow. Accustomed to use force to knock down opposition—force being the power he knows best how to direct—the toils of investigation, deliberation, and judgement, are seldom had recourse to by a Naval Governor."

The following is from the Doctor's second tract, "the poisonous publication and vicious pamphlet," referred to by Sir Richard Keats. If these ancient admirals could only have lived to see our local press at

[1] He mentions in his second pamphlet, 1813, that he had been dismissed from his offices of surgeon to the volunteers and the gaol, an office now held by his grandson, Dr. Henry Shea.

electioneering time, how would they feel when 'Dr Carson's papers so' hurt their pride ?—

" I am far, very far indeed, from wishing to impugn the motives of the Governors. I am even disposed to allow, that they have been, for the most part, actuated by the best intentions   It is the habits of Naval Commanders, generating a fondness for arbitrary rule, and thereby requiring a passive submission to their will, utterly unfitting them to preside at the head of a Government not possessing the usual necessary restraints. It is the undertaking a high situation, with the duties of which they cannot be acquainted, that I wish to expose and decide, as inconsistent with just moral conduct, derogatory to the character, and hostile to the privileges of Britons

  " .The inhabitants of Newfoundland are 'truly loyal,' and attached even 'to enthusiasm, to the glory and interest of the British nation. They are uniformly desirous of obtaining the good opinion, and the good will of their Governors. This fact has been strongly manifested, on the arrival of each succeeding Governor; but, no sooner did they become entangled in the Gothic system of pulling down fences, stages, and houses , no sooner did they commence the blasting system of favouritism and proscription, than all hopes of improvement were dissipated, and the mind recoiled into gloomy despondency.

  " The only remedy against the evils flowing from the present system, will be found in giving to the people, what they most ardently wish, and what is unquestionably their right, a civil Government, consisting of a resident Governor, a Senate House and House of Assembly.

  " I shall as briefly as possible, endeavour to point out the advantages that would flow to this island, and the mother country, from the establishment of a civil Government, and from the appropriation and cultivation of the lands. In doing this I shall have to combat some prejudice, and some error   The island of Newfoundland has been represented as destitute of soil; the atmosphere as unfriendly to vegetation , agriculture as injurious to a fishery, and the country colonized as contrary to the interest of the British merchants, and incompatible with the policy of the mother country."

As the result of the action of the merchants and the animadversions of the doctor, Sir Richard Keats' instructions from England

"Directed his attention to the propriety of authorising the cultivation of those lands of the colony which might be applicable to that purpose . He was therefore to consider himself authorised to grant leases of small portions of land to industrious individuals for the purpose of cultivation, taking care, however, to reserve an annual quit-rent, either nominal or real, according to the circumstances. of each individual case. In furtherance of the design contemplated by this instruction, the following notice was published, bearing date June 26, 1813 —

  " ' All resident and industrious inhabitants desirous of obtaining small grants of land for the purposes of cultivation in the neighbourhood of St John's, subject to very moderate quit-rents, are desired to give in their applications to the office of the Secretary to the Governor, before the last day of July.'

  " Before issuing this order, His Excellency had called for a return of all lands that were already claimed outside the town of St John's, with the titles on which the several claims were based, when it appeared that the inhabitants were proceeding rather rapidly to do for themselves what they had tardily received from the Government permission to do, and this without the condition annexed in the latter case. The return showed that between October 25, 1812, and July 10, 1813, twenty-six persons had enclosed plots of land of various dimensions, but amounting in the aggregate to seventy-five acres.

"The following extracts are taken from the letter of the Governor to Lord Bathurst, reporting the success of this measure. They also afford a glimpse of the squatting system which had begun to prevail, and of new ideas which were dawning in people's minds as to the agricultural capacities of the country :—

"'The measure which I was authorised to adopt, of making small grants of land to industrious individuals for the purpose of cultivation, has been generally

FARM SCENE NEAR ST. JOHN'S ABOUT 1790.
From a water colour painting in the B.M., MS. 33233.

received with becoming gratitude, notwithstanding pains have been taken to induce the lower classes to ascribe the bounty of Government to a wrong motive. In proceeding to execute this part of my instructions, it became necessary to make some enquiry into the lands at present enclosed, or in cultivation, and into the titles by which those in occupancy in the vicinity of St. John's are held. And it is evident that the possessors of a considerable portion of them have no other claims than that which occupancy may be permitted to establish. St. John's, with a population of nearly 10,000, seems to have grown out of its original situation, and to be changing its character from a fishery to a large commercial town, and for a considerable time past has offered such advantages to the farmer and gardener, as to overcome all the restraints which nature and the policy of Government have laid on the cultivation of a soil certainly less sterile than it has generally been considered. More than a thousand acres are in cultivation, and as many more perhaps enclosed, the produce of which is confined to hay, potatoes, and vegetables of various kinds, crops of which may be seen as plentiful as in England, whilst the environs of the town, the natural beauties of which are very striking, present to the view several neat, well-cultivated, and productive little farms.

"'It is a circumstance particularly favourable to agriculture that husbandry does not interfere with the fisheries, and that the fisheries supply the farmer with manure. The lands may be prepared, and the crops put in and taken out, before the commencement of, and after the fishery is over. With these advantages, and that of a certain and profitable market, the desire to possess land for several years has been eager and general Proclamations repeated by my predecessors, forbidding persons to take possession of lands, have been disregarded In cases where grants or leases have been obtained from Government, the limits have commonly been exceeded. Pretexts of every sort which ingenuity could devise have been resorted to to found titles, and by paying attention to claims or pretexts of private property, of which they are peculiarly jealous (and they have not been invaded by me) I have found but little land in the neighbourhood of St. John's to dispose of.

"'The total number of grants made this season by the Governor under the authority afforded by his instructions was one hundred and ten small plots of land not exceeding four acres These were subject to annual quit-rents of from 2s. 6d. to 5s per acre, renewable at the expiration of thirty years at moderate fines. The above grants were not equal to the number of applications Many of the latter had yet to be decided on; His Excellency governing himself chiefly by the recommendation of the magistrates, paying attention to character, and considering the circumstances and family of the applicant.

"'The scarcity of provisions which had prevailed in the early part of the year 1813, had been well calculated to stimulate the people to make trial of what the land could produce towards their support. During the first months of 1812, before the declaration of war by America, supplies were in sufficient abundance, and to be had at a moderate price. But after the breaking out of hostilities, the prices gradually advanced to an unprecedented height Fortunately, a seasonable importation was received from Canada, of 12,000 cwt. of bread, and 4,000 barrels of flour, which barely dissipated the prospect of starvation during the winter Even with this welcome addition, so dire was the scarcity, that at one period common biscuit " was retailed out in small parcels of a few pounds as a peculiar favour to the poor, at the rate of £6 sterling per cwt Potatoes were sold at 35s per barrel (two bushels and a half), and the inhabitants were reduced to the most alarming state of need, when a vessel arrived from Greenock with relief" Before the arrival of this vessel, a committee of gentlemen had paid General Moore £7 sterling per barrel as a deposit for flour out of the public stores, to bake up for the poor Even in the summer of 1813, the following high prices prevailed—Biscuit, 70s to 84s per cwt. Flour, 120s to 126s per barrel. Beef, 140s. to 147s. per barrel. Pork, 180s to 200s Potatoes, 22s 6d. to 25s. per barrel. On July 16, the society of merchants reported to His Excellency that the quantity of provisions on hand was not more than sufficient to supply the demand for two months, and there was little prospect of any considerable importations'

"On this subject the Governor made urgent representations to the Secretary of State, and, probably as the result of those representations, though apparently coming in the ordinary way of trade, large imports were received, mostly from Great Britain, which replenished the stores, brought down prices, and removed all apprehensions of famine for the ensuing winter."[1]

[1] From PEDLEY's *History of Newfoundland* and *Newfoundland Records*.

In June 1814 there is a letter in the Records from Hunter & Co. praying permission to export a quantity of flour, "that the market is " now so glutted that it is impossible to sell it, and that if not allowed " to send it away it will be spoiled."

In 1815 both Colclough and Sir Richard-Keats left the Colony The Chief Justice was evidently terrified by the following letter. He put forth a proclamation immediately, offering a reward of £100 for the discovery of the writer or of the person who affixed it to the Court House gate, of course without result.

" To the Honorable CESAR COLCLOUGH, Esq , Chief Judge in the Supreme Court
    of St. John's, and in and over the Island of Newfoundland, &c , &c., &c.

" The humble petition of the distress[d] of St John's in general most humbly sheweth :—

" That the poor of St. John's are very much oppressed by different orders from the Court House, which they amigine is unknown to your Lordship, Concerning the killing and shooting their doggs, without the least sine of the being sick or mad Wee do hope that your Lordship will check the Justices that was the means of this evil Proclamation against the Interest of the poor Families, that their dependance for their Winter's Fewel is on their Doggs, and likewise several single men that is bringing out Wood for the use of the Fishery, if in case this business is not put back it will be the means of an indeferent business as ever the killing the Doggs in Ireland was before the rebellion the first Instance will be given by killing Cows and Horses, and all other disorderly Vice that can be comprehened by the Art of Man.

" Wee are sorry for giveing your Lordship any uneasines for directing any like business to your Honour, but Timely notice is better than use any voilance What may be the cause of what we not wish to men' at present, by puting a stop to this great evil. Wee hope that our Prayrs will be mains of obtaining Life Everlasting for your Lordship in the world to come

" Mercy wee will take, and Mercy wee will give "

The Chief Justice should have known, as one experienced about his countrymen, that the threatening letter is a common Hibernian device ; that, whilst it is sometimes malignant, often enough it is the mere wanton trick of some idle vagabond who can write, and wants to worry his neighbour. Magistrates of any standing, either in Ireland or amongst Irish people, could " paper a trunk " with such epistles This one is in very mild tone; it has not got even the traditionary coffin and cross bones at the head of it; it is more of a respectful remonstrance than a threat of murder, as the affrighted Colclough translated it. During the troublous times that were coming on the Colony, it was a good thing he left. Colclough was succeeded in the Chief Justiceship by Francis Forbes, Esq , a distinguished barrister of Lincoln's Inn. He was appointed on the 4th August 1816, and commenced the discharge of his duties on the 15th July 1817, and remained resident in the Colony up to the 6th of May 1822 Chief

Justice Forbes won golden opinions from all classes, the pages of "The Select Cases in the Supreme Court of Newfoundland" are an abiding monument to his profound learning and serene intelligence.

The faction fights went on for many years after Colclough left. "Yallow-belly Corner," on the east side of Beck's Cove, commemorates the spot where the wounded in the melee used to be washed in the little brook flowing into Beck's Cove. The Tipperary "clear airs," the Waterford "whey bellies," and the Cork "dadyeens" were arrayed against the "yallow belly" faction—the "Doones" or Kilkenny boys, and the Wexford "yallow bellies" There were besides the "young colts" and a number of other names for the factions. They fought with one another "out of pure devilment and divarsion," as an old Irishman explained it to me Besides these scrimmages there were plenty of fights when the "fools" or mummers came out from Christmas to Twelfth Day These men were dressed up with high paper caps of a triangular form, ornamented with ribbons They wore white shirts, sewn all over with ribbons and streamers A good "rig-out" cost both time and money. The "swabs" were made of a bladder, covered with canvas or a switch, made sometimes of a cow's tail fastened to a stick Some were dressed as women, with long garments, known as "eunchucks." They were all masked, and ran at passengers with an Indian yell, and spoke in a falsetto voice. Men were often beaten badly for old grievances by the fools. I remember, as a boy, how proud I used to be to shake hands with a fool, and to know what "rigs" Noah Thomas or Mick Toole were going out in. Each company had one or more hobby-horses, with gaping jaws to snap at people. The fools had to be put down by Act of Parliament Mummers and fools were English customs, dating back to the Saxon time, brought to this Colony by the old Devonshire settlers

The returns for the year 1814 show unexampled prosperity—an enormous fishery, a large catch of seals (a hundred and twenty thousand) and splendid prices; 1815 was also a good season,[1] the fish exported amounted to one and a quarter million quintals. Fish was quoted in St. John's at nineteen and twenty-one shillings' per quintal, cod oil at thirty-three pounds, and seal oil at thirty-six pounds per ton. 1814 is, wrongly, generally stated to have been a regular *annus mirabilis*, nine hundred and fifty thousand quintals of fish having been reported to have been taken and sold, at

---

[1] In 1815, 1816, and 1817, Newmans built several fine vessels at Great Jervois, which were highly commended by Trinity House for their excellent models and staunch construction, all constructed out of timber obtained in Bay Despair.

two pounds sterling per quintal, the whole exports being valued at the enormous sum of over two million pounds sterling.[1] With the close of the year 1815 came the crash.[2] In December 1815 Mr. Coote, the Supreme Surrogate, and Captain Buchan, R.N., on whom the whole judicial business of the capital devolved, wrote to Sir R. G. Keats :—

"In November 1815 there have been upwards of seven hundred writs issued since the closing of accounts in October [in all over nine hundred summons], and forty declarations of insolvency ; notwithstanding which we are happy to inform your Excellency that the public peace has not in any material degree been interrupted, nor do we perceive the smallest ground for apprehension of any change of sentiment likely to disturb the present tranquillity."

What a contrast between these calm words of two brave cool-headed men in the midst of dire calamity and the fears and forebodings of Colclough. Peace had come after the crushing defeat of Waterloo,

WEXFORD HERRING COT.[3]

18th June 1815 ; the United States had made peace with England by the Treaty of Ghent ; American and Norwegian fish flowed into the Mediterranean markets ; produce was selling abroad for less sometimes

[1] The official returns of exports for this year, from October 1813 to October 1814, do not show either such high prices or quantities. Fish is put down at 20s. to 26s. per quintal ; value of seal oil, &c. and furs at £38,570 ; salmon, 3,425 tierces, at £4 per tierce. There is a significant item of 2,049 quintals of fish *exported to the Brazils*. James Stewart is credited with being the first merchant in Newfoundland to inaugurate this important business. In one of his letters he writes, "30,000 quintals of fish, well handled, should make any man's fortune."

[2] PRICES, 1812–1816.

"Price of cod oil, Liverpool, 1812, £38 sterling per ton.

"Price of cod oil, Liverpool, 1813, £49 sterling per ton.

"Price of cod oil, London, 1813, £42 10s. sterling per ton.

"Tar in England, 1813, 43s. per barrel, and expected to rise higher.

"April 1816, the price of cod oil continues low at £28 per ton. The introduction of gas light for the streets and shops lessens the consumption very considerably, and will be worse."—*From* NEWMAN & Co.'s *Books*.

[3] It was from this handy little craft that our fishermen got the idea of the boat now in such general use all over the Colony ; it displaced the lug-sails towards the end of last century.

The fishing boats in the cod and seal

than one-third of its cost to the merchant   A panic ensued, and nearly all the houses in the trade went down.   The catch of 1816 was considerable[1]—over a million quintals were exported   Prices, however, had become abnormally low—fourteen, twelve, and even ten shillings per quintal

The winters of 1815, 1816, and 1817–18 are memorable in the annals of the Colony.   In the winter of 1815 the capital and all the outports were in a state of actual starvation   The losses and insolvencies referred to by Coote had ruined the credit of our merchants.   Importations of provisions were quite inadequate, and, to add to the general misery, emigrants were flocking in from Ireland [2] By Christmas 1816, when communication with the outside was virtually shut off, the dread spectre of famine threatened our unfortunate Colony.   Fortunately, at this terrible crisis, the virtual control of the Colony was in the hands of Captain David Buchan, R.N.   The most fulsome panegyric is really but faint praise for the cool courage, able management, and humane exertions of the heroic commander. During this trying winter he put his own men on H.M S *Pike* on short allowance, when the following address was presented to him by the Grand Jury —

"You, sir, were seen conspicuous in public exertions to afford the only refuge to which those suffering the calamities of impending famine could address themselves for succor "

fishery were formerly called shallops and shalloways, these words often occurring in our history. The shallop was a large boat, decked at both ends and open in the centre, with moveable deck-boards and pounds, there were cuddies both fore and aft where the fishermen could sleep   There were never less than three men in a shallop, their dimensions were—30 to 40 feet keel, 10 to 40 feet beam, many of the larger shallops had five men, and would carry 200 qtls. dry fish   The shalloways were open boats, what are now called punts.   The sails in common use until after 1780 were lug sails   The sprit-sail boats were probably copied from Irish models, like the picture of the Wexford herring cot.   There was no fire below deck, the cooking apparatus, or galley, was built of stone, and was generally on the forecastle   The fishermen's clothing was made commonly of whitney and barked swanskin (oiled clothing had not been invented, and the barvel was universally used by the fishermen all over North America) ; for the seal fishery the men had bluchers and buskins; pewter pots were mostly used for cooking and drinking vessels   The first decked vessels for the seal fishery were about the size of ordinary Western boats, 40 to 50 feet keel, and 14 to 15 feet beam.   The

schooners all had deep, heavy keels; both the bottom planking and keel were made of birch and witch hazel.   It took about seven men to haul out the birch stick for a keel   For the boat's frame juniper was generally used, the timbers were about a foot apart, and the planking was about an inch and a half thick, generally of pine, with black spruce for spars.   The schooner rig came into vogue about the time of the commencement of the ship seal fishery   In the early accounts of this industry a distinction is made between the fishery as prosecuted in shallops and in schooners   The only novelty introduced about 1798 was the use of larger vessels in this business.   There was always more or less of a seal fishery carried on by the residents with nets, pursuing them on the ice, and following them up with shallops and punts.

[1] Pedley, in his history, states the catch was small.   The records show that the amount was about 1,083,452 quintals.

[2] Eleven thousand Irish came to St. John's between 1814 and 1815. There is an instructive correspondence between Kent and Morris of Waterford about the cubic space required for an emigrant   Their sufferings in crossing must have been terrible, only exceeded by the horrors of the middle passage on board an African slaver.

If Buchan deserved all these encomiums for his services in 1815–16, what praise shall we give him for his still more difficult task in the terrible season of 1817–18, known in Newfoundland as the "Hard Winter," and still more generally as the "*Winter of the Rals?*" In the former season, starvation alone had to be contended with; now famine, frost, and fire combined, like three avenging furies, to scourge the unfortunate Island. A frost that sealed up the whole coast commenced early in November, and continued almost without intermission through the entire season, and on the nights of the 7th and 21st of November 1817, three hundred houses were burnt, rendering two thousand individuals, in depth of that cruel winter, homeless.[1] Nothing can add to the simple pathos of the grand jury's presentment :—

"Calamities so extensive would have been in our most prosperous times productive of severe distress, but on retrospecting to our situation for the last three years, during which period we have alternately suffered by fire, by famine, by lawless outrage, and numerous mercantile failures, which have greatly injured the commercial reputation of the town, the recent conflagrations seemed only wanting to consummate our misfortunes. Several hundred men in the prime of life, without money, or the means of being employed, without adequate clothing or food, are at the hour of midnight wandering amidst the smoking ruins to seek warmth from the ashes, and food from the refuse of the half-consumed fish. In dwelling-houses the misery is little less. Many families, once in affluence, are now in absolute want. Within these two days, two men have been found perished of cold, and many hundreds must inevitably experience a similar fate if humanity does not promptly and effectually step forward to their relief."

To add to this misery, gangs of half-famished, lawless men everywhere threatened the destruction of life and property; vigilance committees were formed in every settlement. Mr. George Kemp, then residing in Brigus, tells of the confidence and safety the planters felt when Captain Buchan came amongst them. In St. John's and every outport his presence brought tranquillity; all caught the contagion of his splendid courage. The suffering endured during that winter no pen can fully describe.

A vessel with provisions put into Bay Bulls in distress; the people flocked down *en masse* to board her, and they would not let the ship leave the harbour until half her cargo had been unloaded by the authorities and distributed. In Renews, two West Country crews were frozen up; a mob, headed by the village blacksmith, attacked the room, threatening to murder the Devonshire men unless they surrendered their provisions; one of the skippers, an old captain of a privateer, had been expecting an attack, and had his store loopholed for musketry; he fired a volley over the heads of the crowd, and all fled; afterwards the same captain and his merchant shared all their provisions with the Renews

[1] There had also been a very destructive fire in February 1816.

people. Many more incidents could be related about the winter of the
" Rals," or " Rowdies." Near Renews, a lot of Irish emigrants left their
ship at the edge of the ice, and crawled on shore on their hands and
knees, to add more sharers in the already inadequate rations. During
these three unhappy years everything was against us; even the seal
fishery failed in 1817.[1]

In the spring of 1818 this period of calamity came to an end.
The seal fishery was unusually productive, in less than a fortnight

WOODLANDS COTTAGE, ST. JOHN'S.

From a drawing by Lady Hamilton, in the possession of Sir E. A. Hamilton, Bart.

scores of little vessels returned, loaded to the scuppers with fat; hope
revived, the fisheries were good, the markets improved, and the poor
old Colony again began to lift up her head. The Governor, Sir Francis
Pickmore,[2] had been ordered to remain through the winter in Newfoundland. Dr. Carson's pamphlet had shown up the absurdity of
Governors coming out for two or three months in the year. Henceforth
all their Excellencies were perennials, not fleeting annuals. Admiral
Pickmore was a firm, courageous old man, but the toil, exposure, and

[1] 1817 is the worst seal fishery on record,
only thirty-seven thousand seals being killed
over the whole Island.

[2] There appears to be no information
about Sir F. Pickmore beyond what can be
gathered from the Navy Lists. The family
appears to have died out, as none of this
name can be found in the Navy, Army,
Church, &c

anxiety of the last terrible winter told on his enfeebled constitution, and on the 24th of February he died. One can form some idea of the severity of the season from the fact that it took all the crew of H M S *Fly*, with the assistance of civilians, a whole fortnight to cut a channel through the ice, which was between four and five feet thick The faithful admiral's obsequies were carried out with great state, the grandest ceremony ever known in the Colony.

> " So past the strong heroic soul away.
> And when they buried him the little port
> Had seldom seen a costlier funeral."

The sufferings of the Newfoundland colonists called forth humane response from all quarters. The British Government sent £10,000, Halifax contributed liberally, but the most touching and generous gift was from the large-hearted people of Boston A few years before they were fitting out privateers to destroy our fishing vessels, now they sent us a welcome ship-load of provisions In the most inclement month of the year, January, the brig *Messenger* came into St. John's, bearing the following address :—

" To His Excellency FRANCIS PICKMORE, Esq., Vice-Admiral and Governor, &c , President of the Society for the Improvement of the Poor of St. John's

" SIR,—The recent conflagration of a great part of the town of St John's, at a period of the year when it may be impracticable to obtain relief from the parent country, and the calamity which must necessarily ensue to a large number of our fellow-beings, have been felt in this town with all the sympathy which they are calculated to inspire A subscription, for the purpose of affording some immediate aid to the sufferers, has been consequently opened in this place, and the means of purchasing a quantity of such articles as are considered to be best adapted to the exigencies of the moment, have been readily contributed by a number of its inhabitants.

" The American brig *Messenger*, Captain Peterson, having been chartered for the exclusive object of carrying this offering to St John's, we have now the honour to enclose you a bill of lading, and manifest of her cargo, consisting of the following articles :—

174 barrels of flour	125 barrels of meal
11 tierces of rice	27 barrels and 963 bags of bread,

which, on behalf of the contributors, we request that you will have the goodness to receive, and cause the same to be distributed among the sufferers by the late conflagration, in such manner and in such proportions as their respective circumstances may require We beg leave to recommend the bearer, Captain Peterson, to your kind protection. . . The cause of humanity alone has induced him to undertake, at this inclement season, such a voyage which, under other circumstances, he would have felt himself obliged to decline.

" We have the honour to be, with all due consideration, very respectfully, your Excellency's obedient humble servants.   (Signed)

" JAMES PERKINS	ARNOLD WILLIS
' JONATHAN AMORY, Junr.	BENJAMIN RICH
" TRISTRAM BARNARD	JOHN HOUSTON.

" Boston, December 27. 1817."

Bishop Lambert, of the Franciscan order, had succeeded the eminent Dr. O'Donel as Roman Catholic Bishop of Newfoundland, he was consecrated at Wexford, April 1806, Bishop of Chitra *in partibus*. Dr. Lambert was rather an old man when appointed, and of very delicate constitution All his contemporaries speak of him as a perfect gentleman, sometimes a little hasty, but genial, kind, and of pre-eminent social qualities; he dined out a good deal with the Governor and the officers and merchants, entertaining them in return at his own hospitable board.   Dr. Lambert received an allowance from the British Government.[1] In 1811 Dr Scallan came out to assist, and was afterwards his successor   The first three Roman Catholic bishops in this Colony, by their suavity of manner, and their liberal, enlightened policy, contributed perhaps more than any others to promote harmony and peace in the community.

There were two treaties of peace with France—in 1814 and in 1815. St. Pierre and Miquelon had been formally given back to our enemies in 1814, when suddenly, in 1815, Captain Buchan was sent again to retake the islands and plant the Union Jack on the Governor's staff; the taking and retaking of these little islands was a regular "Jack-in-the-box" affair.   Before the peace the merchants of St John's had sent a very strong memorial to the Prince Regent praying that in any future settlement foreigners might be excluded from our fisheries, the Governors vigorously supported the prayer of the memorial.   His Royal Highness promised favourable consideration, but, as usual, our interests were deliberately sacrificed   France had been completely conquered. Why, then, did she recover her position on the Newfoundland coast?   Castlereagh's answer is characteristic: "The European sovereigns wanted to make the Bourbons popular with the French people"   For the sake of the incapable, unteachable Louis XVIII, a galling yoke was thrown round the necks of British colonists   It is the flimsiest and most paltry excuse for a great diplomatic blunder

On the death of Admiral Pickmore, Captain Bowker, of the admiral's ship, was Acting-Governor until the arrival of Sir Charles Hamilton [2] in July 1818   In the beginning of September of that year another fire broke out in St. John's, which consumed twelve houses and part of the

---

[1] A stipend of £75 per annum was granted to Dr Lambert " 1814, April In consideration of the respectability attached to your situation as Head of the Catholic Church in Newfoundland, and of the highly creditable and meritorious manner in which you discharge the duties of your important office, His Royal Highness has been graciously pleased to direct that an annual allowance of £75 shall be paid to you whilst you continue to hold that important situation"

[2] Sir C Hamilton, born 1767, was entered on the books of his father's ship, the *Hector*, in 1776; in 1784 he succeeded to the baronetcy, was captain in 1789 In 1794 he was present at the sieges of Bastia, Calvi, &c He was in command of the *Melpomene* for seven years, serving on the coasts of Holland, Africa, the East and West Indies In 1801

Ordnance property, and in 1819 yet another destructive conflagration, which destroyed one hundred and twenty houses at the western end of the town; the loss was estimated at £120,000 sterling. There can be very little doubt that these fires were the work of incendiaries. Although, for the time, these recurring calamities caused great privations and misery, the result was a great improvement in the laying out of the city; Water Street and Duckworth Street, formerly narrow lanes, were now built up with good substantial houses, and were widened to fifty feet.[1] The new Governor was chiefly remarkable for his stern, unbending Conservatism. The most important event during his tenure of office was the convention of 1818 with America.

SIR C. HAMILTON, BART.

From a portrait in the possession of Sir E. A. Hamilton, Bart.

It was agreed :—

"That the inhabitants of the United States should have for ever, in common with the subjects of His Britannic Majesty, the liberty to take fish of every kind on that part of the southern coast of Newfoundland extending from Cape Ray to

he was returned for Dungannon, and in 1807 for Honiton, which he represented till 1812, though away on active service. Was made rear-admiral in 1810, and vice-admiral in 1814. From 1818 to 1824 he was Governor of Newfoundland; became admiral in 1830, a K.C.B. in 1833, and died at Iping, Sussex, in 1849. Lady Hamilton was the first Governor's wife to reside in the Colony; she lived in Fort Townshend, St. John's, for four years, and drew the portrait of Mary March.

[1] THE ST. JOHN'S FIRES OF 1817-20.

1 Geo. IV. Cap. li.

AN ACT TO REGULATE THE RE-BUILDING OF THE TOWN OF ST. JOHN'S, IN NEWFOUND-LAND, AND FOR INDEMNIFYING PERSONS GIVING UP GROUND FOR THAT PURPOSE.
[15th July, 1820.]
WHEREAS the Town of *Saint John*, in the Island of *Newfoundland*, hath recently been visited by very great and destructive Fires, the ravages whereof have been chiefly occasioned by the narrowness of the Streets, and the difficulty of arresting the progress of the flames; And whereas it will greatly contribute to the convenience of the said Town, as well as to its future security, if

certain regulations be made for the rebuilding of such parts thereof as have been destroyed, and also for the erection of any Houses or Buildings in the said Town hereafter; Be it therefore enacted by the King's Most Excellent Majesty, by and with the advice and consent of the Lords Spiritual and Temporal, and Commons, in this present Parliament assembled, and by the authority of the same, that the Lower Street in the said Town, commonly called *Water Street*, shall not be less than Fifty Feet in width in every part thereof, extending from the house and stores occupied by *Brown, Hoyles & Co.*, at the East end, to the public Ships Room, commonly called the *Western Ships Room*, at the West end thereof; and that the Upper Street, commonly called *Duckworth Street*, shall not be less than Forty Feet in width; and that all and every Houses, Stores, Erections and Buildings whatsoever, built and erected since the first day of *June* One Thousand Eight Hundred and Eighteen, or which shall at any time or times hereafter be erected and built in the said street or either of them, whether the same be upon any vacant spot of Ground or upon the site of any former Building, shall be made to conform to the width of the said

the Rameau Islands; on the western and northern coast, from Cape Ray to the Quirpon Islands; on the shores of the Magdalen Islands, and also on the coasts, bays, harbours, and creeks, from Mount Joli on the southern coast of Labrador to and through the straits of Belleisle; and thence northwardly, indefinitely along the coast, without prejudice, however, to any of the exclusive rights of the Hudson's Bay Company."

The convention further provided :—

" That the American fishermen should also have liberty for ever to dry and cure fish in any of the unsettled bays, harbours, and creeks of the southern part of the coast of Newfoundland above described, and of the coast of Labrador; but so soon as the same, or any portion thereof, should be settled, it was not to be lawful for the said fishermen to dry or cure fish at such portion so settled without previous agreement for such purpose with the inhabitants, proprietors, or possessors of the said ground."

LADY HAMILTON.
From a portrait in the possession of Sir E. A. Hamilton, Bart.

Streets, as the same is respectively hereby established and directed; Provided always, that nothing herein contained shall be construed to extend to any House, Store, Erection or Building, which since the said first day of *June* One Thousand Eight Hundred and Eighteen, may have been or at any time hereafter may be erected in *Water Street* aforesaid, the same being built and made entirely of Stone or Bricks, and covered with Slates or Tiles, and always having a clear width in the said Street of not less than Forty Feet.

II.—*And be it further enacted*, That there shall be Four Cross Streets or open spaces to serve as Fire-breaks, and intersect the said Streets called *Water Street* and *Duckworth Street* as nearly as might be at right angles; and that all and every of the said Cross Streets shall not be less than Sixty feet in width, and shall run in the following directions, that is to say, the first or western Cross street from the Water Side, in a line with the corner of *Dinah Elliot's* Shop and *Maddock's Lane* to *Duckworth Street*; the second from the Water Side running in a line with the corner of *James Clift's* and *Perkins and Winter's* tenements leading up the *Church Hill*; the third to run from the Water Side between *Clapp's* and *Keen's*

Properties, lately held by *George Niven* and *A. Chambers*, the middle of the Cove to be the centre of the Street, through the Ground lately occupied by *William Barnes* and others; and the last or Eastern Street from the Ordnance Wharf up to the *King's Road*; and that no House, Store, Erection or Building whatsoever, shall be erected or built so as to front above *Water Street*, upon any or either of the said Cross Streets, but that the same shall be and remain open and free from any Buildings whatsoever, other than the inclosures thereof; and also, that in case any other Cross Streets may be hereafter required as a security against Fire, upon the same being marked out and presented by the Grand Jury, and approved by the Governor for the time being, there shall be such other Cross Streets or Fire-breaks, of the like dimensions of those hereinbefore mentioned, and according to the Boundaries so presented and approved; and the Ground and Property necessary to be taken shall be estimated and paid for in like manner as is herein-after mentioned; Provided always, that nothing herein contained shall authorise the taking of any Fishing Room, Flakes, or any part thereof, which may be actually occupied and employed for the purpose of curing Fish.

The agitation for representative government in the year 1819 received great impetus from the well-known case of Butler and Lundrigan. At a surrogate court held in Harbour Grace, before Captain David Buchan, H.M.S. *Grasshopper*, and the Rev. John Leigh, Episcopal Missionary, Lundrigan, not appearing upon a summons, was held to be guilty of contempt of court, and sentenced to receive thirty-six lashes on his bare back. Lundrigan was tied up and flogged by the boatswain of the ship until he fainted under the severity of the punishment.[1] At a meeting held in St. John's on the 14th of November 1820, Patrick Morris chairman, the following resolutions were passed :—

" Resolved that we yield to no body or class of men in loyalty to our King, in obedience respect and support of the laws of our country, or in love and veneration to our glorious constitution.

" Resolved that we have beheld with abhorrence and detestation the cruel and ignominious punishment inflicted on the bodies of Philip Butler and James Lundrigan for the trifling causes elicited in evidence on the late trial in our Supreme Court.

" Resolved that we shall pursue such legal and constitutional means as may be within our power to have the law repealed which, it appears, sanctions such arbitrary proceedings in the Surrogates, and that a committee be appointed to carry our intentions into effect.

" Further resolved that we defray Butler's and Lundrigan's expenses and maintenance and that thanks be passed to the Lawyers Dawe and Geo. Lilly for their disinterested conduct in conducting the cases in the Supreme Court.

" WILLIAM CARSON, M.D.,	PATRICK DOYLE,
" PATRICK MORRIS,	JOHN RYAN,
" JOHN ROCHFORT, M.D.,	GEO. GADEN,
" GEORGE NIVEN,	THOMAS BECK,
" HENRY SHEA,	THOMAS BURKE,
" TIMOTHY HOGAN,	ROBT. R. WAKEHAM,
" LEWIS W. RYAN."	

The case of Butler and Lundrigan was taken up solely for the purpose of being used as a lever to obtain a legislature for the Colony. Petitions were presented to both Houses of Parliament, and Dawe was sent to England to work up the case. There is no doubt that this agitation very much forwarded the demand for local government. The immediate result of the appeal, which was warmly supported by Lords Holland and Darnley in the Lords, and by the celebrated Sir James Macintosh and Dr. Lushington in the Commons, was the Judicature Act and the suppression of surrogate courts.

---

[1] Sir Charles Hamilton was so disgusted with the way that Government suits were conducted in the courts, that he requested the Government to send him out a lawyer who could act as attorney-general ; a gentleman called Westcott was accordingly sent out to His Excellency. Sir Charles found his new law adviser very glib at recommending measures in the Council, but utterly incapable of defending their legality in the courts ; the imported adviser made the last state of things worse than the first, and he was soon sent back again to England ; both Westcott and his wife enjoyed a pension for the valuable services he rendered the Colony.

APPENDIX TO CHAPTER XIII.

I. The Recapture of St. John's in September 1762.

FROM THE "LONDON GAZETTE."

Whitehall, October 12 This morning arrived Captain Campbell, of the 22nd regiment, from St John's, Newfoundland, being dispatched by Lieutenant-Colonel Amherst with the following letters to the Earl of Egremont

(*a*) COL AMHERST to the EARL OF EGREMONT

St. John's Newfoundland,
MY LORD, Sept 20 1762

According to the orders I received from Sir Jeffery Amherst at New York, of which your Lordship will have been informed, I proceeded from New York to Halifax with the transports, to take up there the troops destined for the expedition I got into the harbour the 26th of August; and finding Lord Colvill sailed, determined to embark the troops there, and at Louisbourg, as expeditiously as possible, and proceed after his Lordship The men-of-war being sailed, who were to have taken part of the troops on board, I was obliged to take up shipping to the amount of 400 tons. I had everything embarked, ready to sail on the 29th, but contrary winds kept us in the harbour till the 1st of September, when we got out and arrived at Louisbourg on the 5th The next day the troops were embarked, and we sailed out of the harbour the 7th in the morning

I had the good fortune to join Lord Colvill's fleet on the 11th, a few leagues to the southward of St John's, and by the intelligence his Lordship had received, I was obliged to change my resolution of landing the troops at Kitty Vitty (a narrow entrance close to the harbour of St John's), the enemy having entirely stopped up the passage in, by sinking shallops in the channel From the best information I could get, it appeared that Torbay, about three leagues to the northward of St John's, was the only place to land the troops at, within that distance. Lord Colvill sent the *Syren* man-of-war into Torbay with the transports, and it was late at night on the 12th, before they all came to an anchor. Capt Douglas, of His Majesty's ship *Syren*, went with me to view the bay, and we found a very good beach to land on. It blew hard in the night, and one of the transports, with the provincial light infantry corps on board, was driven out to sea

I landed the troops early the next morning, at the bottom of the bay, from whence a path led to St. John's a party of the enemy fired some shots at the boats, as they rowed in. The light infantry of the regulars landed first, gave the enemy one fire, and drove them towards St. John's. The battalions landed, and we marched on, the path for four miles very narrow, through a thick wood, and over very bad ground. Capt M'Donell's light infantry corps in front came up with some of the party we drove from the landing place they had concealed themselves in the wood, fired upon us, and wounded three men A part of Capt. M'Donell's corps rushed in upon them, took three prisoners, and drove the rest off.

The country opened afterwards, and we marched to the left of Kitty Vitty It was necessary to take possession of this pass to open a communication for the landing of artillery and stores, it being impracticable to get them up the way we came. As soon as our right was close to Kitty Vitty river, the enemy fired upon us from a hill on the opposite side I sent a party up a rock, which commanded the passage over, and under cover of their fire, the light infantry companies of the Royal and Montgomery's, supported by the grenadiers of the Royal, passed, drove the enemy up the hill, and pursued them on that side towards St John's, when I perceived a body of the enemy coming to their support, and immediately ordered up Major Sutherland, with the remainder of the first battalion, upon which they thought proper to retreat, and we had just time before dark to take post Capt Mackenzie, who commanded Montgomery's light infantry, was badly wounded We took ten prisoners The troops lay this night on their arms

The next morning, the 14th, we opened the channel, where the enemy had sunk the shallops; they had a breast work which commanded the entrance, and a battery not quite finished Lieutenant-Colonel Tulliken, who had met with an accident by a fall, and was left on board, joined me this day, and Captain Ferguson, commanding the artillery, brought round some light artillery and stores from Torbay, in the shallops The enemy had possession of two very high and steep hills, one in the front of our advanced posts, and the other near to St John's, which two hills appeared to command the whole ground from Kitty Vitty to St John's. It was necessary that we should proceed on this side, to secure at the same time effectually the landing at the Kitty Vitty; from the first hill the enemy fired upon our posts

On the 15th, just before daybreak, I ordered Captain M'Donell's corps of light infantry, and the provincial light infantry, supported by our advanced posts, to march to surprise the enemy on this hill. Captain M'Donell passed their sentries and advanced guards, and was first discovered by their main body on the hill as he came climbing up the rocks near the summit, which he gained, receiving the enemy's fire. He threw in his fire, and the enemy gave way. Captain M'Donell was wounded, Lieutenant Schuyler of his company killed, and three or four men, and 18 wounded. The enemy had three companies of grenadiers, and two picquets at this post, commanded by Lieutenant-Colonel Belcombe, second in command, who was wounded ; a captain of grenadiers wounded and taken prisoner, his lieutenant killed, several men killed and wounded, and 13 taken prisoners. The enemy had one mortar here, with which they threw some shells at us in the night ; a six-pounder not mounted, and two wall pieces. This hill, with one adjoining, commands the harbour.

The 16th we advanced to the hill nearer St. John's, which the enemy had quitted. Twenty-nine shallops came in to-day with artillery and stores, provision and camp equipage, from Torbay, which we unloaded. I moved the remainder of the troops forward, leaving a post to guard the pass of Kitty Vitty on the other side. Last night the enemy's fleet got out of the harbour. This night we lay on our arms.

The 17th a mortar battery was completed and a battery begun for 4 twenty-four-pounders and 2 twelve-pounders ; about 400 yards from the fort made the road from the landing for the artillery, and at night opened the mortar battery with one 8 inch mortar, seven cohorns and six royals. The enemy fired pretty briskly from the fort and threw some shells.

The 18th in the morning I received a letter from Count D'Haussonville, of which I do myself the honour to enclose your Lordship a copy, with copies of other letters that passed and of the capitulation. As Lord Colvill at this time was some distance off the coast and the wind not permitting his lordship to stand in, to honour me with his concurrence in the terms to be given to the garrison, I thought no time should be lost in so advanced a season and therefore took upon me to determine it, hoping to meet with his Lordship's approbation ; and he has given me the greatest pleasure by entirely approving of everything that I have done.

I must beg leave to say, my Lord, that every assistance we could possible desire from the fleet has been given us, Lord Colvill upon the short notice he had of our joining him having laboured to get together all the shallops he could and with which we were amply supplied ; it was a measure of essential service and without which our opera-

tions must have been considerably retarded. The indefatigable labour and persevering ardour of the troops I have the honour to command, so necessary towards completing the conquest before the bad season set in, did indeed exceed what I could have expected. Lieut.-Col. Tullikin seconded me in everything that I could wish. Captain McDonell of Col. Fraser's regiment having Sir Jeffrey Amherst's leave to go to England, was to have delivered this to your Lordship, but his leg was broken by the wound he received, which keeps him here. May I humbly presume, my Lord, to recommend this gentleman to your Lordship's protection as a real brave and good officer.

Lord Colvill intends sending H.M.S. *Syren* immediately to England. I send Capt. Campbell of the 22nd Regiment with these despatches who will inform your Lordship of any particulars you may desire to know. I do myself the honour to transmit to your Lordship such returns as I can possibly get in time, to show the true state of the French troops and garrison here.

I am, &c.
                              WILLIAM AMHERST.
Capt. Campbell has brought with him the French colours which were hoisted on the fort at St. John's.

(b.) COL. AMHERST to the FRENCH COMMANDER.

                              Camp before St. John's,
SIR,   Sept. 16, 1762.

Humanity directs me to acquaint you of my firm intentions. I know the miserable state your garrison is left in and am fully informed of your design of blowing up the fort on quitting it ; but have a care, as I have taken measures effectually to cut off your retreat, and so sure as a match is put to the train, every man of the garrison shall be put to the sword. I must have immediate possession of the fort in the state it now is, or expect the consequences.

I give you half an hour to think of it.

I have the honour to be Sir,
Your most obedient humble servant,
                              WM. AMHERST.
To the officer commanding in St. John's.

(c.) COUNT D'HAUSSONVILLE to COL. AMHERST.

                              16 Sep. 1762.
With regard to the conduct that I shall hold, you may, sir, be misinformed. I wait for your troops and your cannon ; and nothing shall determine me to surrender the fort unless you shall have totally destroyed it and that I shall have no more powder to fire.

I have the honour to be Sir,
Your most humble and most obedient servant,
                      The COUNT D'HAUSSONVILLE.

(d) Count D'Haussonville to Lieut.-Col Amherst

Sir,

Under the uncertainty of the succors which I may receive either from France or its allies, and the Fort being entire and in a condition for a long defence, I am resolved to defend myself to the last extremity. The capitulation which you may think proper to grant me, will determine me to surrender the place to you, in order to prevent the effusion of blood of the men who defend it. Whatever resolution you come to, there is one left to me, which would hurt the interests of the Sovereign you serve.

I have the honour to be Sir
Your most obedient humble servant,
Le Compte D'Haussonville.

Fort St. John,
Sept. 17, 1762

[N B —This date should be the 18th]

(e)

Camp before St John's,
Sept. 18th 1762

Sir,

I have just had the honour of your letter His Britannick Majesty's fleet and army co-operating here will not give any other terms to the garrison of St. John's than their surrendering Prisoners of war. I don't thirst after the blood of the garrison but you must determine quickly or expect the consequences for this is my final determination.

I am Sir &c
Wm Amherst

To Count D'Haussonville.

(f) Count D'Haussonville to Col Amherst

Sept 18, 1762

I have received sir your letter which you did me the honour to write to me I am as averse as you to the effusion of blood. I consent to surrender the fort in a good condition as I have already acquainted you, if the demands which I enclose herewith are granted to my troops

I have the honour &c.
Le Compte D'Haussonville.

(g) Articles of Capitulation.

Demands of the garrison of St. John's, and, in general, the troops that are in it

The French troops shall surrender prisoners of war —Agreed to

The officers and subaltern officers shall keep their arms to preserve good order among their troops —Agreed to.

Good ships shall be granted to carry the officers, grenadiers, and private men, either wounded or not, to France in the space of one month, on the coast of Britanny.—Agreed to
(Lord Colvill will, of course, embark them as soon as he can)

The goods and effects of both the officers and soldiers shall be preserved —His Britannick Majesty's troops never pillage

The gate will be taken possession of this afternoon, and the garrison will lay down their arms.

This is to be signed by Lord Colvill, but it will remain at present, as afterwards, in full force

Camp before St John's, 18 Sept. 1762.
Wm Amherst
Le Compte D'Haussonville

(h) Total of the French Troops made Prisoners in St. John's Fort

1 colonel, 1 lieut -colonel, 13 captains, 13 lieutenants, 4 ensigns, 27 serjeants, 45 corporals, 40 sub-corporals, 12 drummers, 553 fusiliers.

Staff Officers.

M. Le Compte D'Haussonville	Colonel.
M. De Bellecombe	Lieut -Colonel.
M De Mongore	Major and Adjutant
M. Seire	Engineer
Henry	Surgeon Major
Michel	Chaplain

(i.) English Killed and Wounded

Return of the killed, wounded, and missing of the troops under the command of Lieut.-Col. Amherst, from the 15th Sept. inclusive.

Captain Maxwell's light infantry —3 rank and file killed ; 10 rank and file wounded

Captain McDonell's light infantry —3 rank and file killed ; 1 lieutenant, 1 serjeant, 5 rank and file killed ; 1 captain, 15 rank and file wounded

Captain Barrow's provincial light infantry —1 rank and file killed ; 3 rank and file wounded

First battalion—
2 captains, 1 serjeant, 1 drummer, 3 rank and file wounded.

Second battalion—
1 rank and file killed , 1 rank and file wounded

Provincial battalion—
1 rank and file killed

Total, 1 lieutenant and 11 rank and file killed , 3 captains, 2 serjeants, 1 drummer, 32 rank and file wounded

Names of the Officers.

Lieut Schuyler, of the Royal Americans, killed

Captain McDonell, of Frazer's -
Captain Baillie, of the Royals } wounded.
Captain McKenzie, of Montgomery's -

Wm Amherst.

St. John's,
Sept. 20, 1762

(k.) Lord Colvill to Mr. Clevland.

Copy of a letter from Lord Colvill, Commander-in-Chief of His Majesty's ships in North America, to Mr. Clevland. Dated on board the *Northumberland*, in St. John's Harbour, Newfoundland, Sept. 20, 1762.

Sir,

I had the honour of sending you an account of my proceedings until the 18th of August by a vessel which sailed from Placentia for England at that time, and on the 22nd I sailed with his Majesty's ships the *Northumberland*, *Antelope*, *Gosport*, and *Syren*, and the *King George*, belonging to the province of Massachusetts Bay.

On the 25th we chased a schooner off St. John's, and took her close to the harbour's mouth. She had been an English privateer, taken by the enemy, had eight carriage guns mounted, and was manned with thirty Frenchmen, commanded by an ensign de Vaisseau.

The enemy had sent away great part of St. John's men, women and children, by giving them vessels and provisions to carry them where they pleased; two of these, a sloop and a schooner, we met with on the coast, and took twenty-three Irishmen that were single men out of them, to replace in part the marines of the squadron that were left in the garrison at Placentia and the Isle of Boys. These Irishmen said, that if I would go into the Bay of Bulls, numbers of their countrymen would resort to me and enter on board the squadron; but during two days which I stayed in that bay, not a man joined me. The few inhabitants that remained there, quietly followed their business of fishing, and it is possible the enemy prevented any others at St. John's from coming.

Mr. Garland and Mr. Davis, two of the principal inhabitants of Harbour Grace and Carboners, in Conception Bay, having acquainted me that a number of men in their neighbourhood were willing to serve in the squadron during the present exigency, I sent the armed schooner for them, and she returned with fifty men, which I have distributed among the ships. And the same gentlemen, representing that the enemy sometimes sends small parties by land to Portugal Cove, which have threatened to molest them in shallops from that place, desired, in behalf of themselves and all their neighbours, that the schooner might be stationed in Conception Bay, for their protection and defence, which request I complied with.

The island of Carbonera, in Conception Bay, has had no other garrison for many years but a few old men of the artillery, to take care of the guns and ordnance stores. Had some of the inhabitants of the adjacent coast taken post here, they might easily have defended it against any force, as the island is inaccessible on all sides, except one narrow landing place, and no safe road in the neighbourhood for great ships; but the enemy landed in boats, and destroyed the whole without resistance. And the island of BOYS, near Ferryland, would probably have shared the same fate, had it not been possessed in due time by the *Syren's* marines.

In frequently passing the harbour's mouth of St. John's, we could plainly see that the fort, which fronts the entrance, was fortified all round with new works; and that a redoubt, or something like one, was raised at the little Harbour of Kitty Vitty. The old battery at the south side of the harbour's mouth was repaired with additional works, and a new one erected on the same side nearer the entrance. All these were to be seen from the sea; and I could not learn that the enemy intended any thing more than the finishing these works.

On the 8th of September I received, by a sloop express from Halifax, letters from Sir Jeffery Amherst at New York, acquainting me that he had come to a resolution to send a body of troops, in order to dislodge the enemy as soon as possible from St. John's; and that Lieutenant-Colonel Amherst was to command these troops. The same conveyance brought me letters from Colonel Amherst, acquainting me with his arrival at Halifax on the 26th of August, his departure from thence on the 1st of September, and with his intention to call at Louisbourg for the troops there, and then proceed round Cape Race, to join me on this coast. Upon receipt of these letters, I sent the sloop which brought them to look out for Colonel Amherst and the transports off Cape Race, and in order to join them the sooner, to concert measures for the ensuing operations, before the enemy could have notice of their arrival, I dropped down with the squadron to Cape Broyle; but Mr. Gill of St. John's, who had been sent out of the town in a cartel schooner, sending off advice from Ferryland, that he was sure the enemy intended to sail in a very little time, I returned with the squadron to our station off St. John's.

On the 11th we were joined by Colonel Amherst, with the troops in ten transport vessels; and I proposed Torbay as the proper place to land at; it is to the northward of St. John's, about seven miles by land, and the roads pretty good, but the bay is not reckoned safe anchorage, being open to the easterly winds, which usually begin to prevail at this season.

By one of the transports from New York I received a duplicate, the original not yet come to hand, of their Lordships' order of the 7th of June, directing me to repair myself or send a sufficient force, to enable Captain Graves of the *Antelope* to defeat the designs of the squadron commanded by M. de Ternay.

On the 12th we proceeded to Torbay. I sent Capt. Douglas in the *Syren* to anchor with the transports, accompanied by the boats of the squadron, and a number of shallops, or fishing boats, which I collected from different parts for the king's service. With the rest of the ships I returned to my station close to St John's harbour

Next morning Col Amherst landed with the troops in the head of the Bay, having only four men wounded from the distant bush firing of the enemy; he marched directly to Kitty Vitty and made himself master of that important post in the evening without having a man killed, and only two or three wounded. Everything belonging to the army was carried from Torbay to Kitty Vitty in shallops escorted by boats from the squadron. And this service was conducted with diligence and care by Mr Dugdale, my first lieutenant, Captain Douglas having joined the squadron again

The enemy's fleet was to have sailed the morning I passed the Harbour with the transports; and three hundred men only were to be left in St John's for the winter—but upon seeing us they landed the grenadiers again.

The 15th it being strong from E to E S E with duck rainy weather In the evening the wind shifted to the westward, light breezes and thick fog At six next morning, it being calm with a great swell, we saw from the mast head, but could bring them down no lower than half-way to topmast shrouds, four sail bearing S S E distant seven leagues, the mouth of St John's Harbour at the same time bore W. four leagues. We lost sight about seven, though very clear, and some time after a small breeze springing up from the S W quarter I stood towards Torbay in order to cover the shallops that might be going from thence to Kitty Vitty.

In the afternoon I received a note from Col Amherst acquainting me that the French fleet got out last night Thus after being blocked up in St John's Harbour for three weeks by a squadron of equal number, but smaller ships with fewer guns and men, M de Ternay made his escape in the night by a shameful flight I beg leave to observe that not a man in the squadron imagined the four sail when we saw them were the enemy, and the pilots were of opinion that they must have had the wind much stronger than with us to overcome the easterly swell in the Harbour's mouth. I sent the King George as far as Trepassy to bring me intelligence if the enemy should steer towards Placentia; and I directed Captain Douglas of the Syren to get the transports moved from Torbay, a very unsafe road, to the Bay of Bulls

A bomb battery was opened against the fort, in the night of the 17th, and next day it capitulated before any other batteries had begun to play; and I herewith enclose a copy of the capitulation.

The squadron got into the harbour yesterday morning; and in the evening I received their Lordships' order of the 2nd of

August, sent me by Captain Palliser of the *Shrewsbury*, who with the *Superb*, *Bedford*, and *Minerva*, had just arrived on the coast I have directed Captain Palliser, with the other ships, to come into the harbour as soon as convenient opportunity offers for so doing

We have about 800 prisoners, grenadiers picquets, and some marines, being a very fine body of men and nearly equal in number to the regulars of our army I am now preparing transports to carry them to Brest The enemy did not intend to leave so great a part of their force here, their grenadiers were ready for embarking, but M. de Ternay seemed determined at all events to grasp an opportunity, which if once lost might never be regained, therefore in the utmost confusion he left behind his grenadiers, anchors, and turned his boats adrift, when they had towed him out The fog was so thick that Lieut. Col Tulikin who was posted on an eminence in the narrowest part of the harbour's mouth could hear their noise but could not discern any of the ships, the fog even altered the direction of the sound, which seemed to come from another part of the Harbour whilst they must have been directly under him

There is a considerable quantity of provisions and other goods at this place collected and tumbled promiscuously into different storehouses by the enemy. Many of the Irish servants have also been robbing and plundering their masters. To ascertain properly in order to make restitution as far as can be, and to restore regularity to a country so long distracted by being in the enemy's possession, will be the particular care of Governor Graves who in my opinion is well qualified for such an office, and as he will stay here he will be able in a great measure to restore the affairs of this country. Captain Douglas of the Syren has behaved with spirit and activity and exerted every talent of a good officer during the expedition, (and without adding any more officers to the corps) I am happy in the opportunity of sending him to wait on their Lordships

II. Bermudians in the Bank Fishery.

(a) Messrs HULL & HARVEY to JOHN BRICKWOOD, Public Agent for the ISLAND OF BERMUDA

Newfoundland Aug 11th 1788

Since arrival of Governor Admiral Elliot are confirmed by him, in indulgence of making and drying fish on any part of the coast of Newfoundland for present year; but he is of opinion that the clause in the Act of 14th Parliament 15th year of Reign of present Majesty is against us, insomuch that they may not in future land, to cure and make their fish on any part of coast, unless a different explanation of that clause take place Notwithstanding by Act of William III 10 & 11 c xxv His Majesty's subjects residing within the realm of England or dominions belonging, trading to Newfoundland have equal right to making and husbanding &c. of fish on the shores, as well as taking it on the Banks—appears to be no repeal of that Act, unless the explanatory clause of Act alluded to be construed to repeal so much of Act of William III.

By the Boston Port Bill, Bermudians are particularly named encouraged and licensed to engage in this business. The force of that law was done away by change of Government in United States so far as respected them only, and as no repeal has taken place, conceive no doubt, but that it still has effect with all subjects therein described who continued subjects to the Crown of Great Britain. Act [Boston Port Bill] speaks not of landing or curing fish, but of general licence of taking it on the Banks; Query! will not landing and curing be considered as a natural consequence of taking? Otherwise indulgence of law will not avail them, for if forbidden to Bermudians to land fish for drying and husbanding in Newfoundland ports, it would be little short of total prohibition of indulgence granted—distance from Banks to Bermuda being too great to carry green fish, with security, and if carried safe, the severity of the weather in all the fishing season will not admit husbanding and curing fish in their island fit for market—the attempt would be preposterous.

There are many reasons for indulging Bermudians in present pursuit. They have no staple commodity for exporting, they are altogether supported by our Navigation. All supplies of Cordage Sail canvas, nails &c. for ship building are mostly received from England. Before the War they were carriers of a large proportion of the produce of America from thence to the Sugar Colonies, but now that trade is loaded with difficulties and expenses, they cannot continue it with any advantages. We apprehend great exertions will be made by Merchants from the West of England to prohibit them in their present pursuit, and we request that their [Bermudian] agent loses no time nor exertion to get Acts alluded to explained, or anything contained that tends to obstruct them in making and husbanding fish on shore in harbours and bays about Newfoundland, or in bringing into port for curing and manufacturing oil on shore, either whales or blubber, killed and taken in and about Coast, to get such obstruction removed by most certain means possible. We shall take the earliest opportunity of laying before the Legislature of Bermuda a representation of their difficulties. They have now employed in their Bermuda Vessels upwards of 200 men, four-fifths of whom are natives, and a large proportion raw inexperienced men, and but few blacks. May not Bermuda be said to become a nursery for seamen for America, with good affect that fewer will be encouraged to leave His

Majesty's dominions in Europe. We further hint that the difficulties that are started are founded on the expression in the 4th Clause of the first Act alluded to.

(b.) Governor Elliot to the Governor of Bermuda.

St. John's, Newfoundland,
Sir,   20th August 1788.

On my arrival here a few days since, I was surprised to find a number of vessels belonging to Bermuda engaged in the fishery of this island contrary to an Act of Parliament past in the 15th year of His present Majesty, entitled " An Act for the encouragement of the fisheries carried on from Great Britain, Ireland, and the British Dominions in Europe, and for securing the Return of the Fishermen, Sailors, and others employed." [As] I am inclined to believe [they came] without any intention on their part of infringing the law, I shall allow them to continue till the end of the present season, but must request of your Excellency to warn them against coming here next year, as the most positive orders will be given to the Custom House not to admit them upon any consideration whatever, to land and dry their fish contrary to the before-mentioned Act of Parliament.

I have the honor to be, Sir,
Your Excellency's Most Obedient
and Most Humble Servant,
Elliot.

His Excellency
The Governor of Bermuda.

(c.) G. Elliot, Governor, to Lord Sydney.

St. John's, 26th Oct. 1788.

Soon after my arrival from England this year I was informed that Bermudian ships were engaged in the Newfoundland fishery, and in course of ten days nineteen sail of them came into the port of St. John's with their second cargoes of fish from the banks. Had I arrived in time I should have thought it my duty to refuse them the privilege of landing and drying, but in consideration of the vessels being owned and navigated by British subjects, and understanding they had been misled by Act 15 of His present Majesty, which although it deprived them of most of the privileges enjoyed by vessels arriving from our British Dominions in Europe did not preclude them from catching fish on the Banks and bringing them into harbours of Newfoundland for sale, I permitted them to compleat their voyages, and I hope my conduct therein, together with my letters to the Governor of the Bermudas upon the subject, will meet with H.M. approbation.

(d.) (From the Bermudian Records.)

Friday, June 27th, 1788.
Colonel Tucker, Mr. James Tucker, and Mr. George Bascome [were appointed]

D D

a committee in conjunction with a committee of council to correspond during recess of assembly with John Blackwood, Esq , public agent at Lamlin

---

(e) Tuesday, November 11th, 1788

EXTENSION ADDRESS OF THE GOVERNOR (HENRY HAMILTON) ON THE OPENING OF THE SESSION

The promotion of the Newfoundland fishery appears to me an object calling for your immediate attention if any obstacles have occurred which have rendered the first adventure less profitable than might have been expected, your prudence will surmount them or weaken their effect by legal restrictions or adequate encouragement Should it appear to you advisable to resort to the favour and protection of the British Legislature, the earliest intimation must be given to the principal agent whose endeavours, I am persuaded, will not be wanting to advance a branch of commerce in the said fisheries to the said Ports thereof at the end of the Fishing Season which by the following Clause (" and in order to obviate any doubts that have arisen or may arise to whom the Privilege or Right of drying Fish on the Shores of Newfoundland does or shall belong under the before mentioned Act made in the 10th and 11th years of the Reign of King William III. which Right or Privilege has hitherto only been enjoyed by His Majesty's Subjects and the other British Dominions in Europe be it enacted and declared by the authority aforesaid that the said Right and Privilege shall not be held and enjoyed by any of His Majesty's Subjects arriving at Newfoundland from any other Country except Great Britain or one of the British Dominions in Europe") of course incapacitates the Bermudians and all other His Majesty's Subjects arriving there in vessels not fitted in letters of the said Act from landing and drying their Fish But in consideration of their having been at considerable expense and the very great loss they would sustain if at this period they were to be prohibited from prosecuting their voyages, which were undertaken so advantageous to "these Islands"

(f) EXTRACT FROM REPLY OF THE HOUSE OF ASSEMBLY TO THE GOVERNOR'S ADDRESS AT THE OPENING OF THE SESSION.

To people destitute of a staple, nothing can be more desirable than the establishment of some productive substitute In this point of view, the cod fishery demands our immediate and serious attention. We shall therefore endeavour to promote such measures as shall [tend] to remove the difficulties which have arisen to the prosecution of the first adventure, and to afford in future a greater probability of success

III.—The Conspiracy in St. John's in 1799–1800.

St John's, Newfoundland,
SIR, July 2, 1800.

I am sorry to inform you, that a spirit of disaffection to our Government has manifested itself here last winter and in the spring The first symptoms made their appearance about the latter end of February, by some anonymous papers posted up in the night, threatening the persons and property of the magistrates, if they persisted in enforcing a proclamation they had published, respecting hogs going at large, contrary to a presentment of the grand jury We advertised a hundred guineas reward for the discovery of the author or authors, and the inhabitants viewing it in a very proper light, as the commencement of anarchy and confusion, and destruction of all order, handsomely came forward in support of the magistrates, and offered two hundred guineas more, but I am sorry to say without effect The next step, still more alarming, was a combination of between forty and fifty of the Royal Newfoundland Regiment, to desert with their arms, with a declared intention, as appeared by a letter left behind them, of putting every person to death who should attempt to oppose them. This they put in execution on the night of the 24th April Their place of rendezvous was the powder shed, back of Fort Townshend, at 11 at night, but were not joined in time from Fort Townshend or Fort William. We know not the reason why the party from Fort Townshend did not join them, but at Fort William Colonel Skinner happened to have a party at his house very late that night, preventing the possibility of their going out unperceived at the appointed hour, and the alarm being made at Signal Hill for those who quitted that post, the plot was blown, when only nineteen were met, who immediately set off for the woods, but from the vigilance and activity used in their pursuit, in about ten days or a fortnight, sixteen of them were taken, two or three of whom informed against the others, and implicated upwards of twenty more, who had not only agreed to desert, but had also taken the oaths of United Irishmen, administered by an archvillain Murphy, who belonged to the regiment, and one of the deserters, who with a sergeant Kelly, and a private, have not as yet been taken We do not know, nor was it possible to ascertain, how far this defection and the united oaths extended through the regiment General Skerret ordered a general court martial upon twelve of those taken, five of whom were sentenced to be hanged, and seven to be shot; the former were executed on a gallows erected upon the spot where they met at the powder shed, the other seven were sent to Halifax, to be further dealt with as His Royal Highness should think proper, those also implicated by the king's evidence

were sent in irons to Halifax; and the Duke
of Kent has at length removed all the regiment,
except two companies of picked men, to head
quarters, and has relieved them by the whole
of the 66th regiment, who are now here.
Various have been the reports on this business;
the town to the amount of 2, 3, or 400 men
mentioned as privy or concerned in this
business, and of acting in concert with them,
at least so far as to destroy, plunder, and
set off for the States, but no names have
been particularly mentioned, so as to bring
the proof home. In fact, we were at one
time in such a situation, as to render the
policy of acting very doubtful, until more
force should arrive, as we knew not who we
could depend upon for support in case of
resistance, having every reason to believe the
defection was very extensive, not only through
the regiment, but through the inhabitants of
this and all the out harbours, particularly to
the southward, almost to a man have taken
the United Oaths, which is "to be true to
the old cause, and to follow their heads of
whatsoever denomination." Although those
heads are not to be known to them till the
moment a plan is to be put in action, all
this one of the evidences has declared
originated from letters received from Ireland.
Although a United Irishman, he was yet but
a novice, and was not so far let into the
secret as to know who the letters were addressed to, or who from. Although we are at
present without any immediate apprehension
of danger, we have no reason to suppose their
dispositions have changed, or that their plans
of plunder, burnings, &c., are given up, but
only waiting a proper opportunity to break
forth. The most probable time for such an
event would be towards the close of the
winter, when the ships of war are absent, the
peaceable and well-disposed part of the community off their guard, and no possibility of
succour for two or three months, or of even
conveying intelligence of our situation. If
such has been their plan, of which there is
little room left for doubt, though I believe
more for motives of plunder than of conquest,
either of which would be equally destructive,
it would be absurd to suppose it might not
take place again—I should therefore imagine
it behoves Government not to risk another
winter without obviating its possible effect;
and I am firmly of opinion, after taking the
whole of what has passed into view, that the
security of the trade and fishery, nay, the
security and salvation of the island itself, will
entirely depend upon a proper military force
at this place with sufficient strength to afford
small detachments to some of the out harbours
to the southward to watch their motions, and
assist the magistrates when necessary. This
force to render security effectual cannot be
less than 800 or 1,000 men, particularly
while Ireland is in such a state of ferment as
it has been and is likely to continue till the
business of the union is settled, for the events

of Ireland have heretofore and will in a great
measure govern the sentiments and actions
of the far greater majority of the people in
this country.

I omitted observing that the regiment now
here (the 66th) have but little more than half
their complement of men, and are mostly
composed of drafts from the Irish brigade
sent three or four years ago to Halifax, of
course not so well adapted for the protection
required, as a full and complete regiment from
England, staunch and well-affected.

I have thus ventured to offer my opinion
upon the public situation of affairs in this
island, and have only to regret in common
with the real well-wishers to its prosperity,
that by the triennial mode of appointing
governors we are to be deprived of the aid of
your influence and counsel, at a time when
from your real knowledge of the island and
its internal affairs, they might be of such
essential service.

I have the honour to be, &c.
J. OGDEN.
To the Hon. Vice-Admiral Waldegrave,
&c. &c. &c.

IV.—The Early Seal Fishery.

Described by J. BLAND, of Bonavista, in a
Letter to Governor GAMBIER.

SIR, Bonavista, 26th September 1802.
Your Excellency has been pleased to
request of me some information respecting
our seal fishery, and as far as my own
experience and general observation can lead,
I shall endeavour to comply with that request.

This adventurous and perilous pursuit is
prosecuted in two different ways—during the
winter months by nets, and from March to
June in ice-skiffs and decked boats, or
schooners. The fishery by nets extends from
Conception Bay to the Labrador, and in the
northern posts there is most certainty of
success. About fifty pounds weight of strong
twine will be required to make a net, the half
worn small hawsers, which the boats have
used in the summer fishery, serve for foot
ropes; new ratline is necessary for head
ropes, and each net is required to be about
forty fathoms in length, and nearly three
in depth. I am thus minute that your
Excellency may form some idea of the expense attending this adventure, as well as of
the mode in which it is conducted.

Four or five men constitute a crew to
attend about twenty nets, but in brisk sealing
this number of nets will require a double
crew in separate boats. The seals bolt into
the nets while ranging at the bottom in quest
of food, which makes it necessary to keep the
nets to the ground, where they are made to
stand on their legs, as the phrase is, by means
of cork fastened at equal distances along the
head ropes. The net is extended at the
bottom by a mooring and killock fixed to
each end, and it is frequently placed in forty

D D 2

fathoms water, for we observe that the largest seals are caught in the deepest water. To each end of the head-rope is fixed a line with a pole standing erect in the water to guide the sealers to the net, and when these poles are torn away by ice, or other accident, they are directed by landmarks and find their nets with creepers. The seals, in their efforts to get free, cable the nets at the bottom, and none but experienced sealers can disengage them without cutting the net. This description, sir, may not be interesting, but it will convey to your Excellency a correct idea of this laborious business, and show that none but men active and inured to hardship, can be qualified to engage in it. On the Labrador coast the seal fishery begins in November and ends about Christmas, when the nets are taken up. With us, it begins about Christmas and continues through the winter, the ice in this quarter being seldom stationary for any considerable length of time.

Should strong East and N E winds prevail through the months of December and January, the seals towards the end of the latter month never fail to appear in large companies, always going before the wind and ice till they find themselves inbayed The seals upon this coast are of many species, they are classed and distinguished by names only to be found in the Newfoundland nomenclature, and only understood by the Newfoundland naturalists *Tars, Doaters, Gunswauls,* and many others, breed upon the rocks in the summer season, and may be called natives, but these make but little part of our fishery, our dependance rests wholly upon *Harps* and *Bedlemers,* which are driven by winds and ice from the north-east seas The harp in its prime will yield from ten to sixteen gallons of oil, and the bedlemer, a seal of the same species, only younger, from three to seven About the middle of March the female harp whelps upon ice, and, in the course of a few days, becomes reduced to less than half of her largest bulk The male, also, from this period reduces, but not in the same proportion There is, therefore, an evident advantage in catching the seals in the winter

I will now, sir, proceed to bring into view the produce of this fishery in Bonavista Bay for some years back, in doing which I shall be as precise as the nature of the case will now admit of In the winter of 1791-2, a succession of hard gales from the north-east brought the seals in great numbers, before the middle of January, unaccompanied by any ice, a circumstance that rarely occurs In Bonavista about two hundred men might have been employed in attending the nets, and the number of seals caught amounted to about seven thousand The entire catch at Bonavista Bay may be taken at ten thousand, and two-thirds of the whole reckoned *Harps.* The harps yielded thirteen shillings each, and the bedlemers seven shillings and sixpence,

which at that time afforded the merchant a large profit in the English market.

The winter of 92-3 the nets were unproductive, but the ice-skiffs in the spring were generally successful, killing from five to six thousand seals, principally young, which yielded five shillings each.

For the winter and spring 93-4, we may reckon about five thousand.

In 95 the nets were successful in the prime part of the season, and the numbers taken about six thousand, two thirds of which were harps

The five succeeding years may be averaged at six thousand each, and three-fourths of these may be reckoned young seals In the spring of 1801 we may count about twenty thousand, the greatest part of which were dragged on the ice by men, women, and children, with incredible labour These seals were principally of the *hooded* kind, and about nine-tenths of them young. The old yielded about fourteen shillings and the young seven. The last season may have produced six thousand, yielding on an average about seven shillings each I do not know, sir, if what I have written will be thought satisfactory I have confined myself to the district in which I live, not having materials from which to give anything like a correct statement of the other sealing ports of the island and of Labrador It may, nevertheless, be proper to say, that your Excellency ought not to form an estimate of these, from the foregoing sketch The ports on ' the coast of Labrador, on the northern shore, now possessed by the French, and southward to Fogo, have been out of all comparison more successful in this fishery by nets.

The sealing-adventure by large boats, which sail about the middle of March, has not been general longer than nine years It has been pursued with various success, and unquestionably has a tendency to promote the first intention of government beyond any other. From two to three thousand men have been employed in this perilous adventure, and it may excite surprise that so few fatal accidents have happened It is, however, in my opinion, for various reasons, upon the decline, and it may properly become a question whether Government ought to suffer it to fall, if it can be supported to its full extent through the medium of a premium or bounty Out of the harbour of Saint John's this adventure has been followed with uncommon spirit, and your Excellency, it is likely, may obtain useful information on this subject from the merchants of that quarter

I have the honour to be with great respect, Sir, ⁚

Your Excellency's obedient humble servant,

JOHN BLAND.

His Excellency
James Gambier, Esquire

CHAPTER XIV.

REIGN OF GEORGE IV

1820-1830

1822 —Richard Alexander Tucker, Esq , Chief Justice

1823.—The last of the Red Indians of Newfoundland seen; Indian women brought to St John's Newfoundland School Society established Mr. Cormack crossed the Island Dr Scallan, Bishop of Drago, and Vicar Apostolic of Newfoundland and Labrador. Chamber of Commerce, St John's, instituted 26th December.

1824 —Imperial Act, 5 Geo IV. cap 67, for the better Administration of Justice in Newfoundland, appointing Supreme Court, with Chief Justice and two assistant judges First fire company, Eastern Ward, St John's

1825 —Sir Thomas Cochrane Governor First roads constructed

1826 —Supreme Court of Newfoundland constituted by Royal Charter. First assistant judges, with Chief Justice Tucker, were John William Molloy and A. W Des Barres, Molloy soon removed, E B. Brenton appointed

1827.—Bishop Inglis, Anglican Bishop of Nova Scotia and Newfoundland, first visited Newfoundland and consecrated St John's Church. Beothic Institution W E Cormack, President

1828 —Publication of P. Morris's pamphlet. Great agitation for representative institutions

1829 —Bishop Fleming consecrated Bishop of Carpasia *in partibus.*

REIGN OF WILLIAM IV.

1830-1837.

1831 —First coach road opened to Portugal Cove

1832 —Representative Assembly granted to Newfoundland

1833 —1st January, first Session of the Newfoundland House of Assembly opened by Sir Thomas Cochrane, Governor.

1834.--Captain Prescott, R N, Governor. George Lilly, Esq, appointed Acting Judge, Supreme Court, first native judge. Savings Bank constituted.

1836 —First Light erected on Cape Spear Bank of British North America established in St John's.

In 1820 the long reign of George III. came to a close. The agitation about Butler and Lundrigan caused the British Government to consider the whole question of the administration of justice, and the formation of constitutional government in the Colony. Sir Charles Hamilton was recalled, for the purpose of consulting with the Ministry, Chief Justice Tucker[1] acting as Governor during his absence. As the result of these deliberations, the Royal Charter, the Imperial Act 5 George IV cap. lxvii.—An Act for the better administration of justice in Newfoundland—was passed.

The preamble states :—

" Whereas it is expedient to make further provision for the administration of justice in the Colony of Newfoundland, it is therefore enacted by the King's Most Excellent Majesty, by and with the consent and advice, &c., in this present Parliament assembled, and by the authority of the same, that it shall and may be lawful for His Majesty by his charter, or letters patent, under the Great Seal, to institute a Superior Court of Judicature in Newfoundland, which shall be entitled ' The Supreme Court of Newfoundland,' and the said court shall be a Court of Record, and shall have all civil and criminal jurisdiction whatever in Newfoundland and in all lands, islands, and territories dependent upon the government thereof, as fully and amply to all intents and purposes as His Majesty's courts of King's Bench, Common, Pleas, Exchequer, and High Court of Chancery, in that part of Great Britain called England have, or any of them hath, and the said Supreme Court shall also be a Court of Oyer and Terminer, and general gaol delivery in and for Newfoundland, and all places within the Government thereof, and shall also have jurisdiction in all cases of crimes and misdemeanours committed on the banks of Newfoundland, or any of the seas or islands to which ships or vessels repair from Newfoundland for carrying on the fishery "

The principal provisions of the Act were to the effect that the Supreme Court shall be—

" Holden by a chief judge and two assistant judges, being respectively barristers in England or Ireland of at least three years' standing, or in some of His Majesty's colonies or plantations, that it shall be lawful for the Governor to divide the colony into three districts, as may appear best adapted for enabling the inhabitants to resort with ease and convenience to the circuit courts to be therein established,—that it shall be lawful for His Majesty to institute circuit courts in each of the three districts, such courts to be holden at least once every year by the chief judge, or one of the assistant judges of the supreme court; that the circuit courts shall have the same jurisdiction within the district in which they were severally held, as is vested in the supreme court for the whole colony, with the exception of trying certain crimes specified, or of hearing or determining any suit arising out of a violation of any Act of Parliament, relating to the trade and revenue of the British colonies in America Such crimes and such suits to be tried, heard, and determined only in the supreme court. To persons who feel themselves aggrieved by any judgment given in the circuit court, there is granted power of appeal to the supreme court, for a reversal of such judgment Authority is given to the Governor to institute a court of civil jurisdiction on the coast of Labrador "

Although the Act was passed in 1824, the Supreme Court was not duly constituted until the 2nd January 1826, when it was opened with

[1] Chief Justice Forbes resigned in 1822.

the following imposing ceremonies by His Excellency Captain Sir Thomas Cochrane :—

" The honourable judges, the honourable Lieut. Colonel Burke, C.B., commanding His Majesty's forces, the magistrates and heads of all the public departments, civil and military, the clergy, the chamber of commerce, the grand jury, and most of the principal inhabitants assembled at the Government House, when the oaths of office were administered to the chief judge and assistant judges, after which His Excellency delivered to the chief judge His Majesty's Royal Charter, which was handed by the judge to the chief clerk of the Supreme Court, to be borne by him to the Court House, and to be there read.

" After these preliminaries were over, the assembled parties formed themselves into a procession, the order of which had been fixed by a programme previously issued. The constables (two and two)—fort-major—gentlemen of the learned professions (two and two)—clerks of the central, southern, and northern circuit courts—magistrates (two and two)—the chief magistrate, &c.

JUDGE DES BARRES.
From a photograph taken in 1861.

&c. On arriving at the Court House, the Charter was solemnly read; at the conclusion of which proceeding, all the prisoners confined in the gaol (with the exception of five) were called to the bar, and, after a suitable admonition from the chief judge, were informed that His Excellency the Governor had been graciously pleased to exert on their behalf the prerogative of pardon entrusted to him by the Crown."

The judges appointed under the Act were Chief Justice Tucker, and Assistant Judges John William Molloy and Augustus Wallet Des Barres.[1] Molloy was soon removed, and Judge Brenton appointed in his stead. The full dress of the chief justice, as superior civil officer, was appointed by the king—a blue coat, but no epaulettes nor lappets, button-holes upon the cuff and collar only, but the same pattern as worn by Lords-Lieutenants. The chief magistrate was ordered to wear a blue coat,

[1] The two puisne judges first appointed to the Supreme Court in 1826 presented a marked contrast. John William Molloy was a reckless, gay, squandering squireen, who soon ran into debt, and was got rid of. The Hon. Augustus Wallet Des Barres was, on the contrary, a most prudent and correct man. His father, Governor Des Barres, was a distinguished French engineer officer in the English service; his surveys of the Maritime Provinces were celebrated; he is alleged to have been present at the battle on the heights of Abraham when Wolfe was killed; and was Governor of Cape Breton and Lieut.-Governor of Prince Edward's Island. He was a man of consummate ability and immense influence; he is reported to have danced on a table when he was a hundred. He died at Halifax, N.S., in 1824, aged 102. His son, A. W. Des Barres, was so young when he received his first appointment —I believe as Attorney-General of Cape Breton—that, by the advice of his friends, he wore a pair of false whiskers when he went to receive his commission. He was celebrated for his ready wit and repartee. Once when the late Judge Hayward was quoting Chitty to the Bench, his Lordship retorted : " Chitty, Mr. Hayward! Goodness me, what does Mr. Chitty know about this country? He was never in Newfoundland."

with red cuffs and collar, buttons with crown, and G. R. cockade on the side of the hat. Constables were to wear blue coats and buttons, with the crown and G. R., a red waistcoat with the same buttons, and a cockade on the hat, and were required always to carry the insignia of

N. W. HOYLES.

From a portrait in the possession of Mrs. A. O. Hayward.

office. His Excellency had a great taste for official forms and ceremonials. Lieut.-Col. W. Haly, Thomas H. Brooking, John W. Dunscombe, and Newman W. Hoyles, were in 1825 appointed His Excellency's colonial aides-de-camp, with the rank of lieut.-colonels of militia.

Sir Thomas Cochrane is now universally admitted to have been the best Governor ever sent to Newfoundland; everywhere are monuments erected to his memory. He inaugurated our system of roads, promoted agriculture, and laid out the beautiful grounds of Virginia as his country seat. Cochrane Street and the Military Road remind us of the great administrator. I cannot say much in praise of His Excellency's taste in the erection of Government House. The site is an admirable one, the grounds are well laid out, but the building

COLONIAL BUILDINGS AND GOVERNMENT HOUSE IN 1856.
From Mullaly's Trip to Newfoundland.

itself looks more like a prison than a vice-regal residence; the ditch all round is a trap to catch snow, and in winter the north entrance is as cold as Siberia. I can give him credit for every other improvement, but am compelled to say that Government House is a huge pile of unredeemed ugliness.

The two great leaders in the struggle for a local legislature in New-foundland were Doctor William Carson and Patrick Morris. Both were distinguished, able men, but in marked contrast to each other. The Doctor, the originator of the movement, was a stiff-mannered, pedantic old gentleman; dogmatic, self-opinionated, and independent, a very clever man both in his profession and the conduct of public affairs. Morris, on the other hand, had all the qualities of a popular tribune; you can see both in his writings and his speeches that he was an impetuous Irishman; everything was done with a rush; in place of the doctor's calm reasoning and carefully polished periods, his pamphlets are full of go, flashes of Irish wit and sarcasm; when he comes down to person-

HON. P. MORRIS.
From an old portrait.

alities he is as truculent and scur-rilous as a Western editor. Morris once tried to cross swords with the great tri-bune O'Connell; the arch-agitator annihi-lated his colonial antagonist simply with a wink. At a great repeal meeting near Waterford, Morris, who was opposed to O'Connell's views, attempted to address the meeting; O'Connell called out in his broadest Kerry brogue, " Well, Pat, when did you come across, was there much fog on the Banks ? " and then with his finger to his nose said : " Boys, do you smell the fish." Amidst the roar of laughter that followed, Morris quietly disap-peared.

Sir Thomas Cochrane's government lasted from 1825 to 1834. During the first part of his administration his popularity was un-bounded ; he was the first civil Governor, the first real administrator and ruler of the Colony. An eminently practical man, he not only organised improvements, he personally superintended their execution. His activity was unbounded; in the early mornings he was out on horseback inspecting the roads, directing his workmen, laying out the grounds at Virginia, having interviews with the farmers, giving them practical hints about agriculture ; everywhere he impressed his strong personality on Colonial affairs. He was very sociable, and his hospitality

was unstinted; no Governor ever entertained in the style of Sir Thomas
Cochrane. Mr. Morris in his pamphlet thus speaks of him:—

" Our present Governor is allowed, I understand, about £4,000 per year,
out of which he has to support the splendour of 'vice-regal authority,' a large
retinue of servants, entertain the principal inhabitants of Newfoundland at his
table, and all strangers who visit the seat of his government, to subscribe to all
public charities and institutions. A great part of his income is expended in the
country, so that if the author of this pamphlet [2] only just takes an enlarged view
of the subject, he will find that he was egregiously in error in supposing that his
favourite *Admiral-Governor* was a *cheaper governor*, for it appears that the matter
of pounds, shillings, and pence, is his only criterion of judgment. If a comparison
be made between the relative systems, the difference will appear more striking;
our present Governor has been, since his arrival, improving the condition of the
country and the people; and . . . I maintain that he has done more real
good to the colony, since his appoint-
ment, than all his predecessors put
together.

SIR THOMAS COCHRANE.
From a photograph by Maull and Polyblank.

He has, as far as his limited authority
permitted him, given every encouragement to the cultivation of the *soil,* and
has himself shown the example; he has
encouraged every measure calculated to
promote the internal resources of the
country; he has made roads, some of
them at his own expense; he has been
the patron of education for the poor and
the rich; and he had scarcely landed
on our shores when he recommended
the establishment of a university for
the education of our respectable youth,
to prevent the necessity of sending
them to the United States and other
parts; in short, he has felt a sympathy
for the country and the people beyond
what was ever felt by his predecessors,
and the country feels grateful to him
for it."

Both Bishop Fleming [3] and Doctor Carson were equally loud in their
praises of His Excellency.

[1] The salary was only £3,000 per annum.
[2] *A View of the Rise, Progress, &c. of
the Newfoundland Fishery.* Poole, 1828.
[3] Dr. Scallan, the third Roman Catholic
bishop of Newfoundland, was appointed in
April 1815 bishop of Drago *in partibus,* and
in 1816 coadjutor to Dr. Lambert; he was
consecrated the same year at Wexford; he
had been labouring as a priest in St. John's
since 1812. No man was more beloved in
his diocese than Bishop Scallan; he was in
every sense a gentleman. Both Bishop Mullock and Bishop Howley censure him for
his extreme liberality. The Right Rev.
Michael Anthony Fleming was appointed his
coadjutor, and consecrated in the old chapel
Bishop of Carpasia *in partibus* in 1829. Car-
pasian, the Bishop's farm, now owned by
John Duder, Esq., was named after his titular
episcopate.

All the great improvements around St. John's may be said to date from Sir Thomas Cochrane's time. The roads to Topsail, Bay Bulls, Torbay, and Portugal Cove had been commenced before his arrival; it was, however, his energy that pushed them forward. At this time officials and merchants vied with each other in creating country residences and farms—Mount Pearl, cleared by Sir James Pearl, Holbrook's Farm, cultivated by Surveyor-General Holbrook, and the finest of all, Brookfield, the property of William and Henry P. Thomas. Everywhere around the capital land was being cultivated; a perfect *furore* seemed to have seized everyone to become landed proprietors. The great pioneer in this movement was Dr. Carson, though it must be remembered to their honour that Major Griffith Williams, Col. Skinner, and Lieut.-Col. Haly had been farming before he cleared "Rostellan,"

H. P. THOMAS.
From an old photograph.

formerly known as "Billies." Amongst the public-spirited merchants of that day the chief place must be given to the Thomases, and especially to the senior partner, William Thomas.[1]

During the whole of the first part of Sir Thomas's administration, there was a continued agitation for a local legislature; whilst the Irish were probably the most busy workers for reform, many of the leading Protestant merchants took an active part. Besides the committee, the most conspicuous supporters of the movement were William Thomas, Thomas H. Brooking, his partner, G. R. Robinson (afterwards member of the English House of Commons), Benjamin Bowring, founder

[1] The family of the Thomases are probably the most ancient in this Colony; their connection can be traced back to the Shapleighs (one of whom was grandfather to John Treworgie, the Cromwellian Governor of the Colony), thence through the Bevils to William Bevil Thomas.

The Thomases carried on business at Dartmouth and St. John's in partnership with a Mr. Stokes, as Thomas & Stokes. William Bevil Thomas was born in St. John's in 1757; he married Elizabeth Way, in 1785, at Dartmouth, and had two sons, William Thomas and Henry Phillips Thomas.

William Thomas was foremost in every benevolent work. As a very young man he was secretary to the society for improving the condition of the poor; he was equally distinguished as a merchant and a politician. He filled all positions well, whether presiding at a religious meeting or as president of the Chamber of Commerce. Though a professedly religious man, sometimes the old leaven broke out in him. He was very active, and fond of directing everybody. Often, as he paced his long wharf, if one of his ships was beating in the Narrows, say his fine brig the *Cynthia*, Captain Goldsworth, he could be heard muttering, "Luff, confound you, Goldsworth, luff, you lubber!" Brookfield, the fine house at Devon Row, their Water Street premises, and the beautiful cottage at Topsail, are monuments of the large progressive ideas of the Thomases, and especially of the constructive ability of Henry Phillips Thomas.

of the firm of Bowring Brothers, a very active, intelligent Liberal (cousin of Sir John Bowring), Charles T. Bowring, who afterwards filled

THE LATE C. T. BOWRING, ESQ.
*From a photograph by
Hart, Exeter.*

a high position in the Corporation of Liverpool (father of William Benjamin Bowring, recently Lord Mayor of Liverpool), R. R. Wakeham, the genial secretary of the committee (brother-in-law of Sir W. V. Whiteway, K.C.M.G.), and Henry Winton, the able and independent editor of the *Public Ledger*. The opposition consisted of all the officials and those dependent on the Governor's good will; James Simms — afterwards Judge Simms — seems to have been their mouthpiece at all public meetings.

The bitterest antagonists of the measure were, however, the old West Country merchants; the idea of Newfoundland having a legislature was to their minds simply outrageous. One of them—Peter Ougier—stated in his evidence, "they are making roads in Newfoundland, next thing they will be having carriages and driving about." In his pamphlet Mr. Patrick Morris scarifies the author of a work entitled, "A view of the rise and progress of the Newfoundland Fishery." The whole object of this writer was to recommend a return to the rule of the fishing admirals; the pamphlet was published in Poole, and the writer declared his object was to give an *enlarged* view of the fisheries and trade of Newfoundland.

ALDERMAN W. B. BOWRING.
*From the Illustrated London News.
Photo. by Brown, Barnes, & Bell.*

There can be no doubt that it was the influence of these West Country merchants that retarded the grant of a local legislature; a good deal could be said against the movement. Bishop Fleming, in a letter to Lord Glenelg, declared that he never approved of it; but the reply to every objection was the unanswerable argument that all the British Colonies, even to little

Bermuda, had a local government, Nova Scotia had obtained it in 1758, the older American Colonies had always governed themselves, and Newfoundland could no longer be denied. English statesmen clearly saw that, with all its defects and possible evil consequences, it was the only way in which free men could be governed under the British constitution, and it came at last as a matter of course[1] In July 25th, 1831, Mr. Robinson objected to the Vote for Newfoundland in the House of Commons, adding, "that if a local "legislature were granted, the colonists would never ask the House "for another farthing." Lord Howick, in reply, stated "that the time had come for such a boon to be granted" In January 1832, Mr. Brooking, Chairman of the Newfoundland Committee in London, writing to William Thomas, Deputy Chairman in St. John's, stated that Viscount Goderich informed him that it was the intention of His Majesty to give Newfoundland a representative government similar to that of Nova Scotia and New Brunswick The agitators had hit upon a fortunate time in English politics—the era of the great Reform Bill. In 1832 the Bill was passed in the House of Commons granting a representative assembly to Newfoundland, on August 26th of that year Sir Thomas returned to St. John's armed with full powers to carry out the great constitutional change The general election took place in the autumn of 1832

The first House of Assembly seems to have been a very respectable body. The only contest in which there appears to have been any excitement was in St. John's, the candidates were Dr. Carson, Mr Patrick Keough, Mr. William Thomas, Mr John Kent (a relative of Bishop Fleming's, from whom he received strong support), and Mr. W. B Row, who does not appear to have gone to the poll. The great Doctor was defeated, the author of the new constitution was the first to test the proverbial fickleness of the public : —

> " Fantastic as a woman's mood
> And fierce as frenzy's fevered blood."

He had been the pioneer of the new movement, had suffered in the people's cause, and yet the public, "that many-headed monster thing —the mob"—were the first to cast aside their leader in the fight for Home Rule, and to give their votes and support to a new and

---

[1] Note the items of expenditure under this government of officials ; the whole revenue swallowed up in enormous salaries, and only £300 allowed for roads, show that it was high time to make a change (See in the statistics the expenditure in 1830, 1831, and 1832, prior to grant of Legislature.)

untried man. Carson was a veteran in the Liberal cause; compared with him, Kent was a mere neophite. The Doctor's defeat was due, so the story goes, to an old electioneering trick. An Irishman called Bennett came into the booth where a number of Wexford men were casting their votes. "Well," he said, "I hear the Doctor say he did not "care how it went, so long as he could bate Keogh and them blooming "yallow bellies." Mr. Keough was a Wexford man, and after that he got every Wexford vote. The story was a barefaced lie, but it served its purpose.

Our old friend Mr. John Kent, who then fleshed his maiden sword, was a very young man. His address shows how thoroughly he had grasped the political situation, that there was no finality about the existing Legislature; it was merely a lever to force greater concessions from the British Government.

MR. JAMES SIMMS.

From a portrait in the possession of J. Simms.

In his address to the electors of St. John's, 4th September 1832, he states :—

"Our constitution has, as yet, only half developed itself ; but in that partial development, a sufficient evidence is given of the desire of power to hedge round its prerogative with a force ductile to its will, but irresponsible to the people. In a council nominated by the Governor, composed of those holding offices under Government, or expectants for place, and in which the leading interests of the country are unrepresented, oligarchical principles must prevail. The task of prostrating those principles, or of so modifying them as to make them useful, now devolves on the people. . . . Your extensive franchise, amounting almost to universal suffrage, will enable you to do this."

Mr. James Simms, who had been a merchant, carrying on business in St. John's, was appointed Attorney-General of Newfoundland on the 2nd of January 1826. The first law officer of the Crown was one of the most prominent opponents of the new Legislature, and, as senior member of the Council, his conduct towards the Lower House was most overbearing. Many of us can remember him as a handsome, gentlemanly old man, very stiff in his opinions, and of fearless courage, in his own house hospitable and generous. He had a very high-pitched voice, and very slow, measured speech, which gave more point to his sarcasms. Once, in the Amalgamated House, Mr. Kent declared : "I will "attack Her Majesty's Attorney-General." Simms rose, slowly, to reply : "I know not," said he "with what weapon the Honourable Member will "attack me, except it be with the jawbone of an ass"

On the 1st of January 1833, with all due pomp and ceremony, the first House of Assembly was opened. The newspaper report says :—

" His Excellency the Governor left Government House a little before two o'clock, attended by some of the principal military officers and by his staff, and proceeded to the Court House, at the doors of which he was received by a guard of honour and was saluted with nineteen guns from the fort. Having been conducted to the door of the High Sheriff's house, His Excellency was received by the High Sheriff and the Sergeant-at-Arms to the Council, who led the way to the throne, &c. . . ."

The speech of the Governor dwelt at considerable length on the new era which had arisen in the political condition of the island, and the new responsibilities imposed thereby, concluding with the following declaration of His Excellency's own sentiments :—

" The experience of the past will afford the best criterion by which to judge of my wishes and feelings towards those you are here to represent. Uninfluenced by any local prejudices, and without a single personal desire to gratify, I can have but one object before me—their happiness and prosperity; and I assure you, gentlemen, from the bottom of my heart, that it will be my most anxious and increasing endeavour to co-operate with you in every measure that can best attain those objects, for which the privileges now about to be enjoyed have been solicited by the people, and graciously conceded to them by their sovereign."

The following members were elected for the nine districts to the first House of Assembly of Newfoundland in 1832 :—

St. John's -	- Patrick Keough.	Bonavista	- William Brown.
,, -	- John Kent.	Trinity -	- John Bingley Garland.
,, -	- Wm. Thomas.	Ferryland	- Robert Carter.
Conception Bay	- Peter Brown.	Burin -	- Wm. Hooper.
,, -	- James Power.	Fortune Bay	- Newman W. Hoyles.
,, -	- Charles Cozens.	Placentia	- Roger F. Sweetman.
,, -	- Robert Pack.	,, -	- John Hill Martin.
Twillingate and Fogo	Thomas Bennett.		

The House of Assembly of 1833 was the youngest constituent body in America, but it was not one whit behind any of them in stately parliamentary pageant and grandiloquent language. H. B. (Doyle) in London caricatured it as the "Bow-wow Parliament," with a big Newfoundland dog in wig and bands as Speaker putting the motion : "As many " as are of that opinion say—bow ; of the contrary—wow ; the " bows have it." The Clerk of the first House of Assembly, appointed by the Crown, was Mr. E. M. Archibald [1]; he had been admirably trained in his father's office, and he kept the Speaker and the new House

---

[1] E. M. Archibald, afterwards Sir Edward Archibald, Consul-General in New York, a very able man, was one of the younger sons of the celebrated Hon. S. G. W. Archibald, the most distinguished Nova Scotian of his day, a man with influence enough to secure for himself the position of Attorney-General of Nova Scotia, Speaker of the House of Assembly, and subsequently Chief Justice of Cape Breton ; his son, Charles Dixon Archibald, was Clerk of our Supreme Court, and was succeeded in this office by his brother Edward, who afterwards became Attorney-General.

straight on all questions of parliamentary form; his journals are
admirably written.

The first journal contains election petitions from Dr. Carson and
Hugh Alexander Emerson. The former shows some queer ways of

THE BOW WOW PARLIAMENT.
From a drawing by H. B. (Doyle).

working a contest. It appears there were at first only four candidates,
John Kent, William Thomas, William B. Row, and Patrick Keough,
afterwards the Doctor came forward. Each candidate agreed to bring
his voters to the poll in tallies of ten; Carson alleged that Kent and

C. D. ARCHIBALD.
By Bowness, Ambleside.

SIR E. ARCHIBALD.
By Antony, New York.

Keough broke this agreement by both of them bringing forward two
fictitious candidates, who crowded out his voters. The Doctor also
contended that as Mr. Keough had been employed "filling up several
" places and appointments in the court house for the opening convenience

" of the local Legislature, the said Patrick Keough is therefore utterly
" disqualified for being a member of this Honourable House. Elections
" are fountains from whence flow the purity of parliaments; if the
" sources are permitted to be impure the accumulated mass will soon be
" corrupt." The complaint of Hugh Alexander Emerson, candidate for
Bonavista, is all directed against Peter Le Messurier, the returning
officer. The House of Assembly dismissed both petitions.

John Bingley Garland was elected Speaker In 1834, on the removal
of Mr. William Thomas to the Legislative Council, and Garland's retirement, William Carson was elected for St.
John's, and William Bickford Row for
Trinity. There was a sharp contest between Dr. Carson and Mr. Thomas Bennett
for the speakership; Bennett won.

The most absurd thing about the constitution was the creation of a Colonial
House of Lords—the Legislative Council.
It looked as if it had been formed on purpose to render the whole machinery unworkable; it consisted wholly of officials.
The Governor's instructions, besides directing him to summon a House of Assembly,
commanded him also to call together the
following persons appointed to be members of His Majesty's Council in the Island, viz.:—

J. B. GARLAND.
*From a portrait in the possession of
Mrs. Murray Cookesley.*

"The chief justice for the time being, the officer in command of the land
forces for the time being, the attorney-general for the time being, the colonial
secretary for the time being, the collector or other chief officer of the Customs for
the time being, and William Haly, Esq. 'With all due and usual solemnity' the
Governor was to cause his commission to 'be read and published before the
' Council, and to administer to each of the members thereof the oaths therein
' required.' He was also to communicate to the said Council such of the instructions wherein their advice and consent were mentioned to be requisite, and to
permit the members to have and enjoy freedom of debate, and vote in all affairs of
public concern submitted to their consideration in council."

The two bodies, as might be expected, immediately disagreed; Chief
Justice Tucker, a Bermudian, contended that the Assembly had no *right
to pass a Revenue Bill*. The matter was referred to England, and, as a
matter of course, the Ministry supported the Lower House; Richard
Alexander Tucker resigned his office, and left the Colony in disgust.

Chief Justice Henry John Boulton succeeded Mr. Tucker; he had
been Attorney-General of Upper Canada.[1] The difficulties between the

---

[1] Subsequent to his dismissal from the Chief Justiceship in 1838, Boulton returned to Toronto, and afterwards represented Niagara, and also Norfolk, in Parliament. He was taken prisoner during the year 1811 by a French privateer called the *Grand Duke of Bey*, when crossing the Atlantic in the *Minerva* and kept a prisoner until 1815 at Verdun.

House and the Council were rendered much more bitter by his appointment. He was most overbearing to the Lower House, always calling himself—most improperly—*The Speaker*.[1] With him were associated in the Council Colonel Sall, Commandant; James Crowdy, Colonial Secretary; James Simms, Attorney-General; the Collector of the Customs; and Lieutenant-Colonel William Haly. Next year (1834) J. B. Bland and William Thomas were added.

Carson and Kent, in the House of Assembly, kept up a continual quarrel with Boulton and Simms. They fought over the most trivial details. When the lower branch styled themselves the *Commons* House of Assembly in *Parliament* assembled, they were ordered to strike out the word "*Parliament.*" Their controversies were of the most puerile character; each side displayed vile temper and utter incapacity. The essence of politics is compromise, a principle that neither side seems to

CHIEF JUSTICE BOULTON.

have understood. On the whole, the Council were the most cantankerous. Boulton had undoubted ability, but he was the worst possible selection for both the Council and the Bench. His views, both of law and legislation, were most illiberal; as a technical lawyer he was mostly right and sublimely independent, but his harsh sentences, his indecent party spirit, and his personal meanness caused him to be hated as no one else was ever hated in this Colony. Forbes and Tucker were both able men, especially Forbes; they were not only learned, but, better still, they were shrewd men of the world, thoroughly polished, courteous gentlemen.

Apropos of Boulton's character for inhospitality, a good story is told by Bishop Strachan, the genial old Anglican Bishop of Toronto. Boulton, in a hot argument with a young lawyer, committed the unpardonable crime of stopping the bottles at the Bishop's table. Strachan stood it for a few minutes; at last he called out, in his broad Scotch: "Henry John, pass the bottles; ye're nae in yer own hoose noo, mon."

The fiercest controversy between the two bodies was over the Contingency Bill of the Lower House. These contingencies were swelling up each session; the Council tried to cut them down; strictly speaking they had no authority to touch them at all. They could throw out the

[1] This shows Boulton to have been a very small minded man, and either ignorant or presuming. The presiding officer in all Colonial Legislative Councils is styled the President. When rebuked by the Secretary of State for using the term Speaker, he signed himself Henry John Boulton in full, with a very small P.C.

Bill, which would include their own charges, but they could not amend it. The Council not only refused to pass the Contingency Bill, but year after year, also, threw out the Supply and Revenue Bills. In the meantime, the Governor drew warrants on the Colonial Treasury for the civil expenses of the Government, an extremely high-handed proceeding. The quarrel between the House and the Council was inflamed by the press and the mercantile body. I give two examples of the amenities of the press :—

"And we believe a greater pack of knaves does not exist than that which composes the House of Assembly for the Colony. Take them for all in all, from the Speaker downwards, we do not suppose that a greater set of low-life and lawless scoundrels as Public men can be found under the canopy of Heaven.

"As for the arrogant scoundrelly House of Assembly with which the country is cursed, His Excellency will in this instance do well to, as far as possible, wash his hands clear from it, and take upon himself a judicious responsibility, in which all honest men will bear him out. And let the House of Assembly take any course which it may deem fit."

The men to be pitied in all these childish squabbles were the English Ministry ; they were worried to death with long memorials from each side, volumes of despatches ; the Colonial Legislature they had called into existence was a veritable political Frankenstein, that unceasingly haunted and disturbed them.

Viewing the events between 1833 and 1838—an unfortunate time for the Colony—we see clearly that free institutions never had a fair trial. The upper and mercantile classes were on the whole bitterly opposed to them : the Legislative Council, with Chief Justice Boulton at its head, was an uncompromising opponent ; Boulton brought his powerful but narrow mind in antagonism to the Lower House on all questions ; he was almost invariably wrong in his constitutional doctrines, as he was astray in his decision about servants' wages not having a prior claim on the fish and oil. As I have shown, the custom of giving the fishery servants the first claim on the voyage had existed in the Colony since the fishery began.

We had also another element that worked against our infant assembly—the violence of the mob ; this gave support to all the arguments of the Tory and mercantile party, and it helped to kill out some of the very best blood in the Colony—the very cream of the most important element in the community—the Irish middle-class Liberals (afterwards designated with the odious name of "mad dogs"). How these men and their families were insulted, attacked, and many driven from the Colony, is one of the most deplorable chapters in our political history. The worst effect, however, of free government was the sectarian discord it produced. Previous to the introduction of the Legislature the community was harmonious and united ; for years

afterwards there was nothing but strife and discord. The House gave
a handle to their opponents by providing little jobs and pickings for
their supporters, as their Contingency Bills show, they were not very
large The new Government was, after all, preferable to the ring of
officials

In the politics of this period the Roman Catholic bishop always played
a prominent part It is told, as an example of Bishop Fleming's skill and
sagacity, that when a delegation, consisting of Messrs. Nugent and
O'Brien, were sent to the Colonial Office, he suggested that the Hon
Lawrence should always go first, as a very handsome Colonial specimen,
but, when it came to speaking, Nugent, who was a scholar, should do
the work. At the close of his life, Bishop Fleming deeply deplored the
unhappy divisions politics had produced in the Colony, he held out the
right hand of fellowship to all who had been at enmity with him, his
friendship with Dr. Carson was warm and sincere On all matters,
both public and private, his confidant, friend, and legal adviser was
Mr Wakeham In the latter part of his episcopate, which extended
over the long period of twenty-one years, he was ably assisted by
Dr Mullock

In 1834 Sir Thomas Cochrane was rather suddenly called home.
The Ministry seemed to have entertained the idea that he was in some
way responsible for the unsatisfactory state of affairs in the Colony It
is painful to relate that many of those who had been loud in his praises
as the best Governor ever sent to the Colony, had now turned against
him, and loaded him with abuse. The conduct of the mob was most
disgraceful When His Excellency sailed for England they hooted, and
actually threw dirt at Sir Thomas and Miss Cochrane as they passed
down Cochrane Street to embark at the Queen's wharf Every respectable
man in the community, except a few political agitators, regretted his
departure, and addresses were presented to him from the leading
inhabitants all over the Colony[1] 1835 witnessed the barbarous outrage
on Mr. Henry Winton, editor of the *Public Ledger*[2]

Captain Prescott, R.N, was sent out to succeed Sir Thomas Cochrane
in 1834 No doubt the idea of the Ministry was that Sir Thomas might

[1] In 1834 an Act was passed for the
creation of a savings bank. Newman
W Hoyles was appointed first treasurer and
cashier, at his death, Patrick Morris succeeded
to both positions. J. R M Cooke, a son-in-
law of Mr. Hoyles, was clerk to the bank

[2] Henry Winton, on whom this most
disgraceful outrage was perpetrated, was a
man of remarkable intrepidity, an able and
most independent editor He was one of a
very convivial circle, which included Mr.

John Boyd, whose Bailie Nicol Jarvie was
considered by good judges the best amateur
acting ever seen either here or elsewhere.
Boyd was being sharply cross-examined
about Winton's habits in a libel suit Winton
was of rather a saturnine habit, except when
under the influence of good liquor, which
brought out all his talents. " Now, sir," said
Mr. Emerson, pointing at Boyd, " did you
never see Mr Winton the worse for liquor?"
" Nae, nae,' said Boyd, " never I often saw
him the better of it "

have been too rigid in his views, and that, with a new man at the helm, matters might work smoother in the distracted colony. After all Governor Cochrane's great services, he was superseded in a discourteous and shabby manner; his first intimation of the change of government was the arrival of Captain Prescott, with a fresh commission. During the new Governor's stay, from 1834 to the summer of 1840, the political condition of the Colony did not improve, the quarrels between the Council and the Assembly were rather intensified. In 1838 an

PORTUGAL COVE ROAD, OPENED IN 1831.
From a photograph by Sir T. N. O'Brien, K.C.M.G.

attempt was made to infuse a more popular element into the Council; then consisted of the following (the Hon. Patrick Morris was added 1840):—

"Lieut. Col. William Sall, Commanding the troops.
James Simms, Attorney-General.
James Crowdy, Colonial Secretary.
James Morton Spearman, Collector of Customs.
John Dunscombe.
William Thomas.
John Bayley Bland.
John Sinclair.
Patrick Morris, Colonial Treasurer."

The first House of Assembly by statute, ended in 1836. The elections of this year were very hotly contested ; there were riots at Harbour Grace and all around Conception Bay, and great disturbances in St. John's. The Attorney-General indicted a number of persons for riot and assault ; six of these were members of the House of Assembly.[1] There was not a tittle of evidence to sustain the charges against the members, and they were acquitted. In the other cases, the sentences passed by Chief Justice Boulton were considered so unnecessarily severe that they were remitted by the Home Government. The most preposterous proceeding of all was the disannulling of the 1836 elections, on the ground that one returned writ was *unsealed*.[2] Both Boulton and Attorney-General Simms declared the elections invalid. New writs were ordered ; at the second contest the Conservatives or Protestants made no fight, and a very inferior set of members were returned, one of them being the cele-brated Tom Fitz-Gibbon Moore, of Dildo.[3] The new House contended for its right to appoint its own officers. Mr. E. M. Archibald, the clerk, and other officials had been ap-pointed by the Crown. The new House, however, appointed its own clerk, Mr. R. R. Wakeham. Between the Legislative Council and the Assembly there was war to the knife. The Council threw out Supply, Re-venue, and Contingency Bills ; as fast as the Lower House enacted measures the Upper House annulled them. There was only one way out of the deadlock : the Ministers at home had to be appealed to.

P. H. GOSSE.[4]
From an old photograph.

---

[1] One of the parties indicted was the Hon. Patrick Morris. The only evidence of violence at the great political meeting held at Rae Island was that young Mr. John Kent rode a spirited blood horse, and a man called Power sang out " Bah." The rioting and disturbance in Conception Bay was disgrace-ful. Nearly all the election fights were between rival Roman Catholic candidates. The Hon. T. Talbot, in his pamphlet on Newfoundland, gives a graphic description of one of these scenes. Some of the Con-servatives who could not be frightened were bullied and threatened ; another member, however, who was not to be intimidated in any way, they punished by setting fire to his house. Lord John Russell sharply rebuked Governor Prescott for his laxity in not sending troops to Carbonear in 1840. His Lordship said this place, Car-bonear, should be disfranchised. An old

man named Farrell, who was one of the leaders of the mob, complained that " after all the murdering and blackguarding he had done in these elections, he had no berth, whilst the man he put in had a fat office, and was aiting and drinking the best in the land."

[2] In the elections of 1836 and 1837 to the House of Assembly there was a com-plete change ; nearly all the leading men seem to have retired. Peter Winsor replaced Mr. Carter in Ferryland ; Peter Brown, John McCarthy, Anthony W. Godfrey, and James Power were elected for Conception Bay ; John V. Nugent and Patrick Doyle were returned for Placentia ; Trinity was represented by Tom Fitz-Gibbon Moore, Fogo by Edward James Dwyer, Bonavista by the Solicitor-General, Hugh A. Emerson, Fortune Bay by W. B. Row, whilst the St. John's members were Dr. Carson, John Kent, and Patrick Morris.

[3] Tom Fitz-Gibbon Moore used to walk from his home to the Assembly every session, carrying his "nunny" bag on his back; a wild, eccentric individual, he was as excited as an Indian bravo over the arrest of Judge Lilly. Only one of his many speeches has come down to us. His father was a soldier, and Tom had been a drummer in the Navy, in one of his famous orations he described himself "As born in the Glorious British Army, reared in the Navy, and Musician under our Most gracious Sailor King." A rival of Moore's—Dwyer—was the Hon Member for Lion's Den, Fogo.

[4] A very interesting sketch of the social and political history of the Colony from 1827 to 1835 is given in the life of Philip Henry Gosse (1810-1888), the eminent naturalist, by his son, the well-known author and critic, Edmund Gosse It appears from this biography that William Gosse, an elder brother (who survived until 1893), went out to Carbonear in 1822 to the old firm of Pack, Gosse and Fryer; the youngest brother, Philip, later on became a clerk in the house of Slade, Elson & Co A graphic account is given of the outfitting, tallying, seals, and settling the shareman's accounts, the wrangle over what was "took up," all the phases of out-harbour life in the thirties are admirably told The firm had a branch establishment at St Mary's, ruled by a pompous little West countryman, John Hill Martin, one of the first members for Placentia Gosse was packed off to this out of-the-way place, so we get a description of St Mary's, of Phipard and his pretty daughters, and a very graphic account of the journey overland from St. Mary's to Carbonear with Byrne, prototype of Tom Kelly, at the Head, and other noted country guides Gosse was living at Carbonear when the dastardly attack was made on his friend Henry Winton He mentions the name of the surgeon who cut off Winton's ears Philip Henry Gosse's character, with all its faults and foibles, is admirably portrayed—his generosity, his high sense of honour, his absorbing passion for natural history, and his rigid religious convictions In these days Carbonear was the most turbulent district in the colony. It is not, therefore, to be wondered at that Gosse's views of his religious and political opponents are unfavourable. A few persons still living in Carbonear and Harbour Grace remember him, his mania for collecting, his friendship with the talented St John family, the Elsons, and many other Carbonear worthies, whose memory is fast fading away from the present generation In 1833 P H Gosse wrote and copiously illustrated a volume which he entitled *Entomologia Terræ Novæ* This was the earliest attempt made to describe the insects of Newfoundland, but the young naturalist did not find a publisher, and his work has never been printed

APPENDIX TO CHAPTER XIV

The Tariff and Contingency Bill, 1835

THE TARIFF

A Table of Duties upon Goods, Wares, and Merchandize (except Wines and Spirits) imported into Newfoundland and its Dependencies

	£	s.	d
Beef and pork (salted) the cwt -	0	0	9
Flour, the barrel, not exceeding in weight 196 pounds - - -	0	0	9
Oatmeal, the barrel, not exceeding in weight 200 pounds - -	0	0	6
Bread or biscuit, the cwt - -	0	0	3
Butter, the cwt - - - -	0	1	6
Molasses - - - - -		Free	
Salt - - - - - -		Free	
Implements and materials fit and necessary for the fisheries,—videlicit, lines, twines, hooks, nets and seines - - - -		Free.	
Coin and bullion - - - -		Free	
Apples, the barrel - - -	0	0	6
Coals, the ton - - - -	0	0	6
Horses, mares, and geldings, each -	0	10	0
Neat cattle, each - - - -	0	5	0
Calves - - - - -		Free	
Sheep, each - - - - -	0	0	6
Hogs, each - - - - -	0	0	6
Lumber, one inch thick, the thousand feet - - - -	0	1	0
Ton timber, and balk, of all kinds including scantling, the ton -	0	0	6
Shingles, the thousand - -	0	0	4
Goods, wares, and merchandise (except wines and spirits), not otherwise enumerated, described or charged with duty in this Act, and not herein declared to be duty free, for every £100 of the true value thereof - -	2	10	0

CONTINGENCIES

The sum of £3,137 17s 2d to be applied towards remunerating the officers of the Legislature for their services, and towards defraying the contingent expenses of Her Majesty's Council, and of the House of Assembly, as follows —

The clerk of Her Majesty's Council for his services, £100.

The master in Chancery attending Her Majesty's Council, £100

The usher of the Black Rod, for his services, £70.

The door-keeper of Her Majesty's Council, £35

The assistant door-keeper and messenger of Her Majesty's Council, £10

The clerk of Her Majesty's Council, for preparing and superintending the printing of the Journals for the present session, £25

The clerk of Her Majesty's Council, to defray the expenses contingent on his office, £9 13s 3d

Probable amount of printing and binding the Journals of Her Majesty's Council for the present session, £100.

The usher of the Black Rod, to defray the expenses contingent on his office, £11 13s 10d.

Richard Perchard, house-keeper, for cleaning the Council Room the present and last sessions, £10

The librarian of the Legislature for salary of one year and a quarter, omitted in Contingency Bill of last session, £18 15s

The librarian of the Legislature for salary of the current year, £15.

To the Hon. the Speaker of the House of Assembly, £200

To the chairman of the Committee of Supply, towards defraying the charges of attendance during the present session, at the rate of £1 per diem, for forty-two days, travelling charges, postages, and extra expenses of the members of the House of Assembly (exclusive of the Speaker) resident at St. John's, and in the out-ports, £743.

The clerk of the House of Assembly, £100

Hugh W Hoyles, Esq, for preparing and superintending the printing of the Journals, £50

The Serjeant-at-Arms, for his attendance during the present session, £70

John Delancy, door-keeper, for his attendance this session, £35, and a further sum of £10 for extra services

David Walsh, messenger, for his attendance, £35, and a further sum of £5 for extra services

Philip Brown, under door-keeper, for his attendance, £25, and a further sum of £5 for extra services

John B Cox, assistant door-keeper, for his attendance, £25, and a further sum of £5 for extra services

Mortagh Dunn, assistant messenger, for his attendance, £25, and a further sum of £5 for extra services

The solicitor of the House of Assembly, for his services, £100

The solicitor of the House of Assembly, for extra services, £50.

Richard Holden, assistant clerk, for his services, £80.

The chairman of Supply and Finance, for his services, £50

Alexander M'Iver, for stationery, £32 1s 9d

William Firth, for coals, 15s 4d.

William Freeman, for fitting up the Assembly for the present session, £24 17s 2d

David Walsh, for his services as special messenger to Conception Bay, £5

Ryan and Withers, for account of the Legislature, £18 1s

Stephen J Daniel, for stationery and engrossing, £3

Robert R Holden, for engrossing petitions in 1837, £10 18s. 4d

The chairman of the Committee of Audit, for his services, £50

The proprietor of the *Newfoundlander*, for balance due for printing the journals, £53 9s. 9d.

The proprietor of the *Newfoundlander*, for printing the Journals of the present session, £150

The proprietor of the *Patriot* newspaper, for the general printing of the House of Assembly during the present session, £279 18s.

The representatives of the late Timothy Kelly, for painting the Court room, £4 3s 4d.

The assistant clerk, towards paying for the newspapers of the Colony, £7 18s 2d.

The reporter of the House of Assembly, £50

The door-keeper, for expenses contingent on his office, 7s.

Henry Winton, for stationery, £1 3s 1d

Richard Holden, junior, for copying since the last, and during the present, session, £30

Robert R Wakeham, for office rent and coals, £13 10s

Richard Holden, assistant clerk, for extra services, £50

Ambrose Shea, for binding the Journals of the two last sessions, £19 10s 2d

The under door-keeper and the assistant door-keeper, to defray the expenses of cleaning the House of Assembly, £10

And a further sum of £50 to Thomas Beck, Esq, for his services during the present session

And a further sum of £130 to the acting clerk of the House of Assembly towards the defraying of law charges incurred by order of the House of Assembly.

And a further sum of £10 to Walter Dillon, Esq, for his services the present session

CHAPTER XV.

REIGN OF VICTORIA.

1837–1857.

1838.—First geological survey by J Beete Jukes Boulton, C J., removed, and Bourne appointed. Great case of Kielly v. Carson.

1839.—Newfoundland constituted a separate see; Bishop Spencer, first Anglican Bishop.

1840.—Regular fortnightly sailing packets established between St John's and Halifax H M S. *Spitfire* first steamer to visit St John's

1841.—Foundation stone of the Roman Catholic cathedral laid

1842.—Amalgamated Assembly constituted by Act of Parliament First Presbyterian kirk established. Agricultural Society formed. Captain Fabvre and Mr. W. Thomas, President Chamber of Commerce, appointed Commissioners on French Fishery Question.

1843.—Amalgamated House opened by Sir John Harvey. Act for the Encouragement of Education passed by Richard Barnes.

1844.—Edward Feild, D D , appointed Bishop of Newfoundland The first steam packet, the S.S *North American*, arrived in St. John's from Halifax, N.S. sixty hours' passage. Chief Justice Norton, first Roman Catholic Chief Justice.

1846.—Public meeting on 26th May in the Court House, St John's, in favour of Responsible Government; petition sent to Queen and Parliament. Terrible and destructive fire consumed the town on the 9th June. Tremendous gale on 19th September Colonel Law, Administrator.

1847.—Sir Gaspard Le Marchant, Governor. Chief Justice Brady appointed. Foundation stone of English Cathedral of St. John the Baptist laid; also Colonial Building and Custom House, St John's.

1848.—First Session of Legislature, after return to Constitution of 1833, opened on December 14th by Sir Gaspard Le Marchant. Bishop Mullock arrived on 6th May. Free Kirk established.

1849.—Customs' Department placed under control of the local Government.

1850.—Death of Bishop Fleming

1851.—Public meeting to promote direct steam communication from St John's to England

1852.—Ker Baillie Hamilton, Governor. First steamer in Conception Bay. Hon. J. Crowdy, Administrator. Electric telegraph introduced into St. John's by F. N. Gisborne. Terribly disastrous seal fishery ; "Spring of the Wadhams."

1854.—Reciprocity treaty between British America and the United States. New York, Newfoundland, and London Telegraph Company incorporated.

1855.—Governor Darling. Responsible Government introduced ; Hon. P. F. Little first Premier. Roman Catholic Cathedral consecrated.

1856.—Direct steam by the Galway Line. The American steamer *James Adger* arrived in St. John's ; endeavoured to lay the cable across the Gulf.

1857.—Hon. L. O'Brien, Administrator. Sir Alexander Bannerman appointed Governor. The Anglo-French Convention about the Newfoundland fishery ; indignation meetings ; delegates sent to Canada, Nova Scotia, &c. Gulf cable laid by S.S. *Propontis.*

On the 20th of June 1837 begins the reign of Victoria, Her present Majesty, the noble Queen whose virtues have won the hearts of all English-speaking people, whose fine character and statesmanlike ability have done so much to quicken the loyalty of her subjects, to—

> " Keep her throne unshaken still,
> Broad based upon the people's will."

Her accession ushered in the dawn of a happier era of peace and marvellous progress. To treat of all the important events that have occurred during the Victorian age, even in this small portion of Her Majesty's dominions, is quite beyond the space at my disposal.[1]

The very first subject brought under the notice of the English Ministry in the year of the Queen's accession concerning our Island was the old trouble and dispute between the Council and Assembly. In 1837 the House of Assembly sent home delegates on the complaints against Chief Justice Boulton, and respecting the disputes between the House and the Council. The Assembly was represented by Dr. Carson,

---

[1] The first Anglican Bishop of Newfoundland, Aubrey George Spencer, was appointed in 1839—a most amiable and godly prelate. He founded the Theological College, and laid the first stone of the Cathedral. His feeble health soon gave way under the strain of his arduous episcopal labours. The successor of Bishop Spencer was the Right Rev. Edward Feild, our great Anglican prelate, whose life has been admirably written by the Rev. H. W. Tucker, M.A. A striking personality, his powerful influence changed the whole character of the Church and the clergy in the Colony. The ministers had all belonged to the Evangelical or Low Church type ; one of this school is now a *rara avis* in the diocese. The Bishop's predominant trait was the true missionary spirit ; to the service of his Divine Master he was consecrated, body and soul. He scorned popularity and all the pomps and vanities of the world. To his opponents he seemed narrow and intolerant ; but to his admirers, and they now embrace the whole Anglican Church, he was the embodiment of all that is saintly and holy. In social life the Bishop was a delightful companion, full of pleasantness and humour, a dear lover of children. The marvellous work he performed in his great diocese is well known ; one of the results of his powerful influence was the sub-division of the Protestant educational scheme. With all my admiration for the great prelate, I cannot say that it was a good movement ; I believe its influence in dividing the grant, and in giving many localities two poor schools in place of one good one, has been very detrimental to the progress of education in the Colony.

P. Morris, and J. V. Nugent. As the result of this appeal in 1838, the Queen recommended the adoption of the Appropriation Bill by the Council. The Assembly in the main succeeded; both Houses, however, were severely blamed for their discourteous and improper conduct

J. V. NUGENT.
By Lyon, St. John's.

towards each other, and were informed that they ought to show each other proper consideration. The success of the British Constitution, as the best Government in the world, is largely dependent on the fact that it is worked out by gentlemen and men of honour, who, notwithstanding all the acerbities of party, are governed by the rules of courtesy and propriety. As a result of the appeal, the Chief Justice was dismissed. With all Boulton's faults, he was shabbily treated by the Home Government. In the first place his appointment was an injudicious one; he was an extreme partizan, a rigid Tory, and too fresh from the heated political strife of Upper Canada to suit the calm atmosphere of the Bench; in order to make amends for the loss of the Attorney-Generalship of that province, the Ministry had appointed him Chief Justice of Newfoundland; his pecuniary loss by the change was a very great one. The popular attacks on Boulton were most disgraceful and unfair. The serious charges, that his judgments were biassed by his political views, and that his decisions were corrupt, were all proved to be untrue. The Privy Council should have considered his anomalous position as President of the Council and Chief Justice; they were wholly incompatible offices. There was, however, sufficient evidence of his party speeches, his attendance at political meetings, and of his intemperate and injudicious behaviour, to warrant the Privy Council in advising his removal. As he was made the scapegoat for an unworkable political system, he should certainly have been pensioned, and not cast adrift penniless after filling such high office.

The advice of the English Ministers does not seem to have been acted on, for in 1838 we find the House and the Council more seriously at variance than ever; this was largely due to the celebrated case of Kielly v. Carson. On Tuesday, 7th August 1838, Doctor Kielly met Mr. John Kent on the street; both were very high-spirited gentlemen. Mr. Kent declared that Dr. Kielly had put his fist up to his face and had then and there threatened to pull his nose. This amounted, as anyone can see, to an ordinary case of assault, and the remedy lay in proceedings before the magistrates or the Supreme Court; that, however, would not have suited the insulted and impetuous Kent; he

appealed to the House.[1]   The Assembly sat with closed doors, and finally
decided to summon Dr. Kielly to the bar.   Mr. Speaker Carson informed
him that he had been brought there on a charge of having violated the
privileges of the House by making an attack on one of their members.
The clerk was ordered to read the report of the committee appointed
to consider the matter with the evidence.   The report declared "the
" conduct of Dr. Kielly is a gross breach of the privileges of the House,
" and, if allowed to pass unnoticed, would be a sufficient cause for
" deterring members acting in the independent manner so necessary for

WATER STREET, ST. JOHN'S, LOOKING WEST, IN 1837.
From a drawing by William Gosse, Esq.

" a free Assembly." The doctor requested to be allowed to produce
witnesses on his own behalf; this was refused. The Speaker informed
him that his only course was to plead ignorance of the privileges of the
House, to express regret, and to throw himself on the clemency of the
Assembly. Far from apologizing, the doctor pointed his finger at
Mr. Kent who was sitting in the House, and said he was a liar and a
coward. For this ebullition of temper Kielly next day sent a written
apology. When brought to the bar the second time he was ordered to

[1] John Kent, examined, said : " He was
a member for the District of St. John's; he
and Dr. Kielly had some difference, pro-
voked by him [Dr. Kielly], about 12 o'clock
that day. Dr. Kielly had put his hand
clenched up to his [Mr. Kent's] face several
times and said, ' he had it in him for him, the
lying puppy, and his privileges should not
protect him,' alluding to certain statements
made by him [Mr. Kent] in his place in the
House upon the subject of the St. John's
Hospital."

apologise in the following terms: " I exceedingly regret that I have
" been guilty of any act or expression which has been considered by
" your Honourable House to be a gross breach of its privileges." The
prisoner refused to make this apology. With the Conservative party,
the doctor now became the hero of the hour.[1] In charge of the
celebrated Tommy Beck, Serjeant-at-Arms, with the mace, Dr. Kielly
was marched down to the prison, situated on the east side of
Church Hill (now Market House Hill). Mr. Bryan Robinson,[2] then
a rising young barrister, applied to Judge Lilly for a habeas

DR. KIELLY.

corpus, on the grounds that the House
of Assembly had no such rights and
privileges as were assumed in their late
extraordinary proceedings, and that the
warrant for Kielly's arrest was informal.
Judge Lilly[3] decided that the commit-
ment was deficient in those essentials
necessary to constitute it legal. Three
days afterwards his lordship delivered a
long and very able judgment.

The House of Assembly seem to have
completely lost their heads; instead of
submitting to the law, and thus setting
a good example, they were guilty of
the most outrageous absurdities. It was the Wild Westerner—Tom
Fitz-Gibbon Moore—and Mr. Kent who proposed that Mr. Robinson,
for taking up Dr. Kielly's case, should not be permitted to communicate with the House as Master in Chancery of the Legislative
Council.[4] Another motion proposed was that the *Newfoundlander's*

[1] " Oh! Did you see Dr. Kielly, oh!
       With his boots and spurs and styly oh."

[2] Mr. B. Robinson was charged by John
O'Mara and Edward Morris that, in his
argument before the court on the habeas
corpus for Kielly, he had compared the
privileges of the House to those of the
Mechanic's Society. He had said that the
House had simply the power of turning
people out that disturbed it.

[3] In their address to the Queen, the House
of Assembly made a most unjustifiable attack on Judge Lilly. They spoke of him as a
judge who had rendered himself conspicuous
by publicly subscribing to most outrageous
calumnies on the persons and political
character of the members; Mr. E. M. Archibald, the Clerk of the Court, and Clerk of the
Assembly who assisted the judge in the
preparation of the judgment, was also
denounced as a violent partizan.

[4] The House, considering " that B. Robinson, Esq., Master in Chancery, attendant on
H.M. Council, by contemptuous language
and observations respecting the House of
Assembly and the Members thereof, and
by the issuing out of certain writs at the
suit of one Edward Kielly for alleged damages
against the Speaker, &c., has been guilty of
a gross breach of the privileges of this House,
and the said B. Robinson being an officer
of H.M. Council, this House cannot proceed
against him for such contempt.

" Resolved, That the said Bryan Robinson be not admitted as the bearer of any
message to this House until a message be
dispatched to H.M. Council acquainting the
Council with their resolution."

Two days later the House of Assembly
came to their senses and rescinded the
resolution against the obnoxious Master in
Chancery. Of all their absurd proceedings
this is the most humorous of all.

proprietors and printer should be brought to the Bar *for publishing Judge Lilly's judgment*. These, however, were mild outbreaks of legislative insanity compared with their last act. The Speaker issued his warrant to arrest Dr. Kielly, who had been discharged from custody, also to arrest the High Sheriff, who had liberated him under a judge's order, and, lastly, to arrest Judge Lilly. The spectacle was seen in the town of Tommy Beck, with the mace, dragging a highly respected judge of the Supreme Court through the streets, with a great mob hurrahing and following the cortège. After being taken to the Speaker's room the judge was confined in the house of the Serjeant-at-Arms. Governor Prescott immediately prorogued the Legislature, and thus promptly and properly put an end to these undignified proceedings. In the autumn the case of Kielly *v.* Carson came up before Chief Justice Bourne, in the Central Circuit Court, for adjudication. The decision of the court was reserved for the opinion of the three judges in the Supreme Court. The judges differed; Assistant-Judge Lilly decided that the plea of justification, on the ground of privilege, had not been made out, and that the plaintiff should have judgment on the demurrer, Des Barres, A.J., and Bourne, C.J., gave judgment in favour of the defendants. This judgment was appealed against to the Privy Council, and the final decision was pronounced as follows, on the 11th of January 1841, by Chief Baron Parke :—" The House of Assembly of Newfoundland " is a Local Legislature with every power reasonably necessary for the " proper exercise of their functions and duties ; but they have not, what " they erroneously supposed themselves to possess, the same exclusive " privileges which the ancient law of England has annexed to the " House of Parliament." The fantastic tricks of our legislators furnished the leading case on the question of the powers of colonial parliaments ; Kielly *v.* Carson established the law on the subject for all time.

One word more and we have finished with the legislatures of 1833 and 1836 and the short-lived parliament of 1841. The terrible election riot at Carbonear, in the autumn of 1840, so disgusted the British Ministry with Newfoundland affairs, that Governor Prescott was ordered to dissolve the Legislature, which he did on the 26th April 1841,[1] and the

---

[1] GOVERNOR PRESCOTT'S Speech in Closing the HOUSE OF ASSEMBLY, 26th April 1841.
" Mr. President and Hon. Gentlemen of the Council, Mr Speaker, and Gentlemen of the House of Assembly,
" As a Committee of the House of Commons has been appointed to enquire into the state of Newfoundland, before which Committee I shall have to appear, I will on the present occasion confine myself to the expression of my regret that such a proceeding should have become indispensably necessary to the tranquillity and welfare of the Colony."

Constitution was suspended from that date until the 17th January 1843. In 1842, under the Conservative ministry of Sir Robert Peel, a new constitution was given to the Colony—the Amalgamated Legislature. The members of the Legislative Council sat with the fifteen elected members; the Acts were worded, "Be it therefore enacted by the Governor, Council, and Assembly in General Assembly convened." It was one of the queerest forms of a statutable parliament ever invented; there was an executive council, but it did not contain a single one of the popularly elected members. As usual, the whole patronage of the Government was in the hands of the Executive.

SIR H. PRESCOTT.[1]
From an old photograph.

In the summer of 1841 Captain Henry Prescott, C.B., ceased to govern us. He is universally acknowledged to have been a polished gentleman, his speeches are able and above all concise, but the last of the naval administrators, with all his good qualities, was neither a strong Governor nor a good diplomatist; the whole period of his rule was troubled with political squabbles and sectarian animosities. He disliked Boulton, but appears to have been either unable or unwilling to control him. The dawn of a brighter day, however, was already breaking; our old friend Byrne, most able and practical of road surveyors, was laying out the great roads to Placentia, the road around Conception Bay and the Bay Bulls line. Mr. James Douglas and Mr. O'Brien—named the "Colossus of roads"—were busy getting all the ways to Outer Cove, Middle Cove, and all the other coves

---

[1] Admiral Sir H. Prescott, G.C.B. [1783–1874], was the only surviving son of Admiral Isaac Prescott (who was on the Newfoundland station in 1781) and was born at Kew Green, Surrey. He entered the navy at the usual age; was engaged in action with four ships that escaped from Trafalgar; was employed off Sardinia from 1808 to 1810, and took part in the defence of Sicily. He was promoted to the rank of Captain, after distinguishing himself in the destruction of several vessels at Amatia; was Governor of Newfoundland from 1831 to 1844; was a Lord of the Admiralty during the later half of 1847 and was Admiral Superintendent of Portsmouth Dockyard from December 1847 to the end of 1852. In 1862 he became Admiral of the Blue and was a magistrate for Surrey. He was created a G.C.B. in 1869. (*Men of the Reign*, 1885.) Further full details of Sir H. Prescott's early life will be found in O'Bryne's Naval Biography.

about the capital improved. Sir Bryan, then Mr. Robinson, was also what my friend Justice Harney would call an enthusiastic "projector of viaducts."

The arrival of Sir John Harvey, on the 16th of September 1841, marks an important point in our history; for the first time the control and management of the Colony were placed in the hands of two able politicians, two statesmen of consummate tact and ability, Sir John and his colleague, the Hon. Jas. Crowdy, for fourteen years the Colonial Secretary. Crowdy had been for many years endeavouring to smooth over difficulties and to make peace, but Boulton was too overbearing and the House too extreme. From this time forward the political wheel ran smoother.

Sir John had one rather awkward habit, he always wrote his speeches, and, though excellent, they were uncommonly long. He had been known in the Army as "the handsome Colonel Harvey"; his manners were the perfection of courtesy, nothing disturbed him. In those days Cassidy the tailor was a great sporting man, and prided himself on his knowledge of farming in general. At the great agricultural meeting at Mount Pearl,

SIR JOHN HARVEY.
From Bonnycastle's Newfoundland.

when His Excellency made the speech memorable in every history of the Colony, the irate tailor came in to complain of Murray, another sporting tailor, who insisted on judging a ploughing match. Cassidy, very excited and inebriated, strode up to the head of the table where His Excellency was being entertained by the magnates of the land; " Your Excellency," says he, " is a shoemaker to be a judge of a tailor's " work, your Excellency, or a tailor to be a judge of a shoemaker's work, " your Excellency ? " With a bland bow, " Mr. Secretary Templeman,"

F F

said Sir John, turning to that fat official, "be good enough, sir, to take "a note of these most valuable suggestions of Mr. Cassidy."

The Amalgamated House was a makeshift assembly, but under the presidency of its admirable speaker, Mr. Crowdy, it worked better than the former arrangement; there was fierce debate, scurrility, and vituperation, but at any rate the Acts were passed, and the public service was not embarrassed. In the first session Mr. Richard Barnes introduced and passed a valuable Education Act, and large grants were made each year for roads. All the country was prosperous—the seal fishery had immensely increased; exports of all kinds were very large; in 1840 over nine hundred thousand quintals of fish and over six hundred thousand seals rewarded the labours of our hardy fishermen; taxation was very light, the revenue for 1840 being only £43,863, and the whole civil expenditure £39,347—dear, delightful days of Arcadian simplicity! when we had no debt, and port wine was a shilling a bottle!

HON. J. CROWDY.
By Southwell.

The Governments of Captain Prescott and Sir John Harvey mark the parting of the ways, the interregnum between the last days of the cook-room [1] and the fishing ships and the new departure.

The wonderful growth of the spring seal fishery just about this period completely changed the social habits of the people; the work

---

[1] On every large mercantile establishment the cook-room was a necessary institution. All the planters and servants were boarded and lodged on the premises during their stay in the capital; the men slept in bunks ranged round the cook-room like the berths in a ship; generally an ancient retainer of the house, with an assistant, often a man and his wife, cooked for all.

I have heard an old Newfoundland merchant describe his experiences. When he came out, as a young man, to the Colony in 1808, he became great friends with Mrs. Dollard, the presiding genius of the cook-room on John Hill & Co.'s premises; as the smallest clerk in the shop he had the privilege of getting the ends of listing off the West of England cloth, which were used to make moccasins; he generally bartered his listing with Mrs. Dollard for sweets—bull's-eyes.

A great institution on the merchant's premises, always called in the vernacular "The Room," was the periodical serving out of grog; morning, eleven o'clock, noon, and in the afternoon, all employed in the room had a glass of rum; on the Jersey and on Newman's place this continued up to my own time. Various attempts were made by reformers to alter this practice. A most worthy Scotchman—Mr. Johnson, familiarly known as Wullie Johnson (managing partner of the old firm of Baine Johnson)—tried to improve it by watering the grog; he went on diluting it until he raised a rebellion. Mr. Robert Job was the first man to make a firm stand against the practice; he was execrated at the time, but he stood steadfast, and lived to see his example followed by all his brother merchants. Mr. Job and his brother, Mr. Thomas Job, were zealous promoters of all civic improvements. Mr. Robert Job was largely instrumental in getting the Long Bridge, known as Job's Bridge, built; he introduced gas, and helped greatly to form the first Water Company.

required for fitting out the vessels, building punts, repairing and strengthening the sealing schooners, kept masters and crews at work all through
the winter; what had formerly been a carnival of drinking and dancing
now became a season of hard, laborious toil.[1]   The seal fishery, besides

MR. T. JOB.   MR. J. MUNN.   MR. RIDLEY.
By Sarony, Scarborough.   By Negretti & Zambra.   By Silvy, Bayswater.

altering social customs, largely increased the importance of the out-ports;
the statistics of the early part of the century show us that there was a
considerable foreign trade in the Island outside of St. John's.   Many
resident merchants carried on a large business in such places as Trinity,
Greenspond, Twillingate, Fogo, Bonavista, King's Cove, Harbour Grace,
Carbonear, Brigus,[2] Port de Grave, &c.   Some of these men were
Catholic Liberals; injured by politics, many of them later on left the
Colony, others were ruined.   The effect of the seal fishery was to add
materially to the wealth of the various settlements where it was
carried on.   First of all there was the building of the ships, as prior to
about the Forties, when the Conception Bay merchants began buying the
slop-built vessels from the Provinces, nearly every vessel in the seal
fishery was native built; the crews belonged to the place; in many
cases the seals also were manufactured into oil in the same harbour—
Twillingate, Fogo, Greenspond, Trinity, besides the Conception Bay

[1] From Mr. Daniel Ryan, of King's Cove,
and from other sources of information, it
appears that sharemen were always clear of
service by 20th September; after that there
was dancing, drinking, and card-playing every
night, from house to house in the out-ports,
often ending in a fight; when the Hibernian
element was present, generally a faction fight.
On the first of May all hands set to work
again.   A large number of English and Irish
went home every autumn, and returned in
the spring; Jersey men always left.   From
about 1820 the spring seal fishery changed
all this.   There was always, however, a
carnival of dancing, mumming, and, of course,
drinking, from Christmas to Twelfth day.

[2] Brigus in the Forties, as we can see
from the returns, was the head-quarters of a

great seal fishery.   In 1844 Mr. and Mrs.
Gilbert Harrison (brother of Mrs. T. Ridley)
were making a tour of the bay, accompanied
by Mr. Addison, chaplain to Bishop Spencer.
They were people of great refinement and
culture.   Mr. Brown tells the story how he
took them over to see old Billy Rabbits; of
course the "broke" sugar and the hot water
and spirits were immediately produced, and a
toast had to be proposed.   "Bloody decks to
en," said Billy, as he raised his glass.   Addison was horrified.   "Really, my dear sir, as
a minister of religion, I could not drink to
such a sanguinary wish as that."   Mr. Brown
had to explain it was a customary toast of
success to the seal fishery, and homicide was
not intended.

F F 2

ports, had vats.   All this, as my readers can readily understand, brought
strength and wealth to the out-harbours, and nourished the growth of a
great middle class—the traders and sealing skippers ; the two occupations
were often combined.   Enormous amounts of money were made in those
days.   Steam completely changed the whole aspect of affairs.   The men
now get much smaller shares ; the big bills of the Forties and the
Fifties are no longer earned ; a man's share to-day hardly ever goes over
£8 or £10, and the great army of sealing skippers and great planters,
where are they ?   Their descendants, the Ashes, Dawes, Delaneys,
Blandfords, Kanes, Knees, Jackmans, Bartletts, and others, are still the

KILLING SEALS.

most skilful ice masters, and their crews of Newfoundlanders the best
sealers in the world.   Dundee has splendid sealing steamers, but her men
can never have the same aptitude as ours for this perilous pursuit.
The following anecdote of the late Mr. Smith Mackay's, apropos of
copying (jumping from pan to pan of ice), shows how much at home the
Newfoundlander feels on the ice floe :—

" There was a Canadian on board one of our sealers who was very smart at
going on the ice; there were also some boys on half their hand; a great rivalry
existed between them.   One day the master called out that there were seals on the
starboard bow ; over the side went the Canadian, followed by the boys ; there was a

channel just caught over, which the Canadian did not see, and down he went ; as
he rose the boys, seven in number, came to the edge, and successfully copied over
the Canadian's head and shoulders. Well might a Dundee captain exclaim
' barbarous ! ' when he heard the story."

PANNING SEAL.
From a photograph by Walter Monroe.

When Mr. Walter Grieve sent the first sealing steamer to the ice it was
a poor day for Newfoundland. The only consolation we can lay to our
hearts is that steam was inevitable ; it was sure to come, sooner or later,
the pity of it is that it did not come later. Politics and steam have done
more than any other cause to ruin the middle class, the well-to-do dealers
that once abounded in the out-ports. Contrast the statistics of 1848
with 1878. It was as bad for the merchants as for the men.

Another aspect of our trade, which is almost forgotten by the
present generation, was the great influx of Spanish vessels between
1840 and 1860 ; the direct cause was the Spanish duty known in the
Peninsula as " el derecho de la bandera."—the deferential duty in favour
of the Spanish flag, amounting to over a dollar a quintal. For several
years there were often sixty and seventy Spanish vessels loading fish in
this port, and a large number in Harbour Grace. C. F. Bennett & Co.
had thirty-two in one year. The most numerous at first were our old
acquaintances the Biscayans : their ships, however, compared with the
Spaniards' from the Mediterranean, were small and poorly equipped,
a great many of them simply luggers of sixty and seventy tons
Barcelona, Malaga, and Valencia vessels were splendid craft ; many of

them were slavers ; you could see the ring-bolts in the hold to which the poor Africans were chained   Mr. Henry Le Messurier informs me that one beautiful vessel of this class upset, and in getting her up a number of secret places were found in her hold   The captains of these ships nearly always brought gold Spanish onzas and Mexican dollars to pay for their cargoes and Mr. Le Messurier speaks with gusto of the cart-loads of Spanish bullion sent up to the bank   Whilst it lasted it must have been a large source of profit to the trade   For many years these Spanish vessels carried away between one hundred and sixty and one hundred and seventy thousand quintals of fish [1]   The alteration of the tariff—doing away with the preference given to Spaniards—ended this trade.[2]

Under both Captain Prescott and Sir John Harvey there was great activity both in agriculture and road making [3]   In 1838 the first geological survey was commenced under the distinguished J. Beete Jukes, who arrived in St John's in Mr. John Stuart's clipper brig

[1] In 1850 there were seventy Spanish and Portuguese vessels in St John's alone, aggregating 8,673 tons, navigated by 678 men, they loaded 154,415 qtls of cod-fish and 378 tons of oil   In the same year American vessels loaded 16,582 qtls of fish , a German and Danish vessel took 200 tons of oil and 6,430 seal skins

The trade with Hamburg in oil continued for many years , Munns sent as much as 500 tons of pale seal oil in a year to Hamburg, the greatest factory of adulterated goods in the world, there to be converted by German science and dexterity into the finest quality of "*Pure Cod-liver Oil*"

[2] PORTUGUESE FISHING COMPANY

"In 1835, a Portuguese company was formed in Lisbon, under the title of the Compañía Piscarias, for the prosecution of the Bank fishery , they sent to England and purchased seven English schooners, of about 100 tons each, and shipped in Devonshire, at high wages, men who had been accustomed to the Bank fishery   After being fitted out at a large expense with all the luxuries they thought Englishmen were fond of, such as cheese, brandy, porter, &c (and fine feasting these old Bunkers had), the vessels proceeded to Lisbon, and on arrival there, an equal number of Portuguese were put on board, to be instructed in the method of fishing , then taking in sardines for bait, they proceeded to the Banks, and when they had completed their first trip, they returned to Fayal, in the Western Islands, where they landed their fish and then went on a second voyage, on the return from which those who had been successful landed the second cargo, and proceeded on their third voyage, the catch of which they took green to Lisbon, where it was sold in the same condition   In Fayal the fish was taken in waggons to the tops of the mountains, where flakes had been previously made, covered with boards, as a screen to protect the fish from the scorching rays of the sun, and it was there cured by the winds and heats, which in those climates are very drying, and when cured the fish was thence exported to Portugal, where it is admitted at a nominal duty   At the end of the season the Englishmen so employed were discharged and sent home, the Portuguese having thus obtained from them all the information they required (they now fish with bultows) , the Company, however, is not in a flourishing state, having laboured under many disadvantages   So ignorant were many of the Directors, at the time the Company was formed, that at one of their meetings, the Vice-President proposed drying the fish on the Banks !   Their Government, I believe, have made overtures to Great Britain to take off a portion of the heavy duties they now impose upon our fish, on condition of having granted a portion of the Newfoundland coast, for them to form a settlement for the cure of fish , if such is the case, the Portuguese Government not having the means of granting bounties, it would be wise policy in Great Britain to accede to the proposal, as the consumption is much curtailed by the high prices the consumers have to pay, the duties being in many instances more than the price we obtain for the fish itself, and the quantity consumed would increase in a greater ratio than the difference of quantity the Portuguese would catch "—(WARREN's *Lecture*, pp 17, 18)

[3] In two years, 1837 and 1838, the Legislature voted $175,000 for roads.

Diana, in company with the celebrated Plantagenet Harrison. Two very important elements in the commercial life of the Colony—a bank [1] and regular postal communication with Halifax—were established during this period. The first steamer to visit our waters was H.M.S. *Spitfire*, a paddle steamer, in 1840; she put into St. John's with a detachment for the Royal Newfoundland Company. J. B. Jukes returned to England in her. In 1842 the steamship *John McAdam* arrived, and several pleasure trips were made to Trinity and Conception Bay, and duly astonished the natives. By 1844 we had a regular packet steamer plying between St. John's and Halifax, Nova Scotia; most of us can remember the excitement caused in the town when the *North American*, with her huge walking beam and a figure-head of an Indian

J. B. JUKES.
From an engraving.

painted white, first came into Mr. Matthew Stewart's wharf; she had made a wonderful passage of *sixty hours* from Halifax, and her captain,

MR. J. W. SMITH.
By S. H. Parsons.

MR. R. BROWN.
By S. H. Parsons.

Richard Meagher, was duly congratulated on his remarkable voyage. From this time forward the sailing packets which had been run by

[1] The Bank of British North America commenced business about 1836. Mr. Andrew Milroy, father of Lady Thorburn, was the first manager. For many years they carried on business in Tobin's Building, Water Street, below Mr. Stott's; for some reason the Legislature refused for several years to grant the bank a charter. In April 1844 the Newfoundland Bank was incorporated, the capital was £50,000, half paid up. The following were the principal shareholders : Charles Fox Bennett, William Bickford Row, Lawrence O'Brien, Robert Prowse, George H. Dunscombe, Richard Barnes, John Dillon, John Kent, Richard O'Dwyer, John P. Mullowney, Robert Roberts Wakeham, Lawrence Maccassey, James B. Wood, John Stuart, Edward Kielley, Thomas Ridley,

Bland & Tobin were discarded, and we have had continuous steam communication ever since. The service for many years was carried out by Cunard & Co., in conjunction with their Liverpool line, and, though several vessels were lost, it was maintained very efficiently by the well-known Captain Corbin, and afterwards by the dashing Guildford, two as fine seamen as ever trod a deck.

The Amalgamated House[1] lasted all through Sir John Harvey's administration; it worked far more harmoniously than the first House; a glance at its composition will show us that it contained nearly all

NARROWS, OR ENTRANCE OF THE HARBOUR OF ST JOHN'S, NEWFOUNDLAND
WITH THE FLIN TOWN
London, Published by H. Colburn & C? Marlborough Street 1842.

the best and ablest men in the Colony. In the memorable year of the fire (1846), an agitation was set on foot to obtain responsible government; it was not entirely successful, but in 1848, when the

William Walsh, and Charles Loughlan. The money was returned to the shareholders. The very existence of the new concern probably influenced the existing bank, and made it discount with more liberality and less favouritism, and the *raison d'être* for the Newfoundland Bank ceased. . . . Nearly the same proprietors founded, in 1854, the Union Bank of Newfoundland; the success of this institution was due, in the first place, to the able management of Mr. J. W. Smith, manager, carried out afterwards by his successor, Mr. Goldie. The Commercial Bank was established in 1857; the first manager was Mr. R. Brown, under whose careful ad-

ministration the bank was a marked success. He was succeeded by Mr. Henry Cooke.

[1] The last session of the House of Assembly, under the first constitution, was closed by Governor Prescott on the 26th April 1841, His Excellency making the shortest speech on our parliamentary records, the constitution being suspended until 1842, when an election was held on the 20th December of that year. Sir John Harvey opened the new Legislature, the Amalgamated House, on the 14th January 1843 with the longest speech on record.

The House consisted of the 10 following members appointed by the Crown:—Hon. J.

world was agitated with revolution, and crowns were falling in a very promiscuous manner all over Europe, our original constitution of Queen, Lords and Commons, was restored to us. I should have mentioned that Chief Justice Boulton was succeeded in 1838 by John Gervase Hutchinson Bourne; he was a scholar, a Fellow of Magdalen, Oxford, and an able lawyer He was, however, unfortunately cursed with a violent temper; at the bar he was uniformly favourable to Mr George Henry Emerson and antagonistic to Mr. Robinson (afterwards Sir Bryan)[1] Many stories are told of Bourne's temper, the best one I know is in connexion with the crier of the court, Lambert. The old man was helping the chief with his gown, the sleeve was inside out, and Bourne could not get his arm through; in his wrath he swore, " The devil's in the gown", old Lambert, who was getting the sleeve right, said, quite innocently, " Not yet, my Lord, not yet." Sir John Harvey dismissed the Chief Justice in 1844, he was succeeded by Thomas Norton, a most accomplished Irish gentleman, who had been sent out as assistant judge to Demerara[2] Norton was the first Roman Catholic Chief Justice, he was a universal favourite, an able, impartial judge, a most humorous and fascinating companion off the Bench. he only remained in Newfoundland a few years, he loved gay society, and had most influential friends to promote his advancement.

During the Governorship of Sir John Harvey, St John's was devastated by the " Great Fire ", what the Hejira is to the Mussulman, the 9th of June 1846 was to Newfoundlanders, a date constantly referred to. The previous year, 1845, had been remarkable for the disastrous fire at Quebec, and a month later the terrible conflagration at St. John, New Brunswick. St. John's, to its honour, had contributed

---

Simms, Attorney-General, Hon Jas. Crowdy, Colonial Secretary, Honbles Jro. Dunscombe, Wm. Thomas, P. Morris, Colonial Treasurer, W B. Row, Jas Tobin, Jo Noad, Surveyor-General, C. F Bennett, Jno Kent The 15 members elected were.—

    For St John's Dr Carson, L O'Brien, J. V Nugent.
    Conception Bay : Thos Ridley, John Munn, J L Prendergast, E Hanrahan.
    Trinity Richard Barnes
    Bonavista Robt Carter.
    Ferryland T. Glen
    Placentia Jno Dillon, Simon Morris
    Fortune Bay · B Robinson
    Fogo J Slade

In 1846 there were three sessions, and members and officers got three sessions' pay. H. W. Hoyles, Solicitor to the House In June 1846, owing to the absence of Mr Speaker Crowdy, Mr Kent was appointed

Speaker. The House sat in the Eastern Chamber of the Orphan Asylum School House

[1] Chief Justice Bourne was terribly antagonistic to Mr Robinson, who petitioned the Imperial Government against him. The Chief Justice then made charges against the Colonial Secretary, Mr Crowdy, and Sir John Harvey, his complaints were shown to be unfounded, and he was quietly removed. He was a man of ability and learning, but his ungovernable temper utterly unfitted him for a position requiring calmness and cool judgment

[2] Chief Justice Norton was an intimate convivial friend of Sir Alexander Cockburn. One day on circuit Cockburn sent him a note, " Master in Lunacy dead, will this suit you luck, Tom ?" Norton answered at once, " Your servant Tom will accept this crumb that falls from your Lordship's table "

liberally to the sufferers by both calamities. Our fire was the most disastrous of all ; it began in Hamlin the cabinet maker's shop, about 8 a m., and by nightfall it had destroyed the city, the suburbs, then very unimportant, were left; by sundown nothing but a forest of chimneys remained to mark the site of our flourishing town. The citizens and the fire brigade worked manfully ; Sir John, Major Robe, Colonel Law, and the military were untiring in their exertions, His Excellency was everywhere An attempt was made at Messrs. E. & N Stabb's, now Blair's premises, to blow up the corner building, and thus make a break. One artilleryman and two citizens were killed, many had narrow escapes By mid-day the heat of the fire became so intense that no one could do anything. The conflagration reached everywhere; the beautiful new convent at the head of Long's Hill, far away from the flames, was destroyed by sparks carried by the high wind ; when the huge wooden building, St John's Church, caught, the heat to leeward became overpowering. With the burning of the many substantial wooden buildings and seal vats on Water Street, and with several ships on fire in the harbour, it seems now almost miraculous that the south side escaped. Out of sixty large mercantile warehouses, Newman's old premises at River alone remained [1]

[1] A plan of the town, showing the extent of this fire, will be found at p. 522.

(*Newfoundlander, June 18, 1846*)

" The fire broke out at 8 30 a m on Tuesday, 9th June 1846, in the shop of Hamlin the cabinet maker, in George Street, off Queen Street, and was caused by the overboiling of a glue-pot. The fire immediately communicated to Queen Street, and in a short time the whole collection of stone and wooden houses in the locality were on fire It was hoped that a stand might be made at the corner of Queen Street and Water Street, but the fire spread on, consuming Messrs. Rogerson's, Stewart's, and C. F Bennett's premises, it was stopped by an heroic effort at Newman's premises, River Head. The wind began to blow from the westward The terrified cry now arose that Bennett's and Stewart's oil vats were on fire, at that sound despair seized on every mind and paralysed every nerve; it was then seen that the total annihilation of the town was inevitable, and the scene of consternation that arose defies description. Sir John Harvey ordered Mr. Stabb's house (O'Dwyer's corner) to be blown up The break, however, was not of sufficient extent, and the wind, which was strong at first, seemed to act here with redoubled violence, hurrying on the flames with fearful rapidity to the back of Stone Buildings, commencing with Mr Pierce Grace's house, and ending with Messrs. McBride and Kerr's, and the entire range of wooden dwellings at the opposite side The next suites of buildings at both sides were soon enveloped, and the fire, now rendered all powerful by the immense quantities of oil and combustible materials of every description which it had consumed, and with which it had been fed, hastened on the work of destruction with inconceivable rapidity, laying waste completely every erection at both sides, stone and wood without distinction, as far as the break at Messrs. Douglas & Co's The Custom House next took fire, and lured the flames forward to Messrs Gill's premises, hence they extended rapidly along, consuming everything intermediate to the premises of Messrs Robinson, Brooking & Co These fine buildings were soon involved, and the ravages continued with unabated violence even to the premises of Messrs Parker and Gleeson, at the extreme end of Magotty Cove, after the consumption of which, it might with truth be said, the fire died out from the utterness of exhaustion, having left nothing to sustain it, and having laid the entire way for more than a mile in extent a barren waste, its two principal streets. The loss of life, if the extent of the havoc be remembered, is inconsiderable, we believe there were but three—one artilleryman and two civilians—who met death on this occasion. The public buildings consumed were, besides the Custom House above mentioned, the beautiful convent of the Presentation Nuns, and schoolroom opposite, St John's Church,

Not one of us who witnessed the terrors of that awful fire will ever forget the 9th of June 1846. The weather was fortunately warm, otherwise the misery of the poor families who were huddled together on the Barrens for the first night or two would have been still greater;

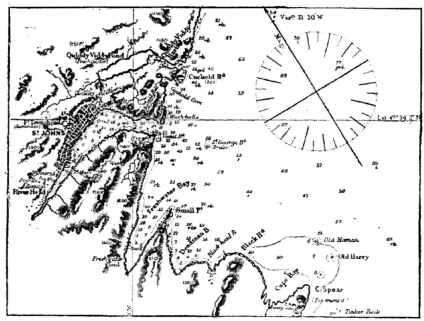

PLAN OF THE APPROACH TO ST. JOHN'S HARBOUR.

with military promptness, tents were provided for their shelter, and in the course of a very short time long lines of wooden sheds were erected, called "the camps." The leading men in St. John's showed great spirit

the Court House and jail, the theatre, the Commercial Buildings, the Bank of British North America, the Colonial Treasurer's Office, and Savings Bank. The public moneys fortunately were all saved and deposited in Government House. The Roman Catholic Chapel, the Orphan Asylum School, the Native Hall, and the Factory were immediately thrown open for the shelter of the many houseless and destitute of our fellow creatures, who had been in the short space of a few hours deprived of their homes and means of subsistence.

"We cannot speak in too high terms of praise of the conduct of His Excellency Sir John Harvey in these melancholy circumstances. He was to be seen during the day in the midst of the scene of horror, aiding the people by the suggestions of a superior judgment and experience, counselling against the commission of irretrievable errors, and evincing all that sympathy for the afflicted which is so strikingly characteristic of his humane and tender heart. To Lieut.-Col. Law and M. A. Robe and every officer of the garrison we feel an expression of public thankfulness is a just debt. Their actions were judiciously directed, and most energetically continued, and the troops under their command have ably sustained the high character they had achieved on many and similar occasions of public distress.

"The fire destroyed the premises of Messrs. Hounsell, Schenk & Hounsell, Stabb Row,

and alacrity in taking measures to relieve the distressed, and to re-construct the town The very next morning some of the citizens were at work excavating amongst the ruins of their dwellings, and preparing to erect temporary sheds, thousands were ruined, but everywhere there was a hopeful, determined spirit that St John's should rise again. Sir John and his advisers acted with great promptitude and good judgment, an admirable relief committee was appointed; property was carefully guarded by the military. On the very next day His Excellency adopted measures to meet the pressing emergency of the situation.

Pedley says —

"He issued a proclamation convening the local legislature to meet in six days. He laid an embargo for a limited period on the exportation of provisions. He addressed a circular letter to the Governor-general and the lieutenant-governors of all the British American colonies, and the British consuls at Boston and New York, making known the deplorable disaster and the immediate wants arising from it. He authorised the chartering of two vessels, one to Halifax and one to New York, for provisions. Lastly, he called a meeting, held on the 10th, at which he presided, of all the heads of the mercantile establishments, as well as of the principal inhabitants, the clergy, judges, and officers of the Government One of the resolutions passed at the public meeting deserves to be recorded, as evincing the strong brave heart of the citizens amidst the still smouldering embers of the fell ruin which had suddenly come upon them —

"'Resolved. That this meeting is aware that the well-established credit and stability of the trade of St. John's, coupled with the natural and inexhaustible resources of its fisheries, will speedily enable it to recover its usual current, but that in the meantime it is necessary that publicity should be given to the demand for provisions and building materials which at present exists in this market'

"Great sympathy was displayed, accompanied by a bounteous liberality, towards the inhabitants of St. John's suffering under such a fearful calamity, in the neighbouring colonies and in the United Kingdom. Halifax was the first to exhibit its practical charity At a meeting of the citizens held the day after the news arrived, a subscription was commenced which in a very short time reached £1,500 This munificent contribution was expended in provisions. which were forwarded by the steamer, and was in addition to £1,000 transmitted in specie by the Government of Nova Scotia. Prince Edward's Island also forwarded a large sum, as did also the towns of St John and Fredricton. The Government of Canada sent £2,000. and the citizens of Quebec subscribed even a larger sum for the same object The news arrived in England at the time when Mr Gladstone was holding the office of Colonial Secretary only until the appointment of his

and Holmwood William Grieve & Co, Wilson & Meynell, Robert Alsop & Co, Rennie Stuart, & Co, Wm Warren, Boyd & McDougall, P Rogerson & Son, J & W Stewart, C F. Bennett & Co, John Warren, Langley & Tessier, P. & W Carter, E Taylor, Shea & Murphy. Thomas Glen, John McWilliam, E & N Stabb, Pierce Grace, I & I Kent, R O'Dwyer & Co, Neil McDougall, Begg Kerr, & Co, Bowring Bros, R & A Rutherford M Stewart & Co. Robt Finlay, McBride & Kerr, Michel Nowlan, John Renouf, Richard Hovley,

Saml Mudge, Warren Bros, Baine Johnston & Co, Edward Smith, Wilson & Co, James Clift, Richd. Perchard, S G Archibald, J Fox & Co, R Prowse, R N Gott & Co, W & H Thomas & Co, J M Rendell & Co, Gilbert Clapp, J B Barnes & Co, Job Bros & Co, Hunters & Co, Jas Tobin & Co, L O'Brien & Co., James Douglas & Co., Parker & Gleeson, Edward Morris, Nicholas Gill, G F. Bown, Walter Dillon, J Cusack & Sons, Duncombe & Harvey, Robinson Brooking & Co, John Brockle-bank, John P. Mullowney, Richard Hillman"

successor: but he at once sent present relief to the extent of £5,000, and immediately afterwards the new secretary, Earl Grey, with the sanction of Parliament, added to that sum £25,000 Besides this large public grant, the Queen issued a letter to the Archbishops of Canterbury and York, authorising them to bring before the clergy and congregations under their charge the case of the sufferers in Newfoundland, in the manner that might seem best calculated to draw forth the liberality of the benevolent." [1]

The year of the fire was a most unfortunate one for the Colony. On the 19th of September a terrific gale destroyed an immense amount of property, both by land and sea, the unfinished Native Hall was blown down, St Thomas's Church was moved bodily, a large number of houses in St. John's, partly built, were injured; there was also an extraordinary high tide, the water came up to the floors of several houses on the south side of Water Street. [2]

There were addresses and most sincere and universal regret from all classes when Sir John Harvey left this Colony to assume the Government of Nova Scotia, in August 1846, he went there, as he went everywhere, to calm the troubled sea of politics His success in promoting peace and harmony among the able but excitable politicians of that province was the final achievement of his long and active life Lady Harvey, to whom he was tenderly attached, expired rather suddenly in 1851. Sir John never rallied from this blow, in March 1852 he also died, at Halifax. [3] His merits as an able diplomatist and politician were rightly appreciated in Nova Scotia, but he has received scant justice from our local politicians and historians. We have only to

[1] PEDLEY's *History of Newfoundland*

[2] In the June session of the House of Assembly (1846) Mr Glen proposed to spend £100 to increase the gas lamps in Water Street; clergymen, doctors, and out-harbour planters complained of the dangers and darkness of the streets. R J Parsons, E Hanrahan, R Carter, and Hon. W B. Row voted against it; Parsons vehemently denounced the expenditure.

[3] Major-General Sir John Harvey, K C B, entered the army in 1800; he served with great distinction in India and in Egypt. As Deputy Quartermaster General he went through the American war of 1812. On one occasion, when opposed to General Wingfield Scott, U.S.A., his opponent admired his gallantry so much that he gave orders to his soldiers not to fire at the handsome, dashing colonel After the war, Sir John was appointed Inspector-General of the Police in Ireland; even in this difficult position his became a universal favourite. In 1835 he was made Lieut -Governor of Prince Edward's Island, and two years later was promoted to the larger governorship of New Brunswick. His Excellency had to inaugurate responsible government in the province, and it need

not be said that he carried out the liberal policy of the English ministry in an eminently satisfactory manner. During his tenure of office, there was great excitement over the Maine Boundary question; Sir John and his old opponent General Scott, by their wise and pacific measures, kept peace between England and the United States. For his action in opposition to the Commander-in-Chief in Canada, Sir John was dismissed; after explanations, his valuable services were rewarded by a K C B. and promotion to the Governorship of Newfoundland.

In 1845 the Cunard steamer *Hibernia* struck near Cape Race, she got off all right, and the passengers came on to St. John's. One of them wrote to the *Fredericton Loyalist*, "St. John's Harbour is quite a business place, the harbour full of shipping, everybody actively employed, and apparently profitably so . Political feuds have vanished, religious differences are unknown, Protestants and Catholics are living in Christian charity and perfect harmony with each other, the society is excellent, and the people hospitable in the extreme, and this state of things, I am happy to say, is mainly attributed to the propitious administration of

contrast the violence and party animosity that existed under his predecessors, both excellent Governors, to rightly value the tact and the ability with which Sir John Harvey managed all parties. Both sides have always declared that, with his infinite grace and smooth speech, he humbugged them all ; perhaps he did, at any rate he was a skilful peace-maker, one of the first duties of a Governor.[1]

Sir John Harvey was succeeded in 1847 by Sir Gaspard Le Marchant, a distinguished soldier.[2] His Excellency will long be gratefully remembered in this Colony for the deep interest he took in promoting agriculture. He was a thoroughly practical man and not a diplomatist, like his august predecessor ; Sir John talked admirably about farming, Sir Gaspard acted. He introduced Ayrshire and Jersey cows, and in a few years completely transformed the breed of cattle throughout the Colony. He liked to see after everything personally ; when he heard that the mob were burning him in effigy, he went down to see if his

SIR G. LE MARCHANT.
By Bassano.

Sir John Harvey, their present Governor, and the former Governor of New Brunswick ; he is certainly the most kind-hearted, hospitable, excellent man ; he is doing a great deal of good here, and is respected and beloved by by all classes, I believe. . . ."

[1] Mr. Timothy Mitchell, afterwards the well-known Inspector of Police, had been in the police force, under Sir John Harvey, in Ireland and New Brunswick, and at His Excellency's suggestion he came on to St. John's. In the old days the Inspector did splendid work, both in the detection of crime and in the capture of criminals. I remember on one occasion when he was attempting to arrest a rioter in Catalina, the man caught up an old picket with a long rusty nail in it ; as he was going to make a blow at Mitchell the Inspector drew from his pocket the case of a long French pipe he had borrowed from me ; the man thought it was a revolver, and dropped his weapon at once. In the witness-box Mitchell showed as much ability as in the performance of his other duties. Judge Robinson had rather a sharp way of cross-examining police and magistrates ; he was asking the Inspector, rather peremptorily, about the confession made to him in an arson

case. " You searched the prisoner, sir, what did you find on him ?" " His insurance policy in one pocket, my Lord, and the Key of Heaven in the other," was the imperturbable reply.

[2] Sir John Gaspard Le Marchant, Knt. Bachel. (creat. 1838); G.C.M.G., 1860; K.C.B., 1865. Entered the army in 1821; became a colonel in 1851, and held local rank as a major-general till fully promoted to that rank in March 1858; retired from the command of the 85th foot in 1846 on proceeding to Newfoundland; was Governor and Commander-in-Chief of Newfoundland from February 1847 to June 1852; Lieut.-Governor of Nova Scotia from June 1852 to December 1857, when he was appointed Governor of Malta, and received local rank of lieut.-general there, 1859; was a brigadier-general in the service of Her Catholic Majesty; a knight of the 1st class and a knight commander of the orders of San Fernando and of Charles III. of Spain; received the honour of knighthood from the Queen, with permission to wear his foreign orders, which were conferred for services in Spain. He died in 1874.

image was properly got up, and if his bold aquiline nose had been successfully copied [1]

In December 1848 the first session of the new Legislature was opened under the old Constitution of 1832, with separate Council and Assembly. 1848 was a year of revolution in Europe, with the exception of Her Gracious Majesty the Queen's, every throne in Europe was tottering and tumbling. The wave of political excitement which Thackeray describes—

> ' When pursuing of their shindies,
> They broke the lovely windies,
> Upon the Shannon shore "—

reached our Island home. Responsible government was the war cry of our modest rebellion, and the only outbreak of violence, burning the Governor's image. The revolutionary fever has so far always attacked us in a mild form. Both the Whig Earl Grey and the Conservative Sir John Pakington refused point blank to grant the Colony local self-government. Earl Grey wrote —

"Until the wealth and population of the Colony shall have increased considerably beyond their present amount, the introduction of what is called Responsible Government will by no means prove to its advantage. . . . . . The institutions of Newfoundland have been of late in various ways modified and altered, and some time must unavoidably elapse before they can acquire that amount of fixity and adaptation to the colonial wants of society which seems an indispensable preliminary to the future extension of popular Government "

Sir John Pakington, in 1852, also took the same view, in a despatch of April 3, he says —

"Her Majesty's Government see no reason for differing from the conclusions at which their predecessors had arrived in the question of the establishment of Responsible Government, and which were conveyed to you by Lord Grey. . . I consider on the contrary that the wisdom and justice of these conclusions are confirmed by the accounts since received from Newfoundland "

---

[1] POSTAL COMMUNICATION, 1847

"James Hodge begs to acquaint the Public at large that he intends to run a four-sail boat between Kelligrews and Brigus and Port de Grave during the winter months, a steady and confidential man will leave St. John's every Wednesday morning, with the packages and letters for transmission, which will be forwarded to their destination as regularly as the weather will permit single letters 1s, double letters 2s, packages in proportion to their bulk and weight.

"Mr. Doyle begs to announce to the communities of St. John's, Harbour Grace, and Carbonear, that he has engaged a confidential packet man to travel around the Bay during the winter months and while the boat is necessarily laid up . .

In 1841 Messrs. W. Thomas and Jos. Noad recommended that there should be no postal communication outside of St John's and Conception Bay.

			$
The Postal Revenue in 1841 was	1,084
"	"	1851 ,,	4,329
"	"	1861 ,,	5,170
"	"	1871 ,,	10,000
"	"	1878 ,,	15,609
"	"	1892 ,,	44,000

The agitation still went on, notwithstanding Earl Grey and the sturdy Sir John Pakington. Responsible government had been conceded to every one of the North American Colonies; the Home Government ought to have had wisdom enough to see that it was inevitable, and conceded it gracefully, instead of having it wrung from them. Each successive House of Assembly had pronounced in favour of executive responsibility; even the Amalgamated House, in which two-fifths of the members were nominees of the Crown, had voted in favour of the same principle.

This political agitation, begun at the May meeting in 1846, continued up to the introduction of our present form of government in 1855. The actors in the final scenes of our great constitutional drama, however, were new men. Mr. John Kent, in 1849, became Collector of the Customs in place of Mr. Spearman (who retired with a pension). Dr. Fleming, worn out with incessant toil and labour in his diocese, in 1848 obtained as coadjutor Dr. Mullock, who arrived in St. John's on the 6th of May 1848. From this time forth the leaders of the Liberal and Catholic party were Mr. P. F. Little and the new Bishop. Both were men of great ability, liberal and enlightened in their views.[1] Dr. Mullock was a scholar, full of wit and eloquence; he did much to forward the interests of the Colony, and was one of the first to promote telegraphic communication, local steam, and practical agriculture.

P. F. LITTLE.
By Lafayette, Dublin.

Mr. P. F. Little, afterwards Assistant Judge of the Supreme Court, and brother of the present excellent judge, J. I. Little, came from Prince Edward's Island, where he was born in 1824; he began practice as a lawyer about 1845. He had a very up-hill fight, but his ability, his attention to business, with his shrewdness and knowledge of affairs, soon

---

[1] Bishop Mullock's good sayings, however, are quite eclipsed by the wit of his brother, familiarly known as Tom, organist of the Cathedral, the "Parish Piper" as he styled himself. On one occasion there was a discussion at the Bishop's table about the interior of the Colony; Dr. Mullock, in his impetuous way, said it was a wilderness, only fit for the bears. "That's what I was saying," said Tom, "it was *barely* known." On another occasion, Tom, for want of a better conveyance, sent down to Don Hipolito De Uriarte, the Spanish Consul, a piano he had purchased for him, on a hearse. The Don was very indignant; a crowd had collected before his door to witness this novel method of moving a piano. "What for, Mr. Mullock," said Uriarte, "you send down my piano on the funeral cart?" "Sure," said Tom, "I wanted to convince you that you had a *dead bargain*." Tom's peculiar drawl and brogue, and his rubicund countenance, gave a fine flavour to his jokes, which is lost in the telling.

brought him clients; from the first to the last he enjoyed the complete confidence of Dr. Mullock. He was elected to the Legislature in 1850, and almost at once became the real leader of the Catholic and Liberal Party in the House.[1] In the agitation for responsible government Mr. P. F. Little was the leader, the organiser, and by far the most powerful man in the movement; he was not so polished a speaker as Mr. Robinson, or as eloquent and ornate as Mr. Kent, but in astuteness, in assiduity, in political sagacity, in the management of his party, and in constitutional knowledge, he was a match for all his opponents.

Sir Gaspard was appointed Governor of Nova Scotia, and left the Colony on July 28, 1852. His last speech at the close of the House of Assembly was neither courteous nor dignified, and was accordingly assailed by a portion of the local press in very scurrilous terms; his enemies specially sneered at his devotion to agriculture; the introduction of cocks and hens, cows, horses, and sheep were the subjects of infinite ridicule. Administrations come and go, politics pass away, but an improved breed of cattle is a permanent benefit to the country that possesses it; the fight between the Governor and his political enemies has long been forgotten, but many an old farmer in the country even to-day will point out with pride a beautiful cow as " of ould Sir Gaspar's breed." The rough old soldier was a very poor politician, but he was loyal, honest, and sincere; he did far more practical work in encouraging the cultivation of land, and especially the breeding of cattle, than any former Governor.

His Excellency Ker Baillie Hamilton,[2] who assumed the reins of the government in December 1852, was in marked contrast to his predecessor. Sir Gaspard went about everywhere, and knew every farmer around St. John's; Mr. Hamilton was an exceedingly shy, taciturn man; he wrote well, and was very pious and good, but he never

---

[1] LEGISLATIVE COUNCIL.

Hon. Col. Law, President.
,, E. M. Archibald, Attorney-General.
,, Jas. Crowdy, Colonial Secretary.
,, W. B. Row.
,, Jo. Noad, Surveyor-General.
,, C. F. Bennett.
,, J. J. Grieve.
,, L. O'Brien.

HOUSE OF ASSEMBLY.
Speaker, Hon. J. Kent.
St. John's: John Kent, Little, Parsons.
Placentia: G. Hogsett, A. Shea.
Burin: C. Benning.
Fogo: G. H. Emerson.
Ferryland: P. Winsor.
Conception Bay: Hayward, Nugent, Talbot, and Hanrahan.

Fortune Bay: H. W. Hoyles.
Bonavista: J. H. Warren.
Trinity: S. March.

[2] Ker Baillie Hamilton, C.B., was educated for the Army at the Royal Military Academy at Woolwich; entered the Indian military service in 1822; appointed a writer in the civil service of the Mauritius in 1826, and assistant private secretary to Governor Sir Lowry Cole there; appointed clerk of the council, at the Cape of Good Hope, in 1829; afterwards acted there as colonial secretary; appointed Lieut.-Governor of Grenada in 1846; administrator of the Government of Barbados and the Windward Islands in 1851; Governor of Newfoundland in 1852; Governor-in-Chief of Antigua and the Leeward Islands in 1855 to January 1863.

tried to please the public; he could not speak, and in the crisis and agitation for responsible government he was about as unfit a man as the British Government could possibly have selected to fill a difficult position. Lord Dufferin humorously compared himself to the humble individual in a paper cap who goes about with a long-spouted tin can oiling the machinery, and his Lordship's marvellous success as an administrator is largely due to his tact and good judgment, and his

GOVERNOR BAILLIE HAMILTON.
From an old photograph.

faculty as a political lubricator. Poor Ker Baillie Hamilton, excellent, good, honest man, had not this gift; he never tried to conciliate parties or to make the government work smoothly; as a Governor he was a complete failure: at the same time nothing can palliate the indecent manner in which the majority of the House of Assembly assailed him.

It is not necessary to go over all the long discussion about responsible government. When the British Cabinet, represented by the Duke of Newcastle, finally agreed to grant the Colony Home Rule, they attached two main conditions—the old office holders should receive fair treatment, and there should be a proper Representation Bill. The Secretary of State for the Colonies wrote to Governor Hamilton that—

"Her Majesty's Government had come to the conclusion that they ought not to withhold from Newfoundland those institutions, and that civil administration, which, under the popular name of Responsible Government, had been adopted in all Her Majesty's neighbouring possessions in North America, and they were prepared to concede the immediate application of the system as soon as certain preliminary conditions had been acceded to on the part of the Legislature."

On the question of the pension to the retiring officers, there was a most contemptible wrangle; a Committee of the House, consisting of A. Shea, Little, Benning, Hogsett, and Hanrahan, decided to give E. M. Archibald, Attorney-General, after twenty years' good service as a public officer, and now compulsorily retired, £140 per annum. Governor Hamilton very properly refused to accede to such an unfair allowance, and the Home Government approved of his conduct. Finally, the pensions were fixed as follows :—J. Crowdy, Colonial Secretary, £400; Archibald, Attorney-General, £350; Noad, Surveyor-General, £285; H. A. Emerson, Solicitor-General, £90 Over the Representation question both sides fought bitterly; Mr. Little's party wanted to "gerrymander" the districts to secure his party majority, whilst the Conservative with equal pertinacity opposed him. In such a difficulty a wise and diplomatic Governor would have stood between the opponents and have endeavoured to work out a fair compromise; during the three years' struggle he certainly should have had a census taken. Responsible government was brought in in 1855, and the only return of population that both sides had to work on was the imperfect census of 1845; it was owing to the Council, ruled by the Governor's friends, that a census Bill passed by the Assembly had been thrown out. We know now that if a census had been taken in 1853 or 1854 it would have shown a very different basis from the one on which representation was ultimately carried. The most disagreeable feature in this interminable discussion was the desire for sectarian ascendency evinced by both sides. Subsequent history shows that the Conservative party were in the main right in their contention that Bonavista and Twillingate with one member each were under-represented, whilst less important and less populous districts, like Placentia and Ferryland, had each two members. It is clear, however, that the Protestant Party were unwise in stolidly resisting any change. They should have known that responsible government was sure to come sooner or later, and have stood out firmly for a census before the Representation Bill was agreed to, and endeavoured to make the best of the coming event. Too much importance was given to the personal

HON. T. R. ROW.
By Cox and Durrant.

interests of the office holders, and too little regard to the future good government of the Colony. There should have been a fairer distribution of offices. No one can doubt now that the Roman Catholics had been unfairly treated; under the new Government that came into office in 1855 [1] there was a complete change. After a lapse of forty years we can now view the whole matter dispassionately, and it must be admitted that Mr. Little played his hand in the political game artfully, and the Conservatives' stolid opposition to any change in the

[1] LEGISLATIVE COUNCIL.

Hon. L. O'Brien, President.
  ,, Jas. Tobin.
  ,, John Roehfort, M.D.
  ,, Geo. H. Emerson, Solicitor-General.
  ,, John Munn.
  ,, S. Carson, M.D.
  ,, T. R. Row.
  ,, J. J. Rogerson.
  ,, T. H. Ridley.
  ,, Jas. Furlong.
  ,, P. Duggan.

HOUSE OF ASSEMBLY ELECTED 7TH MAY 1855.

The first House of Assembly under responsible government consisted of the following members :—

St. John's West : Hon. P. F. Little, Attorney-General and Premier ; Hon. A. Shea, Speaker; John Fox.

St. John's East : Hon. J. Kent, Colonial Secretary ; R. J. Parsons ; Peter Winsor.

constitution was a political blunder. We may give them credit for honesty of purpose, but all the same they committed a grave mistake.

It is due to Governor Hamilton's memory to record that when important questions of telegraphic and steam communication arose during his administration he showed both liberal and enlightened views; he also wrote very able despatches on the French fishery question. On the subject of the telegraph, I have carefully consulted the records of the time, and, as far as possible, endeavoured to state the history of its introduction into the Colony correctly in Chapter XXI.

In 1855 the new administration under responsible government was appointed, with the Hons. P. F. Little, Premier and Attorney-General;

R. PROWSE.

J. Kent, Colonial Secretary; T. Glen, Receiver-General; E. Hanrahan, Surveyor-General; G. H. Emerson, Solicitor-General; and L. O'Brien, President of the Legislative Council. It was purely and entirely a Liberal administration, all the members of the Government representing Roman Catholic constituencies; Mr. Emerson did not count, as he had been defeated in Twillingate, and now sat in the Council. The three principal officers, Little, Kent, and Glen, were able men; in the words of Mr. Hanrahan, as an administration " *it was as near perfection as possible.*" They had the rare good luck of prosperous years, " the sunshine of prosperity," in the words of Mr. Kent, beamed on the Government. 1855, 1856, and 1857 were years of plenty; the new Cabinet, under the firm hand of the Premier, was able, liberal, and progressive.

In 1854, the cholera was brought into St. John's by infection from a sailor's clothes: it spread destruction with frightful rapidity; all the efforts

Carbonear : Hon. E. Hanrahan, Surveyor-General, and Chairman of the Board of Works.
Holyrood : Talbot and Byrne.
Port de Grave : R. Brown.
Ferryland : Hon. T. Glen, Receiver-General; E. D. Shea.
Burin : Benning and Morris.
Bonavista : R. Carter, Warren, and Walbank.
Fogo and Twillingate : Ellis and Knight.
Fortune Bay : H. W. Hoyles.
Burgeo and La Poile : R. Prowse.
Placentia : Hogsett, Delaney, and Kelly
Trinity : F. Carter, March, and Winter.
Bay de Verds : Bemister.

The first administration under responsible government was composed of able and enlightened politicians; the Governor guided their footsteps, and was their firm ally and supporter. The Attorney-General, P. F. Little, very wisely associated himself with members from the opposite side ; Messrs. Walter Grieve, Munn, Ridley, Rogerson, G. H. Emerson, and Hayward (afterwards Judge Hayward), were amongst his Protestant supporters. Mr. Little was an able leader, and always kept his party well in hand; from first to last he enjoyed the unbounded confidence of Bishop Mullock. Mr. Kent made an excellent Colonial Secretary, and T. Glen was a heaven-born Receiver-General, one of the best party men that ever sat in a cabinet. At a political meeting an out-harbour member, who was under obligations to the Government, said to Glen, in a patronizing tone : " I believe you are right, Mr. Receiver-General; I will support you." " Confound you," said Glen, " I don't want your support when I am right; it is when I am wrong you must back me up."

of medical skill, the humane exertion of the clergy and of self-devoted women, were powerless to stay the plague; however, it was practically confined to the lowest and dirtiest parts of the city. Whilst the cholera lasted, the number of deaths was appalling. Bishops Mullock and Feild and Archdeacon Bridge were conspicuous during the epidemic by their heroic, self-sacrificing labours for all—Catholics and Protestants alike were personally attended by these devoted servants of God. Bishop Feild lived to a good age, but Archdeacon Bridge, the idol of his congregation, almost equally adored by rich and poor of all creeds, fell a victim to duty soon after. No one who has ever seen his beautiful countenance, or heard his magnificent tones in the sublime service for the dead, will ever forget Thomas Finch Hobday Bridge, the most beloved Anglican minister that ever set foot on our soil; his place has never been filled; generous, warm-hearted, and deeply religious, Nature had endowed him with every gift and grace, even the divine gift of humour; religion had purged away all the earthly dross of selfishness and ambition from a truly noble character, and made him one of the most lovable of men. After escaping the deadly peril of the cholera, he died from fever contracted whilst attending one of the very poorest of his congregation. Readers of to-day may think this language exaggerated, but the generation that heard that earnest voice will bear witness to the deep affectionate feelings of all St. John's for the Archdeacon.

ARCHDEACON BRIDGE.

From a miniature in the possession of his son, Admiral Bridge.

Direct steam to England by the Galway line, the completion of the telegraph, and finally, in 1858, the laying of the first Atlantic cable, are the striking events of this period. In 1858 Judges Des Barres and Simms were pensioned, and Hons. P. F. Little and B. Robinson became the assistant judges of the Supreme Court.

Sir Charles Darling, who inaugurated responsible government in 1855, remained only until 1857.[1] He was a remarkably able man, of

---

[1] Sir Charles Henry Darling, K.C.B. (created 1862), entered the Army as ensign on the 7th December 1826, by recommendation from the Royal Military College, Sandhurst, after public examination; became, in 1827, assistant private secretary to the late General Sir Ralph Darling, then Governor of New South Wales and Major General com-

vast experience; he taught his new ministry how to work the new constitution, and ruled them like a pack of schoolboys. The Conservative party came into collision with him, first as regards his authority to inaugurate the new constitution, and again when they insisted on naming members of their own party for the new legislative council; on both these questions Sir Charles was clearly and constitutionally right.

VIEW OF VIRGINIA WATER, ST. JOHN'S.

It will be remembered that Louis Napoleon was just about this time, after the Crimean War, our "good ally," and the English Government were most anxious to please the French, and for that purpose the interests of this Colony were as usual to be sacrificed. There can be

manding the Forces in that colony and Van Dieman's Land; and was also appointed military secretary to that officer in 1830. In 1833, while a student in the senior department of the Royal Military College, was appointed secretary to the late Lieutenant-General Sir Lionel Smith, upon that officer's nomination to be Governor and Commander-in-Chief of Barbados and the Windward Islands, and was employed in that capacity until 1836; Sir Lionel Smith having been in that year nominated to the government of Jamaica, Mr. Darling was appointed Governor's secretary for that colony, and retained the appointment until the termination of Sir Lionel Smith's Government in 1839; in that year obtained an unattached company, and retired from the army in 1841; in 1843 appointed by the Earl of Elgin, then Governor of Jamaica, Agent-General of Immigration for the colony, and held also the office of Adju-

tant-General of Militia, was a member of the assembly and of several executive boards; was again appointed Governor's secretary during the ad-interim administration of the government of Jamaica by Major-General Sackville H. Berkeley, and continued to hold that office during the earlier period of the government of the Right Hon. Sir Charles Grey in 1846-47; in 1847 was appointed Lieutenant-Governor of the island of St. Lucia; in 1851 appointed Lieutenant-Governor of the Cape of Good Hope, an office specially created for the conduct at Cape Town of the civil government while Sir George Cathcart, the Governor and Commander-in-Chief, might be engaged in his military and civil duties on the frontier. After the departure of Sir George Cathcart, administered the government of the Cape from May 1854 to December 1854, during which period the parliamentary constitution of the settlement was

no doubt that Governor Darling, eager to please the Home Government, lent himself to this policy, his famous No. 66 Despatch was a strong argument, ably put no doubt, but entirely in the interests of the French, and opposed to the rights and claims of the Colony. There was much indignation in St John's when it was published with the other papers concerning the great Convention with the French of 1857

In order to comprehend the wild outburst of popular indignation which arose in 1857, it is necessary to go back for some time, and also to understand the character of the previous negotiations which had been going on between the representatives of the two Governments for several years, all these various discussions and draft settlements have one unvarying characteristic the French gain all the advantages, and the Colony gets nothing in return. The principal English negotiator, Sir Anthony Perrier, appears to have been either a French tool or thoroughly incapable official. All the fine diplomacy of France was directed to three principal points first, to secure an unlimited supply of bait; second, to get the right to arrest and remove Colonial fishermen and their vessels, third, to get a secure territory and to extend their rights on the treaty shore It is a fortunate thing for us that the French were so over-reaching and so covetous of territory that even Perrier could not concede all their demands, and that the final Draft Convention of 1857 was an outrageous abandonment of our fishery rights Labouchere and Perrier were aghast when they heard of the excitement these unfair propositions created in the Colony, the Newfoundlanders held indignation meetings as hot and fiery as the Tea riots of Boston, not only was Newfoundland aroused, all British North America rose with her.

The Earl of Derby, the Secretary of State for the Colonies, in a despatch in 1884 to Sir John Glover, summarized the negotiations resulting in the Convention of 1857 as follows.—

"In the year 1844 the French Government proposed negotiations to be held in London, and previous to opening them it was determined to appoint a British and French Commissioner in Newfoundland to report upon the question

"Captain Fabvre, commander on the French naval station, and Mr Thomas, President of the Chamber of Commerce at Newfoundland, were, in consequence, appointed by their respective Governments.

inaugurated and established, was nominated to the government-in-chief of Antigua and the Leeward Islands, previously to his sole administration of the government of the Cape, but never assumed the duties of that Government, having shortly after his arrival in England been required to proceed to Newfoundland as Administrator of the government of that colony, of which he was subsequently appointed Governor and Commander-in-chief in February 1857 was appointed Captain

General and Governor-in-Chief of Jamaica, an office which embraces the general superintendence of the affairs of British Honduras and the Turks' Islands, and at that time included also the government-in-chief of the Bay Islands, received the Order of the Bath (K C B) 1862, for his "long and effective public services" Appointed Governor of Victoria, 1863, recalled, March 1866, died in 1870

"On the 30th July 1844, Mr. Thomas made his report to the Governor. In this report he suggested with regard to the French claim of 'exclusive rights,' that the respective fishermen of both nations should be kept separate and distinct in their fishing places He also suggested the extension of the French fishery limits to Belle Isle North, and made suggestions with regard to the sale of bait to French fishermen

"This report resulted in negotiations being held in Paris in the month of March 1846

"The British Commissioner, Sir A Perrier, was authorised to offer, in exchange for the French cession of all rights between Cape Ray and Bonne Bay, the following concessions —

"Admission of *exclusive* right of fishery from Bonne Bay to Cape St. John, going round by the north,

"Exclusive right of French fishery, drying, and curing at Belle Isle North,

"Permission for English fishermen to sell bait at St. Pierre

"At preliminary conferences held in Newfoundland, these measures had nearly been agreed to by Mr Thomas and Captain Fabvre, but Captain Fabvre was desirous of retaining for France, in addition to the exclusive rights above mentioned, her rights of fishing, curing fish, &c. at Cod Roy, Red Island, Port-a-Port, and Lark Harbour, and to acquire for the French a 'concurrent' right of fishery on the coast of Labrador.

"The instructions, however, to the French Commissioner did not admit of his negotiating on the above-mentioned principles, and as no new propositions were brought forward by the French Government up to the month of May 1847, the negotiations fell through

"On the application of the French Government in 1854 negotiations were renewed, Sir A Perrier being again directed to proceed to Paris to act as British Commissioner, M de Bon being appointed on the part of France.

"The British Commissioner was instructed to invite proposals from the French Commissioner such as might form a starting point in the negotiations

"M. de Bon accordingly proposed, on the part of France, to admit the right of British subjects to inhabit the Bay St George, or, in other terms to give up the exclusive right of fishery in that bay, to which they considered themselves entitled by the Treaty of 1783 In return for this concession he demanded—

"1 The right to fish for bait (herring and caplin) on the south coast of Newfoundland, without restriction

"2. The right to fish during two months of the year (without curing or drying on shore) on that part of the coast of Labrador situated between the Isles of Vertes and the Isles St. Modeste, both included ; and

"3 The right of fishery at Belle Isle North, in the Straits, which the French Commissioner asserted was enjoyed by the French up to 1841, without any demur on the part of Great Britain

"The concessions demanded by the French negotiator were not considered admissible, and the British Commissioner, in order to overcome the difficulties arising out of the claim of Great Britain to a concurrent right of fishery, suggested that the question would be best settled if the rights of the fishermen of the two nations were kept separate and distinct In order to carry out this suggestion, he proposed that the French rights should be made exclusive as against British subjects from Cape St. John to some point on the western coast, such as Cape Verde (Green Point, to the north of Bonne Bay), the French, on the other hand, to renounce their right altogether on the remainder of the coast, which would be that part where the British had been in the habit of carrying on the herring fishery and other fisheries incidental to the requirements of a fixed population

"The French negotiator offered no objection to the plan of recognising the French 'exclusive right' on a diminished extent of coast, but he contended for the retention of a 'concurrent right' on that portion on the coast on which the exclusive claim might be renounced, and for other advantages as well, such as admission, concurrently with British fishermen, to the fisheries of Labrador and North Belle Isle, and to the 'bait fishery' on the southern coast, all of which, he maintained, were necessary, as an equivalent for admitting British subjects to a free 'concurrent right' on the lower portion of the western coast

"The British Commissioner was disposed to accept the demands of the French so far as to extend the French fishery to North Belle Isle, and also to remove all restrictions on the purchase of 'bait,' on condition that the French should entirely renounce their rights between Cape Verte and Cape Ray, and in June 1855, he forwarded to the Foreign Office the above suggestions in the form of a counter proposal to those which had been made by France.

"Mr. Labouchere, Her Majesty's Secretary of State for the Colonies, concurred in the adoption of the British negotiator's project of a 'compromise' as the basis of negotiation to be offered to the French Government It corresponded, he believed, with the views of the Colonial authorities, deprived neither nation of any advantage of real value, and there would only be a reciprocal abandonment of barren rights and useless or nominal restrictions, and he prepared a draft treaty which might be substituted for the whole of the existing engagements on the Newfoundland Fisheries question.

"The negotiations were continued in the year 1856 by Captain Pigeard, who arrived in London in the month of July of that year, and by Mr. Merivale, the Under Secretary of State for the Colonies The basis of these negotiations was founded upon the counter proposals made by Sir A Perrier, and also upon the draft of the treaty proposed by Mr Labouchere. The negotiations finally terminated by the signature of a Convention in London on the 17th January 1857.

"According to the stipulations of this Convention, an exclusive right of fishery and the use of the strand for fishery purposes was conceded to the French from Cape St John, on the east coast of Newfoundland, to the Quirpon Islands, and from the Quirpon Islands, on the north coast, to Cape Norman, on the west coast, in and upon the following five fishery harbours, namely, Port-au-Choix, Small Harbour, Port-a-Port, Red Island, and Cod Roy Island, to extend, as regarded these five harbours, to a radius of three marine miles in all directions from the centre of each such harbour On other parts of the west coast (the five harbours excepted) British subjects were to enjoy a 'concurrent' right of fishing with French subjects, but French subjects were to have the exclusive use of the strand for fishery purposes from Cape Norman to Rock' Point, in the Bay of Islands, north of the River Humber, in addition to the strand of the reserved harbours.

"A 'concurrent' right of fishing was also granted to French subjects on the coast of Labrador, from Blanc Sablon to Cape Charles, and of North Belle Isle."

The excitement in the Colony over the Convention of 1857 was most intense and wide spread, the British flag was hoisted half-mast, other excited citizens flew American flags, everywhere there was burning indignation over this proposal to sell out birthright for a mess of pottage. The proceedings of our Legislature in 1857 are a guide to us as to what our conduct should always be in dealing with the fisheries, "there none were for a party but all were for the State." Government and Opposition united to maintain our rights. Our Chief Justice.

Sir F. B. T. Carter, K.C.M.G. Sir A. Shea, Hons. E. D. Shea, P. F. Little, Mr. Prendergast, Mr. J. J. Rogerson, and Mr. Kelly, alone survive of those who took a leading part in that famous struggle. Sir Frederick (then Mr. Carter, M.H.A.) went with Hon. John Kent as a delegate to Canada, and won golden opinions for himself by his ability in this matter. Immediately the House closed, Hon. P. F. Little and H. W. Hoyles were sent as delegates to England; all worked unitedly and with a will to destroy the convention. H. W. Hoyles (leader of the Opposition), P. F. Little (the Attorney-General), J. Kent (Colonial Secretary), R. Prowse, W. H. Ellis (Opposition members), and

HON. E. D. SHEA.
By S. H. Parsons.

J. J. ROGERSON.
By S. H. Parsons.

R. J. PARSONS.
From an old photograph.

R. J. Parsons, were the committee appointed to draft resolutions and addresses on the subject. The resolutions adopted by the Newfoundland Legislature were worthy of the occasion. I will quote only the concluding paragraph :—

"We deem it our duty, most respectfully, to protest in the most solemn manner against any attempt to alienate any portion of our fisheries or our soil to any foreign power, without the consent of the local legislature. *As our fishery and territorial rights constitute the basis of our commerce and of our social and political existence, as they are our birthright and the legal inheritance of our children,* we cannot, under any circumstances, assent to the terms of the convention; we therefore earnestly entreat that the Imperial Government will take no steps to bring this Treaty into operation, but will permit the trifling privileges that remain to us to continue unimpaired."

The result was a great triumph for the Colony. Before Governor Darling left in May 1857, he had received and laid before the Legislature the celebrated despatch known as " The Labouchere letter " :—

"The proposals contained in the Convention having been now unequivocally refused by the Colony, they will of course fall to the ground; and you are authorised to give such assurance as you may think proper. That the consent of the community of Newfoundland is regarded by Her Majesty's Government as the essential preliminary to any modification of their territorial or maritime rights "— (H Labouchere.)

Mr. Darling had informed the House during the winter of his promotion to Jamaica The publication of His Excellency's own despatch (No. 66, July 23rd, 1856) created a very strong feeling against him, on a careful perusal of this document, I think the irritation it produced was rather extreme He states emphatically, in regard to the French proposals —

"Their proposition may be, indeed, justly described, when regarded in its national bearing, as one of which *the advantage is wholly on the French side* "

The objectionable paragraph in the paper is on the question of French exclusive rights

Governor Darling's letter is in marked contrast to his predecessor's communication of September 1853 (No 57)[1] Governor Hamilton's views are both more logical and more correct, they are founded on a more complete knowledge of the history of the fishery. The despised and insulted Ker Baillie Hamilton was really a far more sincere and loyal friend of the Colony, and a far abler defender of our fishery rights than Sir Charles Darling, the popular introducer of responsible government and the patron of the Liberal party We must give both of them credit for honesty of purpose, but it is clear that Hamilton had the advantage of superior information on the subject. This, I think, was largely due to his advisers, Messrs Archibald and Crowdy, as well as his mercantile friends

On the question of "fixed settlements," the correct definition of the term is undoubtedly given by Governor Hamilton. It is clear, that under the administration of our naval Governors, the fishery carried on by both French and English on the coast was a *ship* fishery without permanent stages, &c, under these arrangements each ship as she arrived selected a fishing place for her crew and made the necessary erections for carrying on their operations Owing to the French being driven off the coast during the wars between 1756 and 1818, English fishermen had monopolised all the north-east coast; but long before this, as far back as 1698, Newfoundland "planters" had extended themselves from Bonavista gradually as far north as Quirpon It was the permanent establishments of the English fishing ships which interfered with the free exercise of French rights, when the French fishermen came back in such overwhelming numbers after the last treaty of peace in 1815, the English ship fishermen had to be forced away, but the real permanent settlers were never interfered with, the French encouraged their presence as guardians and keepers of their fishing establishments,

1 These despatches unfortunately are found in the Journals of the House of

originally they never claimed a right to interfere with these small farmers and permanent settlers on the coast, whose occupations in the winter were furring and sealing, and it is to this direct encouragement that the present English settlements on the north-east and west coasts are largely due. The English fishery at this time was changing its character from a ship fishery into a shore fishery, and the men who had been using the west and north-east coasts now betook themselves to the more lucrative fishery at Labrador. The fight made against the French by one of these old ship fishermen is told in the narrative of the stubborn old West Countryman Tory.[1] Fixed settlements only referred to the permanent establishments of their rivals, the English ship fishermen. Governor Hamilton's advisers were well aware of this historical fact; Governor Darling seems to have entirely ignored it.

The treaties on this subject must be construed according to their real legal meaning, and the principles of International law, and also by the *expositio contemporanea* showing how they were interpreted and understood. Whatever was not given to France remains with the proprietor and Sovereign Power, England; we have therefore the right to clear and cultivate land, to work mines, to carry on a salmon fishery, and any other business that does not actually interfere with the French cod fishery. Our opponents may claim that either or any of these interferes with their limited fishery rights, but the injury must be proved, their claim for damages must be a reasonable claim, and the question must be decided in a reasonable and rational manner by the British Government, the only authority who can execute a treaty on English territory. For instance, on the west coast of Newfoundland there are several small settlements on rivers. These streams are barred at their mouths by sand banks, and are therefore entirely unsuited for a ship cod fishery; for a century and more Englishmen have cleared and cultivated land at these places, and latterly some lobster factories have been carried on in these localities; will any reasonable man contend that we cannot occupy these places? We have done so, and will continue to do so.

---

[1] The case of the firm of Richard & Mellam Tory, of Poole, carrying on a large business at Sop's Arm, White Bay, for twenty-four years (set forth very fully in a long memorial to Governor Elliott in 1786), represents very high-handed proceedings on the part of the French naval officers. First, two bateaux with fifty men attempted to take possession of Tory's premises, but they would not allow them to land; next day two French men-of-war came to Sop's Arm, and officers and men armed came ashore, drove the Torys from their premises, took away two-thirds of their dwelling house, dragged another English planter, Craze, on board the French sloop-of-war, and kept him prisoner for two hours; they also took possession of a salmon fishery up a brook which had been occupied and used by an Englishman, named Craze, for thirty years, made him leave the brook and take up his nets, &c. The French let the Newfoundland planter Craze remain in possession of his dwelling-house and premises. The great antagonism of the French at the time was against their rivals the English ship fishermen, the fixed settlements referred to were their rooms, not the humble establishments of the resident fishermen, which the French rarely disturbed.

It may be asked, is there no fair solution and settlement possible of this venerable international difficulty? The French, as business men, are the most reasonable, clear-headed people in the world. If this question could be once approached in a fair and reasonable spirit, it might be amicably settled. At the present time the French fishery is a ship fishery, carried on principally on the banks; their sedentary or shore fishery is relatively insignificant;[1] as a French friend of mine explained, it is "an affair of a dozen old fishing brigs." The first requisite for a successful bank fishery is a certain supply, at reasonable prices, of the three varieties of fresh bait—herring, caplin, and squid. Our

HON. A. G. CUZON-HOWE.

[1] "LIST OF FRENCH LOBSTER FACTORIES AND COD FISHING ROOMS ON THE TREATY COAST OF NEWFOUNDLAND DURING THE SEASON OF 1893.

LOBSTER FACTORIES.

Where situated.	Number of Men approximately.	Manager.	Where from.	Remarks.
Brig Bay	—	Belin	——	Not worked since 1892.
Bartlett's Harbour	32	Bandgren	France.	
St. John's Island	30*	Marie	France.	
Port au Choix	12*	Vilala	France.	
Port au Choix	17*	Belin	France.	
Black Duck Brook	15	Tajan	St. Pierre.	
Les Vaches	24	Farvacque	St. Pierre.	
Red Island	(All lobsters canned at Les Vaches.)			

COD FISHING ROOMS.

Red Island	60	Poirier	St. Pierre.
Tweed Island	28	Hacala	St. Pierre.
Port au Choix	80*	Belin	France.
Savage Islands	35	Belin	France.
Port au Choix	80*	Vilala	France.
Port au Choix	34	Budeau	France.
Berbice Cove	34	Budeau	France.
St. John Island	70*	Marie	France.
Fishot Islands	46	Foliard	France.
St. Juliens	68	Eyon	France.
Rouge	35	Dollo	France.
Rouge	35	Perdon	France.

* The numbers marked * vary according to the fishing, as their services are most required for either cod or lobsters."

Commodore the Hon. A. G. Curzon Howe, the most efficient officer ever sent on this service gives me the table of French fishermen and lobster factories for the following years. The numbers have been increased by bounties of 50 francs per head from the Municipal Council of St. Pierre, by squatters, and by deserters from the French service.

	1892.	1893.	1894.	1895.
Men	678	735	933	983
Lobster factories working	8	8	9	11

Gallic neighbours know well that Fortune Bay, in close proximity to St Pierre, furnishes the best possible supply of bait in the world, it is abundant, easily accessible, and reasonable in price. Without a certainty of this supply at a moderate rate the bank fishery is unremunerative, every French fisherman thoroughly understands and appreciates this great fact.[1] This supply is entirely in our hands, we can at any moment paralyse the movements of the whole French fishing fleet by stopping their supplies of bait. We did so in 1888. Their full complement for their first baiting on herring amounts to fifty-four thousand barrels; by the 4th May in that year the French had only obtained four thousand and forty barrels, their spring fishery was in consequence a complete and disastrous failure. The effect of the Bait Act, which began in 1888, is clearly shown by the tables given below[2]. That year was a favourable one in the bank fishery, as both the English and American fishermen made good voyages in 1888.

There can be no possible doubt about the effect of the Bait Act on the French fishery; besides the convincing proof of the returns, we have the following extract from a letter published at Paris, in the *Petit Journal*, dated St Pierre and Miquelon, July 15th, 1889 :—

" Our Colony is very severely tried this year, the cod fishing, which constitutes its principal—we might say its only—industry, has, up to this date, given deplorable results. During the first trip, seven-eighths of the fishermen have barely paid for their wine, all have returned from this trip with an average of from four to eight thousand fish, sixty-five to one hundred and thirty quintals for

---

[1] The value of our bait is shown by the following —

" According to the report of Captain Loch, of H M S *Alarm*, in 1848 there were 360 French Banking vessels, of from 150 to 300 tons each, carrying from 16,000 to 17,000 Frenchmen, which vessels caught annually 1,200,000 quintals of fish on the Banks. He also states that Monsieur Delucluse, the French Governor of St Pierre's, had the honesty to tell him, it was the supply of bait obtained from the Newfoundland fishermen that alone enabled them to carry on the Bank fishery. Captain Loch also remarks :—' It is obvious that, by withholding from the French the supply of bait from our shores, their catch on the Banks would sensibly diminish, and their trade could not increase beyond the limits controlled by the comparatively very scanty supply of bait afforded by their own coasts and islands.' All naval officers who have been on the Western station, as well as all disinterested persons who are acquainted with that coast, unite in stating that it is only by means of the bait supplied to them by British subjects, that the French are enabled to carry on the Bank fishery. Is it not, then, a source of

wonder, that our Legislators are so blind to the interests of the country as to permit this evil to continue ? Is it not surprising they should be so supine as to neglect their great and important duty of passing such laws, and adopting such measures, as will effectually check and prevent our foreign rivals from obtaining their supplies of bait from our shores ? "—(WARREN'S *Lecture*, p 14)

[2] EXPORTS OF FRENCH FISH, FROM OFFICIAL RETURNS.

	Total catch calculated in dry qtls	Bounty paid Francs
1878	.201,982	
1879	233,923	
1880	...254,939	
1881	236,250	
1882	.255,671	.2,056,619
1883	304,580	2,528,443
1884	404,601	3,342,114
1885	497,284	.3,849,221
1886	579,390	5,109,680
1887	453,658	4,673,240
1888	338,126	
1889	300,000	

each craft, which represents nearly nothing. The whole of this fish has been sent to Bordeaux, and we have nothing left, and the future prospects look almost like a complete failure, consequently consumers will have to pay very dearly for the fish which they have hitherto been able to buy at a low price. *The schooners from St Pierre are obliged to go to the east coast on the French shore of Newfoundland in search of bait, which means a month's fishing lost*"

And from the French journal, *Le Progrès*, of June 2nd, we get the following incontrovertible testimony —

" This bait is made of small fish, which is only to be found in any quantities in the warmer waters of the south coast of the island, and is the necessary bait for cod-fishing, and which, until 1887, the French could buy, according to their want, at St Pierre, Miquelon *The law forbidding its sale was thus a great blow for them*, as they were reduced to bring from France a salted bait less liked by cod, or else to find for themselves, on the French Shore a fresh bait which would always be costly, and the supply of which would be irregular. *Thus the Bait Bill entailed both loss of time and money to the French, and they found their fishing much less productive than before* "

The French are a very shrewd people, in each and all the various commissions to frame a settlement, one of their principal demands was a free supply of bait from our waters It is clear then that we have something exceedingly valuable to give the French ; what should we ask in return for this immense boon of free bait ? I think, if the French would be reasonable, we could settle the whole question something after this manner, or at least have a *modus vivendi* : —

1. Let the French have exclusive possession for the fishing season within the three-mile limit around each harbour which they actually occupied with their fishing ships and crews last season, one or two guardians to be allowed in each harbour to protect their property ;

2 Concurrent rights of fishing over the whole north-east coast, and on the west coast as far south as Cow Head ;

3. An absolute right to purchase, paying port charges and light dues, a full supply of bait at anchor in any port of entry in Newfoundland during the fishing season, subject only to the same regulations as our local fishermen

In return for these valuable privileges, what should we ask ? I think we might demand —

1. That the French give up their impracticable and absurd claims, and give us a free and uninterrupted right of fishing on all the north-east and west coasts of the treaty shore, except where

the French are allowed exclusive rights ; and should also give us—

2. An English consul at St. Pierre ;

3. And an undertaking to prevent the export of intoxicating liquors in their fishing vessels except for ship's use

This simple arrangement would solve a great many of the present difficulties It would not wound French pride, they would have the inestimable advantage of obtaining at all times a sure and certain supply of bait fresh from the nets, it would prevent the present wanton destruction of the bait fishes, and put an end to smuggling The plan could be easily carried out. Some Newfoundlanders might object to it, and no doubt the St. Pierre shopkeepers would strongly oppose any arrangement which would put an end to their lucrative trade of smuggling. This suggestion is entirely my own; it is a good working arrangement, and should be acceptable to all but the extremists on both sides. Under no circumstances should bait be allowed to be exported to St. Pierre. Recent experience has taught the bait dealers that the indiscriminate sale of bait to the French is suicidal folly even for them. Every sensible man in Fortune Bay will approve of my proposal.

CHAPTER XVI.

REIGN OF VICTORIA.

1857–1895.

1858.—First Atlantic cable landed in Trinity Bay, but soon ceased to act.

1860.—Prince of Wales visited the Island. Formation of the Volunteer Corps.

1861.—H. W. Hoyles became Premier; political riots in St. John's, Harbour Grace, and Harbour Main.

1862.—Great distress owing to bad fisheries. Steamers used in the seal fishery.

1863.—Hon. L. O'Brien, Administrator. Revenue collected at Labrador.

1864.—Sir A. Musgrave, Governor. Confederation of the Dominion of Canada. Copper mining commenced at Tilt Cove. The Currency Act confirmed.

1865.—Present Geological Survey commenced. F. B. T. Carter became Premier, and Sir H. W. Hoyles, Chief Justice.

1866.—Second Atlantic Cable successfully landed at Heart's Content.

1867.—Fishery very successful. The British North America Act for the Confederation of the Provinces is passed. Dominion of Canada proclaimed.

1868.—Proclamation issued by the Carter Administration suppressing able-bodied poor relief.

1869.—Sir Stephen Hill appointed Governor. General Elections; Confederation candidates defeated. Census taken. Dr. Mullock died.

1870.—Hon. C. F. Bennett became Premier.

1871.—Garrison withdrawn from Newfoundland. Treaty of Washington.

1873.—Direct Steam to England by Allan Line commenced. General Election; Bennett Government defeated.

1874.—The largest cod-fishery ever known in Newfoundland. Sir F. B. T. Carter became Premier. The Royal Commission; Sir B. Robinson, J. Goodfellow and J. Fox, Esquires.

1875.—The first Government Railway Survey under direction of Sandford Fleming, Civil Engineer.

1876.—Sir J. H. Glover, G.C.M.G., Governor. Halifax Fishery Commission met; $5,500,000 awarded as compensation to be paid by the United States to the British Provinces; Newfoundland's share, one million; Sir W. V. Whiteway, Commissioner for Newfoundland. Bishop Feild died, in Bermuda.

1877.—Sir F. B. T. Carter appointed Acting Assistant Judge. Commander W. Howorth, R.N., appointed first Stipendiary Magistrate, West Coast, by Imperial and Colonial Governments; duties first collected there.

1878.—Sir W. V. Whiteway became Premier.

1880.—Sir F. B. T. Carter appointed Chief Justice; Colonial Government allowed to make grants of land on the West Coast or "French Shore" so-called. Sir F. B. T. Carter, K.C.M.G., Administrator. First Railway Bill passed.

H H

1881.—Serious disturbance on the railway line (Battle of Fox Trap). Sir Henry Fitz-Hardinge Maxse, Governor. First Railway under construction in Newfoundland; St John's to Harbour Grace.

1882.—An Act passed for the construction of the Great American and European Short Line Railway. Charter granted for the construction of a Graving Dock. Sir W. V. Whiteway became Premier.

1883.—St Stephen's Day Harbour Grace riots. Sir F. B. T. Carter, Administrator. Sir H. Maxse died in St John's. Sir John H Glover, G C M G, appointed Governor. Dry Dock at Riverhead, St. John's, opened. H M S *Tenedos* docked. Fishery Exhibition held in London; Sir A Shea, K C.M G, Commissioner for the Colony. Railway to Harbour Grace opened for passengers. Hon E. Morris, Administrator in absence of Sir F B T Carter, K C M G.

1885.—Ford-Pennell Convention on French fishery claims. Sir F. B. T. Carter, Administrator. Sir Robert Thorburn, Premier. General Election.

1886.—Report of Joint Committee on Fishery question. Placentia Railway commenced. Sir F. B T Carter, Administrator. Sir G W Des Vœux appointed Governor.

1887.—The Bait Act became Law. Sir H. A Blake, Governor. Ballot Act passed. Queen's Jubilee; Service in English Cathedral attended by all denominations of Protestants. Sir A. Shea, K.C M.G, appointed Governor of the Bahamas. Colonial Conference held in London; Colony represented by Sir R. Thorburn, Premier, and Sir A. Shea.

1888.—Second Washington Treaty negotiated; Hon. J S Winter represented the Colony. *Modus vivendi* established for two years. Bait Act put in operation in March. Placentia Railway opened for traffic. Act to provide Municipal Council for St. John's passed. Sir T N O'Brien appointed Governor. Sir F. B. T Carter Administrator to January 1889.

1889.—General Election; Thorburn Government defeated by an immense majority. Sir W V. Whiteway, Premier.

1890.—Act authorising new Railway Line North. Agitation concerning the *modus vivendi* with the French about Lobster Factories West Coast. Reciprocity Treaty with United States by Hon. R Bond, Colonial Secretary; prevented being carried into effect by Canada. Delegation to England on difficulties with the French.

1891.—Municipal Council Act amended. Delegation to England on difficulties with French. International arbitration on Lobster question to be held at Brussels. Hall's Bay Railway completed to Trinity and Bonavista Bays. Celebrated case of Baird v Walker, arising out of *modus vivendi*, determined by Supreme Court in favour of plaintiff; confirmed by the Privy Council. Newfoundland Bill in the House of Commons.

1892.—Death of the Duke of Clarence, January 14th. Terrible calamity and loss of life in Trinity Bay, February 28th. Great fire in St John's on 8th and 9th of July.

1893.—General election; Sir W. Whiteway's Government returned by a large majority.

1894.—Election petitions, sixteen members unseated. Goodridge Government formed. Failure of the Commercial and Union Banks and many mercantile houses. Greene Government formed.

1895.—Disability Bill sanctioned by the Imperial Government. Sir W. V. Whiteway, Premier.

I am conscious of many sins of omission and commission in the preparation of this most difficult part of my subject; whilst endeavouring to write a true history of the period, I have had also to walk, like Agag before Saul, delicately, in order to avoid offence. Many minor events which I have not included in the text will be found in the notes and the chronology. The history of St. Pierre and Miquelon, one of the most amusing episodes in our Island story, and an account of the Labrador, will be found in a separate chapter.

Many persons have imagined that the frequent election rows in Newfoundland, about this period, were the outcome of religious bigotry, but a better understanding of the facts will show us that this is an incorrect view. There is no real bigotry or sectarian intolerance in Newfoundland; all these riots were made to order. Dr. Johnson has defined

ANGLICAN CATHEDRAL AND THE NARROWS, ST. JOHN'S, IN 1835.
From a drawing by the Hon. and Rev. W. Gray.

patriotism as "the last refuge of a scoundrel." The sham patriots who instigated their dupes to get up these disturbances often made religion a stalking horse for their designs on the Treasury; the blatant demagogues who cried out that the Catholic Church was in danger, or that the sacred rights of Protestantism were being trampled on, always bloomed out after the *mêlée* as fat officials. Instigated by these designing rogues, a few rowdies and bludgeon men led the way, and the simple crowd that followed were led to believe that their rights or their

religion were in danger; in American political slang this is known as
" bulldozing."

For a few years after the inception of the Legislature these tactics
were pre-eminently successful, especially in Conception Bay. We hear
most about riots by Catholic mobs, but the attacks on Catholics by
Protestants, in Bay Roberts and other places, were equally disgraceful.
The riots of 1861 marked the end of this discreditable violence; it was
all caused by unscrupulous politicians, there was no strong popular
sentiment to sustain it; disorder and political rowdyism completely died
away shortly after these events of 1861; it would never have arisen had
the principles of amalgamation[1] and fair play to all parties been carried
out on the introduction of responsible government; but the Protestants
and the Merchants' party blindly resisted the new movement, and the
Liberals and Catholics, being wiser in their generation, and more skilful
politicians, though representing really a minority of the population,
gained the ascendency, and kept it from 1855 to 1861. Having kept
power so long, they were loth to give it up; they made a terrible outcry
when they were turned out in 1861. When the elections were fairly

SIR B. ROBINSON.
By Hughes, Ryde.

contested, the Protestant party, representing a
majority of the people, easily won. In their
turn they kept all the departmental offices for
themselves; it is due to Sir Hugh Hoyles's
memory, however, to state that he offered his
opponents a fair share in the Government—
the Presidentship of the Council, held by Hon.
L. O'Brien, and two departmental offices—but
the Catholics either could not, or would not,
coalesce with him. The principle of amalgamation, giving all classes and creeds a fair share
of the offices and patronage, was not carried into
effect until 1865, under the Liberal Administration of Sir Frederick Carter. Since then, the
relative position of the great religious bodies has completely changed;
formerly their numbers were nearly balanced, now the Protestants out-
number the Catholics by nearly two to one.

Sir Alexander Bannerman's administration of the Government lasted
from 1857 to 1863; the period was marked by prosperity. In the year
following his arrival, Hon. P. F. Little, the able leader of the Liberal

---

[1] Mr. Little offered Mr. Hoyles the
Attorney-Generalship if he would assist in
the movement for responsible government;
Hoyles refused. No offers were made on the
formation of the first Ministry in 1855.

party, retired from politics, and was appointed an assistant judge of the Supreme Court; the Hon. A. W. Des Barres and J. Simms, assistant judges of the Supreme Court, having been pensioned, Mr. B. Robinson and Mr. Little were appointed in their places; two more able and efficient judges never graced the Bench.

One of the most notable events in 1859 was the hotly contested election of that year. Burin was what the Americans call the pivotal district; there has never been in this Colony anything like the struggle which took place there; every office holder of the old Assembly, and every Liberal supporter, was requisitioned for the campaign fund. Mr. Glen, who managed this part of the business, was inexorable; members and officials fought against the demands of the stern old Receiver-General, but all had to pay down their money. Hoyles and Evans were the Conservative candidates, the Liberals were represented by A. Shea and J. J. Rogerson; they were well matched opponents. Mr. Shea, now Sir Ambrose, was the greatest politician of his party, one of the most able men the Colony has produced, and amongst his co-religionists far away the greatest of them all; he had an opponent worthy of his steel in the Conservative leader, Sir Hugh Hoyles. What the contest cost has never been made public, purity of election was then undreamt of. The Liberals were credited with spending about

JOHN STUART.[1]
By S. H. Parsons.

£2,000; Mr. Hoyles paid all his own expenses. The contest was exceedingly close, but the tactics of Mr. Shea, and the intimidation of electors by the celebrated Cody ("who had a claim") at Flat Islands and elsewhere, helped materially to gain the day.

The Liberals again carried the Government—the Hon. J. Kent was Premier and Colonial Secretary; Hon. G. J. Hogsett, Attorney-General; Mr. Shea, Speaker. The new administration was inferior in strength to Mr. Little's cabinet. Mr. Kent, as Premier, was a most honest and capable official, but his temper was uncertain, he never enjoyed the complete confidence of the Catholic party and of Dr. Mullock

---

[1] John Stuart, of the old firm of Rennie Stuart & Co., was the most popular man in Newfoundland; for over 30 years he performed the duties of the two responsible offices of clerk to the House of Assembly and the Board of Works. A most able official, kindliest and most genial of men, his death left a void in the House and our hearts which can never be filled.

like his predecessor; the real leader was Mr. A. Shea. Though the sunshine of prosperity had risen upon them, it did not last; from 1860 to 1861 there were serious divisions in the party, the strong and skilful hand of Mr. Little was no longer felt, and the great Liberal party began to fall to pieces. Shea and Kent did not work harmoniously together. In 1860 the fisheries partially failed, there was consequent distress, and a lavish expenditure of relief to able-bodied poor; Mr. Kent, I believe, was opposed to this indiscriminate expenditure. In the autumn of 1860 there was a special session of the Legislature held before Christmas; it was soon manifest to outsiders that there was war in the Liberal camp.

HON. JOHN KENT.
By Chisholm.

A serious conflict had arisen earlier in the year, between Bishop Mullock and the administration, which called out the celebrated letter given below.[1] His lordship and Mr. Justice Little, on a visit to New York, had virtually made a contract with the owners of the steamer *Victoria* to run this vessel

[1] "To the Catholic people of the Diocese of St. John's.

"My dear people,   June, 1860.

"I address you this letter on a matter of vital importance to your interests, and I consider that my advocacy of everything connected with the improvement of the country gives me a right to offer you a few words of advice. The great and paramount want of Newfoundland is a facility of communication between the capital and the outports; as long as the outports are left isolated, so long will education, religion, and civilization, be left in the background. Newfoundland must remain in that state of darkness to which ages of bad government have reduced it. I solemnly declare that without steam communication the people must remain poor, degraded, and ignorant. Forced by the indignant voice of the people, those whom you call your representatives passed a Bill granting £3,000 a year for five years for out-port steam. It appears that by a dishonest quibble, intended to defeat the project, two steamers were smuggled into the Bill so as to render the offer illusory, in plain English a humbug.

"A beautiful steamer, in every way adapted for the purpose, engaged to do the service north and south twice a month, was offered in New York; I visited the ship myself, and if she was not all that was specified, the contract could be terminated at three months' notice. She had every accommodation for passengers, and would have done more to develop the interests of the out-harbours than all the Houses of Assembly that ever met on the Island.

"The Government, when they saw the matter brought to a point, refused to engage her. What was intended only to delude the people was about to become a reality, and the contract was repudiated. How does it happen that an enormous revenue, wasted in providing useless places for *State paupers*, cannot afford the sum of £3,000 a year for outport accommodation? Year by year every improvement is put off for want of means, though every infant even in Newfoundland pays in taxes £1 a head. Will strangers believe that in a British Colony the shire town of Fortune Bay is in reality further from us than Constantinople? but then we have the satisfaction of seeing thousands upon thousands of pounds distributed amongst our *locust-like officials*. We pay heavy taxes, but get comparatively no return; almost all goes in salaries and pretended compensations, and I have no hesitation in saying that the collection of a revenue under the present system is nothing but *legalized robbery*. I am aware

twice a month north and south. An Act had been passed granting £3,000 a year for local steam, and the bishop,[1] a most vigorous supporter of improved communications both by steam and telegraph, was terribly wroth when his own particular Government refused to recognise his authority to commit them to a contract; when his lordship found that the Government firmly refused to charter the *Victoria*, he denounced Mr. Kent's administration in this scathing epistle.

The year that marked the publication of Bishop Mullock's letter is also distinguished in our annals by the arrival of His Royal Highness the Prince of Wales on his way to Canada and the United States. The visit, which lasted from the 22nd to the 25th July 1860, was a complete success; the town was given up to festivity and rejoicing, the young heir apparent won all hearts by his grace and courtesy. We did honour to our future sovereign by a grand ball, a regatta, a review, and the gift of a dog[2] from the breed of the celebrated Bat Sullivan. Much of the

THE PRINCE OF WALES.

success of the Prince's visit was due to Sir Alexander and Lady Bannerman, the Duke of Newcastle's tact, and the geniality and refined courtesy of old Earl St. Germains, the excellent management of General

that my name has been made use of to prop up the supporters of this system, but I consider it due to myself, and to those whose interests I advocate, to repudiate any connexion with a party who take care of themselves, but do nothing for the people. This is not a political or a religious question, it is one of civilization, in which Catholics and Protestants, priests and ministers, are equally interested."

[1] Newfoundland owes a deep debt of gratitude to Dr. Mullock; he was not only the active, earnest promoter of steam communication, both local and transatlantic, for the Colony, he was the first to advocate a railway to Harbour Grace and telegraphic communication. The steamer *Victoria*, Captain Cudworth, eventually inaugurated local steam communication north and south; she was

utterly unfitted to the service; in September 1861 she completely broke down, and had to return to New York. In 1863, the S.S. *Ariel* was put on the route north and south, by her owner, Hon. Captain Cleary; under her most careful commander, Hagan, she did excellent work, until she was finally replaced by the steamers *Tiger* and *Leopard*. In 1877 the *Curlew* and *Plover* began a very efficient service. In 1888 the fine steamers *Volunteer* and *Conscript* of the Coastal Steamships Company performed the work. These splendid boats were a vast improvement on the former coastal steamers.

[2] This dog, " Cabot," was afterwards the subject of an amusing law suit. Cabot was a very fine animal, and Sullivan charged a royal price for him, which the committee thought exorbitant.

Bruce, the Prince's Governor, and the popular gay young Captains Grey and Teesdale; the hero of Kars. All went merry as a marriage bell during the three lovely summer days of the Prince's stay amongst us; one and all did their best to make the auspicious occasion a truly joyous time; our volunteer turn-out and review was a great success.

The spring session of 1861 was marked with more dissensions in the Government ranks about poor relief.[1] An injudicious utterance of the Premier brought matters to a climax; the strife in the party was so keen that there would have been a split even if this untoward event had not happened. Mr. Kent, in his place in the House of Assembly, openly accused Sir Alexander Bannerman of conspiracy with the judges,[2] the lawyers, and the minority in the House of Assembly, to defeat the

SIR W. HOYLES.

By the Stereoscopic Company.

Government Bill fixing the value to be given to sterling money in the payment of official salaries. This accusation appeared in the newspapers. The Governor wrote to the Colonial Secretary asking for an explanation; Mr. Kent replied that he did not consider himself called upon to give an account of his utterances as a member of the Legislature to His Excellency.[3] Immediately on receiving this communication, Sir Alexander dismissed his ministry and called upon the leader of the Opposition, Mr. Hoyles, to form a new administration. Mr. Hoyles selected his Government, and announced its formation to the Assembly.

The House was immediately dissolved, and a general election took place in April 1861.[4] There was no contest in Burin, and no conflict or

[1] Bishop Mullock wrote an indignant letter about the distribution of poor relief. Mr. Kent tried honestly to curtail and regulate the expenditure. He found a conspiracy against him, headed by Mr. Shea. Mr. P. Nowlan brought in a resolution "that any regulations made on the subject of poor relief should not ignore the just influences of the representatives of the people." Mr. Kent declared he "was attacked by a miserable faction who sought his political destruction; a set of frozen serpents, which having been warmed into life had stung the breast which gave it vitality. There was no doubt a Judas at the bottom of all these proceedings . . . It was well known who was the person behind the scenes, some designing, cozening, cunning rogue who for ambition or vindictive purposes had devised this treason against the Government."

[2] Judge Robinson had always contended that *sterling* could only mean British sterling, *i.e.*, dollars at 4s. 2d. It had been the practice to use two sterlings, one a colonial sterling dollar at 4s. 4d. and another, designated as British sterling, at 4s. 2d. Judge Robinson petitioned the House against the passage of this Bill, urging his claim to be paid his official salary in British sterling.

[3] In a debate on this question, Mr. Hoyles stated that Mr. Kent had not consulted his colleagues before replying to the Governor. Mr. Hogsett contradicted him; "He consulted me," said the ex-Attorney-General. "Then if he consulted you," replied Mr. Hoyles, "he would be sure to put his foot in it."

[4] For the result of the election, see p. 664.

riot, except in the districts of St. John's, Harbour Grace, and Harbour Main The result completely changed the position of political parties. There was a serious disturbance in Harbour Main between the rival Catholic candidates, Hogsett and Furey, on one side, Nowlan and Byrne on the other. The attempt to invade Cats Cove (now Conception Harbour) with a strong Harbour Main contingent caused terrible bitterness, the death of one man, and the looting and destruction of property After a protracted contest before the election committee, Nowlan and Byrne were subsequently declared duly elected

On the 13th of May 1861, the Governor opened the new House of Assembly, His Excellency was hooted, and a violent mob surrounded the Colonial Building and attempted to break through the doors[1] Messrs Hogsett and Furey, who claimed to be elected for Harbour Main on a certificate from the returning officer, which it was afterwards stated was obtained by intimidation, took their seats in the House. They were ordered to withdraw from the Assembly, they refused, Mr. Hogsett was then removed by the police, and Mr Furey followed.

Later on the same day, there was a serious riot in St John's, a mob broke into the premises of Messrs. Nowlan and Kitchen (relatives of Mr. P. Nowlan, the member for Harbour Main), on Water Street The soldiers were ordered out, Col Grant and Judge Little and Father Jeremiah O'Donnell did all in their power to calm the violence of the mob and to persuade them to retire; the magistrate read the Riot Act, but all to no purpose, stones were thrown at the military, an attempt was made to drag Colonel Grant from his horse Finally, it is alleged, a shot was fired at the soldiers, and reluctantly the commander was then compelled to give the order to fire.[2] Three people were

[1] I remember looking at the mob from the windows of the House of Assembly A crowd tried to break in at the lower western door, a tall Irishman, whose name was never known, put his back against the door and defended it against the whole excited rabble

[2] It is but fair on this question to place side by side with my own views the arguments put forward on the Liberal side They contend that the Governor should not have dismissed his Ministry for the act of one member, that it was unlawful to exclude Hogsett and Furey from the House of Assembly, that the police force and special constables should have been used to stop the riot—to all who were present at the *mêlée* of 13th May this idea of the police maintaining order is simply absurd, in presence of such a mob the small police force of that day were utterly powerless A review of the whole evidence given on the inquest clearly exonerated the authorities from all blame, there is not a shadow of a case against either

Mr Carter or Mr Bennett, the magistrates The behaviour of Col Grant was most forbearing, for nearly two hours he endeavoured to make the mob retire peaceably. The *Newfoundlander* that attacked Mr. Hoyles and the Governor so bitterly on this subject, made the same attack on the Government about the Harbour Grace election. What was the result there when order was restored and the election fairly conducted? Both Messrs. Hayward and Moore were returned by double the number of votes received by Prendergast

No one can doubt now that Sir Alexander was fully justified in dismissing the Premier and his Ministry when he made such a charge against the Queen's Representative, and refused to withdraw or apologise Hon. T Talbot, sheriff (the Protector of the District Judges), an eminent and devout Catholic, says, in his short History of the Colony "No Governor fit for his position would have taken any other course than the one adopted

killed and twenty wounded; amongst the injured was the estimable Father O'Donnell, for whom great sympathy was expressed among all classes.

The whole trouble was due to the turbulence of the defeated candidate Hogsett and the violence of a few rowdies. The unfortunate riot in St. John's was the direct outcome of the Harbour Main election. For a time it appeared like an organised attempt to make parliamentary government impossible; thanks, however, to the exertions of Bishop Mullock and his clergy, and the general good sense of the community, order was completely restored. The next day the town was as quiet as usual; Colonel Grant walked up through the city alone with his cane and a little dog to attend at the inquest. It was fortunate for us at this stage of our history that the reins of government were in the hands of one who, in this terrible crisis, showed a firmness, and cool, undaunted courage that won the admiration of his fiercest opponents. Sir Hugh Hoyles, the leader of the new Government, and, we may say, the whole Administration rolled into one, soon after 1861, when the angry passion of this evil time subsided, became not only the most respected, but the most popular, man in the Colony, beloved by all classes.[1]

HON. T. TALBOT.

---

by Sir Alexander Bannerman." After all, the best answer to all objections made against both the Governor and Mr. Hoyles is the result of the appeal to the constituencies; when the elections were fairly conducted a good working majority of their own party, over and above their Catholic allies, was obtained to sustain their action.

[1] THE RIOTS OF 1861.

Newfoundlander, May 14th, 1861.

"The military should never be called out, and never are called out, where prudence and good order prevail, until the civil powers of repression have been proved insufficient, and this was notoriously not the case here, for the means of increasing them to efficiency in the way we suggest had been neglected. Well, what might have been anticipated followed; the presence of the troops excited anew the fury of some of the townspeople. Those who had been before then dispersing began to collect again; stones were thrown at the soldiers; Colonel Grant was insulted and struck; provocation followed provocation, and the order was given to fire. Then came that terrific discharge which yet thrills with horror every soul who heard it, that sound which told of slaughter to the innocent and

guilty, perhaps to the innocent alone, as the blow might chance to fall; and then was the air rent with such shrieks as the sudden and awful sense of the death summons can alone produce. Seven shots told, three of them mortally; one man, named Clifford, an aged widow's only son and support, died on the instant. The two others, Hunt and Fitz-Patrick, lingered but a short time; the latter was an elderly invalid, who had only the day before come out of the hospital, and though, unhappily for the poor fellow, making one of the crowd, quite incapable of mischief, both from age and infirmity. Amongst the wounded, we grieve to say, was the Rev. Jeremiah O'Donnell, one of the most esteemed and loved priest in the island. Exhausted from his previous labours of the day, he called a respectable man, named Patrick Mirick, whom he saw in the crowd, and took him to lean on and help him through, while he entreated and implored them, for the love of God, to keep the peace and retire to their homes. While thus engaged in the divine work of peace, this most amiable and worthy priest received a shot which passed through his ankle. He was taken into a neighbouring house for a while, and then, in a most painful and prostrate condition, carried home on a bed; poor

Out of evil sometimes comes good ; the direct result of all this rioting and violence, all this storm of violent partisanship and sectarian strife, was to put an end for ever to religious ascendency on both sides. After a short respite, it became the settled rule in the formation of our Government that all religious parties should be fairly represented in the arrangement of an administration and in the distribution of offices. As a direct result, sectarianism in politics, bigotry, and intolerance, have year by year diminished.

The year 1861 witnessed the commencement of the great civil war between the North and South, many of the blockade runners made St John's a port of call on their way to and from the Southern States

The following year, 1862, will always be remembered as " the spring of the *Polynia* and *Camperdown*," two Dundee whalers that were sent out to prosecute the seal fishery. Within the memory of man there has never been such an ice blockade, for weeks and weeks it blew a " solid " north-easter, the sealing steamers did not take a seal The ill wind, however, blew wealth untold into Green Bay, all along our

Minck, who was with him, was shot in the thigh, and, of course, very seriously injured When the alarm rang through the crowd that the priest had been shot down, their strongest feelings were aroused to a degree, seemingly, beyond all control, and infuriated demands for vengeance were heard in every direction. At this critical juncture came again the most praiseworthy services of the Catholic clergy and Judge Little. They positively left no means unemployed to restrain the people, and had they done less than they did, we are assured by undoubted eye-witnesses that direful retaliation would have followed The judge, at imminent peril to his life from stones on the one hand and musket balls on the other, rushed into the middle of the mêlée He called upon the magistrate, Mr. Bennett, to retire the troops for the safety of the town. Mr. Bennett declined The judge then asserted his own superior authority, and assured Colonel Grant of peace if he would withdraw his soldiers This assurance was strongly endorsed by Crockwell, J P, who came up at the moment, and with wise and cool discernment saw and declared the judge's proposed course to be the right one in all respects The Colonel at once consented, with an expression of deep regret for what had taken place, and requested the judge to accompany him and his men to barracks, which was accordingly done. Meanwhile, between eight and nine o'clock, the powerful summons of the cathedral bells bade the terrified and enraged multitude repair from amidst scenes of crime and blood to the House of God, there to hear the voice of their chief pastor The thoroughfares began at once to

empty themselves in that direction, and in a few minutes a vast multitude had assembled within the cathedral The Right Rev Dr Mullock appeared on the altar in pontificals, and, with heartfelt and melting supplications, conjured the people to be calm, to keep the peace, and to go to their homes He then presented to them the Chalice containing the Most Holy Sacrament, and exacted a promise from all present that, for the honour of the Divine Presence, they would obey his instructions, and endeavour to induce all within their influence to do the same Soon after this all externally was restored to tranquillity, and no disturbance or breach of the peace took place in the night His Lordship, on the following evening, repeated his exhortation to peace, and with such excellent effect that, thank God, all is well up to the time we write The present is not the moment for recrimination or for any other words than those which may tend, with Heaven's help, to soften down passion stimulated to madness.

" At a more fitting period responsibility for the present state of the community will doubtless be fixed upon its causes and accessories But now the immediate and paramount duty of all is to strain every nerve for the conservation of peace and order, and to avoid, as far as possible, every subject or proceeding calculated to freshen or keep alive the bitter aching memories of those events we have endeavoured to describe We are happy to be enabled to add that Father O'Donnell, for whom such universal sympathy exists, is satisfactorily recovering from the effects of his accident."

northern coast the catch of seals by shore men was the largest on record; £25,000 was made by one firm, Muir and Duder, out of this

remarkable windfall. The cod fishery of this year was a partial, and the ship seal fishery almost a complete failure [1] — the worst season since 1845—the whole export of seal skins amounting only to two hundred and sixty thousand.

In the following year Sir Alexander Bannerman [2] resigned his Governorship; he was a man well stricken in years, and died in the year following his retirement from Newfoundland. He will long be honoured in our memories as an honest, straightforward administrator; a genial, kindly, liberal old Scotchman, with a dry, pawky humour, essentially Aberdonian. I do not remember that he had any prejudice in the world except against the Galway line.

The early spring of this year was marked with the terrible shipwreck of the S.S. *Anglo-Saxon* at Clam Cove on 27th, accompanied with great

---

[1] The season of 1862 was unprecedented; for fifty-two days the wind was inshore, N.E. to E.N.E., and for more than two months not a drop of rain fell. The papers of the day speak of the certain decline of the seal fishery. They attribute the losses made in this industry to the large size and expense of the more modern vessels. The *Newfoundlander*, of 7th April, 1862, says:—

"New capital will certainly not be invested to any amount in the costly ships that have been in vogue of late years, and it looks as though the choice will lie between the vessels of the olden time and screw steamers. We think, whether we will or no, the trade will come to be carried on by means of steamers. Their failure in the present year [*Polynia* and *Camperdown*], when all have failed from causes without precedent, and beyond all human control, will, perhaps, not deter the same parties from another attempt; and should the adventure succeed, we must go to work with all the same means, or be content to abandon the enterprise altogether."

LETTER FROM CAPTAIN E. WHITE TO JOB BROS, 6th April 1862.

Evanthes at Sea.

After referring to the wind, N.N.E. and E.N.E., and sea, he says:

"As to losses, I am afraid the number will be fearful. I have seen some six or eight go down the last few days, among which are the *Emily Tobin*, *Melrose*, and the *Margaret*, besides several others I cannot name. While I am writing there is so much sea, and the ice is so heavy, that I cannot tell the minute the sides of my vessel will be driven in. I have driven from the Funks since the 28th ult. tightly jammed. We are now off Cape St. Francis and expect to drive to Cape Race before getting clear. . . . . . The young harps are all in Green Bay and White Bay, the vessels cannot enter more than half a mile in the jam of ice, and then they subject themselves to damage and loss from the fearful sea." The spring of 1894 very much resembled this extraordinary season.

[2] Sir Alexander Bannerman, Knt., born 1783, died 1864, a cousin of the baronet of that name, was for many years an extensive shipowner, merchant and banker of Aberdeen, and M.P. for Aberdeen in the Liberal interest from 1832 to 1847. He was elected Dean of the Faculty in Marischal College, Aberdeen, and appointed, by Lord Melbourne, Commissioner of Greenwich Hospital; knighted in 1851 on his appointment as Governor of Prince Edward's Island, thence to Bahamas in 1854, Newfoundland in 1857 to 1863. Lady Bannerman, *née* Margaret Gordon, survived her husband several years; she was an intimate friend of the great General Gordon, and the celebrated Margaret beloved by Thomas Carlyle.

loss of life. The steamer *Bloodhound*, belonging to Baine, Johnston & Co., commanded by the late Captain Alexander Graham, and the *Wolf*, belonging to Walter Grieve & Co., William Kean master, inaugurated the employment of steam in the seal fishery. The first attempt was a comparative failure ; the *Bloodhound* arrived, 22nd April, with three thousand, and the *Wolf*, with thirteen hundred seals, on the 28th.[1]

WALTER GRIEVE.
By Moffatt, Edinburgh.

A limited supply of water was provided for St. John's by the water company instituted in 1848. The flow was derived from George's Pond, Signal Hill, and was found very beneficial ; later on there was a demand for a larger and fuller supply. In 1863 the town was at length furnished with an almost unlimited quantity of water from Winsor Lake, by the General Water Company. A great blunder was made in the engineering by an official whom the company had distinctly refused to employ. Sir A. Shea and the other directors

HON. L. O'BRIEN
From an old photograph.

weakly gave way, and the works cost the Colony about $120,000 more than they should have done. However, we cannot grumble ; the supply of pure water is simply invaluable, and, if properly managed, it offers a complete protection against fire. No town in the world has such a water supply as St. John's, in proportion to its population. The natural pressure is sufficient to reach the highest points in the city. The supply is beautifully soft, clear, cool, and absolutely pure drinking water ; much of the success of the water company is due to the good management of our veteran sportsman, John Martin.

During the interval between the departure of Sir Alexander in 1863, and the arrival of Governor Musgrave in 1864, Hon. Lawrence O'Brien,

---

[1] The next trip of the SS. *Bloodhound* is commemorated in a local poem :—

"The *Mary Joyce*
Is stuck in the ice,
And so is the *Bloodhound* too,
Young Bill Ryan left Terry behind
To paddle his own canoe."

President of the Council, administered the government with dignity and efficiency. During the four years of Mr. Musgrave's tenure of the

SIR A. MUSGRAVE, K.C.M.G.
By Duryea, Adelaide.

Governorship there were great changes, progress, and poverty. Sir Anthony was an amiable and painstaking administrator; he was thought a great deal of at the Colonial Office as an able writer of despatches, and no doubt he made the Home Government believe that he was able to carry confederation in the Colony; he never, however, had any real power or influence in Newfoundland.[1] By the end of 1864 Sir Hugh Hoyles' health had so completely failed that he was no longer able to bear the heavy burthen of his office; he had literally worked himself to death's door. In 1865 he became Chief Justice of the Supreme Court, a position of comparative ease—as a lawyer Sir Hugh was unrivalled. He made a model judge, the most painstaking, able and impartial administrator of justice that ever graced the bench of any British colony—an indefatigable worker, he gave no complaints for the law's delays. His decision of character, his amiable manners, and his extreme courtesy endeared him to all. We were all proud of Sir Hugh as the most distinguished Newfoundlander of our day. The leadership of the party naturally fell on the shoulders of the present Chief Justice. In the election of 1865 Sir Frederick's Government was sustained by a large majority.

SIR F. B. T. CARTER, K.C.M.G.
By S. H. Parsons.

The great political movement of the time was the confederation of British North America. To complete the union our Island was necessarily included in the scheme; Sir Frederick and Sir Ambrose Shea were sent as our delegates to the great confederation conference, and returned

---

[1] Sir Anthony Musgrave, K.C.M.G. (1875) (C.M.G. 1871), was Private Secretary to Mr. Mackintosh when Governor-in-Chief of the Leeward Islands, 1850–51; entered as student at the Inner Temple, 1851; appointed treasury accountant at Antigua, 1852; resumed legal studies at the Temple in 1853; appointed Colonial Secretary of Antigua, February 1854; administrator of the Colony of Nevis, October 1860; Administrator of Government of St. Vincent, April 1861; appointed Lieutenant-Governor of St. Vincent, May 1862; Governor of Newfoundland, April 1864; Governor of British Columbia,

with a draft of the terms on which we might become united with the Dominion. The proposals to unite our destinies with Canada, were not received with enthusiasm. The main question was one of terms, what would Canada give us in return for surrendering our independence? The offer from the Dominion on the all-important subject of a railway and a steam ferry has hitherto been vague and uncertain, but even if any such tangible offer had been made before 1869, looking back now at the excited condition of our population on the subject, I very much doubt if any terms would have been accepted. The anti-confederate party were strong in numbers, powerful in organisation, and their leader, Mr Charles Fox Bennett, showed himself a most able and indefatigable political campaigner. The awful tales that were told about taxation, about ramming the new-born babes down Canadian cannon, "bleaching their bones on the desert sands of Canada," had a tremendous effect on the simple out-harbour people. There still lingers amongst them a traditionary remembrance of the sufferings their forefathers endured from the French Canadian and Indian raids made in the seventeenth and eighteenth century, and this partly accounts for their dread of Canada; Irish national feeling, their hatred of the Union, brought about by fraud and bribery, was also appealed to. The result was an overwhelming defeat for the Confederate party; they were simply annihilated, and from that day to this Confederation has never been put forward before the country as a practical political question.[1]

Both from an Imperial and Colonial point, the union of the British North American Colonies is a consummation devoutly to be wished, it is all a question of terms. There are, however, some objections to union. Since the death of the great Sir John A McDonald there is no statesman in Canada strong enough to guarantee us such terms as we would accept. There are also great drawbacks in Canada's protectionist tariff, the Dominion is a fish producer and not a fish consumer; our business relations and our future market lie with the United States, the customers and consumers of our inexhaustible fisheries are the sixty-three million Americans. Canada's latest move on the Blaine

June 1869; Lieutenant-Governor of Natal, May 1872; Governor of South Australia, 1873; Governor of Jamaica, 1877; Governor of Victoria, where he died. He married the only daughter of David Dudley Field, of New York. Sir Anthony came to this Colony with the full assurance of carrying confederation. He was a good writer, and an amiable man, who made few enemies.

[1] Our modern Newfoundland legislators have earned fame in various ways. Sir W V Whiteway will be handed down to posterity as the introducer and successful promoter of the railway; Sir Robert Thorburn is immortalized by a great road — the Thorburn turnpike; Mr Goodridge as the Rupert of debate; Sir James Winter for his connexion with the Chamberlain-Blaine Treaty; Mr. Murray for his amusing campaign literature; but all these celebrities sink into insignificance compared with the first introducer of the public grindstone, where every man could grind his own axe at the public expense. Skipper John Bartlett, the anti-

Bond Convention has alienated the feelings of many Newfoundlanders who were formerly Confederates.

Great impetus was given to mining by the operation of C. F. Bennett and Smith McKay in the great Tilt Cove Mine in 1864, to-day one of the finest copper deposits in the Colony. The geological survey was commenced under the late Mr. Alexr. Murray, C.M.G., in 1865, continued by his able successor, Mr. Jas. Howley, F.R.G.S. In 1866 the telegraph cable was successfully landed in Hearts Content; in August the end of the 1865 cable was picked up, and the gulf cable repaired by McKay in the *Bloodhound.* 1867 is noted as the year of the "great fishery" and the great Labrador gale; the destruction of boats, shipping, and stages was enormous. The large firms had most of their losses covered by insurance; to the poor settlers and small planters it was a terrible calamity. In 1868 a vigorous

HON. JOHN BEMISTER.
By S. H. Parsons.

effort was made by the Carter Government to suppress able-bodied poor relief; it was a bold move, all the best men in the party supported the measure, and it was pre-eminently successful.

Sir Frederick's administration and all his party were overthrown in 1869, and Mr. Bennett formed an administration, which in its turn was again defeated in 1873, through the defection of three of its supporters. Mr. Bennett's tenure of office corresponded with the Governorship of Sir Stephen Hill, K.C.M.G. In July 1869, direct steam to England by the Allan Line was permanently established. Vessels of the same line had been making calls each year since the S.S. *North American* first came to St. John's in January 1862.

HON. C. F. BENNETT.
By Lenthall.

The Bennett Government was a most able and progressive administration. The Premier had always been an indefatigable promoter of

confederate member for Brigus, was the prime mover in this great public improvement—a most popular move. Besides the public grindstone at Brigus, there are subsidiary public grindstones at Bareneed, Port de Grave, Clarke's Beach, and Pick Eye. The late T. D. Scanlan is my authority; he says: "I have used the public grinder myself, and ground my own hatchet at the public expense."

roads; the present efficient police is due to Mr. Bennett's statesmanlike sagacity; during his tenure of office there were successful fisheries, good harvests, and general prosperity; the revenue rose in 1871 to $831,160. In the mining industry, the increase was very marked under the fostering care of the great pioneer of this industry (Mr. Bennett); the large expenditure of wages in Green Bay to the copper workers added largely to the resources of our working population, and helped to diffuse general prosperity throughout the Colony.

SIR STEPHEN HILL.

The most exciting subject in 1872–73, next to the all-absorbing question of confederation, was the right of our Government under the Charter to pre-empt the New York, Newfoundland and London Telegraph Company's rights and plant. With the exception of a few cool-headed individuals, everyone went mad about monopoly and pre-emption. Mr. H. Labouchere, M.P., a leading shareholder in the Direct Cable Company, has always had the credit of engineering this great financial dodge. Our telegraph company's stock, known amongst financiers as "Dogs," stood at a high figure (above par); as it was a highly speculative stock, it probably was rated above its real value. A shrewd operator discovered this point about *pre-emption*. He saw that if sufficient pressure or influence could be gained over the Newfoundland Government to get them to decide that they would pre-empt, or that they would not waive their right of pre-emption, the stock could be beared to a large extent. To accomplish this end the great writer Lawrence Oliphant was sent to influence Governor Hill The Duke of Buckingham wrote to the Premier on the subject; the Hon. J. Tobin and a Mr. Cole were also sent out to the Colony. Lawyers' opinions were published that the Newfoundland Company's plant might be taken over by our Government as so much old wood and iron; we were to receive a handsome yearly revenue for the right to land on our shores; even ministers of the Gospel were dragged from their sacred functions to go sounding in Placentia Bay; money was spent like water, and at last the desired result was obtained. At the moment that it suited the stock-jobbers, a telegram was sent by our Government that "they would not waive their right of pre-emption," "Dogs" declined 9*l.* a share, and a ring of speculators who had prepared this elaborate plan pocketed £400,000 sterling. Pretty nearly all the influential men in the Colony were drawn into this clever, unscrupulous game, and the most respectable individuals amongst us were paid agents in working out this great financial dodge.

Pre-emption was the wildest, maddest, most absurd proposal ever entertained by a Government; to commit us, with our small revenue, to the purchase of a speculative concern like a cable and a telegraph; to risk our revenue for about ten years on a thing that might be gold to-day and utterly worthless to-morrow;—George Law's Mississippi scheme was not more fantastic.

THE EAST END OF WATER STREET BEFORE THE FIRE OF 1892.
From a photograph by S. H. Parsons.

The most humorous thing about the whole affair was the way in which it was managed; that the agents, the paid pamphleteers, the subsidized press and the whole army of claqueurs should gird at the monopoly and attack the Anglo-American Company, was only meet and right. They were paid for it, and I am bound to say they did it well, they earned their money; but that the whole outside public, unpaid and disinterested, should clamour for the same object, that virtually the whole Colony should aid and abet a great stock-jobbing trick, seems really too absurd; however, there are men amongst us, even to this day, who will not believe that the offers made to our Government were a sham and the whole affair a delusion and a snare.

The high moral tone assumed by Labouchere and all these financing agents is quite delightful. Our Government was quite prepared to pre-empt if they could obtain a good guarantee for reimbursement in case of loss; they applied for this purpose to the British Government but none could be obtained, and so Sir F. Carter's Government very properly, therefore, refused to entertain the subject.

The following extract of a letter from Mr. Labouchere to Governor Hill shows the kind of vague promises on which our Government were requested to run so enormous a risk :—

"Should you, Sir, terminate the existing monopoly in 1874, and take over the land lines of the island, for the value of their plant and material, I am informed by responsible capitalists that they will be ready, if it be wished, to take over your lines at a rental, agreeing to lower the tariff, and to allow all cables to land on your shores, and to advance money on the guarantee of the rental to enable your colony to pay off Mr. Field. In fact, they are ready to enter into any arrangement with you which may facilitate the operation, so anxious are all commercial houses and our daily press to reduce the heavy cost of transatlantic telegrams.

"I have the honour to be, Sir,

"Your Excellency's most obedient humble servant,

"To Sir S. Hill, K.C.M.G. HENRY LABOUCHERE."

One of the most humorous things was the final result. The big telegraph monopolist, John Pender, of the Anglo-American, gained a controlling influence over the Direct Cable Company, and the balances due to the lawyers and claqueurs against the Anglo-American and their monopoly were all ultimately paid through the company's agent, A. M. Mac Kay ; so ended the farce.

The election returns of 1873 gave a small majority to the Bennett Government, but it was of a doubtful character; by a series of intrigues well understood at the time, Mr. T. R. Bennett, Member for Fortune Bay, and the Surveyor-General, Hon. Henry Renouf, took office as District Judges, and Mr. C. Duder joined Mr. Carter; this left the Government in a minority of one.[1] Mr. Carter was called on to form an Administration, and he worked along through the session of 1874 with only the Speaker's casting vote; in the autumn he dissolved the House, and a general election gave him a good working majority. To this period belongs the incident of the Royal Commission, consisting of Sir B. Robinson, James Goodfellow, and J. Fox, Esquires. The evidence was not taken on oath, only the Report was published. The Opposition demanded the evidence, which was never produced. From the known high character of the Commissioners, we may rest assured that the inquiry was honestly conducted; the non-production of the evidence, however, seriously impaired its value; it is known in our annals as

[1] If Bennett's party had remained steadfast he had a majority of three. When T. R. Bennett and Renouf took office, and C. Duder left his party, Mr. Carter had fifteen to fourteen, with the Speaker. The return of 1875 shows the immense advantage of going before the country with the control of the Executive machinery.

the "Jim Dobbin" Commission.[1]   Sir Frederick's Administration in 1874 was happily favoured with prosperity and the largest fishery ever known in the Colony.

SIR A. SHEA.
By Bassano.

In 1875, Sir Stephen Hill, in his speech at the opening of the session of the Legislature, said :—

"The period appears to have arrived when a question which has for some time engaged public discussion, viz., the construction of a railway across the Island to St. George's Bay, should receive a practical solution. . . . . . As a preliminary to this object, a proposition will be submitted to you for a thorough survey to ascertain the most eligible line, and with a view to the further inquiry whether the Colony does not possess within itself the means of inducing capitalists to undertake this great enterprise of progress."

A sum of money was voted for the preliminary survey; it was completed during the summer of 1875 by a number of Canadian surveyors under the superintendence of Sandford Fleming, the eminent Canadian engineer. The result of the survey, which was carried out in a very rapid manner, and over quite a different course from the one followed in the actual construction of the railway, clearly demonstrated that a line was feasible, that there were no great engineering difficulties to be overcome, and that a light railway might be constructed at a very reasonable rate per mile. Mr. Bellairs' previous survey established the same result.

Sir Stephen Hill's term of office having come to a close in 1876, he was succeeded by Sir John H. Glover, G.C.M.G.[2] The new administrator proved himself a most energetic ruler.

---

[1] This nickname was given to it by the sheriff, Hon. T. Talbot, a member of Mr. Bennett's Government; he stated that the Commission was got up entirely for party purposes. He compared it to a dispute between two neighbours who had fallen out—Jim Dobbin and Pat Ellard—and Jim Dobbin got all the friends on his side to blacken the character of Pat Ellard. Badinage apart, there are very grave objections to the appointment of a judge on a political inquiry of this character.

[2] Sir J. H. Glover, R.N., G.C.M.G. (1874), entered the navy in 1841 on board the *Queen*, bearing the flag of Vice-Admiral S Edwaird Owen, in which ship he sailed to the Mediterranean; transferred, in May 1842, to the Mediterranean Survey until 1850; for two years commanded the cutter *Auxiliar*;

in 1841 served on the West African station until promoted to lieutenant in October of that year; in 1852 served in the *Winchester* frigate on the East Indian station; transferred to the steam sloop *Sphinx*, shared in the attack and capture of Pegu, and in the action at Donihew, was especially mentioned in despatches on both occasions; senior lieutenant in the steam sloop *Rosamond* in the Baltic in 1854; commanded the *Otter*, steam, 3 guns, from 1st March 1855 to March 1857, and was employed in her on " particular service " in the rivers Elbe and Weser, in 1855; from March 1857 to March 1861 was employed on the service of the Niger Expedition, surveyed the lagoons at Lagos, and that portion of the River Niger comprised between Boressa and the sea; during 1861-2 he commanded the *Handy* gunboat on the lagoons

In the following year, 1877, after protracted negotiations, and repeated applications to the Imperial Government, Commander W. Howorth, R.N., was appointed the first stipendiary magistrate on the west coast, and, in accordance with the undoubted rights of the Colonial Government, Custom House officers were appointed and duties collected there.

In 1877 Sir Bryan Robinson was compelled by age and increasing infirmities to retire from the Bench; Sir Frederick Carter took his place, and Sir W. V. Whiteway became acting Attorney-General. One of the important subjects that required the attention of the new Cabinet was the Washington Treaty, ratified between England and the United States on the 8th of May, 1871.

Under the compensation clause of this treaty a Commission was arranged to sit in Halifax, Nova Scotia, which commenced on the 15th June and closed on the 23rd November 1877, after the examination of some hundreds of witnesses, and the production of a vast quantity of documentary evidence.

There had been much controversy, negotiations, and correspondence before the arrangements for the assembling of the Commission were finally concluded.

Both in the Newfoundland Cabinet and amongst outsiders very influential people ridiculed the idea of our ever getting anything out of the Americans. Notwithstanding, however, these opposite views,

at Lagos, until promoted to the rank of commander; first commission as Administrator of the Government of Lagos, 21st April 1863; Colonial Secretary, Lagos, 5th May 1864; Administrator of the Government from 21st February 1866 until the 9th of July 1872; received the thanks of the Secretary of State for Foreign Affairs and of the Secretary of State for War for services rendered on different occasions; also received the thanks of the Administrator and Council of the Government of the Gold Coast for his survey of the River Volta, from the rapids to the sea, and for the assistance he rendered in destroying the pirates of the island of Duffoe on that river in 1870; Special Commissioner to friendly native chiefs in the eastern district of the protected territories on Gold Coast, 18th August 1873; engaged and defeated the Ahoonah tribes, December 1873, and having left Mr. Goldsworthy in command in that quarter, marched with about 700 Houssas into Ashanti, and made his way to Coomassie, through the ruins of which he passed on the 12th of February 1874. Received the Grand Cross of Saint Michael and Saint George for these services. Sir John succeeded Sir Stephen Hill as Governor from 1876 to 1881. On the death of Governor Sir H. Maxse, he was reappointed in 1883. Sir John died in London in 1885. A monument to his memory was erected in the Anglican cathedral of St. John's. No more honourable, generous, kind-hearted, or active ruler ever presided over our Government.

Sir William Whiteway, then Solicitor-General, held strongly to his opinion that we were now entitled to, and would receive, compensation. He accepted the position of British counsel for Newfoundland at the Commission. Messrs. Doutre, S. Thompson, Weatherbee, and L. H. Davies, all eminent lawyers, were appointed British counsel to conduct the Canadian branch of the inquiry.

HON. W. J. S. DONNELLY.
By Notman.

In conjunction with the Hon. W. J. S. Donnelly, Mr. J. O. Fraser, Judge Bennett, and Mr. W. Kelligrew, Sir William prepared our case. In this important work his assistants were not only experienced and able men, but probably the best that could be selected in the Colony. Judge Bennett's practical knowledge of the fishery on the southern and southwestern parts of the island, and the operations of American and French fishermen on our shores, was unequalled; both Mr. Donnelly, Mr. J. O. Fraser, and Mr. Kelligrew were thoroughly versed in the general trade in the Colony. Their duty in assisting to prepare the evidence and select witnesses was very well performed. Whilst we give them every credit for their valuable labours, their work does not in the least detract from the eminent services before the Commission of our counsel. Sir A. Shea, who was always pre-eminently clear and lucid in his statements, whilst praising their work, put Sir W. V. Whiteway's services in the right light when he declared that they were rendered *in a case of greater importance and involving larger responsibilities than have ever fallen to the lot of any public man in connexion with the affairs of this Colony.* Addresses to Sir W. V. Whiteway from both Houses were passed in the following complimentary terms :—

JUDGE BENNETT.
By S. H. Parsons.

MR. J. O. FRASER.
By S. H. Parsons.

" Resolved, That the Legislative Council has pleasure in recording its thankful appreciation of the services of the Hon. William Vallance Whiteway, as counsel for Newfoundland, before the Halifax Fisheries Commission, in the year 1877.

" The Council feel assured that the successful issue of the inquiry there held into the claim of Newfoundland was in large measure due to Mr. Whiteway's able and zealous exertions in behalf of the interests of this Colony

" EDWARD MORRIS,

" Legislative Council,   " President.
  ' April 18th, 1879

" Resolved, That the thanks of the House be accorded to the Hon William V. Whiteway, Premier of the Colony, for the ability and energy displayed by him in successfully conducting the case of this island before the Fisheries Commission which sat at Halifax in 1877, appointed as a Tribunal of Arbitration under the terms of the Washington Treaty

" A. L. W McNeily,

" April 18th, 1879   " Speaker."

The result of the Halifax Commission is well known, its great success was largely due to the tact and ability of the secretary, Sir Henry G. Bergne Five-and-a-half million dollars were accorded by the Commissioners, and out of this amount the handsome sum of one million to Newfoundland under the following award —

" The undersigned Commissioners, appointed under Articles XXII and XXIII. of the Treaty of Washington, of the 8th of May 1871, to determine, having regard to the privileges accorded by the United States to the subjects of Her Britannic Majesty, as stated in Articles XIX and XXI of the said Treaty, the amount of any compensation which, in their opinion, ought to be paid by the Government of the United States to the Government of Her Britannic Majesty in return for the privileges accorded to the citizens of the United States under Article XVIII. of the said Treaty, having carefully and impartially examined the matters referred to them according to justice and equity, in conformity with the solemn declaration made and subscribed by them on the 15th day of June 1877, award the sum of five millions five hundred thousand dollars in gold to be paid by the Government of the United States to the Government of Her Britannic Majesty, in accordance with the provisions of the said Treaty.

" Signed at Halifax this 23rd day of November 1877.

" MAURICE DELFOSSE
" A. T. GALT."

A number of gentlemen in the Council and Assembly took part in the discussion when the award was considered Speeches were made by Hon A W Harvey, Sir Ambrose Shea, and Sir William Whiteway, they throw light on the subject, and bring out in a very distinct and emphatic way the immense value of our fisheries— the greatest cod-fishery in the world—and the magnitude of the interests at stake before the Commission

The Hon. A. W. Harvey spoke as follows on this occasion :—

" The amount of the award made by the Commission is declared by the Americans to be out of all proportion to the privileges of fishery they have obtained, and to no part of the award did they object so vehemently as to the

HON. A. W. HARVEY.
By S. H. Parsons.

portion allotted to Newfoundland; in fact, they insisted that Newfoundland should be ruled out of court altogether. By reference to the terms of the Washington Treaty it will be seen that they do not specify what the remuneration, if any were awarded, was to be paid for. They do not say, for instance, that if the fishery privileges granted are ten times more valuable than those given to us on the coasts of the United States, the award should be proportioned to that. Nor do they say that the extent to which the United States fishermen used those fisheries over and above the extent to which British fishermen used the United States fisheries, should be the gauge of compensation. It is the value of the privilege of fishing the claim was based on, which was a very difficult and intricate matter to get hold of and decide upon. If the value of the fisheries were to be a basis, then five million dollars would not be a tithe of what the United States should have to pay for their use of the fisheries of Newfoundland, New Brunswick, and Nova Scotia: and he should have said that one million dollars would be utterly inadequate to represent the value of our fisheries, if that were to be the standard, as we contended they were worth more than all the fisheries the United States fishermen were admitted to participate in on the coasts of the other provinces. There would be hardly a disputation that the fisheries between Cape Ray and Cape John were of more worth than the combined fisheries of the neighbouring colonies; and if upon that principle the award had been decided, we should have received more than two million five hundred thousand dollars of the whole sum. But as that would have been manifestly unfair, I consider the ends of justice were more conserved by paying this Colony one million dollars than the larger amount. No doubt the Nova Scotia fisheries are far more interfered with by the United States fishermen than are ours, and the extent to which they use, and will use them, is four times greater than the use they will make of ours; therefore I consider we had made an uncommonly good bargain in securing the proportion of the award that has been paid to us."

The Hon. A. Shea said :—

" He regarded this issue as involving much more than the money consideration, for it established the value ascribed by an impartial authority to a right to participate in our fisheries for 12 years, and the House would see the importance of this decision in the event of any future negotiation in which it became necessary to appraise the worth of the fisheries of this country. And it had this further great value, that looking at the temper of the American people on the subject of the award, they would not be likely to ask for a renewal of the case, and in thus becoming rid of the presence of active competition in our fisheries, we should be gainers in a degree far beyond any supposable amount to be desired as alleged compensation for the privilege of participation."

Sir W V Whiteway, the Attorney-General, after acknowledging the vote of thanks, concluded by saying :—

"For some years after the signing of the Washington Treaty it appeared to be very doubtful whether or not the Halifax Commission would ever sit. The question was international between Great Britain and the United States. Numerous despatches were interchanged between the two Governments in reference to the subject At length, in the year 1876, official information reached us to the effect that the Commission would probably sit in 1877, and we were required by the Imperial Government to prepare our case. Two members of the Executive the Hon. Mr. Donnelly and myself, were nominated to perform this duty We did so, and had our case ready to submit to the British Agent, Mr Ford who with Mr. Bergne visited St John's on his way to England from Canada, where they had been engaged for about two months with the fishery officials of the Dominion and several eminent counsel in the preparation of the Canadian part of the case. The stay of Messrs Ford and Bergne here was short, some two weeks only, as our prepared case needed little or no alteration, a re-arrangement being all that was required to make it accord with the case of Canada And here it affords me infinite pleasure to refer to the eminent services rendered by the hon. Surveyor-General. Mr Donnelly. The services rendered by Judge Bennett, Mr Fraser, and Mr Kelligrew may be gathered from the records of the Commission. By their evidence and by about twenty affidavits our case was sustained, and there was not a point which was not secured I may say it was not only nailed home, but each nail was clinched, and our position rendered invulnerable On the part of the United States there were about seventy witnesses examined and a similar number on behalf of Canada, in addition to which they each produced between two and three hundred affidavits. A treaty had been entered into between Great Britain and the United States, by which the United States had conceded to Great Britain the right of fishing upon a certain part of the American coast and a free market in the United States for Canadian and Newfoundland caught fish and produce, and in return Great Britain had conceded to the United States the right of fishing in Canadian and Newfoundland waters in common with British subjects We alleged that the value of our concession was greater than that made by the United States This Commission, appointed by virtue of the treaty, was to try that question, and to award the difference in value, if any, to Great Britain. Now, the United States counsel candidly admitted, first, that the concession to us to fish in American waters was of no value to us, as we could never use it; and secondly, it was our argument at the trial and clearly proved that for us to have the right of importing into the United States our fish and fish produce duty free was an advantage to the United States as a nation , it gave them a cheaper article, upon the principle that the consumer always paid the duty, and in this case it was shown by conclusive evidence that, duty or no duty, the Canadian exporter of mackerel had averaged about the same returns in his account sales A duty simply operated as a protection to the United States fishing interests as a distinct business To take it off was an injury to that interest, but a benefit to the United States as a nation It was with the nation that Great Britain was dealing . therefore the concession of a right of fishing on the American coast was admitted to be valueless, and the right of free market was shown to be a benefit to the United States and no additional value to us. On the other hand, Newfoundland conceded to the United States a free right of fishing on the coast from Ramea Islands by Cape Race to Cape John What was the value of this concession ? Had the Commission found nothing in our favour what would have been the effect hereafter in British negotiators with the United States and with France ? Let us for a moment suppose the case of Great Britain proposing to us to give the French a free right of fishing all along our coast, with a view to the solution of our so-called French Shore difficulty. We know that this course would prove our ruin, but the argument of Great Britain to us would have been unanswerable :—' You have had

SIR W. V. WHITEWAY, K.C.M.G.
By S. H. Parsons.

'the opportunity of a solemn inquiry before a 'disinterested tribunal sitting in the very centre 'of your fisheries, where every facility was at 'hand for fully investigating their value, and the 'conclusion arrived at, after six months inquiry 'by that tribunal, was, that a right to fish along 'your coast was not worth anything." I venture to say that probably the true position and importance of this inquiry was not generally appreciated here at the time of this Commission, or we should not have had loose, ill-considered opinions expressed. The decision had established that which would for all time endure to the benefit of the country. It has been decided after a most rigid investigation that the right to fish along a portion of our coast for 12 years, under the facts given in evidence, is worth one million dollars. We have now an established basis, and I look upon this as of the greatest importance, and that upon which we cannot set too high a value."

Sir Frederic Carter having taken his seat upon the Bench, first as Assistant Judge, and in 1880 as Chief Justice, in succession to Sir Hugh W. Hoyles, who had been compelled to retire by failing health, the conduct of affairs devolved on Sir William Whiteway, K.C.M.G.; he showed himself most progressive in his ideas. In 1880 he passed the first Railway Bill for a light railway from St. John's to Hall's Bay.[1]

---

[1] THE HALL'S BAY RAILWAY.

The Bill was founded on the following report, prepared by a Joint Committee of the Legislative Council and the House of Assembly, and is an admirable résumé of the reasons for building the railway :—

"April 2nd, 1880.

"The Joint Committee of the Council and House of Assembly appointed to consider the question of constructing a railway in this island, have to report that they have given the most careful consideration to this matter, and beg to state the result of their deliberations.

"The question of the future of our growing population has for some time engaged the earnest attention of all thoughtful men in this country, and has been the subject of serious solicitude. The fisheries being our main resource, and to a large extent the only dependence of the people, those periodic partial failures which are incident to such pursuits continue to be attended with recurring visitations of pauperism, and there seems no remedy to be found for this condition of things but

that which may lie in varied and extensive pursuits.

"This reflection would apply with force to the present population, but when we contemplate it in relation to our increasing numbers, the necessity of dealing with the subject urgently presses itself on our consideration.

"Our fisheries have no doubt increased, but not in a measure corresponding to our increase of population. And even though they were capable of being further expanded, that object would be largely neutralised by the decline in price which follows from a large catch, as no increase of markets can be found to give remunerative returns for an augmented supply.

"It is evident, therefore, that no material increase of means is to be looked for from our fisheries, and that we must direct our attention to other sources to meet the growing requirements of the country. Our mining industry may now be regarded as an established fact. Large areas of geological formation similar to that in which the mines are being successfully worked are known to

In the autumn of 1880 the survey was completed from St. John's to Harbour Grace. Tenders were received from various capitalists

exist, and there is every reason to believe from recent explorations that a great amount of wealth in copper and other ores is waiting the application of enterprise and capital to bring them into profitable use Our agricultural industry, though prosecuted to a valuable extent, is yet susceptible of very enlarged development. Vast stretches of agricultural land, extending from Trinity Bay north, along the heads of Bonavista Bay, Gander Bay, and Exploits River, as well as on the west coast, need only the employment of well directed labour to convert them into means of independent support for thousands of the population

" We have in this town a large market for agricultural produce and live stock, which at present is mainly supplied from abroad, and as an illustration of what may be done by the cultivation of the land when a market is within reach, we have the fact that amongst the most prosperous of our labouring people are those who live by the land in the vicinity of St. John's, though the average conditions of fertility are far below those which exist in the interior of the Island There are indications, moreover, leading to the conclusion that we shall hereafter be more dependent than before on home supply of live stock, for in those places from which we have hitherto received our meat supplies, attention is being given to the English market, which is supposed to offer better prospects, and an advanced value may therefore be reasonably anticipated

" With an improved market on the spot the inquiry is further suggested whether this Colony should not become an exporter of live stock to England, and we have little difficulty in affirming this position For grazing purposes we have large tracts that, we believe, cannot be surpassed in British North America, and when we regard our proximity to England, and the all-important consideration of a short voyage for live stock, the advantages we possess in this connection are too manifest to be subject of question or argument

" But to what end do these elements of wealth exist if they continue to remain neglected? For they will as before be outside the reach of the people if some energetic effort be not made to render them accessible to our centres of population. We have means of remunerative employment in those dormant resources, coincident with the spectacle so often about us of unemployed labour, and we cannot but feel that the Government fails in its duty if it have the power and does not employ it in connecting those resources with that industry, which ought to receive its satisfactory reward

" Your Committee believe that no agency would be so effective for the promotion of the objects in view as that of a railway, and when they consider that there is no Colony of equal importance under the Crown without a railroad, and the advantages thereby conferred elsewhere in the enhancement of the value of property and labour, it is felt that in our circumstances no effort within the means of the Colony should be wanting to supply this great desideratum.

" They are not unmindful of the financial considerations involved, but having regard to the influence of such a work in elevating the people and enlarging the area of profitable industry, the Committee are convinced that ample compensation will be found in the improved condition of the country for any outlay the undertaking may require.

" We do not regard it per se as an enterprise that will pay, or as one that offers attraction to speculators, but as the work of the country, and in its bearing on the promotion of the well-being of the people, in which the returns are alone sought and will be found, it eminently commends itself to our judgment In this sense we believe that, in time, it will amply pay its cost, and that the consequent advance in the comfort and independence of the people will fully attest the wisdom of its establishment.

" The Committee are of opinion that the present financial condition of the Colony makes the time favourable for entering on the project, and that it may be undertaken on conditions which will not unduly press upon our resources

" The Committee believe that a narrow gauge road might be constructed at a comparatively moderate cost, and that it would be found well adapted to the circumstances of this Colony, as well in regard to our means as to the physical condition of the country. The road should be made from St John's through the peninsula of Avalon, and the favoured agricultural and timber regions north, to the mineral district, connecting the principal towns and settlements in Conception Bay and along the proposed line. Your Committee have had reference to the survey made in 1875, and it would seem to be ample for preliminary purposes, so far as it affects the district of Avalon and along the route already examined to the northern point indicated, but a further survey would be required to establish the immediate location of that, as well as of such branch lines as shall seem to be necessary and practicable for the carrying out of the proposed project

" Your Committee therefore recommend the introduction and passage of an Act to construct the line The Premier moved a resolution to refer the consideration of the various proposals to a joint committee of both Houses. On the recommendation of this committee, a provisional contract was made and a charter afterwards granted to the Newfoundland Railway Company. The principal points in the contract provided that the company were to build a substantial, reliable, and efficient railroad of three feet six inches gauge, subject to the approval of the Government engineer, and were to continuously operate and maintain the same, and to complete the whole line to Hall's Bay within five years, the Government to pay an annual subsidy of $180,000 per annum for thirty-five years, the subsidy to attach as each five miles of road was completed and passed by the Government engineer, a large land grant of five thousand acres per mile was to be given for each completed mile It is due to Sir William Whiteway to say that he was always in favour of the Government constructing the line themselves

On the 9th of August 1881 the railway was actually commenced, and at the close of the working season twenty miles were graded, and ten miles metalled, very large sums of money were expended in labour on the line. During the ensuing winter hundreds of men were employed north and south cutting sleepers. The money thus spent in construction and in purchase of the right of way was found most beneficial, it came on the whole community like the gentle rain from Heaven, its refreshing dews descended alike on the friends and opponents of the new enterprise, its rills trickled into everyone's pocket—merchant, trader, small shopkeeper, all alike experienced the good results of this large outflow of money to the railway labourers. In his opening speech to the Legislature in 1882, Sir

---

authorising the raising by loan of the required amount in sums not exceeding five hundred thousand dollars in any one year, and providing an organisation for carrying out the object in accordance with the views contained in this Report The Committee further recommend that the Executive Government apply to Her Majesty's Government, requesting that they will guarantee the interest on the bonds of the Colony for such amount as may be required for the purpose of constructing the railroad, within the sum of one million pounds sterling, and we cannot doubt that this will meet with a favourable response when Her Majesty's Government are made aware of the exceptionally sound and healthy condition of our finances

" All of which is respectfully submitted

" (Signed)   W V WHITEWAY,
                        " Chairman.

      " P G TESSIER
      " C R AYRE
      " ROBT THORBURN
      " A SHEA
      " JOHN RORKE
      " JOSEPH I LITTLE
      " ROBT J KENT
      " A M MACKAY."

Ordered, That the said Report be received

Frederic Carter, Administrator of the Government, announced to the Legislature :—

"That the leading industries of the country had, during the previous year, been prosecuted successfully on the whole, and that mining showed a considerably enlarged export of copper ore, and prospects of a further development in the immediate future. He referred to the railway as progressing satisfactorily in construction, conferring important benefits on the people, and causing a large monetary expenditure in the country. This great work, he said, is an enterprise which, in the increase of commercial and social communication, and the development of our agricultural and mineral resources, contains the elements of solid and lasting prosperity for Newfoundland.

"The revenue was found to be in a very flourishing condition, amounting to $1,003,803, being the largest ever received.

THE DRY DOCK, ST. JOHN'S.

From a photograph.

"The Administrator further informed the Legislature that the imperial authorities had at length authorised the local Government to make land grants, and issue mining licences on that part of the coast on which the French have fishery privileges. This was the boon for which the Colony had been pleading in vain for many years. Its importance to the people of Newfoundland can hardly be overrated. It is a virtual settlement of the vexed French Shore question, and a removal of a serious and long-standing grievance. It opens the half of the island, which had hitherto been closed to the people, to settlement and industrial enterprise. It enfranchises the population of this part of the island, who are in future to have two representatives in the local Legislature, and removes all restrictions on the exercise of territorial rights. The Administrator very justly connected this concession with the name of Sir William Whiteway, to whose able and persevering representations the country is largely indebted for a settlement of this vexed question.

" The coincidence, said the Administrator, of the improved conditions to which I have adverted with the inauguration of the Newfoundland railway, marks an era of progress which is a meet subject of congratulation to the country."

1882 was a period of enterprise, a shaking up of the dry bones; besides the railway, two other great works were initiated, the construction of the dry dock at River Head and the Rope Walk. The dock is over 600 feet long, one hundred and thirty-two at its widest part, with twenty-five feet over the gate sill at high water; it is large enough to admit the largest ocean steamer afloat. It was built by the patentees, J. E. Simpson & Co., of New York. The work began in May 1883, and in December 1884 H.M.S. *Tenedos* was docked, and the great work formally occupied. The patentees agreed to lease the dock for ten years at $15,000 per annum. Owing to a dispute between the lessees and the Government about the cost of dredging and the nonpayment of rent, the dock has been taken out of Messrs. Simpson's hands, and is now under lease to Messrs. Harvey & Angel for $11,000 per annum. The dock has been a magnificent success; it is of very great benefit and convenience to the trade, gives almost constant employment to tradesmen, and keeps in the colony thousands of dollars which would be otherwise expended abroad.

The most important social industry in St. John's is the Rope Walk. As a great fishing country Newfoundland uses an enormous amount of lines and twines, netting, cordage, and cables; until quite recently all these articles were imported, principally from the West of England, latterly from New England. The Colonial Cordage Company was founded by the energy and enterprise of the Hon. M. Monroe, a brother of the distinguished Judge Monroe, of the Higher Court in Ireland. Aided by local and foreign capital, he inaugurated a work which gives employment to a large number of workpeople, and circulates money in the

HON. M. MONROE.

Colony. The goods turned out by this company are all of the very finest quality. Instead of importing all our cordage from abroad, the bulk of the lines, twines, nets, and cables used in our fishery are now made in the country. Whilst the initiation of the enterprise was the work of the Hon. M. Monroe, its successful working is mainly attributed to the practical skill, tact, and good judgment of his brother, the sole managing partner, James H. Monroe.[1]

THE COLONIAL CORDAGE COMPANY'S MILL.

The events of the next succeeding years, from 1883 forwards, are fresh in the memories of all, and it is not needful to dwell with minute particularity over circumstances with which all Newfoundland readers are familiar. One unpleasant subject I should like to pass over, the virulence, mendacity, and misrepresentation with which the promoters of the railway and the graving dock were assailed. The most monstrous fictions were invented to set the people against these new enterprises. This resulted in a very serious disturbance.

In 1881 the inhabitants of the south shore of Conception Bay, believing that all unutterable evils would happen to them if the line

[1] The Rope Walk is owned and operated by a local joint stock company, the Colonial Cordage Company, Limited, of St. John's, Newfoundland. It gives constant and steady employment to upwards of 500 people—men, boys, and girls—in the manufacture of cables and cordage of all kinds, fishing lines of every description, and all sorts of netting, sieves, and cod traps. It is situate at Monday Pond, convenient to the railroad.

This concern was originally built in 1882, and burned down in December 1885. The present buildings are of a more substantial nature in brick and stone. They were pushed forward with great energy, operations being commenced the following July, only six months after the destruction of the old buildings. The machinery is of the most improved description, and the goods manufactured are quite equal to anything produced in England or the United States.

went through their lands, stoned the engineers, took away their instruments, and drove them from their work. The inspector of police, Mr. Carty, and the police magistrate, with only eleven men, were left to contend with a mad, excited crowd of about five hundred men and women armed with guns and every variety of weapon. The arrest of the ringleader at the point of the bayonet, and the firm action of the police authorities, eventually restored order. All this unseemly,

THE ROPE WALK.

dangerous disturbance was directly caused by the unscrupulous fabrication of falsehoods to stir up these poor, ignorant people to oppose the railway.[1]

For five days the whole population from Topsail to Indian Pond were in an insane state of excitement. Though it was the busiest time of the year, they never did a stroke of work; all day long they watched

[1] This riot has been generally known as the "Battle of Fox Trap." The people of the south shore were told by a leading merchant in the west end of St. John's that if the railway were carried out a "tall gate" (toll gate) would be erected near the Long Bridge, and every man going into town with a horse and cart would have to pay fifty cents; that their little farms and horses would be taxed, and they would be ruined. They further believed that if the tape was once carried over their ground, it would be taken from them.

the engineers and the small posse of police, and followed them from place to place. From Topsail to Indian Pond the whole population believed the advent of this terrible monster, the railway, meant their ruin. Thanks to the wise counsels of the Rev. Jeremiah O'Donnell, the people of Holyrood and Harbour Main never made the slightest opposition to the line.

It is not necessary in the present day to say anything in favour of one of the greatest factors in the promotion of modern civilization and progress—the railway; however useful and beneficial it may be in an old settled country, it is a positive and absolute necessity for the development and settlement of new territory. Looking at the position of our most important northern out-ports,

SIR HENRY MAXSE.

with their great timber and mineral wealth, developed and undeveloped, communication with them by railway, especially in winter, is the only

HON. J. I. LITTLE.
By S. H. Parsons.

possible means of intercourse. It was one of the insuperable objections to the line that it could never run in severe winter weather; however, experience shows us that by good management the railway will never be retarded, even by the worst weather, beyond a few hours. When the coast is blocked by ice, when all travelling by road is impossible, the trains to Whitbourne and Placentia have run their course almost as punctually as in the finest summer weather. So far the railroad is the most complete, the most safe and convenient road and mode of communication the wit of man has been able to devise; no other enterprise of modern times so benefits the working man or distributes labour in so generally beneficial a manner.

The year 1883 is distinguished for the painful episode of the Harbour Grace riot; it was not only a most regrettable incident, owing to

K K

the deplorable loss of life, but also for the dire feelings of revenge and hatred it called forth. Three men were killed belonging to the Orange procession and one on the Catholic side. The police authorities at Harbour Grace . . . . ng, yet no . . . . en to keep the rival fac . . . . fatal . . . . disastrous effects, both so . . . . It upset . . . . Assembly and the trials, ... xhibition of . . . . prejudice, were by no means edifying. The whole trouble was begotten of fanaticism, and it ended in a complete fiasco.

In 1885 there was a new deal of the political cards, and considerable shuffling. Sir W. V. Whiteway, who had been Premier during two parliaments, resigned, and a new party was formed, known as the "Thorburn Administration." It was intended at first to be a

genuine Protestant Government, worked on sound commercial principles; it was to inaugurate a new reign of moderate progress, economy, and no amalgamation; it ended by building the expensive railway to Placentia, and the Thorburn turnpike road to Broad Cove, the best constructed and the most costly road in the Colony. Its stern principles of "no amalgamation with Catholics" soon died away.

SIR R. THORBURN.
By Bassano.

The Thorburn Administration will ever be memorable for their bold policy in the inauguration of the Bait Act, the construction of the Placentia Railway,[1] and the inception of the new line to Hall's Bay. They added one fine touch of humour to the annals of our constitutional history, the construction of the Placentia Railway under the disguise of a road. One member of the Executive, when attacked in the Legislative Council on this subject, solemnly declared that he was not aware that the Government were building a railway, and when he found out that the so-called road was the veritable Placentia Railway he resigned.

---

[1] This railway was built, so it is said, to obtain the adhesion of the two Members for the district, Hon. W. J. S. Donnelly and the Speaker, G. H. Emerson. Each of these eminent legislators cost the Colony $250,000. Another account of the reasons for building the Placentia Railway and the admission of Catholics to the ministry is given by a friend of Sir G. Wm. Des Vœux. He and the Governor were standing on Colinet Bridge; they were on their way to Placentia; they could plainly hear the sound of the railway whistle at Whitbourne. The Governor then and there determined to use his influence to build the Placentia branch railway. My informant also states that it was the Governor's objection to the gentleman named as Colonial Secretary that caused the Ministry to seek for Catholic allies.

To some of the stern unbending Tories of Water Street, the railway was the unclean thing, hence this thin disguise; it was altogether too transparent to deceive the public.

The convention between England and France, made in 1884 relative to French fishery rights in Newfoundland, was submitted to the Newfoundland Government in 1884, by Sir Clare Ford and Mr. E. B. Pennell, C.M.G.; with certain modifications it received a qualified approval, but the Whiteway Cabinet absolutely refused to hold a special session of the Legislature to recommend its adoption. In 1885, on the change of Government, Mr. E. B. Pennell, C.M.G., of the Colonial Office, was again sent out to Newfoundland with an amended convention to confer with the local authorities on the subject, and to endeavour to make an arrangement. The negotiations resulted, however, in the Joint Committee of the House of Assembly and the Council absolutely refusing to ratify the Ford-Pennell Convention, unless the French would agree to withdraw or modify their bounties; concurrently the committee drafted, and both Houses passed, the first Bait Act of 1886. In substance it empowered the Executive to prohibit the capture in our waters for exportation or sale of bait fishes, except under special licence to be issued by the Receiver General under the authority of the Governor in Council.

SIR G. W. DES VŒUX, K.C.M.G.

If carried out efficiently it would stop all the supply of bait to the French from our south coast. The French made every effort to induce the Imperial Government to refuse their sanction to the Act, and in the Governor's speech of 1887 Sir G. W. Des Vœux informed the Legislature that Her Majesty would not sanction the Bill. The Governor's despatch in favour of the proposed measure, and the address from the House of Assembly sent home with the second Bait Bill in 1887, are both very able and well-written documents.

Sir G. W. Des Vœux wrote on January 14, 1887, to Sir H. Holland; after referring to the matter generally, he concluded :—

"25. Though this measure, if allowed, would to a large extent place the fish production in this neighbourhood within the control of the people of this Colony, they have no desire to monopolize it, and I feel satisfied that they would willingly modify the provisions of the measure in favour of such Governments as would grant a proportional reciprocity

"25. Without of course being able to speak with certainty as to the amount of concession that would be granted by the Legislature in any particular case, I have very good reason for believing that, as regards the United States, the right of obtaining bait would be restored on the opening of the American markets to Newfoundland fish, or (if common cause be made with Canada) to all British fish, while in view of the greater expense involved in maintaining the fishery from head-quarters on the other side of the Atlantic, I believe that in the case of the French the abolition or a substantial reduction of the export bounties would alone be held sufficient, even though the other bounties and the prohibition of the import of British fish were still retained   In a word, the principle that the colonists desire to maintain is, 'Live and let live,' and they merely object to that of 'Let others live by killing us'

"26. But whether the views of the colonists on this subject are just or not (and after much and anxious consideration of the subject I am bound to say that, in my opinion, they are based on very substantial grounds), the proposed measure of prohibition, as in no way affecting the Treaty rights of foreign Powers, can scarcely be contended to be otherwise than such as is within the competence of the local Legislature under the existing constitution of the Colony, and, indeed, if the same object had been aimed at by more indirect means, and a Bill had been passed imposing a prohibitive duty on bait exported in foreign vessels, it appears open to doubt whether, under my existing instructions, I should have been justified in refusing assent to it

"27. But however this may be, any question as to the competence in the mat of the Colonial Legislature has been practically set at rest by the recent allowance of the Canadian Bill, which, I am informed, adopts almost precisely similar means for procuring an analogous object   And as the importance of the fisheries to the Dominion is moreover incomparably less, for the reasons above given, than to this Colony, it may be presumed that the disallowance of the Newfoundland Bill, which would appear probable from the long delay of decision, is due to some Imperial consideration which applies either not at all, or in a considerably less degree, to the case of Canada.   If this be so, as indeed there are other reasons for believing, I would respectfully urge that in fairness the heavy resulting loss should not, or at all events not exclusively, fall upon this Colony, and that if in the national interest a right is to be withheld from Newfoundland which naturally belongs to it, and the possession of which makes to it all the difference between wealth and penury, there is involved on the part of the nation a corresponding obligation to grant compensation of a value equal, or nearly equal, to that of the right withheld.

"31 I would respectfully urge that, in the absence of a fixed decision against this measure, the delay which has already taken place in respect of its allowance should not be further prolonged.

"32. Now that I fully comprehend the present position of the Colony, it is to me no longer a matter of wonder that the Legislature has hitherto failed to ratify the proposed Arrangement with France, indeed, I can scarcely conceive it possible that this Arrangement will ever be accepted so long as the Bait Clause remains in it, and no security is taken that the export bounties will not be maintained on their present footing.

" 33 For though all the other articles have the appearance of concession on the part of the French, and some are, no doubt, substantial concessions, they are all immeasurably outweighed by the single concession required on the part of this Colony For if there were granted to the French an inalienable right to procure bait here, the future, not only of the coast where they already have fishing rights but of the whole Colony, would practically be placed within the control of their Government Even if the present bounties should prove insufficient, it would require but a slight addition to them, involving an exceedingly small cost by comparison with the enormous expenditure of France, to destroy the trade of this Colony altogether, and at once, and in view of the great importance attached to these fisheries by the French, as the means of maintaining the strength of their navy, it would appear by no means improbable that such an attempt would be made if there were thus withdrawn the only means of preventing its success And this probability appears the greater, when it is considered that the cessation of British productions with the cause in operation that would render its recovery impossible would, in all probability, produce a rise in the market value of fish, which would eventually render unnecessary the continuance of any bounty, so that the additional expenditure on the part of France would be only a temporary sacrifice that would secure a permanent economical gain

" 34 As the matter at present appears to me, it seems deserving of the consideration of Her Majesty's Government whether it would, under any circumstances be politic to place in the hands of the French a weapon capable of being used with such terrible effect against British interests, and whether, without the security for the discontinuance of the bounties on their present footing as above referred to, it would be wise to make further effort for the passing of the Arrangement while the Bait Clause is included in it.

" 35. In conclusion, I would respectfully express, on behalf of this suffering Colony, the earnest hope that the vital interests of 200 000 British subjects will not be disregarded out of deference to the susceptibilities of any foreign Power, and this especially when the privilege which that Power desires to retain cannot be pretended to be matter of right, but is a benefit which may be lawfully withdrawn, as in the nature of a tenancy at will, and may now be justly withdrawn as being used for the infliction of fatal injury on those who have hitherto permitted its enjoyment. Sincerely hoping that the fulfilment of the desire of Newfoundland may be no longer delayed, and that I may be able to meet the Legislature next month with the announcement that this important Bill has already received Her Majesty's gracious allowance and confirmation, I have, &c

" G. William des Vœux "

The House declared :—

" It was with feelings of profound disappointment and regret that we learned from His Excellency's speech, at the opening of the present Session of the Legislature, and from your despatch to him of the 3rd instant, that Her Majesty will not be advised to give her sanction to this Bill.

" This announcement awakened a public sentiment that has had its expression in the immediate passage of another similar Bill, which took precedence of all other business in the Legislature, and will be transmitted immediately for the approval of Her Majesty's Government. We most earnestly trust that the result of this renewed effort in support of our rights may not be another disappointment with its ruinous consequences.

" When we learn from your despatch that the main reason for the refusal of our Bill is that its present adoption would ' inflict grave loss on the French fishermen,' we cannot forbear from the expression of our surprise at this apparent disregard of the sufferings of our fishermen, and of the British interests which are thus made subservient to the purposes of foreigners The people of this Colony have the right in our fisheries, and foreigners have not, and we cannot see those rights surrendered in defiance of our appeals without expressing our deep sense of the injustice to which our people are thus called on to submit.

"Your despatch sets forth that further information is required to enable Her Majesty's Government to appreciate the true character and bearings of our Bait Bill. The Address of the Legislature, already referred to, in possession of Her Majesty's Government, is pregnant with facts in justification of that measure, and appears to us to exhaust the whole subject. But while we fail to see any want of completeness in the evidence already supplied, every desire is felt to satisfy any further reasonable requirements in this respect.

" It would further appear from your despatch that, in support of the objections to the measure, much importance is given to the fact that the bait traffic has been long recognised, and has only of late been resisted We thought the reasons for this change of view had been fully explained in the representations recently made to Her Majesty's Government The traffic was permitted so long as the bounty-assisted fisheries of France found a market in that country for their produce. But within the last three years the great increase in their fisheries has gone far beyond the requirements of their home markets , and we find them meeting us in Spain, Italy, and other European countries, and, with the bounty equal to 60 per cent. of the value of the fish, they are fast supplanting us ; the reduced value of our staple industry from this cause already representing a fairly estimated sum of £250,000 per annum, under conditions that menace us with a still more serious decline. In these facts, our change of view of the bait traffic is but too well warranted, and we have abundant reason for the application of the remedy provided in the Bait Act. In furnishing our rivals with bait, we promote the evils we have to contend with, and our only course is to terminate this suicidal traffic.

"We are but too conscious that, from the causes referred to, the condition of our trade awakens a sense of great anxiety at the present moment; while we have full trust in the future, if only permitted by Her Majesty's Government to legislate as we see fit for the protection of what belongs to us We regret we cannot safely accept your view of waiting to test, by further experience, the question how much longer and to what further extent our trade will bear up against the adverse influences that now prevail. Our ability to sustain ourselves against undue competition would be no argument for obliging us to contribute to its continuance, while the perils of such an experiment are too obvious to warrant its acceptance.

"Her Majesty's Government, in proposing that they should be the judges of the effect of our measures on our local interests, are not, we humbly submit, in a position to discharge that duty with safety or advantage. When it is suggested that, as regards our Bait Act, a consultation with the French may lead to a remedy being found in some other direction for the admitted evils, this proposal would appear to have originated with a want of knowledge of the situation A free supply of bait to the French from our coasts means the effacement of our British trade and the exodus of our population, and forbids all thought of possible equivalents. We, moreover, must decline respectfully to accept the view that the French, or any other foreign Power, has a status or consultative claim in the control or disposition of our property, and we humbly demur to any recognition of their pretensions in this respect We acknowledge no authority but that of the Imperial Government, and their rights of dominion are wisely limited by our constitutional powers, which secure for us the free exercise of our instructed intelligence in the management of our local affairs.

"The decision of Her Majesty's Government leaves us to deal with disheartening prospects for another year, the effects being already seen in the restriction and abandonment of proposed enterprise; but we cannot believe that any alleged difficulties will be allowed further to supersede the rights and mar the fortunes of the loyal people of this Colony struggling to maintain their position as an independent and honourable appendage of the British Crown."

In 1887, when our delegates were sent to England to press on the sanction of the Bait Act, their arrival, most fortunately for our interests, coincided with the holding of the Colonial Conference in London. Our Premier, then Mr. Thorburn, soon made Sir Robert, represented the most ancient colony; he was the premier of colonial premiers. In claiming our rights to control and legislate for our own fisheries we had all the colonies on our side but Canada; she demanded from the Colonial Office that the Act should be disallowed, and even if allowed, the penal clauses should be altered. Our representatives gave an assurance that Canadian fishermen were "to be placed upon the same footing as our own." Whilst we must all do justice to the able and earnest efforts of our delegates, Sir A. Shea and Sir R. Thorburn, the fortunate coinci-

dence of their visit and the conference of all the Colonial Premiers gave great weight to our demand for the Imperial sanction to the Bait Act; in the Jubilee Year of Her Majesty's accession, the Colonial Office dare not be so ungracious as to refuse us the exercise of a right in which we would be sustained by every Colonial statesman then in London.

The British Government, having most reluctantly assented to the Bait Act, made it a condition that the Act should not be put in force until the following spring (1888).

The year 1887 will be ever me-

HER MAJESTY THE QUEEN.
By Bassano.

morable as the Jubilee of our Gracious Sovereign Queen Victoria. The occasion called out a grand exhibition of loyalty over the vast Empire whose drum-beat now encircles the world. In St. John's an impressive Jubilee service was held in the Anglican cathedral of St. John the Baptist, and was attended by all denominations.

The subsequent history of this important question of the Bait Act is well known to Newfoundland readers. I was requested by the Thorburn Government to put the Act in operation. In March 1888 I found myself one morning suddenly transformed from a peaceful District Judge into the commander of a fleet; the French called me "Bombarde Admiral," and our tugs "the Ironclads." We had very great difficulty in getting free from the ice; the old *Hercules*, however, butted her way round Cape Spear, and the S.S. *Lady Glover* followed in her wake; we managed to "clear our skirts," whilst the *Curlew* and *Portia* were detained for a long time at Trepassy. The initial difficulties attending a very arduous undertaking were thus overcome.

The year 1892 will ever be memorable in the Colony as a period of calamity, beginning with the great disaster in Trinity Bay, and followed by the fire of July. In January all the English-speaking world mourned for the death of the Duke of Clarence; sincere and widespread sympathy was felt for the bereaved prince and for the mother, the beloved Danish princess, endeared to all English hearts. In February occurred one of those terrible calamities and loss of human life which vividly impress us with the terrible dangers to which our hardy fishermen, who earn their bread upon the waters, are daily and hourly exposed.

Saturday, the 28th of February 1892, is a dark day in the annals of Trinity, a day to be ever remembered and mourned. The morning sun ushered in a lovely dawn, the sky was clear, a soft, bright, balmy air blew from the land over the treacherous sea, the light breeze scarcely ruffled its bosom. From Trinity, and every harbour adjacent, boats were out by early dawn in pursuit of seals, which had been seen the previous evening. From Trinity, Ship Cove, Trouty, English Harbour, Salmon Cove, and other

SIR HENRY BLAKE, K.C.M.G.
By W. & C. Downey.

small places, the daring ice-hunters set off with high hopes and buoyant spirits to chase the wary seal; in this most exciting and dangerous pursuit the Newfoundlander recks not of danger; difficulties and perils that would affright one unaccustomed to the icefields are mere sport to the hardy native. On this eventful day seals were few and scattered; in the fierce excitement of the chase many went far out into the bay, heedless of the coming tempest; a few of the older fishermen, especially those from Trinity, more wary, and probably less vigorous, noticed the first signs of the storm, and before the icy blast came down with full force they were under the lee of the

land and could row in. Two hundred and fifteen men were out on that
day ; the majority got safe to land after a tremendous struggle for their
lives ; the rest of the unfortunate fishermen, in spite of their heroic
exertions, were finally overpowered ; with strong arms they rowed for
their lives, but the freezing icy tornado swept down upon them and
paralysed their efforts ; they had done all that men could do against the
blizzard ; they fought with the gale whilst instant death appeared on
every wave. One bold crew from English Harbour, seeing all their
attempts to stem the tempest were in vain, made for the ice ; so chilling
was the blast that before the boat had reached the floe, flying before
the wind, one young fellow became paralysed with the cold ; however,
Newfoundlanders in a difficulty are never without resource. They
climbed on to a pan higher than the rest, where they made a rude
shelter ; their boat was broken up to make a fire ; with this and some
seals they managed to live through that awful night. Thirteen fishermen were found frozen to death in their little punts ; eleven others
were driven up the bay and perished in that dark cold night of death.
The hardships that were endured, the sufferings of the poor fellows
that were saved, the agony of suspense for the dear ones on shore, the
heroism of these poor humble souls in their hour of agony is known
only to the Almighty Power " that rules the raging of the sea."   All that
could be done was done to alleviate the distressed ; a gallant crew from
Heart's Delight saved the sixteen men on the ice ; the generous Captain
Fowlow put out in the schooner and succoured some and brought them
home to their agonised families. Charity flowed in to the widows and
orphans ; kindness, open-handed liberality, tender human sympathy was
called forth for the mourners, for those, alas, whose sorrow for the
dead will never die, who all life long will grieve over the death and
destruction of that dark day of storm.

In the course of this History I have often had to chronicle the
ravages of fire ; thrice our capital has been destroyed by the devouring
flame ; the conflagration of the 8th and 9th of July 1892 far exceeded
all former calamities in suddenness and in the immense value of the
property destroyed. The great fire of 1846 began with the upsetting
of a glue-pot in the shop of Hamelin the cabinet-maker, the still greater
fire of July 1892 commenced in a stable, and was, in all probability,
caused by the spark from a careless labourer's pipe. Commencing on a
fine summer's evening, fanned by a high wind, the fire burnt all through
the night, and in the bright dawn of that ever-memorable 9th of July,
ten thousand people found themselves homeless, a forest of chimneys and
heaps of ashes marking where the evening before had stood one of the

busiest and most flourishing towns in the maritime provinces.   Lest I should be accused of prejudice, I prefer giving an account of the disaster

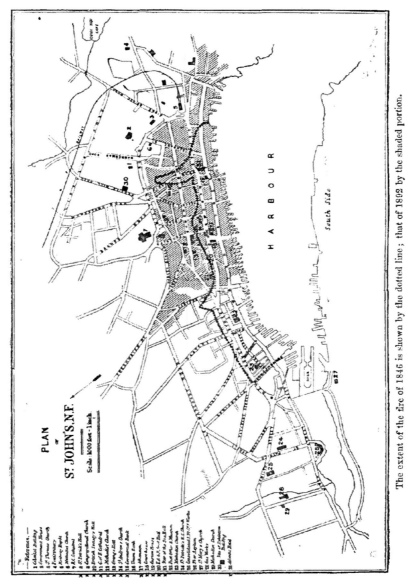

PLAN
OF
ST. JOHN'S, N.F.

Scale 1200 feet - 1 inch.

The extent of the fire of 1846 is shown by the dotted line; that of 1892 by the shaded portion.

from another pen.   Nearly all the following description is taken from the *St. John's Evening Herald* of 10th September 1892 :—

Ever memorable in the annals of St John's will be the 8th day of July 1892. For generations to come the great fire of this year will form a subject for conversation, a period to date from, in the same manner as for the past forty-six years the great fire of the 9th of June 1846 has been. Exactly forty-six years and one month had passed away since the great fire of 1846, and the inhabitants of St John's had come to look upon the fire demon as one that would never again destroy any great portion of our city. We felt secure in the great water power we had, and the almost unlimited quantity which was stored in the natural reservoir at Windsor Lake. In fact, such was our faith in the power of the fire department, and in the supply of water, that when a fire occurred, even at night, but few people ever troubled to arise from their beds to ascertain its whereabouts.

Such was the feeling of security, that when the bells rang the double alarm on Friday, the 8th July, but few people paid any attention to it. The weather had been extremely hot for some weeks before; so much so, that the grass had withered on the high lands, and vegetables were being dried up. Forest fires prevailed in the surrounding country, and for days the air had been laden with the smoke and heat of burning bush and moss Friday was one of the hottest days of the summer, the thermometer registering 87° in the shade at 2 p m. Although the thermometer ranged so high, an unusually strong breeze of wind prevailed all day, decking the harbour with "white caps," and the dust flew about in blinding showers. About five o'clock the Central fire bell rang out an alarm, which was quickly responded to by the firemen, who proceeded to the scene of the conflagration at the junction of Freshwater and Pennywell Roads By the careless handling of a match the stable of Mr. T. Brien had caught fire, and there is not the least doubt that it might have been easily extinguished in its incipient stage, but that not a bucketful of water could be had, for the water-pipes had been undergoing repairs that day, and although the water is said to have been turned on at 3 p m , the water at 5 had not reached the higher levels of the town, and the reservoir, close to the scene of the outbreak, was found to be empty, having been pumped out by the fire brigade at a practice about one month previously With no water to check the devouring element, and a stable full of hay to feed, and a gale of wind to fan the flames, the fire spread with incredible rapidity, leaping from house to house It was speedily seen that the fire was going to assume large proportions, and a call was made for extra aid, which brought many townsfolk to the spot, but although there were many willing hands, there was no water This fact seemed to paralyse the firemen, and the leaping flames flying with such rapidity from house to house, passing over an occasional one, demonstrated the fact that no human effort could stay their onward rush. Whilst one stream of fire rapidly descended Carter's Hill, another swiftly destroyed the buildings on the south side of Harvey Street, and those on Long's Hill, taking in its course the magnificent Methodist College Hall, School, and Home , the Masonic Temple, a comparatively new building, and one that was justly looked upon with great pride by the Masonic fraternity. The destruction of Presbyterian Manse and building near by followed

People began to realise that the fire was going to be one of huge proportions , household goods were hastily packed and taken to places which were thought to be safe, such as the Church of England Cathedral, the Gower Street Methodist Church, and the St. Patrick's Hall. Soon flying pieces of shingle and light wood were scattered over the city, and in less than two hours fires had started in several places. Scotland Row, on Church Hill, was on fire before the Masonic Temple had caught, and a building inside of Chain Rock was burnt down before the fire reached Water Street. The Court House and W. Campbell's supply store caught simultaneously, and before Gower Street Church was on fire. Standing near the Synod Hall one could see a mass of flames rushing down Long's Hill and across the road from the Fire Hall, licking up the brick buildings in front of Victoria Hall as though they were chips. A few firemen, with a short hose, through which feebly filtered a small stream of water, endeavoured to put out a spark of fire which fell on the building north of Mr. Mariott's house; presently it was seen that the Clergy House adjoining Bishop Jones's residence was on fire, and then the roof of the Synod Hall caught. A ladder and some water would have saved these buildings, but there was none at hand, and the chief of the Municipal Council stood and gazed in a helpless manner at the empty hose and the burning buildings.

The fire had now reached that noble edifice the Church of England Cathedral, a work of art, of Gothic design, by Sir Gilbert Scott. Although not quite complete, it was the pride of the city. It had been erected at a cost of about $500,000, the transepts and chancel having been lately added to the nave, which latter had been built forty years previously. Alas, it now lies a magnificent ruin. With the onward sweep of the fire, the heat and the wind increased. Sweeping down over Gower and Duckworth Street, the brick and stone buildings, warehouses, stores, halls, public buildings, and houses on Water Street fell before the flames as speedily as did the wooden buildings higher up. The Union Bank had a narrow

VIEW OF THE ANGLICAN CATHEDRAL AND THE UNION BANK AFTER THE FIRE.

From a photograph.

escape, due no doubt to the fact that it was protected in the front by the large poplar trees standing in the Cathedral grounds.

By 8 o'clock the fire had reached Water Street, and Messrs. Harvey and Co.'s premises, Campbell's, Job Bros. and Co.'s, were on fire in the east, and the Court House to the west of Market House Hill. People on the upper levels were fast hurrying away with their household goods, those who could employing teams and paying exorbitant prices for their hire. Many deposited their belongings in the streets, only to be consumed by the relentless flames, or stolen from them. As the night advanced, the fire swept on from Long's Hill west down over Playhouse

Hill to Beck's Cove, where a vigorous stand was made, which was effectual in stopping its progress west. On Playhouse Hill, near Bates Street, a vigorous effort was made by some noble workers, who formed a fire break by tearing down Dougherty's Forge, thus saving the upper part of the town. The fire, which had taken possession of the buildings on Garrison Hill, was communicated to the St. Patrick's Hall, and notwithstanding the great efforts made by the Christian Brothers and others to save this fine building, it was soon one mass of flames. It was then feared that the fire would spread to the Convent and buildings on Military Road, and a stand was made to save the houses on the north side of Queen's Road. All on the south side were in flames, but the stone chapel belonging to the Congregationalists stood intact. It was here that great want of tact was displayed by those in charge of the fire department. A hose which was engaged in playing on some wooden buildings further to the eastward, and which could not possibly do any service at the time, should have been employed in wetting the side of the Congregational Church. Had such been done, this building, the one opposite, and in all probability the houses of Mr. Greene and of Maxse Terrace, would have

THE ANGLICAN CATHEDRAL AFTER THE FIRE.

From a photograph.

been saved. The fire which had swept down Gower, Duckworth, and Water Streets, crept slowly up Prescott Street, and at the top of King's Road a great effort was made to save the Eastern Fire Hall, which was successful. Had this taken fire all the buildings on Military Road would have been destroyed. Another anger menaced Military Road in the presence of a stable to the south-east of the

Drill Shed, which could not be reached by the hose   On this building for over half-an-hour three of the members of the force worked right valiantly, being supplied with water by a body of citizens, who vied with each other in carrying buckets   It was here that Constable Manning fell, injuring himself somewhat. Owing to the exertions of these policemen and citizens, the Military Road Buildings, the Methodist School on Carew Street, and the Church of England Academy Buildings were saved

The fire had now reached Cochrane Street, and it was hoped that the upper portion of this fine street might be saved   A few lengths of hose were obtained, but not sufficient to reach the burning houses, and the water supply was not what it ought to have been   Several attempts were made to pull down buildings, but as they were supplied with very staunch chimneys, the efforts proved futile until the fire had reached next door to the Hon G T Rendell's residence   The house to southward was partially torn down whilst on fire, saving Mr Rendell's, the only house now standing on the east side of Cochrane Street

About two o'clock, the fire had reached the buildings west of Devon Row   The waterside premises, stores, warehouses, wharves, &c, from Bowring's to Murray's were a mass of ruins   Pitts' Tobacco and Soap Factory was in flames, and it was feared that Devon Row would go, but a vigorous effort on the part of its residents saved it, and the destroying element swept past, consuming the stores of Hon A M McKay, The Tannery, Messrs John Woods & Son's premises, Harvey's Tobacco Factory and Bakery, the Coastal Company's Wharf and Stores, a portion of Hoyles Town, including the Convent School, and the buildings on Signal Hill including the Bavarian Brewery, Lindberg's, W. Canning's, and the American Consul's residences. The preservation of that part of Hoyles Town adjoining the Railway Depôt is due to the hard work done by Manager Noble, of the Railway Company, and his men, who successfully fought the sparks and flames   The St. George's Barracks, which was used as a fever and diphtheria hospital, and several buildings on the crest of the hill had taken fire, and were destroyed early in the evening.   Several vessels lying at the wharves had narrow escapes   The *Nelly, Ethel,* and *Prince Le Boo* moved into the stream, and their rigging and sails caught fire several times   The steamer *Sharpshooter,* brig *Dovre,* the coal hulk *Huntress,* and a number of small boats were burned

About 5 30 a m of the ninth the fire had completed its work of destruction ; fully three-fourths of the city lay in ruins $20,000,000 worth of property had been destroyed, only covered by an insurance of $4,800,000.[1]   Nearly eleven thousand people were homeless, some two thousand houses and stores had been destroyed, and the following public buildings. Church of England Cathedral, Rectory,

---

[1] AMOUNT OF INSURANCE EFFECTED ON PROPERTY IN ST JOHN'S DESTROYED BY THE FIRE		Brought forward	- 3,555,000 $
	$	Manchester - - - -	- 100,000
Liverpool, London, and Globe	- 375,000	Commercial Union - -	- 200,000
Phœnix, London - - -	- 750,000	Imperial - - - -	- 240,000
Atlas - - - -	- 100,000	Lion - - - -	- 50,000
Queen - - - -	- 550,000	City of London - -	- 37,000
Northern - - -	- 300,000	Lancashire - - -	- 30,800
Royal - - -	- 500,000	General - - - -	- 120,000
Norwich Union - - -	- 45,000	Phœnix of Hartford (U S) -	- 38,000
Guardian - - -	- 200,000	Citizens - - - -	- 20,000
North British - - -	- 235,000	London Assurance - -	- 50,000
London and Lancashire - -	- 500,000	Sun (London) - - -	- 150,000
Carried forward -	- 3,555,000	Total - -	- 4,590,800

Clergy House, Synod Hall, Orphanage and Sunday School House; Gower Street Methodist Church, Parsonage, College Hall, School and Home; Presbyterian Church (St. Andrew's), Manse and School House, the Congregational Chapel, Queens Road, Colonial and Continental Church Society's School and Dwelling; the Old Factory, the following public halls St. Patrick's, Athenæum (including the offices of the Savings Bank, Surveyor-General, Government Engineer, and Fisheries Commission), Star of the Sea, Masonic, Victoria, Total Abstinence, Temperance, Mechanics and British, Commercial Bank, City and Academia Club Houses, Temple Billiard Room, Court House and Custom House; St John's Laundry; Hotels: Atlantic, Waverly, Central, and Gordon, City Skating Rink; Factories: Harvey's Bakery and Tobacco, Pitts' Tobacco and Soap, Terra Nova Boiler Works, Lindberg's Brewery, Boot and Shoe Company's Tannery, Printing Offices. *Herald*, *Times*, *Gazette*, *Advocate*, *Telegram*, *Colonist*, and Bowden and Sons; every lawyer's office; all the offices and residences of the principal physicians, the druggist shops of McMurdo & Co, J T O'Mara, Kavanagh, and Hatton, the S.P.G. Depôt, and principal stationers' shops, the business premises and wharves from Bowring's hardware shop to Chain Rock, including Bowring Bros' dry goods shop and eastern store, J & W. Pitts, Goodfellow & Co, Ayre and Sons, G Knowling, Prowse and Sons, J. Baird, Baine Johnston & Co, Clift Wood & Co, S. Woods, W. Frew, Thorburn and Tessier, West and Rendell, Marshall and Rodger, T J Edens, W. Campbell & Co, J H Martin & Co, Job Bros & Co, Rothwell and Bowring, Hearn & Jo, J Stott, Harvey, & Co, Gleeson, S March and Sons, W P Walsh, W. and G. Rendell, Shea & Co, H J Stabb, J Murray, J. Woods and Son, and A J. Harvey, were among the principal ones burnt

The boundaries of the burnt district may be thus particularly described: from Beck's Cove, up Beck's Hill, along Bates Street to New Gower, west along New Gower, up Carter's Hill to corner of Wickford Street, thence west to back of houses on east side of Good View Street, thence north to Cabot Street, thence up Carter's Hill to Le-Marchant Road, and on to Freshwater Road, thence east along Freshwater Road and down Harvey Street to Roman Catholic Cathedral. Down Garrison Hill and along Military Road, thence along Queen's Road, south to Fire Hall, thence south of Church of England Academy, and east along Bond Street. Up Cochrane Street and along Military Road to King's Bridge Road, thence south down Ordnance Square to Temperance Hill, up Signal Hill Road (the fire destroying many detached houses in the neighbourhood), thence west along Water Street, including all the waterside premises.

The loss of life was comparatively small It is known that Ellen Molloy, Mrs. Stevens, daughter and servant were burnt. All the shipping at the wharves had to make for the stream, and there anchor out of reach of the flames, and all the wharves, in many instances with valuable contents, were destroyed All through the long night the crowds continued passing and repassing, those who had friends gladly availing themselves of the welcome shelter of their houses, while those who had no better places, settled themselves with their belongings in Bannerman Park, the Roman Catholic Cathedral grounds, and even by the road sides waiting for day to break Few there were who closed their eyes in sleep that night—the homeless too heartsick and weary to seek relief in slumber, while those more fortunate found themselves burdened with relatives and friends, or gave way to the natural excitement engendered by such an occasion, and wandered aimlessly from place to place fascinated by a scene at once magnificent and awe inspiring The misery of that awful night will long be borne in the memories of the witnesses, and the scenes of utter desolation and hopeless ruin which became evident at every step were sufficient to unman the strongest nerves. When morning broke the thick clouds of smoke still ascended from the burning ruins, and it was hours before it had cleared sufficiently to admit of a view of the track or the desolating scourge.

A walk through the deserted streets demonstrated that the ruin was even more complete than seemed possible at first. Of the whole easterly section scarcely a building remained. In the extreme north-east a small section of Hoylestown was standing protected by massive Devon Row, but the remainder of St. John's east had vanished. Of the immense shops and stores which displayed such varied merchandise and valuable stocks gathered from all parts of the known world; of the happy homes of artisans and middle classes, where contentment and prosperity went hand in hand; of the comfortable houses where the labouring man sought rest and refreshment; and of the costly and imposing structures and public buildings which were the pride and glory of our people, scarcely a vestige remained; and St. John's lay in the morning sun as a city despoiled of her beauty and choicest ornaments, presenting a picture of utter desolation and woe. But hungry months were to be fed; houseless people provided with shelter, and with the advent of the morning the work commenced. Temporary shelters were erected in Bannerman Park, and substantial provisions provided.

The temporary telegraph offices enabled us to communicate the details to the outside world, and on Saturday the first offers of relief came pouring in. To

ENCAMPMENT NEAR QUIDI VIDI FOR FIRE SUFFERERS.

From a photograph.

Halifax belongs the glory of first assisting us, and that evening H.M.S. *Blake* started from there with a large stock of provisions and tents. The *Ulunda* left about the same time, and the *Portia* followed her on Monday. Subsequently the s.s. *Havana*, with a full cargo of relief stores, arrived from Halifax, followed by the Dominion steamer *Newfield* with a contribution of $10,000 worth from the Dominion Government, and the s.s. *Newfoundland* from Montreal, with a cargo of relief stores. Besides the large amount collected for the relief of the city throughout the length and breadth of the Dominion, the Ontario Government voted $10,000 towards our needs, and the Dominion Government $20,000. We cannot too highly extol the magnificent spirit of charity which pervaded our fellow subjects in the Dominion . . . . . All honour to the noble-hearted and generous people of the Dominion, and may they never meet such a dire calamity as we have passed through. From Great Britain generous donations poured in, and by the influence of our Governor.

Sir T. N. O'Brien, K.C.M.G., and Lady O'Brien were in England, enjoying a brief holiday; the moment they heard of the great calamity they at once cancelled all their engagements, and during the remainder of their stay at home devoted themselves to the relief of the sufferers. By their personal influence and untiring zeal in the cause of the distressed, very large and generous donations were sent from England, both in money, clothes, and materials; all these Lady O'Brien, with a committee of ladies in St. John's, afterwards dispensed to the fire sufferers; only those who have been concerned in such work of relief can realise the time, the trouble, the worry and anxiety involved in such labours. In his exertions on behalf of the Colony Sir Terence was ably assisted by the Newfoundland colonies in London and Liverpool,

SIR T. N. O'BRIEN, K.C.M.G.
By Bleber, Hamburg.

also by Sir J. S. Winter, the Honourable A. W. Harvey, and afterwards by Bishop Jones. A Mansion House fund was started, which reached £20,000 sterling. From the United States many contributions were received, notably the gift from Boston, raised principally among our fellow-countrymen there by the zeal and energy of two warm-hearted Newfoundlanders, Messrs. Taylor and Whittle.

On the 12th July a Relief Committee was appointed by His Excellency the Administrator of the Government, the Hon. Sir F. B. T. Carter, K.C.M.G., consisting of the following gentlemen:— Hon. Judge Little, President; Honbles. Sir W. V. Whiteway, H. J. B. Woods, E. P. Morris, J. S. Pitts, E. D. Shea, G. T. Rendell; J. J. Rogerson, Sir R. Thorburn, J. Outerbridge, H. C. Burchell, Thomas Mitchell, J. R. McCowan, W. P. Walsh, A. Marshall, C. Tessier, Col. Fawcett; J. B. Sclater, Secretary and Alfred Pike, Clerk.

The most important event in the year 1893 was the general election in November. Both sides entered into the contest with the greatest enthusiasm; the utmost vigour and energy was displayed in the contest; it was the most stubbornly-contested party fight in our annals. Both the Whiteway party and the Opposition everywhere had good candidates, the Conservatives being largely composed of the mercantile party, with a powerful wing of the Catholic or old Liberal Party. The contest was so keen, the chances appeared so evenly balanced, especially in St. John's

LADY O'BRIEN.

By S. H. Parsons.

that no one, under the Ballot Act, could foretell the result. Mr. Monroe, one of the ablest politicians in the island, conducted his own election in the west end of St. John's with immense spirit, leaving no stone unturned to gain his seat; Mr. Walter Baine Grieve made an equally determined fight against Sir William and the Hon. R. Bond in Trinity. The merchants used their influence to the full, and the Whiteway party employed the machinery of Government to the very utmost extent; both sides were sure of victory. The old leaven of prejudice against the mercantile monopolists of a former time has still immense influence in the Colony; antagonism between capital and labour shows in a very pronounced degree under the Ballot Act. This feeling, and the unlimited use of the machinery of Government, gained the day for the Whiteway party.

The prejudice against the merchants, however reasonable and natural in olden times, should not exist now; employers and employed are mutually dependent on each other. We have seen the effect of the withdrawal of large mercantile houses from the outports. No one has filled their places; their beneficial influence in giving labour and employment to the people has been entirely lost.

It should always be remembered that a fishery business like ours is a most precarious enterprise; it is exposed to a thousand accidents, from the dangers and perils of the sea, from the chances and changes of a variable climate, quite apart from the risks of markets abroad. Whatever great fortunes were made in the old days, they are not gained now; occasional large profits are a necessity in such an exceedingly risky business. The men who stir up strife between capital and labour in the Colony are no true friends of Newfoundland; what we require is more money introduced into the Colony, more patriotism and less politics.

The election campaign of 1893 was marked by a remarkable out-burst of personal abuse ; both the political parties vied with each other in keeping up this indecent carnival of scurrility. There was not even a stray gleam of coarse humour to palliate the nauseous dose ; the one and only comic element in the campaign literature of 1893 was the political manifesto of Mr. Murray, who posed as " the fisherman's friend."

SIR R. J. PINSENT, D.C.L.
By S. H. Parsons.

The year 1893 was saddened by the untimely deaths of Sir R. J. Pinsent, D.C.L., on April 28th, and the Most Rev. Dr. T. J. Power, Roman Catholic Bishop of St. John's, on December 4th. Sir Robert was a native that any Colony might be proud of ; he was not only an able lawyer and a distinguished judge, he took a deep interest in all that con-cerned the welfare of the Colony, and was active in every good work to promote the best interests of his native land ; his mild, amiable character and his polished courtesy made many friends ; few men in the Colony were more beloved, few who are more missed. His clear intellect, his untiring industry, and his intense love of his profession, combined to make a lawyer who would have been an ornament to the Bench and the Bar of any portion of Her Majesty's dominions. Sir Robert's courtesy and kindness to the Bar were proverbial. He had all the qualities of an able judge, strong in his law, clear in the marshalling of his facts ; always prompt in his decisions, no charge could ever be laid against him of that terrible delay which is a practical denial of justice.

SIR J. S. WINTER, K.C.M.G.

The period between 1884 and 1894 was marked by a number of negotiations with other countries. Besides the Ford-Pennell Conventions of 1884 and 1885, and other questions concerning the Treaty shore and the lobsters, we had the Washington Treaty of 1888, in which England and Canada were represented by Mr. Chamber-lain, M.P., and Sir Charles Tupper, Newfound-land by Sir James Winter, K.C.M.G. An admir-able Reciprocity Treaty was arranged between the United States, Canada, and our Colony ; it was not, however, ratified. The United States treated us in rather a dishonourable manner; they obtained the benefit of a *modus vivendi* for two years, and then repudiated the solemn international engagement.

In 1890 we had the *modus vivendi* about the lobster controversy with France. Two delegations were sent to England; the one from the Patriotic Association consisted of Sir James Winter, P. Scott, and A. B. Morine, Esqrs. (also one to Canada, composed of D. Morrison, P. R. Bowers, and D. J. Greene, Esqrs.); the other was the official delegation of Sir W. V. Whiteway and the Hon. A. W. Harvey (who went first to England), and the Hons. R. Bond and G. H. Emerson, Speaker, who followed later on. In the same year the Hon. R. Bond was sent to Washington to negotiate the Blaine-Bond Reciprocity Treaty. In 1891, again, a delegation, consisting of Sir W. V. Whiteway, the Speaker, G. H. Emerson, and A. B. Morine, with Honbles. A. W. Harvey and M. Monroe, was sent by the Legislature to oppose the French Fishery Treaty Bill, known in popular parlance as the "Coercion Bill," then before the House of Lords. These were all very important questions for the Colony; they brought us a good deal into public notice, and it is necessary for the due elucidation of our history to state the leading points in each question. I will take first the abortive Convention with the United States, known as the Blaine-Bond Treaty, leaving the French Fishery dispute to be dealt with in a separate chapter.

According to the Parliamentary papers laid before the House of Assembly, the Colonial Secretary went to Washington with the concurrence and at the request of Lord Knutsford. The terms of the Convention to be made between Newfoundland and the United States were approved of by the Colonial Office, and it was only after the whole matter was definitely arranged that the Imperial Government intervened at the instance of Canada and refused to ratify the Treaty. Sir John A. McDonald's opposition to the arrangement, and his imperious order to the Home Government to put an end to it, was given on the eve of an election; it was done to secure his Government's return. For the English Government to act as election agents for Canada seems a very extraordinary proceeding; our rights as an independent Colony have been made entirely subservient to the political exigencies of the Dominion. Because Canada could not get a suitable Reciprocity Treaty with the United States, she should not have stopped our Convention with America.

D. MORRISON, ESQ.

Nothing did more to stir up a hostile feeling against the great Dominion than this interference in our affairs. A conference met at Halifax, Nova Scotia, in 1893 to endeavour to arrange in an amicable manner matters between the two Colonies. One of our demands was that Canada's opposition to the Blaine-Bond Treaty should be withdrawn. Matters still remain *in statu quo.* Canada has a considerable trade with Newfoundland, but our Colony sends very little produce to the Dominion. She is not one of our consumers, but our rival in the fish trade, our great market of the future lies in the United States. The American deep-sea fishery is a decaying industry; the consumption of salt-water fish is very small compared with Europe. We can supply the great Republic with all the fish she can consume from our most abundant and extensive cod and herring fisheries. We have immense advantages to offer the Americans in the pursuit of their own bank fishery, we are not like Canada, rivals with the States in manufacturing and agriculture America, from its position and its immense population, is our best customer Every West India island is allowed to make an arrangement with the States, why should we alone be forbidden to carry on our trade in a way which is most beneficial to ourselves? The position of the British Government on this subject was rather undignified. The points of our case against both Canada and the British Government were very clearly set forth in the Resolutions proposed in the House of Assembly on March 6th, 1891, by the Hon. R Bond, Colonial Secretary, and adopted by that body.

Any fair-minded person reading the correspondence on the intended Treaty will be convinced, first, that the Secretary of State for the Colonies authorised Mr Bond to negotiate for the Blaine-Bond Convention, that England made no objection, that the only opposition to the proposed Treaty emanated from Canada. If after the Colonial Minister submitted the Convention to the Dominion Government it was then to entirely fall to the ground, the Secretary of State should have stated that such was his decision clearly to the Newfoundland Cabinet, that his sending Mr. Bond again to Washington, after hearing Canada's objections, could have only one meaning and intention, viz, that the Imperial Government, notwithstanding Canada's objections, proposed to allow Newfoundland to carry out the proposed Convention, and this is further proved by the despatch from the Colonial Office to Canada that the Convention could not be indefinitely postponed Colonists are wont to rely upon the honour and word of an English Minister If he was not all the time playing with Newfound-

land, if he really meant serious business, then the only obvious meaning
and true intent of his words, the only construction that any honourable
man can put upon his language and action, is that he intended and
determined that this Colony should be allowed to make a Convention
with the United States. In the negotiations now going forward between
the Governments respecting the union of Newfoundland with the
Dominion, it is to be hoped that the Canadian statesmen will show
themselves liberal, and even generous, towards the Colony, otherwise
they will make the path of the Island delegates very thorny and
difficult. No terms whatever will satisfy the opponents of the Newfoundland Government, but if the conditions are eminently reasonable, all sensible men in the Colony who are now disposed towards
confederation as the best available way out of our difficulties will be
satisfied

The other alternative, making the Island into a Crown Colony,
which is put forward very earnestly by many persons and the
Opposition, is really not a practical solution ; we must remember that
an English Cabinet would never take away a constitution from its
British subjects unless there was tremendous pressure brought to bear
in its favour, the least opposition to it on the part of the Colony or the
Assembly would decide against it. The Home Government would also
object to administer the government and make themselves responsible
for its finances and general control. The Crown Colony idea is obsolete
and impracticable.

The whole of this chapter was printed in 1894, and the book was
intended to end with that year, owing, however, to my absence from
England, final publication was delayed until 1895, and in order to bring
this History up to date it becomes my very unpleasant duty to comment on the disasters and disgrace of 1894 These events are too near,
some of the details are still *sub judice*, and the whole circumstances are
too recent, to be calmly discussed and impartially considered, all the
facts want to be brought forward, and a certain distance of time and
space allowed, before we can fairly adjust the blame for all these
disasters and humiliations. One thing, however, comes out very
clearly, that merchants and politicians on both sides have helped to
bring the unfortunate Colony into disrepute by the fierce rancour
and bitter personal hate which characterised their party struggles,
in their mad desire for revenge on each other true patriotism disappeared, and the vital interests of our unfortunate Colony were entirely
ignored

The merchants' party having suffered ignominious defeat in the General Election of 1893, were determined to be revenged on the Whiteway side, their avowed object being to ruin its leader: for

HON. A. F. GOODRIDGE.
By Bradnee, Torquay.

this purpose petitions were filed in the Supreme Court under the Corrupt Practices Act against seventeen members of the majority. The English opinion that measures all political questions in the Colonies by its own imperial bushel has been extremely severe on the Whiteway party, and laudatory of their opponents. Persons well acquainted with Newfoundland politics see clearly that there was no real principle involved, that there was not a pin to choose between the Goodridge and the Whiteway politicians, that this clever political trick to kill Sir William, all the turmoil, disorder, and bad feeling caused by these election petitions and the contests they created, the disgrace and degradation of the Colony, were simply the outcome of rage and vindictiveness.

The Corrupt Practices Act is a very severe and drastic measure, but standing alone it is quite an inadequate remedy for the rotten method of electioneering pursued everywhere in North America. The spoils system lies at the root of all political corruption at contests. It is only, therefore, by the reform of the Civil Service on the English model that elections can be carried out in a fairly decent and honourable way. In the distribution of patronage and the allocation of public work to their supporters the Whiteway party continued the bad practices of their predecessors, and the Goodridge party did much the same. It was acknowledged at the election trials by the judges that the public road-money had been fairly well spent, and that no charge of personal dishonesty could be brought against the unseated members.

How any set of politicians, aware of the condition of the Colonial finances, and, as directors of the banks, cognisant of the state of the trade, could have ventured on this wild career and rushed the Island down headlong to ruin, seems utterly unintelligible, except on the supposition *quum Deus vult perdere, prius dementat.* The real interests of the Colony were never considered.

No one can deny that the findings on the election petitions were technically right, but the manner and mode of delivering the first judgment was, to put it in the mildest way, not judicious. The first decision, which was to govern all the cases, should certainly have been the

act of the full Court ; the judgment should have been delivered by the
Chief Justice as the united act of the Bench, not as the isolated opinion
of the one judge, who had only recently been an extreme opponent of
the Whiteway party

Our successive disasters, the fire of 1892, and the jarring of the
political factions, seemed enough to fill up the cup of our woe,
but worse was in store for us. Up to fatal Black Monday, 10th December 1894, Newfoundland credit stood high Our principal monetary institution, the Union Bank, had for forty years maintained
the highest reputation at home and abroad, suddenly credit, financial
reputation, confidence in both mercantile houses and banks, fell like
a house of cards.   For several days we were the most distracted
country in the world—a community without a currency, the notes of
the banks had been the universal money of the Colony— circulating as
freely as gold on Saturday, on Monday degraded to worthless paper.

It would be too painful a task to enumerate all the causes that
led to this terrible financial crisis   The death of a commission merchant in London disturbed nearly the whole monetary affairs of the
Colony If his executor had gone on accepting, probably the crisis
might have been postponed for some months   The only excuse that
can possibly be alleged for the directors of the banks, their large
borrowings and crass mismanagement, was that, like Micawber, they
were waiting for "something to turn up"—some rise in the fish
markets, or some other lucky chance that would lift them out of the
mire of insolvency.

The misery caused by these failures of banks and mercantile
houses was as disastrous, as widespread, and as universal within our
border as the bursting of the South Sea bubble was in the United
Kingdom   All our prospects still seem black and gloomy, and in most
countries such disastrous events could have but one result—irretrievable ruin, the prospects of Newfoundland, however, cannot be
judged by outside standards   Once before, in 1817, she suffered far
more severely and rose again, may we not, therefore, reasonably hope
that Newfoundland and her bold and adventurous sons will once
again emerge from her present unhappy condition ? Populations that
live by the sea and earn their bread upon its treacherous waters
are always liable to dire disaster, but the same spirit that leads
them to face the dangers of the troubled waves, nerves them also
with a spirit to rise again from calamities that would for ever daunt
the courage of a landsman.   One change was inevitable ; the dishonest
credit system on which the business of the Colony was transacted
had to die out, demoralising to the people and disastrous to the

merchant, there could be no genuine prosperity whilst this old truck system existed recent events have effectually banished it, we may hope, for ever Terrible misery will be caused before the change can be effectually carried out, but in the end it will be beneficial. If commercial gambling finally ceases, trade and finance will rest on a firmer and safer foundation. Not only must there be a new mercantile method of carrying on the fish business, the old antiquated system of curing and handling our staple product must also be superseded by modern ideas, and newer and more scientific methods adopted both in preparing, packing, and transporting

We must remember that whilst much of the working capital of the Colony has been lost in recent failures, the wealth-producing power of the Island has not been seriously impaired Fish must always remain one of the staple foods of the world, but the products of the sea, which have hitherto been our chief, we may almost say our only resource, should in time be augmented by the labours of the lumberman and the miner Newfoundland is still almost an unexplored country: her geological formation points to much hidden wealth, which we may fairly hope the development and completion of the railway will help to bring forth; the natural result of speedy and convenient communication is to attract capital and start new enterprises

On the morning of the 24th June 1897 four hundred years will have rolled away since John Cabot first sighted the green Cape of Bonavista. four centuries will have elapsed since the stem of the *Matthew's* boat grated on the gravelly shore of Keels, and since King's Cove witnessed the setting up of the Royal Ensign, the feudal ceremony that proclaimed to the world the possession of a new continent for England, the grandest field for the expansion of our race. May we not confidently hope that when the morning sun shines out again on the anniversary of that great Baptist's day in 1897 evil times will have passed, and our Island, closely united with her prosperous younger sisters, will once again become a happy and contented New-found-land ?

CHAPTER XVII

THE PRESENT POSITION AND FUTURE PROSPECTS OF THE COLONY

In my original introduction I mentioned that this work was only an attempt to write the History of Newfoundland No one recognises more forcibly than I do the imperfections of this volume, especially the modern portion. One of my American reviewers, says " The Fishing " Admiral was the dire enemy of the early Newfoundland settler. " We are, however, bound to confess that when this truculent mariner " disappears from her annals, all the light and glow, and romance, fade " away out of Newfoundland history."

To write of the events of to-day, to record the annals of our own time with absolute candour and impartiality is a most difficult task , to one situated as I am, it is not only a hard task, but an unpleasant one. Once, however, having put my hand to the plough, I cannot now turn back , to make this book in any sense complete the history must be written up to date In this chapter, therefore, will be found a chronicle of events continued to the commencement of 1896

The year 1894 ended in gloom Almost universal despondency prevailed throughout the Colony. the shadow of the awful disaster, the " crash " lay like a dark pall over the land The stoppage of the banks, the run on the savings bank, and the failure of seven large mercantile houses, had a most widespread effect, almost universal distrust prevailed In one form or another, as note holders shareholders, or depositors, the whole population of the Colony lost by the banks. The narrow resources of widows and orphans the painful savings of a lifetime, gathered in by rigid frugality, earned, a good deal of it, in constant danger and peril on the sea, all was lost in this tremendous failure.

Newfoundland trade had been considered sound. The Union Bank was a time-honoured respectable institution , its credit stood high, both at home and abroad , what caused this sudden downfall this awful crash The actual immediate occasion of the disaster was the death of Mr Morris a commission agent in London, who had financed several

Newfoundland firms, this wrecked the Commercial Bank. The fall of the Commercial closed the doors of the Union, and broke down seven large firms, the whole fell together like a house of cards

All students of history must readily see that the decease of Mr. Hall was only the proverbial last straw that breaks the camel's back. The true origin and cause of this terrific financial wreck lay much deeper and further back. It was unsound banking and unsound trade that injured Newfoundland on this fatal "Black Monday." We know now that for several years past the Newfoundland fish trade has been conducted, with some exceptions, wholly on credit. A business whose sole basis rests on such a frail foundation is liable to sudden overthrow. The crash of 1894 was a terrible catastrophe to the trade, but worse happened in the Waterloo year, 1815

Immense fortunes had been made in the business, but of late years there has been a cheapening all round of articles of food, and general stagnation in commerce. Our staple article, like wheat and sugar, has gone down in the principal markets of the world. The truck system on which the merchants do their business, at its best, is a dishonest and degrading method of conducting trade. It is a direct encouragement to idleness and fraud on the part of the fishermen, and, as sad experience has shown, disastrous to the merchant.

It now appears that for the last few years markets have been so bad that the shippers have been losing money continually on cargoes sent abroad When merchants, therefore, fell behind and had to pay heavy interest to the banks, their swift descent to insolvency was only too rapid and too sure. It has been the practice of their opponents to rail at the Newfoundland merchants, and accuse them of robbing and oppressing the poor toilers of the sea Now that all the secrets of their business are laid bare, we find that the fishermen had the best of the bargain, lately, at any rate, they have been paid prices for their fish far beyond its market value, and far in excess of what the merchant has received Some of these old firms who have now gone under have been standing for a century. Through fish shipments and other losses, all their own capital has disappeared, and the borrowed money along with it. The conduct of the bank directors is now *sub-judice*, and it would be highly improper to comment on their management. One fact, however, comes out clear and distinct. With the exception of Mr Pitts, in the Commercial Bank, and Mr. Harvey, in the Union Bank, all the rest of the Directors owed very large sums to the banks The overdrafts and liabilities to the bank of three directors of the Union amounted to double the capital The liabilities of the Commercial Bank Directors were even larger. These enormous overdrafts were unsecured, unrealisable, and, although one firm in each Directorate will probably pay 70 cents in the dollar, and, if not thrown into liquidation would, with time, have paid in full, the larger portion of these debts is absolutely lost to the shareholders. It is an extraordinary exhibition of unsound banking and crass mismanagement.[1]

The crash produced, as it might naturally be expected, a great deal of destitution. During the winter of 1895 the wants of the poor were relieved by a Relief Committee at the West End, by Lady O'Brien and a number of benevolent ladies, and by Mrs. Edgar Bowring, and her Committee. Friends of the Colony—Bowrings and others in England assisted. The United States and Canada contributed liberally to the funds distributed by the philanthropic workers in St. John's. The government, the general public in the city, and especially the clergy of all denominations, were active in the good work.

It is pleasant to turn from these melancholy themes to a brighter subject. Amidst the general depression there were many who looked on the crash as a blessing in disguise, and there were several firms, like good weatherly ships, who rode out the gale without losing a rope yarn. The first banking facilities came from the Bank of Nova Scotia, brought to the Colony through the instrumentality of Mr J. S Pitts; the great Bank of Montreal soon after established an agency in St John's, and a branch of the Merchants' Bank of Halifax also commenced business in the Colony. These Canadian Banks largely assisted in promoting trade, and in helping the Local Government to tide over its difficulties.

As the spring advanced the horizon began to brighten, steamer after steamer came in loaded with seals. The first arrival was the *Aurora*, Captain Jackman, on the 27th of March, with nearly thirty thousand young harp seals, closely followed by the *Neptune*, Hon Captain Blandford, with over thirty-two thousand. A good seal fishery always puts heart into the merchants to supply for the summer codfishery. Owing, however, to so many firms being in liquidation, the advances for this important business would have been very inadequate were it not for the generosity of the British Government in advancing a large sum for relief. We were fortunate in getting this generous gift, we

---

[1] The banks are now in the hands of liquidators and lawyers. It is expected that a good dividend of about 75 cents in the dollar will be got out of the Union, the dividend from the Commercial will be a small one, 20 to 25 cents. Two suggestions were made at the time to save the Union Bank, the Commercial was long past redemption, one was to get a strong bank, like the Bank of Montreal, to take over its business and carry out the liquidation. It is unmistakeably advantageous for a bank to liquidate a bank; the other was for the shareholders to advance on preferential stock about $400,000, which would have tided over the difficulty. It is believed that, under either of these arrangements, the Union would have paid in full. If, as most people consider, the crash was inevitable, then we have the one miserable consolation of knowing that it did not come at the worst time of the year; if it had happened in May it would have stopped a large proportion of the fitting out of the fishing fleet, a disaster too awful to contemplate.

were still more fortunate in the Commissioner who was sent out to distribute it. A happier selection for this difficult work than Sir Herbert Murray, K.C.B., could not have been made.

Money was advanced to the farmers for the purchase of seed potatoes ; useful public works were instituted, and, above all, numerous deserving planters and fishermen were assisted in the hire of schooners, the purchase of salt, and the supplies of food and fishery gear. It is very satisfactory to know that almost to a man the outharbour fishermen have honourably repaid their loans.

HON. D. J. GREENE.

The political events of the year 1895 can be very briefly chronicled. The Legislature met early in January ; on the 21st of the month an Act was passed removing the disabilities of the members unseated by the decisions of the Supreme Court.[1]

On the 31st of January the Hon. D. J. Greene, Premier, who had conducted the government with marked ability, resigned. Sir William Whiteway and his colleagues were sworn in, and all re-elected without opposition.

On the 27th February a message had been sent by Sir T. N. O'Brien to the Governor General of Canada, on the question of reopening negotiations for union between the two Colonies ; a favourable reply

---

[1] Some members of the present Government are of opinion that my views of the election petitions are rather unjust towards them. In order to show both sides of the question, therefore, I give the following extract from the " New York Herald " of March 1895. My own views are still unchanged. I am still of opinion that the decisions of the judges under the Act, though possibly too severe in disqualifying, were right in unseating the members petitioned against. I still consider Sir William and his colleagues' resignation in 1894 was poor play ; he should have remained in office, and trumped Morine's election petition's trick with a repealing Act, as he did in January 1895. All the time the Whiteway party had the country at their back. In March 1895 the " New York Herald " wrote :—

"The people at the polls defeated the Winter-Morine party, but A. B. Morine, a lawyer of considerable ability, with a Canadian political education, worked an old Canadian election dodge on the unsuspecting Whitewayites successfully. Under the Bribery and Corruption Act it is illegal to do a lot of little things Newfoundland politicians have been doing from time immemorial. For instance, in some cases the member representing a constituency visits his electors very seldom, the elections being held in the spring or fall, when all the fishermen are home. Constituents embrace the opportunity afforded by the presence of their representative to obtain grants or promises of grants for road repairs, &c. This kind of thing was construed into bribery and corruption, and accordingly 17 election petitions were prepared secretly, all in the same form, and filed in court on January 6, 1894, at 3 o'clock, on the last day and at the last hour which, under the law, an election petition could be filed.

having been received, the delegates were appointed on the 17th March, and on the 4th April, Honourables R. Bond, E P Morris, Geo H Emerson, and W H Horwood, the representatives of Newfoundland, met the Dominion Delegates in conference at Ottawa After many protracted sessions negotiations were finally broken off, the Dominion Government refused to accede to the only honourable terms which the Newfoundland Delegates could venture to propose for the acceptance of the Colony. The main difficulty was the refusal of Canada to take over the whole debt of the Colony They believed at Ottawa that our Island was in such financial straits that we would accept any terms they might offer The greatest of all Canadian statesmen, Sir John A McDonald, and the ablest of his successors, Sir Charles Tupper,[1] held firmly to the opinion

This prevented any of the Whiteway party petitioned against from filing counter petitions to contest the return of their opponents, and also prevented the introduction during these trials of any recriminatory evidence against the other side. The whole of the Whiteway Cabinet were included in the petitions filed

"The first case tried was that of Hon Mr. Woods, Surveyor-General, before Sir James Winter, who had just retired from the leadership of the opposition, and accepted a seat on the Bench Mr Woods was unseated and disqualified Every charge in the petition, and all the particulars in it, were in connection with the expenditure of public money on public works There was no charge, direct or implied, that any private means had been used to bribe and corrupt any elector Nor was there one solitary case of personal bribery proven in all of the 17 election trials. The charge was that the candidates, after the dissolution of the Legislature in 1893, continued to administer up to polling day, November 6, the affairs of the districts they had, in most cases, previously represented.

"To properly appreciate this it must be borne in mind that the duties of a Member of Parliament in Newfoundland are not alone legislative, but executive and administrative, in other words, there being no municipal form of government in the various districts, towns, and settlements, on the Member devolves all the duties which, in the United States, England, and Canada, properly attain to the county council and overseers of the poor It was, therefore, for the allocating of the various grants voted by the Legislature for railway connecting roads, for the repairs of public highways and bridges, construction of launchways, lighthouses, and generally looking after their district and doing, in the autumn of 1893, the identical work they had done in 1889, 1890, 1891, and 1892, and all the years they had stood in a representative capacity that the Whiteway Members were unseated and disqualified. And so nicely was the distinction drawn that, in delivering his judgment on the Trinity petition filed against Sir William Whiteway, Hon Robert Bond, and Mr Watson, who represented that section, Mr. Justice Little took occasion to make use of the following remarkable language 'Nevertheless, although under the law there 'is nothing left for me to do but unseat and 'disqualify Sir William Whiteway, Mr Bond, 'and Mr. Watson, I deem it only due to them 'to say that they leave this court without a 'stain on their honour, integrity, or morality'"

[1] The foregoing was written before the delivery of Sir Charles Tupper's able speech at Sydney, Cape Breton, during his election tour Sir Charles is recognized as the ablest man in his party—wonderfully vigorous and energetic—a Canadian grand old man

"Regarding the admission of Newfoundland as a member of the Confederation, Sir Charles said he had always attached great importance, and had told Sir John Macdonald, when the question first came up, that the rounding off of the confederacy by its entrance was an all-important one He did not for a moment wish that the island should be brought into confederation unless it be accomplished on terms that would substantially benefit the people of Newfoundland He believed that union would contribute to the happiness and well-being of that people He had no desire to see them enter the confederacy except with their hearty concurrence, and he deeply regretted the collapse of the recent negotiations He was vain enough to think that if he had been consulted earlier in those negotiations, the result would have been different The stumbling block in the recent negotiations was the financial question—the refusal of the Imperial Government to contribute $5,000,000 towards the colony's indebtedness Lord Ripon consulted him (Sir Charles), but it was a case of locking the stable door after the horse had been stolen Lord Ripon pointed out that it was utterly impossible for the Home Government to give the desired aid to Newfoundland, because it would create a dangerous precedent, and similar aid could

CANADIAN AND NEWFOUNDLAND CONFEDERATION DELEGATES.

that the union of our Island with the Dominion was absolutely necessary for Canada, and if the negotiations had been in their hands, the
terms of union would have been settled   Quite a reaction of feeling
on the subject has since taken place in Ottawa, Montreal, and Quebec,
men of all shades of opinion now deplore the failure of the late Conference   Canada would be in the long run a greater gainer by the union
than Newfoundland   In the Appendix will be found a correct statement
of the terms proposed on both sides   The facts are condensed from a
very able speech delivered by the senior delegate (in the absence of
Mr. Bond) Hon E P. Morris, in the House of Assembly, 16th May,
1895.

    The consolidation of British North America is an Imperial as well as
a Colonial question ; it was unfortunate that at this particular juncture
of affairs both Canada and Newfoundland had to deal with a moribund
Liberal Government in England   Had the present enlightened chief of
the Colonial Office been at the head of affairs with his large views of
Imperial Federation, Mr. Chamberlain would not have allowed such a
favourable opportunity to unite British North America to elude his grasp.
All the older statesmen of Canada have repeatedly declared that the
Atlantic terminus of the Canadian Pacific Railway should be in Newfoundland.   In these negotiations the railway across our Island should
have been considered as part of the great Imperial highway, a Dominion,
not a local road.   After the Trent affair, the Intercolonial railway was
built through Canadian territory entirely for strategetic and Imperial
purposes   The Canadian Pacific Railway is used for Imperial purposes
to transport the Imperial forces over English territory to the Pacific
By the completion of the Newfoundland route, English naval and
military forces could be landed at Montreal under five days from
Plymouth   By fast transports like the *Campania* or *Teutonic*, they
could be placed on English territory in America in three and one half
days steaming from Plymouth.   Warlike operations in modern days

not be given to other colonies in similar
financial difficulties   But Sir Charles pointed
out to Lord Ripon the peculiar circumstances
which surrounded this case, inasmuch as
under the old French treaty Newfoundland
had suffered most severely, and that about
six hundred miles of its coast line was
practically in the possession of a foreign
power   He also pointed out the difficulty of
making France believe that a little island of
two hundred thousand people could override
the wish of the Imperial Government   The
matter would be entirely different, however,
were Newfoundland a portion of half a continent with five millions of a population, and
were Newfoundland a portion of the great
confederation the question could be settled

without much inconvenience   Equally strong
reasons for Imperial assistance could not be
given by any other colony   Another point
which would justify such a precedent was
the Imperial guarantee of the cost of the
intercolonial railway at the time of confederation, on the ground that it was in Imperial
interests   Sir Charles expressed his belief
that Mr Chamberlain would lend his powerful
assistance in consummating this very desirable
object   He emphasised the importance of the
union from commercial and financial considerations, and above all for the idea of
consolidating all the British American colonies, and he believed that before long he
would find means of solving it "

are swift and sudden, and the advantages to England and to Canada of possessing the quickest route across the Atlantic and through their own territory, are simply incalculable in case of war. In the two last conflicts between England and America, Newfoundland was the head quarters of the North American squadron, as many as thirty-two British men-of-war were at one time in St. John's Harbour. With abundant coal supply, splendid harbours on her east coast, an English naval force operating from St. John's or Trepassey, commands within easy range not only the Gulf of St. Lawrence, but of the whole trade of the Atlantic. St John's and Cape Race are the most important strategetic points in North America. Newfoundland is the advanced outpost, the guardian and sentinel of Canada. This was Sir John A. McDonald's strongly expressed opinion, every naval expert will endorse the view. Our country will be a great outlet for Canadian trade, but to connect the two countries, to make commerce flourish, to promote traffic between the Dominion and Newfoundland, to unite them in a real union, the railway to Port-aux-Basque, and the steam ferry across the gulf are absolutely essential. The connexion between the two countries cannot be made either complete or profitable without these new lines of communication.

Viewing this question in its larger aspect, and as it should be looked at, from an Imperial point of view, it seems a reflection on the capacity and statesmanship of the Canadian and English politicians concerned in these negotiations for union, that, after such protracted discussion, for the sake of a few paltry thousands a year, the whole matter ended in such a lame and impotent conclusion.

On May 11th 1895, the Newfoundland Government received a final answer from the Executive of Canada, declining to accede to the only possible terms on which Newfoundland could, with honour, have entered the Dominion. At this juncture of our affairs, the future of the Colony seemed dark and gloomy, a heavy floating debt, and the large amount of interest due in July had to be met; our credit had been so injured by lying despatches from the enemies of the Island, that many believed money could not be borrowed on any terms whatever, there seemed no alternative in this unfortunate state of affairs but to make default on our bonds, or become a Crown Colony.

A meeting of the Executive Council was convened on the day the despatch was received, and sat all day in anxious council. Mr. Bond, the Colonial Secretary, volunteered at once to proceed to the money markets in England and America, to try and obtain the required loan of $2,500,000. His offer was accepted by the Government, and the same

evening he left for Pictou, Nova Scotia, in the S.S. *Tiber*, arriving in
Montreal on the 15th May.

Whilst the enemies of the Government scornfully derided his mission
as a predestined failure, even his friends thought his venture a forlorn
hope. At every step new obstacles beset his path, new calumnies, new
falsehoods, and new misfortunes, whilst he was in Montreal there was
a run on the Newfoundland Savings Bank, the Bank of Montreal and
Bank of Nova Scotia were appealed to in vain for assistance. In this
untoward state of affairs a total collapse seemed inevitable, and unless
a temporary loan of $150,000 could be obtained within forty-eight hours
the Savings Bank would have to close its doors, and then all hope of
obtaining the required loan for the Colony had flown. An effort was
made by Mr. Bond, through a leading firm of brokers in Montreal, to
obtain the sum required. As a consequence of the crash, and of the
defamation of the Colony that had been so persistently practised by its
enemies here, the Government securities held by the Savings Bank
would not be accepted as sufficient security by lenders, and, as a last
resource, the Colonial Secretary had, with the deposit of the Debentures,
to pledge his personal security in order to procure $100,000. The
Savings Bank for the time was saved, it was fortunate for the Colony
that our envoy had not only the high-minded patriotism, but also
sufficient means and credit to avert a dire calamity.

Mr. Bond discovered that it was useless to try and obtain the larger
loan for the Colony in Canada, so he at once proceeded to the United
States, first, however, having put himself in communication with leading
financiers in London, through their agents in Montreal. He found, after
a time, that he could do better for the Colony in England, so, on the
5th June 1895, he left New York, and arrived in London on the
15th June, and a few weeks later he succeeded in obtaining a loan for
the Colony of £550,000 sterling, at four per cent., inscribed stock for
forty years, this amount was subscribed for nearly twice over. Whilst
Mr. Bond was in London, busy with bankers, arranging the terms of the
loan, information reached him that the Savings Bank was again
embarrassed; the Directors cabled him to try and raise a temporary
loan of $850,000, after much labour he succeeded in obtaining this
sum, at three and a half per cent, thus placing our local monetary
institution beyond all peril for the future.

Now that the Colony is again floating in the calm waters of solvency
and sound finance, it is easy for scoffers to make light of Mr. Bond's
labours, but when one thinks of the angry sea of trouble through
which our envoy had to pass, the vile slanders, the abuse, the villanous

M M

attacks that were made at the time both on our agent and the Colony, one feels astonished at his marvellous success.

On Mr. Bond's return from his mission, he was welcomed with enthusiasm, even his bitterest opponents came forward and thanked him for his exertions on behalf of the Colony [1]

Immediately after Mr. Bond's return, the Executive began arranging their Retrenchment Scheme. Our Government is not an ideal Government, and the Retrenchment Act was not an ideal measure, it was a rough and ready method of equalising revenue and expenditure, a measure absolutely necessary to stabilitate the credit of the Colony, in many cases it pressed harshly and severely, especially on the poorest class of public servants, the school teachers. The reduction amounts to $494,000, and estimating the revenue for 1895-96 at $1,725,022, and the expenditure at $1,331,000, a surplus is anticipated of $394,022. For the last six months of 1895, from July to December, the revenue was quite equal to the revenue received during the same period in 1894. [2]

The Council of Higher Education in this Colony has been a long time forming, but since its constitution it has done splendid work. In September of this year the results of the Matriculation Examinations were made known, the results show that our scholars have attained a very high general average in these examinations. These contests produce a wholesome rivalry, and they have done more in a few years to advance education in the Colony than all that has been done in this generation. The three denominations in St. John's, the Church of England, the Roman Catholics, and the Wesleyans, have each been fortunate in the selection of masters for their colleges. Mr. Blackall, of Bishop Field's College, has had the most up hill work, but under his able and energetic management, with the aid of good assistants, the school under his charge has marvellously increased in numbers and

[1] The Rev. D M Harvey, LL D, the ablest opponent of Sir W. Whiteway's Government, in the January number of the "Canadian Bankers' Journal," thus writes of Mr Bond's mission —

"The Hon Robert Bond, Colonial Secretary, did not despair of the colony, and resolved to make an attempt to negotiate a loan. His efforts were crowned with success. He obtained in the London money market, on behalf of the colony, a loan of two millions and a half of dollars at 4 per cent, to be repaid in 40 years. He also obtained a million of dollars for the savings bank at $3\frac{1}{2}$ per cent, so that this institution was rendered absolutely safe in any emergency. This loan was an immense boon to the colony. Not only was the floating debt paid off, but the credit of the colony was greatly strengthened It furnished a proof that the kings of finance had formed a favourable opinion of the resources of the colony, and did not despair of its future" The directors of the savings bank unanimously passed a resolution thanking Mr. Bond for pledging his own credit and for his valuable services to the institution.

[2] On the 19th May Newfoundland sustained a grievous loss in the death of the Hon Moses Monroe For years he had been one of the most prominent figures in our commercial, social, and political life, a man of fine intellect, far seeing, energetic, and enterprising in business. No one in his class was more popular, no one had more friends Warm hearted, generous, courteous, his place amongst us will never be filled.

efficiency. It is not necessary that I should sing the praises of the Christian Brothers, they have completely revolutionized Catholic education in the Colony, enthusiastically devoted to teaching, they now possess noble school buildings, fitted with every modern appliance, and their schools both for discipline, system, and teaching, are simply unrivalled. Mr. R. E Holloway is too well known throughout the length and breadth of the Colony to need any encomium from me As a scholar, and a many sided scientific teacher, he would fill the highest position in any college It is satisfactory to know that the great religious body, who benefit so immensely by his manifold gifts, appreciate fully his moral and intellectual worth

The great Navigator, Cook, first made his mark as a scientific observer in Newfoundland ; he was a man far in advance of his age In his letters and reports he dwells upon the great industrial resources of Newfoundland, and especially mentions the coal which he discovered in his exploration of the rivers and lakes of the West Coast. At the time he was treated as a visionary and wild enthusiast, but after a lapse of nearly a century and a half, Cook s views are now proved to be correct. Between 1838 and 1840 the celebrated John Beete Jukes was Geological Surveyor of Newfoundland, and he discovered seams of coal at St George's Bay and Grand Lake Later on they were explored by Mr. James P Howley, the present head of the Geological Survey. The most important coal areas lie close to the railway track, at the head of Grand Lake and in St George's Bay. They have been thoroughly explored by Mr. Howley, and numerous workable seams of coal have been discovered ; one seam has been traced for eleven miles, and indications of coal have been found over an area of fifty square miles The coal area at St. George's Bay is not quite so extensive as the one at Grand Lake, but it is of immense value, and the coal is of a very superior character.

This discovery has revolutionized the whole state of affairs in Newfoundland, everything is possible to the country that has coal and iron in abundance Lying as it does right alongside the track of the railway,[1] close to good shipping ports on the West Coast, and eighty miles from salt water on the North Coast, it will supply the thousands of tons of coal now produced from Cape Breton and elsewhere , employment will be given to our labouring population, not only in mines, but also in pulp factories and the manufacture of paper from wood We

[1] Mr R G Reid intends building immediately substantial and commodious shipping wharves and stores at Bay of Islands ; it is hoped that the railway will be completed this year (1896) to Port aux-Basques , every effort will be made to push it through

have all the ingredients for the successful prosecution of this industry, abundance of spruce and other wood, cheap labour, and finally coal.

On the 1st November 1895, a car load of coal from the Grand Lake coal fields was brought over the railway to St. John's, by Mr. R. G. Reid.

MR. R. G. REID.
By S. H. Parsons, St. John's, Newfoundland.

It was tested, both for steam and household use, and found superior to Cape Breton coal. Some of the coal in the George's Bay area is hard steam coal, but, as this particular seam has not yet been fully opened out, the quantity available is at present unknown.

Iron ore exists in large quantities in the Island, but so far no mine had been worked until the Nova Scotia Steel Company([1]) of New Glasgow, N.S., began their operations at Belle Isle, Conception Bay, about twelve miles from St. John's. Work was begun in the summer of 1895, on a large scale, extensive tramways and a loading pier constructed. It was very late in the season before the company began shipping cargoes of ore to Nova Scotia. In Mr. Howley's report will be found an accurate description of this immense deposit of iron, the two veins alone which are now being worked containing forty millions tons of iron. Hematite iron of a very superior quality has recently been discovered to the northward, and there can be no doubt that there is abundance of this most useful mineral in the Island. The iron mine at Belle Isle is now in full operation; next spring will witness the full opening up of the coal fields.

Coal is an important factor both in civilisation and war; a coal supply for a great naval power is one of the most essential ingredients in modern warfare. Great Britain is well supplied; from British Columbia to Newfoundland she now possesses an inexhaustible supply, and as Sir William Dawson points out, our Newfoundland coal fields are the nearest to Europe.

Sir Terence O'Brien retired from the governorship of the Colony on a well-earned pension in May 1895. For some months Sir F. B. T.

[1] This summer (1896) the Company will ship 100,000 tons of ore. They also intend laying ... to Belle Isle. There is another valuable ... iron ... the Island, and arrangement ... have ... made between the syndicate of owners and a Nova Scotia Company to work these new lodes. Another valuable deposit of iron at Port-aux-Port is also to be operated this season.

GOLD MINES, BRIER N.S.

Carter, K.C.M.G., who holds the dormant commission, most efficiently administered the government. Owing to the salary having been so reduced under the retrenchment scheme there was considerable curiosity about the next occupant of Government House. Fortunately for the

SIR H. MURRAY, K.C.B.
By Lombardi & Co., London.

Colony, Mr. Chamberlain was able to draw Sir Herbert Murray from his retirement, and to persuade him to become the Ruler of Newfoundland; everywhere the new Governor was cordially welcomed. Since Sir John Harvey's time no such high official in the English service, a Knight Commander of the Bath, has been the Queen's representative in this Island. From his well-known character, and his great influence with the Colonial Office, our new Governor is a powerful influence for good in Newfoundland. Sound finance, economical management, and the development of the resources of the Colony, can be depended on whilst he has control of our affairs; he has no ambition to gratify, no ulterior objects to serve, and he is too cool and clear headed ever to become partizan. All we can hope is that his Excellency will stay with us, he is far too good to lose.

During all the late summer of last year there were constant rumours of large smuggling operations being carried on in St. John's. A most efficient officer of the customs got word of a quantity of spirits being stowed away in a store on O'Dwyer's premises; a search revealed a number of barrels of rum. This discovery led to further developments. Under the skilful management of Inspector O'Reilly the whole conspiracy to defraud the revenue was laid bare; two of the smugglers turned informers, and in consequence a number of licensed publicans in St. John's were arrested and tried, and their licenses suspended. However, through a defect in the law, they all eventually escaped

[1] Sir Herbert Harley Murray, K.C.B., son of the Right Rev. George Murray, Bishop of Rochester, educated at Christchurch, Oxford; entered the Civil Service in 1852; private secretary to Lord Derby, Prime Minister 1866 to 1868. In 1870 appointed Treasury Remembrancer in Ireland, where he served until 1882. In that year appointed to the Board of Customs, of which he became chairman in 1889; retired on superannuation in 1894. In the spring of 1895 appointed Commissioner to Newfoundland; made K.C.B. in 1895. Sir Herbert's brother-in-law was the well known Sir John Pakington, raised to the peerage as Lord Hampton; he is best remembered in Newfoundland as the stern opponent of responsible government in this colony.

without punishment. Other smugglers in Burin, Burgeo and elsewhere were arrested through the exertions of the ubiquitous inspector; only a small number of the real culprits were brought to trial, but enough is now known to the authorities to warrant me in saying that since the great fire of 1892, over fifty thousand dollars a year have been robbed from the revenue by this bold smuggling band. The activity of the Government in this matter will do good; eternal vigilance is the price of liberty, and eternal watching is the only safeguard against smuggling The criminal neglect of duty shown by this investigation was a constant invitation to defraud the revenue. Now that every officer of the customs is on watch and guard, smuggling may decline, but whilst St Pierre exists, it will never die out. Mr. Emerson and Mr E P. Morris, who prosecuted for the Crown, were determined to root out this evil : their efforts were crowned with success ; there must, however, be no relaxation of vigilance.

What the future will bring forth for Newfoundland is the subject of much anxious thought. Someone said lately Newfoundland must be a great country to have survived such a series of disasters, like a staunch old ship she has weathered the gale, some of her top hamper and rigging have gone, but her hull and spars are sound I, for one, believe that Newfoundland has a bright future in store for her Last year there was a great recovery, sea and land yielded their increase abundantly ; the opening up of new enterprises in coal and iron, the good revenue, and the stability of our credit abroad, inspired new hope One serious obstacle stands in the path of progress, our political animosities and partizan hatred have done and are still doing us incalculable injury both at home and abroad. The strife of 1893, and the election petitions seem to have fanned the unholy flames of party rancour into a furious blaze of hatred To ensure progress and prosperity for Newfoundland we must have peace within our borders ; the foul tongues of slander and scurrility must be hushed, all good men must work together to cast out from us the evil demon of political strife. Already the public are becoming nauseated with venomous lies and sensational slander. When once newspaper editors feel that the people no longer delight in lies, and their appetite for slander has ceased, when they further encounter the anger of the decent public, above all, when they find these kind of fictions cease to pay, they will adopt a different policy I know my countrymen well, and I can bear testimony to their character, in the whole world I do not believe there exists a more quiet, orderly population than in Newfoundland ; strangers who come amongst them are delighted with their courtesy their simple kindness. There is no other country so free from crime as this Colony, the denominational system of education has not done them justice, but for mother wit, for dexterity as boat builders, house carpenters, railroad men, and all avocations of the sea, they have few equals. As daring sailors, as sealers on the shifting ice floes, ask the Dundee whalers or those who have gone to the Arctic with a Newfoundland crew. They have no compeers in the world, and these are the people who have been foully slandered as thieves, wreckers, and cowards. Contrast the heroism and hardihood of the Newfoundlander, Gudger, in the late wreck on the Nova Scotia coast with all the rest of the unfortunate crew.

The future success of Newfoundland lies in the path where Canada and America have gained their prosperity; new enterprizes, new industries, improved communications have mainly contributed to their welfare and progress, and in that direction we must follow. In this stormy month of winter, whilst the steam engine and the snow-plough dash through the drifts and keep up communication, with the cable ship at Riverhead bringing employment and wealth to the city, every intelligent man can now understand the wisdom and the statesmanship of Sir William Whiteway and his government in inaugurating the railway and the dock.

I know that I should be looked on as a visionary if I were to speak of all the possibilities and increased prosperity the coal mines will bring forth; I therefore pass forward to a new enterprize, in which the results are sure, the success is certain. Mines and minerals may "peter out," the gold and tin which experts say abound may all vanish away, but the fish around our shore is an everlasting harvest, ever ready for the benefit of man, the free gift of the Almighty ruler of the sea. With old methods, the great winter fisheries at Bonne Bay, Bay of Islands, and around the western shore might remain as they now are, stagnant and neglected, but, with collecting steamers and cold storage, the fish harvest can be gathered in three times a week, and delivered punctually at the fish markets all over Canada and the continent. When New Zealand mutton is carried fresh sixteen thousand miles through the tropics, and now comes in competition even with the cheap food products of Canada, what cannot be done with our abundance of fish? Trade in fresh fish is one of our great enterprizes for the future, it is in safe hands, and it will be carried out efficiently by Mr. R. G. Reid. Our salt fish business is overdone, this new departure will help to make better prices. With coal, iron, and copper, timber, agriculture, and the fisheries, Newfoundland should prosper. That she may have every success, that her sons and daughters may grow and multiply, that their garners may be full with all manner of store, is my earnest hope, my heartfelt wish.

APPENDIX TO CHAPTER XVII

I—Proposed Terms of Union between Canada and Newfoundland.

ABSTRACT.

The first conference with the Canadian representatives took place on the 4th day of April; nine conferences altogether took place The conference closed on the 16th of April, having been 12 days in session altogether

On the 9th day of April, the following terms were submitted by Canada and discussed by the conference :—

1 Canada will assume of present debt of Newfoundland - -	$8,350,000
Canada will assume an excess of debt over the $8,350,000 amounting to $2,000,000 - -	2,000,000
Total - - -	$10,350,000

This is equal to $50 per head of her population of 207,000

On the excess of $2,000,000, Canada will pay interest at 5 per cent per annum half yearly.

2 Canada will pay as a yearly allowance to Newfoundland the following sums :—

Allowance for legislation -	50,000
Subsidy of 80 cents per head of her population up to 400,000—which at present population of 207,000 equals - - -	165,600

The payments to be made on the population of each decennial census after the union

Allowance for Crown lands and right of minerals and metals and timber thereon and thereon -	150,000
Interest at 5 per cent on $2,000,000 excess debt - -	100,000
Total - - -	$165,600

3 Canada will maintain all that class of services in Newfoundland which fall under the head of general or Dominion services These comprise—Governor's salary, Customs, Excise, Savings' Banks, Public Works (of a Dominion character), Crown Lands, Administration of Justice, Post Office, Steamship Services, Marine and Lighthouses, Fisheries, Penitentiaries, Weights and Measures, and Gas Inspection, Arts, Agriculture, and Statistics, Quarantine and Immigration, Insurance Inspection, Geological Survey.

4. Canada is to maintain, in regard to steamship services, passenger and mail communication in at least as efficient a manner as at present, as follows —Between the Mainland and Newfoundland, between Newfoundland and Great Britain, the Coastal Steam Service, east and west, between Labrador and Newfoundland.

. 5 In lieu of expenditure on militia in Newfoundland, until such time as Parliament may deem it necessary to introduce therein a more general militia system, Canada will grant $40,000 annually towards the maintenance of a police constabulary, to consist of — men, and to be as to efficiency, equipment, and discipline, up to standards approved by the Minister of Militia This force is to be at the disposal of the Dominion Government for use anywhere in Canada in cases of general and serious emergency

6 The fishermen of Newfoundland are to participate equally with those of Canada in any bounties to fishermen which may be granted by the general Government at any time

7 Canada will take over, at a fair valuation, the S S *Fiona*, now in use by the Government of Newfoundland for fishery service

8 Newfoundland shall be represented in the Senate of Canada by four Senators, and in the House of Commons by 10 representatives

It will be remembered that in 1888, on the visit of Sir Charles Tupper, certain informal terms were discussed, but not officially These terms, however, were made public, and it was generally understood that Canadian statesmen were prepared to favour such terms for the accomplishment of the union.

The following counter-proposals of the Newfoundland delegates were therefore based, to some extent, on the proposals of 1888

No 1 The Registrar General fixed the population of the Colony on the 30th September 1894, at 206,614; it is therefore safe to assume that at the end of the year it was 207,000 The subsidy would, therefore, be $165,6000.

No 2 Bounties to fishermen, $150,000.

No 3 Canada's net public debt is $250,000,000. Her population is 5,000,000; the per capita debt is therefore $50. The population of Newfoundland, as mentioned in No 1, is 207,000, which, at the Canadian per capita debt of $50, would represent a total indebtedness of the Colony of $10,350,000

The funded public debt of Newfoundland is - - - $ 9,116,534.73
And under Loan Act, 58 Vict. cap. 2 - - - 1,456,000 00
Floating debt - - - 675,000 00
Amount required to complete railway to Port aux Basque - - - - 3,620,000 00
Amount required to cover cost, of Brigus branch R Road - - - - 312,000 00
Amount to capitalize liability to Newfoundland R. R. Co , viz , $45,000 at 4 per cent for 22 years - - - 650,300 00

Total - - $15,829,834 73

Less Debt represented by railway system of the Colony, as follows, viz —
Cost of N and W. Railway to date, 31st Dec. 1894 - $ 4,146,000 00
Placentia Railway - - 525,000 00
Brigus branch, completion 312,000 00
Western Railway - - 362,000 00
Consolidated liability to N F R R Co - - - 650,300 00

$9,553,300 00

Or $4,073,465 27 less than the proportion This at 5 per cent. will yield an annual amount of $203,673 35 , the annual subvention to be paid Newfoundland under No 3

No 4 Salary, Lieut -Governor - - - - $ 12,000 00
Customs - - - - 75,295 00
Judicial - - - - 18,500.00
C D C Judges - - 6,440 00
Postal - - - - 70,545 00
Block House - - - 550 00
Custom House, Harbour Grace, St John's Penitentiary - - - 7,850 00
Interest on public debt - 371,245 00
Steam subsidies - - 185,360 00
Shipwrecked crews - - 3,000 00
Pension, P O - - - 231 00
Fog and noonday guns - 948 00
Signal Station - - - 610 00
Inspector, weights and measures - - - 100 00
Examiners of masters and mates - - - - 2,300 00
Encouragement, ship-building - - - - 10,000 00
Maintenance, lighthouses - 46,850 00
Observatory - - - 160 00
Medical attendance, Labrador - - - - 800 00
Protection of fisheries - 500 00
Inspector, pickled fish, Labrador - - - - 1,000 00
Fishery bureau - - - 19,000 00
Treasury Office in connection with Customs - - 4,700 00
Government engineers - 4,628 00

Travelling expenses of Harbour Grace Judge - - $ 240 00
Maintenance of telegraph lines - - - - 18,000 00
Inspection, railway construction - - - 4,000 00

$862,858 00

No 5 In lieu of contemplated allowance for battery of artillery, it is considered that an amount to be agreed upon should be allocated towards the Police Force, who could be trained and equipped as a military force

No 6 By reference to No 3, it will be observed that the cost of the railway systems of the Colony has been deducted from the net public debt

No 7 This only had reference to the ungranted Crown lands within the island , but whereas the dependency of the Labrador embraces an area of at least 160,000 square miles, the mineral and timber and mineral lands, of which have not been disposed of, it is claimed that $100,000 per annum should be added to the amount above named

No 8 It should be understood by this that similar expenditures as are made in the other provinces of the Dominion, should be carried out in Newfoundland, and that the Fishery Commission, at present established, should be the medium of expenditure

No 9 STEAMSHIPS SUBSIDIES — A Efficient mail and passenger accommodation between Canada and Newfoundland weekly ; and upon the completion of the railway to Port aux Basque, a first class steamer shall be put on to connect that port with the nearest terminal railway port in the Dominion B East and West postal service equal in efficiency to the present steamship service C Communication between St John's and Liverpool by steamers direct D. Postal service upon the large bays by steamers, viz , Green Bay, Bonavista Bay, Trinity Bay, and Placentia Bay

No 10 That the fishermen of Newfoundland shall be exempted from the payment of any licenses, fees for fishing, or for use of cod-traps.

No 11. At the present time there are a number of local industries which have been established by protection Those industries, under confederation, would be considerably hampered, if not closed It is submitted that as these particular interests would be thus injured in the general interests of the Dominion, that compensation in the way of aid for a limited period should be allowed. The establishment of a naval brigade in the Colony, which will take the form of a naval training ship

No 12 Precious metals to be reserved to the Colony

No 13 Fifty thousand dollars to be allowed for legislation

SERVICES TO BE BORNE BY THE COLONY OF NEWFOUNDLAND

	$
Government House - -	3,301 00
Provincial Secretary - -	5,924 00
Financial Secretary - -	2,562 00
Board of Works - -	8,850 00
Colonial buildings - -	1,500 00
Legislative contingencies -	35,000 00
Attorney-General - -	2,400 00
Solicitor-General - -	1,200 00
Sheriff, Central District -	1,385 00
„ Northern District -	1,385 00
„ Southern District -	923 00
Bailiff, Central District -	650 00
Chief Clerk and Registrar -	2,000 00
1st Clerk, Registrar's Office	800 00
2nd Clerk, Registrar's Office	600 00
3rd Clerk, Registrar's Office	600 00
Stationery - - -	200 00
Crier of the Court - -	500 00
Crown prosecutions - -	5,000 00
Magisterial inquiries - -	400 00
Circuit Court of Supreme Court, and hire of steamer	5,500,00
Clerk of the Peace - -	1,570 00
Constabulary - -	60,000 00
Keeper, Court House, Harbour Grace - -	50 00
Magistrates, outports -	22,048 00
Court houses and goals -	10,000 00
Ferries - - -	5,076 00
Repairs to public buildings -	11,300 00
Relief, poor - -	209,611 00
Pension, Inspector Carty -	1,440,00
Other pensions - -	1,296 00
Education - - -	151,891.00
Roads and bridges - -	129,300 00
Keeper, half-way house, Salmonier - -	162 00
Repairs, clocks in public buildings - -	200 00
Inspector of meats - -	250 00
Public Works - -	36,000 00
Education, deaf and dumb -	900 00
Education, blind - -	1,050 00
Registration jurors - -	350 00
Rent, public offices - -	2,500 00
Fuel and attendance, public offices - - -	350 00
Dry docks, water rates -	100.00
Rent, Bannerman Park -	80 00
Insurance - - -	800 00
Promotion, agriculture -	10,000 00
Conveyance of sick fishermen from Labrador -	400 00
Registration, births, deaths, and marriages - -	1,500 00
Sheep Preservation Act -	100 00
Total - - -	$835,794 00

And on the 10th day of April the Newfoundland delegates submitted their counter proposals, which were as follows —

What Newfoundland asked was, in subsidies —

		$
1 Eighty cents per head of 207,000 population - -	-	165,600 00
2 Bounties to fishermen -		150,000 00
3 Difference in public debt		203,673 35
4 Crown lands - - -		250,000 00
5. Legislation - -	-	50,000 00
		$819,273.35

This sum would go to defray the local services left by Canada to the colony, some of which subsidies were, of course, subject to some slight reduction, the said services amounting to $738,591, according to the latest estimate of the Newfoundland Receiver General

What Canada offered us to defray the above services was $505,600, as follows —

	$
1. 80 cents per head of population of 207,000 - - -	165,600 00
2 Interest at 5 per cent. on $10,000,000 being the difference between the funded debt of Newfoundland, and $8,350,000 00 which Canada would assume	100,000 00
3 Crown lands - - -	150,000 00
4 Legislation - - -	50,000 00
5. Contribution towards police or militia - -	40,000 00
	$505,600 00

It will be seen by this statement that the subsidies offered by Canada to defray the cost of the services left to and to be borne by Newfoundland would leave a deficit against the colony to be raised by direct taxation or otherwise of $232,991, thus —

	$
Local services as per 1894 estimate - - -	738,591 00
Canadian subsidies to defray same - - -	505,600 00
Deficit against colony - -	$232,994 00

Added to this would be the interest on $7,497,334 73 the portion of the public debt of Newfoundland which Newfoundland would have to assume, which at 4 per cent would be $299,193

In other words, if Newfoundland joined the Dominion under the above terms, and maintained the various services as they are now maintained, she would have to raise by direct taxation for local purposes $532,187

And even supposing these local services could be reduced to come within the Canadian subsidies of $505,600, there would still be $299,193 interest on balance of public debt left the colony to be met.

It must also be borne in mind that on the expiration of Mr. R G Reid's operating contract, the colony would have to operate her whole system of railways, this would have to be borne by direct taxation, which for maintenance and operation over and above income, may be put down at $150,000.

Further, maintenance of telegraph lines, $18,000.

Inspectors of railways, $4,000; Government engineers, $4,628 would also have to be borne by the colony; it would then be—

	$
Shortage on subsidy	232,994 00
Interest on public debt	299,193 00
Operating railway	150,000 00
Telegraph maintenance	18,000 00
Government engineers office	1,628 00
Inspectors of railways	4,000 00

To be raised by direct taxation - - - $708,915 00

Such terms as these were out of the question, could not be entertained, much less recommended. The Newfoundland delegates said that a *sine quâ non*, a first condition to the discussion of terms, was the assumption of the public debt of Newfoundland by Canada. If the Dominion Government would assume the total debt and obligations, and operate the railways and telegraph lines, the Newfoundland delegates were prepared to reduce the amount of $738,594 00, asked for local subsidies to $650,000 00, or a reduction of $88,594 00.

The Dominion delegates, however, could go no further as regards the assumption of the public debt than they had done, viz., $8,230,000, but they were prepared if the Imperial Government would assume the difference between our debt and obligations and the Dominion of Canada, viz., $5,479,834 74, to further consider the raising of the annual subsidies from $505,600 to $650,000, the minimum amount asked by the Newfoundland delegates for annual subsidies.

Negotiations were then entered into with the Imperial Government by the Dominion Government to ascertain if aid could be had in that quarter. On Saturday, the 11th day of May, the following proposal was made by cable from Sir Mackenzie Bowell —

To Sir Wm V Whiteway

St John's, Newfoundland,
Ottawa, May 11th, 1895.

Lord Ripon's despatch, 9th May, to Lord Aberdeen, forwarded to Governor of Newfoundland, will inform you of position taken by British Government. If Newfoundland adopt Ripon's proposal, terms may be modified by aid from Home Government, if not, Canada can only supplement proposal made to your delegates by agreeing in adding to aid in construction of Newfoundland Railway from River Exploits to Port-au-Basque by a subsidy of $6,000 per mile and to add $35,000 to yearly allowance.

BOWELL

It will be seen by this that the Canadian Government are prepared to raise the annual subsidy, $35,000, and contribute $6,000 per mile towards the construction of the railroad from River Exploits to Port-au-Basque, which is equivalent to the assumption of a little over the cost of one-third of the railway from these points.

As regards the Imperial Government, they are not prepared, so far, to contribute in any way —(*Evening Telegram*, May 17, 1895.)

II. An Account of the Newfoundland Coal Fields.

By J P HOWLEY, FCS, DIRECTOR OF THE GEOLOGICAL SURVEY OF NEWFOUNDLAND.

In 1889, the coal seams already known to exist on Robinson's Head and Middle Barachois Rivers were first visited, and thoroughly uncovered, so that accurate measurements, and good average specimens of their quality could be obtained. The Howley seam was uncovered for 150 feet along its outcrop, and was found to attain a thickness of 4 feet 2 inches good solid coal. The Jukes seam was traced over a quarter of a mile, and various openings made across the strike of the seam. It was found to vary from 3 to 8 feet in thickness, and averaged 4 feet 6 inches. It is a beautiful quality of coal, of a brittle nature, presenting a brilliant, sometimes iridescent lustre, and would seem to be somewhat analogous in appearance to what is known in Scotland as cherry coal, though it partakes more of the nature of caking coal. The Cleary seam above this gave a thickness of 2 feet 2 inches. It is a good solid coal, breaking out in oblong blocks, and much resembles Glace Bay coal. Twelve other seams, varying in thickness from a few inches to 6 feet, were discovered on the Middle Barachois River. Two others besides the Howley seam on Robinson's Head River, and four more, including the Shears' seam on the Northern Feeder, a tributary of the latter river. The principal seams in the section, the actual existence and dimensions of which have been so far ascertained beyond question, are —

	Ft.	In.
The Jukes Seam	4	6
The Cleary Seam	2	2
The 18-inch Seam	1	6
The Slaty Seam	1	4
The Clay Seam	1	8
The Rocky Seam	1	5
The Murray Seam	5	4
The Howley Seam	4	2
The Shears Seam	1	2

The Murray Seam, which shows the greatest average thickness of coal, is made up of alternate layers of coal and shale. It is a tough, rather slaty coal, much inferior, at least, at its out-crop to the others It was named after the late Director of the Survey, Alex Murray, C M.G , F G.S The Sheal seam, though so small, is a very superior quality of coal, approaching a semi anthracite in hardness and brilliancy of lustre It is a very clean coal, remarkably free from impurities Altogether the coal seams contained in the St George's Bay trough, that have been as yet discovered, aggregate about 27 feet in thickness. They are all repeated by being again brought to the surface on the opposite side of the trough, where several of them were seen and uncovered The area occupied by these coal seams has not as yet been definitely ascertained, nor is it my intention now to make any haphazard assertions as to what it may probably amount to. I shall not go beyond an actual statement of the facts observed. Were I permitted to continue the exploration of this region, I have little doubt that long ere this I should have been in a position to furnish reliable information on this head To illustrate the importance of what such information would mean, it may be stated that an aggregate of 27 feet of coal, provided the seams maintained their ascertained thickness throughout, should, for every square mile of superficial area they may be found to underlie, contain about 25,920,000 tons of coal All that is known with certainty at the present time is, that on the Middle Barachois River, the trough has a width of at least two miles, while in its longitudinal extent coal has been found to outcrop at points five miles apart in a straight line, from the most easterly to the most westerly known limits In 1891, the Government were pleased to adopt the suggestion of giving the Humber River area a more thorough search for coal, especially in view of the contemplated extension of the railway system to the western side of the island On leaving the scene of operations, the Colonial Secretary, Hon R Bond, said to me, "If you "can find a workable coal seam at Grand "Lake, it will be the means of insuring the "construction of the railway to the West "Coast" I replied that I would do my utmost, and if it were there I believed I could find it The result of this and the succeeding season's work is contained in the published report of the Geological Survey for 1891–92, under one cover. As many of those interested in this subject may not have seen these reports or cared to wade through the geological details, I shall only give a summary of the actual facts ascertained from an economic point of view The existence of a long, narrow, trough of true coal measures on the south side of Grand Lake was established, commencing at a point about four miles from its head, which was traced easterly as far as Kelvin Brook, a distance of over six miles Here it was lost to view, being covered over by an immense accumulation of superficial drift, which spread over a large area of flat country lying between Grand and Sandy

Lakes on the southern branch of the Humber River. Several small streams flowing into Grand Lake afforded the only sections of the strata which were at all accessible, and these only after an immense amount of labour in removing the dense forest growth, and then costeaming the banks wherever any prospect of reaching the bedrock presented itself The principal brooks thus explored were Aldery Brook, Coal Brook, and Kelvin Brook, which occur at intervals of about two miles and a half, succeeding each other from west to east as named above Two other small rivulets, unnamed, were also explored. Very perfect sections of the coal measures were obtained on Aldery and Coal Brooks On the former, in a horizontal distance of about one-quarter of mile, 30 separate outcrops of coal were observed, crowded together, with but a comparatively small amount of intervening rock strata Owing to the doubling up of the strata composing this section, there is, of course, a repetition of the different layers, and in reality the 30 outcrops only represent 15 actual distinct coal seams Most of these are quite small, varying from a few inches to a foot in thickness Those over a foot are as follows —

				Ft.	In.
No	6 outcrop contains coal		-	2	0
No	7	,,	,,	-	1	6
No	8	,,	,,	-	1	8
No.	12	,,	,,	-	1	3
No	15	,,	,,	-	3	0
No	16	,,	,,	-	2	5

Another section of the same measures, on the opposite side of the brook, gave a better showing in some respects No six seam was about the same, but Nos 10, 11, 12, and 13 seemed to have come together, forming one large seam, containing 14 feet of coal No 14 outcrop showed 2 ft 10 in coal, No 15, 2 ft. 2 in ; No 16, 2 ft. 6 in , and No 25, 1 ft 7 in The coal contained in Nos 6, 7, 16, and 25, is of excellent quality, as is also that of some of the smaller seams, but the 14 foot seam, and also No 15th outcrop is soft, and rather impure on surface exposure On Coal Brook the same section is exposed in part, and here the trough has a wider spread, measuring about 30 chains across in a horizontal line Eighteen outcrops of coal were uncovered here representing nine separate seams The remainder of those seen on Aldery Brook, if they exist, could not be reached, owing to the great depth and toughness of the superficial deposits Only four of these seams showed over 1 foot of coal, viz. —

				Ft	In
No.	2 outcrop contains coal		-	1	4
No	4	,,	,,	-	3	5
No.	11	,,	,	-	1	6
No.	12	,,	,,	-	2	4

No 4 is a good seam, and the coal is of excellent quality It was from this outcrop the Messrs Reed obtained the ear load of coal On Kelvin Brook but a very small section of the measures is exposed It contains however, six outcrops of coal No 1 consists of soft coaly and shaly layers alternating, 3 ft. 8 in of which is coal No. 5, contains 2 ft 6 in of rather impure coal, but No. 6 is made up of two layers of excellent bright black coal, divided by a layer of carbonaceous shale The lower coal is 3 ft. 6 in thick, and the upper 2 ft 8 in , making in all 6 ft 2 in of good coal The shaly layer in the middle is about one foot in thickness, but appeared to become somewhat thinner as the seam was sunk upon As it was impossible to go beyond a few feet down at the time, owing to the influx of water from the river, it could not be clearly ascertained whether it maintained this same character to any extent In all probability the shale in the middle may thin out entirely, or become more and more real coal, as the seam is developed In either case it will be seen that this is one of the most promising coal seams so far discovered in the Grand Lake district, though, perhaps, not the best coal as regards quality During the past season of 1895, our knowledge of the more southern trough has been greatly increased by the discovery of two seams of coal, and indications of others at a point on the line of railway, 4½ miles to the eastward of the Kelvin Brook section, and on the same line of strike This discovery places beyond all reasonable doubt the fact that the coal measures form a continuous trough from about one mile to the west of Aldery Brook, to the point on the railway line, a total distance in a straight line of 11 miles Certain observations made during this past season also, seem to point towards a widening of the trough in its easterly extension, but much yet remains to be accomplished before any definite conclusion can be arrived at as to what may be the full extent and importance of this promising coal field.

JAMES P HOWLEY

Coal Analysis.

By WILLIAM H FILTON, F G S ,
F.S Sc., Leeds, England

No 20 Seam.

ALDERY BROOK, GRAND LAKE

Moisture = 7 41 | Volatile matter = 30 73
Fixed Carbon = 53 49 | Ash = 7 71
Sulphur = ·66
Coke (in closed vessel) 61 86 per cent
Colour of ash - - Light pink

No. 16 Seam.

ALDERY BROOK, GRAND LAKE

Moisture = 7 41 | Volatile matter = 38 62
Fixed Carbon = 55 28 | Ash = 4 49
Sulphur = 79
Coke (in closed vessel) 60 58 per cent
Colour of ash Brown

No. 6 Seam.

ALDERY BROOK, GRAND LAKE

Moisture = 5 80 | Volatile matter = 31·44
Fixed Carbon = 57 86 | Ash = 4 08
Sulphur = 82
Coke (in closed vessel) 62 76 per cent
Colour of ash - - Light pink

No 17 Seam

ALDERY BROOK, GRAND LAKE

Moisture = 4 32 | Volatile matter = 16 84
Fixed Carbon = 72 66 | Ash = 5 33
Sulphur = 85
Coke (in closed vessel) 78 84 per cent
Colour of ash - - Light brown

The Iron Mines at Belle Isle.

III —EXTRACTS FROM THE REPORT OF THE DIRECTOR OF THE GOVELNMENT GEOLOGICAL SURVEY OF NEWFOUNDLAND MADE TO THE COLONIAL SECRETARY, DATED ST JOHN'S, DECEMBER 12TH, 1895

The third and fourth ore beds are confined to the upper shales, above the quartzite, the former, occupying an area of about 1½ square miles, the latter of a little over a quarter of a square mile. The outcrops of those two bands have been thoroughly traced out by Mr Chambers, and they are all contained within the company's leases, except a mere corner of the lower band. They are both perfectly parallel to each other, forming a gentle curved line, and are separated by about 150 feet of strata The lower band, No 3, ranges in thickness from 4 to 12 feet, averaging about 6 feet 6 inches The upper band, No 4, ranges from 3 feet 6 inches to 6 feet 6 inches, averaging about 5 feet 6 inches. According to a rough estimate made by Mr Chambers, the two together are believed to contain about 40,000,000 tons of ore. Several thin irregular layers occur between the two main bands, as well as above the upper, and below the lower one But these are not considered of much economic importance Most of the associated strata are more or less impregnated with iron, though not sufficiently rich to be considered as ore

The general character of all these deposits is pretty much the same, though varying somewhat in the percentage of metallic iron they contain The uppermost, No 4 band, is the richest, averaging 56 per cent of metal No 3 averages about 50 per cent But one analysis of No 2, that I am aware of, has been made, it gave 18 per cent of metal. No 1 has not been analysed as yet. They are all a variety of brown hematite ore, of a dull colour, with a somewhat steely lustre on a fresh fracture, and having a peculiar fine granular structure The bands are all distinctly stratified, conforming in every respect with the associated strata. Fossil shells, Lingula, are abundant on the top of No 1, and are found more rarely in all the others The ore partakes of the same cleavage as the sandstones of the section, being, if anything, even more jointed. It breaks out in rhomboidal junks of all sizes. often nearly square, more frequently oblong It thus affords most unusual facilities for mining, and owing to its lying so near the surface, and being covered only with a thin coating of soil, it can be easily stripped, and the ore bed laid bare for acres in extent Its jointed cleavage renders blasting unnecessary, except an occasional shot to loosen up the ore. Half a dozen men with mining picks could raise several hundred tons per diem without difficulty The principal workings at present in operation are situated on No 4 band.

Although not a high grade ore by any means, the abundance of it, so near the surface, with the unusual facilities for raising and shipping, should render it a most valueable property Its chief value to the present company, I understand, consists in its ready fusibility, thereby acting as a flux for the less tractable ores of Nova Scotia Moreover, as these latter ores contain little or no phosphorus, and the former rather more than is necessary, a mixture of the two in the furnace affords about the requisite quantity of this substance in the resultant pig for the production of a good class of steel. The Nova Scotia Steel Company, Limited, of New Glasgow, are but the lessees of the property They pay a royalty of 5 cents per ton on all ore raised, to the original holders of the grants The grants are four in number, comprising an area of 1 square mile each The remainder of the Island is held under licenses to search for minerals by several parties The facilities for working and shipping ore from these claims are equally as favourable as those described above. Were it hereafter considered advisable to smelt these ores on the spot, the island is admirably situated for the purpose, and many eligible sites for the erection of such works are available

In conclusion I may add that I know of no more promising deposits of this class of iron ore in this country, nor do I think there are many in North America more favourably situated in every respect

I have the honour to be,

Sir,

Your obedient Servant,

(Signed)   JAMES F. HOWLEY, F G S,

Director

CHAPTER XVIII.

CHRONOLOGY, JUSTICIARY, HOUSE OF ASSEMBLY

I. Chronology.

GEORGE III., 1760 to 1820

1760 —**Captain WEBB** captured French vessel *Tavignor*, with 3,500 quintals fish, which was sold in St John's for £2,570 sterling.

1761.—**Captain (afterwards Lord) GRAVES** sailed in December, 1761, with convoy to Spain and Portugal, seventy sail of vessels, 7,000 tons, 680 men and 200 guns.

1762 —St. John's, Carbonear, and Trinity captured by French squadron under Admiral de Ternay, re-captured same year, in September, by Colonel Amherst, brother of Sir Geoffrey Amherst, Capt McDonel, with Highlanders and Provincials (Loyal Americans) Light Infantry, battle of Quidi Vidi.

1763 —War with Spain, importation of fish from Newfoundland prohibited R. Carter, Esq, garrisoned Isle Bois, Ferryland, C Garland, Carbonear Treaty of Paris, St. Pierre and Miquelon confirmed to France, all the rest of North America given up to England Survey of the Island by the immortal navigator Cook Labrador re-annexed to Newfoundland Population 13,112; 386,274 qtls fish, 106 fishing ships, 123 going foreign voyages; 142 vessels from New England and other parts of British North America, Cork, Waterford, Belfast, and Glasgow, engaged in Newfoundland trade.

1764.—**Sir Hugh PALLISER** Governor. Collector of Customs appointed in St John's, under the Commissioner of the Custom House in Boston, Mass; soon after Comptroller appointed Court of Vice-Admiralty, St. John's, Major Griffith Williams, R A, resident in St John's and commanding Royal Artillery, published an account of the Newfoundland fishery

1765 —Large increase in fishery, total catch for this year 493,654 qtls. 1763—348,294 qtls. 1764—470,118 qtls. Rev. Laurence Conghlan, Church of England minister, introduced Wesleyanism into the Colony Sir H. Palliser's report very severe on Newfoundland

1766 —Riots in St. John's and Harbour Grace Lieut Cartwright made an unsuccessful attempt to effect friendly intercourse with Beothies, first European to visit Red Indian Lake; wrote a history of the Red Indians, or Beothies of Newfoundland. Repeal of the obnoxious American Stamp Act.

1769 —**Commodore BYRON**, grandfather of Lord Byron, the poet, Governor.

1770 —John Stretton, Wesleyan minister, has hot dispute with Rev David Balfour, Episcopal Minister, Harbour Grace, about the right to preach in Carbonear chapel.

1772 —**Commodore MOLYNEAUX** (afterwards Lord Shuldham) Governor. Rev John Hoskins Wesleyan minister. Governer issues Proclamation 24th June, regulating river salmon fishery for the Colony, French not mentioned.

1773.—Engineer Pringle began to build Fort Townshend, and to construct King's Road and Military Road.

1774 —Placentia Court House built . Continental Congress in America   All exportation to Newfoundland from North America States prohibited 17th September, 1774 , caused great distress in Newfoundland.   Imports from colonies £345,000 stg prior to Revolution.   Quebec Act, 14 Geo III. cap 83, Labrador annexed to Canada

1775 —Rev John Jones first Congregational Minister in St John's. — Heaviest storm ever known in Newfoundland , 300 persons drowned   Palliser's Act, 15 George III Bounty for bankers to continue eleven years, first Act requiring written agreement between masters . and servants in the fishery , wages first charge on fish, &c , all cases to be tried summarily by Court of Sessions or Court of Vice-Admiralty.   Duty of one shilling per gallon on rum from America , caused excitement in New England   **Commodore DUFF**, Governor, issues Proclamation about salmon fisheries at Exploits, Gander Bay, &c

1776 —4th July, Declaration of Independence, United States   7th May, **Rear-Admiral MONTAGUE**, Governor, arrived.

1777 —July   Admiral Montague fitted out several armed vessels in Newfoundland seas to cruise there against the American privateers, by which measure he kept the coast clear, so that vessels might sail without danger

1778 —Independence of the United States recognised by France   France declared war against England   Admiral Montague captured St. Pierre.

1779 —Spain declared war against England   **Rear-Admiral EDWARDS**, Governor, completed Fort Townshend   New Anglican Church on site of present cathedral being built

1781 —The lower road (Water Street) and the upper road (Duckworth Street) ordered to be kept twelve feet wide   First regiment formed in St John's, under Colonel Pringle , Wm Lilly, Ensign   Smart fitting out of H M S *Pluto*, in St John's, and capture of two American privateers at Petty Harbour, one called *The George* , part of her timber now in the Museum, St John's

1782 —**Vice-Admiral John CAMPBELL** Governor   Independence of United States acknowledged by England

1783. —N Gill, D'Ewes Coke, George Williams, Archibald Buchanan, Magistrates, St John's   Treaty of Versailles, French allowed from Cape John to Cape Ray , declaration of King George III that English not to interrupt French fishery by their competition.

1784 —Royalist province of New Brunswick created ; divided from Nova Scotia 1784 Religious freedom established in the Colony , Dr. O'Donel, first Roman Catholic Prefect Apostolic, arrived.   Lease for 99 years to Rev J (Bishop) O'Donel, and certain trustees, of the premises known as "Parson Langman's Garden" (Old Chapel) , Rev. Walter Price appointed Episcopal minister, St John's

1785. —Judges of Oyer and Terminer, D'Ewes Coke, Geo. Williams, Wm Gaden, Richard Hutchings, Richard Routh, Nicholas Lechmere and Thos Dodd   John McGeary, Wesleyan missionary, arrived in Newfoundland   Permission given to import bread, flour, and livestock from United States in British bottom

1786 —Act 26 George III cap 26, continuing bounty to Bank fishery for ten years Jurisdiction of Courts of Vice-Admiralty to try fishery cases transferred to Sessions Courts.   Rev. Jno. McGeary Wesleyan minister. — **Rear-Admiral ELLIOT** Governor   Prince William Henry, afterwards William IV , arrived in Newfoundland as Captain H M S *Pegasus*, presided in Court at Placentia , instrumental in building present English Church, Placentia, towards which he contributed fifty-five guineas and the present handsome communion plate

1787 —Wm. Carter, grandfather of Sir F B T Carter, appointed Judge Vice-Admiralty Court, *vice* N. Gill, deceased   Bishop Inglis appointed as Anglican Bishop of Canada (formerly Rector Trinity Church, New York), New Brunswick, Nova Scotia, and Newfoundland   John Jones allowed to erect Meeting House (Old Congregational Church).   Dr. John Brown appointed J P Placentia (grandfather of Sir H W Hoyles).   Year of peace and plenty , no prisoners in the jail

1788. —Many Bermudian vessels fishing in Newfoundland , complaints against them by West of England adventurers   Serious riot at Ferryland   McAuslan appointed Deputy Postmaster, October, 1778.

1789   **Admiral Mark MILBANKE** Governor   French Revolution   Court of Common Pleas established for the Colony   Seal fishery prosecuted in small decked vessels and open boats.

1791.—**Chief Justice REEVES** presided in Court, designated as "the Court of Civil Jurisdiction of Our Lord the King at St. John's, in the Island of Newfoundland," appointed by Act 31 George III Canada divided into two Provinces Rev W Black, Wesleyan minister, arrived in the Colony

1792 —"Supreme Court of Judicature of the Island of Newfoundland," presided over by C. J. Reeves, opened 7th Sept, 1792; first case tried—Andrew Thomson v. George Williams This Act was renewed annually until 1809 Surrogate Courts established The Floating Surrogates Cottage Farm, Quidi Vidi, cleared by Captain Skinner, R E **Admiral KING** Governor

1793 —Louis XVI, King of France, beheaded Chief Justice, **D'EWES COKE**

1794.—Murder of Lieut Lawrie, R N Farrell and Power convicted of the murder. H.M S *Boston* pressing men for Navy in St. John's France declares war against England

1795 —Royal Newfoundland Regiment embodied, Commander, Colonel Skinner

1796 —**Admiral Sir James WALLACE** Governor. All St John's under arms. French under Admiral Richery destroyed Bay Bulls. England and Spain at war Newfoundland fishery very prosperous £1,500,000 invested in fisheries Dr O'Donel consecrated, at Quebec, Bishop of Thyatira *in partibus*, and Vicar Apostolic of Newfoundland, first Roman Catholic Bishop. George Williams appointed Chief Magistrate

1797 —Battle of Cape St. Vincent Mutiny of the Nore The ringleader, Parker, hung Bishop O'Donel received a grant of land 500 yards frontage at River Head. Governor, Hon. **Wm WALDEGRAVE**, Vice-Admiral, afterwards Lord Radstock R. ROUTH Chief Justice

1798 —Irish Rebellion. Nelson's great victory over French fleet. Battle of the Nile.

1799 —First Grammar School opened, Rev L Anspach Head Master Census of St. John's this year (1799), 3,132 inhabitants, besides military, General Skerett in command of the troops

1800 —Mutiny in the Garrison at St John's. Ringleaders captured and punished **Admiral POLE** Governor of Newfoundland. Richard Routh, Chief Justice, drowned on his passage to England

1801 —Union of England and Ireland. **J. OGDEN** Chief Justice

1802 —**Admiral Lord GAMBIER** Governor. Treaty of Amiens, signed by England, France, Spain, and Holland

1803 —Regiment of Volunteers, under the name of "The Newfoundland Light Infantry," formed 1,000 strong, Colonel Skinner in command Former regiment Newfoundland Fencibles disbanded, 1802 Saint John's Charity School Society instituted, August 1803 **Thomas TREMLETT** Chief Justice. Thomas Coote Chief Magistrate, vice Williams, deceased.

1804 —Phoenix Insurance Company, of London, presented a fire-engine to the town, British and Imperial Insurance Companies gave 35 fire-buckets Sunday schools re-established **Sir Erasmus GOWER**, Governor, opened Gower Street.

1805 —Post Office established in the Colony Simon Solomon Postmaster-General Battle of Trafalgar Death of Nelson. Population of St. John's, 5,564.

1806 —Benevolent Irish Society formed at the London Tavern by Jas McBraire, Esq, Major Commandant of the St John's Volunteer Rangers; President Captain Winckworth Tonge. Dr. Lambert, Roman Catholic Bishop, arrived, consecrated in Wexford Bishop of Chitra *in partibus* Volunteer Corps Newfoundland Rangers embodied, officers—Captains Parker, J Williams, Boucher, T Williams, Batten, Lieuts Shea, Solomon, Lilly, Stevenson, Haire; Ensigns Parker, Gill, Thomas, Mellege, Parsons, Surgeon Coughlan; Quarter-master Beenlan

1807.—Four actors ask permission to open a theatre **Admiral HOLLOWAY,** Governor, arrived July 26th, 1807. The "Royal Gazette and Newfoundland Advertizer," first published, 27th August 1807, under most careful restrictions. John Ryan, editor and publisher Abolition of the slave trade by England

1808.—Formation of Volunteer Corps for defence of the capital and island. Lieut. Spratt, R N, sent with paintings to the Beothics.

1809.—Labrador and Anticosti re-annexed to the Government of Newfoundland by Act 49 Geo III, which also established permanent Courts of Judicature in Newfoundland

1810.—Proclamation to protect Red Indians   Sir John Thomas **DUCKWORTH** Governor. Magistrates for St. John's—T Coote, J. Broom, R Sconce, James Blaikie, Esqrs , and Rev. D Rowland Population, St John's, 6,000. Major-General Moore in command of the troops.

1811.—Lieut Buchan's expedition to Beothics   Two marines killed   Waterside in St. John's cleared of ships' rooms , leased by auction to the public. Permission first granted to erect permanent houses.

1812.—Second American War. St John's in a flourishing condition. North American fleet consisted of 3 sail of the line, 21 frigates, 37 sloops, brigs, and schooners of war   Harbour of St. John's full of prizes   Napoleon's retreat from Moscow.   Volunteer Force re-organised , Major McBraire, commanding ; Captains—Bouchier, T. Williams, Lilly, McAllister, G R Robinson, Crawford, Haynes, Ryan, Trimingham, Thomas , Lieutenants—Melledge, Broom, Steward, McLea, Simpson, Livingston, Grieve, Arnott, Clift, Shannon . Ensigns—Morris, McCalman, Rendell, Scott, Willis, N Gill, Niven Laug; Adjutant—Hughes ; Quarter-master—Barnes , Surgeon—Duggan

1813.—June 1st, Capture of the *Chesapeake*, American frigate, off Boston, by H M.S. *Shannon*.   Twenty-two Irishmen, bound to Newfoundland, were in *Shannon*   Coming out in Newman & Co 's brig, *Duck*, they had been captured by American privateer, *Governor Plummer*, recaptured by English privateer brig, *Sir John Sherbrooke*, and then put aboard *Shannon*   **Cæsar COL-CLOUGH** Chief Justice, from Prince Edward Island, in place of Tremlett, who was sent there in a King's ship   **Sir Richard Godwin KEATS**, Governor, laid foundation stone of St John's Hospital, Riverhead   First grants of land ; 110 grants issued the year   Decisive victory of Wellington at Vittoria, Spain. French driven across the Pyrenees   Publication of Dr William Carson's pamphlet , agitation for Colonial Parliament   The following magistrates were appointed this year —Coote, Broom, Roland, Blaikie, for St. John's , Carrington and Lilly, Harbour Grace , Rev J Church and Burrell, Trinity ; Edgar, Greenspond , Ford, Bonavista , McKie and Angell, Bay Bulls ; W. Carter, Ferryland ; Bradshaw and Blackburn, Placentia , Gosse, Carbonear , Jackson, Trepassey , Butler and Bishop, Burin ; Spooner and Anthoine, Fortune Bay , Bryant, Ferryland , Phippard, St. Mary's , Pinson and S. Prowse, Labrador ; and for the Island, Captains R N. Elliott, Cooksley, Skekel, Campbell, Holbrook, Buchan, and Rev F Carrington and P C Le Geyt, the Governor's Secretary.   Major-General Campbell commanding troops numbering 750.

1814.—Battle of Lundy 's Lane, between Loyal Canadians and Americans.   Treaty of Ghent , end of second American War   First Treaty of Paris ; allies enter Paris 1,200,000 qtls fish exported , whole value of exports, $11,144,000   Newfoundland Mercantile Journal established   P. W. Carter, Esq , Registrar Vice-Admiralty Court

1815.—Battle of Waterloo   Abdication of Napoleon , banished to St. Helena   Second Treaty of Paris   Last Treaty made between England and France about the Newfoundland Fishery.   Confirms Treaty of Versailles, 1783   Numerous failures, caused by peace and depreciation of fish in foreign markets.   Wesleyan Mission Stations organised into districts   26th August, Captain David Buchan, R N , took possession of St. Pierre and Miquelon.

1816.—12th February, St. John's nearly destroyed by fire; great distress , loss, £100,000 sterling ; cargo of provisions sent in winter by benevolent people of Boston, U.S **Francis FORBES**, Esq , afterwards Sir Francis, Chief Justice, arrived ; a most able and competent Judge ; continued on the Bench six years   First visit of an Anglican Bishop to Newfoundland by Dr Stanser, Bishop of Nova Scotia   Dr Scallan, third Roman Catholic Bishop, consecrated Bishop of Drago *in partibus*, and Vicar Apostolic of Newfoundland   Church at Harbour Grace burnt   H M S. *Comus* and transport *Harpooner* lost at St Shott's, November 10th   Admiral **PICKMORE** Governor.

1817.—St John's again visited by fires, November 7th and 21st ; 200 houses destroyed. Great distress; severe winter , riots ; known in Newfoundland history as "The Winter of the Rals," and the Hard Winter.

1818.— Convention with the United States respecting the Fisheries   Admiral **PICKMORE**, first resident Governor, died in St John's.   Captain **BOWKER** Administrator. Coldest winter ever experienced in Newfoundland. Arrival of brig *Messenger* in January with cargo of provisions, sent by the benevolent people of Boston   Sir C. **HAMILTON** Governor.

1819.—Queen Victoria born, 24th May. Red Indian woman, Mary March, brought to St John's Celebrated case of Butler and Lundrigan Great fire in St John's

1820.—Death of George III , aged 81, his reign of 60 years being the longest of any English sovereign.

GEORGE IV., 1820 to 1830.

1822.—**Richard Alexander TUCKER**, Esq , Chief Justice, appointed 1st October

1823.—The last of the Red Indians of Newfoundland seen ; Indian women brought to St John's Newfoundland School Society established by Samuel Codnor, Esq , of Dartmouth, Devon Mr Cormack crossed the Island St John's Library Society instituted February 14th , President, Hon R A. Tucker ; Librarian, James Clift Surrogate Courts abolished J Broom Chief Stipendiary Magistrate, vice Coote resigned James Blakie and P. W. Carter, Esqrs., Stipendiary Magistrates, St. John's Dr. Scallan Bishop of Drago and Vicar Apostolic of Newfoundland and Labrador. Chamber of Commerce, St. John's, instituted 26th December , Newman Hoyles first President, Secretary, John Boyd Naval establishment removed from St John's.

1824.—Imperial Act, 5 Geo. IV. cap 67 Act for the better Administration of Justice in Newfoundland , appointing Supreme Court with Chief Justice and two Assistant Judges First fire company, Eastern Ward, St John's , N W. Hoyles, Captain St John's Dorcas Society instituted October 29th ; Mrs. Ward, wife of Rev. D. S. Ward, Congregational minister, first president ; Mrs R Job, second President. Peace of Ghent between England and the United States, December 24th.

1825.—**Sir Thomas COCHRANE** Governor. First roads constructed.

1826.—Supreme Court of Newfoundland constituted by Royal Charter, and opened with great ceremony by the Governor January 2nd, 1826. First Assistant Judges, with **Chief Justice TUCKER**, were Jno William Molloy and A. W. Des Barres. Molloy soon removed E B Brenton appointed. Orphan Asylum erected , Orphan Asylum school instituted February 17th , 1826 , Chairman, T. Hogan , Master, Henry Simms. Fire Company, Middle Ward, St John's, October 16th, 1826 , P. Kough, Captain Lieut.-Governor of St John's, Col. Sir George Elder, Knt ; Lieut -Governor, Placentia, Col. George Reeves.

1827.—Bishop Inglis, Anglican Bishop of Nova Scotia and Newfoundland, first visited Newfoundland and consecrated St. John's Church Mechanics' Society formed 3rd March, 1827. J. Crowdy Colonial Secretary. Beothic Institution, W. E. Cormack, President

1828.—Publication of P. Morris's pamphlet Great agitation for representative institutions ; movement led by Dr. W Carson and others

1829.—Roman Catholics emancipated Bishop Fleming consecrated Bishop of Carpasia in partibus Duel fought on Robinson's Hill between Captain Rudkin and Lieut Phillpotts , the latter killed ; Rudkin tried and convicted of manslaughter. Shawnandithit, a captive Boethic, died in St John's

WILLIAM IV., 1830 to 1837.

1830.—Liverpool and Manchester Railway opened September 15th. Bishop Scallan died. Government House completed

1831.—First coach road opened to Portugal Cove

1832.—Representative Assembly granted to Newfoundland Opening first Parliament under Reform Bill in England. Great fire in Harbour Grace. Factory opened by benevolent ladies of St John's

1833.—1st January, first Session of the Newfoundland House of Assembly opened by Sir Thomas Cochrane, Governor John Bingley Garland first Speaker ; Chief Justice Tucker President of the Legislative Council , he resigned this year, and was succeeded by **Hy. John BOULTON**, Chief Justice. First Convent of Presentation Nuns in St John's founded by Bishop Fleming

1834.—**Captain PRESCOTT**, R N , Governor George Lilly, Esq , appointed Acting Judge Supreme Court, first native Judge. August 1st, Abolition of Slavery in the British Colonies. Heavy Criminal Calendar ; four persons convicted of murder. Savings Bank constituted, N. W. Hoyles, Colonial Treasurer, Cashier.

1886.—First light erected on Cape Spear Bank of British North America established in St John's Second General Election.

VICTORIA, 1837.

1837.—Accession of Her Majesty to the Throne, June 20th. First Session of Second General Assembly commenced, 3rd July. Father Matthew's Temperance Missions. Daguerrotype process discovered

1838.—First Geological Survey made by J Beete Jukes, who arrived in St John's, in company with the celebrated Plantagenet Harrison, by the brig *Diana*, belonging to Stuart and Rennie. Chief Justice Boulton removed, and **John Gervase Hutchinson BOURNE** appointed. Legislature voted $175,000 in two years for roads. Great case of Kielly v Carson

1839.—Newfoundland constituted a separate see; Bishop Spencer, first Anglican Bishop

1840.—First regular sailing packet established between St John's and Halifax, N S, trips once a fortnight. H M S *Spitfire*, paddle steamer, arrived with troops; Jukes left in her, first steamer in St John's. Native Society formed St Thomas's Church consecrated. Penny Postage established in England

1841.—Legislative Union of Upper and Lower Canada. Foundation Stone of Roman Catholic Cathedral laid by Dr. Fleming. **Major-General Sir John HARVEY**, K C B, appointed Governor

1842.—Sisters of Mercy arrived in St John's, 10th June. Amalgamated Assembly of Newfoundland constituted by Act of the Imperial Parliament—5 & 6 Vict cap cxx, passed August 12th; Hon. J. Crowdy, Colonial Secretary, first Speaker. First Agricultural Society formed. S S *John McAdam* arrived. Steamship Company incorporated in St John's to run steamer between St John's and Halifax, N S. First Presbyterian kirk established; Rev Donald A Fraser minister. Captain Faybre and Mr W. Thomas, President Chamber of Commerce, appointed Commissioners on French Fishery Question. General Election of Members to the Amalgamated House held on 20th December. The Assembly consisted of 15 elected members and 10 nominees of the Crown. Hon J Crowdy Speaker

1843.—Act for the Encouragement of Education introduced by Richard Barnes. Death of Dr Wm Carson. Nugent introduced Bill to abolish oath of supremacy and abjuration, and to substitute oath of allegiance. Amalgamated House opened by Sir John Harvey on 17th January, longest opening speech on record. St Andrew's Kirk opened December 3rd

1844.—Edward Feild, D D, appointed Bishop of Newfoundland. The first steam packet arrived in St John's from Halifax, N S, S S *North American*, commanded by Captain Richard Meagher, sixty hours' passage. Non-denominational Academy at Castle Rennie, St John's, Charles D Newman, M A, Oxford, Principal, J Nugent and T Talbot, Masters. **Chief Justice NORTON** first Roman Catholic Chief Justice, most excellent Judge.

1845.—Prince Henry, son of the King of the Netherlands, in war steamer *Rhine*, visited St John's, great demonstration. Gas introduced into St. John's. Geo Lilly appointed Judge, Supreme Court.

1846.—26th May, public meeting in Court House, St John's, in favour of Responsible Government, petition sent to Queen and Parliament. 9th June, terrible and destructive fire consumed the town. 19th September, tremendous gale. Sir John Harvey appointed Governor of Nova Scotia. **Col. LAW** Administrator.

1847.—**Sir Gaspard LE MARCHANT**, Governor, arrived 23rd April. **Chief Justice BRADY** appointed. Foundation Stone of English Cathedral of St. John the Baptist laid, also Colonial Building and Custom House, St John's

1848.—Great Revolution in Europe. December 14th, first Session of Legislature, after return to Constitution of 1833, opened by Sir Gaspard Le Marchant. Bishop Mullock arrived, May 6th, in S S *Unicorn*, Captain R Maher. First Water Company, supply from Signal Hill. Free Kirk established

1849.—Discovery of gold in California. Customs Department placed under control of local Government, J Kent first collector; Mr Spearmen retired on a pension. Steamer *Kestrel*, Captain Maher, lost

1850.—Death of Bishop Fleming. Market House opened. Free Kirk opened.

1851.—Public meeting to promote direct steam from St John's to England. The great Exhibition of the Industries of all Nations held in London, May 1st. Great demonstration of Sons of Temperance, St. John's. General Election

1852—**Ker Bailie HAMILTON** Governor. Death of the Duke of Wellington
Louis Napoleon Emperor of the French. First Steamer in Conception Bay.
Hon J. Crowdy Administrator. Electric telegraph introduced into St John's
by F. N Gisborne; St John's and Carbonear Electric Telegraph Company;
R Prowse Managing Director. Terribly disastrous seal fishery; "Spring of
the Wadhams"

1853—English and French fleet enter the Dardanelles   Turkey declares war against
Russia   The Electric Telegraph Company, Gisborne's Company, incorporated,
1853

1854—Union Bank established   Outbreak of cholera in St John's   Crimean War
Victories of the English and French   Battles of Alma, Balaclava, Inkerman.
Reciprocity Treaty between British America and the United States
F. B. T Carter appointed Acting Judge, Supreme Court   New York,
Newfoundland, and London Telegraph Company incorporated

1855—**Governor DARLING**   Increased Representation Act, giving 30 members,
including Burgeo and La Poile   Responsible Government introduced   Taking of
Sebastopol; great rejoicings over the British Empire   First General Election
under Responsible Government.   Hon **P. F LITTLE** : first Premier
Roman Catholic Cathedral consecrated. The American steamer *James Adger*
arrived in St John's with Mr. and Mrs. Cyrus Field, Peter Cooper, Bayard
Taylor, and a distinguished company , endeavoured to lay the cable across the
Gulf; failed owing to bad weather , cable parted , forty miles paid out.

1856—Newfoundland divided into two Roman Catholic dioceses, St John's and Harbour
Grace; Dr Dalton first Bishop of Harbour Grace   Telegraphic communication
established with the American continent.   First message sent across Gulf from
J and W Pitts to A. and M Cameron, Baddeck   Foundation Stone Gower
Street Methodist Church laid   Fire in St John's (Tarchin's Town)   Direct
steam by the Galway Line   Gulf cable laid by S.S *Propontis* , Sir Samuel
Canning , T D Scanlan represented New York, Newfoundland, and London
Telegraph Company.

1857—**Hon. L O'BRIEN** Administrator, on the promotion of Sir C Darling to
the Governorship of Jamaica.   **Sir Alexander BANNERMAN** appointed
Governor   The Indian Mutiny   The Anglo-French Convention about the
Newfoundland fishery; indignation meetings   Delegates sent to Canada, Nova
Scotia, &c   Gower Street Wesleyan Church completed   Commercial Bank
established

1858—First Atlantic Cable landed at Bay Bulls Arm, Trinity Bay , great rejoicings in
St John's in honour of Cyrus Field, to whose indefatigable energy final success
was due   First cable soon collapsed   Hon. P. F Little and B Robinson
appointed Judges Supreme Court, and the Hons J Simms and A. W Des Barres
retired on pensions

1859—News boat placed at Cape Race by the New York Associated Press to intercept
ocean steamers   First ship intercepted, *Vigo*, of Inman Line   General
Election , great contest at Burin   Act for Local Steam passed   **Hon. John
KENT** Premier

1860—His Royal Highness the Prince of Wales visited the Island   Formation of
Volunteer Corps

1861—**H W. HOYLES** Premier   Time of great political excitement   Political
riots in St John's, Harbour Grace, and Harbour Main.   Commencement of the
American Civil War between North and South

1862.—January, first Allan Steamer, *North American*, left St John's   S S *Polynia*,
S S *Camperdown*, total failure at seal fishery   Great haul of seals at Green
Bay   Colonial and Continental Church Society incorporated   Great distress
owing to bad fisheries   S S *Victoria* inaugurated local steam north and south

1863.—27th April, loss of *Anglo-Saxon*, Clam Cove ; great loss of life   St John's
provided with water from Windsor Lake   S S *Bloodhound*, Captain Graham,
arrived 22nd April, 3,000 seals, S S. *Wolf*, W. Kane, arrived 28th, 1,340 seals.
Fire Brigade established   Revenue collected at Labrador. Hon. L O'Brien
Administrator.   S S *Ariel* put on route, north and south.

1864—**Sir Anthony MUSGRAVE** Governor   Confederation of the Dominion of
Canada   Meeting of Delegates in Maritime Provinces and Quebec to inaugurate
Confederation , Sir F B T Carter and Sir A. Shea represented the Colony.

Copper mine opened, Tilt Cove, by C F. Bennett, the pioneer of mining in the Colony, and Smith McKay, the discoverer   Three steamers, *Bloodhound, Wolf,* and *Osprey,* at the seal fishery   The Currency Act confirmed   Hon. J. Hayward appointed Acting Assistant Judge

1865 —Present Geological Survey commenced. American Civil War ended with the complete conquest of the Southern States, and abolition of slavery.   F. B. T. CARTER Premier   Sir H. W. HOYLES Chief Justice.   General Election

1866 —Second Atlantic Cable successfully landed at Heart's Content, Newfoundland, by the *Great Eastern,* August 1866 ; the end of 1865 cable also picked up, and successfully landed at Heart's Content same year   A M Mackay successfully repaired Gulf Cable in S S *Bloodhound.* First business message sent across the Atlantic by W J S Donnelly, fee £20 sterling

1867.—Fishery very successful.   Great gale at Labrador, much shipping destroyed.   The British North America Act for the Confederation of the Provinces is passed   Dominion of Canada proclaimed   Bishop Kelly consecrated coadjutor to Bishop Feild

1868 —Proclamation issued by the Carter Administration suppressing able-bodied poor relief. 7th August, Hon J. Hayward appointed Assistant Judge Supreme Court, on the retirement of P F. Little.   Cunard contract ceased and Inman Company carried mails and passengers from St John's to Halifax, N S , during winter months

1869 —Large increase in the Public Debt caused by the bad fisheries   Sir Stephen HILL appointed Governor in July   Central District Court constituted   General Election ; Confederation Candidates defeated.   Census taken   Dr Mullock died

1870.—The Most Rev. T. J Power, consecrated at Rome Bishop of St John's, arrived in St John's 9th September.   Diocesan Synod of Church of England established. Hon. C. F. BENNETT Premier

1871.—Garrison withdrawn from Newfoundland.   Increasing prosperity consequent on good fisheries, &c   Treaty of Washington   S S *Ariel* discontinued coastal service, carried out by S S *Tiger* and *Leopard.*

1872.—First Exhibition held in Newfoundland, opened by the Governor ; Rev E Botwood, R D , projector   Agitation about pre-emption of the New York, Newfoundland, and London telegraph lines , continued through 1873

1873 —Direct steam to England by Allan Line commenced   George Street Methodist Church opened.   General Election , Bennett Government defeated by the withdrawal of three members.

1874.—The largest catch of cod fish ever taken in Newfoundland.   Sir F. B. T CARTER Premier   Newfoundland Conference of Methodist Church of Canada organised, Rev G. S Milligan President   The Royal Commission , Sir B. Robinson, J. Goodfellow, and J Fox, Esquires

1875 —The first Government Railway Survey under direction of Sandford Fleming, Civil Engineer

1876 —Christian Brothers arrived in St John's   Sir J. H. GLOVER, G C.M.G , Governor. Dr. J B. Kelly, D D , appointed Bishop of Newfoundland   Halifax Fishery Commission met , $5,500,000 awarded as compensation to be paid by the United States to the British Provinces , Newfoundland's share one million; Sir W. V Whiteway Commissioner for Newfoundland   Bishop Feild died, in Bermuda. Both Presbyterian kirks burnt.

1877.—Sir F B. T. Carter appointed Acting Assistant Judge, on the retirement of Sir B. Robinson.   Commander W. Howorth, R N , appointed first Stipendary Magistrate, West Coast, by Imperial and Colonial Governments , duties first collected there. St Andrew's Kirk built by United Presbyterians.   Trinity, Catalina, and Bonavista connected by telegraph.   S S *Curlew* and *Plover* on coastal service.

1878 —Dr Ll Jones, D.D , appointed Bishop of Newfoundland   Sir W. V. WHITEWAY Premier.   Telegraph extended to St. George's Bay, Bay of Islands, Bonne Bay, Betts Cove, Tilt Cove, and Little Bay Mines.

1879 —First issue " Evening Telegram "

1880.—Sir F. B. T. CARTER appointed Chief Justice, and R J. Pinsent Judge Supreme Court.   Colonial Government allowed to make grants of land on the west coast. or " French Shore " so-called.   Sir F. B. T. CARTER, K C M G , Administrator.   First Railway Bill passed.

1881.—Serious disturbance on the Railway line (Battle of Fox Trap) **Sir Henry Fitz-Hardinge MAXSE** Governor First railway under construction in Newfoundland, St John's to Harbour Grace

1882 —First issue " Evening Mercury." An Act passed for the construction of the Great American and European Short Line Railway Charter granted for the construction of a graving dock. **Sir W. V. WHITEWAY** Premier. Inauguration of St. Patrick's Hall, B I Society

1883.—St Stephen's Day, Harbour Grace Riots **Sir F. B. T. CARTER** Administrator. Hon. J I Little appointed Assistant Judge, Supreme Court, in place of Hon Judge Hayward, retired. Sir H Maxse died in St. John's Fishery Exhibition held in London , Sir A Shea, K C M G , Commissioner for the Colony. **Hon. E. MORRIS** Administrator, in absence of Sir F. B T. Carter, K C.M G.

1884.—Union of Methodist Bodies in Canada. Newfoundland Conference of Methodist Church organised in Gower Street Church ; Rev. Dr Milligan, President July, **Sir J. H. GLOVER** arrived in St John's as Governor Dry Dock at Riverhead, St John's, opened H M.S Tenedos docked in December. Railway to Harbour Grace opened for Passengers in December

1885 —Ford-Pennell Convention on French Fishery claims **Sir F. B. T. CARTER** Administrator **Sir Robert THORBURN** Premier General Election. Choir and transepts of English cathedral consecrated by Bishop Jones First issue " Daily Colonist " Great Storm in Newfoundland and Labrador Atlantic Hotel opened, May Telegraph extended to Greenspond and Twillingate, also Burin, St. Lawrence, Lamaline, Grand Bank, and Fortune Sir W. V Whiteway resigned Premiership in October General Election November. **Sir R. THORBURN** Premier Death of Sir J H. Glover in London

1886 —**Sir F. B T. CARTER** Administrator **Sir G. W. DES VŒUX** Governor. Building of New Post Office. Corner Stone of Methodist College laid by Sir G W Des Vœux Report of Joint Committee on Fishery question; approved of Bait Act and refused to sanction the Ford-Pennell Convention. Placentia Railway commenced

1887.—The Bait Act became Law. **Sir H. A. BLAKE** Governor. Ballot Act passed Queen's Jubilee , Service in English Cathedral attended by all denominations of Protestants. Sir A Shea, K C M G , appointed Governor of the Bahamas Methodist College and Alexander Street Methodist Church opened. Colonial Conference held in London ; Colony represented by Sir R. Thorburn, Premier, and Sir A Shea

1888.—Second Washington Treaty negotiated , Hon J S Winter represented the Colony. Modus vivendi established for two years Methodist College Home opened. Bait Act put in operation, March Placentia Railway opened for traffic Act to provide Municipal Council for St John's passed. S.S. Volunteer and Conscript on coastal service Governor Blake appointed to Jamaica **Sir F. B T CARTER** Administrator to January 1889

1889.—**Sir T. N. O'BRIEN** appointed Governor ; arrived in January 1889 General Election Thorburn Government defeated by an immense majority. Roman Catholic Cathedral, Harbour Grace, burnt Act granting manhood suffrage passed

1890.—**Sir W. V. WHITEWAY** Premier Act authorising new Railway Line North Agitation concerning the modus vivendi with the French about Lobster Factories West Coast The modus was accepted by French Ambassador, 11 March Protest from both Houses 14 March. Meeting of Patriotic Association, Bannerman Park, 26 March. Tax on all Canadian vessels purchasing bait Reciprocity Treaty with United States by Hon R Bond, Colonial Secretary , prevented being carried into effect by Canada Delegations to England on difficulties with the French, consisting of Sir W. V. Whiteway, Hon A W. Harvey, Hon R Bond and the Honble The Speaker, G H. Emerson (official) , from the Patriotic Association Sir J S. Winter, P. J Scott, and A B Morine to England, and D J. Greene, D Morison, and P. R Bowers to Canada.

1891.—Municipal Council Act amended Delegation to England on difficulties with French, consisting of Sir W V. Whiteway, Hon A. W. Harvey, G. H. Emerson Hon. M Monroe and A. B Morine International Arbitration on Lobster Question to be held at Brussels. Hall's Bay Railway completed to Trinity and

Bonavista Bays Celebrated case of Baird ι Walker, arising out of *modus vivendi*, determined by Supreme Court in favour of plaintiff, on appeal to Privy Council, judgment confirmed Newfoundland Bill in the House of Commons; Temporary Act (Treaty Bill) passed for two years

1892 —Death of the Duke of Clarence, Jan 14th Terrible calamity and loss of life in Trinity Bay, Feb 28th, death of 24 men caught in a northerly gale, driven to sea, and frozen to death Visit of Deep Sea Mission to Labrador Conference at Halifax, N S, between Canadian Ministers and Members of the Newfoundland Government. Great fire in St John's on July 9th

1893 —Bait Act suspended in April by Proclamation Temporary French Treaty Bill extended to end of 1895. April 28th, death of Sir R J Pinsent, D C L November, General Election The Whiteway Government sustained by a large majority December 4th, the most Rev T Jos. Power, D D, Roman Catholic Bishop of St John's, died Dispute with the French about payment of duty on goods landed on West Coast not carried in fishing vessels.

1894 —January 6th, nine petitions against 17 members Whiteway party filed under Election Act February 16th, Houses of Assembly opened. March 27th, two members for Bay de Verde unseated and disqualified April 2nd, judgment communicated to the House of Assembly April 3rd, deputation of 20 members of Whiteway party waited on Governor asking for a dissolution April 4th, counter deputation of Goodridge party protested against dissolution April 10th, dissolution refused April 11th, Whiteway Government resign **A. F GOODRIDGE** Premier, Whiteway party withdraw Supply and Revenue Bills April 14th, House of Assembly prorogued to 23rd, April 21st, prorogation extended till 23rd May May 5th, two members of St John's East unseated and disqualified. May 22nd, Bay de Verde bye election resulted in return of one Government and one opposition candidate May 23rd, prorogation extended to 7th June May 31st, three members St John's West unseated and disqualified June 7th, prorogation extended to 7th July June 11th, Revenue Act expired June 14th, one member for Burgeo and La Poile unseated and disqualified June 23rd, H R H the Duchess of York safely delivered of an infant Prince July 7th, prorogation extended to 7th August July 25th, two members for Trinity unseated and disqualified and a third member unseated only July 31st, two members for Placentia unseated and disqualified August 2nd, House of Assembly opened August 9th, House of Assembly closed September 10th, Burgeo and La Poile election resulted in return of a Government candidate October 2nd, Bonavista bye-election, Colonial Secretary and Attorney-General returned Fogo election, Duder, Government candidate, returned Twillingate election, 16th October Foote, Opposition candidate, returned Three Opposition members elected for Trinity 10th November, Placentia, St John's, and Burin all returned Whiteway candidates Carty, Government candidate, returned for St George's, 12th November, 20th, severe storm December 10th, Black Monday; failure of Commercial and Union Banks and several mercantile houses, December 12th, resignation of Goodridge Government; 13th, appointment of Cabinet with **D. J. GREENE** Premier

1895 —January 27th, Act passed removing the disabilities of members unseated by decisions of Supreme Court January 31st, new administration formed, **Sir W. V. WHITEWAY** Premier February 22nd, Bishop Howley, first native Catholic bishop, arrives Relief committees formed, liberal contributions from England March 27th, Confederation delegates appointed. Arrival of SS *Aurora*, with 27,000 seals April 2nd, House of Assembly re opened April 3rd, arrival of Sir H. H Murray, K C B, Relief Commissioner April 4th, first meeting Union Conference at Ottawa April 16th, Conference broken off May 19th, death of Hon M Monroe June 15th, Hon R Bond obtains loan, 550,000*l* July 2nd, Retrenchment Act passed. July 27th, departure of Sir T N. O'Brien September 13th, Rt Rev Neil McNeil appointed Roman Catholic Bishop of West Coast September 24th, Sir H H Murray, K C B, appointed Governor October, prosecution of smuggling syndicate. November 25th, judgments in smuggling cases overruled by Supreme Court November 28th, **Sir H. H. MURRAY** arrives.

II.—Judiciary.

CHRONOLOGICAL TABLE OF THE CHIEF JUSTICES, AND ASSISTANT JUDGES OF THE SUPREME COURT.

1. **JOHN REEVES**, C J, 1791–1792. Appointed in 1791, under Act 31 Geo III c xxix., sole Judge of the Court of Civil Jurisdiction of Our Sovereign Lord the King, at St John's, Newfoundland, next year, by 32 Geo III c lvi, the Supreme Court of Judicature of the Island of Newfoundland was created, Reeves, C J, sole Judge, D'Ewes Coke and AARON GRAHAM assessors

2. **D'EWES COKE**, C J, 1792–1797 Coke, originally a surgeon in the navy, settled in Trinity, was afterwards supreme surrogate at St John's

3. **RICHARD ROUTH**, C J., 1797–1800 Was formerly collector of the customs, on his appointment as Chief Justice he was required to reside permanently in the Colony, in 1800 he requested permission to visit England, and was drowned on the passage; his widow enjoyed a pension for many years

4. **JONATHAN OGDEN**, C J, 1801–1803. Surgeon, R N, sent as assistant surgeon to hospital by H R H. Duke of Kent, commanding in Nova Scotia, became naval officer and supreme surrogate, appointed acting C J in 1801, received his commission in May 1802, resigned in 1803, and was pensioned

5. **THOMAS TREMLETT**, C J, 1803–1813 Was an insolvent merchant of Poole, became naval officer and supreme surrogate in succession to Ogden, and, on the latter's retirement from ill health, Chief Justice, he was translated to Prince Edward's Island as Chief Judge, in exchange for Judge Colclough, 1713.

6. **CÆSAR COLCLOUGH**, C J, 1813–1815 An Irish gentleman of good family, an amusing writer, but a very inefficient judge, and no lawyer, salary increased to £1,000, retired on a pension.

7. **FRANCIS FORBES**, C J, 1816–1822 Appointed by commission bearing date 4th August 1816; took his seat on the bench 1st July 1817, resigned 30th September 1822, resided on the Island during the whole of the period, a most able and popular judge.

8. **RICHARD ALEXANDER TUCKER**, C J, 1822–1833 Commission dated 1st October 1822, took his seat on the Supreme Court Bench 5th May 1823, sole Judge until 2nd January 1826, when the Royal Charter granted by His Majesty to the Supreme Court of Newfoundland, under the provisions of the Act 5 Geo. IV cap lxvii s 17, was promulgated, and the bench then filled by—

HON. R A TUCKER, Chief Judge
HON. JOHN WILLIAM MOLLOY -
HON AUGUSTUS WALLET DES BARRES } Assistant Judges

On 26th September 1826 HON EDWARD BRABAZON BRENTON was appointed A J in the room of Mr. Molloy, who had been removed from his office JAMES SIMMS was sworn in, 2nd January 1826, as H M Attorney-General. In September 1826, during the absence of the Governor, Sir T. Cochrane, Tucker, C J, was Administrator of the Government, Brenton Acting C J., and JAMES COCHRANE Acting Assistant Judge, until Sir Thomas's return on 12th August 1828.

9. **HENRY JOHN BOULTON**, C.J., 1833–1838. Was formerly Attorney-General of Upper Canada; removed from office and appointed C.J. of Newfoundland; removed by order of the Privy Council in 1838. Charges having been made against Judge Des Barres, he retired temporarily, and E. M. ARCHIBALD, Clerk of the Court, was Acting Assistant Judge in December 1833, and in part of 1834.

10. **JOHN GERVASE HUTCHINSON BOURNE**, C.J., 1838–1844.
DES BARRES and BRENTON, A.J's.
Bourne was dismissed by Sir John Harvey in 1844.
J. Simms, Attorney-General, made Acting Chief Justice on 10th June 1844, and continued to act until the arrival of C.J. Norton.

11. **THOMAS NORTON**, C.J., 1844–1847. Commission dated 5th November 1844.
Des Barres and Brenton, A.J's.; Brenton died in 1845; and
GEO. LILLY was appointed A.J.; Lilly died in 1846; and
J. Simms was appointed Assistant Judge on 27th November 1846.
Des Barres was Acting Chief Justice from 3rd September 1847 to 29th November 1847.

12. **SIR FRANCIS BRADY**, C.J., 1847–1865. Sworn in 29th November 1847.
F. B. T. CARTER became acting A.J. on 6th April 1854, in place of Des Barres, A.J., who resumed in the fall term of the same year.
G. H. EMERSON, Acting Judge in 1856.
Des Barres and J. Simms, A.J's. until November 1858.
P. F. LITTLE appointed A.J. on 1st November 1858.
BRYAN ROBINSON appointed A.J. on 2nd November 1858.
P. F. Little was Acting Chief Justice on 30th November 1858.
CHARLES SIMMS was acting A.J. on 30th November 1858, and again on 7th February 1859.

13. **SIR HUGH WILLIAM HOYLES** C.J., 1865–1880. Sworn in on 20th May 1865. P. F. Little retired, 20th November 1866, when Geo. Hy. Emerson was appointed acting A.J. on 19th August 1867.
JOHN HAYWARD was appointed A.J. on 7th August 1868.
F. B. T. Carter, Attorney-General, was acting A.J. on 20th May 1865, on 20th May 1868, and again on 20th May 1878.

14. **SIR FREDERIC BOWKER TERRINGTON CARTER**, C.J., K.C.M.G., 1880, present Chief Justice. Sworn into office 20th May 1880.
SIR R. J. PINSENT, D.C.L. Made Judge of the Supreme Court on 20th May 1880; died April 1893.
J. I. LITTLE. Made Acting Judge on 27th November 1883, and Judge on 7th May 1884.
SIR J. S. WINTER. Made Judge on 27th May 1893.

III.—House of Assembly.

District.	1832.	1837.	1842.	1848.	1852.
Bonavista	Wm. Brown	H. A. Emerson	Robert Carter	Robert Carter	J. H. Warren.
Burin	Wm. Hooper	Henry Butler	C. Benning	J. G. Falle	C. Benning.
Ferryland	Robert Carter	Peter Winser	T. Glen	P. Winser	P. Winser.
Fogo	T. Bennett	E. J. Dwyer	J. Slade	G. H. Emerson	G. H. Emerson.
Fortune Bay	N. W. Hoyles	W. B. Row	B. Robinson	H. W. Hoyles	H. W. Hoyles.
Conception Bay	Peter Brown	Peter Brown	Thomas Ridley	J. L. Prender-gast.	J. Hayward.
"	James Power	James Power	John Munn	Nicholas Mol-loy.	J. V. Nugent.
"	C. Cozens	John McCarthy	J. L. Prender-gast.	Richard Rankin	T. Talbot.
Placentia and	Robert Pack	A. W. Godfrey	E. Hanrahan	E. Hanrahan	T. Hanrahan.
St. Mary's	R. F. Sweetman	J. V. Nugent	John Dillon	A. Shea.	G. J. Hogsett.
St. John's	J. H. Martin	Patrick Doyle	Simon Morris	J. Delaney	A. Shea.
"	P. Keough	W. Carson	W. Carson	J. Kent	John Kent.
Trinity	John Kent	John Kent	J. O'Brien	L. O'Brien	P. P. Little.
"	Wm. Thomas	Patrick Morris	J. V. Nugent	R. J. Parsons	R. J. Parsons.
"	J. B. Garland	T. F. Moore	Richard Barnes	T. B. Joh	S. March.

District.	1855. 7th May.	1859.	1861.
Bay de Verde	J. Bemister	J. Bemister.	J. Bemister.
Bonavista	K. Carter	S. March.	S. March.
"	J. H. Warren	J. H. Warren.	J. H. Warren.
"	M. W. Walbank	M. W. Walbank.	M. W. Walbank.
Burgeo & La Poile	R. Prowse	James Seaton.	D. W. Prowse.
Burin	C. Benning	A. Shea.	H. W. Hoyles.
"	P. Morris	I. J. Rogerson	Ed. Evans.
Carbonear	E. Hanrahan	E. Hanrahan	E. Hanrahan.
Ferryland	T. Glen	T. Glen	T. Glen.
"	E. D. Shea	E. D. Shea	E. D. Shea.
Fortune Bay	H. W. Hoyles	Capt. Carter, R.N.	Capt. Carter, R.N.
Harbour Grace	J. Hayward	J. Hayward	J. Hayward.
"	J. L. Prendergast.	J. L. Prender-gast.	H. Moore.
Harbour Main	T. Talbot	P. Nowlan	P. Nowlan.
"	T. Byrne	C. Purcy	A. Shea.
Placentia & St. Mary's	G. J. Hogsett	G. J. Hogsett	R. McGrath.
"	J. Kelly	J. Delaney	W. G. Flood.
"	R. Brown	J. English	J. Leamon.
Port de Grave	J. Kent	J. Kent	J. Kent.
St. John's East	R. J. Parsons	J. Leamon	J. Kavanagh.
"	Peter Winser	R. J. Parsons	R. J. Parsons.
St. John's West	P. F. Little	J. Casey	J. Casey.
"	A. Shea	T. S. Dwyer	T. Talbot.
"	John Fox	J. M. Barron	Henry Renouf.
Trinity	F. B. T. Carter	F. B. T. Carter	F. B. T. Carter.
"	S. March	S. Rendell	John Rendell.
"	J. Winter	J. Winter	John Winter.
Twillingate and Fogo	W. H. Ellis	W. V. White-way.	W. V. White-way.
"	T. Knight	T. Knight	T. Knight.

HOUSE OF ASSEMBLY—*continued.*

District.	1865.	1869.	1873. November.	1874. November.	1878. November.	1882. November.	1885. October 31st.	1889. November 6th.
Bay de Verde	J. Bemister	J. Bemister	J. J. Rogerson	J. J. Rogerson	A. Penny	E. Garland	S. R. March	E. White.
Bonavista	J. T. Oakley	J. L. Noonan	C. Bowring	J. H. Warren	F. Winton	W. B. Grieve	A. J. W. McNeily	H. J. B. Woods.
"	J. H. Warren	F. Winton	A. J. W. McNeily	C. Bowring	G. Skelton	G. Skelton	J. L. Noonan	D. Morison.
"	J. T. Burton	W. M. Barnes	J. T. Burton	A. J. W. McNeily	J. Saint	F. Winton	A. Kean	S. Blandford.
Burgeo & La Poile	B. W. Prowse	P. Emerson	P. Emerson	P. Emerson			E. White	A. B. Morine.
Burin	Ed. Evans	F. B. T. Carter	C. R. Ayre	C. R. Ayre	A. M. McKay	A. M. McKay	A. M. McKay	A. M. McKay.
"	P. R. T. Carter		J. S. Winter	J. S. Winter	J. S. Winter	J. S. Winter		J. Murray.
Carbonear	J. Rorke	J. Rorke	J. Rorke	J. Rorke	J. J. Rogerson	J. E. P. Peters	H. E. P. Peters	E. Rothwell.
Ferryland	T. Glen	J. Glen	J. Glen	R. Raftus	J. Rorke	A. Penny	A. Penny	Dr. Tait.
"	M. Kearney	T. Battcock	R. Raftus		D. J. Greene	D. J. Greene	D. J. Greene	W. Duff.
Fogo				J. G. Conroy	J. G. Conroy	A. F. Goodridge	G. Shea	G. Shea.
Fortune Bay	T. R. Bennett	T. R. Bennett	W. O. Wood	R. Alexander	J. O. Fraser	J. O. Fraser	R. Bond	D. J. Greene.
Harbour Grace	J. Hayward	J. Munn	A. Shea	A. Shea	C. Dawe	A. Shea	J. Rolls	J. Rolls.
"	W. S. Green	W. S. Green		J. Godden	A. Shea	C. Dawe	J. S. Winter	J. Studdy.
"							C. Dawe	W. H. Whitely.
Harbour Main	G. J. Hogsett	J. I. Little	J. I. Little	J. I. Little	J. I. Little	J. I. Little	J. Godden	E. Dawe.
"	Charles Furey	J. Kennedy	P. Nowlan	P. Nowlan	P. Nowlan	R. McDonnell	J. Veitch	R. S. Munn.
Placentia and St. Mary's	A. Shea	C. F. Bennett	J. Collins	C. F. Bennett	W. J. S. Donnelly	W. J. S. Donnelly	R. McDonnell	E. J. Morris.
"	P. M. Barron	H. Renouf	H. Renouf	M. E. Dwyer	J. Collins	A. Bradshaw	J. F. McGrath	W. J. Woodford.
"	T. O'Reilley	R. J. Parsons, Jr.	C. F. Bennett	N. Rabbits	M. E. Dwyer	M. Tobin	W. J. S. Donnelly	G. H. Emerson.
Port de Grave	J. Leamen	J. K. Wood	J. Bartlett		N. Norman	J. Bartlett	G. Emerson	R. O'Dwyer.
St. Barbe						J. H. Boone		J. F. McGrath.
St. George					M. J. O'Mara	M. H. Carty	G. A. Hutchings	J. A. Clift.
St. John's East	J. Kent	W. P. Walsh	R. J. Dearin	R. J. Kent	R. J. Kent	R. J. Kent	M. H. Carty	G. C. Pearn.
"	J. Kavanagh	J. A. Jordan	R. J. Parsons	R. J. Parsons	R. J. Parsons, Jr.	J. J. Dearin	A. Shea	M. H. Carty.
"	R. J. Parsons	R. J. Parsons	R. J. Kent	J. J. Dearin		R. J. Parsons, Jr.	M. J. O'Mara	T. J. Murphy.
St. John's West	T. Casey	T. Talbot	L. Tessier	L. Tessier	L. Tessier	P. J. Scott	E. P. Morris	Dr. Dearin.
"	T. Talbot	H. Renouf	P. J. Scott	M. Fenelon	M. Fenelon	P. D. White	P. J. Scott	J. Hollaren.
"	H. Renouf	P. Brennan		P. J. Scott	P. J. Scott	P. J. Callanan	J. J. Callanan	E. P. Morris.
Trinity	P. Brennan	P. Rendell	J. Steer	W. V. Whiteway	W. V. Whiteway	W. V. Whiteway	R. Thorburn	J. Day.
"	S. March	T. H. Ridley	J. H. Watson	J. Steer	J. H. Watson	R. Bond	W. B. Grieve	L. Gearin.
"	S. Rendell	R. Alsop	W. V. Whiteway	J. H. Watson	J. Rendell	J. Boyd	E. Watson	W. V. Whiteway.
"	F. J. Wyatt							K. Bond.
Twillingate	W. V. Whiteway	S. McKay	C. Duder	P. B. T. Carter	A. J. W. McNeily	S. McKay	A. P. Goodridge	D. C. Webber.
"	T. Knight	C. Duder	P. B. T. Carter	C. Duder	S. B. Carter	R. P. Rice	S. McKay	E. R. Burgess.
"			S. McKay	W. Killigrew	L. P. Rice	J. P. Thompson	M. T. Knight	J. P. Thompson.
"								T. Peyton.

* By Redistribution Act three members were given to Twillingate and one to Fogo.

STATISTICS, CLIMATE, SOIL, TIMBER, MINES, MINERALS, SPORT, AND GAME LAWS.

I.—Table of Trade, Revenue, and Expenditure from 1805 to 1860.

Year	Revenue £	Expenditure £	Public Debt £	Imports £	Exports £	Qtls Fish Exported No	Tuns of Cod and Seal Oil Exported No	Seal Skins Exported No.	Ships Entered No	Ships Cleared No
1805*	—	—	—	231,200	590,490	566,922	4,084½	81,085	550	467
1810*	—	—	—	447,089	743,350	778,557	4,478½	118,090	619	600
1815*	—	—	—	650,290	1,183,800	1,247,503	7,632	126,315	852	871
1820*	—	—	—	580,090	947,000	961,159	6,292½	213,579	730	752
1822	9,174	11,900	—	467,732	728,198	881,476	1,520	306,982	749	718
1823	14,290	11,753	—	523,329	693,196	864,711	6,400	289,410	753	741
1826	25,611	20,260	—	862,443	789,305	963,942	9,343	252,007	831	823
1835	42,207	91,482	—	671,374	765,177	—			810	833
1830	46,387	38,019	—	633,576	850,534	840,354	9,319½	394,321	851	735
1837	40,471	34,489	—	769,295	806,705			—	925	890
1838	44,587	47,172	—	639,288	829,005	724,515	8,025½	375,861	817	852
1839	42,640	42,822	—	710,557	901,385	835,577	8,905½	437,501	801	834
1840	43,563	39,347	—	788,045	983,961	915,791	12,724½	633,385	1,005	952
1841	44,143	40,787	—	806,423	932,52?	1,090,725	10,600½	417,115	964	920
1842			—			1,007,980	1,300	344,683		
1843	50,684	59,830	—	741,965	960,461	932,202	12,344½	651,370	1,171	1,071
1844	60,233	66,874	—	770,016	882,905	852,162	10,230	685,530	1,190	1,045
1845	66,483	62,703	—	801,330	989,436	1,000,233	8,504½	332,702	1,189	1,123
1846	76,740	74,050	—	802,247	799,103	879,065	6,703	265,160	1,219	1,223
1847	69,040	74,873	—	943,409	806,565	837,973	9,595	496,831	1,155	1,151
1848	67,300	62,071	—	769,628	897,581	920,396	10,321½	521,604	1,101	1,040
1849	69,405	96,262	—	770,160	876,987	1,173,167	8,597½	306,672	1,149	1,077
1850	92,652	71,807	106,701	807,316	975,770	1,089,188	10,302	598,860	1,220	1,102
1851	80,395	73,770	103,713	943,191	950,751	1,017,158	10,852½	511,630	1,230	1,080
1852	83,025	90,409	111,712	795,758	965,772	972,921	11,633	534,378	1,246	1,015
1853	98,857	93,006	114,820	912,095	1,170,503	922,718	12,299½	521,783	1,221	1,050
1854	81,007	77,492	113,558	961,527	1,019,372	774,117	3,272	388,870	1,073	923
1855	120,446	120,826	151,804	1,112,801	1,142,212	1,107,388	8,056	293,083	1,077	963
1856	118,631	105,845	167,257	1,271,604	1,388,797	1,268,384	9,650½	361,317	1,327	1,140
1857	149,324	116,748	176,706	1,413,432	1,651,171	1,882,322	12,487½	496,113	1,558	1,314
1858	141,128	178,863	175,630	1,172,862	1,318,836	1,088,080	12,097½	507,624	1,440	1,254
1859	124,799	114,589	177,018	1,323,298	1,357,113	1,105,293	10,577½	329,185	1,423	1,278
1860	133,603	120,728	182,139	1,254,128	1,271,712	1,338,544	9,892½	444,292	1,421	1,296

* For these years the returns do not furnish the *value* of the goods *imported* or *exported*, only the quantities of each article, so that the sterling amount for either the imports or exports is only an approximation, being based upon the prices paid and given, for the various articles at the present time.

II.—Table of Trade, Revenue, and Expenditure from 1861 to 1893.

Year	Revenue	Expenditure	Public Debt	Imports	Exports	Qtls. Fish Exported	Tuns of Cod and Seal Oil Exported	Seal Skins Exported	Ships Entered	Ships Cleared
	£	£	£	£	£	No.	No.	No.	No.	No.
1861	90,043	126,753	180,988	1,152,837	1,092,251	1,021,720	8,062	375,282	1,337	1,139
1862	110,929	138,058	173,642	1,007,083	1,171,723	1,080,069	16,637	283,424	1,345	1,159
1863	103,174	106,967	172,795	1,072,272	1,253,353	811,777	7,389	387,151	1,327	1,090
1864	116,770	116,707	177,202	1,067,062	1,111,330	849,339	4,315	125,050	1,115	941
	$	$	$	$	$	No.	No.	No.	No.	No.
1865	508,170	684,424	942,133	6,299,608	5,403,605	801,359	6,776	242,471	1,088	918
1866	675,947	634,043	1,001,395	5,784,849	5,494,305	716,690	6,978	203,629	1,161	949
1867	568,945	625,816	994,154	5,551,008	5,008,803	815,088	8,418	599,041	1,250	1,014
1868	815,025	803,576	1,047,681	4,314,423	4,926,650	688,063	7,634	385,856	1,115	955
1869	921,976	628,899	1,161,317	5,254,159	6,026,199	874,160	9,438	334,958	1,263	953
1870	836,321	670,077	1,162,818	6,733,849	6,231,270	970,176	8,575	263,189	1,276	1,015
1871	788,006	691,518	1,157,439	6,030,227	6,252,983	957,488	10,688	486,282	1,170	965
1872	805,578	891,309	1,151,676	6,716,068	6,707,012	906,843	8,248	231,244	1,144	998
1873	807,470	942,051	1,149,865	6,766,603	6,290,750	909,687	10,148	449,727	1,246	937
1874	819,897	895,048	1,149,100	7,314,649	7,336,089	1,248,326	7,224	392,228	1,173	961
1875	920,729	797,749	1,258,710	7,058,372	6,482,003	888,489	7,961	344,924	1,157	906
1876	917,291	912,197	1,319,390	7,295,907	6,962,190	737,218	6,951	341,292	1,264	1,060
1877	905,143	970,996	1,339,653	7,383,634	6,841,582	740,443	9,029	431,373	1,392	1,202
1878	1,019,033	1,148,573	1,317,692	6,988,723	5,630,891	694,339	8,851	419,220	1,332	1,104
1879	1,250,950	1,065,651	1,451,200	7,261,002	6,918,924	394,334	10,512	457,855	1,270	1,027
1880	985,311	1,040,741	1,450,933	6,966,243	5,635,707	985,134	9,027	281,508	1,341	1,098
1881	1,096,389	1,040,741	1,350,508	6,863,708	7,818,880	1,178,510	10,498	406,470	1,327	1,048
1882	1,274,734	1,234,597	1,498,777	8,359,322	7,001,222	1,027,269	7,134	175,812	2,362	1,107
1883	1,265,882	1,334,421	1,549,313	9,131,464	7,035,738	1,163,934	8,176	322,603	1,357	1,478
1884	1,236,913	1,312,917	2,194,153	8,075,792	6,567,135	1,197,637	7,650	266,280	—	—
1885	1,009,222	1,376,184	2,288,302	6,020,036	4,962,051	913,145	6,491	290,355	1,982	1,037
1886	1,739,970	1,693,663	3,005,040	5,307,408	5,176,730	953,537	5,854	298,464	1,431	1,022
1887	2,040,690	1,738,252	3,355,680	7,490,440	6,589,013	889,574	7,759	335,827	1,533	1,590
1888	1,730,929	1,831,441	4,138,268	6,607,065	6,122,985	774,294	6,914	220,863	1,502	1,598
1889	2,102,963	2,208,735	4,138,627	6,368,855	6,089,686	774,294	3,195	220,321	—	—
1890	1,681,536	1,293,288	4,188,627	6,868,858	7,457,158	947,575	2,992	—	—	—
1891	1,973,275	1,831,432	5,222,383	5,012,977	5,651,116	—	—	—	—	—
1892	1,983,790	1,608,120	6,383,367	7,572,569	6,380,912	900,743	2,950	175,217	—	—
1893	1,764,781	2,110,012	8,053,127							

Records destroyed by fire.

XXXV.—Climate and Soil.

There has been a fierce controversy waged over the climate and soil of our island. I am not writing a Government guide-book, and I therefore state definitely that Newfoundland does not rejoice in the balmy airs of California, and her soil is not equal to the black loam of Manitoba. On the other hand, old Terra Nova is not a barren waste and howling wilderness, and her temperature is by no means arctic. On the east coast, where there has been the earliest settlement and most cultivation, the earth is frequently thin, with underlying gravel. This naturally poor soil is wonderfully productive; grasses and all vegetables grow with astonishing quickness. Connoisseurs declare that the Newfoundland peas, beans, turnips, potatoes, cabbage, and cauliflower, are the sweetest and the richest they have ever tasted. Wheat has been ripened over and over again; barley, oats, and all leguminous plants come to perfection. The greatest drawback to our climate is the tardy and uncertain spring, caused by the presence of ice on the coast. The summer is always delightful, and, except in the extreme north of the island, there is generally no severe weather before Christmas. During the winter, when the cold is much less severe than either in Canada or Maine, there are a few very extreme days, and a few snowstorms, but very seldom a continued hard frost. We are quite free from the violent thunderstorms and tornadoes that devastate other countries. We have no venomous reptiles. The hardy, robust appearance of our stalwart fishermen, the blooming complexions of our girls, all bear testimony to the healthiness of our sea-girt isle. On the west coast, after Cape Ray is turned, there is some excellent land about the Codroy Valleys and St George's Bay; with the rudest and most primitive farming fine crops are raised. That a large portion of Newfoundland is rocky and barren is unfortunately too true; both Nova Scotia, New Brunswick, Maine, and Canada, also contain some of the most barren and sterile soil in the world. Our country has been condemned because the rocky and sterile parts, the haunts of the deer-stalker, are known, whilst large portions of the good soil lies up river valleys and amidst forests, mostly unexplored and unknown except to the surveyor and the lumberer. Newfoundland contains many fine stretches of grazing land. Even about the comparatively shallow soil of Avalon cattle and sheep become wonderfully fat and flourishing. The truth about the country lies between the picturesque enthusiasm of our own writers and the fierce depreciation of some English and American travellers, who, from hasty observation of the most unfavourable portions, have cursed the whole country.

XXXVI.—Timber.

Whatever questions may arise about our soil, there can be no question about our forest wealth, the best answer to all our detractors is the price of our pine lumber in London, Newfoundland Yellow Pine fetching the very highest price in that market. The principal varieties of our forest timber are :—

White Pine, Yellow or Red Pine, Scrub Pine, Black Spruce, White Spruce, Red Spruce, Fir, called here Var, Larch, called Hackmatack in New Brunswick, Tamarack in Canada, and very erroneously Juniper in Newfoundland.

White Birch, Yellow Birch, called Witch-hazel, Black Birch, Low and Alpine Birches, two inferior varieties.

White Ash, Black Ash, Mountain Ash or Rowan Tree, called here Dogwood.

Balsam Poplar or Balm of Gilead, Aspen Poplar.

Willow in several varieties, Alders, Choke, and Wild Cherry.

XXXVII.—Mines and Minerals.

The mineral wealth of Newfoundland has only been developed very partially. Large deposits of copper have been found principally in Nôtre Dame Bay. Whilst so much of the country is unsurveyed, it is only reasonable to suppose that there is much latent wealth over a wide and unknown area, displaying much the same geological formation as Tilt Cove and Bett's Cove Mines. Every facility is given to explorers, licence fees to secure a large mining area are only $20. Valuable information can be obtained on the subject of our mineralogy from the yearly geological reports furnished to the Government. The following account is taken principally from Mr. Howley's Geography.

The metals and economic minerals known to exist in Newfoundland are as follows :—Gold, found only in traces in quartz veins, and associated with iron ore, native silver is found in Fortune Bay. Silver, associated with galena, nickel ores, viz., copper nickel, cloanthite, and millerite. Copper in various forms, viz., native copper, variegated copper ore, grey and yellow sulphurets, copper pyrites, &c., galena, or sulphuret of lead, graphite, or plumbago, molybdenum. Iron ores in great variety, viz., magnetic, chromic, specular, iron pyrites, or sulphuret of iron, iron sand, hæmatite, vivianite, or phosphate of iron, manganese and zincblende, coal, and several other less important minerals. Various other important substances, such as marbles, white, black, and variegated, limestone in abundance, barytes, gypsum, shell marl, kaolin clay, brick clays, roofing slates, granites, syenites, serpentines, sandstones, whetstones, steatite, asbestos, petroleum, &c., and many others. The following are the localities where the more important of these substances have been found. Copper ores, at Shoal Bay, south of St John's, in the neighbourhood of St John's Town; at Holyrood, Turk's Gut, and Crow's Gulch, in Conception

Bay; at Tickle Harbour, and head of Random Sound, in Trinity Bay; at Pit Sound Island and Bloody Bay, Bonavista Bay; at Twillingate Island, Trump Island, New Bay Head, Pilley's Island, Sunday Cove Island, Three Arms, Green Bay, Burton's Pond, Bett's Cove and Tilt Cove, in the Great Bay of Nôtre Dame In Mings Bight, Bay Vert, or Little Bay, on Groais Island, in St Julien Harbour, in Goose Cove and Howe Harbour, Hare Bay, in St Mary's Bay At Placentia Harbour, and La Manche, in Placentia Bay, at Bennoits Brook, Lewis Brook, and Serpentine River, Port-à-Port Bay, and several other localities

Lead is known to exist near St John's Harbour, in Conception Bay, Trinity Bay, St Mary's Bay, Placentia Bay, principally at La Manche, in Fortune Bay, Bay Despair, on the west coast, at Red Rocks, near Cape Ray, in East and West Bays, Port-à-Port, and other parts of Port-à-Port Peninsula, besides various other localities Iron ores are found on every side of the island, and in all the bays A valuable supply of the finest ore is now being worked by a Nova Scotia Company at Belle Isle, Conception Bay Nickel is almost invariably found in the serpentines, but has only been developed in workable quantity at the Union Mine, Tilt Cove. Coal, as already mentioned, in St George's Bay It is stated to exist in workable seams, but its commercial value has not yet been fully ascertained, some of the seams are on the new line of railway, and will be opened up by the Construction Company. Petroleum, in Port-à-Port Bays, at Cow Head, and Cape Rouge Peninsula, gypsum, in immense volume in St. George's Bay, and at Great Codroy River. Excellent roofing slates in Smith's Sound, and on Random Island, Trinity Bay, white and variegated marbles at the mouth of the Humber River, at Canada Bay, and other places An immense deposit of asbestos is now being worked very successfully by a company on the west coast · Building stones of every description and good quality, limestones, &c, are found in vast profusion at many parts of the island, the latter especially on the north-eastern and western shores There are only a few places where the more valuable ores were worked to any extent so far, viz, at the Union Mine, Tilt Cove, and at Bett's Cove and Little Bay, Nôtre Dame Bay At the former nickel and copper are mined to a large extent, at the latter, only copper as yet. Lead has been worked at La Manche Mine, Placentia Bay, and at Lead Cove, Port-à-Port Bay

XXXVIII.—Sport.

As a sporting country Newfoundland has no rival in North America The whole interior of the island, unvisited by man, is the home of immense herds of Caribou (*Cervus Tarandus*); a species of reindeer peculiar to this Colony Soon after the birth of their young

in the spring, the Cariboo herds migrate north and return again to the milder southern coast in the autumn, many deer also remain in the woodlands about the Gander River and other northern streams all the winter. Throughout the interior the deer-paths abound, even the stones in places are worn smooth by the countless herds who have been making their pilgrimage through endless years At some places lakes and streams lie across their track. At one of these crossing places, Gander Lake, fifteen hundred deer, so Garrett Kelly informed some tourists lately, had been killed, his original statement to me was seven hundred The very best deer grounds in the island can now be reached quite easily by the new railway or by coastal boats, north and south. With camp and canoe, the deer-stalker can be transported in a few hours to grounds that formerly could only be reached by three and four days, often a week, of most laborious toil and travel Deer-stalking, the sport of princes in Europe, the common occupation of Newfoundland fishermen, requires endurance, nerve, and straight shooting, with these qualifications and sufficient leisure, nowhere in North America can better sport be obtained. Grouse-shooting comes next to deer-stalking in the Terra-Novian sporting bill of fare, and is a most fascinating, health-giving amusement Whilst the best deer-stalking is at the north and west, by far the most extensive moors and the largest number of broods are found in the south-east part of the island, Avalon Peninsula, St. Mary's, and Placentia Bay The local game laws are well observed, and by the 15th September grouse are generally to be found in fair numbers, even around St John's, ten or a dozen miles from the capital, bags of eight and ten brace are made on the first day by good shots and hard walkers For successful grouse-shooting, next to straight powder, the most important factor is a well-trained setter, with these concomitants and fine weather, a good Newfoundland barren affords glorious sport I have heard Admiral Kennedy, R N, a very prince amongst shooters, declare that he preferred the wild shooting in Newfoundland to any other sport in the world. To ensure success a knowledge of the habits of your game is also essential The grouse, a semi-arctic bird, takes no heed of cold, but is extremely sensitive to wet and north-east winds, in fogs they are found on the highest and barest rocks, always, as the fishermen say, "standing," on the alert, hard to get at. There are two distinct species of grouse, the Willow Grouse (*Tetrao salicensis*), and the true Ptarmigan, known amongst the fishermen as the rock partridge; this latter bird is found on the highest and barest hills, west of Fortune Bay It is entirely unknown on the east coast, where the Willow Grouse, the great sporting bird of Newfoundland, is most abundant Besides grouse, there are geese, ducks, and snipe, &c Salmon fishing has been specially good during the season of 1894, one commander killed thirty fair-sized salmon and grilse for his own rod in one day. Sea trout are even more abundant than salmon in some streams, they run small, from a ½ pound to 2 pounds, but in all the good rivers, both north and south, the average is from 1 lb to 3½ lbs. I have never seen a sea trout over 5 lbs., though I understand they run much larger at Labrador, up to 7 lbs. Brown and fresh-water trout are of all sizes, and marvellously abundant. Recently rainbow trout and Loch Levens have been introduced, many of these fish were caught this season near St John's weighing 4 lbs to 5 lbs, and one 6¾ lbs (a beautiful fish) The American or blue hare, as it is known in Scotland, s extraordinarily abundant. The large arctic hare is common, but never in large numbers. Our local natural history is very incomplete. A good catalogue of indigenous plants has been made by the Rev. Mr Wagborne. The one and only list of birds was made by Mr Henry Reeks, F.L S, and published in the *Ornithologist*, it applies more especially to the west coast of the island. Valuable notes on Newfoundland natural history were also made by Philip H Gosse, but have not been published.

The following graphic description of a deer-shooting episode in Newfoundland is copied from a recent work on caribou shooting in the Colony by Dr Davis —

"On the plain below us were more than a hundred caribou, moving about among the little moss-covered knolls, rocks and tufts of scraggy evergreens of fir and juniper. As I brought my field-glass to bear upon the scene, I beheld a picture which I shall never forget. About half-a-mile down the slope, in a small open marsh, were at least fifty caribou gathered in a crowd, and right in the centre was a battle royal between several great stags for supremacy and possession of the favoured does. The battle seemed to be waged principally against one great kingly-looking fellow with magnificent antlers. The does with their fawns and the yearlings (prickets) and younger stags had apparently formed a ring or circle round the half-dozen or more fierce combatants in their great struggle for the survival of the fittest—the does venturing in near them now and then seemingly to encourage the fighters by their presence. The clashing of their horns could be easily heard as they plunged and reared at each other in deadly strife. The weaker gradually succumbed one by one, and were eventually driven off, leaving the 'king' master of the situation. But his glory was destined to be short-lived, little did he know that there was danger near, and that his kingly head should soon fall, as a specimen and trophy of the noblest of his kind. It was now quite late in the afternoon, and as we were about five miles from camp as the raven flies, and several more by the roundabout way we were obliged to take to reach our cabin, Le Buffe thought it was too late to begin shooting; the weather was mild, and the deer could not travel,

better go to camp and return in the morning with the whole outfit, put up a temporary camp, and remain until we had filled out our string of heads allowed by law. But what sportsman could turn his back on such a picture without making an attempt to secure the head of the king? I suggested that we should try for it; even at the risk of camping out. This was easier said than done, as there were several small groups of deer between us and the herd in which he was presiding, and many sharp eyes and noses to be feared. Le Buffe was fearful that if they should detect us either by sight or scent we might stampede the whole party and lose all, though he was willing to make the effort.

"We started out very cautiously, creeping through the low cover and keeping as well to windward of them as possible, gradually getting nearer the point of attack. When within about 400 yards we thought all was lost, as a big stag close by, which had been whipped discovered us and created quite a disturbance by his loud grunts as he kept trotting backwards and forwards from group to group, trying to give the alarm, but as there was another fight on below him, the main herd's attention was attracted to that, and no stampede occurred just then. From this point forward the cover was so light that we had to worm along very close to the ground part of the way, through water and muck, regardless of wet knees and elbows, but finally succeeded in getting within about 225 paces of the 'king', but here the cover ended and our position on sloping ground exposed us to the deer, and I was obliged to try my hand again at long range. I raised the sights for the estimated distance as well as I could, and as I was lying down took very careful aim from an elbow rest, military style. I fired, and as the rifle cracked I saw that the ball had struck him, too far back, it seemed, to make him perfectly ferocious, as he crippled around in the herd with a broken thigh, still holding the fort against all comers. He soon turned a broadside, and I fired again with better results, he made a few wicked lunges in the direction of one of his late rivals, and fell dead. We then broke cover and ran down to where the fallen hero lay; and strange to say, the herd seemed to be panic-stricken at the downfall of their leader—some of them trotting around close by, and others standing as if paralyzed within easy shot. Just then I noticed a large stag standing about eighty yards off with a magnificent head of antlers. I shot him down in his tracks. At this stage of the game all seemed to be in confusion, as the deer did not seem to know what all the shooting meant. As Le Buffe did not carry a gun, to keep out of my way and out of sight of the game he had taken shelter behind a large rock, about the size of an old fashioned Pennsylvania bake-oven (such as our ancestors used), about 200 yards from where I was doing the shooting. Here he almost came to grief, as he was attacked by a fierce caribou with most vicious horns. His cry for help attracted my attention just in time to save him, as the maddened beast was grunting and charging at him as he was running round and round the rock. I ran down to within 20 yards of the circus, when the enraged animal caught sight of me and immediately squared off to give me battle on open ground, and looked as if he asked no other favour under the circumstances. But I had him well covered with the rifle, and called out to Le Buffe to lie flat behind the rock as I was going to shoot. Just as the great savage deer lowered his head to make a rush at me, I fired a ball into his breast, and he fell dead within six feet of Le Buffe, who is a brave man and used to danger, but at this moment was as white as a sheet as he again took me by the hand.

Game Laws of Newfoundland.

For WILLOW GROUSE, locally named partridge, and other varieties of grouse and eggs of same, close time begins 12th January, ends 15th September; birds, however, may be sold up to 22nd January, provided they are shot in season.

CURLEW, PLOVER, SNIPE, or other wild or migratory birds, or eggs of same, close time 12th January to 20th August.

WILD GEESE may be shot at any time or their eggs taken.

CARIBOU, close time 15th February to 15th September.

MOOSE or ELK (imported), close time 10 years from 1st January 1886.

OTTER and BEAVER, close time 1st April to 1st October.

RABBITS and HARES, close time 1st March to 15th September.

SALMON, close time from 11th September to 30th April.

TROUT, land-locked salmon and other fresh water fish not to be taken in any lake, river, or stream, between 15th September and 31st December.

CARIBOU. Note.—Licence is required by non-residents to shoot deer, fee $100; only five stags and three does can be killed by each sportsman. The licences are granted by Justices of the Peace and Custom House officers in the form prescribed by the Act.

CHAPTER XIX.

THE CHURCH OF ENGLAND IN NEWFOUNDLAND

By Rev. W. Pilot, D D,

Superintendent of Church of England Schools

The history of the Church of England in Newfoundland may be said to date from the first attempt to colonize the Island by Sir Humphrey Gilbert in 1583, when by authority of Queen Elizabeth he ordained that the laws and policy of the Island should not be "against the true Christian faith or religion now professed in the Church of England" This attempt at colonization failed, and it was not till 1611 that the first clergyman landed on these shores This was the Rev. Erasmus Stourton who came out with John Guy on his second visit to the island His headquarters were at Cupids and his mission extended around Conception Bay, and from Cape St. Francis to Ferryland. He left this country in 1628, and became chaplain to the Earl of Albemarle.

Just before the period of D'Iberville's invasion, 1696–97, a petition was presented to the Home Government by the Newfoundland settlers, praying, "that a sufficient number of ministers should be sent to the " principal harbours, and that they might be paid from England " There had been many earnest appeals to the same effect without avail In 1697, when the Government of William III were endeavouring to repair the terrible injuries inflicted on the Colony by the French, an order was made that the men-of-war should carry chaplains The Rev. Mr. Jackson was one of these chaplains, with the consent of the Bishop of London in 1699, he remained on the island, accepting from the inhabitants a guarantee of 50*l* a year for three years. A small yet handsome church was soon built within the precincts of the newly erected Fort William. The population of St. John's at that time was about eight hundred In 1701 Mr Jackson was taken on the list of the "Society for Promoting Christian Knowledge," and in 1703 was accepted as the first missionary of the "Society for the Propagation of the Gospel in Foreign Parts" in Newfoundland.[1]

---

[1] In April 1703 the Society took into consideration the deplorable condition of Mr. Jackson, a painful minister in New foundland, who had gone upon a mission into those parts with a wife and eight children " In 1705, when Mr Jackson was recalled by

The attacks made on the new minister by the notorious Major Lloyd are fully set out in the former part of this history. The Rev John Jackson, though a very poor man, burthened with a family of eight almost helpless children, showed himself both a God-fearing missionary and a bold opponent of immorality and corruption in high places. The needs of his family, the poverty of the living, finally drove him from his post, it is satisfactory, however, to know that after his trials in Newfoundland he was finally presented to an English living by Queen Anne in 1709. The small garrison church was in existence, so we find from the records, in 1708, it gradually fell into decay, subsequently, in 1720, a larger wooden church was built near the site of the present cathedral,[1] by 1759 this also had fallen into decay, and in this year, as described,[2] a new and finer edifice was erected by the determined effort of Governor Richard Edwards.

The successor to Jackson was the Rev. Jacob Rice, appointed by the Bishop of London. Our information about his ministry is very meagre, like his predecessor he was very much distressed through want of means. In 1730 Mr Fordyce succeeded Mr. Rice, he was sent out by the Society on the faith of a promise from the inhabitants of St John's to provide him with a small annual stipend and an allowance of a quintal of merchantable fish from every shallop, of the salary only three-fourths of the promised amount was paid, another fourth was soon lost through the death and removal of some of the subscribers, and the promised quintal of fish was either refused or paid in the worthless quality of dried cod, known in this Colony as "Madeira." About three years after his arrival everything in the shape of payment was withheld, until he erected a gallery in the church, costing thirty guineas, at his own personal expense. After manfully discharging his onerous duties for five years under circumstances of unparalleled difficulty he was at last compelled in 1736 to return to England from sheer inability to procure a subsistence for his family. Whilst the inhabitants of St. John's treated

the Bishop of London, he was wrecked on the voyage home, and lost all his effects In 1709, in reporting on his case, the Committee of the Society for the Propagation of the Gospel "were of opinion that the said Mr Jackson is an object of the society's favor and compassion, that he, having been in Her Majesty's service, as well by sea as in the plantations, and having therein suffered many unreasonable hardships, and being a man of good deserts, he is worthy to be recommended to the favour of the Lord Keeper'

[1] The first wooden church built on the site of the present Anglican Cathedral was erected in 1720 The Rev Thomas Walbank, chaplain of H M S *Sutherland*, whilst at St John's in 1742, mentions that he "ministered for four months to a congregation of 500 people, in a large church built of firr and spruce by the inhabitants, in the year 1720, the building was well furnished, and a poor fisherman of Petty Harbour had recently given the church a decent silver Patten and Chalice with gold." New England was not satisfied with supplying Newfoundland with cattle and grain, she also wished to supply us with her dissenting minister. The West Country men clung with tenacity to the old Church of England, and refused all religious aid from America

[2] At p 295

this most deserving minister with such incredible meanness, after his departure they forwarded to the Society a public testimonial that the Rev. John Fordyce was a most diligent and faithful pastor.

Fordyce was presented with a gratuity of 30*l* to pay his debts, and was appointed in 1736 to the society's mission at Prince Frederick, in South Carolina, where he died in 1751, fully maintaining the same character for ministerial activity and zeal which had met with so ill a requital in Newfoundland.

In 1736 the mission of St. John's was given up for nine years, when the inhabitants, having fully realized the loss they had sustained by their own niggardliness, in refusing to fulfil their stipulated agreement to pay their clergyman, again petitioned the Society for a missionary. This time they alleged that they had purchased a house for the missionary, and bound themselves to an annual payment of 40*l* towards his maintenance. Trusting to these assurances, the Society, unable to procure a missionary in England, consented to the removal of the Rev M. Peasley, M A, who had been sent to carry forward the work so successfully begun by Mr. Jones at Bonavista Peaseley remained in St John's for seven years, discharging his duties diligently. In his letter, dated November 1745, he says his congregation, which was larger on his arrival, continued to increase, insomuch that the church could scarcely contain it Besides attending to his own flock in St. John's, he was in the habit of making periodical visits by water during the summer months to Petty Harbour. But Mr Peaseley was destined, like his predecessor, to experience the non-fulfilment of the promises of his people, which made his longer residence among them impossible His embarrassed condition led him to petition the Society to be removed, which was done, and he was appointed to St. Helena, Beaufort, in South Carolina.

The next missionary of St. John's and the out-harbours, which embraced the whole of the province of Avalon, was the Rev. Edward Langman, M.A., of Baliol College, Oxford, appointed at the request of the inhabitants, to whom he had been favourably known from a former residence among them, and who were therefore well able to appreciate the value of his services On his return thither to take charge of his cure in 1752, he reported that his congregation was numerous, and the number of communicants thirty. Of one hundred families which, exclusive of the garrison, formed the entire population of the town, forty were of the communion of the Church of England, fifty-two Roman Catholic, and eight Dissenters.

In 1759 he undertook a missionary voyage to Placentia, where he remained ministering to a congregation of sixty or seventy fishermen, and performing the several offices of the church   During his visit he baptised fifty persons, some forty, some thirty, some twenty years of age, and fifteen infants.   And further, he stimulated the people to repair their church, which at this time had fallen into decay.   The next summer he paid a similar missionary visit to the harbours of the south-east

Mr. Langman found in Reneuse twenty-five families, of which nine were Protestants, and sixteen Irish Catholics, the whole population amounting to one hundred and forty   In Fermeuse nearly the whole population, amounting to one hundred, were Roman Catholic   In Ferryland there were sixty-four Protestants and eighty-six Roman Catholics.   In this visit he baptised thirty-eight children, and distributed copies of the Bible, Book of Common Prayer, and Catechism.

At St. John's his ministry was marked with diligence, especially in the work of catechising the children in the face of the congregation, which he did every Wednesday and Friday, and during the season of Lent, and frequently reading one of the Homilies, with which the people seemed well pleased, and were edified   In 1761 he extended his missionary visits again along the southern shore, and found in the Bay of Bulls forty-five families, of which thirty-seven were Roman Catholic from Ireland, the remainder Protestant.   Eleven families whom he found living in Witless Bay were almost all Irish.

Thus far Langman's ministry had proceeded without any serious impediments, but in the year 1762 it was destined to receive a severe shock   On St John's Day the French landed at Bay of Bulls,[1] marched their troops towards St. John's, which not being in a condition of defence, speedily surrendered by capitulation , the garrison were made prisoners, and the French seized every kind of property within their reach   In the general plunder, Mr Langman was a sufferer to the extent of 130l , and the losses sustained by the rest of the inhabitants now rendered it more difficult for them to do all that they had promised towards his maintenance   Still much that might have been done on his behalf was left undone.   The house promised to him, as to his predecessor, Mr Peasely, was never provided, and to eke out the needful substance for himself and his family the only provision on which he could reckon was an allowance of 50l a year from the Society.   The offerings of the people were scanty, and niggardly given, and for the little gratuities he

---

[1] In the attack on Bay Bulls in 1796 by the French, they proceeded through the woods half way to Petty Harbour, discouraged by the difficulties of travelling, they returned and burned the Anglican and Roman Catholic churches in Bay Bulls, and every house in the harbour, except Nowlan's.   When the French broke into his hut, the unfortunate mother ran for her life, but the sight of poor Nowlan, with his infant twins on his knees, excited such commiseration that the invaders left him in peace

did receive, he was compelled to go and beg as a poor man would for an alms. Notwithstanding these heavy drawbacks, Langman persevered as a "faithful dispenser of the Word of God" to discharge his laborious duties until his death in 1783 He had been particularly zealous in allaying religious strife in St John's, and could write with satisfaction to its absence, and to the fact that several families of Dissenters were in the habit of joining in the public worship of the church, and of receiving the Holy Communion. The Reverend Edward Langman is one of the most important figures in the early history of the Church of England in the Island, he resided continually in the Colony for about forty years, he was conspicuous for his culture, broad and liberal views, his upright life and his earnest devotion to his Master's work; he was the first minister to occupy the magisterial bench, a man of strong and decided views, he asserted his opinions with the vigour and force of an uncompromising layman. He was truly the rector of the whole parish, and seems to have been very well liked, both within and without his own communion. Parson Langman was in his day nearly as popular and beloved as his more modern successor Archdeacon Bridge. The good old clergyman died full of years in 1783, and was succeeded by the Rev. Walter Price, curate of Dartmouth, Devon, who had been recommended to the Society by the principal merchants and shipowners of Dartmouth, then carrying on an extensive trade in Newfoundland In the first year of his ministry we find that, besides the care of his own parish of St John's, where he had already merited the regard and esteem of his congregation, he occasionally visited Petty Harbour, Bay Bulls, and other surrounding settlements. He represented to the Society in striking terms the spiritual destitution of the Island. "There are some places," he says, "where there are many English settlers who have never heard the word of God preached among them for thirty years past." His congregation at St John's was numerous and respectable, and gradually increased, "many adorning their profession by an exemplary life." In his time the question of a parsonage house for the minister was at last satisfactorily settled Mr Price mentions, with great respect and gratitude, the kindness of Governor Elliott, who "has done everything in his power to carry out the pious designs of the Society," and by his own good example and precept to promote the attendance on public worship. Through the Governor's liberality and the subscriptions of the naval and military officers and general body of churchmen a suitable parsonage house was procured for the minister. In 1788 Mr Price opened a free school in his new residence, where he taught himself, and paid the salary of an assistant; he continued in the mission for seven years, when the parent Society offered him the new mission of

Nashwalk, in New Brunswick. In 1790 Mr. Harries, who had been minister at Placentia, was transferred to St. John's, at the particular request of the inhabitants. Mr. Harries remained as minister in the capital from 1791 to 1810, when he was succeeded by the venerated Rev. David Rowland. On October 19th, 1800, a new church was opened. His successor was the Rev. Thomas Grantham, who had been the first missionary at Burin. He remained in St. John's only one year. In 1818, the Reverend Frederick Carrington, missionary for many years at Harbour Grace and a chief magistrate, became rector of St. John's;

BISHOP INGLIS.
From an engraving.

some now living can remember his noble presence and the roll of his fine sonorous voice in prayer and praise.

In the year 1787 the See of Nova Scotia was constituted, and Newfoundland, which up to this time had been nominally under the care of the Bishop of London, was included in the letters patent, but Bishop Inglis was never once able to visit the Island. It was not till twenty years later that it received its first Episcopal visit from Bishop Stanser, when five clergymen and seven schoolmasters formed the missionary staff. In 1822 the Rev. John Leigh was appointed Episcopal Commissary to Bishop Stanser, and made a visitation of the whole of the Island [1] in 1822 and 1823.

Dr. Stanser's successor, Bishop John Inglis, made his first visitation of Newfoundland in 1827; he was received with every mark of respect, and amongst his earliest visitors was the Roman Catholic Bishop, the courtly Dr. Scallan. In the course of five thousand miles of travel he consecrated eighteen churches, and twenty burial grounds, and confirmed nearly two thousand four hundred candidates. The Bishop saw much to gratify him in the labours of the few clergy in the Island, but declared that "it was impossible to be unmoved by the " deplorable insufficiency of religious instruction in large portions of " the Island." He was glad to find a general observance of Sunday,

---

[1] Rev. John Leigh was missionary at Twillingate and Fogo from 1817 to 1818; Harbour Grace, 1819 to 1822; he died in 1823.

and even in the height of the fishing season a readiness on the part of the men engaged in it to present themselves on that day for instruction and Christian teaching.

No sketch of the Church of England in Newfoundland, however brief, would be complete without reference to the pioneer work in education of the old "Newfoundland School Society," first called also "The Society for educating the poor of Newfoundland," now merged into "The Colonial and Continental Church Society." This Society owes its existence and its successful working entirely to the labours of a Newfoundland merchant, Samuel Codner. Every Newfoundlander should

SAMUEL CODNER.
From a portrait in the possession of the C.C.C. Society.

revere his memory; no single individual has ever done so much for this Colony as this plain West-country merchant. Mr. Codner himself describes how the Society came into existence. At a meeting at Margate in 1821, to inaugurate a branch of the Bible Society, Lord Liverpool made some forcible observations on the duty and responsibility of Great Britain to give to her extensive colonies the blessings of religious instruction; his words sank deep into the heart of Samuel Codner, and he determined, with the blessing of God, to found a society for educating the poor in the Colony where he had

made his fortune. For this purpose he canvassed the whole of England, Ireland, and Scotland; everywhere he enlisted the sympathy of the religious and benevolent. He formed branch societies in all the principal towns. The Liverpool branch had for its president Sir John Gladstone, the father of the great statesman, and John Job, grandfather of Mr. T. R. Job, for its active committeeman. The great Earl of Liverpool gave invaluable aid to the infant society; 500*l.* for building the Central School, St. John's, 100*l.* annually for its first master, and free passages for all its teachers in H.M. transports, besides grants of land for schools in all parts of Newfoundland; all these boons were obtained from the Imperial Government through his influence.

The Society's operations in Newfoundland were commenced in September 1824, seventy years ago; the first school, taught by Mr. and Mrs. Jeynes, was held in the one stone building then existing in

Duckworth Street (occupied before the fire of July 1892 by the
newer houses of Mr. St. John). Mr. Willoughby, the assistant secretary,
who superintended the schools in Newfoundland, was of invaluable help
in forwarding the interests of the infant institution, an earnest worker
with broad and liberal views on the subject of education; his skill, tact,
and energy largely helped forward the good work. The schools were
supported by generous contributions from all denominations, Protestant
vied with Catholic in promoting their success. Sir Thomas Cochrane
was a constant friend of the Society; Chief Justice Boulton and
Archdeacon Wix largely contributed to its initial prosperity. The first
teachers of the Newfoundland School Society were admirably suited for
the work, well-trained, earnest, religious men; their enthusiasm and
their success soon excited a universal desire for the Society's schools all
through the Colony; their non-sectarian plan of education, founded on
Bell's system, and their honest and conscientious desire to avoid offence
on denominational questions produced universal confidence in their
teachers and schools. Year by year new fields of labour were opened
up; liberal support was given to the Society, both in England
and Newfoundland; by 1830, six short years after its commence
ment, a wonderful work was accomplished by the devoted Samuel
Codner.[1]

[1] Principal Stations, with their Branch Schools.	When established.	Principal and Branch Teachers.	Day Schools.		Sunday Schools.		Adult Schools.	
			Total admitted.	Now on the Books.	Total admitted.	Now on the Books.	Total admitted.	Now on the Books.
St. John's	September 1824	Mr. and Mrs. Jeynes	772	150	——	——	221	40
Portugal Cove	November 1828	Branch teacher	80	40	——	——	——	——
River Head	July 1828	Ditto	102	60	——	——	——	——
Quidi Vidi	February 1825	Ditto	90	30	90	30	——	——
Signal Hill	August 1828		50	30	——	——	——	——
Torbay	July 1828	Suspended	——	——	20	——	——	——
Trinity	June 1825	Mr. Benjamin Flect	166	75	178	50	69	23
North Side	—— 1828	Branch teacher	33	33	33	33	——	——
Ship Cove	—— 1828	Ditto	33	33	33	33	——	——
Cuckold's Cove	—— 1828	Ditto	24	23	24	23	——	——
Old Bonaventura	—— 1829	Ditto	48	30	48	30	——	——
Harbour Grace	September 1825	Mr. and Mrs. Kingwell	311	144	251	139	68	36
Mosquito	August 1828	Suspended	63	——	——	——	——	——
Spaniard's Bay	July 1829	Branch teacher	88	48	90	80	42	42
Island Cove	Ditto	Ditto	85	45	——	——	——	——
River Head	May 1830	Ditto	90	90	——	——	——	——
Carbonnierre	October 1825	Suspended	116	——	85	——	20	——
Petty Harbour	September 1825	Mr. and Mrs. Martin	135	105	95	69	55	22
Maddox Cove	August 1828	Suspended	36	——	——	——	——	——
Bonavista	November 1826	Mr. and Mrs. Meek	298	130	120	99	50	50
Green's Pond	October 1828	Mr. and Mrs. King	117	98	151	111	69	45
Swain's Island	September 1829	Branch teacher	20	8	20	20	——	——
Fool's Island	—— 1829	Ditto	20	20	27	27	——	——
Port de Grave	October 1829	Mr. and Mrs. Lind	150	150	84	60	54	36
Bay Roberts	December 1829	Branch teacher	40	35	——	——	——	——
Cupids	May 1830	Ditto	26	26	——	——	——	——
Twillingate	October 1829	Mr. William Walker	60	60	74	74	50	50
Herring Neck	March 1830	Branch teacher	50	50	54	54	——	——
		Total	3,123	1,513	1,477	932	680	344

Most of the early teachers of the Society became ordained ministers of the Church of England in the Colony; the saintly memories of these teachers and missionaries, Meek, Kingwell, and others, will always be revered amongst us. To the last Samuel Codner[1] took the warmest interest in the Colony; his life was devoted to the Society he had so successfully founded. In one of his last letters to Mr. Bond (father of the Hon. R. Bond) he makes inquiries as to whether Mr. Robert Prowse, who has been recommended as unpaid manager of the institution in Newfoundland, would be a suitable person for the work. During the long period that the Newfoundland School Society has been at work in the Colony its teachers have been almost invariably good instructors, and the schools prosperous and well managed; for a great many years 500l. has been granted to them by the Local Government, and to-day twenty schools are in full operation in the Island.

In 1829 Bishop Inglis constituted the two archdeaconries of Newfoundland and Bermuda, and the Rev. Mr. Coster became the first archdeacon of the former. The venerable George Coster, our first archdeacon, was a missionary at Bermuda from 1822 to 1824. He was then appointed visiting missionary to Newfoundland and Ecclesiastical Commissary. He resided chiefly at Bonavista, where he laboured earnestly and faithfully in his Master's vineyard. He is well remembered as the constructor of the first three miles of road around the settlement. The Rev. Edward Wix, first stationed at Bonavista in 1826, in 1830 succeeded the Rev. George Coster as archdeacon, and removed to St. John's; Archdeacon Wix visited all around the island, and even made an extended visitation to the Labrador. The history of the Church of England would be very incomplete without some reference to his life and labours. In his very interesting work, "Six months of a Newfoundland Missionary's Journal," February to August 1836, he mentions that he had then been ten years in the service of the Society, two of which he had spent in Nova Scotia and eight in Newfoundland. In 1839 the Ven. Aubrey George Spencer, who had been successively missionary in Newfoundland, and the first archdeacon of Bermuda, was consecrated the first Bishop of Newfoundland, which

ARCHDEACON WIX.

was then severed from the See of Nova Scotia. By the appointment of a bishop and the separation of Newfoundland from the See of Nova Scotia, an immense impetus was given to Church feelings,

[1] Samuel Codner was connected with the Newfoundland trade until March 30th, 1844, when he sold his business to Wilson and Meynell.

principles, and interests. The Rev. Aubrey George Spencer came to Newfoundland as a missionary in 1818. He was first stationed at Placentia, 1818, Ferryland, 1819, and in 1820 at Trinity. It is related that when he first preached in St. John's, Sir Charles and Lady Hamilton were so much taken with his earnest and eloquent sermons that they determined to have him promoted ; the future bishop, however, would not give up his missionary work. Bishop Spencer was a very elegant and accomplished man and, although a born aristocrat, he was most simple and unpretending in his habits.   Many of the older generation can remember his residing in Cochrane Place, the marriage of his daughter to Sir John

BISHOP SPENCER.

From an engraving.

Harvey's son, and the kindly genial manners that endeared him to all hearts. The new Diocesan was an Evangelical of the old school of Wilberforce and Bickersteth ; he promoted the work of the Newfoundland School Society, the British and Foreign Bible Society, and throughout his episcopate both the Church and the Clergy in the Colony were distinctly of the Evangelical or Low Church School. When he was appointed to the see of Newfoundland as the first bishop, in 1839, he was at the time Archdeacon of Bermuda.[1] "At my consecration," said the Bishop, "to the see of Newfoundland, I found only eight clergymen of the Church of England in the whole Colony." The Church was in a most disorganized and dispirited condition ; the schools were languishing, many of them broken up, and all were destitute of that spirit of unity and order so essential to real efficiency. Within a brief episcopate of a little over four years,[2] some of these evils were remedied,

[1] Bishop Spencer resided in Bermuda from 1822 to 1838, and was Archdeacon of Bermuda from 1825 until his elevation to the See of Newfoundland in 1839.

[2] Bishop Spencer was a grandson of the second Duke of Marlborough. In his letter to the Society for the Propagation of the Gospel in 1841, he says, "I have travelled this year 1,188 miles, visited 35 stations, confirmed 1,136 persons, consecrated six churches, organised, or assisted in the building of 21 new churches, ordained two priests and eight deacons, founded or restored more than 20 day schools or Sunday schools. Bishop Spencer left the Colony in 1843. On his appointment as Bishop of Jamaica, he thus wrote about the qualities necessary for his successor : " He must have strength of constitution to support him under a climate as rigorous as that of Iceland, a stomach insensible to the attacks of sea sickness, pedestrian powers beyond those of an Irish

the most crying deficiencies supplied, and the foundations laid of that
church organization upon which his successor, Bishop Feild, subsequently
built with so much success.   In all his work he was largely aided
by Archdeacon Bridge.[1]   Bishop Spencer divided the diocese into
rural deaneries ; established, with the aid of the Society for the Propagation of the Gospel, a theological institution for the training of
divinity students, helped and encouraged the erection of more than 20
new churches, originated and revived Sunday schools everywhere,
increased the number of clergymen to twenty-
five, with lay readers and schoolmasters under
them ; established a mission to the Micmac
Indians, and raised a considerable sum of
money, with the hope of building a cathedral,
the first stone of which he laid before quitting
the diocese.   These were the legacies he left
to his successor in the See, and it is with
that successor, the Apostolic Bishop Feild,
that the progress of the Church in Newfoundland will ever be closely associated.

BISHOP FEILD.
By Kilner, St. John's.

The story of the labours and successes of
the long episcopate, of thirty-two years, of
this remarkable man, must of necessity, in this
brief sketch, be incomplete and imperfect.   We can only summarize
them.   He doubled the number of clergy ; churches and parsonages were
multiplied in a like proportion.   The theological institution was
enlarged and endowed, and now exists under the name of Queen's
College.   He established separate seminaries for boys and girls, which
have been highly successful ; founded distinct orphanages for destitute

gossoon, and an ability to rest occasionally
on the bed of a fisherman or the hard boards
in a woodman's tilt.   With these physical
capabilities he must combine a patient temper
and energetic spirit, a facility to adapt his
speech to the lowest grade of intellect   .   .   .
.   .   together with the discretion and charity
which will induce him to live, as far as may
be possible, at peace with all men   .   .   ."

[1] Mention has been made at page 469 of
the labours of Archdeacon Bridge.   He came
out to Newfoundland in 1825, first as tutor to
Sir Thomas Cochrane's sons, Charles and
Baillie Cochrane (afterwards Lord Laming-
ton).   Prior to his appointment, as rector of
St. John's, in 1840, he had been curate to the
Rev. F. Carrington ; he was a most earnest
and devoted minister, the first promoter of
temperance in the Church, and specially
energetic in the cause of education ; at one

time he was superintendent of the Newfoundland School Society, and all the older generation have lively remembrances of his admirable
school and his marvellous gifts as a teacher ;
his congregation literally worshipped him.
In 1840 he visited England to take his M.A.
degree at Oxford, and to obtain funds for the
erection of the new cathedral, the cost of
which Bishop Spencer modestly estimated at
£4,000 sterling.   Mr. Bridge died in 1856.
Contemporaneous with Archdeacon Bridge
was the Rev. C. Blackman, for many years
incumbent of St. Thomas's, a most able and
eloquent preacher ; he came out to the Colony
as private secretary to Sir Charles Hamilton,
was ordained in Newfoundland, and after serving several years as minister at Port de Grave,
became second incumbent of St. Thomas's,
in succession to Archdeacon Wix, mainly
through whose exertion the church was built.

children of both sexes; designed and partially built the beautiful cathedral of St. John the Baptist in the Capital; originated and provided an endowment for the future support of the Episcopate; reduced an unorganised and feeble ecclesiastical system to one of synodical order and unity; and year by year, in the church ship *Hawk*, visited and comforted his clergy and their flocks, scattered along a rugged shore of over three thousand miles.

REV. J. MOUNTAIN.
From an old photograph.

REV. MR. HUTCHINSON.
By S. H. Parsons.

REV. W. W. LE GALLAIS.
By Adams and McKenney.

In all these enterprises and labours he was helped by a staff of fellow-labourers, like-minded with himself, whom his noble example attracted to the oldest of England's colonial possessions. The names of Boland, Le Gallais, Mountain, Hutchinson, White, Cunningham, Johnson, Colley, Curling, Botwood, and a roll of others too numerous to unfold, were

REV. THOMAS WOOD.
By Gowland, York.

ARCHDEACON BOTWOOD.
By S. H. Parsons.

REV. DR. PILOT.
By S. H. Parsons.

among those who flocked to his standard, and with him fought the battle for the Master. The salvation of souls and the honour of God and of His Church, were the mainsprings of his life and work, and when these were concerned he knew no compromise. He entered into his rest on the 8th June 1876 at Bermuda.

The Right Rev. James Butler Kelly succeeded him by virtue of a vote of the Synod in 1873, but his health did not admit of his continuing

REV. G. R. JOHNSON.
By Braduce, Torquay.

his labours, in which for nine years he had so heartily shared with Bishop Feild as his co-adjutor, and on his resignation in 1877 the Synod remitted to delegates in England the choice of his successor, which resulted in the consecration, on May 1st, 1878, of the Rev. Llewellyn Jones.

His Lordship, the present Bishop of Newfoundland, is a sound High Churchman, a man of broad and liberal views; in St. John's he has won all hearts by his cheery manner, his unfailing courtesy. The bishop is imbued with the true missionary spirit; although the labours of his great diocese have seriously injured his health, he declined to accept easier work, and a more advantageous position as Anglican Bishop of Nova Scotia. On all platforms and by all creeds the bishop is welcomed; he has endeared himself to the whole Colony by his exceeding gentleness;

one of the most modest of men, he shrinks from all puffing and praise. He is a most methodical and energetic worker, a good platform speaker, a very earnest and able preacher; the keynote of all his sermons is sincerity, an overmastering desire to win souls for his Master. One of the foremost of his missionaries, writing of him, says "He shares with his clergy their " perilous work, and no less than his prede- " cessor is enkindled with the same spirit of " zeal for the diocese. He has done much to " forward the work of the church in New- " foundland. Improvements, material and

BISHOP JONES.
By Russell and Sons.

" spiritual, are manifest in all directions." Besides the care of all the churches in Newfoundland and Labrador, the bishop is ordinary over the English Colony in St. Pierre and Bishop of Bermuda. By the devotion of the churchmen in these lovely islands, and by the special labours of Mr. Reid, the church has prospered exceedingly. In organization and in church building the later episcopate of Bishop Jones has been specially distinguished, both in Newfoundland and Bermuda.

It has also been marked by the completion of the noble cathedral, now, unhappily, in ruins from the disastrous fire of July 1892; by the erection of new and enlarged orphanages in St John's, and of many beautiful and commodious churches throughout the diocese, and the establishment of a sustentation fund for the future maintenance of the clergy; by prolonged visitation voyages to all parts of his extensive diocese; and by a more generous support of all church institutions by the laity than had heretofore obtained.

In the great fire of July 1892 the Church sustained losses amounting to $60,000, exclusive of the beautiful cathedral. By the energy of Bishop Jones, appeals were made to the Church at large for help towards making these losses good. These appeals have been liberally responded to, and in a few years, with the help of a willing laity, it will be found that the dreaded fire was but an angel in disguise.

Even in this short sketch mention should be made of the deep debt of gratitude which the church in Newfoundland owes to Mrs. O. Johnson, a widowed lady who took up her abode in St. John's, though infirm in body, she was most energetic in the Master's service, and contributed

ANGLICAN CATHEDRAL, ST. JOHN'S.

liberally to the diocese. Rev. C. Palairet, another friend of the Bishop, will always be devoutly remembered for his deep devotion, and his liberal gifts to Topsail. In Bishop Feild's episcopate the missions to White Bay and Bay of Islands were commenced, the first by the earnest and devoted missionary, Mr. Temple, the second by the Rev. U. Z. Rule. After Mr. Rule's resignation the church was provided with one of her most remarkable and devoted missionaries. The Rev. J. Curling, whilst serving as an engineer officer in Bermuda, was brought under the holy influence of Bishop Feild; he resigned his commission in the army, and after due preparation was ordained in 1873. He was appointed to the

REV. J. J. CURLING.
By Debenham, Cowes.

mission of Bay of Islands. Out of his large means he presented the diocese with his yacht "Lavrock." No more humble, devoted servant of the Church has ever laboured more abundantly to win souls than did this young engineer officer.

In 1879 Mr. Curling was made rural dean of Belle Isle Straits. After sixteen years of such constant toil and labour as falls to the lot of few, Mr. Curling gave up his mission to prosecute his further studies at Oxford. His liberal benefactions to the Church of England in Newfoundland have been distributed all over the Island. Generous as Mr. Curling has been in distributing his wealth to benefit the diocese, still more good has been done by his spiritual influence and his deep devotion to duty; his noble example of self-denial has helped to strengthen many feeble knees, to support the weak, and to deepen their faith.

BAY OF ISLANDS.
From a photograph by the Rev. J. J. Curling.

Time would fail to tell of many interesting features of the Newfoundland diocese: the hardest missionary labour of all is in Arctic Labrador.

Archdeacon Wix visited the coast but appointed no clergyman. Mr. Gifford was the first missionary at Forteau in 1847, remaining there ten years. Mr. Gifford went afterwards to New Zealand, where he

NEWFOUNDLAND CHURCH SHIP "LAVROCK."
From a photograph by the Rev. J. J. Curling.

still resides. Rev. H. P. Disney, an Irish clergyman, gave up his living in Ireland to plant the church at St. Francis Harbour. Our present archdeacon succeeded Mr. Gifford in Forteau, and laboured most abundantly in that dreary region for three years. Rev. F. Colley, and latest of all, Rev. Mr. Quinton, combines in his clerical work the hardihood of the typical Newfoundlander with the devoted zeal of an apostolic missionary.

THE CHURCH IN THE OUTPORTS.

BONAVISTA.

In 1722 the Rev. Henry Jones was settled at Bonavista by the liberality, as it would appear, of the inhabitants of that settlement. For although the journals of the S.P.G. in 1726 show that he was in correspondence with the Bishop of London, and its Committee, and received at different times gratuities of money, and books for use in the school which he had established there, there is no statement that any regular allowance was made to him, as it is always in the case of those who were upon the list of the Society's missionaries. He wrote in 1730 that his church, which was built it would seem from sources altogether independent of any which the Society supplied, was nearly finished, and that a gentleman of London had given him a set of vessels for the Communion and a handsome stone font. In 1734 he represented his congregation to be in a flourishing condition, and the number of his communicants increasing. Within a period of eight years he baptized one hundred and fourteen persons, of whom five were adults. His ministrations were faithfully carried on, and gratefully received among an affectionate and willing people, and these evidences of his usefulness led the S.P.G. in 1741 gladly to appoint him its missionary in their more important settlement of Trinity Bay, as successor to one who had already begun a good work there. The proximity, however,

FORTEAU CHURCH, LABRADOR.

From a drawing by the Hon. and Rev. W. Gray.

of Trinity Bay to Bonavista enabled him to still keep up some intercourse with his former congregation, as, indeed, he was requested by the S.P.G. to do, until the services of a regular minister could be obtained for them, and these were soon afterwards secured by the appointment of the Rev. Mr. Peasley, a graduate of Trinity, Dublin. Mr. Jones continued to discharge his duties as the missionary for Trinity Bay for a period of six years, but in 1744, finding the winters too severe for his constitution, he asked leave, after twenty-five years of hardness endured

Q Q

for his Master's sake, to be sent to a warmer climate, and was accordingly appointed to a mission among the Indians in the Moskito country. On his way thither he put into Jamaica, and was persuaded by the Governor of the Island to accept the living of St. Anne's.

TRINITY.

Trinity Bay is one of the deepest bays which indent the shores of Newfoundland, and had been one of those earliest settled by fishermen from the mother country. So numerous had they become in 1729 that they represented to the S.P.G. their earnest wish to have a clergyman settled amongst them, pledging themselves to contribute 30*l.* a year towards his maintenance and to build a Church. The Society accordingly sent to this extensive district the Rev. Robert Killpatrick, on a salary of 30*l.* a year.

The discouragements which he encountered, particularly in the inconsiderable contributions of the people notwithstanding their promise to the Society, led him after a few months' residence to request that he might be transferred to a settlement in New York. He was accordingly sent to New Windsor, in that Colony, but so far was he from improving his condition by the change, that he applied for and obtained leave to return to his first mission. In New Windsor he could meet with no one who would give him a lodging on any terms.

On his way back to Trinity Bay his course brought him to Placentia, where he was detained three months. Here he did what he could to repair the evils which he describes prevailing in that settlement, from the absence of all religious ordinances, and from the inculcation of the principles of infidelity to which many of the inhabitants had abandoned themselves.

He preached here for six Sundays and baptized ten children   It may be of interest to mention that while the French held possession of the Island, Placentia was the seat of Government and was a place of great importance as a military post of the French. In 1689, there had been established a branch of the Convent of our Lady of Angels of Quebec, on the site of the present Church of England church and burying ground, and a few of the French and Basque tombs of the date of 1680 and 1690 are still preserved in the chancel of this church to mark out the place where it stood. As on the acquisition of this place by the English the French were allowed to dispose of their titles to properties here, it seems probable that the site of the recent convent was purchased by the English settlers, and converted into a church for the use of the Church of England. This was only twenty-one years before the visit of Killpatrick, who probably held service in it on the six Sundays referred to

The joy caused in Trinity Bay by Killpatrick's return to his flock proves that his services had more than a transient effect upon their minds, and that he had too hastily judged with respect to their supposed lack of sympathy and goodwill. He reported that his congregations were numerous, and at Old Perlican he had about two hundred hearers.

" By a strange coincidence the land formerly in the possession of the church at Old Perlican, and upon which at one time stood a building for the conduct of divine service, has during this year 1889, after its alienation from the church for over sixty years, been purchased and a church erected thereupon."

In 1737, being under the necessity of returning to England, he brought with him a letter from the justices of the peace, church-wardens and inhabitants of Trinity Bay, in which they gratefully and humbly thanked the S.P.G. for their great favour in sending a missionary to be their spiritual director according to the usage of the Church of England Subsequently Commodore West, then in command of the station, wrote to the Bishop of London to say that having a full knowledge of the vigorous work of clergyman of Trinity Bay, he recommended him to the favour of his Lordship, and characterizes Killpatrick in the word, the most comprehensive of all others, as a good Christian These testimonies of this early missionary afford evidence of the stedfastness and success with which he had continued to discharge his duties.

HARBOUR GRACE AND CARBONEAR

The Rev. James Balfour was appointed missionary at Trinity, with the out-harbours of Old and New Perlican, Bonaventure, in 1765. In acknowledgment of his services, his parishioners, soon after his arrival, built him a house, but after nine years spent in this mission, which was not less than forty leagues in circuit, he was removed to the more important station of Harbour Grace and Carbonear, vacant by the resignation of Mr. Coughlan in 1773. Mr. Balfour set himself to establish a school in Harbour Grace, and having secured the services of William Lampen, he recommended him to the favour of the Society, who were pleased to confirm the appointment, and make a grant of 15l a year towards his salary, on condition that he taught the children of the poor free of charge. The whole of Conception Bay was his mission, and with indefatigable zeal he made a tour around it four times in each year. In 1788 he wrote: " that he had visited every small harbour in " that bay · that he was in the habit of publicly catechizing the children

" in church, in face of the congregation, and that they gave great
" satisfaction in the performance." In a letter dated 1789, he reports
that the population of the Bay was three thousand seven hundred and
seventy-three Protestants, and two thousand six hundred and fifty-four
Roman Catholics In the following year he laments the great increase
of Popery , he reports that he had administered the Lord's Supper every
Sunday, and that the number of communicants was two hundred.
Mr. Balfour continued to discharge his many duties with unabated
vigour for thirty years, when age or infirmity compelled him to retire,
the Society continuing his salary in consideration of lay and active
services, and the destitute condition of himself and his family.   From
the record of the foundation of St. Paul's, Harbour Grace, we learn that
the first Anglican church in the town was built in 1764 , it was burnt
down on 18th August, 1832, and the present stone edifice was commenced on the 28th July 1835, the corner stone being laid by Governor
Prescott   The first Anglican clergyman in Harbour Grace was Laurence
Coughlan, next David Balfour, succeeded by G. C Jenner   From 1802
the place was filled for several years by the historian, Rev L A.
Anspach   Another well-known Anglican rector of Harbour Grace was
the Rev F. Carrington

The S.P.G., which had been for some time solicitous to fill the mission
of Trinity, which had been vacant since the removal of Mr. Balfour to
Harbour Grace in 1773, appointed the Rev. James Barker to proceed to
that place in 1782. He had already been in the service of the Society
as Missionary at Providence, in the Bahamas, but upon the capture of
these Islands by the Spaniards, a year or so before, he was compelled to
leave it, and return to Ireland, his native country , no record, however,
of his long work is to be found in any of the Society's publications, and
it is probable that Mr Barker never reached his destination.

PLACENTIA.

In 1787 a memorial from the principal inhabitants of Placentia was
laid before the S.P.G., setting forth the great want of a clergyman in
that settlement, and their willingness to contribute to his support.
Placentia had attracted the notice of His Majesty King William IV.,
then Duke of Clarence, when in early life he was engaged in the
honourable service of his country as Commander of the *Pegasus,* and he
was not slow in recommending the claims of the ancient seat of Government of Newfoundland to the favourable notice of the Society   He further

showed his interest in the work of the Church here, by contributing the sum of fifty guineas towards the erection of the Church, to which also he presented a handsome set of vessels, which are still used, although now very occasionally, at the celebration of the Holy Communion. The S.P.G. had not been unmindful of the condition of the neighbouring settlements as represented by Killpatrick and Langman, and had made several attempts to procure a suitable man for the post, but as no decent provision was assured towards his maintenance, by the people, they did not feel justified in taxing their scanty income for his entire support. Now, however, upon the faith of their promised contributions, they were enabled to send the Rev. John Harris, who had already proved himself an able and useful minister as curate of Haverford West. After a passage of nine weeks, Mr. Harris arrived at Placentia. He found that the original church, formerly the Chapel of our Lady of Angels, had been removed, that the population had nearly all become members of the Roman Catholic Church, only a remnant of one hundred remaining members of the Church of England in Placentia, and thirty in the out-harbours. After the first year of his ministry here, he was enabled to state that by the activity and diligence of Mr. Brown, the first

ANGLICAN CHURCH AT HERMITAGE BAY

magistrate of the place, a new church was nearly completed, and that he had visited Burin and Fortune Bay, performing the various offices of the church. In 1790, upon the removal of Mr. Price from St. John's, he was transferred thither on the particular request of its inhabitants, and the Rev. Mr Evans, a curate in the vicinity of Haverford West, was appointed to succeed him.

Mr. Evans speaks, in 1790, of the civility and attention shown him by the principal inhabitants, one Mr. Waldron, at no little inconvenience to himself, placing a boat at his disposal, and accompanying him in his missionary excursions. His visits to Burin were highly appreciated. Here he procured from the Governor a grant of land for building a church, and established a school under a Mr. Sanders, who discharged his duties with great attention and diligence, to whom the Society made an allowance of £15 a year. He also made excursions into Fortune Bay, which then had a population of about a thousand settlers, extending the knowledge of God, as he says, among a people who had hitherto lived in lamentable ignorance and darkness, and content to endure risk, fatigue, and hardship, if so be he might answer the end of his mission On one of these voyages—"voyages of discovery" the apostle of fishermen, Bishop Feild, used in later years to call them ––he was shipwrecked, and to the surprise of all who knew the coast, he managed to escape to shore, having lost everything except what he had on. After ten years of labour such as this, Mr. Evans left the mission of Placentia, since which, no resident of the Church of England has been stationed there.

APPENDIX TO CHAPTER XIX.

I.—Chronological List of Clergy.

RECTORS OF ST JOHN THE
BAPTIST, ST JOHN'S, NEW-
FOUNDLAND.

1699 Rev John Jackson.
1705 Rev Mr. Rice.
1730 Rev. Mr. Fordyce
1741 Rev M Peaseley, M A
1752 Rev Edward Langman,
    M.A , Baliol College,
    Oxford
1783 Rev Walter Price
1791 Rev John Harries, M A.
1810 Rev. David Rowland,
    M A
1817 Rev Thomas Grantham,
    M A
1819 Rev. Fredk. Carrington,
    B A.
1840 Rev Thos Bridge, M A ,
    C C. Oxford.
1854 Right Rev Edward Feild,
    D D
1876 Right Rev J B. Kelley,
    D D , D.C.L
1878 Right Rev Llewellyn
    Jones, D D
1894 Rev. Arthur Heber
    Brown, M A., St Ed-
    mund's Hall, Oxford

ST THOMAS'

1836 Ven Archdeacon Wix,
    M A.
1840–1852 Rev Charles
    Blackman, M A
1853–81 Rev. Thomas Martin
    Wood, R.D , incum-
    bent 1853, rector 1877.
1881 Rev Arthur Charles
    Fitzgerald Wood, M A ,
    Curate, Rev Henry
    Dunfield, 1881.

ST MARY'S

1856 Rev. John Pearson, In-
    cumbent
1864 Rev. Charles Medley,
    B.A., Incumbent.
1867 Rev Edward Botwood,
    Incumbent, 1867,
    Rector, 1877, R.D ,
    1879, Archdeacon,
    1894.

RECTORS OF HARBOUR
GRACE

1766 Rev. Laurence Coughlan.
1773 Rev James Balfour,
    M.A.

1795 Rev G C Jenner
1802 Rev. Lewis Amadeus
    Anspach
1813 Rev. Frederick Carring-
    ton, B A.
1818 Rev John Leigh, Episco-
    pal Commissary
1822 Rev. John Burt.
1833 Rev James Shreve.
1837 Rev S Musson
1842 Rev George J Addison,
    B A.
1843 Rev George Baring
    Cowan
1845 Rev. John Chapman.
1850 Rev. Henry Purden
    Disney.
1851 Rev Bertram Jones
1877 Rev John Monk Noel

MISSIONARIES OF TRINITY.

1729 Rev. Robt Killpatrick
1748 Rev. Henry Jones
1750 Rev. Benjamin Lindsay.
1764 Rev James Balfour,
    M A.
1782 Rev Mr. Barker
1786 Rev John Clinch, M D.
1820 Rev. Aubrey George
    Spencer, D D.
1822 Rev William Bullock,
    D D.
1830 Rev. William Nisbett,
    Curate.
1842 Rev Mr Martine
1842 Rev. H J Fitzgerald,
    M A.
1848 Rev Bertram Jones
1850 Rev. Thomas Martyn
    Wood
1853 Rev. Benjamin Smith,
    R D
1877 Rev. Henry Dunfield
1881 Rev. Henry Foster.
1883 Rev. Henry Chas H.
    Johnson
1889 Rev. William Weaver.

MISSIONARIES AT FERRY-
LAND

1610 Rev. Erasmus Stourton
1748 Rev Edward Langman,
    M A.
1791 Rev. Samuel Cole
1799 Rev. John Dingle
1802 Rev. Henry Wood
1819 Rev. Aubrey George
    Spencer, B A
1823 Rev Charles Blackman,
    M.A.
1827 Rev Peter Perring.
1839 Rev William Bowman.

1843 Rev. William J. Hoyles.
1847 Rev. Henry Harris
    Hamilton, B A
1857 Rev Augustus E. C
    Bayly
1861 Rev Robert Temple
1864 Rev. John Monk Noel.
1868 Rev. Henry Maynard
    Skinner
1870 Rev. Charles Rock
    West.
1873 Rev Cornelius Martin
    Ellingham.
1875 Rev. Arthur Charles
    Waghorne

TWILLINGATE

1816 Rev — Lee
1819 Rev. — Langhorne
1822 Rev. — Bullock
1823 Rev — Chapman

PLACENTIA

1787 Rev — Harries
1790 Rev — Evans
1819 Rev — Spencer ?

HEART'S CONTENT

1827 Rev Otto Weeks
1829 Rev. J Moore
1836 Rev — Hamilton
1840 Rev — Lind.

BAY ROBERTS.

Rev. Oldvald Howell

CARBONEAR.

1820 Rev — Burt
—— Rev — Fitzgerald

BURIN

1815 Rev. — Grantham

ST. JOHN'S OUT-
HARBOUR

1822 Rev. C. Blackman
1823 Rev. — Langhorne.
1829 Rev — Perring
1829 Rev T. Boone.
1832 Rev. T M Wood
1840 Rev. — Addison

GREENSPOND

—— Rev. — Coster.
—— Rev. T. M. Wood
—— Rev. — Gilchrist.

PORT DE GRAVE

1827 Rev C Blackman.
1839 Rev — Vicars.

II.—Church of England.

Church population, as per census,
1891 - - - - - 69,823

Number of Missions and
Parishes - - - 51
Number of Clergy - - 51
Number of Lay Readers and
Catechists - - - 141
Number of Communicants - 12,000
Number of Churches conse-
crated - - - - 135
Number of Parsonages - 51
Number of Sunday Schools - 172
Number of Sunday Scholars - 11,000
Number of Sunday Teachers 931
Number of Day Schools - 213
Number of Day School
Scholars - - - 11,949

One Theological College endowed

	$
Amount collected for General Church Fund	20,000
Amount collected for Home and Foreign Missions	2,400
Amount collected by Women's Home Mission	700
Amount collected for support of Orphanages	1,500
Endowment for Bishoprics	60,000
Endowment for Queen's College	46,500
Endowment for Sustentation Fund	12,000
Endowment for Special Missions	1,000
Endowment for Clergy Pension Fund	6,500
Endowment for Widows of Clergy Fund	21,000
Value of Cathedral and Churches	500,000
„ Schools	80,000
„ Parsonages	65,000
„ Glebes	20,000

DIOCESE OF NEWFOUNDLAND

Former Prelates—Aubrey George Spencer, D D , 1839 Edward Feild, D D , 1844 James Butler Kelly, D D , 1876.

Present Bishop—Right Reverend Llewellyn Jones, D D , Lord Bishop of Newfoundland, Consecrated in St Paul's Cathedral, London, on Festival of SS Philip and James, 1878, by the late Archbishop Tait, of Canterbury, the Bishops of London and Hereford, and Bishop Kelly.

Archdeacon of Newfoundland—Rev. Edward Botwood

Commissaries in England—Rev. Canon Jones, M A , Barneside, Kendal, Rev J J Curling, B A , Hamble, Southampton

Commissary in Bermuda—The Ven. J. Lumley Lough

DEANERY OF AVALON.

Rev Edward Colley, Rural Dean
St. John's Cathedral
Rev. A H Browne, Rector
Rev A G Bayly, B A , Senior Curate
Rev J H Bradford, Junior Curate
Rev. W. Pilot, D D , Succentor
St Thomas'—Rev A C F Wood, M A , Rector, Rev H Dunfield, Curate
St. Mary's—Rev Edward Botwood, Rector
Topsail and Fox Trap—Rev E Colley, Rev H. Marriott, B.A
St John's Outports—Rev H Elmington
Portugal Cove—Rev W R Smith
Non-Parochial—Rev Wm Pilot, D D , St John's, General Inspector of Church of England Schools
Theological College—Rev C Knapp, M A

DEANERY OF CONCEPTION BAY.

Rev John M Noel, *Rural Dean*
Brigus—Rev G H Bolt, M A
Salmon Cove—Rev. J Darrell.
Port-de-Grave—Rev T. G Netten
Bay Roberts—Rev. Wm Shears
Spaniard's Bay—Rev John Godden
New Harbour, Trinity Bay—Rev E K H. Caldwell
Upper Island Cove—Rev J S Sanderson.
Harbour Grace—Rev. J M Noel.
Harbour Grace (South Side)—Rev. James White
Carbonear—Rev F W. Colley
Bay-de-Verds—Rev J G Cragg

DEANERY OF TRINITY BAY.

Rev H C H Johnson, *Rural Dean*
Heart's Content—Rev. H C H Johnson.
Random—Rev G R Godden, B A
Trinity West—Rev. Frank Smart
Trinity East—Rev G H Field
Catalina—Rev. John Antle.

DEANERY OF BONAVISTA BAY.

Rev Augustus E C Bayly, *Rural Dean*
Bonavista—Rev. A. E C Bayly, R D , and Rev. Henry Petley.
Kings Cove—Rev William Kirby
Goose Bay—Rev. T. R. Nurse
Salvage—Rev. Harold F. Wilson, B A
Greenspond—Rev H J Read

DEANERY OF NOTRE DAME BAY.

Rev Robert Temple, *Rural Dean*
Fogo—Rev. W. C. White
Twillingate—Rev Robert Temple, R. D.

DEANERY OF NOTRE DAME BAY—*cont.*

Herring Neck—Rev. G. S. Chamberlain

Exploits—Rev. C. Wood
Little Bay—Rev. A. Pittman
White Bay— ———— ————, Mr A Coffin, Catechist.

DEANERY OF PLACENTIA BAY.

Rev. John Hewitt, *Rural Dean.*
Harbour Buffett—Rev. Arthur Shorter
Burin—Rev. John Hewitt
Lamaline—Rev. F T. E. Smith, B.A
Whitbourne and Placentia—Rev. J H Bull.

DEANERY OF FORTUNE BAY

Rev George Bishop, *Rural Dean*
Harbour Briton—Rev T. P Quinton
Hermitage Bay—Rev George Bishop, R.D.
Bellevram—Rev William A Haynes.
Burgeo—Rev T A. R Allsopp.
Rose Blanche—Rev T. E. Wilson, B.A
: *Channel*—Rev. Llewellyn Godden.
St. Pierre—Rev. T W. Temple (under licence of the Bishop of London).

DEANERY OF STRAITS OF BELLE ISLE.

———— ———— ————, *Rural Dean*
St George's Bay—Rev Charles Jeffery.
Bay of Islands—Rev. Arthur Waghorne
Bonne Bay—Rev Charles W. Hollands
Battle Harbour— ———— ————, Mr. W. Pitcher, Catechist.
Sandwich Bay— ———— ————, Mr. L. Dicks, Catechist
Strait of Belle Isle—Rev. William Weaver, Mr G Mifflin, Catechist.
Rev. H. Petley, Senior, M.A., retired
Rev. J. Godden, unattached.

THEOLOGICAL COLLEGE.

Visitor—The Lord Bishop.
Principal—Rev. C. Knapp, B A.
Council—The Lord Bishop, Rev E Botwood, Rev A C. F. Wood, Rev. E. Colley, R.D, Rev. W. Pilot, Sir J. S Winter, K.C.M.G, Messrs. J. Outerbridge, W. H Horwood.

DIOCESAN SYNOD OF NEWFOUNDLAND

Executive Committee—The Lord Bishop, Revs. E. Botwood, F Colley, H Dunfield, Wm. Pilot, A. C. F. Wood, W. R. Smith, and Hon. A. W. Harvey, K.C M G, Hon G. T. Rendell, J. W. Withers, Hon. Sir W. V. Whiteway, K.C.M.G., Hon W. H. Horwood, Hon Dr Skelton.

Secretary—Hon. G. T. Rendell

CHAPTER XX.

THE ROMAN CATHOLIC CHURCH IN NEWFOUNDLAND

By the Most Rev. M. F. Howley, D.D ,

Bishop of St John's.

The daring explorers of the fifteenth century were animated alike by the spirit of discovery and an ardent desire to spread the gospel of Christ and to convert the heathen We have notices of catholic priests and friars accompanying many of these early voyagers.

Italian monks (Augustinians) went with Cabot on his second voyage, there were priests with the Portuguese, and in the early part of this volume will be found notices of Biscayan clergymen accompanying the Basque fishermen to Terra Nova Cartier mentions having mass celebrated at Brest, Labrador, in 1534.

There are no other records of Catholic worship in Newfoundland until we come down to Lord Baltimore's settlement at Ferryland in 1623 He expended a very large sum of money on his colonization scheme. In 1627, when he first visited Ferryland, he was accompanied by three priests, named Smith, Hackett, and Longville. These priests " said " mass every Sunday at Ferryland and used all other ceremonies of the " church of Rome, in the ample manner as it is used in Spain," so says the Puritan divine, the Rev. Erasmus Stourton. Baltimore's colony failed like all its predecessors, and the next event in the history of the Catholic Church in the Colony is the establishment of the French in Placentia, 1662. We gather from the English records, and from French sources, that there was a small chapel, several priests, and one at least always in residence during the winter from the early foundation of Plaisance.

The formal establishment of the Franciscan Friars at Placentia by Bishop St. Vallier of Quebec took place in 1689. In 1686 Governor Parat, in sending to France for his winter supplies, mentions " 10 lbs " of wax candles for the altar." In the official letter of Bishop St. Vallier to the Franciscans he speaks of " the chapel which has been " consecrated to God in the said town."[1] The Franciscan Church in

---

This chapel appears in the early plan of Placentia facing p 248

Placentia seems to have disappeared with the evacuation of the place by the French after the Treaty of Utrecht in 1713, and all further attempt at forming any permanent religious settlement seems to have been abandoned A *Memoir* of the diocese of Quebec at the year 1794 contains the following remark, " Since the peace of 1763 the Islands of " St Pierre and Miquelon have been subject to a Prefect Apostolic. *Some " travellers report* that there is one also in Newfoundland." Quebec had evidently lost all *rapport* with Newfoundland in ecclesiastical matters. About the middle of the century (1750) the immigration from Ireland (principally from Waterford, Kilkenny, and Tipperary) began to assume considerable proportions, and though they had no regularly organised ecclesiastical government, we learn from the penal enactments of the governors of the times, against acts of Catholic worship, that there were priests in the Island.

We find that towards the last decade of the century the Catholic population of the country had increased to nearly twenty thousand, and there were some six or seven priests in the country. Hence, by the year 1784, it was thought that the population had taken sufficiently permanent root to demand an official recognition from Rome

In this year then, 1784, we may date the birth of the Catholic church in Newfoundland. The Rev. James Louis O'Donel, O.S F , a native of Knocklofty, co Tipperary, Ireland, was appointed Prefect Apostolic of the Island by Pope Pius VI He was a wise and prudent man, and though his assumption of a dignity conferred by the Pope was naturally considered an audacious act of " Papal aggression " by the over-zealous governors of the time, yet by his mildness and firmness he lived it all down, and became a great favourite with all classes. He was elevated to the Episcopal dignity in 1796, and consecrated in Quebec by Bishop Hubert. He built the "Old Chapel" and "Old Palace," visited the diocese, and drew up a set of diocesan statutes. By his prudence he more than once quelled the turbulent spirits of his flock, goaded by persecution, and his services were acknowledged and rewarded by the British Government. After a laborious pastorate of twenty-two years he retired to Ireland in 1806. He received a most complimentary address and presentation from the merchants and people generally on leaving, and his departure was universally regretted

He was succeeded by the Right Rev Patrick Lambert, also a member of the Order of St Francis, who held the reins of Ecclesiastical Government for ten years. During this time the penal restrictions were considerably relaxed, and the population of the place rapidly increased, and society generally began to advance in all the amenities of civilized and social life schools of various denominations were established In the year 1807 the Benevolent Irish Society was formed, and, though non-denominational in character, it soon became practically a Roman Catholic body. Its object was two-fold, charity and education. Under its auspices the Orphan Asylum was built, and schools opened, which have never ceased down to the present day to diffuse the benefits of a sound moral and religious education. Dr. Lambert made a visitation of Conception Bay and the southern shore. He enlarged the "Old Palace" and increased the number of priests to seven, and several small churches were erected during his episcopacy. He returned to Ireland in 1817 and died there.

He was succeeded by Right Rev. Dr. Thos. Scallan, O.S.F., a native of Wexford, who was the first bishop who died in Newfoundland (1829). He increased the number of priests to ten. He visited Rome in 1827, and made a visitation of the diocese as far west as Burin.

ROMAN CATHOLIC CATHEDRAL, ST. JOHN'S.

On October 28th, 1829, Father Michael Anthony Fleming, O.S.F., was consecrated as coadjutor and successor to Dr. Scallan, in the "Old Chapel." This was the first time this religious function had been performed in Newfoundland. Bishop Fleming immediately set to work to divide the Island into regular missions or parishes. He secured nine additional priests from Ireland. He visited as far west as Bay Despair, and gave a great impetus to educational matters, especially by the introduction of the Presentation Nuns in 1833. He had built for them a beautiful convent, which was burnt in the fire of 1846. After a hard struggle with the Imperial authorities, he secured the plot of land on which the Cathedral now stands, and on the 20th of May 1841 he laid the foundation stone of that magnificent building, which before his death was so far advanced towards completion that he celebrated the first Mass in it on the festival of the Epiphany (January 6th), 1850. In 1842 he introduced the Sisters of Mercy Nuns, whose object is to visit the poor and sick, and to teach a higher order of education He built the monastery of Belvedere, where he died full of works and merits on the 14th July 1850. In 1825 there were sixty thousand inhabitants in the Island, of whom twenty-five thousand were Catholics.

Dr. Fleming's health beginning to fail, he asked for a coadjutor, and Father John Thomas Mullock, of the same Seraphic Order, was appointed. He was consecrated in Rome, by Cardinal Franzoni, on the 27th December 1847, and arrived in St. John's the 6th May 1848. He was a man of rare ability, vast erudition, and great strength of character. He ruled the Church for twenty years, and it may be said that the ecclesiastical affairs took giant strides under his energetic government. He made several episcopal visitations to the remotest parts of the Island, visiting St George's Bay and the French shore, for the first time, in 1849, and circumnavigating the Island in 1850 Under his episcopate the cathedral was completed, and adorned with its grand altar, its numerous statues, paintings, and other rare works of art. He built the New Palace, Episcopal Library, St. Bonaventure's College, the two convents for the Presentation and Mercy Nuns, the whole forming a group unique for grandeur of site and beauty of architecture The cost of these splendid buildings was not less than 120,000*l* ($600,000) When he came to the country there were twenty-four priests in the Island, at his death there were thirty-five priests, fourteen convents, and sixty-five churches and chapels The cathedral was consecrated on September 9th, 1855, on which occasion Archbishop Hughes of New York and several of the Canadian bishops attended At this time, also, the foundation stone of the Church of St. Patrick, at River Head, St. John's was laid by the distinguished American Prelate. In 1856 Dr. Mullock had the Island divided into two dioceses, St. John's and Harbour Grace. Father John Dalton was consecrated by Bishop Mullock, in the Cathedral of St. John's, as first bishop of Harbour Grace. The number of Catholics in the Island in 1857 was fifty-seven thousand.

In St. Bonaventure's College, besides the secular school which took the place of the old Roman Catholic Academy, there was an Ecclesiastical Department and soon several natives of the country were prepared for the priesthood Dr Mullock was author of many learned and interesting lectures and pamphlets, which were published from time to time.   He also is credited with being the first to originate the idea of the Transatlantic Telegraph Cable, and the Harbour Grace Railway.   He died in St. John's on Easter Monday, 29th March, 1869.

Bishop Mullock was succeeded by the late Right Rev. Thos. Jos. Power, who was consecrated by His Eminence Cardinal Cullen,

BISHOP POWER.
By S. H. Parsons.

Archbishop of Dublin, at the Church of St. Agatha's, Irish College, Rome, on Trinity Sunday, June 12th, 1870.   The new bishop had already passed a distinguished career in Ireland.   He was born in New Ross, co. Wexford, in 1830.   He was Canon of the Cathedral in Dublin, and President of the Diocesan Seminary at Clonliffe.   He had acquired great renown as a powerful and eloquent pulpit orator, and had gained University honours in London.   He was a most polished and courtly prelate, and well fitted to fill the now important See of St. John's.   He found before him a church flourishing in all its ecclesiastical departments, a grand cathedral, a palatial residence, a devoted, zealous, and distinguished body of clergy, convents, schools, orphanages, and all the institutions of a thoroughly organised diocese, all of which were worthily maintained, increased, and developed during his long and successful episcopate.

He arrived in St. John's on September 9th, 1870.   By a happy coincidence the Church was *en fête* in honour of the anniversary of the consecration of the cathedral.   The triumphant reception which he received was worthy of the noble and faithful people of Newfoundland. He died on the 4th December 1893, thus his episcopate lasted over twenty-three years, being the longest on the list of our hierarchical tree. During this long reign he encouraged all ecclesiastical and educational matters.   He raised to a height of particular grandeur the music and ritual of the cathedral, and while thus caring for the æsthetic beauties of the catholic worship he did not neglect the material needs of the edifice and comforts of the congregation, having secured at a large expense the heating of the vast building by a hot-water system.   He completed and dedicated the Gothic church of St. Patrick's, River Head, and several substantial and elegant churches were erected in different outports.   The great glory of his episcopate is the introduction of the Christian Brothers as teachers of the Benevolent Irish Society's schools, and the erection by the same Society of their hall and schools on the site of the old Orphan Asylum. This hall was burnt down in the great fire of 1892, but is again nearing complete restoration on a still grander scale. The brothers have also schools at River Head, and teach at present some nine hundred boys. The group of ecclesiastical buildings in the capital has also been increased by the fine residence of the brothers at Mount St. Francis, the commodious Orphanage at Belvedere, the Presbytery and Convent at River Head, and the beautiful Chapel of the Sacred Heart at the Mercy Convent; in all respects the diocese has made great progress. There are thirty priests, sixteen convents, two orphanages. The Catholic population is forty-five thousand.

Catholicity [1] in Newfoundland owes a deep debt of gratitude to the old priests of the diocese; these devoted pioneers had to suffer hardships as good soldiers of Christ, to conquer difficulties unknown to the present generation. Fifty years ago the toils of travel were such as would appal the present generation, accustomed to railways, fine coastal steamers, good roads and the telegraph. Amongst the pioneers of the Holy Faith, the best remembered in our day was Dean Cleary, familiarly known all over the southern shore as the "Dane." He was not only a devoted priest, an eminent church builder, you could tell you were entering his parish by the splendid roads; every public work in his great parish was under his personal superintendence. For over half a century he ministered to the spiritual wants of his flock, rich and poor; Protestants and Catholics had equal love and esteem for the good dean; the noble churches and convents

DEAN CLEARY.
By J. Vey.

erected by his unwearied zeal are the perennial monument to his sainted memory. The dean was fond of recounting his labours and toil in the old days. Once when he was telling of his conversions Bishop Mullock said to him, "What's the use of your telling us about Witless Bay and " the Williamses, and all the converts you made? why, if you had stayed " in King's Cove you would have made all Bonavista Bay Catholic."

Time would fail to speak of all the good work done by Father Troy, builder of the churches at The Cove and Torbay, of Father Dalton or Dean Mackin in Brigus, of Father Kyran Walsh and his amiable successor Rev. Jeremiah O'Donnell in Harbour Main, of Father Condon's

---

[1] The following paragraphs down to the commencement of the description of Harbour Grace Diocese have been added by me to Bishop Howley's excellent paper on the Catholic Church in Newfoundland with his full approval —D.W.P.

great works in Placentia, and Father Richard O'Donnell's eminent
service to the church at St. Mary's, of Father Hearn, the zealous apostle
to the Micmac Indians, of Father Ward and Father Brown in Tilton
Harbour and Fogo, and of other devoted priests known to our fathers.
I must hasten on to recount some of the good work performed for our
Holy Church by the younger clergy.   Amongst the great church
builders of our own time, three young native priests are eminently
distinguished.   Bishop Howley has very modestly ignored his own work
at the Belvidere Orphanage and on the west coast, but his praise as an
energetic and devoted priest is in all the churches.   The most remarkable example of zeal and successful carrying out of Catholic institutions
in the colony is the career of Father Morris, cut off in the midst of his
labours ; never since the apostolic age was there a priest who gave
himself so entirely body and soul to the service of the Church ; no
difficulty daunted him, obstacles that would have paralysed a feebler
worker never quenched his zeal or stopped his onward path.   The noble
Church at Oderin, the beautiful Chapel at Manuels, Villa Nova, all bear

SALMONIER CHURCH.
Photo by Parsons.

testimony to his devotion to the sacred cause of religion.   No man ever
so literally fulfilled the Divine injunction " Be not weary in well doing."
The most unselfish of men, he literally wore himself out ; the worries, the
perplexities, the incessant labour he imposed on his enfeebled frame
paralysed at last the unselfish zeal and fiery energy that only death
could conquer.   Father Morris was a liberal of liberals, one of the
earliest promoters of the railway ; his lectures and his literary remains
all bear the hall mark of genius.

Father St. John of Salmonier, amongst the younger clergy, is a worthy
follower of Dean Cleary ; he attends both to the spiritual and temporal

needs of his parishioners with unbounded generosity. He has expended from his private means on the building and improvement of the beautiful churches that adorn the lovely estuary of Salmonier, and has been equally energetic in the promotion of roads and the improvement of agriculture amongst his flock. Father Clarke's good work at Torbay is well known to all. Both in the erection of churches and the moral improvement of his people his Reverence is another signal example of the benefits conferred on our Catholic people by a pious, amiable, and energetic priest.

A short time before the decease of Bishop Power, the Right Rev. Thomas F. Brennan, D.D., was sent here as his assistant. The young prelate is distinguished for his great learning; his amiable and unassuming manner won for him many friends in the diocese. At Bishop Power's death the spiritual welfare of the flock was entrusted by the Holy Father to the care of the Very Rev. J. Scott, as administrator of the diocese pending the advent of a new bishop. The genial and pious administrator is a universal favourite, and under his wise counsels the affairs of the diocese will be well directed. We still happily retain the Venerable Archdeacon Forristal; may he long be spared to aid us by his deep learning and profound experience. Of the eloquence and popularity of Dean Ryan, the devoted pastor of St. John's, West, and the younger clergy, Dr. Ryan and Dr. O'Reilly, it would be superfluous to dwell on their good qualities. They are well known to all the Catholic people of St. John's, to whom they are endeared by the cherished ties which link together for time and eternity the devoted Catholic priest and the Catholic people.

The Catholic Church in this Colony was founded by poor Irishmen, and by Irishmen only, with no extraneous help; it was begun in an evil

BISHOP HOWLEY.

time of persecution and penal laws, when the Catholic priest was hunted like a bandit, when all outward observances of the faith were prohibited under the direst pains and punishments; for years it was only amidst the lonely rocks and under the canopy of heaven that the Holy Sacrifice of the Mass could be offered up by the sorely persecuted clergy. To human eyes the Catholic Church in the Colony seemed a very poor institution, despised and rejected of men. Outwardly she might appear feeble and failing, but she was growing strong with a Divine strength resting on the sure foundation of the eternal Rock of the Faith. The puny seed planted by these poor Catholic Irishmen in Newfoundland, watered by Divine grace, has grown into a great tree, a devoted and noble branch of the Holy Church, under whose beneficent influence, piety and charity, pure religion, morality and the blessings of a Christian education have been spread over our land. Since this paper was in print, Bishop Howley has been appointed to the diocese of St. John's, the first native Catholic bishop.

In 1856[1] the northern part of the Colony was erected into a diocese under the title of Harbour Grace. The Right Rev. Dr. Dalton,

BISHOP DALTON.

By Adams, Harbour Grace.

as mentioned above, was its first bishop. He died in May 1869, five weeks after Bishop Mullock. His episcopate of thirteen years was peaceful and full of good works, the principal of which was the erection of the fine cathedral at Harbour Grace. Bishop Dalton was succeeded by the Right Rev. Henry Carfagnini, an Italian friar of the Order of St. Francis. He had been previously President of St. Bonaventure's College, St. John's. A man of great talent and learning, his Lordship was promoted, after ten years of episcopate, to the diocese of Gallipoli, in Italy. He completed and embellished the cathedral of Harbour Grace, adding the cupola and transepts. This fine building was burnt down in September 1889, but has been rebuilt on a new and improved plan by the present energetic bishop.

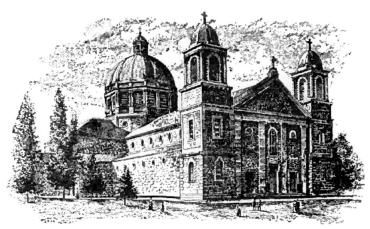

FIRST ROMAN CATHOLIC CATHEDRAL, HARBOUR GRACE.

The Right Rev. Dr. Ronald McDonald, the third bishop of the See, came to Newfoundland in 1879 from Pictou, N.S., where he had

Bishop Howley's narrative recommences here.

been for many years parish priest. His great learning and administrative ability, zeal and indefatigable energy, his prudence and charity, were not unknown to the authorities in Rome, and he was chosen as the one best fitted to remove the difficulties which had distracted the

CATHEDRAL, HARBOUR GRACE.
From a photograph by J. Vey.

diocese of Harbour Grace. The hopes then cherished were fully realised. He soon succeeded in restoring peace, with all its blessings. Of his episcopate, in which he still holds honoured and active rule, it is

BISHOP McDONALD.
Photo by Notman.

enough to say that he has displayed in a still more marked manner, in his new and wider sphere, those virtues and energies already alluded to. He has studded the diocese with churches, schools, and institutions, and is still actively engaged in the work. There are in the diocese twenty-one priests, forty-four churches, eighty-five stations, five convents, twenty-five nuns, ninety schools and a population of twenty-nine thousand.

The western part of the island, comprising the French shore, had been obliged to depend, up to the year 1850, on the chaplains of the French navy and fishing fleet for its spiritual attendance. Occasionally a priest was sent to visit it from Quebec. In 1849 Bishop Mullock visited it for the first time, and in the following year secured for the people the services of a stationary clergyman in the person of the Rev. Alexis Belanger, who was appointed Vicar-General of the diocese of St. John's. He died at Sandy Point, St. George's Bay, on the 7th September 1868,

P P 2

and was buried at Quebec. He was succeeded by the Right Rev. Monsignor Sears, of the diocese of Antigonish, who, in 1870, was created Prefect Apostolic, thus taking the region out of the jurisdiction of St. John's. Monsignor Sears was a most energetic and enthusiastic prelate. Besides building several churches, schools, and presbyteries, and establishing a regular staff of clergy on the shore, he was the first who, by his lectures and vigorous letters to the press, drew the attention of the Government officials of St. John's and England to the state of that part of the Island, to its great natural resources and future prospects. He was the pioneer of the system of public roads on the coast, and by his efforts secured

ST. PATRICK'S CHURCH, CARBONEAR.
From a photograph by E. Parsons.

for it representation in the Legislature, the establishment of mails, police, and custom service, &c. He died at Stellarton, N.S., on November 7th, 1885, and is buried in the family vault at Lochaber, Antigonish. He was succeeded in the Prefecture Apostolic by the Rev. Dr. M. F. Howley, of St. John's. In April 1892 the Prefecture was elevated another step in the hierarchy and made a Vicariate, the Prefect being appointed Vicar Apostolic and Titular Bishop of Amastris. The Right Rev. Dr. Howley was consecrated by Bishop Power, of St. John's, in the cathedral of that place, on St. John's Day (June 24th) 1892, being the first native of Newfoundland elevated to the episcopal dignity. During the past eight years the French shore has developed rapidly; several churches, presbyteries, and schools have been erected, and in 1893 a community of Sisters of Mercy was introduced. There are now in the Vicariate six priests, two convents, ten sisters, thirty-four churches, sixty-nine stations, twenty schools, and about six thousand five hundred of a population. The total Roman Catholic population of the Island, by the census of 1891, is over seventy-two thousand.

The group of islands comprising St. Pierre, Langlade, Miquelon, and Ile-aux-Chiens was fully ceded to the French by the Treaty of Paris, 1763. In that year there was a *curé* there, the Rev. M. Paradis, who was sent from Quebec. In 1770 the Rev. M. Bequet was there as

Prefect Apostolic. At the time of the French Revolution (1793) there were two priests in St. Pierre and one in Miquelon. The oath of allegiance to the Republic was tendered to them, two (Pères Jamtel and Allain) refused to take the oath and escaped to Arichat. Père Longueville took the oath and remained. At this time the island was taken by the English, and occupied by them till 1816, when it was again ceded to France by the treaties of Paris and Vienna. A priest of the diocese of Rennes, France, the Rev. M. Olivier, was sent out in 1815 as Administrator; since then there have been four Prefects Apostolic. In 1842 the *frères des écoles Chrétiennes* were introduced They have a very fine building, and about three hundred pupils in the communal schools There is also a *pension* for young ladies, under the Sisters of St. Joseph de Cluny, an asylum for children, maritime hospital, girls' asylum, industrial home, &c., all under charge of the Sisters. The present Prefect Apostolic is the Right Rev. Monseigneur Tibéri. There are four priests. The Catholic population is, in summer, twenty thousand, in winter, eight thousand.

Roman Catholic Church.

DIOCESE OF ST JOHN'S.

Former Prelates—Right Rev. Dr. O'Donel, died 1811 Right Rev Dr. Lambert, died 1817 Right Rev. Dr Scallan, died 1830 Right Rev Dr Fleming, died 1850 Right Rev. Dr Mullock, died 1869 Right Rev Dr Power, died 1893.

Present Bishop—Right Rev Dr M F Howley

Administrator of the Diocese—Very Rev John Scott.

Archdeacon— ————

Dean of the Diocese —Very Rev John Ryan

Cathedral, St John's—Very Rev John Scott Rev. Charles H O'Neill, Rev J O'Rielly, D D, Rev M Ryan, Ph D

St Patrick's, Riverhead—Very Rev Dean Ryan, Rev Edmund Crook, Rev Wm Jackman

Topsail and Kellygrews—Rev J McGrath

Petty Harbour—Rev Roger Tierney, P P

Torbay—Rev M J Clarke, P P

Portugal Cove—Rev John Walsh, P P

Witless Bay—Rev N Roach, P P, Rev. M. P O'Driscoll

Ferryland—Rev Laurence Vereker, P.P

Renews—Rev John Walsh, P P

Trepassey—Rev William Born, P P

St Mary's—Rev Vincent Reardon, P P.

Salmonier—Vacant

Placentia—Rev M A Clancy, P P

St Bride's—Rev Stephen O'Driscoll.

Little Placentia—Rev J St. John, P P.

St Kyran's—Rev W, P Doutney, P P.

Burin—Rev P M. O'Connor, P P

St Lawrence—Rev James Whelan, P P

Institutions

St Bonaventure's College—In charge of the Christian Brothers

St Patrick's Schools—In charge of the Christian Brothers.

Holy Cross School, Riverhead—In charge of the Christian Brothers.

Convents—Presentation Order, 9, Mercy Order, 5.

St. Michael's Orphanze at Belvidere for girls

St Thomas's Home for boys—at Villa Nova, Topsail.

St Bride's Academy—for boarders at Waterford Bridge, in care of Sisters of Mercy.

DIOCESE OF HARBOUR GRACE

Bishop—Right Rev Dr. Ronald McDonald, Consecrated at Pictou, N S, August 21st, 1881

Harbour Grace—Right Rev Bishop McDonald, Rev J March

Holyrood—Rev I Murphy

Harbour Main—Rev P O'Donnell, P P

Conception Harbour—Rev W Veitch, P P

Brigus—Rev E F Walsn, V G, Rev P. W Browne

Whitbourne—Vacant

Carbonear—Rev F D McCarthy, C C

Northern Bay—Rev John Roe, P.P.

Baye-de-Verds—Rev J Donelly, P P.

Trinity—Vacant

Bonavista—Rev R M Walker, P P

King's Cove—Rev T E Lynch, P P

St Brendan's—Rev J. G Batteock, P P

Tilton Harbour—Rev W P Finn, C C

Fortune Harbour—Revs Richard Walsh and Walter Tarahan

Little Bay—Rev S O'Flynn, P P

Coachman's Cove—Rev M Sheehan, C.C

Couche—Rev John Lynch

Labrador (Blanc Sablon)— ————

Labrador (North)—Attended by Priests from Harbour Grace in summer

Convents—Three of the Presentation Order and two of the Order of Mercy

VICARIATE APOSTOLIC OF WEST NEWFOUNDLAND

Vicar Apostolic—Right Rev Dr Neil McNeil

Sandy Point, Bay St George—Right Rev Dr McNeil, Rev Charles Renouf.

Highlands—Rev G Hawkins

Stephenville—Rev M. O'Rourke.

Porte-à-Porte—Vacant

Codroy Valley Rev. D McInnes

Bay of Islands—Rev A Sears.

Bonne Bay Rev P. W Brown

Harbour Briton Rev. C O'Regan, D D

St. Jacques—Rev. W. J. Browne.

CHAPTER XXI.

THE METHODIST CHURCH IN NEWFOUNDLAND.

By Rev. James Dove, D.D.

The history of Methodism in Newfoundland dates from the year 1765, one year earlier than its epoch in the United States. The story of its rise, progress, and present position is briefly told in the following paragraphs. It is a noteworthy fact that it was the first mission ground ever occupied by the Methodist Church. Mr. Wesley, having heard of the spiritual destitution of the colonists, was very desirous to furnish religious instruction for them. At his instance, supported by the Countess of Huntingdon, Laurence Coughlan was sent to Newfoundland by "The Society for the Propagation of the Gospel in Foreign Parts." He was born in Ireland, and after his conversion, being called to the work of the ministry, he laboured ten years as a travelling preacher in connexion with Mr. Wesley. Complying with Wesley's request, the Bishop of London ordained Coughlan, who sailed from England and arrived at Harbour Grace, Conception Bay, Newfoundland, in 1765. Though now a clergyman under the auspices of the aforenamed Society, he was still a Methodist preacher, both in doctrine and discipline, and to his evangelical labours Methodism owes its origin in Newfoundland.

When he entered upon his missionary work not a school was known in the Island, nor was a single temple raised to the worship of Almighty God, except one in St. John's, more especially for the use of those employed in the military and naval services. "Men who had come "from England had never seen a minister since they left their native "shores; and most of those who had been born on the Island had "never known one in their lives; the need of a zealous missionary "was great, and few men were better adapted for the work than the "man now sent." During seven years Mr. Coughlan pursued his solitary labours, suffering, much of the time, severe persecutions. He was prosecuted in the highest court of the Island, but was acquitted; abusive letters were written to England against him; a physician was engaged to poison him, but, becoming converted, exposed the diabolical design. Meanwhile, as the success of the missionary increased, the fury of his enemies became more violent. They had him summoned before the Governor, a discerning and resolute officer, who not only acquitted him, but made him a justice of the peace His opposers were now reduced to silence, and the persecuted preacher pursued his labours with increased effect. His health at last failed and he returned to England, leaving behind him two hundred communicants, little thinking that besides their conversion he had also kindled a fire in the land that should never be extinguished, that a large Methodist community should arise therein as the result of the seed which he had sown; that the little church he had planted should be cared for, watched over, and edified; that in after years its members should be counted by thousands; that its influence should be felt in the government, and its representatives should sit in the councils of the country, and that by the preaching of his successors, multitudes should be "turned unto the Lord" and be for ever saved

After Coughlan's departure the Methodist Church in Conception and Trinity Bays was kept together and ministered to by John Stretton, an Irish merchant and local preacher, Arthur Thomey, and J. Pottle, who were converted under Coughlan's ministry; and by John Hoskins from England, who settled as a schoolmaster in Old Pelican. In 1785 Mr. Wesley sent out John McGeary to occupy the vacant post. In 1791 the Island was visited by William Black, a missionary from Nova Scotia, who remained six weeks. His success was very marked, the drooping cause was revived During his short stay he organized Methodism in the Island, secured its Church property, and obtained new labourers from Wesley. These carried on and extended the work In the year 1808 three missionaries appear in the minutes of the English Conference as stationed in Newfoundland; these were J. Remmington, Wm. Ellis, Samuel McDowell, all Irishmen, noble and faithful men.

In 1811 the English Committee had asked their agents to pay particular attention to St. John's Definite action was, nevertheless, delayed until the autumn of 1814, when those who had been awaiting the appointment of a preacher in St John's (strengthened by the arrival of several families from Conception Bay) resolved to proceed during the ensuing spring with the erection of a small church, which unfortunately was destroyed in the fiery visitation of February 12, 1816, when a thousand human beings were rendered homeless.

In 1815 the six missions of Newfoundland were formed into a district, with William Ellis chairman. In January 1816 an important meeting took place at Carbonear, when John Gosse, Esq., presided at a gathering of the ministers and leading laymen. They unanimously recommended an extension of the work in different parts of the Island, and as a proof of interest in the issue of their representations, several laymen forwarded nearly £31 sterling to the Missionary Committee in England, with a list of the subscribers, which appeared in the report of 1817 as the first money ever forwarded from a British colony for mission work. At the Conference of 1816, no less than six ministers were selected for service in the Island.

This extension of mission work took place at one of the darkest periods in the financial history of Newfoundland. At the close of the war came the inevitable collapse. Famine, as a gaunt spectre, haunted the minds of many at Christmas, 1816. The unusual gloom was deepened by the failure of the seal fishery of 1817; yet greater troubles were in store for one section of the Island; two destructive fires in the fall of the year destroyed vast amounts of property in St John's, and rendered thousands of the inhabitants homeless. Of the distresses of these dark days the Methodist missionaries were not mere spectators. By the destruction of their first church in the fire of 1816, which, however, was rebuilt and opened on Christmas Day of that year, and the two fires of 1817, the congregation was so scattered and financially crippled as to be powerless to aid the trustees in meeting their obligations, which included a debt of nearly $2,000 on the church burned in 1816. At this crisis the financial affairs of the district were further complicated by the destruction of the large new church at Carbonear in 1817. A burning shingle from a building was borne nearly half a mile to a pile of shavings in the churchyard, and in a few moments the townsfolk were sorely startled as they saw their new sanctuary, built almost by themselves at a cost of more than £2,000, in the relentless grasp of the flames. In these distresses an appeal was made to the Methodists of England, which resulted in the noble subscription of over £2,000 sterling.

The aborigines of Newfoundland were not forgotten by the Methodist Missionary Committee in its plans for the evangelization of the Island.

In 1809, at the request of Dr. Coke, John Remmington had gone in search of these real natives, but through lack of preparation for a difficult and dangerous task, failed to find any representatives of a rapidly diminishing race. Eleven years later, when the story of their misfortune was attracting the attention of English philanthropists, they received special mention in the instructions forwarded by the Committee to their missionaries in the Island. These instructions and efforts were to little purpose, for it is quite probable that, with perhaps a few exceptions, " the real aborigines of the Island were sleeping the sleep of death."

For the spiritual welfare of some members of other Indian tribes, it was not too late to devise plans. Attempts were made to establish a mission on the coast of Labrador, from Hopedale, the most southerly station of the Moravian missions, to the Straits of Belle Isle. Different missionaries visited this part of the coast for some years, but in the report for 1829, it was said, "The Labrador Mission is for the present " abandoned, principally in consequence of the removal of the Esquimaux " tribes from the coast into the interior of the country, and their general " dispersion." Thirty years later, however, missionary work on the Labrador was resumed, and is continued at the present time. From the formation of the Newfoundland District in 1815, the Society's

WESLEYAN CHURCH, ST. JOHN'S.

operations were faithfully carried on with growing interest and success, the chair of the district being occupied by such men as Ellis, Bell, Pickavant, Williams, Botterell, whose ability and wisdom commanded for them general respect. In the year 1855 another step in advance was taken, and Newfoundland became a part of what was known as the Conference of Eastern British America, comprising the provinces of Nova Scotia, New Brunswick, Prince Edward Island, Newfoundland, and the Islands of Bermuda.

After the organization of the new Conference, the work in Newfoundland received a fresh impetus. Additional missionaries arrived from England, sent out by the parent Committee, who still regarded the missions in Newfoundland with fostering care. In the year 1873, the work having developed so largely, a re-arrangement of the circuits and missions was deemed necessary, which resulted in the formation of two districts, by the division and alteration of the one previously large district. Then, in 1874, there came another epoch in the history of Methodism in Newfoundland. A plan for a united Methodist Church which should span the continent from ocean to ocean, being approved of by the regularly constituted courts of the uniting churches, and receiving also the cordial concurrence of the British Conference, was

GEORGE STREET WESLEYAN CHURCH, ST. JOHN'S.

carried into effect on September 16th, 1874, when the representatives of ten annual conferences which had been previously organized, of which number "the Newfoundland Conference" was one, met and constituted the General Conference of "the Methodist Church of Canada," formed by the union of the former "Methodist Churches of Canada and Eastern British America" and of the former "New Connexion Methodist Church in Canada."

In 1883 a further union of Methodist bodies in Canada took place, when the representatives of "the Methodist Church of Canada," "the Methodist Episcopal Church in Canada," "the Primitive Methodist Church in Canada," and "the Bible Christian Church in Canada," met in Belleville, Ontario, on September 5th, "to merge their pre- " viously divided interests, and to prepare to go forth with the united " front of one consolidated, influential, and aggressive Church, with the " noble aim of spreading scriptural holiness throughout a vast territory, " and with the high honour of having vanquished obstacles to a " general union, which Methodists in other lands had hitherto deemed " insurmountable."

This completed union of the various branches of the Methodist family assumed the name of "the Methodist Church," and under this new name the first Newfoundland Conference of the Methodist Church was organized, according to Act of Parliament, in Gower Street Church, St. John's, July 1st, 1884. The Conference meets each year in the month of June, and is composed of all the ministers in full connexion and an equal number of laymen, elected by the laymen of the annual district synod. It has only executive powers, all legislation for the Church being enacted by the General Conference, composed of ministers and laymen in equal numbers meeting quadrennially.

HON. J. S. PITTS.

REV. DR. DOVE.

HON. EDWARD WHITE.

Since the union of 1874 the history of Methodism in Newfoundland has been marked by progress. Her financial economy has developed, churches and parsonages have been multiplied, her evangelistic work has been successful, her educational work has advanced.

" Accepting the denominational system so called, which in 1874 and " 1875 was endorsed by the Legislature in accordance with the expressed " wish of the leading denominations," she has striven, co-operating with the Reverend Dr. Milligan, the able and zealous superintendent of Methodist Day Schools, to provide educational advantages for her rising youth, and her efforts have been successful, as is evident from the following figures taken from the last report of the superintendent:—Number of day schools, one hundred and forty-three; of teachers, one hundred and forty; of scholars, nine thousand one hundred and thirty-one. These figures do not include the teachers and students in the College and the Carbonear Grammar School.

The erection of the new College buildings, replacing those destroyed in the great fire of 1892, is indicative of her high purpose to furnish the means for the superior and liberal education of the youth of the denomination, and others who may be wishful to avail themselves of the same. These buildings, comprising College, Principal's Residence, and Home for the accommodation of non-resident students, and costing when complete upwards of $70,000, are most pleasantly situated in a central locality, accessible to every part of the city, and spread out their extensive frontage of two hundred and sixty feet, commanding the beautiful outlook of the incomparable Narrows and South Side Hills.

METHODIST COLLEGE.

The College has spacious class-rooms, well lighted, well heated, well ventilated, and supplied with modern desks, seats, &c. These are for kindergarten and model schools of primary department, also for the use of classes in the College proper, besides laboratory, library, gymnasia, young men's institute, &c. A lecture-hall, with music-rooms and grand organ, is also provided; chemical and scientific apparatus, and other equipments necessary for a liberal education, are arranged for.

Methodism in the Island owes much to the liberality and zeal of her intelligent laymen, working harmoniously with the ministry, aiding in her councils and in many instances making noble and generous contributions to the various departments of her work. A noble bequest of

$15,000 was made by the late Hon. C. R. Ayre, for the erection of an orphanage in St. John's for the Methodist orphans of Newfoundland.

Plans for the same have been adopted, and ere long the building will rise, a monument to his thoughtful and loving care for the fatherless.

The name of Joseph Laurence, Esq., of East Keswick, Yorkshire, an English Methodist layman, deserves to be placed on record as a true friend of Newfoundland. He took a deep interest in the evangelization thereof, kept up a long and intimate correspondence with the officials of the Conference, which was "marked by a simplicity, a saintliness, well nigh apostolic"; it was therefore most

HON. C. R. AYRE.
By S. H. Parsons.

befitting that a part of the service at his grave in October, 1886, should

COCHRANE STREET METHODIST CHURCH, ST. JOHN'S.

be conducted, as it was, by the ex-president of the Newfoundland Conference, then visiting England, to whom it was a privilege to be able to pay the only tribute then possible to one who for years had had the prosperity of the Lord's work in Newfoundland engraven upon his very soul.

Mention may also here be made of the name of John S. Peach, another zealous friend of Methodism, who spent more than fifty years of ministerial toil on the Island, and died in 1891.

Methodism in St. John's is well represented by her four spacious churches, three mission halls, college, day schools, and present orphanage, which will be replaced by the new one, to which reference has been made. Outside the city liberal provision has been made to meet the spiritual need of her fifty-three thousand adherents, scattered around an extensive coast-line.

APPENDIX TO CHAPTER XXI.

Methodist Church in Newfoundland, 1894.

The following Statistics show the present status of the denomination in the Island

Methodist population, as per census of 1891 - -	53,276
Number of Districts - -	4
Number of Ministers - -	63
Number of Local Preachers -	51
Number of Churches - -	106
Number of other Reading Places	99
Number of Preaching Appointments - - - -	338
Number of Parsonages - -	40
Number of Church Members -	10,834
Number of Sunday Schools -	176
Number of Officers and Teachers - -	1,104
Number of Scholars - -	11,539

	$
Amount raised for Missions -	7,195
Amount raised by Women's Missionary Society - -	188
Amount raised for ministerial support - - -	19,859
Value of Churches - - -	250,000
Value of Parsonages - -	100,000

Rev William Swann, *President of Conference*

Rev. John T. Newman, *Secretary*.

1. St John's District

St. John's Centre—Rev. A. D. Morton, M A

St John's West—Revs H P Cowperthwaite, M A, Rev A. E Rowson, James Dove, D D , *Supernumerary*, Geo S Milligan, LL D , *Superintendent of Education by permission of Conference.*

St John's East—Rev George Paine, Rev Mark Fenwick, Guardian and Chaplain of the Home

Pouch Cove—Rev H C Hatcher, B D

Topsail—Rev Anthony Hill

Brigus—Rev. James Wilson

Cupids—Revs. Solomon Matthews, W A. Palmer

Bay Roberts and Spaniards Bay—Rev Charles Lench

Whitbourne—Rev. John Reay

Chapel Arm—Supply under Rev. Geo P. Story.

Sound Island—Rev George Burry

Flowers Cove—An Agent

St. Anthony—Rev Edgar Jones

Red Bay—Rev. Aykroyd Stoney

Hamilton Inlet—Supply

Labrador Coast—Rev. C. W. Follett (summer months) ; Student at College.

Chairman—Rev. H P Copperthwaite, M.A.

Financial Secretary—Rev Mark Fenwick.

2. Carbonear District

Carbonear—Rev. James Nurse, Rev W J Luscombe.

Harbour Grace—Rev Wm Swann

Freshwater—Rev Jesse Heyfield

Blackhead—Rev Samuel Snowden

Western Bay—Rev. Wm. Kendall

Lower Island Cove—Rev Wm. R. Tratt

Old Perlican—Rev. R W Freeman.

Hant's Harbour—Rev W T D Dunn.

Heart's Content—Rev James Pincock

Green's Harbour—Rev Wm J. Bartlett

Shoal Harbour—Rev. W J. Hutcheson.

Northern Bight—Rev Wm Patterson

Britannia Cove—Rev Charles Flemington

Musgrave Town—Rev. W. H. Dotchon.

Chairman—Rev. Wm Swann.

Financial Secretary—Rev. Wm. Kendall.

3. Bonavista District

Bonavista—Rev Thos. W. Atkinson.

Bird Island Cove—Rev. J J. Durrant.

Catalina—Rev A. A Holmes.

Trinity—Rev Edgar Taylor

Glover Town—Rev Chas. K Hutson.

Greenspond—Rev F G Willey

Wesleyville—Rev Jabez Hill

Musgrave Harbour—Rev. T B Darby, B A

Indian Islands and Seldom Come-By—Rev H J Indoe, B A (Indoe)

Fogo—Rev. W H Browning.

Herring Neck—Rev. Wm Harris

Twillingate—Rev. Levi Custis, B A., Rev A Hoskins

Moreton's Harbour—Rev. S. J Russell

Exploits—Rev Henry Scott.

Laurenceton and Burnt Bay—Rev Selby Jefferson.

Little Bay Island and Pilley's Island—Revs John J Wheatley, C Squires

Little Bay—Rev. John Pye.

Nipper's Harbour and Tilt Cove—Revs John C Sidey, E Moore.

White Bay—Rev. James Opie.

Chairman—Rev Jabez Hill

Financial Secretary—Rev. T. W. Atkinson

4 Burin District.

Burin—Rev. Thomas H. James.

Spoon Cove—Supply

Flat Island—Rev. James Smith, B A.

St Pierre—One wanted.

Fortune—Rev. John Pratt.

4 BURIN DISTRICT—*cont*

Grand Bank—Rev. G. C. Frazer.
Garnish, Fortune Bay—Rev. R. K. Peck.
Burgeo—An Agent.
Petites—Rev. Charles Howse.
Channel—Rev. John T. Newman
St George's Bay—Rev. T. K. Kelly.
Bay of Islands—Rev S. Halfyard.
Bonne Bay—Rev J K Curtis.
French Shore—An Agent
    Chairman—Rev Thos H. James
    Financial Secretary—Rev. John T.
Newman.

Students permitted to attend Mount Allison College, Sackville.

John E Peters	Henry Clegg.
W. B. Ambrose	George Storey.
J. C. B. Peck.	

Wesley College, Montreal.

J. T. Blyth.	C. W. Follett.
George E. Heal	T. E. Roberts.

Toronto University.

F G Drake.

CHAPTER XXII.

THE CONGREGATIONAL AND PRESBYTERIAN CHURCHES, AND THE SALVATION ARMY.

THE CONGREGATIONAL CHURCH IN NEWFOUNDLAND.

The small body of Christians in Newfoundland now officially designated as " The Congregational Church " is one of the oldest dissenting bodies in the Colony, though its numbers have always been very limited, it has had considerable influence and has ever been distinguished for the learning and ability of its ministers. It is stated in the Congregational Hand Book that in Queen Elizabeth's time some of the English separatists (Independents) were banished to Newfoundland : this is inherently probable; our Island was then the best known and most accessible portion of America In the small scattered settlements then existing about St. John's and Conception, these victims of Elizabeth's ecclesiastical tyranny could easily hide themselves away The separatists were the extreme branch of the Puritans, who had broken away from the Church and the Hierarchy.

Guy's colonists and their zealous Puritan pastor, Erasmus Stourton, would join with these exiles, and in this manner a small independent body may have been formed, and their numbers would be increased during the reign of Charles I In 1645 we have certain proof of their existence, George Downing, the first graduate of Harvard, Cambridge, Mass, on his visit to Newfoundland, received an invitation from the Newfoundland Independent Church to become their pastor, and a similar offer was made to the Rev. Richard Blinman, an English divine, who visited Newfoundland in 1660. Probably owing to the want of organisation, this body as a separate denomination died out, and we hear no more of Congregationalism until 1775, when the present church was established by an artillery sergeant, John Jones, a Welshman

From the old records of the church still preserved in St. John's we gather many particulars about this God-fearing old soldier—how first the little congregation met together every Sunday in the Court House. Nathan Parker, a New Englander, one of the founders of the present house of Job Brothers, soon became an elder afterwards Wallis Lang, a carpenter and builder, also became an elder. In the spring of 1777, in twenty-eight days, under the skilful management of Wallis Lang, a small building was put up Governor Montague tried to stop their progress and ordered John Jones to Placentia, but, says the devout old soldier, ". The Lord put his hook in his nose and turned him back by the way " he came, so that he did them no harm, but good, inasmuch as it " made them fast and pray. . . . And the Lord was pleased to bless " and increase them" Soon after this Mr. Jones was ordained in England The little church strengthened and increased, notwithstanding the opposition of the Rev. Edward Langman, a magistrate and episcopal minister, even the stronger opposition of Governor Edwards did not stay their progress All restraints were removed under the genial Admiral Campbell in 1784.[1] In 1789 the Meeting House (existing up to 1892 as the old Temperance Hall) was built. Much of the work was voluntary labour The articles are signed and sealed by John Jones, Henry Phillips, the High Sheriff, Nathan Parker, Wallis Lang, Joseph Lowman, Edward Freeman, James Barnes.

At this period in Newfoundland history every event was inaugurated with copious libations of wines and spirits · the worship of Bacchus was universal; we are not surprised therefore to learn that the foundations of the old Temperance Hall were laid with the accompaniment of a quarter cask of rum, "Ordered by the committee to be purchased and left in care of Mr. Lang." We can picture to ourselves the scene when the cask was sampled and Freeman and Barnes, Parker and Lang, and Phillips and the jolly old Parson Jones, duly moistened the foundation of the new chapel. They had no fantastic notions of temperance in those jovial days; wine was made to gladden the heart of man, and on all joyous occasions it was considered the correct thing to get decently drunk—parson and priest, bishop and deacon, all drank. I am old enough myself to remember the time when a visit from the clergyman always meant an order to my mother to get out a second bottle of port. In reading over records of both the Anglican and Congregational bodies we are struck with the mean subscriptions to the churches, the paltry pittances to the ministers. Poor old Jones, like Langman of the English Church, had to go round like a beggar, whilst at least two of his congregation were very rich and could have paid the whole cost of the Meeting House without feeling it, Henry Phillips had a large income as sheriff, pickings, and a fine business as a merchant, old Parker made a fortune out of the Newfoundland trade, and had a large income after he retired from the manufacture of peppermint The Congregational Church has always been noted for its fine choir. In the old church the music gallery was ably filled by C. Winton, Mr Brace, and old Mr Stentaford

[1] *See* "History of Newfoundland," pp 361, 362.

In March 1800 John Jones, the faithful minister, passed away to his
everlasting rest. In 1851 the new stone church on Queen's Road was
built; the Rev. George Schofield gave an admirable sermon on the
occasion from the very appropriate text, "Let us go hence." Amongst
the many able divines who have ministered to the church in St. John's,
next to the founder, the most distinguished preacher and pastor was the
Rev. James Sabine; the Rev. Daniel Spencer Ward was another well-

NEW CONGREGATIONAL CHURCH.

known and influential clergyman, his pastorate the longest, and his
social influence the most powerful in augmenting the body which in his
days embraced a large number of leading families in St. John's.
Mrs. Ward was the founder of the St. John's Dorcas Society, and its
first president. The three ministers in succession, Evans, Schofield, and
Pelley, were all admirable preachers, and very able men. Hall, Beaton,
and latterly Hodgkinson, maintained the high reputation of the
Independent ministers in St. John's, which has been fully sustained by

the present pastor, the Rev G. Ward Siddall In preparing this short paper I have been greatly assisted by Mrs. Siddall's pamphlet, "The Origin of Nonconformity in St John's, Newfoundland"

PASTORS OF THE CONGREGATIONAL CHURCH IN ST JOHN'S

Rev John Jones -	-	1775–1800	Rev D. D Evans -	-	1844–1848
Rev Rutton Morris -	-	1801–1805	Rev. George Schofield	-	1849–1857
Rev John Hillyard -	-	1805–1807	Rev Charles Pedley	-	1857–1864
Rev Edmund Violet -	-	1807–1810	Rev. John Maize -	-	1864–1865
Rev. John Sanderson	-	1811–1812	Rev James Howell -	-	1866–1867
Rev Wm Jones Hyde	-	1813–1816	Rev Thomas Hall -	-	1868–1880
Rev James Sabine -	-	1816–1818	Rev David Beaton -	-	1881–1886
Rev Thomas Smelt -	-	1820–1823	Rev T. Hodgkinson	-	1886–1891
Rev. Daniel Spencer Ward	-	1824–1843			

THE PRESBYTERIAN CHURCH.

By Rev WM GRAHAM and others.

The Presbyterian church in St John's was first organised in 1842 On the fly-leaf of the register, in most beautiful characters, these words are written —

"Begun on the Fourteenth day of August, in the year of our Lord One thousand eight hundred and forty-two, by the Rev Donald Allan Fraser, Minister of the Established Church of Scotland."

It was not, however, until the 3rd of December of the following year that St Andrew's Church, which stood on the site recently occupied by the Masonic Temple, was opened for public worship Two years later (in 1845), the labours of the first Presbyterian minister—the writer of the above extract, Mr Fraser—were cut short by death.

The Rev Donald Allan Fraser, the first minister of St. Andrew's Church, was a very able man, a fine speaker, and the best Gaelic scholar in North America. A highlander himself, a native of Torosay, he had a warm heart for his fellow highlanders and islanders ; he made long toilsome journeys from Nova Scotia to Cape Breton to minister to these poor outcasts from all religious instruction The Rev. D. A Fraser was the father of a numerous family of eleven sons and one daughter: at the present time the best-known member of the family is J. O Fraser, C M.G , our genial Postmaster-General

The following admirable account of Mr Fraser has been furnished to me by a member of the Presbyterian Church in Newfoundland.

"Rev Donald Allan Fraser, A M., who was the first Presbyterian minister settled in Newfoundland, was born at Torosay, in the Island of Mull, Scotland, on the 24th of November 1793, and was ordained by the Presbytery of Mull on the 22nd of September 1814 On the 30th October in the same year he married

Catherine Maclean, daughter of the Laird of Coll; and in 1818 he was sent by the Church of Scotland as a missionary to Pictou County, where he ministered to a highland population and their descendants, preaching in Gaelic and English every Sabbath. One of his elders, writing of Mr Fraser after his death, said, ' No minister since his day has gained the affections of his people as he did, nor is it likely that any will ' Mr. and Mrs Fraser may be said to have lived in the hearts of his highland people. Being largely influenced by a missionary spirit, he accepted a call to form a congregation at St John's Newfoundland, which call was dated August 1842 The Scotch population at St John's at that time was not large, but they possessed considerable wealth. A very handsome church was erected on a prominent site in the city, which was opened for public worship on the 3rd of December 1843, the text on the occasion being Gal iv. 18—' But it is good to be zealously affected always in a good thing ' The event was attended by the Governor of the Colony, Sir John Harvey, and suite, by the heads of Departments, and by an overflowing congregation

' Mr. Fraser was a scholar of masterly attainments, a captivating speaker, and an argumentative reasoner His mind was richly stored with imagery, and being, ordinarily, an extemporaneous preacher, his eloquence frequently reached sublime heights. He was, too, of commanding presence, standing six feet two inches In the midst of his usefulness, and in the flower of his manhood, he was cut down, and died of cancer on the 7th of February 1845, in the 51st year of his age and the 31st of his ministry His widow and only daughter and six of his ten sons have followed the father, only four sons being now alive.''

His successors were Rev. Arch Sinclair, Rev. Francis Nicol, Rev. Donald McRae, now the esteemed pastor of St. David's, St. John, N B., and Rev J Dykes Patterson, who died the other year in Australia The last named was pastor of the church when it was destroyed by fire in 1876.

In the meantime, the wave of trouble which swept over the parent church in Scotland, and which rent that church in two, in the year 1843, touched St John's, and Free St Andrew's was erected in 1850, on Duckworth Street, near the Commercial Bank. In 1852 the Rev Moses Harvey received and accepted a unanimous call to this church, and continued a most faithful and acceptable ministry till 1876, when it too fell, destroyed likewise by the devouring flames In 1877 a union of the two congregations was effected, and on the 18th day of June 1878 the corner-stone of St. Andrew's Church was laid, the Rev Dr Muir, of Edinburgh, and the Rev Moses Harvey being the officiating ministers In the same year the Rev. L. G Macneill accepted a call to become minister of the united congregation.

Thirteen years ago, on the 30th November 1879, St Andrew's Church, recently destroyed too, like its predecessors, by fire, was dedicated to the worship of Almighty God. The Rev L G Macneill, pastor of the church, conducted the morning service, and preached an impressive sermon from the text, ' The glory of this latter house shall " be greater than the former, saith the Lord of Hosts." The Rev. Job

Shenton, of the Methodist church, occupied the pulpit in the evening. At each service the church was crowded to its utmost capacity, and collections for the day amounted to $940.

The edifice thus dedicated to the worship of God was a substantial and ornamental structure of brick, faced with white free-stone from the quarries of Scotland. It was capable of seating 700 worshippers. A tower, with lofty and graceful spire, rose on the western end of the

ST. ANDREW'S PRESBYTERIAN CHURCH, ST. JOHN'S.

building. The main entrance was on the same side, through a handsome porch, over which was cut in the stone-work, in bold relief, "The Burning Bush"—the emblem of the Church of Scotland. Although all was plain and chaste about the emblem, yet the appearance of the interior was peculiarly pleasing and impressive. The first object which attracted attention on entering was the desk and platform, occupying the place where, in former days, a pulpit would have stood. The first was of polished walnut, richly carved, massive, graceful, and in the centre approximated to the conformation of a pulpit. It was the work of Mr. Richard Goff and son. A massive pillar at each end

supported a tall gasalier, having five branches gracefully proportioned
The centre gasalier was also of beautiful form and the best workmanship,
and lighted the building perfectly. A spacious gallery occupied the end
opposite the minister's desk. The basement for evening services, Sabbath
school, and other classes, accommodated between 400 and 500 persons,
having a ceiling 14 feet high. The vestry opened off the basement.

The cost of the church was $40,000. The organ cost nearly $4,000,
the fine bell $500. Including the furniture in the basement— cabinet-
organ and piano, mission work on hand, pew fittings, Sabbath school
library, minister's gown, pulpit Bible, and other valuables—the total
loss by the fire exceeded $50,000. In addition to these the adjoining
building, known as "The Temple," and a dwelling-house, both church
property, were consumed by the flames. It may also be mentioned
that the valuable communion plate was likewise lost. Indeed, nothing
was saved. The rapid advance of the fire precluded all attempts, so
that the doors of the church were never opened. The Manse, valued at
$4,000, and St. Andrew's school-room, at $1,000, were also destroyed
making a total loss of church property of over $55,000.

In 1866 the Rev. L. G. Macneill resigned, having received and
accepted a call from St Andrew's, St John, N B. In the following
year the Rev W. Graham, of Edinburgh, received and accepted a call
to St. Andrews, and was ordained and inducted to that charge on the
15th May, the Rev. D. McRae, of St. John, N.B., and the Rev. M.
Harvey being the officiating ministers.

In 1855 a Presbyterian church was opened in Harbour Grace.
There are also Presbyterian churches and missions at Little Bay Mines
and Bay of Islands.

The Presbyterians are a very influential body, though small in
number, by the census of 1874 they amounted to 1,168, by the last
census, of 1891, to 1,449.

THE SALVATION ARMY.

In the year 1886 the first service of the Salvation Army was held
in St. John's, in Barter's field. There was a disturbance, and some
assaults on the women who began the "New Religion." The church
now numbers fourteen hundred members. It has eighty-five officers,
and about two hundred local officers (deacons), who assist in various
duties. There are thirty stations, divided into five corps, from Tilt
Cove to Channel. In May 1891 the Honble E. P. Morris introduced

and passed a Bill authorising staff officers of the Society to celebrate marriage. The staff officers are also district registrars and grant certificates of death. In 1891 the Army was allowed a grant of $1,400 for educational purposes, in accordance with their numbers as shown in the last census

There has been lately formed a Refuge Home in St John's, and the organisation has now a missionary vessel. The visits of Commandant Booth and of General Booth in September 1894 were made the occasions of great demonstrations.